Beginning Metap

B

Beginning Metaphysics

An Introductory Text with Readings

Written and edited by

Heimir Geirsson and *Michael Losonsky*

Copyright © Blackwell Publishers Ltd, 1998. Editorial arrangement and introductions
copyright © Heimir Geirsson and Michael Losonsky, 1998

First published 1998

2 4 6 8 10 9 7 5 3 1

Blackwell Publishers Inc.
350 Main Street
Malden, Massachusetts 02148
USA

Blackwell Publishers Ltd
108 Cowley Road
Oxford OX4 1JF
UK

Library of Congress Cataloging-in-Publication Data

Beginning metaphysics : an introductory text with readings / edited by
   Heimir Geirsson and Michael Losonsky.
         p.   cm.
   Includes bibliographical references and index.
   ISBN 1-55786-728-3 (hardbound). – ISBN 1-55786-729-1 (pbk.)
   1. Metaphysics.   I. Geirsson, Heimir.   II. Losonsky, Michael.
BD111.B35   1998
110–dc21   98-11438
                                                              CIP

British Library Cataloguing in Publication Data

A CIP catalogue record for this book is available from the British Library.

Typeset in 10½ on 12½ pt Ehrhardt
by Ace Filmsetting, Frome, Somerset
Printed in Great Britain by MPG Books Ltd, Bodmin, Cornwall

This book is printed on acid-free paper

Contents

Figures and Tables

Figures

Tables

Acknowledgments

The editors thank Michael Bishop, Pat Francken, Bob Hollinger, Margaret Holmgren, Jane Kneller, Jim Maffie, Bill Robinson, Bernie Rollin, Holmes Rolston, John Taylor, and the students in our classes for all their help on this book. We especially thank our students, who forced us to think about the relevance of metaphysics to the issues they really cared about.

The editors and publishers gratefully acknowledge the following for permission to reproduce copyright material:

Plato, "Crito," from *Five Dialogues*, translated by G. M. A. Grube, 1981. Reprinted by permission of Hackett Publishing Company.

Plato, "Phaedo" (excerpts), from *Five Dialogues*, translated by G. M. A. Grube, 1981. Reprinted by permission of Hackett Publishing Company.

Simone de Beauvoir, from *The Second Sex*, trans. H. M. Parshley. © 1952 and renewed 1980 by Alfred A. Knopf Inc. Reprinted by permission of Alfred A. Knopf Inc.

Bertrand Russell, from *The Problems of Philosophy* (Oxford University Press, 1959). Reprinted by permission of Oxford University Press.

John O'Neill, "The Varieties of Intrinsic Value," *The Monist* (1992). Reprinted by permission of the publishers.

J. L. Mackie, from *Ethics: Inventing Right and Wrong* (Penguin Books, 1977). Reprinted by permission of the publisher.

Richard N. Boyd, "How to Be a Moral Realist," in George Sayre-McCord (ed.), *Essays on Moral Realism* (Cornell University Press, 1988). Reprinted by permission of Cornell University Press.

Anselm of Canterbury, "The Existence of God," from *Proslogion*, trans. John Cottingham, in John Cottingham (ed.), *Western Philosophy: an Anthology* (Oxford: Blackwell Publishers, 1996).

Thomas Aquinas, "Five Proofs for the Existence of God," from *Summa Theologica*, trans. John Cottingham, in John Cottingham (ed.), *Western Philosophy: an Anthology* (Oxford: Blackwell Publishers, 1996).

G. W. R. Leibniz, from *Theodicy: Essays on the Goodness of God, the Freedom of Man, and the Origin of Evil*, ed. Austin Farrer, trans. E. M. Huggard. © Open Court Publishing Company, 1985. Reprinted by permission of Open Court Publishing Company.

J. L. Mackie, "Evil and Omnipotence," *Mind* 64 (1955). © Oxford University Press. Reprinted by permission of Oxford University Press.

Alvin Plantinga, from *God, Freedom, and Evil* (Harper & Row, 1974). Reprinted by permission of the author.

Edward H. Madden, "A Third View of Causality," *The Review of Metaphysics* 23 (1969).

Reprinted by permission of The Review of Metaphysics.

Alan Garfinkel, from *Forms of Explanation* (Yale University Press, 1981). Reprinted by permission of Yale University Press.

René Descartes, from "Principles of Philosophy" and "Passions of the Soul," in J. Cottingham, D. Murdoch, and R. Stoothoff (eds), *Descartes: Selected Philosophical Readings* (1985). Reprinted by permission of Cambridge University Press.

Thomas Nagel, "What Is It Like to Be a Bat?," *Philosophical Review* 82 (1974). © 1974 Cornell University. Reprinted by permission of the publisher.

John Searle, "Is the Brain's Mind a Computer Program?," *Scientific American* January (1990). Reprinted by permission of the publisher.

Paul M. Churchland and Patricia Smith Churchland, "Could a Machine Think?," *Scientific American* January (1990). Reprinted by permission of the publisher.

William L. Rowe, "Two Concepts of Freedom," *Proceedings and Addresses of the APA* 61 (1987 supplement). Reprinted by permission of the publisher and the author.

Harry Frankfurt, "Freedom and the Will and the Concept of a Person," *The Journal of Philosophy* LXVIII (1971). Reprinted by permission of the publisher and the author.

Susan Wolf, "Sanity and the Metaphysics of Responsibility," in F. D. Schoeman (ed.), *Responsibility, Character, and the Emotions* (Cambridge University Press, 1988). Reprinted by permission of the publisher and the author.

Rudolf Carnap, "The Elimination of Metaphysics through Logical Analysis of Language," trans. A. Pap, in A. J. Ayer (ed.), *Logical Positivism*. Glencoe, Illinois: Free Press, 1959. Reprinted by permission of the publisher.

Friedrich Nietzsche, from "Twilight of the Idols," trans. W. Kaufmann, in W. Kaufmann (ed.), *The Portable Nietzsche*. Translation copyright 1954 by The Viking Press, renewed 1982 by Viking Penguin, Inc. Reprinted by permission of Viking Penguin, a division of Penguin Books USA, Inc.

John Rawls, "Justice as Fairness: Political not Metaphysical," *Philosophy and Public Affairs* (1985). Reprinted by permission of Princeton University Press.

The publishers apologize for any errors or omissions in the above list and would be grateful to be notified of any corrections that should be incorporated in the next edition or reprint of this book.

1

What Is Metaphysics?

Introduction

At one time or another all of us find ourselves wondering about what there really is. Perhaps you have just been studying very late into the night for an important examination in physics the next day, and as you are trying to catch some sleep you begin wondering about whether matter and energy are all there is to reality. "What about God?" you think, "Does God also exist in addition to this vast universe of matter and energy?" If you are particularly worried about the examination tomorrow, you might even find yourself wondering about the existence of all the material you need to know about for tomorrow. "Do force and motion exist? Does matter exist? What if my thoughts are all there is, and everything else is just a figment of my beliefs, desires and imaginations?" you think as you begin to fall asleep.

Maybe once again you were trying to learn a whole unit of a course the day before an examination. You are irritated that this always seems to happen and that your most earnest resolutions to study more effectively have no effect whatsoever, except to make you feel guilty. "Maybe there is no freedom after all," you think to yourself, "and no matter how hard I try to change myself, I will end up on this course of life I am forced to follow." Or you might have a more upbeat response to your crisis. Instead of resignation, you might affirm your freedom and your decision not to study more efficiently. You think: "Everyone tells me I have an obligation to study better and perform better in school, but what are obligations anyway! Obligations do not really exist; they are totally subjective," while you reminisce about the fun you had when you were supposed to be studying.

These are examples of metaphysical musings, and all reflective people find themselves thinking about these and similar issues about what there is. These musings bring us very close to metaphysics because when these issues are pursued with some rigor – that is, with some respect for clarity and good reasoning – we are actually doing metaphysics. What distinguishes metaphysics from metaphysical musings, and from what usually passes for metaphysics in the marketplace, e.g. healing crystals and reading palms, is that *metaphysics is a sustained and rational study of what there is and the ultimate nature of what there is*.

What makes a pursuit *sustained*? It seems that this is clear enough. We all know when we are working hard over a period of time at trying to master a technique, and when we are only whiling the time away. Simply "cramming" for a final is not a sustained effort, but studying earnestly and with discipline throughout the semester is a sustained effort. If on a fairly frequent and regular basis you devote the best of your abilities to a project, then your pursuit is sustained. Of course, we can pursue a project in a sustained manner over a lifetime or just for a few months, say the length of a semester, but in either case the pursuit is a sustained one as long as we keep working at it in an earnest and focused manner.

What makes a pursuit *rational* is a bit more difficult to spell out. In fact, it might even be impossible to define rationality adequately. But that need not intimidate us. After all, spelling out in detail what makes a certain kind of animal a horse is not an easy task either. It may even be impossible to spell out the features every horse must have and only horses can have (that is, the necessary and sufficient conditions for being a horse), because maybe there are no necessary and sufficient conditions for being a horse. Nevertheless, we typically can spot horses with ease. What goes for horses goes for many other things, including other animals, plants and even human artifacts such as tables or chairs.

In the same manner, we have a good idea of rationality even if we cannot define it. In part, it involves aiming to have good arguments with premises that are to the best of our knowledge true or probably true, considering all the relevant evidence available to us, being open to objections and counter-arguments, trying to be clear and not obfuscate what one is saying, listening to others and giving them the benefit of the doubt. There are other features, of course. There are times when it is rational to stop arguing and start acting. There are even circumstances when it is irrational and a waste of precious time to continue listening to someone. Knowing what those times and circumstances are is also a part of rationality, and knowing this is perhaps the most difficult feature of rationality.

So far, we have discussed the method or manner of metaphysical study, but what about the subject matter, namely *what there is and the ultimate nature of what there is?* To understand the subject of metaphysics, think about the most basic ways in which we classify or categorize the world around us. Suppose you are starting to study biology. As you begin your studies, you learn to distinguish the subject matter of the biological sciences from the subject matter of the physical sciences. While biologists study the constituents and changes of life and living organisms, physicists and chemists study the constituents and changes of matter and energy. You might also think about how the biological and physical sciences differ from the social sciences, which focus on the changes and constituents of human society.

Since biology tries to understand the vast complexity of life and living organisms, studying biology also involves comprehending various classifications. You must understand many kinds of plants, animals, fungi, and single-celled organisms, their structures and functions, their underlying chemical processes, and the relationships and dependencies of all these living organisms.

Knowledge in any field always involves classifying reality, and typically we turn to the sciences to find out about different natural kinds and processes. However, we turn to metaphysics when we get to the highest levels of classification. To see this, let's start at the top with the broadest category there is: Reality. What should we put next? Let's just try starting with the following categories:

Physical Matter and Energy   Life and Living Things

Are these the only categories we should place immediately below the heading Reality, or do we need more? Do we include another category for non-physical things, such as divine beings, minds and spirits, or moral values, such as right and wrong? If we add such a category, then we are saying that reality consists of things that are not physical, and that is an important metaphysical claim. If we do not find a place for divine beings, minds and spirits, or moral values under the heading Reality, then we are suggesting that they are unreal, and that of course is also a significant metaphysical position.

You might think that there are no divine beings, but you might try to find a place for them in reality as subjects of myths and stories. Myths and stories are real – they are things people write, say, draw, or act out, and they exist as much as the leaf of a plant or the mineral in a rock exist. What do not exist are the

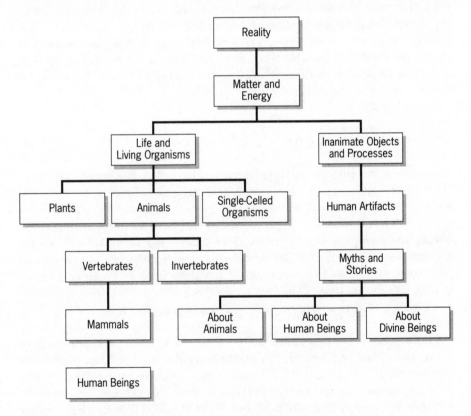

Figure 1   Life as a special configuration of physical matter and energy.

things that myths and stories describe, and so if we make divine beings into what is described in certain kinds of myths and stories, we have indeed found a place for them in reality, but only as something described by fiction. Needless to say, that is an important metaphysical view. While living organisms simply exist, divine beings are just the subjects of myths and stories human beings tell each other.

When thinking about the structure of reality, we are not just wondering about what categories to include in our classification of reality, but how the categories should be related to each other. An important example of this is the question of how Life and Living Organisms are related to Physical Matter and Energy. Should Life and Living Organisms and Physical Matter and Energy be on the same level, or placed one under the other? We can easily imagine someone believing that all life is just a special configuration of physical matter and energy, and so for him or her Life and Living Organisms should be placed under Matter and Energy. This same line of thinking suggests that human beings are just special kinds of living organisms, and so that the classification of reality should look something like that shown in figure 1.

Not everyone will agree with this system of classification, which makes all of reality into some species of matter and energy. Whether or not you do, try to think of alternative classifications. Perhaps you wish to add the category of Mind and Spirit alongside the heading of Matter and Energy. If you find yourself thinking or arguing about the accuracy of this or alternative classifications of reality, you are discussing what there is and the ultimate nature of what there is, and if you are doing it in a somewhat sustained and rational manner, you are, for better or worse, doing metaphysics.

Science and Metaphysics

At this point, it would not be surprising if you have the following two concerns. (1) If metaphysics is about what there is and the nature of reality, how is metaphysics different from science? Don't we go to the sciences to find out what there is? Psychology tells us about minds, physics and chemistry about matter, biology about life, the social sciences about society, and so on. What is left for metaphysics to discuss? (2) Does metaphysics make a difference to how we act? Isn't metaphysics just like counting angels on the head of a pin, and consequently a waste of time? Don't we always have something better to do than metaphysics, even if it happens to be playing a game of chess or going for a walk?

Let us turn to the first concern right away. Metaphysics and science have always had a close relationship. In fact, the roots of science and metaphysics are intertwined. If you look at the historical introduction to your college physics text, you will probably read about Pythagoras (580–500 BCE), Empedocles (490–430 BCE), Democritus (460–370 BCE), and Aristotle (384–322 BCE). These are not only early physicists but also some of the first philosophers and metaphysicians.

Democritus was a contemporary of Socrates, who is perhaps the most famous of all philosophers, because not only did he drink hemlock and die in the name of philosophy, but he is also the star in Plato's well known dialogues. Democritus argued that free space and an infinite number of invisible and indivisible atoms are all there is. Pythagoras and Empedocles were pre-Socratic philosophers concerned with the unchangeable elements of the universe: Pythagoras thought they were numbers and their relations, while Empedocles thought they were fire, air, water, and earth, together with how they are related by love and strife.

Aristotle, like other revered pioneers, held views that we reject today – for example, that heavy bodies fall proportionately faster than lighter ones and that the brain is a thermostat. But like other ancient thinkers, he also made lasting contributions to science and philosophy, and one of his important contributions was that it is not enough to state what there is; we also need to give causal explanations that account for what there is. We need to study the causes of what there is as well as their powers to effect changes in themselves and their environment.

Aristotle's recognition that change is a basic feature of reality was in part motivated by his appreciation for biological phenomena. He appreciated facts such as that an acorn grew into an acorn tree and that acorn trees have a cycle of growth and death. These developmental changes need to be explained, and Aristotle did so by postulating that all things have natures or essences – that is, the potential or power to be something – and what actually is the case is determined by an object's nature.

The various scientific disciplines that emerged from the scientific revolution of the sixteenth and seventeenth centuries have common roots with philosophy. Rene Descartes (1596–1650), who is considered the father of modern philosophy, is an example of the broad scholar who preceded the specialization that comes along with the creation of disciplines and sub-disciplines. Not only did Descartes make great contributions to philosophy; he also invented or discovered analytic geometry and wrote the first textbook in physiology, which was based in part on his own dissections and observations. He is credited with independently discovering that the function of the heart is to pump blood; a discovery that in all likelihood was made possible because of his metaphysical views about the mind.

Robert Boyle (1627–1691), the father of modern chemistry and best known for having discovered the law named after him, namely that at a constant temperature, the volume occupied by a fixed quantity of gas is inversely proportional to the applied pressure, is appropriately called a scientist today, but could just as well have been classified as a philosopher back in his day, along with his life-long friend John Locke (1632–1706), who, along with Boyle, Isaac Newton (1642–1727), Christiaan Huygens (1629–1695), and other notable figures of the scientific revolution, was also a member of the English Royal Society.

But, nevertheless, Locke went down in history as a philosopher while Boyle is remembered as a scientist, and there are good reasons for this. For one thing, Locke did very little experimental work, while Boyle spent most of his working time testing hypotheses and designing experiments. Although philosophers rely on experimental results and confirmed hypotheses, they do not, as philosophers, test hypotheses and design experiments. They leave that to scientists.

What set Locke apart from his fellow scientists is best described by Locke himself. Scientists such as "Boyle . . . , the Great Huygens, and the incomparable Mr. Newton," were in Locke's mind "Master Builders, whose mighty Designs, in advancing the Sciences, will leave lasting Monuments to the Admiration of Posterity." Locke thinks of himself as someone who is employed by these Master Builders as an "Under-Labourer in clearing Ground a little, and removing some of the Rubbish, that lies in the way of Knowledge." The methods and concepts of modern science were not orthodoxies in the seventeenth century and they needed to be defended. This was Locke's task and in many ways continues to be the task of philosophy, including metaphysics.

Behavioral scientists and neuroscientists might think that the right way to study the human mind is to study human behavior and the brain. They mostly assume that this is a good method and go about their work, but the philosopher and metaphysician is needed to defend this assumption. Social scientists might assume that it is appropriate to use the scientific method to study human societies, and they carry out this assumption in their daily work, but it is the philosopher and metaphysician who has the capacity to properly defend this assumption. Life scientists might assume that biological properties and processes – that is, life itself – have special laws that are distinct from the laws of physics, and it is the philosopher and metaphysician who is the defense attorney for this assumption.

So one way in which science and metaphysics can differ is that while the scientist uses certain methods and concepts in her scientific work, the metaphysician is concerned with these underlying assumptions that guide the scientific work, and attempts to defend them against critics. But philosophical metaphysicians can also be critics of science. Locke himself was not just an attorney for science, but also a critic. For instance, consider Locke's relation to the corpuscular world view, namely that matter was made up of small invisible bodies in a void, the predecessors of present-day atoms. Although Locke shared this view with Boyle and the most advanced scientists of the seventeenth century, he also took great pains to emphasize that corpuscularism was only a probable hypothesis and not something we could come to know with certainty. Thus he called on scientists to appropriately qualify their claims about what there is. Locke's critique was successful, in that it led scientists to abandon the idea that they are after certain and infallible knowledge, and instead affirm the nobility of their quest for probable opinions.

More recently, philosophical metaphysicians criticized scientific work on the mind on the grounds that it did not explain consciousness and that consciousness needed to be explained. This critique was first ignored, but eventually it was heard, and now there is much lively and fruitful scientific work being done on the nature of human and other animal consciousness.

In addition to being defenders and critics of science, philosophers and metaphysicians are also interpreters of science. For example, in contemporary physics, the Big Bang is a commonly accepted explanation for important features of the universe. Because around ten or twenty billions of years ago the universe exploded from a concentrated point of energy, the universe now has the density it has and the galaxies recede in the way they do. This of course raises many questions. "But what came before the Big Bang, where was the Big Bang, and what caused the Big Bang?" children and lay adults ask, and the initial task of the metaphysician is to interpret what scientists are up to with this explanation. When we explain a burning forest in terms of an explosion in an old mine, we can legitimately ask for the causes of this explosion, but asking about what caused the Big Bang is often thought to be illegitimate by scientists, and one of the tasks of the metaphysician is to attempt to explain this illegitimacy.

In addition to interpreting, defending, and critiquing science, there is a fourth feature that distinguishes metaphysics and science. Scientists in their work as scientists studying their particular subjects do not step outside of their domain and take a bird's eye view of what all the sciences study, and try to understand how these subjects relate and depend on each other. Doing that is left for the philosopher and metaphysician.

Descartes, for instance, was interested in many subjects: biology, mathematics, algebra, and psychology. But it is as a philosopher and metaphysician that he turned his attention to understanding the relationship between all these domains. Descartes believed that while matter and the properties of matter could explain everything that physicists and biologists are trying to explain, psychologists have a domain that is distinct from matter. Descartes believed that minds and the properties of minds cannot be understood in terms of matter and its properties. The mind, Descartes believed, was immaterial. Of course, not everyone agreed with Descartes. The English philosopher Thomas Hobbes (1588–1679) and the French philosopher and scientist Pierre Gassendi (1592–1655) believed that the mind was material and should to be studied in the way we study the rest of matter. Whether Descartes or Hobbes and Gassendi were right is not something you will find discussed in a textbook of science. Whether matter and energy is all there is and should be the only heading under Reality or whether we should add another heading – for instance, Mind and Spirit – is not a scientific topic. You will not find it discussed in your physics or biology texts, but you will find it discussed in your metaphysics text.

More recently, philosophers and metaphysicians have been raising questions about the relationship between the natural and social sciences. In the first half of the twentieth century, many philosophers assumed that the natural sciences, particularly physics, were fundamental. Eventually, they thought, all other sciences, including the social sciences, would, when fully developed, be just applications of the laws of physics. Today this view is not widely shared anymore. On the other hand, there are today those who suggest that perhaps the social sciences and what they study – the political and socioeconomic relationships – are fundamental, and that physics is better seen as an expression of political or economic power than as something that is guided by natural laws. This issue is not really the subject matter of any of the natural or social sciences, but falls instead within the domain of metaphysics.

We have now considered four features that distinguish the work of a metaphysician from the work of a scientist: the metaphysician interprets, defends, and critiques the work of scientists, and the metaphysician aims for a comprehensive view of the various domains of science. There is still another feature that is of equal importance.

Philosophers in general and metaphysicians in particular are concerned not only with the sciences, but also with other human activities. Human beings not only pursue science, but practice religion, go into politics, and create art and literature. Moreover, we have a common-sense view of us and the world that we use in our practical affairs and that in important respects differs from the scientific perspective. These domains generate their own questions that metaphysicians care about – for instance, the question of God's existence that we mentioned at the beginning. A question generated by our literary activity concerns the nature of fiction and the objects described by fictional works. These issues are not the subject matter of science. Moreover, metaphysicians also care about how these non-scientific subjects are related to the subjects science studies. For instance, the world of common sense is a world of enduring objects, such as rocks and chairs, that have color and texture. It is also a world of value: the mountains are beautiful and the chair is good. How do these common sense features, which seem to be mostly human constructions and projections, mesh with the scientific perspective? Is the world of common sense in conflict with the world of science or do they complement each other? Is perhaps one more fundamental than the other? Trying to understand how the domains of science fit with the domains of common sense is one of the tasks of metaphysical inquiry.

So, in addition to interpreting, defending, and criticizing science and in addition to looking for a comprehensive view of all the sciences, metaphysicians are concerned with problems that emerge outside of the sciences, and they aim to understand how science fits into the much larger pattern of human activity.

Metaphysics and Practice

What is the point of metaphysics? Does it make a significant difference to how we conduct our lives? Is it more than a diversion, like tending a flower garden or playing chess?

We should not discount the point of diversions. Human beings, like their fellow animals, are playful, and this has an important role not only in human development, but in our capacity to face and solve the serious problems and obstacles that come with being alive. We need to find a place and time for playing chess, painting, gardening, playing music, or just going for a walk. Certainly metaphysics can play this role. Thinking about the existence of God or whether moral values are objective can be a pleasant and enjoyable diversion from life's turmoils. Educated people often turn to the history of philosophy or contemporary metaphysics in the same spirit that they turn to gardening or reading a good novel. These activities make life worth living, but they do not provide us with the means of making a living.

Of course, sometimes we can turn these diversions into professional activities. There are professional gardeners who sell flowers or teach students how to garden, and there are professional chess players who make a living entertaining and instructing others with their skills. But at that point, chess or gardening cease to be mere diversions and become means for making a living. If you have ever filed your taxes, you know that tax officials recognize this difference and force you to distinguish between activities you pay for that help you generate your income and activities that do not.

So is metaphysics at best a diversion that some have turned into a profession, namely entertaining and instructing for money those who are interested in this diversion, much like a teacher of chess or gardening? If that is all that can be said for metaphysics, it is a tremendous travesty that metaphysics is one of the major subfields of philosophy, which plays an essential role in the core curriculum of any university. No one would think of requiring university students to learn chess or gardening, but metaphysics is a standard part of required philosophy courses. Is there anything more that can be said for metaphysics?

Consider how we justify other fields we study. Although art for art's sake and science for science's sake is a stance that has some merit, there are times when the arts and sciences are called to justify themselves. Why fund the arts when unemployment and poverty are pressing problems? Why support pure research in the sciences when there are pressing practical concerns? When accountability becomes a serious issue, artists and scientists have serious answers. Not only is art valuable for its own sake, but artists and friends of the arts will also argue that art has practical value. Art improves and educates human beings. Art helps us to maintain a good communal life. Art is cathartic. Art eases the pain of daily life. Art is a powerful commentary on life, and so on. We also know that science claims to improve life. "Better living through science," advertisements proclaim, and pure research is supported because such research is necessary if we are to continue to make technological and medical advances.

Needless to say, metaphysics does not have the kinds of practical consequences science has. But metaphysics is more than a pleasant diversion or a source of income. For one thing, metaphysics has been a fertile ground for new sciences. Physics is rooted in the metaphysics of pre-Socratic philosophers as well as the metaphysical views of Newton, biology in Aristotle's metaphysics, psychology in the metaphysics of Descartes, Locke and Hume, cognitive science in the philosophies of Hobbes, Leibniz, Russell, and Turing.

But more importantly, our own practical lives, even when we are deciding life and death issues, are infused with metaphysical beliefs. When trying to determine what obligations we have to the state, our natural environment, or other animals, or when trying to determine whether individuals or societies are morally responsible for what they do, we will find ourselves in the midst of the domain of metaphysics. We might feel very uncomfortable in these domains because metaphysical issues are not as cut and dried as we might like our lives to be. But no matter how much we dislike this, these confusing issues are woven into the very fabric of our lives, and appear whenever we have to make crucial decisions with far-reaching long-term consequences for us and the world around us.

The pragmatist William James maintained that theoretical differences are important and worthy of our attention only if they make a difference in practice, and this is indeed a good test for determining what is important, what deserves to be studied and taught, and what is worthy of pursuit even in adverse conditions. We believe that metaphysics passes this test. The following chapters aim to show that this is true for the enduring topics of metaphysics: the problem of universals, the reality of moral value, the existence of God, the nature of causality, the mind/body problem, and freedom of determinism.

2

Metaphysics and Political Philosophy

Introduction

Political activity can be motivated by many factors, including sheer hunger for power, but even the vilest politician is guided by views about the nature of society and how it ought to be organized, and this is the stuff of political philosophy. Whether politicians are driven by a noble vision of society or a sinister view that might makes right – whether they are political idealists or political realists – they are working with a political philosophy that helps to shape their political policies and actions.

So political action involves political philosophy, and this takes us to metaphysics because political philosophy overlaps with metaphysics. Metaphysical views make a difference to political philosophy, and political philosophy makes a difference to metaphysics. To see this, let us consider two of Europe's greatest political philosophers and metaphysicians: Plato and Hobbes.

Plato's Politics

Plato was the disciple of another great Greek philosopher, Socrates. In fact, Plato wrote his philosophy mostly in the form of dialogues in which Socrates was the hero. Plato's most dramatic dialogues document the last days of Socrates, who in 399 BCE was condemned by the court of the city of Athens to die by drinking poisonous hemlock. Socrates had been found guilty of the serious charge of "corrupting the minds of the young, and of believing in deities of his own invention instead of the gods recognized by the state." Although he believed that he was innocent on both counts and that the sentence was unjust, Socrates did not try to escape even when given the opportunity to escape by his old friend and neighbor, Crito. Socrates believed that he had a duty to the Athenian state and that he should submit to its authority, even when the state was meting out an unjust sentence.

In Plato's dialogue *The Crito*, one of Europe's first treatises devoted to the question of political obligation, Socrates lays out his reasons for obeying the state. "One must not even do wrong when one is wronged," Socrates believes, and for him to escape the state's sentence would be to do something wrong. He imagines that while he and Crito are preparing to escape, the laws and constitution of Athens confront them with three arguments for why this would be wrong and why Socrates has political obligations to the Athenian state. The first argument is that Socrates agreed to "abide by whatever judgments the state pronounced," and this includes wrong judgments the state might make. The second argument is that disobedience destroys the state's "law and order," which makes the good life possible. The state makes it possible for people to have families, and thus it made Socrates' life possible in the first place, and it also provided for children's education, which is necessary for leading a good life. Finally, the state is like a father or master to its citizens, and citizens should obey the state much like children and servants have to obey their superiors. So if Socrates were to escape, he would violate a willing agreement he made with the state, destroy what makes the good life possible, and show insubordination to his natural superiors.

Socrates considers all these arguments convincing. In fact, he seems to hear these arguments in the same way "a mystic seems to hear the strains of music." These arguments of the laws and constitution of Athens ring so loudly in his head, Socrates maintains in the conclusion of the dialogue, that he cannot hear any objections, and he tells Crito that it would be useless to try to argue with him about this issue. His mind is made up.

Socrates' discussion of political obligation with Crito on the day of his execution makes several assumptions that belong to the domain of metaphysics. For instance, consider that Socrates' first response to Crito is to insist that we should not be guided by popular opinion or "what people in general will say." We need to distinguish between good and bad opinions, and good opinions should guide our actions. Good opinions are the opinions of wise people with expert knowledge, and such expertise is not limited to medicine or athletics. It is possible to have expert knowledge about justice and injustice, goodness and badness, honor and dishonor, or right and wrong. In other words, Socrates maintains that it is possible to have expert knowledge about morality, and consequently morality is not just a matter of opinion. Just because popular opinion agrees that a certain action is right, just, good, or honorable does not make it so.

So what Socrates (and Plato) is after is expert knowledge about morality, and expert knowledge "represents the actual truth." Such knowledge is true, and it is true in virtue of representing something actual or real. For instance, a doctor's knowledge that you twisted your ankle is not only true, but it is true about your actual twisted ankle. In much the same way, Socrates and Plato believe, a moral expert's knowledge "represents the actual truth" about moral values. So the moral expert can know that we have a moral obligation to the state in the same way that a medical expert can know that your ankle is twisted. But this is a metaphysical view: it is a view about the nature of reality. Plato and Socrates believe that there is objective moral value.

A second assumption is expressed with Socrates' metaphor of the laws and constitution of Athens arguing with him and Crito. Of course, Socrates does not believe that the laws and state of Athens are literally persons that can talk and argue, but he does believe that the state is literally a kind of object that exists in addition to all its individual citizens. The state, for Socrates, is not just a collection of individual citizens and their actions, but something over and above these. For example, the wrong decision made by the Athenian court when it condemned Socrates is a decision made by men, not us, the laws and state of Athens tell Socrates. Nevertheless, Socrates has an obligation to obey this decision, but it is not an obligation he has to the people who made the decision, but an obligation he has to the state to obey the decisions of properly constituted courts of Athens.

Third, Socrates assumes that there are eternal objects that do not cease to exist in the way ordinary earthly objects come to be and die. The clearest example of this is Socrates himself. Socrates does not believe that he will not exist any more after his body is killed by hemlock's poison. He will go on to another world with another set of laws and rulers, and he will be accountable to them. The laws of the next world are siblings of the laws of Athens, and they will not give Socrates a kind welcome if he disobeys their brethren, the laws of Athens. This suggests that for Plato and Socrates laws themselves are immortal or timeless. Perhaps the laws of Athens are not timeless, but they are related to the laws of the realm where immortal souls go and to which these souls must answer.

So at least three metaphysical beliefs – that moral value exists, that the state is something over and above its individual citizens, and that some objects are eternal – play a central role in Socrates' discussion with Crito about political obligation. They not only inform their discussion, but they are part of the reasoning that moves Socrates to stay in Athens and drink the hemlock. Here is a clear case of metaphysics not only informing political debate, but influencing political action.

Plato's Metaphysics

Socrates' dialogue with Crito occurred early in the morning of Socrates' day of execution, and while metaphysics is mostly implicit in this dialogue, Socrates addressed it explicitly that evening. While he started the day with a political discussion, Socrates ends the day, and his life, with a discourse on the metaphysics that not only guided his political decision not to escape earlier that day, but guided him throughout his life.

This last discussion and Socrates' death are the topics of the *Phaedo*. Waiting for his death amidst his students, friends, and neighbors – except for a brief appearance of his wife or children, who seem to play no role in Socrates' philosophical thinking – the topic turns to Socrates' immortality. In arguing for the immortality of the soul, Socrates touches on all the central features of his views on what, after all is said and done, there is, and it is this view that Plato develops and refines throughout his long life.

A crucial feature of this metaphysics is the distinction between *appearance and reality*. Some things only seem to be but do not really exist – for instance, a one-eyed ogre of a nightmare – while other things are real and not just parts of dreams, e.g. the heart that keeps pumping blood to your brain while you sleep and dream. Needless to say, people can disagree vehemently about what things should be classified as mere appearance and what things we assign to reality. For instance, some people devote their lives to the proposition that they have encountered space aliens or that they have been cured by spiritual healers, while others see the belief in space aliens and miracle cures as symptoms of widespread derangement.

Although the distinction between appearance and reality may seem very straightforward to us, not all philosophers take this distinction for granted. Some philosophers have argued that only appearances are real, and thus there is no distinction between appearance and reality. In fact, the contemporary philosopher Richard Rorty has claimed that the distinction between appearance and reality has been disastrous for humanity. So even though it may seem very obvious – after all, this distinction is the hallmark of modern science – we must not be blinded to the fact that this is a distinction that we may be called upon to defend.

Whether we think of the distinction as an intellectual achievement of Greek metaphysics or a disaster for humanity, the way Plato draws the distinction is seen as a model for how to draw the line between appearance and reality. For Plato, what we see, hear, smell, taste, and touch belongs to the realm of appearances. Brief reflection on our appearances shows that what we can see and hear is constantly changing. The world we perceive comes and goes with the seasons. The pattern of birth, growth, and death rules all living things. Not even the ocean and its seemingly eternal surf is permanent. Twenty billion years ago there were no oceans on Earth, and in all likelihood in much less time than twenty billion years there will again be no oceans on Earth's surface.

The changing patterns of perception are even more dramatic if you pay close attention to your perceptions. As you blink and move your eyes and head, the perceived scenery changes. Notice how what you see or hear is never exactly the same as you go for a walk. What you see and hear is constantly changing. For Plato, change was the hallmark of appearance, and for that reason appearance is not something we could come to know. Plato believed that knowledge was eternal and unchanging, and consequently what we know had to be eternal and unchanging. Thus for Plato, *empirical knowledge* – that is, knowledge based on our visual, auditory, olfactory, gustatory, and tactile observations – would be an oxymoron.

Plato contrasted the changing stream of appearances with an eternal and unchanging reality that consisted of what Plato called "ideas." Now, it is important to keep in mind that what Plato called "ideas" are very different from what is called an "idea" in English. We think of ideas as something that people have in mind, and without people or beings that think like we do, there would be no ideas. Plato did not think of ideas in this way. For him, ideas were *forms*; that is, more like ideals, abstract blueprints, or models for objects. So to avoid confusing Plato's ideas with what we take ideas to be, it is better to use the term "forms" to refer to Plato's unchanging objects.

Plato had several reason for believing that reality consisted of forms, and not the things we observe. An extremely important reason Plato had for believing that there are forms was his belief that these forms explained an interesting and significant fact. Consider two sticks that are of equal length and two stones that are of equal weight. Both the pair of sticks and the pair of stones have something in common: equality. This example from the *Phaedo* can be multiplied for other things. Consider a red delicious apple and a ripe strawberry. Both have something in common: they are both red. What is it that the apple and strawberry have in common?

The Amazon and Zambezi Rivers are distinct rivers on different continents, but they are both south of the equator. How can two different rivers have something in common? The differences among individual people are striking: people have different parents, different facial features, sizes, and complexions, are born in different states, countries, and nations, speak different languages, have different customs, competing economic interests, and so on. Nevertheless, they are all human beings and deserve to be respected as human beings.

More generally, when any objects have something in common, what exactly is it that they have in common? This question is, in a nutshell, the *Problem of Universals*, and it applies to various ways in which individuals can have something in common. Distinct objects can have properties in common, as in the case of the red apple and strawberry. They both have the same color, and similarly objects can have the same size, texture, weight, and so on. Distinct objects can also belong to the same kind or type, as in the case of human beings, and similarly, different individual horses are all of the same species, distinct from the species to which butterflies or human beings belong. Finally, individuals can share relations: children can have the same parents, be born in the same town, and want the same tricycle.

This may be easily overlooked, but we cannot get around attributing the same thing to different things. Try describing any object around you, and you will see that you will not be able to get around attributing to something what you also attribute to other things. Perhaps you see a tree, but it is not the only object that is a tree. You will attribute the property of being a tree to many different individuals. You might describe it as deciduous, but this is not the only deciduous tree. Perhaps it is an aspen, but it is not the only aspen around. And so it goes for most, if not all, of the ways in which you try to describe it.

In all these cases, diverse individuals share something in common, and the Problem of Universals is to try to explain what this commonality is. Plato's solution to this problem is that, in addition to individuals, there are forms. Different individuals have something in common because they share one common form. For instance, there is a form Humanity which all individual human beings, with all their striking differences, share. The same holds for justice: different actions are just and different states can be just, but the actions or states are just because they share a common form: Justice. What goes for noble properties such as humanity and justice also goes for simpler properties such as having a certain color. Various objects can be red, but they are all red in virtue of sharing a form: Redness. Finally, there are forms for relations, such as Equality for all the relations of equality between equal lengths, weights, and all other equal quantities.

Transcendent Forms

If we grant that there are Platonic forms that exist in addition to individuals, we need to worry about the relation between individuals and forms. What is the relation between the particular red delicious in the fruit basket and the form Redness? What is the relation between individual human beings and the humanity they all share? Plato's and Socrates' answer to this question is not completely clear, but this much seems clear: forms exist independently of individuals. In other words, a form can exist even if no individual has or shares that form. For Plato, Humanity can exist without individual humans, Justice without individual just actions, Redness without particular red apples, and so on.

A good term for this feature of the forms is "transcendence." A form is transcendent when it can exist without any individuals. Plato illustrates his view on the transcendence of forms in the *Republic*, with an allegory about a cave. He describes a cave with prisoners who are forced to watch shadows of puppets and other figures on a wall. When a prisoner is freed and can turn his head, he is blinded at first by the fire that is used to cast the shadows, but after getting used to the light, he can come to see the puppets and other figures directly. Socrates then imagines that if this prisoner is dragged out of this cave, he will be blinded even more by the brightness outside the cave. First, he can only look at shadows and reflections of the real objects outside the cave, but eventually he can look at the actual animals, plants, and so forth. He will then notice that the puppets and figures he saw inside the cave are mere copies of the objects in the outside world. Finally, he will be able to look at the sun itself and see the light that illuminates everything outside the cave.

The shadows and figures inside the cave are the appearances; the shadows are our dreams and illusions, and the figures are like the ordinary objects we can see, hear, touch, and smell. The plants, animals, and other objects outside the cave are the real, timeless forms. The sun is the supreme form, the form of the good, that illuminates all of reality. This realm of forms is not known by observation. It is an intelligible world; that is, a world known by our capacity for abstract reasoning – for example, the capacity we use when doing algebra or drawing conclusions from some given premises.

A central feature of this allegory is that the unchanging forms are outside the cave, separated from the individuals we see, hear, touch, and so on inside the cave. The forms can exist even if they have no copies inside the cave.

The transcendence of form has some important practical consequences for Plato. Knowledge of these forms makes it difficult to live in the shadowy world of appearances. People who aim to know transcendent forms become bungling philosophers who have a difficult time managing their practical affairs. Socrates imagines what would happen if a person who has seen the world outside the cave returns to the cave:

> If such a one should go down again and take his old place in the cave would he not get his eyes full of darkness, thus suddenly coming out of the sunlight?
> He would indeed.
> Now if he should be required to contend with these perpetual prisoners in "evaluating" these shadows while his vision was still dim and before his eyes were accustomed to the dark – and the time required for habituation would not be very short – would he not provoke laughter, and would it not be said of him that he had returned from his journey aloft with his eyes ruined and that it was not worth while even to attempt the ascent? And if it were possible to lay hands on and to kill the man who tried to release them and lead them up, would then not kill him?
> They certainly would, he said.

So not only is the philosopher who comes to know the forms a fool in the eyes of the prisoners still tied to the cave, but if the philosopher tried to take them outside the cave, they would try to kill him, which is just what happened to Socrates.

Making reality distinct from the changing world of nature has grave consequences. For one thing, it denigrates the study of nature. Observing plants and animals, noting their differences – for example, differences in how they reproduce, grow, and die – is not a source of knowledge. Consequently, natural scientists are really just prisoners stuck in the cave, except that they see not only the shadows, but the figures and puppets that cast the shadows. Thus they are one step above artists and writers, who can only see shadows – that is, their own dreams and fantasies – but they are still stuck in the region of appearances.

Moreover, it alienated Socrates from his own body. For Socrates, death is liberation from the shackles of his body, which ties him to the ever-changing world of appearance. As long as he has a body, he is forced to struggle, he is forced to spend most of his time struggling with these pale and constantly changing imitations of reality.

It also denigrates practical politics. For Plato and Socrates, the day-to-day human affairs of political and civic life are not to be taken very seriously. These were only concerned with mere shadows of true justice, which should be the concern of anyone who has a thirst for true knowledge. The *Republic* is not an attempt to discuss a state that was workable, but an attempt to describe a utopia or ideal community – that is, the form of a good state – and actual states, when well organized, are still mere shadows or copies of this form. Only much later in his life, some years before he died, did Plato start taking practical affairs seriously in the *Laws*, a book devoted to the practical affairs of running a country.

Of course, the stance that practical life, particularly practical political action, is unimportant has consequences for how we act in the world. We will ignore opportunities to act politically – whether it is voting in elections or passing out leaflets at a demonstration – because that will be insignificant activity in the realm of appearances. Attempts to bring politics into philosophy or even science will appear to debase these pursuits, which should free us from the shackles of appearance. Perhaps this apolitical stance and diffidence towards practical political and civic affairs is the main difference that Plato's metaphysics can make to how we act in this world. Socrates is ready to die for his principles, but as he himself admits in the *Crito*, he did little to improve the laws of his city.

Reactions to Plato

Plato's metaphysics, particularly his solution to the Problem of Universals, is often called "Platonic realism." It is called "realism" in order to capture the fact that on this view, in addition to diverse individuals, there are forms or universals that individuals somehow share. So if a realist does an inventory of all there are in the world, the list will include not only a column for all the individuals that exist – Socrates, Crito, Plato, you and me, individual red things, and so on – but also Humanity, Redness, Justice, Equality, and so on. We can talk about these things with our language because we have proper names for individuals, e.g. "Socrates," "Crito," or "Plato," and predicates such as "is human," "is red," "is just," or "is equal" to refer to what individuals have in common.

It is called "Platonic" in order to capture the fact that universals on this view transcend individuals. They can exist without any individuals. There are other aspects of transcendence that are important to Plato, particularly that universals are real, while individuals are mere appearances, and that universals are better than individuals, since they are illuminated by the form of the good. But it is the claim that universals can exist apart from individuals that is seen as the root of Platonism and the key to transcendence.

It is this feature of Platonism that bothered Aristotle, one of Plato's students, the most. Aristotle rejected Plato's denigration of the study of nature and civic affairs. The work of the biologist observing the variety of life and practical political work are noble efforts, and not lowly concerns with mere shadows of reality. Aristotle himself was involved in practical political and scientific affairs as an advisor in the courts of Philip of Macedonia and Alexander the Great.

Aristotle takes appearances seriously not only in how he conducts his life, but in his metaphysics. Aristotle was a realist about universals: in addition to individuals there exist forms. But universals do not transcend individuals. Unlike Platonic forms, Aristotle's forms exist in individuals, and good observation, which includes the use of reason, can discern the forms that exist in individuals. For Aristotle, the forms are *immanent* in individuals, and thus Aristotle elevated nature and human affairs by bringing Plato's forms down to earth.

This solution to the problem of universals, about what individuals have in common, is often called "Aristotelian realism." It is a form of realism because it is committed to the existence of universals in addition to individuals, and it is Aristotelian because these universals are not transcendent but immanent in the world of appearances around us. Philosophers concerned with the practical affairs of science and politics often see Aristotle as a breath of fresh air after Plato's dark vision of practical life as a life imprisoned by lowly appearances.

Hobbes's Metaphysics

Another way of responding to Plato is not only to reject the Platonism of Platonic realism, as Aristotle did, but to reject the realism about universals as well. To reject realism about universals is to reject the claim that there are universals in addition to individuals, and to maintain that only individuals exist. This view developed in the late Middle Ages and it has been labeled "nominalism." We will see why this label is appropriate if we turn our attention to the other great political philosopher of Europe, Thomas Hobbes, who wove together a tapestry of nominalist metaphysics and politics no less powerful and influential than Plato's philosophy.

Nominalists cannot get away with just defending their view that there are only individuals and that Plato's and Aristotle's belief that there are universals in addition to individuals is false. Realism about universals is a solution to the problem of universals, and nominalists also need to offer a solution. Since they believe that only individuals exist, nominalists must explain how diverse individuals can have properties or relations in common without appealing to forms or any special objects like that.

The simple answer that Thomas Hobbes defended is that different objects have common properties in virtue of the fact that we use the same word or phrase to describe them. For example, on this view, the red delicious apple and the ripe strawberry are both red not because there is a universal Redness they have in common, but because the same word "red" applies to both of them. I can say "This apple and this strawberry are both red," and I am using one individual word, "red," to describe both objects. So for Hobbes it seemed that we do not need universals in addition to individuals to account for commonality. We can get by with individuals only: in this case the apple, the strawberry, and the word "red."

The basic idea of Hobbes's nominalism is that we can take a word or phrase, say "human being," and let it stand for many things. In this way, all these things come to be thought of as human beings, and that's what accounts for their commonality. For Hobbes, there is "nothing in the world universal but names," and this is why "nominalism" seemed like an appropriate name for this view. *Nomen* is the Latin word for names, and it is the root of the label "nominalism."

Of course, it is not quite right to suppose that names are the only things we use to talk or write about the world. Strictly speaking, "red" in the sentence "The strawberry is red" is not a name, but a predicate. We use predicates to describe individuals, and thus they are our best tools for classifying objects. Since predicates rather than names are typically used to describe individuals, Hobbes's version of nominalism is sometimes called "predicate nominalism," and we will use that term here.

Predicate nominalism about common properties, relations, and kinds has a very important consequence. Universals are human artifacts: commonality is a consequence of how we use language or other systems of symbols. Individuals come to be grouped together and thought of as sharing something on account of the same name or predicate that we use to discuss and think about them. This is a striking contrast to Plato's view that universals are objects that exist independently of how human beings think.

Definitions and Essences

This stark contrast can be seen very clearly if we consider Hobbes's view on definitions. The definition of a word determines what that word signifies; that is, what object or set of objects a person using that word has in mind. For instance, the definition of "triangle" as a closed three-sided figure determines that "triangle" signifies closed, three-sided figures. A consequence of this definition is that any closed, three-sided figure is a triangle and anything that is a triangle is a closed, three-sided figure. In other words, given this definition, a necessary and sufficient condition for being a triangle is that it is a closed, three-sided figure. The definition, then, expresses a set of features common to all triangles and that only triangles have.

Now, we can look at this definition in one of two ways. Aristotle believed that a definition is a phrase that signifies the set of properties that all and only triangles have, no matter how we define our terms and no matter what anyone thinks or says. The objects signified by the word "triangle" really do form a kind or type of object that would be distinguished from other objects independently of anything we do. Such a definition expresses what Plato and Socrates believed to be the form of a triangle, and what for Aristotle was the *essence* or *nature* of a triangle. An important feature of such a definition is that it is either true or false: either the definition correctly describes all the properties all and only triangles have or it does not. For example, if the definition states that all triangles are closed, three-sided figures made of straw, it would be false, because not all triangles are made of straw.

Socrates, Plato, and Aristotle all believed that knowledge begins with such definitions. They believed that to know something was to know its form, essence, or nature, and such knowledge was expressed with definitions. To know what justice is is to know the necessary and sufficient conditions for being just, to know what knowledge is is to know what the necessary and sufficient conditions for knowing something are, and so on.

Another way of looking at definitions is as a phrase that expresses properties that human beings have put together. For the sake of some interests, needs, or desires we have, we classify certain objects together and give them a name. A good example of this is the term "weed," which is defined as a plant that is not desired or cultivated by human beings and that grows profusely. This is not a natural species that would exist even if human beings had never decided to classify some plants as "weeds." Many human beings are interested in having a special category for plants they don't like and that grow abundantly, and they create that category with that name and definition. If human beings had not worried about weeds – for example, either they desired all plants or did not care to have a special category for plants they did not like – then there would not be any weeds.

Of course, there still would be the plants that we now call "weeds," e.g. dandelions and crabgrass, but they would not be weeds. Whether or not there are weeds depends on human beings classifying these plants as weeds. Weeds are not discovered by human beings, they are created by how human beings think, talk, and write about plants. A good label that philosophers have used for a set of properties that are put together by human beings in order to satisfy some of their needs, interests, or desires is "nominal essence." The reason for this name is that in these cases the essence is a product of the names and other labels we use to talk, write, and think about the world. This distinguishes it from a real essence, which exists no matter how human beings classify things.

Hobbes believed that all definitions were like the definition of "weed." There were no real essences: all essences were nominal and created by human beings. A consequence of this is that definitions are neither true nor false. So the test of a definition cannot be whether the definition describes how things really are, because in a real sense you can define words any way you please.

However, this does not mean that all definitions are equally good for Hobbes. Hobbes, like Aristotle and Plato, believed that science began with definitions. In fact, for Hobbes, science is just "knowledge of all the Consequences of names appertaining to the subject in hand." We start with certain definitions – for example, in geometry with definitions of "point," "line," "straight line," "surface," "plane surface," and so on – and, using our reason, particularly the principles of logic, we draw out the consequences from these definitions. In geometry, we call these consequences of definitions "theorems," and Hobbes believed that this term was appropriate for all subjects, not just geometry. In fact, he, along with many other seventeenth-century philosophers, thought geometry was the model for knowledge in all areas, including politics.

For Hobbes, the success of a science is measured by how well it allows human beings to navigate through and control the environment. Consider geometry again. First, we observe a certain individual figure. For Hobbes, this is something we do with our senses, and what we observe is always a particular individual. Then we classify and label this individual; say we try classifying it using our label "circle." Once we have done that, we can use our definition of "circle" and draw consequences from it. It follows from the definition of a circle that any straight line through the center of a circle will divide the circle into two equal parts. So if this observed individual figure is a circle, a straight line through its center will divide it into two equal parts.

This is a prediction and it allows us to exercise some control in our environment. For example, with it we can try to divide the observed object into equal halves. Perhaps, we are trying to divide a meadow, a loaf or a rosette window in a cathedral, and if we succeed, our definition and classification is successful. If our definitions and their consequences increase our ability to navigate through and control the environment, then we have good definitions, and the more control our definitions give us over the individual objects in our environment, the better they are.

Varieties of Nominalism

Although predicate nominalism is the most influential kind of nominalism, there are other important nominalist treatments of properties, relations and kinds.

Instead of trying to solve the problem of universals by relying on names and other linguistic items, some nominalists have thought that our ideas or concepts – what we have in mind, rather than what we say or write – explain universals. The basic idea is that concepts are individual things we have in mind, and we use them to classify diverse objects, and this view is usually called *conceptualism* or *concept nominalism*.

The nature of concept nominalism changes depending on what concepts are. Some philosophers, such as John Locke, thought that concepts were ideas we had in mind, and ideas were like images or pictures we have in mind. In much the same way that Hobbes thought we use an individual name to refer to diverse individual objects, Locke believed that we use an individual idea, say the idea of the color white, and use it to think about all individual instances of white. Other philosophers have thought that this is too simplistic, because not all concepts are like mental images or pictures. They believe that a concept can also be something like a rule or recipe we have in mind that allows us to pick out individual objects. For example, my concept of a chair might just be the rule that a chair is anything that is made for sitting and that I use for sitting. In this case, individuals are tied together by the rule we have in mind for classifying the world.

A subtle brand of nominalism is motivated by the recognition that it is difficult to do without the relation of similarity or resemblance. Even Hobbes sometimes writes that we use names to group objects together that have similar properties. So it seems that in order to account for universals, he cannot get by with only using individual objects and names, but also needs to talk about similarities between objects. Nominalists have sometimes made this explicit by maintaining that individual objects have the same property just in the case that they resemble each other, and a good label for this view is *resemblance nominalism*.

Unfortunately, resemblance nominalism may be too subtle unless it says something about what makes objects similar to each other. Typically, we say that two objects resemble each other because they have a property in common. A ripe strawberry and a red delicious apple resemble each other because they are both red. But resemblance nominalism maintains that they are both red because they resemble each other, not the other way around, and thus we need some account of the bases of these similarities and resemblances if not common properties.

Resorting to common properties would beg the question at hand, namely: what are common properties?

The Austrian philosopher Ludwig Wittgenstein, who was a resemblance nominalist, introduced an idea that many have thought is very useful here: form of life. For Wittgenstein, our individual lives and experiences are tied to our social lives, and our social lives are made up of a variety of features that are difficult to pin down exactly, but they include: various social practices and institutions (such as marriage, schooling, organized sports competitions, elections, and so forth), our interests, needs, and desires (for example, the need to identify edible plants as well as our interest in forming dependable social relations), and the language we have for communicating, engaging in our practices and participating in our institutions (for example, the fact that we have a word that allows us to make promises). All these help to constitute our form of life, and it is this form of life that is the basis of the resemblances. So it is not just language or what we have in mind that classifies the world and accounts for common properties, but our form of life, which includes language and what we have in mind, as well as the activities that sustain our social customs and institutions.

Although there are very important and interesting differences between predicate, concept, and resemblance nominalism, they are all unified by two beliefs: that all there is are individuals and that common properties – universals – are artifacts of what we do: our language, our thinking, or our whole form of life.

Hobbes's Political Philosophy

Like Plato, Hobbes used his nominalism in his political philosophy. While Socrates and Plato aimed to discover the essence of justice as if they were looking for a new star or galaxy, Hobbes tells us how justice is made. For Hobbes, justice is the product of human agreement. Because "the life of man is solitary, poore, nasty, brutish and short," human beings come together and make a pact, contract, or covenant in which they agree to abide by a certain set of rules. This contract defines justice for these people. Without such an agreement, there is no justice and injustice for these people. If they act according to the rules and provisions of their contract, they are just, and if they don't, they are unjust.

People who are not a party to the contract are not bound by it, and they are free to pursue their own individual interest, which for Hobbes means self-preservation. Individuals by nature aim to preserve their own lives, and that is one of the reasons why Hobbes thought individuals without a contract that creates law and order are in a state of war with each other. It is the state of war that makes life without a contract "solitary, poore, nasty, brutish and short," and people attempt to escape it by agreeing to give up the pursuit of self-interest and submit to a set of laws.

Because for Hobbes community is something that is created and naturally people are solitary and only self-interested, Hobbes is often thought of as a social and political individualist. This individualism complements Hobbes's nominalism. If we apply to human beings Hobbes's nominalist view that only individuals are real and commonalities are created by our language, we get the view that there is no real common humanity apart from what we construct with our language. This kind of individualism comes in many variations. An extreme version of it was developed by the Danish philosopher Søren Kierkegaard and existentialist philosophers such as Jean-Paul Sartre. For these philosophers, there is no universal human condition except our complete individuality and uniqueness. We are radically alone in the world, and society and its values are artificial impositions on our individuality.

Hobbes too believes that society, particularly society's standards of justice, are imposed on our individuality. In fact, Hobbes goes so far as to say that we need an absolute sovereign or ruler in order to make society and have justice. He believes that "before the names of Just and Unjust can have a place, there must be some coercive Power, to compel men equally to the performance of their Covenants." For Hobbes, without the "terror of some power" people will not keep to their agreements, because "covenants, without the sword, are but words." People will fall back into their natural state of pursuing their own individual self-interest, and consequently back into a state of war.

Given Hobbes's nominalism about justice, it is easy to see why he thinks we need a sovereign. If justice is a human artifact, there needs to be a power that makes it. Words by themselves are not enough to order the world or the way we think about it. Either we actually need to organize the world in such a way that it makes sense to use the labels we have, or we need some other reason for using the labels. Imagine trying to agree to use the made-up word "smunters" to refer to people that are shorter than five feet or taller than six feet. We would need some reason for classifying people in this odd way.

One thing people could do is to impose this way of classifying people and require that all such people live in special areas or that they are not able to fulfill some important task in society, perhaps by making all clothes, furniture, buildings, and modes of transportation fit only people who are between five and six feet. Another thing we could do is enforce this terminology with some system of rewards and punishments – for instance, people who fail to use this terminology pay fines or do not pass examinations. There could also be more subtle rewards and punishments: perhaps people have a need for scapegoats, and this terminology allows them to fulfill this need.

In all these examples, and you can think of others, human beings need to exercise some power to make sure that there is a reason or motivation people have for classifying the world in that way. Hobbes's sovereign is the power that ensures people have a reason to conform with the laws of the contract, and create justice.

Nominalism and Gender

A contemporary political debate where nominalism has had an important influence is about our gender distinctions; that is, how we classify and distinguish between women and men. While Platonic and Aristotelian realists might argue that being a man and being a woman are real universals shared by all men and women, respectively, nominalists might argue that these categories are only made by how we think, talk or write about people.

Of course, political debates are much messier than metaphysical ones. Sometimes people who are nominalists about gender rest their case on the broader metaphysical position that treats all common properties as human artifacts made by how we think. However, it is also not unusual to find people who think that gender should be treated nominally, although other distinctions should not. For example, someone might not unreasonably argue that although the biological distinction between male and female is real and males and females have real biological essences, our gender distinctions rest on nominal essences. They might argue that for some societies the property of being a woman, for instance, might include the biological property of being female, but also include other properties and relations, such as being emotional, nurturing, weaker and kinder, and more subjective than men, and so on, and this package of properties is a human artifact.

It must be pointed out that nominalists about gender are not necessarily politically liberal, progressive, or radical. A nominalist can argue that the properties of gender are artifacts, but good ones that should be maintained because that kind of classification has good consequences – for example, it increases our abilities to make predictions and in general it increases the power we have over the environment. On the other hand, a nominalist could also argue that this is a poor distinction, because it does not have much predictive success, and insofar as it has such success, it is because individuals have been made to conform to this classification. It is as if you were to take a child and have everyone call him or her "stupid" anytime the child tries to do something new. Eventually he or she will conform to this classification and then will be made stupid.

By the same token, realists about universals need not be conservative about our gender distinctions. For example, a Platonist or Aristotelian could argue the there simply is no universal form of manhood or womanhood. We speak that way and think that way, but this is an error, perhaps one of the shadows in Plato's cave that is not a copy of anything in the real world outside.

Notice, however, that whether they are conservative or not, what will tie nominalists about gender together is how they argue about this distinction. They will not argue about whether there really is a distinction between men and women, but about how useful a tool it is to classify people in that way. In the same way, realists about this distinction are ultimately concerned about whether there really is such a distinction in nature apart from how we think, talk, or write about these issues. Of course, how well we can make predictions using gender classification can be very relevant for a realist, but it will be relevant evidence for showing that there really is such a difference in nature. For a nominalist, on the other hand, it will be relevant only for the practical question of whether or not we should continue using that system of classification.

Who Is Right?

How do we decide between these competing solutions to the problem of universals? Evaluating metaphysical views is a bit difficult, because this is not the sort of issue we could try to resolve with empirical observations and experiments. But there are two important ways in which we can try to evaluate metaphysical views. One way is to try to see how well these accounts fit or cohere with other areas of human knowledge and activity, particularly areas that we think are secure and about which we are quite confident. We can call this the *coherence test*. The other method is to see how well the view solves the problems or puzzles it sets out to solve: does it solve the problem, and does it solve the problem neatly and consistently? We can call this *eureka test*, in honor of the feeling you get when you have solved a problem.

Both nominalism and realism have some difficulties with the coherence test. Let us consider realism first. Realism about universals contends that in addition to individuals there are universals. So, for example, in addition to all individual human beings there is the form of humanity. Now, experience does not seem to reveal such objects to us. We only experience individuals and not real universals. All the objects we experience, it seems, cannot be in two different places at the very same time, and this seems to be a hallmark of individuality. Platonic and Aristotelian forms do not have this property. Your red delicious apple and my ripe strawberry are in different places, but they are both red, and so on the realists' account they share one form: redness. This means that redness is in two different places at the very same time.

Now, it is true that contemporary physics is full of very odd events. For example, according to Einstein's special theory of relativity, two events that occur at the same time for one person can occur at different times for another observer. Moreover, the order in which events occur can be reversed for different observers. While for one observer, event A comes before event B, it is physically possible that for another observer, B comes before A. However, these results of the special theory of relativity are tied to very specific and extraordinary observations made under very controlled circumstances, in this case the observations of a famous experiment first conducted by the British physicists Michelson and Morley. Metaphysical theories are not tied to particular experiments, but to ordinary observations, in this case that distinct objects share properties and relations and are of the same kind. So if a metaphysical theory postulates extraordinary objects or events to explain these ordinary observations, we must be very sure that we have good reasons for accepting this theory.

One good reason would be that it is the best explanation – perhaps the best one by default because it is the only one. However, we know that realism about universals has a competitor. So let us turn to nominalism, and see how well it passes the coherence test.

Nominalism also has some problems passing this test. Nominalism does not cohere very well with some assumptions we make when we rely on common properties and relations in our explanations and arguments. For example, suppose you argue that a certain person and what he did were unjust. It seems that there is something about the person and his action that makes them unjust, and at least worthy of reproach if not more. However, typically for nominalism it is not something about the person or action that makes them unjust, but how we think, talk, or write about them. Thus we would have to say that, in the final analysis, they are unjust because we call them "unjust" or because we think of them as "unjust," not because they are unjust regardless of how human beings happen to classify them.

This problem infects nominalism not just in the social and political domain. Consider the explanation that flowers' bright colors attract insects. If nominalism is right, then flowers have the common properties they have, including the colors they have, on account of how we classify them. But notice that this implies that flowers attract insects because of how we classify them. That is surely an implication that is at odds with how we think this explanation works. It is something about the flowers' colors that attracts insects, apart from how we think, talk, or write about flowers.

So perhaps nominalism and realism about universals are tied with respect to the coherence test. Realism postulates strange objects and nominalism cannot make sense of our explanations. Let us turn to the eureka test to see how the theories fare on this test.

Realism has a very straightforward solution: there are common properties, and that's why an apple and a strawberry can both be red, and why distinct individuals can both be just. Does it leave anything unexplained that it should explain? To pass the eureka test, a solution to the problem of universals must solve it for all diverse objects that have common features.

Plato himself had some concerns in the *Parmenides* that the theory of forms does not pass this test. In a famous argument often called *the third man argument*, Plato worries about the forms themselves. Can the theory of forms explain the common properties of diverse forms? This is an important kind of question that is the hallmark of good philosophy and the pitfall of many theories. Good philosophy always tries to make sure it satisfies the standards that it sets for others. Plato thought that the theory of forms might lead to what is called an "infinite regress." If there are many forms, they will have something in common. For example, they will all be forms, and the forms redness and blueness will both be colors, and so on. So it seems that for any two forms that have something in common there will be another form, and consequently there will be an infinite number of forms.

Is this a problem? This is difficult to decide. Infinity in and of itself is not a problem. The set of natural numbers is infinitely large, the set of grammatically correct English sentences is infinitely large, so why not an infinite number of forms? Moreover, it is not even clear that we need an infinite number of forms. It is true that for any two human beings there is at least one other pair of parents. Human beings cannot be their own parents! But this does not mean that there is an infinite number of human beings or parents. So perhaps in the same way, any two forms will have another form, but that does not mean that there is an infinite number of forms.

These issues deserve more detailed attention, but for now perhaps we can tentatively conclude that realism about universals passes the eureka test. Whatever unease we feel about the realist solution to the problem of universals is probably due to its poor performance on the coherence test: forms just are strange objects. What about nominalism? Nominalism tries to get by with more ordinary things, but does it pass the eureka test?

Nominalism suffers from two problems. The first one is that it seems that nominalism cannot explain all commonalities. You probably noticed that every nominalist theory works with some relation or another. Resemblance nominalism supposes that there is a relation of similarity that different objects share: all red objects are individuals that are similar to each other. Hobbes's nominalism supposes that individual objects are related to the individual names, words, or labels that unify them – for instance, all red objects are individuals that satisfy the predicate "is red." Concept nominalism supposes there is a relation between individuals and concepts or ideas we have in mind: all red objects fall under the concept red we have in mind. So in order to explain common properties, relations, and kinds, nominalism relies on something it is trying to explain: the relations of resemblance, satisfaction, or falling under.

If nominalism is to be successful, it needs to explain these relations in a nominalistic way, but can it do that? This seems difficult. Consider the relation that holds between predicates and objects: satisfaction. This is a relation that many objects and predicates share: apples satisfy the predicate "is an apple," while red objects satisfy the predicate "is red." Predicate nominalism would have to explain this common relation as follows: this relation that holds between all predicates and their objects obtains because there is a term – "satisfy" – that we can use to state things like "Red apples satisfy the predicate 'is red'," "Apples satisfy the predicate 'is an apple'," and so on. So in order for there to be relation of satisfaction, there has to be a term for it: "satisfy" and its cognates, such as "satisfies," "is satisfied," and so on. But the term "satisfy" itself needs to be satisfied, and this leads us into what looks like a vicious circle.

In order for there to be common properties, relations, and kinds, there need to be, according to the predicate nominalist, predicates and a special relation: satisfaction. But in order for there to be satisfaction, there needs to be a predicate – "satisfies" – that is satisfied. Without the relation of satisfaction, predicates cannot make common properties, relations, and kinds, but if predicates cannot make common properties, relations, and kinds, then (if the predicate nominalist is right) there can be no relation of satisfaction, and so the predicate nominalist program cannot get off the ground, and it seems that analogous arguments can be directed against the other forms of nominalism.

Unfortunately, vicious circles are not always easy to see, and not everyone will find such arguments convincing. Perhaps you can find a way to show that the circle is not vicious or that what looks like a circle is not a circle. For this reason, although this first problem raises important questions about the adequacy of nominalism, it is not a fatal problem. Perhaps there are ways around it.

The second problem, however, seems fatal. These solutions to the problem of universals make common properties depend on what people think, speak, or write, or generally how they live, and this seems wrong. Whales would be mammals, ripe strawberries would be red, and Earth would be closer to the Sun than Jupiter even if there were no predicates, concepts, or a form of life for human beings. Now, perhaps this is a mistake and there are some good arguments to show that properties, kinds, and relations do depend on there being thinkers, speakers, and writers who use predicates and concepts, but surely those arguments would have to be very strong and convincing to trump such a fundamental and initially very reasonable belief that if there were no human beings, there still could be whales, planets, and many other things. We will consider such arguments in the next chapter, but until we see some arguments for the view that properties, relations, and kinds are human artifacts, we should stick with what initially seems reasonable to believe. The task of philosophy is not to seek unusual and shocking beliefs, but to search for rational beliefs.

Conclusion

We have concluded that the realist solution to the problem of universals has an edge over nominalism: it passes the eureka test while nominalism does not. This conclusion is open to debate and subject to error. Philosophical conclusions are fallible. Our arguments could be faulty: perhaps our premises are false or our inferences are not valid.

But if we do find that realism about common properties is true, then we should be committed to the practical consequences of this conclusion. For one thing, if justice is a real property, we will have to appreciate Socrates' decision based on the proposition that there is a distinction between justice and the common political practices of his society. The individual decisions of the Athenian courts do not define justice. Justice is not just a function of what people call "just" or agree to consider just. People can make unjust agreements and call things "just" that really are not just. Whole societies can be unjust, and recognizing when this is the case and acting appropriately according to that knowledge is a difficult but noble task.

Moreover, if realism is right, then the human condition as it has come to be understood by many philosophers, writers, artists, and even musicians, namely that we are solitary individuals, radically alone with nothing really in common with others, is false. We share properties with others, especially our humanity. Of course, what humanity is and whether there is something noble about it or not is a difficult question, but visions of our common humanity have played and continue to play an important role in how we organize our social and political lives.

Crito
Plato

Plato (427–347 BCE), the great Athenian philosopher, wrote a series of dialogues that feature Socrates, his teacher, as the protagonist. In his dialogues, Plato raises fundamental philosophical issues that have been the focus of philosophical study to this day, and some philosophers have maintained that all of philosophy is just a footnote to Plato. In *Crito* we encounter Socrates after he has been sentenced to death, and his friend Crito offers to help him escape. The discussion quickly turns to whether or not it is right to escape when one has been sentenced unjustly. Socrates argues that it isn't right; when we are wronged we shouldn't do wrong in return.

SOCRATES: Why have you come so early, Crito? Or is it not still early?

CRITO: It certainly is.

SOCRATES: How early?

CRITO: Early dawn.

SOCRATES: I am surprised that the warder was willing to listen to you.

CRITO: He is quite friendly to me by now, Socrates. I have been here often and I have given him something.

SOCRATES: Have you just come, or have you been here for some time?

CRITO: A fair time.

SOCRATES: Then why did you not wake me right away but sit there in silence?

CRITO: By Zeus no, Socrates. I would not myself want to be in distress and awake so long. I have been surprised to see you so peacefully asleep. It was on purpose that I did not wake you, so that you should spend your time most agreeably. Often in the past throughout my life, I have considered the way you live happy, and especially so now that you bear your present misfortune so easily and lightly.

SOCRATES: It would not be fitting at my age to resent the fact that I must die now.

CRITO: Other men of your age are caught in such misfortunes, but their age does not prevent them resenting their fate.

SOCRATES: That is so. Why have you come so early?

CRITO: I bring bad news, Socrates, not for you, apparently, but for me and all your friends the news is bad and hard to bear. Indeed, I would count it among the hardest.

SOCRATES: What is it? Or has the ship arrived from Delos, at the arrival of which I must die?

CRITO: It has not arrived yet, but it will, I believe, arrive today, according to a message brought by some men from Sunium, where they left it. This makes it obvious that it will come today, and that your life must end tomorrow.

SOCRATES: May it be for the best. If it so please the gods, so be it. However, I do not think it will arrive today.

CRITO: What indication have you of this?

SOCRATES: I will tell you. I must die the day after the ship arrives.

CRITO: That is what those in authority say.

SOCRATES: Then I do not think it will arrive on this coming day, but on the next. I take to witness of this a dream I had a little earlier during this night. It looks as if it was the right time for you not to wake me.

CRITO: What was your dream?

SOCRATES: I thought that a beautiful and comely woman dressed in white approached me. She called me and said: "Socrates, may you arrive at fertile Phthia[1] on the third day."

CRITO: A strange dream, Socrates.

SOCRATES: But it seems clear enough to me, Crito.

CRITO: Too clear it seems, my dear Socrates, but listen to me even now and be saved. If you die, it will not be a single misfortune for me. Not only will I be deprived of a friend, the like of whom I shall never find again, but many people who do not know you or me very well will think that I could have saved you if I were willing to spend money, but that I did not care to do so. Surely there can be no worse reputation than to be thought to value money more highly than one's friends, for the majority will not believe that you yourself were not willing to leave prison while we were eager for you to do so.

SOCRATES: My good Crito, why should we care so much for what the majority think? The most reasonable people, to whom one should pay more attention, will believe that things were done as they were done.

CRITO: You see, Socrates, that one must also pay attention to the opinion of the majority. Your present situation makes clear that the majority can inflict not the least but pretty well the greatest evils if one is slandered among them.

SOCRATES: Would that the majority could inflict the greatest evils, for they would then be capable of the greatest good, and that would be fine, but now they cannot do either. They cannot make a man either wise or foolish, but they inflict things haphazardly.

CRITO: That may be so. But tell me this, Socrates, are you anticipating that I and your other friends would have trouble with the informers if you escape from here, as having stolen you away, and that we should be compelled to lose all our property or pay heavy fines and suffer other punishment besides? If you have any such fear, forget it. We would be justified in running this risk to save you, and worse, if necessary. Do follow my advice, and do not act differently.

SOCRATES: I do have these things in mind, Crito, and also many others.

CRITO: Have no such fear. It is not much money that some people require to save you and get you out of here. Further, do you not see that those informers are cheap, and that not much money would be needed to deal with them? My money is available and is, I think, sufficient. If, because of your affection for me, you feel you should not spend any of mine, there are those strangers here ready to spend money. One of them, Simmias the Theban, has brought enough for this very purpose. Cebes, too, and a good many others. So, as I say, do not let this fear make you hesitate to save yourself, nor let what you said in court trouble you, that you would not know what to do with yourself if you left Athens, for you would be welcomed in many places to which you might go. If you want to go to Thessaly, I have friends there who will greatly appreciate you and keep you safe, so that no one in Thessaly will harm you.

Besides, Socrates, I do not think that what you are doing is right, to give up your life when you can save it, and to hasten your fate as your enemies would hasten it, and indeed have hastened it in their wish to destroy you. Moreover, I think you are betraying your sons by going away and leaving them, when you could bring them up and educate them. You thus show no concern for what their fate may be. They will probably have the usual fate of orphans. Either one should not have children, or one should share with them to the end the toil of upbringing and education. You seem to me to choose the easiest path, whereas one should choose the path a good and courageous man would choose, particularly when one claims throughout one's life to care for virtue.

I feel ashamed on your behalf and on behalf of us, your friends, lest all that has happened to you be thought due to cowardice on our part: the fact that your trial came to court when it need not have done so, the handling of the trial itself, and now this absurd ending which will be thought to have got beyond our control through some cowardice and unmanliness on our part, since we did not save you, or you save yourself, when it was possible and could be done if we had been of the slightest use. Consider, Socrates, whether this is not only evil but shameful, both for you and for us. Take counsel with yourself, or rather the time for counsel is past and the decision should have been taken, and there is no further opportunity, for this whole business must be ended tonight. If we delay now, then it will no longer be possible, it will be too late. Let me persuade you on every count, Socrates, and do not act otherwise.

SOCRATES: My dear Crito, your eagerness is worth much if it should have some right aim; if not, then the greater your keenness the more difficult it is to deal with. We must therefore examine whether we should act in this way or not, as not only now but at all times I am the kind of man who listens only to the argument that on reflection seems best to me. I cannot, now that this fate has come upon me, discard the arguments I used; they seem to me much the same. I value and respect the same principles as before, and if we have no better arguments to bring up at this moment, be sure that I shall not agree with you, not even if the power of the majority were to frighten us with more bogeys, as if we were children, with threats of incarcerations and executions and confiscation of property. How should we examine this matter most reasonably? Would it be by taking up first your argument about the opinions of men, whether it is sound in every case that one should pay attention to some opinions, but not to others? Or was that well-spoken before the necessity to die came upon me, but now it is clear that this was said in vain for the sake of argument, that it was in truth play and nonsense? I am eager to examine together with you, Crito, whether this argument will appear in any way different to me in my present circumstances, or whether it remains the same, whether we are to abandon it or believe it. It was said on every occasion by those who thought they were speaking sensibly, as I have just now been speaking, that one should greatly value some people's opinions, but not others. Does that seem to you a sound statement?

You, as far as a human being can tell, are exempt from the likelihood of dying tomorrow, so the present misfortune is not likely to lead you astray. Consider then, do you not think it a sound statement that one must not value all the opinions of men, but some and not others, nor the opinions of all men, but those of some and not of others? What do you say? Is this not well said?

CRITO: It is.

SOCRATES: One should value the good opinions, and not the bad ones?

CRITO: Yes.

SOCRATES: The good opinions are those of wise men, the bad ones those of foolish men?

CRITO: Of course.

SOCRATES: Come then, what of statements such as this: Should a man professionally engaged in physical training pay attention to the praise and blame and opinion of any man, or to those of one man only, namely a doctor or trainer?

CRITO: To those of one only.

SOCRATES: He should therefore fear the blame and welcome the praise of that one man, and not those of the many?

CRITO: Obviously.

SOCRATES: He must then act and exercise, eat and drink in the way the one, the trainer and the one who knows, thinks right, not all the others?

CRITO: That is so.

SOCRATES: Very well. And if he disobeys the one, disregards his opinion and his praises while valuing those of the many who have no knowledge, will he not suffer harm?

CRITO: Of course.

SOCRATES: What is that harm, where does it tend, and what part of the man who disobeys does it affect?

CRITO: Obviously the harm is to his body, which it ruins.

SOCRATES: Well said. So with other matters, not to enumerate them all, and certainly with actions just and unjust, shameful and beautiful, good and bad, about which we are now deliberating, should we follow the opinion of the many and fear it, or that of the one, if there is one who has knowledge of these things and before whom we feel fear and shame more than before all the others. If we do not follow his directions, we shall harm and corrupt that part of ourselves that is improved by just actions and destroyed by unjust actions. Or is there nothing in this?

CRITO: I think there certainly is, Socrates.

SOCRATES: Come now, if we ruin that which is improved by health and corrupted by disease by not following the opinions of those who know, is life worth living for us when that is ruined? And that is the body, is it not?

CRITO: Yes.

SOCRATES: And is life worth living with a body that is corrupted and in bad condition?

CRITO: In no way.

SOCRATES: And is life worth living for us with that part of us corrupted that unjust action harms and just action benefits? Or do we think that part of us, whatever it is, that is concerned with justice and injustice, is inferior to the body?

CRITO: Not at all.

SOCRATES: It is more valuable?

CRITO: Much more.

SOCRATES: We should not then think so much of what the majority will say about us, but what he will say who understands justice and injustice, the one, that is, and the truth itself. So that, in the first place, you were wrong to believe that we should care for the opinion of the many about what is just, beautiful, good, and their opposites. "But," someone might say "the many are able to put us to death."

CRITO: That too is obvious, Socrates, and someone might well say so.

SOCRATES: And, my admirable friend, that argument that we have gone through remains, I think, as before. Examine the following statement in turn as to whether it stays the same or not, that the most important thing is not life, but the good life.

CRITO: It stays the same.

SOCRATES: And that the good life, the beautiful life, and the just life are the same; does that still hold, or not?

CRITO: It does hold.

SOCRATES: As we have agreed so far, we must examine next whether it is right for me to try to get out of here when the Athenians have not acquitted me. If it is seen to be right, we will try to do so; if it is not, we will abandon the idea. As for those questions you raise about money, reputation, the upbringing of children, Crito, those considerations in truth belong to those people who easily put men to death and would bring them to life again if they could, without thinking; I mean the majority of men. For us, however, since our argument leads to this, the only valid consideration, as we were saying just now, is whether we should be acting rightly in giving money and gratitude to those who will lead me out of here, and ourselves helping with the escape, or whether in truth we shall do wrong in doing all this. If it appears that we shall be acting unjustly, then we have no need at all to take into account whether we shall have to die if we stay here and keep quiet, or suffer in another way, rather than do wrong.

CRITO: I think you put that beautifully, Socrates, but see what we should do.

SOCRATES: Let us examine the question together, my dear friend, and if you can make any objection while I am speaking, make it and I will listen to you, but if you have no objection to make, my dear Crito, then stop now from saying the same thing so often, that I must leave here against the will of the Athenians. I think it important to persuade you before I act, and not to act against your wishes. See whether the start of our enquiry is adequately stated, and try to answer what I ask you in the way you think best.

CRITO: I shall try.

SOCRATES: Do we say that one must never in any way do wrong willingly, or must one do wrong in one way and not in another? Is to do wrong never good or admirable, as we have agreed in the past, or have all these former agreements been washed out during the last few days? Have we at our age failed to notice for some time that in our serious discussions we were no different from children? Above all, is the truth such as we used to say it was, whether the majority agree or not, and whether we must still suffer worse things than we do now, or will be treated more gently, that nonetheless, wrongdoing is in every way harmful and shameful to the wrongdoer? Do we say so or not?

CRITO: We do.

SOCRATES: So one must never do wrong.

CRITO: Certainly not.

SOCRATES: Nor must one, when wronged, inflict wrong in return, as the majority believe, since one must never do wrong.

CRITO: That seems to be the case.

SOCRATES: Come now, should one injure anyone or not, Crito?

CRITO: One must never do so.

SOCRATES: Well then, if one is oneself injured, is it right, as the majority say, to inflict an injury in return, or is it not?

CRITO: It is never right.

SOCRATES: Injuring people is no different from wrongdoing.

CRITO: That is true.

SOCRATES: One should never do wrong in return, nor injure any man, whatever injury one has suffered at his hands. And Crito, see that you do not agree to this, contrary to your belief. For I know that only a few people hold this view or will hold it, and there is no common ground between those who hold this view and those who do not, but they inevitably despise each other's views. So then consider very carefully whether we have this view in common, and whether you agree, and let this be the basis of our deliberation, that neither to do wrong nor to return a wrong is ever right, not even to injure in return for an injury received. Or do you disagree and do not share this view as a basis for discussion? I have held it for a long time and still hold it now, but if you think otherwise, tell me now. If, however, you stick to our former opinion, then listen to the next point.

CRITO: I stick to it and agree with you. So say on.

SOCRATES: Then I state the next point, or rather I ask you: when one has come to an agreement that is just with someone, should one fulfill it or cheat on it?

CRITO: One should fulfill it.

SOCRATES: See what follows from this: if we leave here without the city's permission, are we injuring people whom we should least injure? And are we sticking to a just agreement, or not?

CRITO: I cannot answer your question, Socrates. I do not know.

SOCRATES: Look at it this way. If, as we were planning to run away from here, or whatever one should call it, the laws and the state came and confronted us and asked: "Tell me, Socrates, what are you intending to do? Do you not by this action you are attempting intend to destroy us, the laws, and indeed the whole city, as far as you are concerned? Or do you think it possible for a city not to be destroyed if the verdicts of its courts have no force but are nullified and set at naught by private individuals?" What shall we answer to this and other such arguments? For many things could be said, especially by an orator on behalf of this law we are destroying, which orders that the judgments of the courts shall be carried out. Shall we say in answer, "The city wronged me, and its decision was not right." Shall we say that, or what?

CRITO: Yes, by Zeus, Socrates, that is our answer

SOCRATES: Then what if the laws said: "Was that the agreement between us, Socrates, or was it to respect the judgments that the city came to?" And if we wondered at their words, they would perhaps add: "Socrates, do not wonder at what we say but answer, since you are accustomed to proceed by question and answer. Come now, what accusation do you bring against us and the city, that you should try to destroy us? Did we not, first, bring you to birth, and was it not through us that your father married your mother and begat you? Tell us, do you find anything to criticize in those of us who are concerned with marriage?" And I would say that I do not criticize them. "Or in those of us concerned with the nurture of babies and the education that you too received?

Were those assigned to that subject not right to instruct your father to educate you in the arts and in physical culture?" And I would say that they were right. "Very well," they would continue, "and after you were born and nurtured and educated, could you, in the first place, deny that you are our offspring and servant, both you and your forefathers? If that is so do you think that we are on an equal footing as regards the right, and that whatever we do to you it is right for you to do to us? You were not on an equal footing with your father as regards the right, nor with your master if you had one, so as to retaliate for anything they did to you, to revile them if they reviled you, to beat them if they beat you, and so with many other things. Do you think you have this right to retaliation against your country and its laws? That if we undertake to destroy you and think it right to do so, you can undertake to destroy us, as far as you can, in return? And will you say that you are right to do so, you who truly care for virtue? Is your wisdom such as not to realize that your country is to be honored more than your mother, your father and all your ancestors, that it is more to be revered and more sacred, and that it counts for more among the gods and sensible men, that you must worship it, yield to it and placate its anger more than your father's? You must either persuade it or obey its orders, and endure in silence whatever it instructs you to endure, whether blows or bonds, and if it leads you into war to be wounded or killed, you must obey. To do so is right, and one must not give way or retreat or leave one's post, but both in war and in courts and everywhere else, one must obey the commands of one's city and country, or persuade it as to the nature of justice. It is impious to bring violence to bear against your mother or father, it is much more so to use it against your country." What shall we say in reply, Crito, that the laws speak the truth, or not?

CRITO: I think they do.

SOCRATES: "Reflect now, Socrates," the laws might say, "that if what we say is true, you are not treating us rightly by planning to do what you are planning. We have given you birth, nurtured you, educated you, we have given you and all other citizens a share of all the good things we could. Even so, by giving every Athenian the opportunity, after he has reached manhood and observed the affairs of the city and us the laws, we proclaim that if we do not please him, he can take his possessions and go wherever he pleases. Not one of our laws raises any obstacle or forbids him, if he is not satisfied with us or the city, if one of you wants to go and live in a colony or wants to go anywhere else, and keep his property. We say, however, that whoever of you remains, when he sees how we conduct our trials and manage the city in other ways, has in fact come to an agreement with us to obey our instructions. We say that the one who disobeys does wrong in three ways, first because in us he disobeys his parents, also those who brought him up, and because in spite of his agreement, he neither obeys us nor, if we do something wrong, does he try to persuade us to do better. Yet we only propose things, we do not issue savage commands to do whatever we order; we give two alternatives, either to persuade us or to do what we say. He does neither. We do say that you too, Socrates, are open to those charges if you do what you have in mind; you would be among, not the least, but the most guilty of the Athenians." And if I should say "Why so?" they might well be right to upbraid me and say that I am among the Athenians who most definitely came to that agreement with them. They might well say: "Socrates, we have convincing proofs that we and the city were congenial to you. You would not have dwelt here most consistently of all the Athenians if the city had not been exceedingly pleasing to you. You have never left the city, even to see a festival, nor for any other reason except military service, you have never gone to stay in any other city, as people do; you have had no desire to know another city or other laws; we and our city satisfied you. So decisively did you choose us and agree to be a citizen under us. Also, you have had children in this city, thus showing that it was congenial to you. Then at your trial you could have assessed your penalty at exile if you wished, and you are now attempting to do against the City's wishes what you could then have done with her consent. Then you prided yourself that you did not resent death, but you chose, as you said, death in preference to exile. Now, however, those words do not make you ashamed, and you pay no heed to us, the laws, as you plan to destroy us, and you act like the meanest type of slave by trying to run away, contrary to your under-takings and your agreement to live as a citizen under us. First then, answer us on this very point, whether we speak the truth when we say that you agreed, not only in words but by your deeds, to live in accordance with us." What are we to say to that, Crito? Must we not agree?

CRITO: We must, Socrates.

SOCRATES: "Surely," they might say, "you are breaking the undertakings and agreements that you made with us without compulsion or deceit, and under no pressure of time for deliberation. You have had seventy years during which you could have gone away if you did not like us, and if you thought our agreements unjust. You did not choose to go to Sparta or to Crete, which you are always saying are well governed, nor to any other city, Greek or foreign. You have been away from Athens less than the lame or the blind or other handicapped people. It is clear that the city has been outstandingly more congenial to you than to other Athenians, and so have we, the laws, for what city can please without laws? Will you then not now stick to our agreements? You will, Socrates, if we can persuade you, and not make yourself a laughing stock by leaving the city.

"For consider what good you will do yourself or your friends by breaking our agreements and committing such a wrong? It is pretty obvious that your friends will themselves be in danger of exile, disenfranchisement and loss of property. As for yourself, if you go to one of the nearby cities – Thebes or Megara, both are well governed – you will arrive as an enemy to their government; all who care for their city will look on you with suspicion, as a destroyer of the laws. You will also strengthen the conviction of the jury that they passed the right sentence on you, for anyone who destroys the laws could easily be thought to corrupt the young and the ignorant. Or will you avoid cities that are well governed and men who are civilized? If you do this, will your life be worth living? Will you have social intercourse with them and not be ashamed to talk to them? And what will you say? The same as you did here, that virtue and justice are man's most precious possession, along with lawful behavior and the laws? Do you not think that Socrates would appear to be an unseemly kind of person? One must think so. Or will you leave those places and go to Crito's friends in Thessaly? There you will find the greatest license and disorder, and they may enjoy hearing from you how absurdly you escaped from prison in some disguise, in a leather jerkin or some other things in which escapees wrap themselves, thus altering your appearance. Will there be no one to say that you, likely to live but a short time more, were so greedy for life that you transgressed the most important laws? Possibly, Socrates, if you do not annoy anyone, but if you do, many disgraceful things will be said about you.

"You will spend your time ingratiating yourself with all men, and be at their beck and call. What will you do in Thessaly but feast, as if you had gone to a banquet in Thessaly? As for those conversations of yours about justice and the rest of virtue, where will they be? You say you want to live for the sake of your children, that you may bring them up and educate them. How so? Will you bring them up and educate them by taking them to Thessaly and making strangers of them, that they may enjoy that too? Or not so, but they will be better brought up and educated here, while you are alive, though absent? Yes, your friends will look after them. Will they look after them if you go and live in Thessaly, but not if you go away to the underworld? If those who profess themselves your friends are any good at all, one must assume that they will.

"Be persuaded by us who have brought you up, Socrates. Do not value either your children or your life or anything else more than goodness, in order that when you arrive in Hades you may have all this as your defense before the rulers there. If you do this deed, you will not think it better or more just or more pious here, nor will any one of your friends, nor will it be better for you when you arrive yonder. As it is, you depart, if you depart, after being wronged not by us, the laws, but by men; but if you depart after shamefully returning wrong for wrong and injury for injury, after breaking your agreement and contract with us, after injuring those you should injure least – yourself, your friends, your country and us – we shall be angry with you while you are still alive, and our brothers, the laws of the underworld, will not receive you kindly, knowing that you tried to destroy us as far as you could. Do not let Crito persuade you, rather than us, to do what he says."

Crito, my dear friend, be assured that these are the words I seem to hear, as the Corybants seem to hear the music of their flutes, and the echo of these words resounds in me, and makes it impossible for me to hear anything else. As far as my present beliefs go, if you speak in opposition to them, you will speak in vain. However, if you think you can accomplish anything, speak.

CRITO: I have nothing to say, Socrates.

SOCRATES: Let it be then, Crito, and let us act in this way, since this is the way the god is leading us.

Note

1   A quotation from the ninth book of the *Iliad* (363). Achilles has rejected all the presents of Agamemnon for him to return to the battle, and threatens to go home. He says his ships will sail in the morning, and with good weather he might arrive on the third day "in fertile Phthia" (which is his home). The dream means, obviously, that on the third day Socrates' soul, after death, will find its home. As always, counting the first member of a series, the third day is the day after tomorrow.

Phaedo
Plato

In the *Phaedo*, Plato discusses the issue of immortality, an issue that takes on added significance because Socrates, his spokesperson, has been sentenced to death. Plato argues that it is the presence of the soul that gives a body a life, and that it is the soul that is crucial to personal identity. According to Plato, the body acts as a prison for the soul and the soul forgets what it knew once it enters a body. The true philosopher will therefore welcome death, which is the release of the soul from the body. The soul can then revisit the world of the forms, the unchanging objects that one can have knowledge of.

ECHECRATES: Were you with Socrates yourself, Phaedo,[1] on the day when he drank the poison in prison, or did someone else tell you about it?

PHAEDO: I was there myself, Echecrates.

ECHECRATES: What are the things he said before he died? And how did he die? I should be glad to hear this. Hardly anyone from Phlius[2] visits Athens nowadays, nor has any stranger come from Athens for some time who could give us a clear account of what happened, except that he drank the poison and died, but nothing more.

PHAEDO: Did you not even hear how the trial went?

ECHECRATES: Yes, someone did tell us about that, and we wondered that he seems to have died a long time after the trial took place. Why was that, Phaedo?

PHAEDO: That was by chance, Echecrates. The day before the trial, as it happened, the prow of the ship that the Athenians send to Delos had been crowned with garlands.

ECHECRATES: What ship is that?

PHAEDO: It is the ship in which, the Athenians say, Theseus once sailed to Crete, taking with him the two lots of seven victims.[3] He saved them and was himself saved. They vowed then to Apollo, so the story goes, that if they were saved they would send a mission to Delos every year. And from that time to this they send such an annual mission to the god. They have a law to keep the city pure while it lasts, and no execution may take place once the mission has begun until the ship has made its journey to Delos and returned to Athens, and this can sometimes take a long time if the winds delay it. The mission begins when the priest of Apollo crowns the prow of the ship, and this happened, as I say, the day before Socrates' trial. That is why Socrates was in prison a long time between his trial and his execution.

ECHECRATES: What about his actual death, Phaedo? What did he say? What did he do? Who of his friends were with him? Or did the authorities not allow them to be present and he died with no friends present?

PHAEDO: By no means. Some were present, in fact, a good many.

ECHECRATES: Please be good enough to tell us all that occurred as fully as possible, unless you have some pressing business.

PHAEDO: I have the time and I will try to tell you the whole story, for nothing gives me more pleasure than to call Socrates to mind, whether talking about him myself, or listening to someone else do so.

ECHECRATES: Your hearers will surely be like you in this, Phaedo. So do try to tell us every detail as exactly as you can.

PHAEDO: I certainly found being there an astonishing experience. Although I was witnessing the death of one who was my friend, I had no feeling of pity, for the man appeared happy both in manner and words as he died nobly and without fear, Echecrates, so that it struck me that even in going down to the underworld he was going with the gods' blessing and that he would fare well when he got there, if anyone ever does. That is why I had no feeling of pity, such as would seem natural in my sorrow, nor indeed of pleasure, as we engaged in philosophical discussion as we were accustomed to do – for our arguments were of that sort – but I had a strange feeling, an unaccustomed mixture of pleasure and pain at the same time as I reflected that he was just about to die. All of us present were affected in much the same way, sometimes laughing, then weeping; especially one of us, Apollodorus – you know the man and his ways.

ECHECRATES: Of course I do.

PHAEDO: He was quite overcome; but I was myself disturbed, and so were the others.

ECHECRATES: Who, Phaedo, were those present?

PHAEDO: Among the local people there was Apollodorus, whom I mentioned, Critoboulos and his father,[4] also Hermogenes, Epigenes, Aeschines and Antisthenes. Ctesippus of Paeane was there, Menexenus and some others. Plato, I believe, was ill.[5]

ECHECRATES: Were there some strangers present?

PHAEDO: Yes, Simmias from Thebes with Cebes and Phaidondes, and, from Megara, Euclides and Terpsion.

ECHECRATES: What about Aristippus and Cleombrotus? Were they there?

PHAEDO: No. They were said to be in Aegina.

ECHECRATES: Was there anyone else?

PHAEDO: I think these were about all.

ECHECRATES: Well then, what do you say the conversation was about?

PHAEDO: I will try to tell you everything from the beginning.

On the previous days also both the others and I used to visit Socrates. We foregathered at daybreak at the court where the trial took place, for it was close to the prison, and each day we used to wait around talking until the prison should open, for it did not open early. When it opened we used to go in to Socrates and spend most of the day with him. On this day we gathered rather early, because when we left the prison on the previous evening we were informed that the ship from Delos had arrived, and so we told each other to come to the usual place as early as possible. When we arrived the gatekeeper who used to answer our knock came out and told us to wait and not go in until he told us to. "The Eleven,"[6] he said, "are freeing Socrates from his bonds and telling him how his death will take place today." After a short time he came and told us to go in. We found Socrates recently released from his chains, and Xanthippe – you know her – sitting by him, holding their baby. When she saw us, she cried out and said the sort of thing that women usually say: "Socrates, this is the last time your friends will talk to you and you to them." Socrates looked at Crito. "Crito," he said, "let someone take her home." And some of Crito's people led her away lamenting and beating her breast.

. . .

I want to make my argument before you, my judges, as to why I think that a man who has truly spent his life in philosophy is probably right to be of good cheer in the face of death and to be very hopeful that after death he will attain the greatest blessings from yonder. I will try to tell you, Simmias and Cebes, how this may be so. I am afraid that other people do not realize that the one aim of those who practice philosophy in the proper manner is to practice for dying and death. Now if this is true, it would be strange indeed if they were eager for this all their lives and then resent it when what they have wanted and practiced for a long time comes upon them.

Simmias laughed and said: "By Zeus, Socrates, you made me laugh, though I was in no laughing mood just now. I think that the majority, on hearing this, will think that it describes the philosophers very well, and our people in Thebes would thoroughly agree that philosophers are nearly dead and that the majority of men is well aware that they deserve to be."

"And they would be telling the truth, Simmias, except for their being aware. They are not aware of the way true philosophers are nearly dead, nor of the way they deserve to be, nor of the sort of death they deserve. But never mind them," he said, "let us talk among ourselves. Do we believe that there is such a thing as death?"

"Certainly," said Simmias.

"Is it anything else than the separation of the soul from the body? Do we believe that death is this, namely, that the body comes to be separated by itself apart from the soul, and the soul comes to be separated by itself apart from the body? Is death anything else than that?"

"No, that is what it is," he said.

"Consider then, my good sir, whether you share my opinion, for this will lead us to a better knowledge of what we are investigating. Do you think it is the part of a philosopher to be concerned with such so-called pleasures as those of food and drink?"

"By no means."

"What about the pleasures of sex?"

"Not at all."

"What of the other pleasures concerned with the service of the body? Do you think such a man prizes them greatly, the acquisition of distinguished clothes and shoes and the other bodily ornaments? Do you think he values these or despises them, except in so far as one cannot do without them?"

"I think the true philosopher despises them."

"Do you not think," he said, "that in general such a man's concern is not with the body but that, as far as he can, he turns away from the body towards the soul?"

"I do."

"So in the first place, such things show clearly that the philosopher more than other men frees the soul from association with the body as much as possible?"

"Apparently."

"A man who finds no pleasure in such things and has no part in them is thought by the majority not to deserve to live and to be close to death; the man, that is, who does not care for the pleasures of the body."

"What you say is certainly true."

"Then what about the actual acquiring of knowledge? Is the body an obstacle when one associates it in the search for knowledge? I mean, for example, do men find any truth in sight or hearing, or are not even the poets[7] forever telling us that we do not see or hear anything accurately, and surely if those two physical senses are not clear or precise, our other senses can hardly be accurate, as they are all inferior to these. Do you not think so?"

"I certainly do," he said.

"When then," he asked, "does the soul grasp the truth? For whenever it attempts to examine anything with the body, it is clearly deceived by it."

"True."

"Is it not in reasoning if anywhere that any reality becomes clear to the soul?"

"Yes."

"And indeed the soul reasons best when none of these senses troubles it, neither hearing nor sight, nor pain nor pleasure, but when it is most by itself, taking leave of the body and as far as possible having no contact or association with it in its search for reality."

"That is so."

"And it is then that the soul of the philosopher most disdains the body, flees from it and seeks to be by itself?"

"It appears so."

"What about the following, Simmias? Do we say there is such a thing as the Just itself, or not?"

"We do say so, by Zeus."

"And the Beautiful, and the Good?"

"Of course."

"And have you ever seen any of these things with your eyes?"

"In no way."

"Or have you ever grasped them with any of your bodily senses? I am speaking of all things such as Size, Health, Strength and, in a word, the reality of all other things, that which each of them essentially is. Is what is most true in them contemplated through the body, or is this the position: whoever of us prepares himself best and most accurately to grasp that thing itself which he is investigating will come closest to the knowledge of it?"

"Obviously."

"Then he will do this most perfectly who approaches the object with thought alone, without associating any sight with his thought, or dragging in any sense perception with his reasoning, but who, using pure thought alone, tries to track down each reality pure and by itself, freeing himself as far as possible from eyes and ears, and in a word, from the whole body, because the body confuses the soul and does not allow it to acquire truth and wisdom whenever it is associated with it. Will not that man reach reality, Simmias, if anyone does?"

"What you say," said Simmias, "is indeed true."

"All these things will necessarily make the true philosophers believe and say to each other something like this: 'There is likely to be something such as a path to guide us out of our confusion, because as long as we have a body and our soul is fused with such an evil we shall never adequately attain what we desire, which we affirm to be the truth. The body keeps us busy in a thousand ways because of its need for nurture. Moreover, if certain diseases befall it, they impede our search for the truth. It fills us with wants, desires, fears, all sorts of illusions and much nonsense, so that, as it is said, in truth and in fact no thought of any kind ever comes to us from the body. Only the body and its desires cause war, civil discord and battles, for all wars are due to the desire to acquire wealth, and it is the body and the care of it, to which we are enslaved, which compel us to acquire wealth, and all this makes us too busy to practice philosophy. Worst of all, if we do get some respite from it and turn to some investigation, everywhere in our investigations the body is present and makes for confusion and fear, so that it prevents us from seeing the truth.

"It really has been shown to us that, if we are ever to have pure knowledge, we must escape from the body and observe matters in themselves with the soul by itself. It seems likely that we shall, only then, when we are dead, attain that which we desire and of which we claim to be lovers, namely, wisdom, as our argument shows, not while we live; for if it is impossible to attain any pure knowledge with the body, then one of two things is true: either we can never attain knowledge or we can do so after death. Then and not before, the soul is by itself apart from the body. While we live, we shall be closest to knowledge if we refrain as much as possible from association with the body or joining with it more than we must, if we are not infected with its nature but purify ourselves from it until the god himself frees us. In this way we shall escape the con-tamination of the body's folly, we shall be likely to be in the company of people of the same kind, and by our own efforts we shall know all that is pure, which is presumably the truth for it is not permitted to the impure to attain the pure.

"Such are the things, Simmias, that all those who love learning in the proper manner must say to one another and believe. Or do you not think so?"

"I certainly do, Socrates."

"And if this is true, my friend," said Socrates, "there is good hope that on arriving where I am going, if anywhere, I shall acquire what has been our chief preoccupation in our past life, so that the journey that is now ordered for me is full of good hope, as it is also for any other man who believes that his mind has been prepared and, as it were, purified."

"It certainly is," said Simmias.

"And does purification not turn out to be what we mentioned in our argument some time ago, namely, to separate the soul as far as possible from the body and accustom it to gather itself and collect itself out of every part of the body and to dwell by itself as far as it can both now and in the future, freed, as it were, from the bonds of the body?"

"Certainly," he said.

"And that freedom and separation of the soul from the body is called death?"

"That is altogether so."

"It is only those who practice philosophy in the right way, we say, who always most want to free the soul; and this release and separation of the soul from the body is the preoccupation of the philosophers?"

"So it appears."

"Therefore, as I said at the beginning, it would be ridiculous for a man to train himself in life to live in a state as close to death as possible, and then to resent it when it comes?"

"Ridiculous, of course."

"In fact, Simmias," he said, "those who practice philosophy in the right way are in training for dying and they fear death least of all men. Consider it from this point of view: if they are altogether estranged from the body and desire to have their soul by itself, would it not be quite absurd for them to be afraid and resentful when this happens? If they did not gladly set out for a place, where, on arrival, they may hope to attain that for which they had yearned during their lifetime, that is, wisdom, and where they would be rid of the presence of that from which they are estranged?

"Many men, at the death of their lovers, wives or sons, were willing to go to the underworld, driven by the hope of seeing there those for whose company they longed, and being with them. Will then a true lover of wisdom, who has a similar hope and knows that he will never find it to any extent except in Hades, be resentful of dying and not gladly undertake the journey thither? One must surely think so, my friend, if he is a true philosopher, for he is firmly convinced that he will not find pure knowledge anywhere except there. And if this is so, then, as I said just now, would it not be highly unreasonable for such a man to fear death?"

"It certainly would, by Zeus," he said.

"Then you have sufficient indication," he said, "that any man whom you see resenting death was not a lover of wisdom but a lover of the body, and also a lover of wealth or of honors, either or both."

"It is certainly as you say."

"And, Simmias," he said, "does not what is called courage belong especially to men of this disposition?"

"Most certainly."

"And the quality of moderation which even the majority call by that name, that is, not to get swept off one's feet by one's passions, but to treat them with disdain and orderliness, is this not suited only to those who most of all despise the body and live the life of philosophy?"

"Necessarily so," he said.

"If you are willing to reflect on the courage and moderation of other people, you will find them strange."

"In what way, Socrates?"

"You know that they all consider death a great evil?"

"Definitely," he said.

"And the brave among them face death, when they do, for fear of greater evils?"

"That is so."

"Therefore, it is fear and terror that make all men brave, except the philosophers. Yet it is illogical to be brave through fear and cowardice."

"It certainly is."

"What of the moderate among them? Is their experience not similar?"

"Is it license of a kind that makes them moderate? We say this is impossible, yet their experience of this unsophisticated moderation turns out to be similar: they fear to be deprived of other pleasures which they desire, so they keep away from some pleasures because they are overcome by others. Now to be mastered by pleasure is what they call license, but what happens to them is that they master certain pleasures because they are mastered by others. This is like what we mentioned just now, that in some way it is a kind of license that has made them moderate."

"That seems likely."

"My good Simmias, I fear this is not the right exchange to attain virtue, to exchange pleasures for pleasures, pains for pains and fears for fears, the greater for the less like coins, but that the only valid currency for which all these things should be exchanged is wisdom. With this we have real courage and moderation and justice and, in a word, true virtue, with wisdom, whether pleasures and fears and all such things be present or absent. Exchanged for one another without wisdom such virtue is only an illusory appearance of virtue; it is in fact fit for slaves, without soundness or truth, whereas, in truth, moderation and courage and justice are a purging away of all such things, and wisdom itself is a kind of cleansing or purification. It is likely that those who established the mystic rites for us were not inferior persons but were speaking in riddles long ago when they said that whoever arrives in the underworld uninitiated and unsanctified will wallow in the mire, whereas he who arrives there purified and initiated will dwell with the gods. There are indeed, as those concerned with the mysteries say, many who carry the thyrsus but the Bacchants are few.[8] These latter are, in my opinion, no other than those who have practiced philosophy in the right way. I have in my life left nothing undone in order to be counted among these as far as possible, as I have been eager to be in every way. Whether my eagerness was right and we accomplished anything we shall, I think, know for certain in a short time, god willing, on arriving yonder.

"This is my defense, Simmias and Cebes, that I am likely to be right to leave you and my masters here without resentment or complaint, believing that there, as here, I shall find good masters and good friends. If my defense is more convincing to you than to the Athenian jury, it will be well."

When Socrates finished, Cebes intervened: "Socrates," he said, "everything else you said is excellent, I think, but men find it very hard to believe what you said about the soul. They think that after it has left the body it no longer exists anywhere, but that it is destroyed and dissolved on the day the man dies, as soon as it leaves the body; and that, on leaving it, it is dispersed like breath or smoke, has flown away and gone and is no longer anything anywhere. If indeed it gathered itself together and existed by itself and escaped those evils you were recently enumerating, there would then be much good hope, Socrates, that what you say is true; but to believe this requires a good deal of faith and persuasive argument, to believe that the soul still exists after a man has died and that it still possesses some capability and intelligence."

"What you say is true, Cebes," Socrates said, "but what shall we do? Do you want to discuss whether this is likely to be true or not?"

"Personally," said Cebes, "I should like to hear your opinion on the subject."

"I do not think," said Socrates, "that anyone who heard me now, not even a comic poet, could say that I am babbling and discussing things that do not concern me, so we must examine the question thoroughly, if you think we should do so. Let us examine it in some such a manner as this: whether the souls of men who have died exist in the underworld or not. We recall an ancient theory that souls arriving there come from here, and then again that they arrive here and are born here from the dead. If that is true, that the living come back from the dead, then surely our souls must exist there, for they could not come back if they did not exist, and this is a sufficient proof that these things are so if it truly appears that the living never come from any other source than from the dead. If this is not the case we should need another argument."

"Quite so," said Cebes.

"Do not," he said, "confine yourself to humanity if you want to understand this more readily, but take all animals and all plants into account, and, in short, for all things which come to be, let us see whether they come to be in this way, that is, from their opposites if they have such, as the beautiful is the opposite of the ugly and the just of the unjust, and a thousand other things of the kind. Let us examine whether those that have an opposite must necessarily come to be from their opposite and from nowhere else, as for example when something comes to be larger it must necessarily become larger from having been smaller before."

"Yes."

"Then if something smaller comes to be, it will come from something larger before, which became smaller?"

"That is so," he said.

"And the weaker comes to be from the stronger, and the swifter from the slower?"

"Certainly."

"Further, if something worse comes to be, does it not come from the better, and the juster from the more unjust?"

"Of course."

"So we have sufficiently established that all things come to be in this way, opposites from opposites?"

"Certainly."

"There is a further point, something such as this, about these opposites: between each of those pairs of opposites there are two processes: from the one to the other and then again from the other to the first; between the larger and the smaller there is increase and decrease, and we call the one increasing and the other decreasing?"

"Yes," he said.

"And so too there is separation and combination, cooling and heating, and all such things, even if sometimes we do not have a name for the process, but in fact it must be everywhere that they come to be from one another, and that there is a process of becoming from each into the other?"

"Assuredly," he said.

"Well then, is there an opposite to living, as sleeping is the opposite of being awake?"

"Quite so," he said.

"What is it?"

"Being dead," he said.

"Therefore, if these are opposites, they come to be from one another, and there are two processes of generation between the two?"

"Of course."

"I will tell you," said Socrates, "one of the two pairs I was just talking about, the pair itself and the two processes, and you will tell me the other. I mean, to sleep and to be awake; to be awake comes from sleeping, and to sleep comes from being awake. Of the two processes one is going to sleep, the other is waking up. Do you accept that, or not?"

"Certainly."

"You tell me in the same way about life and death. Do you not say that to be dead is the opposite of being alive?"

"I do."

"And they come to be from one another?"

"Yes."

"What comes to be from being alive?"

"Being dead."

"And what comes to be from being dead?"

"One must agree that it is being alive."

"Then, Cebes, living creatures and things come to be from the dead?"

"So it appears," he said.

"Then our souls exist in the underworld."

"That seems likely."

"Then in this case one of the two processes of becoming is clear, for dying is clear enough, is it not?"

"It certainly is."

"What shall we do then? Shall we not supply the opposite process of becoming? Is nature to be lame in this case? Or must we provide a process of becoming opposite to dying?"

"We surely must."

"And what is that?"

"Coming to life again."

"Therefore," he said, "if there is such a thing as coming to life again, it would be a process of coming from the dead to the living?"

"Quite so."

"It is agreed between us then that the living come from the dead in this way no less than the dead from the living and, if that is so, it seems to be a sufficient proof that the souls of the dead must be somewhere whence they can come back again."

"I think, Socrates," he said, "that this follows from what we have agreed on."

"Consider in this way, Cebes," he said, "that, as I think, we were not wrong to agree: If the two processes of becoming did not always balance each other as if they were going round in a circle, but generation proceeded from one point to its opposite in a straight line and it did not turn back again to the other opposite or take any turning, do you realize that all things would ultimately have the same form, be affected in the same way, and cease to become?"

"How do you mean?" he said.

"It is not hard to understand what I mean. If, for example, there was such a process as going to sleep, but no corresponding process of waking up, you realize that in the end everything would show the story of Endymion[9] to have no meaning. There would be no point to it because everything would have the same experience as he, be asleep. And if everything were combined and nothing separated, the saying of Anaxagoras[10] would soon be true, 'that all things were mixed together.' In the same way, my dear Cebes, if everything that partakes of life were to die and remain in that state and not come to life again, would not everything ultimately have to be dead and nothing alive? Even if the living came from some other source, and all that lived died, how could all things avoid being absorbed in death?"

"It could not be, Socrates," said Cebes, "and I think what you say is altogether true."

"I think, Cebes," said he, "that this is very definitely the case and that we were not deceived when we agreed on this: coming to life again in truth exists, the living come to be from the dead, and the souls of the dead exist."

"Furthermore, Socrates," Cebes rejoined, "such is also the case if that theory is true that you are accustomed to mention frequently, that for us learning is no other than recollection. According to this, we must at some previous time have learned what we now recollect. This is possible only if our soul existed somewhere before it took on this human shape. So according to this theory too, the soul is likely to be something immortal."

"Cebes," Simmias interrupted, "what are the proofs of this? Remind me, for I do not quite recall them at the moment."

"There is one excellent argument," said Cebes, "namely that when men are interrogated in the right manner, they always give the right answer of their own accord, and they could not do this if they did not possess the knowledge and the right explanation inside them. Then if one shows them a diagram or something else of that kind, this will show most clearly that such is the case."[11]

"If this does not convince you, Simmias," said Socrates, "see whether you agree if we examine it in some such way as this, for you doubt that what we call learning is recollection."

"It is not that I doubt," said Simmias, "but I want to experience the very thing we are discussing, recollection, and from what Cebes undertook to say, I am now remembering and am pretty nearly convinced. Nevertheless, I should like to hear now the way you were intending to explain it."

"This way," he said. "We surely agree that if anyone recollects anything, he must have known it before."

"Quite so," he said.

"Do we not also agree that when knowledge comes to mind in this way, it is recollection? What way do I mean? Like this: when a man sees or hears or in some other way perceives one thing and not only knows that thing but also thinks of another thing of which the knowledge is not the same but different, are we not right to say that he recollects the second thing that comes into his mind?"

"How do you mean?"

"Things such as this: to know a man is surely a different knowledge from knowing a lyre."

"Of course."

"Well, you know what happens to lovers: whenever they see a lyre, a garment or anything else that their beloved is accustomed to use, they know the lyre, and the image of the boy to whom it belongs comes into their mind. This is recollection, just as someone, on seeing Simmias, often recollects Cebes, and there are thousands of other such occurrences."

"Thousands indeed," said Simmias.

"Is this kind of thing not recollection of a kind," he said, "especially so when one experiences it about things that one had forgotten, because one had not seen them for some time?"

"Quite so."

"Further," he said, "can a man seeing the picture of a horse or a lyre recollect a man, or seeing a picture of Simmias recollect Cebes?"

"Certainly."

"Or seeing a picture of Simmias, recollect Simmias himself?"

"He certainly can."

"In all these cases the recollection is occasioned by things that are similar, but it can also be occasioned by things that are dissimilar?"

"It can."

"When the recollection is caused by similar things, must one not of necessity also experience this: to consider whether the similarity to that which one recollects is deficient in any respect or complete?"

"One must."

"Consider," he said, "whether this is the case: we say that there is some thing that is equal. I do not mean a stick equal to a stick or a stone to a stone, or anything of that kind, but something else beyond all these, the Equal itself. Shall we say that this exists or not?"

"Indeed we shall, by Zeus," said Simmias, "most definitely."

"And do we know what this is?"

"Certainly."

"Whence have we acquired the knowledge of it? Is it not from the things we mentioned just now, from seeing sticks or stones or some other things that are equal we come to think of that other which is different from them? Or doesn't it seem to you to be different? Look at it also this way: do not equal stones and sticks sometimes, while remaining the same, appear to one to be equal and to another to be unequal?"

"Certainly they do."

"But what of the equals themselves?[12] Have they ever appeared unequal to you, or Equality to be Inequality?"

"Never, Socrates."

"These equal things and the Equal itself are therefore not the same?"

"I do not think they are the same at all, Socrates."

"But it is definitely from the equal things, though they are different from that Equal, that you have derived and grasped the knowledge of equality?"

"Very true, Socrates."

"Whether it be like them or unlike them?"

"Certainly."

"It makes no difference. As long as the sight of one thing makes you think of another, whether it be similar or dissimilar, this must of necessity be recollection?"

"Quite so."

"Well then," he said, "do we experience something like this in the case of equal sticks and the other equal objects we just mentioned? Do they seem to us to be equal in the same sense as what is Equal itself? Is there some deficiency in their being such as the Equal, or is there not?"

"A considerable deficiency," he said.

"Whenever someone, on seeing something, realizes that that which he now sees wants to be like some other reality but falls short and cannot be like that other since it is inferior, do we agree that the one who thinks this must have prior knowledge of that to which he says it is like, but deficiently so?"

"Necessarily."

"Well, do we also feel this about the equal objects and the Equal itself, or do we not?"

"Very definitely."

"We must then possess knowledge of the Equal before that time when we first saw the equal objects and realized that all these objects strive to be like the Equal but are deficient in this."

"That is so."

"Then surely we also agree that this conception of ours derives from seeing or touching or some other sense perception, and cannot come into our mind in any other way, for all these senses, I say, are the same."

"They are the same, Socrates, at any rate in respect to that which our argument wishes to make plain."

"Our sense perceptions must surely make us realize that all that we perceive through them is striving to reach that which is Equal but falls short of it; or how do we express it?"

"Like that."

"Then before we began to see or hear or otherwise perceive, we must have possessed knowledge of the Equal itself if we were about to refer our sense perceptions of equal objects to it, and realized that all of them were eager to be like it, but were inferior."

"That follows from what has been said, Socrates."

"But we began to see and hear and otherwise perceive right after birth?"

"Certainly."

"We must then have acquired the knowledge of the Equal before this."

"Yes."

"It seems then that we must have possessed it before birth."

"It seems so."

"Therefore, if we had this knowledge, we knew before birth and immediately after not only the Equal, but the Greater and the Smaller and all such things, for our present argument is no more about the Equal than about the Beautiful itself, the Good itself, the Just, the Pious and, as I say, about all those things to which we can attach the word 'itself,' both when we are putting questions and answering them. So we must have acquired knowledge of them all before we were born."

"That is so."

"If, having acquired this knowledge in each case, we have not forgotten it, we remain knowing and have knowledge throughout our life, for to know is to acquire knowledge, keep it and not lose it. Do we not call the losing of knowledge forgetting?"

"Most certainly, Socrates," he said.

"But, I think, if we acquired this knowledge before birth, then lost it at birth, and then later by the use of our senses in connection with those objects we mentioned, we recovered the knowledge we had before, would not what we call learning be the recovery of our own knowledge, and we are right to call this recollection?"

"Certainly."

"It was seen to be possible for someone to see or hear or otherwise perceive something, and by this to be put in mind of something else which he had forgotten and which is related to it by similarity or difference. One of two things follows, as I say: either we were born with the knowledge of it, and all of us know it throughout life, or those who later, we say, are learning, are only recollecting, and learning would be recollection."

"That is certainly the case, Socrates."

"Which alternative do you choose, Simmias? That we are born with this knowledge or that we recollect later the things of which we had knowledge previously?"

"I have no means of choosing at the moment, Socrates."

"Well, can you make this choice? What is your opinion about it? A man who has knowledge would be able to give an account of what he knows, or would he not?"

"He must certainly be able to do so, Socrates," he said.

"And do you think everybody can give an account of the things we were mentioning just now?"

"I wish they could," said Simmias, "but I'm afraid it is much more likely that by this time tomorrow there will be no one left who can do so adequately."

"So you do not think that everybody has knowledge of those things?"

"No indeed."

"So they recollect what they once learned?"

"They must."

"When did our souls acquire the knowledge of them? Certainly not since we were born as men."

"Indeed no."

"Before that then?"

"Yes."

"So then, Simmias, our souls also existed apart from the body before they took on human form, and they had intelligence."

"Unless we acquire the knowledge at the moment of birth, Socrates, for that time is still left to us."

"Quite so, my friend, but at what other time do we lose it? We just now agreed that we are not born with that knowledge. Do we then lose it at the very time we acquire it, or can you mention any other time?"

"I cannot, Socrates. I did not realize that I was talking nonsense."

"So this is our position, Simmias?" he said. "If those realities we are always talking about exist, the Beautiful and the Good and all that kind of reality, and we refer all the things we perceive to that reality, discovering that it existed before and is ours, and we compare these things with it, then, just as they exist, so our soul must exist before we are born. If these realities do not exist, then this argument is altogether futile. Is this the position, that there is an equal necessity for those realities to exist, and for our souls to exist before we were born? If the former do not exist, neither do the latter?"

"I do not think, Socrates," said Simmias, "that there is any possible doubt that it is equally necessary for both to exist, and it is opportune that our argument comes to the conclusion that our soul exists before we are born, and equally so that reality of which you are now speaking. Nothing is so evident to me personally as that all such things must certainly exist, the Beautiful, the Good, and all those you mentioned just now. I also think that sufficient proof of this has been given."

"Then what about Cebes?" said Socrates. "For we must persuade Cebes also."

"He is sufficiently convinced I think," said Simmias, "though he is the most difficult of men to persuade by argument, but I believe him to be fully convinced that our soul existed before we were born. I do not think myself, however, that it has been proved that the soul continues to exist after death; the opinion of the majority which Cebes mentioned still stands, that when a man dies his soul is dispersed and this is the end of its existence. What is to prevent the soul coming to be and being constituted from some other source, existing before it enters a human body and then, having done so and departed from it, itself dying and being destroyed?"

"You are right, Simmias," said Cebes. "Half of what needed proof has been proved, namely, that our soul existed before we were born, but further proof is needed that it exists no less after we have died, if the proof is to be complete."

"It has been proved even now, Simmias and Cebes," said Socrates, "if you are ready to combine this argument with the one we agreed on before, that every living thing must come from the dead. If the soul exists before, it must, as it comes to life and birth, come from nowhere else than death and being dead, so how could it avoid existing after death since it must be born again? What you speak of has then even now been proved. However, I think you and Simmias would like to discuss the argument more fully. You seem to have this childish fear that the wind would really dissolve and scatter the soul, as it leaves the body, especially if one happens to die in a high wind and not in calm weather."

Cebes laughed and said: "Assuming that we were afraid, Socrates, try to change our minds, or rather do not assume that we are afraid, but perhaps there is a child in us who has these fears; try to persuade him not to fear death like a bogey."

"You should," said Socrates, "sing a charm over him every day until you have charmed away his fears."

"Where shall we find a good charmer for these fears, Socrates," he said, "now that you are leaving us?"

"Greece is a large country, Cebes," he said, "and there are good men in it;

the tribes of foreigners are also numerous. You should search for such a charmer among them all, sparing neither trouble nor expense, for there is nothing on which you could spend your money to greater advantage. You must also search among yourselves, for you might not easily find people who could do this better than yourselves."

"That shall be done," said Cebes, "but let us, if it pleases you, go back to the argument where we left it."

"Of course it pleases me."

"Splendid," he said.

"We must then ask ourselves something like this: what kind of thing is likely to be scattered? On behalf of what kind of thing should one fear this, and for what kind of thing should one not fear it? We should then examine to which class the soul belongs, and as a result either fear for the soul or be of good cheer."

"What you say is true."

"Is not anything that is composite and a compound by nature liable to be split up into its component parts, and only that which is noncomposite, if anything, is not likely to be split up?"

"I think that is the case," said Cebes.

"Are not the things that always remain the same and in the same state most likely not to be composite, whereas those that vary from one time to another and are never the same are composite?"

"I think that is so."

"Let us then return to those same things with which we were dealing earlier, to that reality of whose existence we are giving an account in our questions and answers; are they ever the same and in the same state, or do they vary from one time to another; can the Equal itself, the Beautiful itself, each thing in itself, the real, ever be affected by any change whatever? Or does each of them that really is, being simple by itself, remain the same and never in any way tolerate any change whatever?"

"It must remain the same," said Cebes, "and in the same state, Socrates."

"What of the many beautiful particulars, be they men, horses, clothes, or other such things, or the many equal particulars, and all those which bear the same name as those others? Do they remain the same or, in total contrast to those other realities, one might say, never in any way remain the same as themselves or in relation to each other?"

"The latter is the case, they are never in the same state."

"These latter you could touch and see and perceive with the other senses, but those that always remain the same can only be grasped by the reasoning power of the mind? They are not seen but are invisible?"

"That is altogether true," he said.

"Do you then want us to assume two kinds of existences, the visible and the invisible?"

"Let us assume this."

"And the invisible always remains the same, whereas the visible never does?"

"Let us assume that too."

"Now one part of ourselves is the body, another part is the soul?"

"Quite so."

"To which class of existence do we say the body is more alike and akin?"

"To the visible, as anyone can see."

"What about the soul? Is it visible or invisible?"

"It is not visible to men, Socrates," he said.

"Well, we meant visible and invisible to human eyes; or to any others, do you think?"

"To human eyes."

"Then what do we say about the soul? Is it visible or not visible?"

"Not visible."

"So it is invisible?"

"Yes."

"So the soul is more like the invisible than the body, and the body more like the visible?"

"Without any doubt, Socrates."

"Haven't we also said some time ago that when the soul makes use of the body to investigate something, be it through hearing or seeing or some other sense – for to investigate something through the senses is to do it through the body – it is dragged by the body to the things that are never the same, and the soul itself strays and is confused and dizzy, as if it were drunk, in so far as it is in contact with that kind of thing?"

"Certainly."

But when the soul investigates by itself it passes into the realm of what is pure, ever existing, immortal and unchanging, and being akin to this, it always stays with it whenever it is by itself and can do so; it ceases to stray and remains in the same state as it is in touch with things of the same kind, and its experience then is what is called wisdom?"

"Altogether well said and very true, Socrates," he said.

"Judging from what we have said before and what we are saying now, to which of these two kinds do you think that the soul is more alike and more akin?"

"I think, Socrates," he said, "that on this line of argument any man, even the dullest, would agree that the soul is altogether more like that which always exists in the same state rather than like that which does not."

"What of the body?"

"That is like the other."

"Look at it also this way: when the soul and the body are together, nature orders the one to be subject and to be ruled, and the other to rule and be master. Then again, which do you think is like the divine and which like the mortal? Do you not think that the nature of the divine is to rule and to lead, whereas it is that of the mortal to be ruled and be subject?"

"I do."

"Which does the soul resemble?"

"Obviously, Socrates, the soul resembles the divine, and the body resembles the mortal."

"Consider then, Cebes, whether it follows from all that has been said that the soul is most like the divine, deathless, intelligible, uniform, indissoluble, always the same as itself, whereas the body is most like that which is human, mortal, multiform, unintelligible, soluble and never consistently the same.

Have we anything else to say to show, my dear Cebes, that this is not the case?"

"We have not."

"Well then, that being so, is it not natural for the body to dissolve easily, and for the soul to be altogether indissoluble, or nearly so?"

"Of course."

"You realize, he said, that when a man dies, the visible part, the body, which exists in the visible world, and which we call the corpse, whose natural lot it would be to dissolve, fall apart and be blown away, does not immediately suffer any of these things but remains for a fair time, in fact, quite a long time if the man dies with his body in a suitable condition and at a favourable season? If the body is emaciated or embalmed, as in Egypt, it remains almost whole for a remarkable length of time, and even if the body decays, some parts of it, namely bones and sinews and the like, are nevertheless, one might say, death-less. Is that not so?"

"Yes."

"Will the soul, the invisible part which makes its way to a region of the same kind, noble and pure and invisible, to Hades in fact, to the good and wise god whither, god willing, my soul must soon be going – will the soul, being of this kind and nature, be scattered and destroyed on leaving the body, as the majority of men say? Far from it, my dear Cebes and Simmias, but what happens is much more like this: if it is pure when it leaves the body and drags nothing bodily with it, as it had no willing association with the body in life, but avoided it and gathered itself together by itself and always practiced this, which is no other than practicing philosophy in the right way, in fact, training to die easily. Or is this not training for death?"

"It surely is."

"A soul in this state makes its way to the invisible, which is like itself, the divine and immortal and wise, and arriving there it can be happy, having rid itself of confusion, ignorance, fear, violent desires and the other human ills and, as is said of the initiates, truly spend the rest of time with the gods. Shall we say this, Cebes, or something different?"

"This, by Zeus," said Cebes.

"But I think that if the soul is polluted and impure when it leaves the body, having always been associated with it and served it, bewitched by physical desires and pleasures to the point at which nothing seems to exist for it but the physical, which one can touch and see or eat and drink or make use of for sexual enjoyment, and if that soul is accustomed to hate and fear and avoid that which is dim and invisible to the eyes but intelligible and to be grasped by philosophy – do you think such a soul will escape pure and by itself?"

"Impossible," he said.

"It is no doubt permeated by the physical, which constant intercourse and association with the body, as well as considerable practice, has caused to become ingrained in it?"

"Quite so."

"We must believe, my friend, that this bodily element is heavy, ponderous, earthy and visible. Through it, such a soul has become heavy and is dragged back to the visible region in fear of the unseen and of Hades. It wanders, as we are told, around graves and monuments, where shadowy phantoms, images that such souls produce, have been seen, souls that have not been freed and purified but share in the visible, and are therefore seen."

"That is likely, Socrates."

"It is indeed, Cebes. Moreover, these are not the souls of good but of inferior men, which are forced to wander there, paying the penalty for their previous bad upbringing. They wander until their longing for that which accompanies them, the physical, again imprisons them in a body, and they are then, as is likely, bound to such characters as they have practiced in their life."

"What kind of characters do you say these are, Socrates?"

"Those, for example, who have carelessly practiced gluttony, violence and drunkenness are likely to join a company of donkeys or of similar animals. Do you not think so?"

"Very likely."

"Those who have esteemed injustice highly, and tyranny and plunder will join the tribes of wolves and hawks and kites, or where else shall we say that they go?"

"Certainly to those," said Cebes.

"And clearly, the destination of the others will conform to the way in which they have behaved?"

"Clearly, of course."

"The happiest of these, who will also have the best destination, are those who have practiced popular and social virtue, which they call moderation and justice and which was developed by habit and practice, without philosophy or understanding?"

"How are they the happiest?"

"Because it is likely that they will again join a social and gentle group, either of bees or wasps or ants, and then again the same kind of human group, and so be moderate men."

"That is likely."

"No one may join the company of the gods who has not practiced philosophy and is not completely pure when he departs from life, no one but the lover of learning. It is for this reason, my friends Simmias and Cebes, that those who practice philosophy in the right way keep away from all bodily passions, master them and do not surrender themselves to them; it is not at all for fear of wasting their substance and of poverty, which the majority and the money-lovers fear, nor for fear of dishonor and ill repute, like the ambitious and lovers of honors, that they keep away from them."

"That would not be natural for them, Socrates," said Cebes.

"By Zeus, no," he said. "Those who care for their own soul and do not live for the service of their body dismiss all these things. They do not travel the same road as those who do not know where they are going but, believing that nothing should be done contrary to philosophy and their deliverance and purification, they turn to this and follow wherever philosophy leads."

"How so, Socrates?"

"I will tell you," he said. "The lovers of learning know that when philosophy gets hold of their soul, it is imprisoned in and clinging to the body, and that it is forced to examine other things through it as through a cage and not by itself, and that it wallows in every kind of ignorance. Philosophy sees that the worst feature of this imprisonment is that it is due to desires, so that the prisoner himself is contributing to his own incarceration most of all. As I say, the lovers of learning know that philosophy gets hold of their soul when it is in that state, then gently encourages it and tries to free it by showing them that investigation through the eyes is full of deceit, as is that through the ears and the other senses. Philosophy then persuades the soul to withdraw from the senses in so far as it is not compelled to use them and bids the soul to gather itself together by itself, to trust only itself and whatever reality, existing by itself, the soul by itself understands, and not to consider as true whatever it examines by other means, for this is different in different circumstances and is sensible and visible, whereas what the soul itself sees is intelligible and invisible. The soul of the true philosopher thinks that this deliverance must not be opposed and so keeps away from pleasures and desires and pains as far as he can; he reflects that violent pleasure or pain or passion does not cause merely such evils as one might expect, such as one suffers when one has been sick or extravagant through desire, but the greatest and most extreme evil, though one does not reflect on this."

"What is that, Socrates?" asked Cebes.

"That the soul of every man, when it feel violent pleasure or pain in connection with some object, inevitably believes at the same time that what causes such feelings must be very clear and very true, which it is not. Such objects are mostly visible, are they not?"

"Certainly."

"And doesn't such an experience tie the soul to the body most completely?"

"How so?"

"Because every pleasure and every pain provides, as it were, another nail to rivet the soul to the body and to weld them together. It makes the soul corporeal, so that it believes that truth is what the body says it is. As it shares the beliefs and delights of the body, I think it inevitably comes to share its ways and manner of life and is unable ever to reach Hades in a pure state; it is always full of body when it departs, so that it soon falls back into another body and grows with it as if it had been sewn into it. Because of this, it can have no part in the company of the divine, the pure and uniform."

"What you say is very true, Socrates," said Cebes.

"This is why genuine lovers of learning are moderate and brave, or do you think it is for the reasons the majority says they are?"

"I certainly do not."

"Indeed no. This is how the soul of a philosopher would reason: it would not think that while philosophy must free it, it should while being freed surrender itself to pleasures and pains and imprison itself again, thus labouring in vain like Penelope at her web. The soul of the philosopher achieves a calm from such emotions; it follows reason and ever stays with it contemplating the true, the divine, which is not the object of opinion. Nurtured by this, it believes that one should live in this manner as long as one is alive and, after death, arrive at what is akin and of the same kind, and escape from human evils. After such nurture there is no danger, Simmias and Cebes, that one should fear that, on parting from the body, the soul would be scattered and dissipated by the winds and no longer be anything anywhere."

When Socrates finished speaking there was a long silence. He appeared to be concentrating on what had been said, and so were most of us. But Cebes and Simmias were whispering to each other. Socrates observed them and questioned them. "Come," he said, "do you think there is something lacking in my argument? There are still many doubtful points and many objections for anyone who wants a thorough discussion of these matters. If you are discussing some other subject, I have nothing to say, but if you have some difficulty about this one, do not hesitate to speak for yourselves and expound it if you think the argument could be improved, and if you think you will do better, take me along with you in the discussion."

. . .

"[A] man should be of good cheer about his own soul, if during life he has ignored the pleasures of the body and its ornamentation as of no concern to him and doing him more harm than good, but has seriously concerned himself with the pleasures of learning, and adorned his soul not with alien but with its own ornaments, namely, moderation, righteousness, courage, freedom and truth, and in that state awaits his journey to the underworld.

"Now you, Simmias, Cebes and the rest of you," Socrates continued, "will each take that journey at some other time but my fated day calls me now, as a tragic character might say, and it is about time for me to have my bath, for I think it better to have it before I drink the poison and save the women the trouble of washing the corpse."

When Socrates had said this Crito spoke. "Very well, Socrates, what are your instructions to me and the others about your children or anything else? What can we do that would please you most?"

"Nothing new, Crito," said Socrates, "but what I am always saying, that you will please me and mine and yourselves by taking good care of your own selves in whatever you do, even if you do not agree with me now, but if you neglect your own selves, and are unwilling to live following the tracks, as it were, of what we have said now and on previous occasions, you will achieve nothing even if you strongly agree with me at this moment."

"We shall be eager to follow your advice," said Crito, "but how shall we bury you?"

"In any way you like," said Socrates, "if you can catch me and I do not escape you." And laughing quietly, looking at us, he said: "I do not convince Crito that I am this Socrates talking to you here and ordering all I say, but he thinks that I am the thing which he will soon be looking at as a corpse, and so he asks how he shall bury me. I have been saying for some time and at some length that after I have drunk the poison I shall no longer be with you but will leave you to go and enjoy some good fortunes of the blessed, but it seems that I have said all this to him in vain in an attempt to reassure you and myself too. Give a pledge to Crito on my behalf, he said, the opposite pledge to that he gave the jury. He pledged that I would stay, you must pledge that I will not stay after I die, but that I shall go away, so that Crito will bear it more easily when he sees my body being burned or buried and will not be angry on my behalf, as if I were suffering terribly, and so that he should not say at the funeral that he is laying out, or carrying out, or burying Socrates. For know you well, my dear Crito, that to express oneself badly is not only faulty as far as the language goes, but does some harm to the soul. You must be of good cheer, and say you are burying my body, and bury it in any way you like and think most customary."

After saying this he got up and went to another room to take his bath, and Crito followed him and he told us to wait for him. So we stayed, talking among ourselves, questioning what had been said, and then again talking of the great misfortune that had befallen us. We all felt as if we had lost a father and would be orphaned for the rest of our lives. When he had washed, his children were brought to him – two of his sons were small and one was older – and the women of his household came to him. He spoke to them before Crito and gave them what instructions he wanted. Then he sent the women and children away, and he himself joined us. It was now close to sunset, for he had stayed inside for some time. He came and sat down after his bath and conversed for a short while, when the officer of the Eleven came and stood by him and said: "I shall not reproach you as I do the others, Socrates. They are angry with me and curse me when, obeying the orders of my superiors, I tell them to drink the poison. During the time you have been here I have come to know you in other ways as the noblest, the gentlest and the best man who has ever come here. So now too I know that you will not make trouble for me; you know who is responsible and you will direct your anger against them.

"You know what message I bring. Fare you well, and try to endure what you must as easily as possible." The officer was weeping as he turned away and went out. Socrates looked up at him and said: "Fare you well also, we shall do as you bid us." And turning to us he said: "How pleasant the man is! During the whole time I have been here he has come in and conversed with me from time to time, a most agreeable man. And how genuinely he now weeps for me. Come, Crito, let us obey him. Let someone bring the poison if it is ready; if not, let the man prepare it."

"But Socrates," said Crito, "I think the sun still shines upon the hills and has not yet set. I know that others drink the poison quite a long time after they have received the order, eating and drinking quite a bit, and some of them enjoy intimacy with their loved ones. Do not hurry; there is still some time."

"It is natural, Crito, for them to do so," said Socrates, "for they think they derive some benefit from doing this, but it is not fitting for me. I do not expect any benefit from drinking the poison a little later, except to become ridiculous in my own eyes for clinging to life, and be sparing of it when there is none left. So do as I ask and do not refuse me."

Hearing this, Crito nodded to the slave who was standing near him; the slave went out and after a time came back with the man who was to administer the poison, carrying it made ready in a cup. When Socrates saw him he said: "Well, my good man, you are an expert in this, what must one do?"

"Just drink it and walk around until your legs feel heavy, and then lie down and it will act of itself." And he offered the cup to Socrates who took it quite cheerfully, Echecrates, without a tremor or any change of feature or colour, but looking at the man from under his eyebrows as was his wont, asked: "What do you say about pouring a libation from this drink? It is allowed?"

"We only mix as much as we believe will suffice," said the man.

"I understand," Socrates said, "but one is allowed, indeed one must, utter a prayer to the gods that the journey from here to yonder may be fortunate. This is my prayer and may it be so."

And while he was saying this, he was holding the cup, and then drained it calmly and easily. Most of us had been able to hold back our tears reasonably well up till then, but when we saw him drinking it and after he drank it, we could hold them back no longer; my own tears came in floods against my will. So I covered my face. I was weeping for myself, not for him – for my misfortune in being deprived of such a comrade. Even before me, Crito was unable to restrain his tears and got up. Apollodorus had not ceased from weeping before, and at this moment his noisy tears and anger made everybody present break down, except Socrates. "What is this," he said, "you strange fellows. It is mainly for this reason that I sent the women away, to avoid such unseemliness, for I am told one should die in good omened silence. So keep quiet and control yourselves."

His words made us ashamed, and we checked our tears. He walked around, and when he said his legs were heavy he lay on his back as he had been told to do, and the man who had given him the poison touched his body, and after a while tested his feet and legs, pressed hard upon his foot and asked him if he felt this, and Socrates said no. Then he pressed his calves, and made his way up his body and showed us that it was cold and stiff. He felt it himself and said that when the cold reached his heart he would be gone. As his belly was getting cold Socrates uncovered his head – he had covered it – and said – these were his last words – "Crito, we owe a cock to Asclepius;[13] make this offering to him and do not forget."

"It shall be done," said Crito "tell us if there is anything else," but there was no answer. Shortly afterwards Socrates made a movement; the man uncovered him and his eyes were fixed. Seeing this Crito closed his mouth and his eyes.

Such was the end of our comrade, Echecrates, a man who, we would say, was of all those we have known the best, and also the wisest and the most upright.

Notes

1 Phaedo was a young friend of Socrates who later founded a school of philosophy at Elis.
2 Phlius was a community in the northeastern part of the Pelopponesus where a Pythagorean society flourished about this time. We are told by Diogenes Laertius (early third century AD) that Echecrates was a member of that society.
3 Legend says that Minos, king of Crete, compelled the Athenians to send seven youths and seven maidens every year to be sacrificed to the Minotaur until Theseus saved them and killed the monster.
4 The father of Critoboulos is Crito, who in the dialogue named after him tries to persuade Socrates to escape from jail. He is also mentioned in *Apology* 33d and

plays a prominent part in the death scene at the end of this dialogue. Several of the other friends of Socrates mentioned here also appear in other dialogues. Hermogenes is one of the speakers in the *Cratylus*. Epigenes is mentioned in *Apology* 33e, as is Achenes. Achenes was a writer of Socratic dialogues. Menexenus has a part in the *Lysis* and has a dialogue named after him. Simmias and Cebes are mentioned in the *Crito*, 45b, as having come to Athens with enough money to secure Socrates' escape.

5 It is interesting to note that Plato makes it clear that he was *not* present on the last day of Socrates' life, whereas in the *Apology* he twice mentions (34a and 38b) that he *was* present at the trial. Whether this has any significance as regards the historical accuracy of the two works is anyone's guess. Probably it just happened to be so, but these are the only instances in which Plato mentions himself in all his works.

6 The Eleven were the police commissioners of Athens.

7 "Even the poets" because poetry concerns itself with the world of sense and appeals to the passions and emotions of the lowest part of the soul in the *Republic* (595a ff), whereas in the *Phaedo* passions and emotions are attributed to the body.

8 That is, the true worshippers of Dionysus, as opposed to those who only carry the external symbols of his worship.

9 Endymion was granted eternal sleep by Zeus, in some versions at the request of Selene (the moon).

10 Anaxagoras of Clazomenae was born at the beginning of the fifth century BC. He came to Athens as a young man and spent most of his life there in the study of natural philosophy. He is quoted later in the dialogue as claiming that the universe is directed by Mind (Nous). See 97c ff. The reference here is to his statement that in the original state of the world all its elements were thoroughly commingled.

11 In the *Meno* Socrates does precisely that. By means of a geometrical diagram and merely by asking Meno's slave questions, he elicits from him the answer that the square on the diameter of a square is double the original square. There, too, this is taken to prove that knowledge is recollection.

12 The plural is puzzling, as only the Form of Equality, on the one hand, and the (imperfectly) equal "sticks and stones" have been mentioned. Commentators suggest that the plural here refers to mathematical equals such as the angles at the base of an isosceles triangle. Plato must have something of the kind in mind, but it is hard to see how he expects a reader who could not be familiar with his later work to realize it, especially as the "equal things" in the next line again refer to the particulars.

13 A cock was sacrificed to Asclepius by the sick people who slept in his temples, hoping for a cure. Socrates obviously means that death is a cure for the ills of life.

Selection from *The Leviathan*
Thomas Hobbes

Thomas Hobbes was born in 1588 on the eve of the battle between the Spanish Armada and the English navy, and so Hobbes liked to remark that "fear and I were born twins." In fact, he experienced social and political strife most of his life, and his best known work, *The Leviathan* (1651) is marked by this fact. Hobbes argued that in order to avoid a life that is "solitary, nasty, brutish, and short," human beings agree to submit to an absolute and powerful ruler. Hobbes was also a materialist and nominalist, who believed that thought is a physical event and that universals were a product of our language. Hobbes died in 1679.

Chapter IV: Of Speech

The Invention of *Printing*, though ingenious, compared with the invention of *Letters*, is no great matter. But who was the first that found the use of Letters, is not known. He that first brought them into *Greece*, men say was *Cadmus*, the sonne of *Agenor*, King of Phænicia. A profitable Invention for continuing the memory of time vast, and the conjunction of mankind, dispersed into so many, and distant regions, of the Earth; and with all difficult, as proceeding from a watchfull observation of the divers motions of the Tongue, Palat, Lips, and other organs of Speech; whereby to make as many differences of characters, to remember them. But the most noble and profitable invention of all other, was that of SPEECH, consisting of *Names* or *Appellations*, and their Connexion; whereby men register their Thoughts; recall them when they are past; and also declare them one to another for mutuall utility and conversation; without which, there had been amongst men, neither Common-wealth, nor Society, nor Contract, nor Peace, no more than amongst Lyons, Bears, and Wolves. The first author of Speech was *God* himself, that instructed *Adam* how name such creatures as he presented to his sight; the Scripture goeth no further in this matter. But this was sufficient to direct him to adde more as the experience and use of the creatures give him occasion; and to joyn them in such degrees, as to make himself understood; and so by succession of time, so much language might be gotten, as he had found use for; though not so copious, as an Orator or Philosopher has need of. For I do not find any thing in the Scripture, out of which, directly or by conequence can be gathered, that *Adam* was taught the names of all Figures, Numbers, Measures, Colours, Sounds, Fancies, Relations; much less the names of Words and Speech, as *Generall, Speciall, Affirmative, Negative, Interrogative, Optative, Infinitive*, all which are usefull; and least of all, of *Entity, Intentionality, Quiddity*, and other insignificant words of the School.

But all this language gotten, and augmented by *Adam* and his posterity, was again lost at the tower of *Babel*, when by the hand of God, every man was stricken for his rebellion, with an oblivion of his former language. And being hereby forced to disperse themselves into severall parts of the world, it must needs be, that the diversity of Tongues that now is, proceeded by degrees from them, in such manner, as need (the mother of all inventions) taught them; and in tract of time grew every where more copious.

The generall use of Speech, is to transfer our Mentall Discourse, into Verbal; or the Trayne of our Thoughts, into a Trayne of words; and that for two commodities; whereof one is, the Registring of the Consequences of our Thoughts; which being apt to slip out of our memory, and put us to a new labour, may again be recalled, by such words as they were marked by. So that the first use of names is to serve for *Markes*, or *Notes* of remembrance. Another is, when many use the same words, to signifie (by their connexion and order,) one to another, what they conceive, or think of each matter; and also what they desire, feare, or have any other passion for. And for this use they are called *Signes*. Speciall uses of Speech are these; First, to Register, what by cogitation, wee find to be the cause of any thing, present or past; and what we find things present or past may produce, or effect: which in summe, is acquiring of Arts. Secondly, to shew to others that knowledge which we have attained; which is, to Counsell, and Teach one another. Thirdly, to make known to others our wills, and purposes, that we may have the mutuall help of one another. Fourthly, to please and delight our selves, and others, by playing with our words, for pleasure or ornament, innocently.

To these Uses, there are also foure correspondent Abuses. First, when men register their thoughts wrong, by the inconstancy of the signification of their words; by which they register for their conceptions, that which they never conceived; and so deceive themselves. Secondly, when they use words metaphorically; that is, in other sense than that they are ordained for; and thereby deceive others. Thirdly, when by words they declare that to be their will, which is not. Fourthly, when they use them to grieve one another: for seeing nature hath armed living creatures, some with teeth, some with horns, and some with hands, to grieve an enemy, it is but an abuse of Speech, to grieve him with the tongue, unlesse it be one whom wee are oblied to govern; and then it is not to grieve, but to correct and amend.

The manner how Speech serveth to the remembrance of the consequence of causes and effects, consisteth in the imposing of *Names*, and the *Connexion* of them.

Of Names, some are *Proper*, and singular to one onely thing; as *Peter*, *John*, *This man*, *this Tree*: and some are *Common* to many things; as *Man*, *Horse*, *Tree*; every of which though but one Name, is nevertheless the name of divers particular things; in respect of all which together, it is called an *Universall*; there being nothing in the world Universall but Names; for the things named, are every one of them Individuall and Singular.

One Universall name is imposed on many things, for their similitude in some quality, or other accident: And whereas a Proper Name bringeth to mind one thing onely; Universals recall any one of those many.

And of Names Universall, some are of more, and some of lesse extent; the larger comprehending the lesse large: and some again of equall extent, comprehending each other reciprocally. As for example, the Name *Body* is of larger signification than the word *Man*, and comprehendeth it; and the names *Man* and *Rationall*, are of equall extent, comprehending mutually one another. But here wee must take notice, that by a Name is not alwayes understood, as in Grammar, one onely Word; but sometimes by circumlocution many words together. For all these words, *Hee that in his actions observeth the Lawes of his Country*, make but one Name, equivalent to this one word, *Just*.

By this imposition of Names, some of larger, some of stricter signification, we turn the reckoning of the consequences of things imagined in the mind, into a reckoning of the consequences of Appellations. For example, a man that hath no use of Speech at all, (such, as is born and remains perfectly deafe and dumb,) if he set before his eyes a triangle, and by it two right angles, (such as are the comers of a square figure,) he may by meditation compare and find, that the three angles of that triangle, are equall to those two right angles that stand by it. But if another triangle be shewn him different in shape from the former, he cannot know without a new labour, whether the three angles of that also be equall to the same. But he that hath the use of words, when he observes, that such equality was consequent, not to the length of the sides, nor to any other particular thing in his triangle; but onely to this, that the sides were straight, and the angles three; and that was all, for which he named it a Triangle; will boldly conclude Universally, that such equality of angles is in all triangles whatsoever; and register his invention in these generall termes, *Every triangle hath its three angles equall to two right angles*. And thus the consequence found in one particular, comes to be registred and remembred, as an Universall rule; and discharges our mentall reckoning, of time and place; and delivers us from all labour of the mind, saving the first; and makes that which was found true *here*, and *now*, to be true in *all times and places*.

But the use of words in registring our thoughts, is in nothing so evident as in Numbering. A naturall foole that could never learn by heart the order of numerall words, as *one, two*, and *three*, may observe every stroak of the Clock, and nod to it, or say one, one, one; but can never know what houre it strikes. And it seems, there was a time when those names of number were not in use; and men were fayn to their fingers of one or both hands, to those things they desired to keep account of; and that thence it proceeded, that now our numerall words are but ten, in any Nation, and in some but five, and then they begin again. And he that can tell ten, if he recite them out of order, will lose himselfe, and not know when he has done: Much lesse will he be able to adde, and substract, and performe all other operations of Arithmetique. So that without words, there is no possibility of reckoning of Numbers; much lesse of Magnitudes, of Swiftnesse, of Force, and other things, the reckonings whereof are necessary to the being, or well-being of man-kind.

When two Names are joyned together into a Consequence, or Affirmation; as thus, *A man is a living creature*; or thus, *if he be a man, he is a living creature*, If the later name *Living creature*, signifie all that the former name *Man* signifieth, then the affirmation, or consequence is *true*; othewise *false*. For *True and False* are attributes of Speech, not of Things. And where Speech is not, there is neither *Truth* nor *Falshood*. *Errour* there may be, when wee expect that which shall not be; or suspect what has not been: but in neither case can a man be charged with Untruth.

Seeing then that *truth* consisteth in the right ordering of names in our affirmations, a man that seeketh precise *truth*, had need to remember what every name he uses stands for; and to place it accordingly; or else he will find himselfe entangled in words, as a bird in lime-twiggs; the more he struggles, the more belimed. And therefore in Geometry, (which is the onely Science that it hath pleased God hitherto to bestow on mankind,) men begin at settling the significations of their words; which settling of significations, they call *Definitions*; and place them in the beginning of their reckoning.

By this it appears how necessary it is for any man that aspires to true Knowledge, to examine the Definitions of former Authors; and either to correct them, where they are negligently set down; or to make them himselfe. For the errours of Definitions multiply themselves, according as the reckoning proceeds; and lead men into absurdities, which at last they see, but cannot avoyd, without reckoning anew from the beginning; in which lyes the foundation of their errours. From whence it happens, that they which trust to books, do as they that cast up many little summs into a greater, without considering whether those little summes were rightly cast up or not; and at last finding the errour visible, and not mistrusting their first grounds, know not which way to cleere themselves; but spend time in fluttering over their bookes; as birds that entring by the chimney, and finding themselves inclosed in a chamber, flutter at the false light of a glasse window, for want of wit to consider which way they came in. So that in the right Definition of Names, lyes the first use of Speech; which is the Acquisition of Science: And in wrong, or no Definitions, lyes the first abuse; from which proceed all false and senslesse Tenets; which make those men that take their instruction from the authority of books, and not from their own meditation, to be as much below the condition of ignorant men, as men endued with true Science are above it. For between true Science, and erroneous Doctrines, Ignorance is in the middle. Naturall sense and imagination, are not subject to absurdity. Nature it selfe cannot erre: and as men abound in copiousnesse of language; so they become more wise, or more mad than ordinary. Nor is it possible without Letters for any man to become either excellently wise, or (unless his memory be hurt by disease, or ill constitution of organs) excellently foolish. For words are wise mens counters, they do but reckon by them: but they are the mony of fooles, that value them by the authority of an *Aristotle*, a *Cicero*, or a *Thomas*, or any other Doctor whatsoever, if but a man.

Chapter V: Of Reason, and Science

When a man *Reasoneth*, hee does nothing else but conceive a summe totall, from *Addition* of parcels; or conceive a Remainder, from *Substraction* of one summe from another: which (if it be done by Words,) is conceiving of the consequence of the names of all the parts, to the name of the whole; or from the names of the whole and one part, to the name of the other part. And though in some things, (as in numbers,) besides *Adding* and *Substracting*, men name other operations, as *Multiplying* and *Dividing*; yet they are the same; for Multiplication, is but Adding together of things equall; and Division, but Substracting of one thing, as often as we can. These operations are not incident to Numbers onely, but to all manner of things that can be added together, and taken one out of another. For as Arithmeticians teach to adde and substract in *numbers*; so the Geometricians teach the same in *lines, figures* (solid and superficiall,) *angles, proportions, times*, degrees of *swiftnesse, force, power*, and the like; The Logicians teach the same in *Consequences of words*; adding together *two Names*, to make an *Affirmation*; and *two Affirmations*, to make a *Syllogisme*; and *many Syllogismes* to make a *Demonstration*; and from the *summe*, or *Conclusion* of a *Syllogisme*, they subtract one *Proposition*, to finde the other. Writers of Politiques, adde together *Pactions*, to find mens *duties*; and Lawyers, *Lawes*, and *facts*, to find what is *right* and *wrong* in the actions of private men. In summe, in what matter soever there is place for *addition* and *substraction*, there also is place for *Reason*; and where these have no place, there *Reason* has nothing at all to do.

Out of all which we may define, (that is to say determine,) what that is, which is meant by this word *Reason*, when wee reckon it amongst the Faculties of the mind. For REASON, in this sense, is nothing but *Reckoning* (that is, Adding and Substracting) of the Consequences of generall names agreed upon, for the *marking* and *signifying* of our thoughts; I say *marking* them, when we reckon by our selves; and *signifying*, when we demonstrate, or approve our reckonings to other men.

And as in Arithmetique, unpractised men must, and Professors themselves may often erre, and cast up false; so also in any other subject of Reasoning, the ablest, most attentive, and most practised men, may deceive themselves, and inferre false Conclusions; Not but that Reason it selfe is always Right. Reason, as well as Arithmetique is a certain and infallible Art: But no one mans Reason, nor the Reason of any one number of men, makes the certaintie; no more than an account is therefore well cast up, because a great many men have unanimously approved it. And therfore, as when there is a controversy in an account, the parties must by their own accord, set up for right Reason, the Reason of some Arbitrator, or Judge, to whose sentence they will both stand, or their controversie must either come to blowes, or be undecided, for want of a right Reason constituted by Nature; so is it also in all debates of what kind soever: And when men that think themselves wiser than all others, clamor and demand right Reason for judge; yet seek no more, but that things should be determined, by no other mens reason but their own, it is as intolerable in the society of men, as it is in play after trump is turned, to use for trump on every occasion, that suite whereof they have most in their hand. For they do nothing els, that will have every of their passions, as it comes to bear sway in them, to be taken for right Reason, and that in their own controversies: betraying their want of right Reason, by the claym they lay to it.

Chapter XIII: Of the NATURAL CONDITION of Mankind, as concerning their Felicity, and Misery

Nature hath made men so equall, in the faculties of body, and mind; as that though there bee found one man sometimes manifestly stronger in body, or of quicker mind then another; yet when all is reckoned together, the difference between man, and man, is not so considerable, as that one man can thereupon claim to himselfe any benefit, to which another may not pretend, as well as he. For as to the strength of body, the weakest has strength enough to kill the strongest, either by secret machination, or by confederacy with others, that are in the same danger with himselfe.

And as to the faculties of the mind, (setting aside the arts grounded upon words, and especially that skill of proceeding upon generall, and infallible rules, called Science; which very few have, and but in few things; as being not a native faculty, born with us; nor attained, (as Prudence,) while we look after somewhat els,) I find yet a greater equality amongst men, than that of strength. For Prudence, is but Experience; which equall time, equally bestowes on all men, in those things they equally apply themselves unto. That which may perhaps make such equality incredible, is but a vain conceipt of ones owne wisdome, which almost all men think they have in a greater degree, than the Vulgar; that is, than all men but themselves, and a few others, whom by Fame, or for concurring with themselves, they approve. For such is the nature of men, that howsoever they may acknowledge many others to be more witty, or more eloquent, or more learned; Yet they will hardly believe there be many so wise as themselves: For they see their own wit at hand, and other mens at a distance. But this proveth rather that men are in that point equall, than unequall. For there is not ordinarily a greater signe of the equall distribution of any thing, than that every man is contented with his share.

From this equality of ability, ariseth equality of hope in the attaining of our Ends. And therefore if any two men desire the same thing, which neverthelesse they cannot both enjoy, they become enemies; and in the way to their End, (which is principally their owne conservation, and sometimes their delectation only,) endeavour to destroy, or subdue one an other. And from hence it comes to passe, that where an invader hath no more to feare, than an other mans single power; if one plant, sow, build, or possesse a convenient Seat, others may probably be expected to come prepared with forces united, to dispossesse, and deprive him, not only of the fruit of his labour, but also of his life, or liberty. And the Invader again is in the like danger of another.

And from this diffidence of one another, there is no way for any man to secure himselfe, so reasonable, as Anticipation; that is, by force, or wiles, to master the persons of all men he can, so long, till he see no other power great enough to endanger him: And this is no more than his own conservation requireth, and is generally allowed. Also because there be some, that taking pleasure in contemplating their own power in the acts of conquest, which they pursue farther than their security requires; if others, that otherwise would be glad to be at ease within modest bounds, should not by invasion increase their power, they would not be able, long time, by standing only on their defence, to subsist. And by consequence, such augmentation of dominion over men, being necessary to a mans conservation, it ought to be allowed him.

Againe, men have no pleasure, (but on the contrary a great deale of griefe) in keeping company, where there is no power able to over-awe them all. For every man looketh that his companion should value him, at the same rate he sets upon himselfe: And upon all signes of contempt, or undervaluing, naturally endeavours, as far as he dares (which amongst them that have no common power, to keep them in quiet, is far enough to make them destroy each other,) to extort a greater value from his contemners, by dommage; and from others, by the example.

So that in the nature of man, we find three principall causes of quarrell. First, Competition; Secondly, Diffidence; Thirdly, Glory.

The first, maketh men invade for Gain; the second, for Safety; and the third, for Reputation. The first use Violence, to make themselves Masters of other mens persons, wives, children, and cattell; the second, to defend them; the third, for trifles, as a word, a smile, a different opinion, and any other signe of undervalue, either direct in their Persons, or by reflexion in their Kindred, their Friends, their Nation, their Profession, or their Name.

Hereby it is manifest, that during the time men live without a common Power to keep them all in awe, they are in that condition which is called Warre; and such a warre, as is of every man against every man. For WARRE, consisteth not in Battell onely, or the act of fighting; but in a tract of time, wherein the Will to contend by Battell is sufficiently known: and therefore the notion of *Time*, is to be considered in the nature of Warre; as it is in the nature of Weather. For as the nature of Foule weather, lyeth not in a showre or two of rain; but in an inclination thereto of many dayes together: So the nature of War, consisteth not in actuall fighting; but in the known disposition thereto, during all the time there is no assurance to the contrary. All other time is PEACE.

Whatsoever therefore is consequent to a time of Warre, where every man is Enemy to every man; the same is consequent to the time, wherein men live without other security, than what their own strength, and their own invention shall furnish them withall. In such condition, there is no place for Industry; because the fruit thereof is uncertain: and consequently no Culture of the Earth; no Navigation, nor use of the commodities that may be imported by Sea; no commodious Building; no Instruments of moving, and removing such things as require much force; no Knowledge of the face of the Earth; no account of Time; no Arts; no Letters; no Society; and which is worst of all, continuall feare, and danger of violent death; And the life of man, solitary, poore, nasty, brutish, and short.

It may seem strange to some man, that has not well weighed these things; that Nature should thus dissociate, and render men apt to invade, and destroy one another: and he may therefore, not trusting to this Inference, made from the Passions, desire perhaps to have the same confirmed by Experience. Let him therefore consider with himselfe, when taking a journey, he armes himselfe, and seeks to go well accompanied; when going to sleep, he locks his dores; when even in his house he locks his chests; and this when he knows there bee Lawes, and publike Officers, armed, to revenge all injuries shall bee done him; what opinion he has of his fellow subjects, when he rides armed; of his fellow Citizens, when he locks his dores; and of his children, and servants, when he locks his chests. Does he not there as much accuse mankind by his actions, as I do by my words? But neither of us accuse mans nature in it. The Desires, and other Passions of man, are in themselves no Sin. No more are the Actions, that proceed from those Passions, till they know a Law that forbids them: which till Lawes be made they cannot know: nor can any Law be made, till they have agreed upon the Person that shall make it.

It may peradventure be thought, there was never such a time, nor condition of warre as this; and I believe it was never generally so, over all the world: but there are many places, where they live so now. For the savage people in many places of *America*, except the, government of small Families, the concord whereof dependeth on naturall lust, have no government at all; and live at this day in that brutish manner, as I said before. Howsoever, it may be perceived what manner of life there would be, where there were no common Power to feare; by the manner of life, which men that have formerly lived under a peacefull government, use to degenerate into, in a civill Warre.

But though there had never been any time, wherein particular men were in a condition of warre one against another; yet in all times, Kings, and Persons of Soveraigne authority, because of their Independency, are in continuall jealousies, and in the state and posture of Gladiators; having their weapons pointing, and their eyes fixed on one another; that is, their Forts, Garrisons, and Guns upon the Frontiers of their Kingdomes; and continuall Spyes upon their neighbours; which is a posture of War. But because they uphold thereby, the Industry of their Subjects; there does not follow from it, that misery, which accompanies the Liberty of particular men.

To this warre of every man against every man, this also is consequent; that nothing can be Unjust. The notions of Right and Wrong, Justice and Injustice have there no place. Where there is no common Power, there is no Law: where no Law, no Injustice. Force, and Fraud, are in warre the two Cardinall vertues. Justice, and Injustice are none of the Faculties neither of the Body, nor Mind. If they were, they might be in a man that were alone in the world, as well as his Senses, and Passions. They are Qualities, that relate to men in Society, not in

Solitude. It is consequent also to the same condition, that there be no Propriety, no Dominion, no *Mine* and *Thine* distinct; but onely that to be every mans
that he can get; and for so long, as he can keep it. And thus much for the ill
condition, which man by meer Nature is actually placed in; though with a
possiblity to come out of it, consisting partly in the Passions, partly in his
Reason.

The Passions that encline men to Peace, are Feare of Death; Desire of such
things as are necessary to commodious living; and a Hope by their industry to
obtain them. And Reason suggesteth convenient Articles of Peace, upon which
men may be drawn to agreement. These Articles, are they, which otherwise are
called the Lawes of Nature: whereof I shall speak more particularly, in the two
following Chapters.

The Second Sex, Introduction
Simone de Beauvoir

Simone de Beauvoir's (1908–1986) publication of *The Second Sex* in 1949 in
her native France established her as one of the leading feminists and philosophers of the twentieth century. This interdisciplinary analysis of women's inequality was widely read right from the start – 22,000 copies were sold in the first
week after publication – and it has achieved the status of a classic text in the
philosophy, psychology, and history of woman.

For a long time I have hesitated to write a book on woman. The subject is
irritating, especially to women; and it is not new. Enough ink has been spilled
in the quarreling over feminism, now practically over, and perhaps we should
say no more about it. It is still talked about, however, for the voluminous
nonsense uttered during the last century seems to have done little to illuminate
the problem. After all, is there a problem? And if so, what is it? Are there
women, really? Most assuredly the theory of the eternal feminine still has its
adherents who will whisper in your ear: "Even in Russia women still are
women"; and other erudite persons – sometimes the very same – say with a
sigh: "Woman is losing her way, woman is lost." One wonders if women still
exist, if they will always exist, whether or not it is desirable that they should,
what place they occupy in this world, what their place should be. "What has
become of women?" was asked recently in an ephemeral magazine.[1]

But first we must ask: what is a woman? "*Tota mulier in utero,*" says one,
"woman is a womb." But in speaking of certain women, connoisseurs declare
that they are not women, although they are equipped with a uterus like the rest.
All agree in recognizing the fact that females exist in the human species; today as
always they make up about one half of humanity. And yet we are told that
femininity is in danger; we are exhorted to be women, remain women, become
women. It would appear, then, that every female human being is not necessarily

a woman; to be so considered she must share in that mysterious and threatened reality known as femininity. Is this attribute something secreted by the ovaries? Or is it a Platonic essence, a product of the philosophic imagination? Is a rustling petticoat enough to bring it down to earth? Although some women try zealously to incarnate this essence, it is hardly patentable. It is frequently described in vague and dazzling terms that seem to have been borrowed from the vocabulary of the seers, and indeed in the times of St Thomas it was considered an essence as certainly defined as the somniferous virtue of the poppy.

But conceptualism has lost ground. The biological and social sciences no longer admit the existence of unchangeable fixed entities that determine given characteristics, such as those ascribed to woman, the Jew, or the Negro. Science regards any characteristic as a reaction dependent in part upon a *situation*. If today femininity no longer exists, then it never existed. But does the word *woman*, then, have no specific content? This is stoutly affirmed by those who hold to the philosophy of the enlightenment, of rationalism, of nominalism; women, to them, are merely the human beings arbitrarily designated by the word *woman*. Many American women particularly are prepared to think that there is no longer any place for woman as such; if a backward individual still takes herself for a woman, her friends advise her to be psychoanalyzed and thus get rid of this obsession. In regard to a work, *Modern Woman: The Lost Sex*, which in other respects has its irritating features, Dorothy Parker has written: "I cannot be just to books which treat of woman as woman. . . . My idea is that all of us, men as well as women, should be regarded as human beings." But nominalism is a rather inadequate doctrine, and the antifemininists have had no trouble in showing that women simply are not men. Surely woman is, like man, a human being; but such a declaration is abstract. The fact is that every concrete human being is always a singular, separate individual. To decline to accept such notions as the eternal feminine, the black soul, the Jewish character, is not to deny that Jews, Negroes, women exist today – this denial does not represent a liberation for those concerned, but rather a flight from reality. Some years ago a well-known woman writer refused to permit her portrait to appear in a series of photographs especially devoted to women writers; she wished to be counted among the men. But in order to gain this privilege she made use of her husband's influence! Women who assert that they are men lay claim none the less to masculine consideration and respect. I recall also a young Trotskyite standing on a platform at a boisterous meeting and getting ready to use her fists, in spite of her evident fragility. She was denying her feminine weakness; but it was for love of a militant male whose equal she wished to be. The attitude of defiance of many American women proves that they are haunted by a sense of their femininity. In truth, to go for a walk with one's eyes open is enough to demonstrate that humanity is divided into two classes of individuals whose clothes, faces, bodies, smiles, gaits, interests, and occupations are manifestly different. Perhaps these differences are superficial, perhaps they are destined to disappear. What is certain is that right now they do most obviously exist.

If her functioning as a female is not enough to define woman, if we decline also to explain her through "the eternal feminine," and if nevertheless we admit, provisionally, that women do exist, then we must face the question: what is a woman?

To state the question is, to me, to suggest, at once, a preliminary answer. The fact that I ask it is in itself significant. A man would never get the notion of writing a book on the peculiar situation of the human male.[2] But if I wish to define myself, I must first of all say: "I am a woman"; on this truth must be based all further discussion. A man never begins by presenting himself as an individual of a certain sex; it goes without saying that he is a man. The terms masculine and feminine are used symmetrically only as a matter of form, as on legal papers. In actuality the relation of the two sexes is not quite like that of two electrical poles, for man represents both the positive and the neutral, as is indicated by the common use of *man* to designate human beings in general; whereas woman represents only the negative, defined by limiting criteria, without reciprocity. In the midst of an abstract discussion it is vexing to hear a man say: "You think thus and so because you are a woman"; but I know that my only defense is to reply: "I think thus and so because it is true," thereby removing my subjective self from the argument. It would be out of the question to reply: "And you think the contrary because you are a man," for it is understood that the fact of being a man is no peculiarity. A man is in the right in being a man; it is the woman who is in the wrong. It amounts to this: just as for the ancients there was an absolute vertical with reference to which the oblique was defined, so there is an absolute human type, the masculine. Woman has ovaries, a uterus; these peculiarities imprison her in her subjectivity, circumscribe her within the limits of her own nature. It is often said that she thinks with her glands. Man superbly ignores the fact that his anatomy also includes glands, such as the testicles, and that they secrete hormones. He thinks of his body as a direct and normal connection with the world, which he believes he apprehends objectively, whereas he regards the body of woman as a hindrance, a prison, weighed down by everything peculiar to it. "The female is a female by virtue of a certain *lack* of qualities," said Aristotle; we should regard the female nature as afflicted with a natural defectiveness." And St Thomas for his part pronounced woman to be an "imperfect man," an "incidental" being. This is symbolized in Genesis where Eve is depicted as made from what Bossuet called "a supernumerary bone" of Adam.

Thus humanity is male and man defines woman not in herself but as relative to him; she is not regarded as an autonomous being. Michelet writes: "Woman, the relative being . . ." And Benda is most positive in his *Rapport d'Uriel:* "The body of man makes sense in itself quite apart from that of woman, whereas the latter seems wanting in significance by itself. . . . Man can think of himself without woman. She cannot think of herself without man." And she is simply what man decrees; thus she is called "the sex," by which is meant that she appears essentially to the male as a sexual being. For him she is sex – absolute sex, no less. She is defined and differentiated with reference to man and not he with reference to her; she is the incidental, the inessential as opposed to the essential. He is the Subject, he is the Absolute – she is the Other.[3]

The category of the *Other* is as primordial as consciousness itself. In the most primitive societies, in the most ancient mythologies, one finds the expression of a duality – that of the Self and the Other. This duality was not originally attached to the division of the sexes; it was not dependent upon any empirical facts. It is revealed in such works as that of Granet on Chinese thought and those of Dumzil on the East Indies and Rome. The feminine element was at first no more involved in such pairs as Varuna–Mitra, Uranus–Zeus, Sun–Moon, and Day–Night than it was in the contrasts between Good and Evil, lucky and unlucky auspices, right and left, God and Lucifer. Otherness is a fundamental category of human thought.

Thus it is that no group ever sets itself up as the One without at once setting up the Other over against itself. If three travelers chance to occupy the same compartment, that is enough to make vaguely hostile "others" out of all the rest of the passengers on the train. In small-town eyes all persons not belonging to the village are "strangers" and suspect; to the native of a country all who inhabit other countries are "foreigners"; Jews are "different" for the anti-Semite, Negroes are "inferior" for American racists, aborigines are "natives" for colonists, proletarians are the "lower class" for the privileged. . . .

. . . The native traveling abroad is shocked to find himself in turn regarded as a "stranger" by the natives of neighboring countries. As a matter of fact, wars, festivals, trading, treaties, and contests among tribes, nations, and classes tend to deprive the concept Other of its absolute sense and to make manifest its relativity; willy-nilly, individuals and groups are forced to realize the reciprocity of their relations. How is it, then, that this reciprocity has not been recognized between the sexes, that one of the contrasting terms is set up as the sole essential, denying any relativity in regard to its correlative and defining the latter as pure otherness? Why is it that women do not dispute male sovereignty? No subject will readily volunteer to become the object, the inessential; it is not the Other who, in defining himself as the Other, establishes the One. The Other is posed as such by the One in defining himself as the One. But if the Other is not to regain the status of being the One, he must be submissive enough to accept this alien point of view. Whence comes this submission in the case of woman? . . .

Notes

1   *Franchise*, dead today.
2   The Kinsey Report [Alfred C. Kinsey and others: *Sexual Behavior in the Human Male* (W. B. Saunders Co., 1948)] is no exception, for it is limited to describing the sexual characteristics of American men, which is quite a different matter.
3   E. Lévinas expresses this idea most explicitly in his essay *Temps et l'Autre*. "Is there not a case in which otherness, alterity [*altéreté*], unquestionably marks the nature of

a being, as its essence, an instance of otherness not consisting purely and simply in the opposition of two species of the same genus? I think that the feminine represents the contrary in its absolute sense, this contrariness being in no wise affected by any relation between it and its correlative and thus remaining absolutely other. Sex is not a certain specific difference . . . no more is the sexual difference a mere contradiction. . . . Nor does this difference lie in the duality of two complementary terms, for two complementary terms imply a pre-existing whole. . . . Otherness reaches its full flowering in the feminine, a term of the same rank as consciousness but of opposite meaning."

I suppose that Lévinas does not forget that woman, too, is aware of her own consciousness, or ego. But it is striking that he deliberately takes a man's point of view, disregarding the reciprocity of subject and object. When he writes that woman is mystery, he implies that she is mystery for man. Thus his description which is intended to be objective, is in fact an assertion of masculine privilege.

Selection from *The Problems of Philosophy*
Bertrand Russell

Bertrand Russell (1872–1970) was a British philosopher and perhaps the greatest philosopher of the twentieth century. He held several university posts and published widely while pursuing his literary, political, and educational interests. He is best known for his contributions to logic and metaphysics, as well as his opposition to the Second World War and the Vietnam War. In the selection below from *The Problems of Philosophy* he argues that universals exist, and compares them to Plato's forms, and further that universals exist independently of the mind. He also discusses the relationship between philosophy and action.

The World of Universals

At the end of the preceding chapter we saw that such entities as relations appear to have a being which is in some way different from that of physical objects, and also different from that of minds and from that of sense-data. In the present chapter we have to consider what is the nature of this kind of being, and also what objects there are that have this kind of being. We will begin with the latter question.

The problem with which we are now concerned is a very old one, since it was brought into philosophy by Plato. Plato's "theory of ideas" is an attempt to solve this very problem, and in my opinion it is one of the most successful attempts hitherto made. The theory to be advocated in what follows is largely Plato's, with merely such modifications as time has shown to be necessary.

The way the problem arose for Plato was more or less as follows. Let us consider, say, such a notion as *justice*. If we ask ourselves what justice is, it is natural to proceed by considering this, that, and the other just act, with a view to discovering what they have in common. They must all, in some sense, partake of a common nature, which will be found in whatever is just and in nothing else. This common nature, in virtue of which they are all just, will be justice itself, the pure essence the admixture of which with facts of ordinary life produces the multiplicity of just acts. Similarly with any other word which may be applicable to common facts, such as "whiteness" for example. The word will be applicable to a number of particular things because they all participate in a common nature or essence. This pure essence is what Plato calls an "idea" or "form." (It must not be supposed that "ideas," in his sense, exist in minds, though they may be apprehended by minds.) The "idea" *justice* is not identical with anything that is just: it is something other than particular things, which particular things partake of. Not being particular, it cannot itself exist in the world of sense. Moreover it is not fleeting or changeable like the things of sense: it is eternally itself, immutable and indestructible.

Thus Plato is led to a supra-sensible world, more real than the common world of sense, the unchangeable world of ideas, which alone gives to the world of sense whatever pale reflection of reality may belong to it. The truly real world, for Plato, is the world of ideas; for whatever we may attempt to say about things in the world of sense, we can only succeed in saying that they participate in such and such ideas, which, therefore, constitute all their character. Hence it is easy to pass on into a mysticism. We may hope, in a mystic illumination, to *see* the ideas as we see objects of sense; and we may imagine. that the ideas exist in heaven. These mystical developments are very natural, but the basis of the theory is in logic, and it is as based in logic that we have to consider it.

The word "idea" has acquired, in the course of time, many associations which are quite misleading when applied to Plato's "ideas." We shall therefore use the word "universal" instead of the word "idea," to describe what Plato meant. The essence of the sort of entity that Plato meant is that it is opposed to the particular things that are given in sensation. We speak of whatever is given in sensation, or is of the same nature as things given in sensation, as a *particular*; by opposition to this, a *universal* will be anything which may be shared by many particulars, and has those characteristics which, as we saw, distinguish justice and whiteness from just acts and white things.

When we examine common words, we find that, broadly speaking, proper names stand for particulars, while other substantives, adjectives, prepositions, and verbs stand for universals. Pronouns stand for particulars, but are ambiguous: it is only by the context or the circumstances that we know what particulars they stand for. The word "now" stands for a particular, namely the present moment; but like pronouns, it stands for an ambiguous particular, because the present is always changing.

It will be seen that no sentence can be made up without at least one word which denotes a universal. The nearest approach would be some such statement as "I like this." But even here the word "like" denotes a universal, for I may like other things, and other people may like things. Thus all truths involve universals, and all knowledge of truths involves acquaintance with universals.

Seeing that nearly all the words to be found in the dictionary stand for universals, it is strange that hardly anybody except students of philosophy ever realizes that there are such entities as universals. We do not naturally dwell upon those words in a sentence which do not stand for particulars; and if we are forced to dwell upon a word which stands for a universal, we naturally think of it as standing for some one of the particulars that come under the universal. When, for example, we hear the sentence "Charles I's head was cut off," we may naturally enough think of Charles I, of Charles I's head, and of the operation of cutting off *his* head, which are all particulars; but we do not naturally dwell upon what is meant by the word "head" or the word "cut," which is a universal. We feel such words to be incomplete and insubstantial; they seem to demand a context before anything can be done with them. Hence we succeed in avoiding all notice of universals as such, until the study of philosophy forces them upon our attention.

Even among philosophers, we may say, broadly, that only those universals which are named by adjectives or substantives have been much or often recognised, while those named by verbs and prepositions have been usually overlooked. This omission has had a very great effect upon philosophy; it is hardly too much to say that most metaphysics, since Spinoza, has been largely determined by it. The way this has occurred is, in outline, as follows: Speaking generally, adjectives and common nouns express qualities or properties of single things, whereas prepositions and verbs tend to express relations between two or more things. Thus the neglect of prepositions and verbs led to the belief that every proposition can be regarded as attributing a property to a single thing, rather than as expressing a relation between two or more things. Hence it was supposed that, ultimately, there can be no such entities as relations between things. Hence either there can be only one thing in the universe, or, if there are many things, they cannot possibly interact in any way, since any interaction would be a relation, and relations are impossible.

The first of these views, advocated by Spinoza and held in our own day by Bradley and many other philosophers, is called *monism*; the second, which was advocated by Leibniz but is not very common nowadays, is called *monadism*, because each of the isolated things is called a *monad*. Both these opposing philosophies, interesting as they are, result, in my opinion, from an undue attention to one sort of universals, namely the sort represented by adjectives and substantives rather than by verbs and prepositions.

As a matter of fact, if any one were anxious to deny altogether that there are such things as universals, we should find that we cannot strictly prove that there are such entities as *qualities*, i.e. the universals represented by adjectives and substantives, whereas we can prove that there must be *relations*, i.e. the sort of universals generally represented by verbs and prepositions. Let us take in illustration the universal *whiteness*. If we believe that there is such a universal, we shall say that things are white because they have the quality of whiteness. This view, however, was strenuously denied by Berkeley and Hume, who have been followed in this by later empiricists. The form which their denial took was to deny that there are such things as "abstract ideas." When we want to think of whiteness, they said, we form an image of some particular white thing, and reason concerning this particular, taking care not to deduce anything concerning it which we cannot see to be equally true of any other white thing. As an account of our actual mental processes, this is no doubt largely true. In geometry, for example, when we wish to prove something about all triangles, we draw a particular triangle and reason about it, taking care not to use any characteristic which it does not share with other triangles. The beginner, in order to avoid error, often finds it useful to draw several triangles, as unlike each other as possible, in order to make sure that his reasoning is equally applicable to all of them. But a difficulty emerges as soon as we ask ourselves how we know that a thing is white or a triangle. If we wish to avoid the universals *whiteness* and *triangularity*, we shall choose some particular patch of white or some particular triangle, and say that anything is white or a triangle if it has the right sort of resemblance to our chosen particular. But then the resemblance required will have to be a universal. Since there are many white things, the resemblance must hold between many pairs of particular white things; and this is the characteristic of a universal. It will be useless to say that there is a different resemblance for each pair, for then we shall have to say that these resemblances resemble each other, and thus at last we shall be forced to admit resemblance as a universal. The relation of resemblance, therefore, must be a true universal. And having been forced to admit this universal, we find that it is no longer worth while to invent difficult and unplausible theories to avoid the admission of such universals as whiteness and triangularity.

Berkeley and Hume failed to perceive this refutation of their rejection of "abstract ideas," because, like their adversaries, they only thought of *qualities*, and altogether ignored *relations* as universals. We have therefore here another respect in which the rationalists appear to have been in the right as against the empiricists, although, owing to the neglect or denial of relations, the deductions made by rationalists were, if anything, more apt to be mistaken than those made by empiricists.

Having now seen that there must be such entities as universals, the next point to be proved is that their being is not merely mental. By this is meant that whatever being belongs to them is independent of their being thought of or in any way apprehended by minds. We have already touched on this subject at the end of the preceding chapter, but we must now consider more fully what sort of being it is that belongs to universals.

Consider such a proposition as "Edinburgh is north of London." Here we have a relation between two places, and it seems plain that the relation subsists independently of our knowledge of it. When we come to know that Edinburgh is north of London, we come to know something which has to do only with Edinburgh and London: we do not cause the truth of the proposition by coming to know it, on the contrary we merely apprehend a fact which was there before we knew it. The part of the earth's surface where Edinburgh stands would be north of the part where London stands, even if there were no human being to know about north and south, and even if there were no minds at all in the universe. This is, of course, denied by many philosophers, either for Berkeley's reasons or for Kant's. But we have already considered these reasons, and decided that they are inadequate. We may therefore now assume it to be true that nothing mental is presupposed in the fact that Edinburgh is north of London. But this fact involves the relation "north of," which is a universal; and it would be impossible for the whole fact to involve nothing mental if the relation "north of," which is a constituent part of the fact, did involve anything mental. Hence we must admit that the relation, like the terms it relates, is not dependent upon thought, but belongs to the independent world which thought apprehends but does not create.

This conclusion, however, is met by the difficulty that the relation "north of" does not seem to *exist* in the same sense in which Edinburgh and London exist. If we ask "Where and when does this relation exist?" the answer must be "Nowhere and nowhen." There is no place or time where we can find the relation "north of." It does not exist in Edinburgh any more than in London, for it relates the two and is neutral as between them. Nor can we say that it exists at any particular time. Now everything that can be apprehended by the senses or by introspection exists at some particular time. Hence the relation "north of" is radically different from such things. It is neither in space nor in time, neither material nor mental; yet it is something.

It is largely the very peculiar kind of being that belongs to universals which has led many people to suppose that they are really mental. We can think *of* a universal, and our thinking then exists in a perfectly ordinary sense, like any other mental act. Suppose, for example, that we are thinking of whiteness. Then *in one sense* it may be said that whiteness is "in our mind." We have here the same ambiguity as we noted in discussing Berkeley in Chapter IV. In the strict sense, it is not whiteness that is in our mind, but the act of thinking of whiteness. The connected ambiguity in the word "idea," which we noted at the same time, also causes confusion here. In one sense of this word, namely the sense in which it denotes the *object* of an act of thought, whiteness is an "idea." Hence, if the ambiguity is not guarded against, we may come to think that whiteness is an "idea" in the other sense, i.e. an act of thought; and thus we come to think that whiteness is mental. But in so thinking, we rob it of its essential quality of universality. One man's act of thought is necessarily a different thing from another man's; one man's act of thought at one time is necessarily a different thing from the same man's act of thought at another time. Hence, if whiteness were the thought as opposed to its object, no two different men could think of it, and no one man could think of it twice. That which many different thoughts of whiteness have in common is their *object*, and this object is different from all of them. Thus universals are not thoughts, though when known they are the objects of thoughts.

We shall find it convenient only to speak of things *existing* when they are in time, that is to say, when we can point to some time *at* which they exist (not excluding the possibility of their existing at all times). Thus thoughts and feelings, minds and physical objects *exist*. But universals do not exist in this sense; we shall say that they *subsist* or *have being*, where "being" is opposed to "existence" as being timeless. The world of universals, therefore, may also be described as the world of being. The world of being is unchangeable, rigid, exact, delightful to the mathematician, the logician, the builder of metaphysical systems, and all who love perfection more than life. The world of existence is fleeting, vague, without sharp boundaries, without any clear plan or arrangement, but it contains all thoughts and feelings, all the data of sense, and all physical objects, everything that can do either good or harm, everything that makes any difference to the value of life and the world. According to our temperaments, we shall prefer the contemplation of the one or of the other. The one we do not prefer will probably seem to us a pale shadow of the one we prefer, and hardly worthy to be regarded as in any sense real. But the truth is that both have the same claim on our impartial attention, both are real, and both are important to the metaphysician. Indeed no sooner have we distinguished the two worlds than it becomes necessary to consider their relations. . . .

The Value of Philosophy

. . . Philosophic contemplation does not, in its widest survey, divide the universe into two hostile camps – friends and foes, helpful and hostile, good and bad – it views the whole impartially. Philosophic contemplation, when it is unalloyed, does not aim at proving that the rest of the universe is akin to man. All acquisition of knowledge is an enlargement of the Self, but this enlargement is best attained when it is not directly sought. It is obtained when the desire for knowledge is alone operative, by a study which does not wish in advance that its objects should have this or that character, but adapts the Self to the characters which it finds in its objects. This enlargement of Self is not obtained when, taking the Self as it is, we try to show that the world is so similar to this Self that knowledge of it is possible without any admission of what seems alien. The desire to prove this is a form of self-assertion and, like all self-assertion, it is an obstacle to the growth of Self which it desires, and of which the Self knows that it is capable. Self-assertion, in philosophic speculation as elsewhere, views the world as a means to its own ends; thus it makes the world of less account than Self, and the Self sets bounds to the greatness of its goods. In contemplation, on the contrary, we start from the not-Self, and through its greatness the boundaries of Self are enlarged; through the infinity of the universe the mind which contemplates it achieves some share in infinity.

For this reason greatness of soul is not fostered by those philosophies which assimilate the universe to Man. Knowledge is a form of union of Self and not-Self; like all union, it is impaired by dominion, and therefore by any attempt to force the universe into conformity with what we find in ourselves. There is a widespread philosophical tendency towards the view which tells us that Man is the measure of all things, that truth is man-made, that space and time and the world of universals are properties of the mind, and that, if there be anything not created by the mind, it is unknowable and of no account for us. This view, if our previous discussions were correct, is untrue; but in addition to being untrue, it has the effect of robbing philosophic contemplation of all that gives it value, since it fetters contemplation to Self. What it calls knowledge is not a union with the not-Self, but a set of prejudices, habits, and desires, making an impenetrable veil between us and the world beyond. The man who finds pleasure in such a theory of knowledge is like the man who never leaves the domestic circle for fear his word might not be law.

The true philosophic contemplation, on the contrary, finds its satisfaction in every enlargement of the not-Self, in everything that magnifies the objects contemplated, and thereby the subject contemplating. Everything, in contemplation, that is personal or private, everything that depends upon habit, self-interest, or desire, distorts the object, and hence impairs the union which the intellect seeks. By thus making a barrier between subject and object, such personal and private things become a prison to the intellect. The free intellect will see as God might see, without a *here* and *now*, without hopes and fears, without the trammels of customary beliefs and traditional prejudices, calmly, dispassionately, in the sole and exclusive desire of knowledge – knowledge as impersonal, as purely contemplative, as it is possible for man to attain. Hence also the free intellect will value more the abstract and universal knowledge into which the accidents of private history do not enter, than the knowledge brought by the senses, and dependent, as such knowledge must be, upon an exclusive and personal point of view and a body whose sense-organs distort as much as they reveal.

The mind which has become accustomed to the freedom and impartiality of philosophic contemplation will preserve something of the same freedom and impartiality in the world of action and emotion. It will view its purposes and desires as parts of the whole, with the absence of insistence that results from seeing them as infinitesimal fragments in a world of which all the rest is unaffected by any one man's deeds. The impartiality which, in contemplation, is the unalloyed desire for truth, is the very same quality of mind which, in action, is justice, and in emotion is that universal love which can be given to all, and not only to those who are judged useful or admirable. Thus contemplation enlarges not only the objects of our thoughts, but also the objects of our actions and our affections: it makes us citizens of the universe, not only of one walled city at war with all the rest. In this citizenship of the universe consists man's true freedom, and his liberation from the thraldom of narrow hopes and fears.

Thus, to sum up our discussion of the value of philosophy: philosophy is to be studied, not for the sake of any definite answers to its questions, since no definite answers can, as a rule, be known to be true, but rather for the sake of the questions themselves; because these questions enlarge our conception of what is possible, enrich our intellectual imagination and diminish the dogmatic assurance which closes the mind against speculation; but above all because, through the greatness of the universe which philosophy contemplates, the mind also is rendered great, and becomes capable of that union with the universe which constitutes its highest good.

3

Values and Reality

Introduction

There is only one person left on planet Earth. In fact, she is the last person in the universe that can think and care about this planet. Earth could not sustain the human species any more and utopian enterprises to settle on other planets or artificial satellites failed miserably, as did attempts to find other persons in the universe or create artificial persons. Human beings turned out to be the only persons in the universe, and now there is only one left.

The red dust settled from her trek across the barren plain to Earth's last oasis. On its edges she finds an abandoned jeep and the corpses of its passengers, as if she needed another reminder that her own end is also very near. There is not enough food here to sustain her for more than a week, nothing to protect her from the bitterly cold nights, and her spells of nausea, dizziness, and shortness of breath are becoming more intense and frequent by the hour. The environment cannot sustain her much longer any more, and this knowledge fills her with terrible anger and disdain for the meager life around her. She curses what is left and in a fit of rage she takes the canister of gasoline from the back of the abandoned jeep and pours gasoline over the vegetation around her and into the spring that sustains it. Her rage turns into a thrill as she reaches for one of the few matches she has left and turns the last oasis into a roaring fire.

Most people confronted with this kind of scenario agree that there is something morally wrong about this action, but what makes this action immoral? Is she destroying something of moral value? As we will see in this chapter, these simple questions lead into the midst of important and far-reaching issues in the metaphysics of morality, issues that are relevant not just to morality, but to questions about the nature of reality itself.

Subjective Value

The example of the last oasis is extreme, but environmental ethicists have argued that although the answer to the questions above is "Yes," modern Western moral theories cannot justify this answer. Moreover, they argue, this failure of Western morality is part of the reason why the environment is in the mess it is today, and consequently we need a new environmental ethic.

An important reason given by environmentalists as to why traditional moral theories are inadequate is that on these views something has moral value just in the case that there are people or creatures much like people in that they have minds and value these things. In other words, these critics believe that traditional morality comes with a metaphysical view about the nature of moral value – that there are no values without valuers – and it is this metaphysics that keeps human beings from properly valuing their environment. Various labels can be attached to this metaphysical view, but a label that is widely used and accurately describes the view is "moral subjectivism." This label captures the idea that something is morally valuable just in the case that there is a person or *subject* that morally values this object.

This means that a necessary condition for something's having moral value is that there are subjects who have a psychological attitude of valuing something. Examples of such attitudes are approving or disapproving of something, recommending or condemning something, prescribing or prohibiting something, or preferring or rejecting something. For a moral subjectivist, without subjects who have these psychological states there are no moral values.

It also means that, for a moral subjectivist, having such a psychological state of valuing something is sufficient for moral value. If a subject morally values something, then it has moral value, period. In short, for a moral subjectivist, the tie between moral value and valuers is very tight. Valuers are necessary and sufficient for moral value. Without valuers, there are no moral values, and wherever there are moral values, there are valuers.

This view about moral values has close relatives for other domains. You probably have heard the popular philosophical question, "If a tree falls in the forest and nobody is there to hear it, does it make a sound?" This question and the negative answer are associated with the eighteenth-century Irish philosopher Bishop George Berkeley, who believed that *esse est percipii*: to be is to be perceived. Berkeley believed that an object existed only if it was thought of or perceived, and he believed this was true of material objects. Tables, trees, and tigers exist only because they are perceived, which, in Berkeley's view, made all material objects into ideas. For this reason, this view about material objects has been called "idealism."

Moral subjectivism is a relative of idealism because the two have this important feature in common: both maintain that something that appears to many people to be part of the fabric of the world that exists independently of any mind really depends on the mind. Idealists maintain this of matter: the existence of material objects depends on someone perceiving these objects, and hence without perceivers there are no material objects. Moral subjectivists maintain this of moral values: to have moral value is to be morally valued, and so without valuers there are no moral values.

Because of this similarity between idealism and moral subjectivism, it is tempting to think that moral subjectivists are idealists, but we need to be careful about this. A little bit of reflection will show that someone can be a moral subjectivist without being an idealist, and in fact many people believe that material objects are independent of minds, while moral values are mind-dependent. Just because you believe that one kind of thing is mind-dependent does not automatically mean that you believe that other kinds of things are mind-dependent.

Objective Value

Environmental ethicists propose that to properly value the natural and non-human environment, we need to reject moral subjectivism and recognize that moral values are objective. In other words, moral value is part of the very fabric of the world.

Someone who believes that moral values are objective believes that something has moral value irrespective of whether anyone values it. On this view, you can say that something is morally valuable, period, without saying anything more about who values it. Compare this to the moral subjectivist, for whom the claim that something has moral value is always, strictly speaking, elliptical. According to moral subjectivism, something always has moral value *for someone*, and it does not make sense to ask about the moral value of something without also asking for whom it has moral value. For instance, for a moral subjectivist, an oasis cannot simply have moral value. If it has moral value, it has moral value for someone, and if it does not have moral value, then it does not have moral value for anyone.

A label widely used for this view about moral value is "moral objectivism." It clearly expresses how it contrasts with "moral subjectivism." However, here too we must be careful to avoid confusion. There are senses of the terms "objective" and "subjective" that refer to ways in which people think and reason. We often claim that people are objective when they try to be rational and impartial about some issue, and we claim that they are subjective when they lack these virtues and are moved by bias or personal inclinations. These are different meanings of the terms "objective" and "subjective," and in this sense of these terms, moral subjectivists can be and in fact are just as objective as moral objectivists.

Another label for moral objectivism is "moral realism," and you may have noticed that this view about moral value is similar in important ways to realism about universals. Both views hold that there are objects that can exist even if no one thinks about them: realists about universals believe that universals exist even if no one thinks or talks about them, and moral objectivists believe that moral values exist even if no one thinks or talks about them. Nevertheless, when using "moral realism" we must be careful not to confuse realism about universals and moral realism. Moral realism is a metaphysical theory about moral value, and Platonic or Aristotelian realism are metaphysical theories about universals, and as we will see, a person can be a realist about moral values while not being a realist about universals.

Intrinsic and Instrumental Value

Sometimes the idea that value is part of the fabric of our environment is expressed by stating that plants or animals of the environment have *intrinsic value*.

However, the term "intrinsic" is confusing because it is ambiguous. Sometimes, "intrinsic value" means objective value, and as we just saw, objective value contrasts with subjective value. But "intrinsic value" can also mean non-instrumental value, which contrasts with *instrumental value*. Something is instrumentally valuable because it promotes something else that is valuable, while something is non-instrumentally valuable because it is valuable in itself, regardless of what other values it promotes or generates.

For example, going to a dentist for most people is only instrumentally valuable. You go because you value health, and if dentistry would not promote health, you would not go. There is nothing valuable in and of itself about sitting in a chair with your mouth wide open for metal high-speed drills and latex covered fingers. Health, however, is a candidate for something that is valuable on its own. It seems that being healthy is valuable no matter what else it promotes, and this would make it intrinsically valuable in the sense of being non-instrumentally valuable.

Nevertheless, people do not agree about what sorts of things are intrinsically valuable. Although ancient Greek philosophers thought health, along with courage and wisdom, had intrinsic value, modern philosophers were inclined to argue that health, courage, or wisdom are valuable only if they promote other values – for example, happiness or rationality. Thus these philosophers believe that health, courage, and wisdom are really only instrumental values while happiness or rationality are intrinsically valuable.

A good test for finding out what you think is intrinsically valuable is to see if a value ceases to be a value in some possible situations where it has bad consequences. For instance, consider a healthy parasite that destroys its host or a healthy tyrant that destroys his community. Here we have health, but this health promotes something bad, and for this reason we might suppose that the health of . the parasite or tyrant is not something that is valuable. If this is indeed the case, health is not an intrinsic value because its value depends on what other values it promotes.

However you decide the question about what values are instrumental and what values are non-instrumental, do not confuse this issue with questions about the subjectivity and objectivity of moral value. Philosophers who claim that all values are subjective can still grant that nature has intrinsic value. This is easy to see. You can value a wilderness because it promotes other values, e.g. cleaner air for human beings, or you can value it for its own sake: wilderness in and of itself is valuable no matter what else it promotes. For a moral subjectivist, if you value the wilderness for other good it generates or promotes, the wilderness has instrumental value for you. If you value it for what it is regardless of what other goods it promotes, it has non-instrumental value for you.

Since a moral subjectivist can distinguish between instrumental and non-instrumental value, it is best to use the term "instrumental value" very carefully and reserve it for a contrast to non-instrumental value, and to use "objective value" for value that is part of the fabric of the world apart from what people think or feel about what is valuable.

Moral Realism and Truth

In addition to the belief that there are objective moral values, moral realists hold that moral statements and beliefs have truth-values. For a statement or belief to have truth-value typically means that it is either true or false. While there are philosophers who believe that there are more than two truth-values, that in addition to truth and falsehood there is, for instance, the truth-value indeterminate, we will stick to two: truth and falsehood.

It is important to notice that moral realism has two components: the view that there are objective moral values and the view that moral statements have truth-values. This second component of moral realism – that moral statements have truth-values – is often called "moral descriptivism" or "moral cognitivism." The motivation for the first label is clear: if moral statements have a truth-value, they describe something. The underlying idea is that something is true or false just in the case that it describes something: what it is, what it does, and so on. The idea behind the second label is that if moral statements have a truth value, then they can express some knowledge, namely knowledge about morality. If moral statements have a truth-value, they are not simply expressions of our feelings, but they can express genuine knowledge about what is and is not morally valuable.

Now, if moral statements have a truth-value, we need to worry about the nature of truth and falsity. What makes a statement or belief true? What makes it false?

One view of what makes a statement or a belief true goes back to Aristotle, who wrote in his *Metaphysics*, "to say of what is that it is not, or of what is not that it is, is false, while to say of what is that it is, or of what is not that it is not, is true." The idea here is simple and appealing. If I state that the sun contains 99.86 percent of the total mass of the solar system, then what I state is true just in the case that the sun indeed contains 99.86 percent of the solar system's total mass, and it is false just in the case that it contains some other percentage of the total mass of the solar system, say 86.32 percent. So, on this view we have on the one hand beliefs or statements: ways in which we can in public or in private describe the way the world is. On the other hand, we have the mass of the sun and the solar system, or, if we are talking about moral realism, moral values. Whether a belief or statement about the sun's mass is true depends on whether the sun has the mass the statement or belief describes it as having. Whether a belief or statement that describes nature as having moral value is true depends on whether nature indeed has moral value.

Because this view of truth assumes that there are things in the world that are the way they are regardless of how anyone or anything thinks or talks about them, it is often called "a realist conception of truth." Sometimes it is also called the "correspondence theory of truth," because this view suggests that there is a correspondence or matching between true judgments or statements on the one hand and the way reality is or is not. Both terms are widely used, but "correspondence theory of truth" is misleading, because it suggests that there is some special relation of correspondence between thought and language on the one hand and the rest of the world on the other. Realists about truth need not assume that there is such a special relation. All they need to maintain is that at least sometimes when we state or believe that something is the case – e.g. that a ball is orange or that an oasis has moral value – then this is true just if this is indeed the case.

Needless to say, there are other views about the nature of truth. Two important competitors to the realist conception of truth, both of which were seriously pursued during the first half of the twentieth century, are the *pragmatic theory of truth* and the *coherence theory of truth*. According to the coherence theory of truth, a belief or statement is true just in the case that this belief or statement coheres with the rest of what we, individually or collectively, believe. So if the statement that an oasis has moral value is consistent with other beliefs we have, then the statement is true. According to the pragmatic theory of truth, at least as defended by the New England pragmatist John Dewey, a statement or belief is true just in the case that it is warranted by the available evidence. So if the statement that an oasis has moral value is supported by evidence – for instance, past observations or the predictive and explanatory success of this statement – then this statement is true.

What the pragmatic and coherence views of truth have in common is that they are *epistemic theories of truth*; that is, they understand truth in terms of how we justify our knowledge. This is the crucial difference between epistemic and realist conceptions of truth. For the realist, how we justify what we believe and state is distinct from what makes our beliefs and statements true: truth and justification are distinct. For defenders of pragmatic and coherence theories of truth, these are not distinct.

It is not surprising that epistemic theories of truth are often defended by idealists. If you believe that minds and properties of minds are all there is, then it makes sense to suppose that truth has to do with how our thoughts are related to each other and how they mutually support each other, which is what coherence and warrant are all about. However, idealists are not the only people who have defended epistemic theories of truth. You can be a pragmatist about truth and still believe that there is more to the universe than what is mental.

Nevertheless, a pragmatist about truth who is not an idealist does have to worry about the following. When such a pragmatist states something about the non-mental world – for instance, that the sun contains 99.86 percent of the total mass of the solar system – what will make that statement true or false, according to the pragmatist, is not a set of facts about the mass of the sun and the solar system, but facts about your beliefs, experience, and what is warranted. So what makes your statement true is different from what it is about. It is about the sun's mass, but what make it true are facts about what we believe and is warranted.

A moral realist who is a pragmatist about truth must face the same kind of consequence. Such a pragmatic moral realist believes that there are objective moral values, but what makes this belief true is not what this belief is about: the existence of objective moral values. Although this belief is about the existence of objective moral value, what makes it true, for the pragmatic moral realist, is the warrant this belief has.

Divorcing what statements and beliefs are about from what makes them true strikes many philosophers as odd. Why not let what a statement or belief is about also determine whether it is true? It is not clear why anyone would claim that there are objective moral values and then divorce these values from the truth of what we state or believe about moral values. Why would someone believe that the sun's mass is independent of what anyone thinks or says, but at the same time maintain that beliefs and statements about the sun's mass are true or false not in virtue of the sun's mass, but in virtue of what you and other people believe? If you believe that something really exists, then what you state or believe about it should be true in virtue of it. At the very least, intellectual honesty and simplicity would require this.

Consequently, a moral realist not only believes that there are objective moral values and that our statements and beliefs about moral values are true or false, but typically also believes that they are true or false in virtue of these objective moral values.

Varieties of Objective Moral Values

Since moral realists believe that there are objective moral values, they have to tell us what these objective moral values might be. The answer is going to place the moral realist in one of two broad categories: *naturalism* or *anti-naturalism*.

Naturalism, in the philosophical sense of the term, is sometimes also called "materialism." Naturalism is the view that nature is all there is and that there are no beings, properties or anything else that transcend or in some other way are distinct from the natural world. Naturalists typically also believe that the scientific method, particularly the reliance on repeatable, empirical, and experimental observation, is the proper way to study nature, and thus all of existence is subject, at least in principle, to scientific study.

Anti-naturalists deny all this. They believe that there are things that are beyond nature and that these things cannot be properly studied by the scientific method. Anti-naturalists are often called "dualists" or even "pluralists" because of their belief that, in addition to natural objects, properties, events, and so forth, there are other kinds of non-natural entities. Religious believers typically are non-naturalists because they believe in non-natural powers and beings that are not subject to experimental and scientific study, God being one such being.

So moral realists who are naturalists identify moral value with some natural value – something that can be located in the realm of nature and subject to empirical and scientific examination. Utilitarians are examples of such philosophers. The English philosopher Jeremy Bentham believed that pleasure and the absence of pain were objective and measurable properties and that these were intrinsic moral values. He even proposed a calculus for measuring pleasure and the absence of pain. For instance, it would measure the duration and intensity of pleasure, as well as its fecundity – that is, how much other pleasure it produces – and this calculus would allow us to measure moral value. He thought this would be especially useful for politicians and civil servants, who could decide on what ought to be done by calculating how much pleasure was produced and pain was avoided by alternative courses of action.

All other values besides pleasure and the absence of pain, such as justice or individual liberty, were only instrumental values; that is, they were valuable not in and of themselves, but because they tended to maximize pleasure and the absence of pain. It follows for the utilitarian that if an apparently just course of action is not instrumental in maximizing pleasure and the absence of pain, then it ought not to be promoted. Needless to say, this consequence, namely that justice ought to be promoted only if it maximizes pleasure and the absence of pain, has generated much criticism of utilitarianism.

One important consequence of the utilitarians' naturalistic approach to value is that we must include non-human animals in our utilitarian calculations. If pleasure and the absence of pain is an objective moral value, it is valuable wherever it occurs. So if cattle or whales feel pleasure and pain (an assumption we will discuss in chapter 6 on the philosophy of mind), we need to put them on the scales when we measure the moral utility of an action. This also means that non-human animals have a moral worth that is independent of what human beings value. If a whale feels pleasure and pain, it feels it no matter what any human being thinks or feels, and consequently it would exhibit moral value – that is, pleasure and the absence of pain – independently of what human beings value or care about.

Another naturalistic approach to objective moral value is to locate it in biological processes. A very simple approach is to identify moral value with evolutionary processes, particularly natural selection. On this sort of view, which is often labeled "evolutionary ethics," something or some action is morally good when it is the product of natural selection or contributes to natural selection. So if something is a product of natural selection or contributes to natural selection, then on this view it is also moral.

Many have thought that this is much too crude, and more complex biological properties are needed if moral goodness is to be a biological property. Many environmentalists believe that biological sense can be made of the notion of flourishing or health, and that moral goodness should be identified with biological flourishing or health. Some feminists maintain that to nurture something is a biological relation, and that nurturing is the fundamental moral good. There are many other proposals for identifying moral goodness with some biological process or property, and naturalists of various stripes and inclinations continue to find this to be a promising strategy.

Plato is the paradigm example of a non-naturalist philosopher. As we saw in chapter 2, Plato had very little philosophical respect for nature, and this carries over into his views on morality. Plato identifies moral value with a timeless and unchanging form: the form of the good. The form of the good is the highest form, and if a person grasps the form of the good, he or she grasps all other forms, including the forms of truth and beauty.

Plato compares the form of the good to the sun: just as the sun makes life on Earth possible and visible for us, the form of the good makes all other forms possible and knowable for us. But the form of the good, like all other forms, is not part of nature. The form Good transcends nature and is a part of a reality of which we and our world are only imperfect replicas, somewhat akin to shadows. Nature can only resemble the form of the good and it can only remind us of the form of the good, which we know not through our senses, but through our intellects.

Arguably the most important non–naturalist moral realist in twentieth-century philosophy is the British analytic philosopher G. E. Moore. In his *Principia Ethica*, Moore took to task naturalistic ethics, particularly utilitarianism, which had become very prominent in the nineteenth century. Moore argued that identifying moral properties, such as moral goodness, with natural properties, such as pleasure and pain, involved committing a fallacy, what he called the *Naturalistic Fallacy*. He argued that although many morally good acts produce pleasure and reduce pain, it is a mistake to think that moral goodness is identical to pleasure and the absence of pain or any other natural property. He defends this claim with the so-called *open question argument*:

1   If moral goodness is identical with natural properties, say maximizing pleasure and the absence of pain, then the statement that pleasure and the absence of pain are morally good is true in virtue of the meanings of its words.
2   If the statement that pleasure and the absence of pain are morally good is true in virtue of the meanings of its words, then we cannot significantly ask whether pleasure and the absence of pain are indeed good.
3   But whether or not pleasure and the absence of pain are indeed good is a significant open question.
4   So, the statement that pleasure and the absence of pain are morally good is not true in virtue of the meanings of its words.
5   So, moral goodness is not identical to the natural properties of pleasure and the absence of pain.

In order to see why premise 3 seemed plausible to Moore and many other philosophers, consider a statement that something is pleasant. We can then always ask the further question, "But is it good?" For example, if I claim that using drugs is pleasant, it is reasonable for you to raise the question of whether it is good. In Moore's words, whether or not the pleasant act is good is an open question. Moore believed that this kind of argument would hold for any natural properties, not just pleasure and the absence of pain, and hence naturalism in morality, he concluded, is false.

Moore does not only argue against ethical naturalism, but offers his own non-naturalistic account of moral value. He argues that when we state that something is morally good, we attribute to it a simple non-natural property; a property that is not of the natural world and that cannot be broken down into any simpler properties. Like Plato, Moore believed that this property is not in space or time, although ordinary objects in space and time could be good. Needless to say, this simple property of moral goodness cannot, in Moore's view, be observed with the five senses. Instead, Moore supposed that there is a special capacity we have – moral intuition – that allows us to know what is and is not good.

Clearly, naturalist and non-naturalist moral realists run in very different directions – as different as Plato and Bentham can be – but this should not blind us to the fact that they are both brands of moral realism. Both believe that moral value is as objective and independent of what anyone thinks as are, for most people, the speed of light or the stars of the universe. Moreover, both can make good sense of the claim that the last person on Earth was wrong to destroy the last oasis. Naturalists can consider the pleasure of the creatures destroyed in this act, the health or flourishing of the oasis, or the evolutionary processes destroyed by this act. Non-naturalists have it easy in this case, perhaps too easy. They can simply justify their critique by saying that the oasis has moral value because it partakes in the form of the good or has the simple property of goodness, and the destruction of the oasis for this reason is evil.

As it turns out, Moore's *open question argument*, at least in the present form, does not seem sound because the first premise seems false. It seems that two terms that refer to the same thing can have different meanings. For instance, "the morning star" and "the evening star" refer to the same thing – Venus – but these terms have different meanings. Another such pair of terms is "vertebrates with kidneys" and "vertebrates with hearts." It so happens that vertebrates with kidneys are vertebrates with hearts, but "vertebrates with kidneys" and "vertebrates with hearts" have different meanings.

Critiques of Moral Realism

There are people who oppose moral realism because they oppose objectivity in any domain: they think *everything* is subjective in the sense that everything exists only because someone thinks about it. This is an extreme metaphysical view – subjectivism with respect to everything there is – but there are less extreme opponents to moral realism. Some people believe that although we should be realistic about light, energy, and other physical things, or even universals, moral value is in a different class and should not be treated realistically, because there are special reasons for rejecting moral realism.

One important argument against moral realism appeals to a principle known as *Occam's razor*. The principle is widely used in the sciences, but it has its roots in medieval metaphysics, particularly in medieval discussions of the problem of universals. William of Occam argued that if we have to choose between two competing theories or explanations, then, all other things being equal, we should choose the simpler theory or explanation. What exactly makes one theory or explanation simpler than another is not that easy to determine, but Occam measured simplicity in terms of the number of kinds of entities a theory or explanations needs. Consequently, Occam's razor has come to be known as the command:

Don't multiply entities beyond necessity.

Occam relied on this principle to argue against realist solutions to the problem of universals. While realists need individuals and universals, nominalists get by with only individuals, and Occam argued using his principle that this meant that nominalism was a better solution to the problem of universals than realism.

Occam's razor can be applied in various ways to moral realism. We can apply it very broadly to the question of whether we need objective moral values: is there another explanation of morality that is as good as moral realism but is not committed to objective moral values? We can also use Occam's razor to settle the dispute between naturalist and non-naturalist moral realism. Let us look at the second issue first.

Ethical naturalism requires only natural entities. Ethical naturalism is committed to moral values, but it identifies them with natural properties – for example, pleasure, health, or natural selection. Ethical non-naturalists require a domain of entities in addition to the natural world, namely the domain of objective but non-natural moral values, such as Plato's form of the good or Moore's simple goodness. So ethical naturalists have simpler explanations of morality, and if naturalism explains morality as well as non-naturalism in all other respects, then Occam's razor requires that we accept ethical naturalism over non-naturalism.

Of, course, this depends on a big "if" – if in all other respects naturalism explains morality as well as non-naturalism – and whether this if clause is true is an issue that is not easy to resolve.

Applied to the question of whether there are any moral values – natural or non-natural – Occam's razor requires that we ask if morality can be explained without any objective moral values. Roughly speaking, a metaphysical theory of morality that says there are objective moral values seems, in Occam's sense, more complex than a theory without objective moral values. This is easy to see. The latter approach takes everything the moral realist claims that there exists, but subtracts moral value from it. So of course this approach has fewer types of things.

Now, this in itself is not convincing. It would be foolish to argue that the metaphysical view that there are no other people besides me – a view called *solipsism* – is better than the view that there are other people because the former is simpler than the latter. Occam's razor requires that we do not multiply entities *without necessity*, and it is very difficult to see how anyone could argue to their own satisfaction that it is unnecessary to suppose that there are other people, and that they can explain all the things that appear to happen to us due to what other people do – for example, our own existence, our pleasures and pains, our perceptions, our loves, and so on – without appealing to other people.

However, when it comes to morality, the view that we do not need objective moral values does not seem so outlandish. Critics of moral realism maintain that it is possible that there are no objective moral values, but that everything else, especially our morality – what we condemn and approve – stays exactly the same. Even without objective moral values, we could still condemn genocide and praise environmental protection, and we could still teach our children to be honest and thoughtful, and so on. If this really were the case and objective moral values were not needed to explain how we act, then it would be better to look for a simpler account of morality that does not rely on objective moral values.

Critics have also been impressed by what appears to be a diversity of moral codes. Moral codes vary from one society to another and within the same society from one period to the next. While homosexuality was approved of by Socrates it was later considered a vice by Aristotle. While 200 years ago slavery was considered moral by many respectable people, today slavery is morally condemned around the world.

Not only are moral codes diverse, but moral disagreements are very hard to resolve. Just consider the endless debate about abortion or euthanasia. If morality rested on objective moral values, then there would have to be more uniformity in moral codes and disagreements would be easier to resolve, non-realists argue. Moreover, the objectivity of morality appears to be undermined by the apparent lack of progress we have made in ethics compared to the various sciences. If there are objective moral facts for ethicists to study as there are, for example, objective facts for psychologists or chemists to study, then how do we explain the lack of progress in ethics compared to the rapid progress of the various sciences?

Finally, it seems that people approve of moral codes because of their way of life and not the other way around: if the society in which you are raised approves of homosexual relations, chances are that its moral codes will find them permissible. But if morality is dictated by one's way of life, and not the other way around, it seems that morality is a product of subjective factors and not some perception, ordinary or extra-ordinary, of objective moral values.

These are important criticisms, but many moral realists remain unconvinced. They are not convinced that subjectivists can explain the full dimension of moral discourse. Moral realists are also inclined to argue that moral differences across cultures are exaggerated, and that moral exemplars, such as Mahatma Ghandi, Martin Luther King or Mother Teresa, appeal across different cultures. Moreover, some moral disagreements have been settled fairly well – for instance, that slavery is immoral. Continuing moral disagreements may be due to disagreements about what the relevant facts are or they may be expressions of real conflicts between objective moral values. Finally, moral criticism often begins by going against the tide of dominant customs and ways of life. After all, moral realists argue, morality and the mores, codes, and customs that prevail in a society are two distinct things.

No matter how good these replies may be, clearly the critics of moral realism have raised some important issues for moral realism that do not have simple answers. Given that moral realism is not without its serious problems, we should try to find out more about moral realism's main competitor: moral subjectivism. Perhaps moral subjectivism has fewer problems than moral realism.

Subjectivists against Moral Truth-value

As we saw above, an important feature of moral realism is that it gives moral statements and beliefs a truth-value; that is, moral realists are moral cognitivists. Although not all moral subjectivists reject moral cognitivism, subjectivism in the twentieth century began with a bold rejection of moral cognitivism, and it has been associated with non-cognitivism ever since.

The most popular and influential proponent of moral subjectivism in this century was the British philosopher Sir Alfred Jules Ayer, who shocked the world by declaring that moral statements do not have a truth-value. Consequently, they really are not even statements; they don't describe anything. Instead they are expressions of feelings of approval and disapproval. For example, if I say that the natural environment has moral value, I am not stating anything, but just expressing my feelings of approval about the environment. We might think of what I am saying as equivalent to:

The natural environment: Yippee! High five!

Notice that this is not really a description of anything. You could describe your emotions by stating that you like your natural environment, by writing, for instance:

I like the natural environment a lot.

But moral statements, according to Ayer, are not such descriptions. They are merely expressions of our feelings, as might be a frown or a happy face.

Of course, when we describe our feelings, we are stating something that has a truth-value. For example, my statement that I like the natural environment a lot is true just in the case that I have the appropriate feelings and inclinations toward the environment. But our fundamental moral pronouncements, such as that it is wrong for the last woman to destroy the environment, are not descriptions of our feelings; they are only expressions of our feelings. Ayer's view is an extreme form of subjectivism called "emotivism"; a name that captures the idea that moral statements are simply expressions of one's emotions.

Why would anyone want to claim that it is neither true nor false that the last person on Earth did something wrong in torching the last oasis, or that it is neither true nor false that Hitler was evil? An important reason Ayer had was a view about the nature of cognitive meaningfulness. A statement was cognitively meaningful just in the case that it was either analytic or synthetic (that is, factually significant), and a statement was synthetic just in the case that it was empirically verifiable. We can sum this up by the following principle:

A statement is cognitively meaningful if, and only if, it is either analytic or empirically verifiable.

This has been called the *principle of verification* and it was a hallmark of logical positivism. Let us take a brief look at what it is for statements to be analytic, synthetic, and empirically verifiable.

If a statement is *analytic*, it is true or false simply in virtue of the definitions or meanings of the terms involved. For example, all we need to do to know that the statement that all triangles are three-sided figures is true is consult the concept of a triangle, and this makes that statement analytically true. We do not need to examine all the triangles of the universe to see if this statement is true.

If an analytic statement is true, it must be true, and if it is false, it must be false. That is, an analytic statement is either necessarily true or necessarily false. For example, not only are all triangles three-sided figures, but it is necessary that triangles are three-sided figures. The definition or meaning of "triangle" entails that a triangle has three sides. So if someone says that a triangle does not have three sides, he or she is saying that something that has three sides does not have three sides, and that is a logical contradiction.

A statement is *synthetic* or factually significant if it is a statement about matters of fact; about the way the world is and not just how we think about the world. For Ayer and the logical positivists, synthetic statements had to be empirically verifiable. Although it proved very difficult to state exactly what it is to verify something empirically, the general idea was that a statement is *empirically verifiable* if it can at least in principle be shown to be true through sensory observation – for example, by seeing, hearing, smelling, touching, or tasting.

The idea that all factually significant statements are empirically verifiable is one of the central ideas of the philosophical movement called *"empiricism."* By endorsing empiricism, Ayer and the logical positivists rejected *rationalism*, which was based on the idea that some claims about the world, especially metaphysical claims, are not verifiable through sensory observation, but can be known in other ways. For instance, a rationalist such as the French philosopher René Descartes claimed to know some things about the world, e.g. that all things are caused and that there is a divine creator of the universe, simply on the basis of pure reason and without relying on sensory observation.

Unlike analytic claims, empirically verifiable statements are not necessary, but contingent. A statement is contingent when it could have been true even though as a matter of fact it is false, or it could have been false even though as a matter of fact it is true. It is, for example, only contingently true that Michael Jordan is a basketball player. It could have been false that he is a basketball player: he might have decided never to play basketball, he might have been born without his right hand, or he might not have been born at all.

According to Ayer, ethical pronouncements fail the principle of verification's test for cognitive meaningfulness. Ayer believed that they are neither analytic nor empirically verifiable. For him, an ethical pronouncement is simply an expression of feeling, or my approval or disapproval, and since such pronouncements lack truth-value, ethical pronouncements cannot be cognitively meaningful. Needless to say, many objections have been raised against this account of ethics. Let us look at four important ones.

First, the principle of verification that lies at the bottom of the emotivists' views about ethics fails its own test for cognitive meaningfulness. On the one hand, if the principle is analytic, then it is, according to the logical positivists, uninformative; something the logical positivists could not accept. On the other hand, if the principle is not analytic, then it has to be verifiable in order to be cognitively meaningful, and, as it turned out, no amount of experience can verify the verifiability principle. It seems, therefore, that the very sentence stating the verifiability principle is not cognitively meaningful, and therefore neither true nor false. With the very foundation of emotivism gone, emotivism, as a metaphysical view, does not have a leg to stand on.

Second, it is doubtful that there is a correlation between morality and emotion. Some people can judge that an action is extremely immoral very calmly and dispassionately, while others judge that the same action is immoral with intense passion and emotion. Does this mean that these people have different assessments of the morality of this action? Emotivists would have to say that the moral assessments are different, but this does not seem right. Some people are more emotional than others, but this need not affect the seriousness of the moral charges they are making. A dispassionate moral judgment does not have less moral force than a passionate moral judgment. In fact, a dispassionate moral judgment that is accompanied by some appropriate action to rectify the immoral situation has much greater moral force than a passionate moral judgment issued from a living room sofa.

Third, emotivism conflicts with our moral practices. When discussing real moral issues – for instance, about our duties to the environment or the poor – we do not treat this substantive moral discourse as expressions of emotions but as statements with truth-values. We believe that certain moral views, say about the morality of abortion, capital punishment, or environmental protection, are false, while other views are true. We argue about what we ought to do and we evaluate people's arguments for their moral views. Since expressions of emotion are neither true nor false and can be neither premises nor conclusions in an argument, it is highly doubtful that moral discourse is just a matter of expressing emotion.

Finally, emotivism gives what looks like the wrong answer to important moral questions. Suppose a massacre of sleeping families takes place and, after it is over, everyone celebrates and no one has any feelings of horror, disgust, or even disapproval about it. Without such emotions, if emotivism is true, there is nothing wrong with this massacre. But there is something wrong with such a massacre no matter what anyone feels, and so emotivism must be false. Similarly, if emotivism is true, there is nothing wrong about the last person willfully destroying Earth's last oasis. For emotivists, morality is just an expression feeling of approval and disapproval, and in the last person scenario there are no feelings of approval for the last oasis or feelings of disapproval for the last person's actions. The only moral feelings there are in this situation are the last person's feelings. All she feels is an aversion towards her environment, which according to emotivism would make the last person's actions moral.

For these reasons, emotivism is not a good account of morality and we should look elsewhere if we are going to be subjectivists about moral value.

Subjectivists for Moral Truth

One of the reasons emotivism failed is that it denied that moral discourse has any truth-value, and consequently, subjectivists have tried to develop theories of morality that do not deny this. In sum, there are subjectivists who are cognitivists. Now, typically there are two truth-values that can be assigned – truth and falsehood – and so there are at least two ways in which subjectivists can be cognitivists: subjectivists can claim that some moral statements are indeed true or subjectivists can claim that all moral statements are false. In this section let us look at the first type of cognitivist subjectivists.

An example of cognitivist subjectivists who hold that some moral statements are true is philosophers who claim that moral statements are really about the individual subjective attitudes of the person making the claim. For convenience, let's label this view *individual relativism*. Good examples of such philosophers are Hobbes, whom we encountered in the previous chapter 2, and the Dutch and Jewish philosopher Baruch de Spinoza. Hobbes and Spinoza suggested that to state that something is morally good is just to say that you desire it. There are other attitudes individual relativists can consider – for instance, approval or preferences – but for the sake of simplicity let's focus on desire.

Individual relativism is different from subjectivism without truth-value because now moral claims are not just expressions of your desires, they are statements about one's desires. If I say that something is morally good and I do not desire it, I am stating something false about myself. If I do desire it, then I am stating a truth about myself.

It follows that whether something has moral value depends on whether someone desires it. It is very important not to confuse this view with utilitarianism. Individual relativism is a brand of subjectivism, but utilitarianism typically is not a brand of subjectivism. For a utilitarian, pleasure and the absence of pain are values no matter what anyone thinks about them. Even if you do not value pleasure and the absence of pain – perhaps you are an ascetic who declines all pleasures and only seeks pain – pleasure and the absence of pain, including your own pleasures, still are moral values. Their status as values does not depend on what attitude you or anyone else has toward them. This is what makes a utilitarian a moral realist.

For an individual relativist, pleasure and the absence of pain are values only if someone desires them. If it should turn out that the universe consists only of true ascetics who desire pain, then pleasure and the absence of pain, on this view, are not values any more. It is in this sense that moral value for the subjectivist is mind-dependent: whether something is a moral value depends on whether someone has a mental attitude toward it.

So, what is it that turns out to be a moral value according to the individual relativist? It would be a mistake to say that on this view moral value is identified with the valuing attitude, such as the desire of the person who is stating that something is morally good. Moral value is a *product* of the attitude, but the attitude itself is not a moral value unless it also becomes an object of the valuing attitude. For instance, if something is morally good only if it is desired, then desire becomes morally good only if it is desired. Needless to say, people have all sorts of desires without having a desire to have those desires. It is not a contradiction to state that moral value depends on desire while denying that desire itself is a moral value.

Another example of moral subjectivism that is committed to moral truth-value and the belief that some moral statements are true is *cultural relativism*. According to cultural relativism, something is only a moral value relative to a society's or culture's attitudes of approval or disapproval. So if your society approves of homosexuality, then it is not immoral; if your society is repulsed by homosexuality, it is not moral. Moreover, the truth of moral statements depends on cultural attitudes. If I state that homosexuality is not morally good, then this statement is true just in the case that my society rejects homosexuality. If my society in fact desires or in some other way approves of homosexuality, what I stated is false.

It is important to recognize that for a cultural relativist, statements such as "This action is morally good" are usually elliptical for "This action is morally good for my culture," and what this means is that this action is approved of by the speaker's culture. When we want to make sure that we are referring to what is morally good according to other cultures to which we do not belong, we typically make this explicit. For example, we might state that although homosexuality was evil for Aristotle's Macedonia, it was not evil for Plato's Athens.

Individual and cultural relativists that try to turn moral statements into statements about attitudes, either the attitude of an individual or the attitude of a culture or society, suffer from a common problem: they cannot make very good sense of moral disagreement.

To see this, consider these two statements:

1   All destruction of life is immoral.
2   All destruction of life is not immoral.

It seems that these two statements cannot both be true. If (1) is true, (2) is false, and if (2) is true, (1) is false. Thus (1) and (2) are contrary to each other. Consequently, if one person, say Ruth, claims (2) and another person, say Dorian, states (1), one of them must be wrong. They cannot both be saying something true. This is why Ruth and Dorian have a genuine disagreement, and if they are arguing about their differences, they are arguing about a genuine difference they have about the morality of the destruction of life.

Cultural and individual relativists cannot make good sense of this because of the way they relativize these statements to particular individuals or cultures.

Consider individual relativism. It would maintain that when Ruth said "All destruction of life is immoral," she really only stated that all destruction of life is undesirable *for her*. Dorian, on the other hand, is really saying that some destruction of life is desirable *for him*. Understood in this way, both statements (1) and (2) can be true. Ruth is simply stating something about her desires and Dorian is stating something about his desires, and their claims are not contrary to each other. So what looked like a significant and genuine disagreement where both people cannot be right is not a genuine disagreement after relativists re-interpret it.

Cultural relativism has the same consequence. If we relativize (1) to certain monastic societies and (2) to typical secular societies, then we don't have contrary statements any more. (1) just states that these monastic societies find all destruction of life undesirable, while (2) states that typical secular societies do not find all destruction of life undesirable. These statements are not contraries anymore – both can be true – but that seems false. Cultures, just like individuals, have genuine disagreements about morality. Monks who venerate all life have a significant disagreement with secular culture, and an accurate moral theory must capture this fact.

Subjectivists for Moral Falsehood

For these reasons, some subjectivists have decided to take moral statements people make at face value and not seek to reinterpret them to make them into truths about individual or social attitudes. Instead, they consider all moral statements to be false! This gives us the basic element for *error theory* for morality. Unlike the moral non-cognitivist, a moral error theorist accepts that moral claims have a truth-value, but unlike relativists or moral realists, the moral error theorists deny that moral claims are true.

Error theories are not limited to ethics. They are found in philosophy of religion, philosophy of mind, and philosophy of science. Your typical atheist, for example, agrees with the claim that there is a truth of the matter when someone makes a claim about God, but thinks that statements about God are false (perhaps with the exception of the statement that God does not exist). So, the atheist is an error theorist when it comes to talk about God.

In the philosophy of science, *instrumentalism* is an example of an error theory. An instrumentalist in the philosophy of science agrees that there is a truth to the matter of whether quarks, muons, and other unobservable things discussed in the natural sciences exist, but claims that there are no pions, quarks, muons, or other such things. Instead, such things are only concepts we have that allow us to make observable predictions on the basis of past observations. In other words, although there are no pions and muons, assuming there are pions and muons allows us to make calculations that yield predictions about the observable behavior of electrons, neutrons, and neutrinos. On this view, the part of a science that gives us equations and other laws for unobservable things is better understood as a complex formal system that allows us to explain and predict observable data, not a description of the way things are.

A significant feature of error theories is that they consider false what many if not most people take to be true. Error theories in morality are a case in point. For instance, the statement that Hitler is morally evil seems true to most people, but moral error theorists will deny this. They maintain that the statement that Hitler was evil is false. Such a shocking claim places a great burden of proof on the shoulders of moral error theorists. They have to show two things: (1) why this moral statement along with all other moral statements is false and (2) why these erroneous statements are so widely adopted. How might error theorists show these two things?

First, let us see why error theorists believe that all moral claims are false. They believe that moral statements, including the statement that Hitler is immoral, are false because they entail that there are objective moral values. They agree with moral realists that when we say that Hitler was immoral, we are assuming that there is some objective moral property – the property of being immoral – and that Hitler or Hitler's actions have this property. However, they reject the moral realist's claim that there are objective moral properties. Moral error theorists are, after all, subjectivists, and subjectivists deny that there are objective moral values. If moral claims entail that there are objective moral values and there are no objective moral values, then all moral claims are false.

The soundness of this argument depends on it being true that there are no objective moral values, and error theorists rely on the critiques of moral realism we discussed earlier. They argue that moral realism violates Occam's razor and that we do not need to posit objective moral values to explain our moral practices. They appeal to the diversity of moral codes: that they vary from one society to another and even within the same society from one period to the next. Finally, they will ask us to worry about the persistence of moral disagreement, the apparent lack of moral progress, and how moral codes seem to be mere reflections of how we live and not guides for living. If we are convinced by these arguments and agree that all moral claims assume that there are objective moral values, the only rational course of action left for us is to accept that moral claims are false.

Once we are convinced that moral statements are all false, we need to explain why it is so easy and natural for people to make such a mistake. Without such an explanation an error theory stands on shaky ground. A general approach for moral error theory is to follow David Hume's suggestion that the mind has a "propensity to spread itself on external objects." This is not an uncommon phenomenon. When you are especially sad, the landscape and the weather around you may also seem sad, and when you are especially happy, you will see a joyful world around you. If you feel intensely patriotic about your nation, you will also see the natural landscape around you – the mountains and the prairies – as sharing in your nationality.

What this means in the case of morality is that we project our subjective moral attitudes onto objects around us. A good reason for doing this with our moral attitudes, error theorists argue, is that these attitudes are very important for a well functioning society. A society runs properly only if people share moral attitudes, and projecting our moral attitudes onto the world around us gives these attitudes authority and encourages others to adopt them. Stating that honesty is a moral virtue has a greater impact in moral education than stating that you approve of honesty. Similarly, stating that Hitler is evil has much more authority and influence than stating that you simply do not approve of Hitler's activities.

We can also see in this explanation of why we project our subjective moral attitudes onto the world around us why we have our moral attitudes. Error theorists will argue that we acquire them by being brought up in a certain way, and that as a consequence of how we are brought up we look at some actions with approval and at other actions with disapproval and even horror. We will only be able to live with ourselves if we conduct ourselves in a way that accords with the values we acquired through our upbringing. This upbringing allows us, for example, to withstand some desires, and our attitudes are strengthened when something we already accept is described in a way that accords with our attitudes.

In short, our moral claims have a subjective source, error theorists argue. For instance, the statement that Hitler is immoral is a projection of our subjective disapproval onto Hitler and his actions. We have such subjective attitudes on account of our upbringing, education, and other forms of socialization. Important tools in this socialization are the moral statements we make, even though they are all false. What makes them false, namely that they entail that there are objective moral values, is also what makes them effective means of inculcating us with the shared moral attitudes that are necessary for the proper functioning of our society.

Subjectivism and the Environment

We have seen that emotivism has problems finding moral value in the scenario with which this chapter began. In that possible scenario, only the last person is capable of feeling approval and disapproval, and she does not feel anything but disgust for the oasis.

Can cognitivist subjectivists get different results? Consider the individual relativists. In this scenario the oasis has moral value only if there is someone who values it; that is, someone who has an attitude toward it, particularly a desire for it. Now, it seems that only creatures with highly developed minds can have such moral attitudes, and in this scenario you are the only one with such a mind.

Plants and inanimate objects clearly do not have such minds. Insects and other small animals that may still be living on this oasis may, with some stretch of the imagination, feel pain and pleasure, but it is not so easy to suppose that they have moral attitudes.

So unless the individual relativist can make a case that in this scenario there is indeed an individual other than the last woman with the appropriate moral attitudes towards the oasis, the oasis has no moral value. If she does not value it, and if no one else values it, it has no value on this subjectivist view of value. Of course, right now you, as someone thinking about this case, may value the oasis, but you are not in the scenario. Of course, if you were part of the story, you might value the oasis, in which case it would have moral value. But that's not the way this story goes. The possibility being considered is one in which you do not exist.

The cultural relativist needs to make a case that there are cultural and social attitudes that value the oasis and disapprove of the last woman's actions. Clearly, when the last woman arrives at the oasis there are no communities any more, and so it is hard to make sense of the idea that there still are cultural and social attitudes. But maybe the attitudes of past cultures are relevant. Perhaps the attitudes of the culture in which the last woman was raised and educated are relevant even if that culture does not exist any more when the last woman torches the last oasis. This raises many important issues about the relevance of the past to the present, but we can make matters very simple by supposing that the last woman's culture had no respect for the environment. After all, that's probably one of the reasons she is the last person on Earth.

Moral error theorists will admit from the outset that strictly speaking the oasis has no moral value and that the last woman's actions are also without moral value. All statements about moral value are false, including the statements that the oasis has moral value and that the last woman's actions are immoral. Moreover, the last woman is not even projecting any positive moral attitudes onto her environment. In fact, since she feels disgust for it, the most one can say is that she projects her negative attitudes onto the environment. So, for the moral error theorist not only are the statements that the last woman's actions are immoral or that the oasis has moral value false, but there are no grounds in this scenario for even making such statements. For someone to make such statements he or she needs to have the appropriate attitude toward the oasis, and the "propensity to spread itself on external objects." The last person has a mind with this propensity, but she does not have the attitude that nature is valuable.

So it seems that the environmentalists are right. None of the subjectivists we have considered, whether cognitive or non–cognitive, can find something in the scenario that makes the last person's action immoral. If the last woman does not have the right moral attitudes, the environment is worthless and there is no moral reason for her to preserve it.

However, moral error theory suggests new ways of thinking about this scenario. As we saw, moral error theory focuses our attention on trying to explain morality. If all moral statements are false, there is no point in trying to justify them. However, we can turn our attention from *justifying* our moral judgments to *explaining* them.

One thing that needs explanation is why we make moral judgments at all, and we saw that the moral error theorist's strategy is to explain that by referring to behavior that one's society recommends and does not recommend. When explaining why people make the particular moral statements they make – for example, why the last person sees no moral value in her environment while others do, and why some people condone homosexuality while others do not – the moral error theorist can look to anthropology, sociology, psychology, biology, and other social and behavioral sciences. Our diverse attitudes are a product of our diverse ways of living, and we need to turn to these sciences to understand this diversity.

It is with the help of these sciences that the moral error theorist can find other values besides moral value with which to evaluate the last woman scenario. For instance, error theorists might discuss the survival value of the last person's attitudes. They might make the case that her attitude was a product of a biologically or socially dysfunctional life that brought about the environmental catastrophe the last person finds herself in. So, although there is no basis in the last woman scenario for morally condemning her actions, the error theorist can find important non-moral values that the last woman fails to satisfy, and perhaps this is good enough. Surely it is good enough to encourage more functional ways of life and attitudes than we find in the last person scenario.

In sum, if we use the last person case to test the viability of metaphysical views about the nature of moral value, two accounts survive as viable alternatives: moral realism and error theory. Deciding which of these two is on the right track is not a simple matter.

The Metaphysics of Morality and Matter

We have spent some time looking at central issues in the metaphysics of morality and their practical consequences. These issues are important on their own, but it is also interesting that the positions on the nature of moral value we have encountered have twins in other areas of metaphysics. To see this, let us return to the metaphysical issue of the existence of matter.

Realists about matter maintain that material objects and processes are not artifacts of the way people think or talk about matter. For instance, causal relations, energy, mass, and other such properties are not artifacts of physical theory, but mind-independent entities. It should be noted that realists about matter are not necessarily materialists or naturalists. Of course, some are, and they hold that matter is all there is, but there are anti-materialist realists who believe that in addition to matter there are non-material things. Typical examples of such non-material things that dualist realists have defended are mind and God.

Subjectivists about matter – that is, idealists – come in various strengths. Non-cognitivist subjectivism, when applied to matter, is a very dramatic position. On this view, there is no matter and claims about matter (with the exception of claims about the existence of matter) have no truth-value; they are mere expressions of the mind's subjective states. Such a view is often attributed to nineteenth-century philosophers such as Hegel, Schopenhauer and Nietzsche, for whom knowledge did not involve representing the way the world is, but expressing states of mind. Contemporary examples of philosophers who carry on this tradition are postmodernists, many of whom seek to understand science as an expression of various desires people and whole cultures have. We will turn to these kinds of views in chapter 8.

Bishop Berkeley's idealism is a good example of a subjectivist theory of matter that is also cognitivist. Statements about matter have a truth-value and in fact many of them are true, but they are not true about mind-independent things. Instead, true statements about matter are truths about ideas. A table is just a bundle of ideas and to say something true about a table is to say something true about this bundle. Since Berkeley's idealism makes matter a construct out of the ideas that individuals have, it is very similar to individual relativism in morality.

Finally, there are metaphysicians who treat matter subjectively but find it highly unlikely that statements about matter are really statements about people's ideas. These metaphysicians have the option of trying to develop an error theory for matter. They will first have to defend the thesis that statements about matter are, strictly speaking, false. Then they will have to explain why we make these false statements and why they are so widespread and successful. If there is no matter, why do people so readily believe that matter exists and that it exists independently of what anyone might say or think?

As we can see, issues and positions in the metaphysics of matter run parallel to issues and positions in the metaphysics of morality. In fact, you can use the views available in the metaphysics of moral value as a template for constructing the available metaphysical views about the subjectivity or objectivity of anything else. Whether you are discussing the nature and existence of mind, meaning, matter, or anything else, you will have to confront the question of whether you are a realist or subjectivist of one sort or another with respect to the things you are talking about.

Conclusion

Many things seem to exist independently of us and continue to exist even when no one thinks about them. Material objects such as mountains and planets are paradigm examples of such things, but moral value is also something that we easily attribute to the world around us. Although most people are not shocked by the claim that beauty is in the eye of the beholder, the idea that morality is in the eye of the beholder is disturbing, especially when we think of the moral horrors human beings have faced in this century and most probably will continue to face. Nevertheless, in metaphysics we have to take seriously the proposition that these things are mere appearances – figments of our minds – without an independent status in reality, and try to determine calmly and rationally the truth-value of this proposition.

Although in the end, after careful reflection, you may still settle on what at first seemed obvious, you will, we hope, do so with new respect for your own beliefs as well as the beliefs you rejected. This is especially true when it comes to moral value. Moral realism captures the belief embedded in our moral practices that moral value is not a mere appearance but an objective feature of reality, but we now see that the rejection of moral realism is motivated by weighty theoretical considerations. Error theory captures a widespread response to increasing familiarity with diverse cultures across the globe and throughout human history, namely that human beings are the makers of moral values, but it leaves us with the great difficulty and discomfort we have in trying to say in earnest that it is false that wanton destruction of people or nature is evil. Deciding between the weighty theoretical considerations on the one hand and our deeply ingrained moral practices on the other is not an easy task, but it is one of metaphysics' central tasks.

The Varieties of Intrinsic Value
John O'Neill

John O'Neill is Lecturer of Philosophy in Furness College, Lancaster University, in England. His philosophical interests are in environmental ethics and economics, socialism and the market, anarchism, and the history and philosophy of science and mathematics. His main non-philosophical activity is climbing rock, snow, and ice.

To hold an environmental ethic is to hold that non-human beings and states of affairs in the natural world have intrinsic value. This seemingly straightforward claim has been the focus of much recent philosophical discussion of environmental issues. Its clarity is, however, illusory. The term "intrinsic value" has a variety of senses and many arguments on environmental ethics suffer from a conflation of these different senses: specimen hunters for the fallacy of equivocation will find rich pickings in the area. This paper is largely the work of the underlabourer. I distinguish different senses of the concept of intrinsic value, and, relatedly, of the claim that non-human beings in the natural world have intrinsic value; I exhibit the logical relations between these claims and examine the distinct motivations for holding them. The paper is not however merely an exercise in conceptual underlabouring. It also defends one substantive thesis: that while it is the case that natural entities have intrinsic value in the strongest sense of the term, i.e., in the sense of value that exists independently of human valuations, such value does not as such entail any obligations on the part of human beings. The defender of nature's intrinsic value still needs to show that such value contributes to the well-being of human agents.

I

The term "intrinsic value" is used in at least three different basic senses: (1) **Intrinsic value**₁   Intrinsic value is used as a synonym for non-instrumental value. An object has instrumental value insofar as it is a means to some other end. An object has intrinsic value if it is an end in itself. Intrinsic goods are goods that other goods are good for the sake of. It is a well rehearsed point that, under pain of an infinite regress, not everything can have only instrumental value. There must be some objects that have intrinsic value. The defender of an environmental ethic argues that among the entities that have such non-instrumental value are non-human beings and states. It is this claim that Naess makes in defending deep ecology:

> The well-being of non-human life on Earth has value in itself. This value is independent of any instrumental usefulness for limited human purposes.[1]

(2) **Intrinsic value**₂   Intrinsic value is used to refer to the value an object has solely in virtue of its "intrinsic properties." The concept is thus employed by G. E. Moore:

> To say a kind of value is "intrinsic" means merely that the question whether a thing possesses it, and in what degree it possesses it, depends solely on the intrinsic nature of the thing in question.[2]

This account is in need of some further clarification concerning what is meant by the "intrinsic nature" of an object or its "intrinsic properties." I discuss this further below. However, as a first approximation, I will assume the intrinsic properties of an object to be its non-relational properties, and leave that concept for the moment unanalysed. To hold that non-human beings have intrinsic value given this use is to hold that the value they have depends solely on their non-relational properties.

(3) **Intrinsic value**₃   Intrinsic value is used as a synonym for "objective value" i.e., value that an object possesses independently of the valuations of valuers. As I show below, this sense itself has sub-varieties, depending on the interpretation that is put on the term "independently." Here I simply note that if intrinsic value is used in this sense, to claim that non-human beings have intrinsic value is not to make an ethical but a meta-ethical claim. It is to deny the subjectivist view that the source of all value lies in valuers – in their attitudes, preferences and so on.

Which sense of "intrinsic value" is the proponent of an environmental ethic employing? To hold an environmental ethic is to hold that non-human beings have intrinsic value in the first sense: it is to hold that non-human beings are not simply of value as a means to human ends. However, it might be that to hold a defensible ethical position about the environment, one needs to be committed to the view that they also have intrinsic value in the second or third senses. Whether this is the case is the central concern of this paper.

II

In much of the literature on environmental ethics the different senses of "intrinsic value" are used interchangeably. In particular senses 1 and 3 are often conflated. Typical is the following passage from Worster's *Nature's Economy*:

> One of the most important ethical issues raised anywhere in the past few decades has been whether nature has an order, a pattern, that we humans are bound to understand and respect and preserve. It is the essential question prompting the environmentalist movement in many countries. Generally, those who have answered "yes" to the question have also believed that such an order has an intrinsic value, which is to say that not all value comes from humans, that value can exist independently of us: it is not something we bestow. On the other hand, those who have answered "no" have tended to be in an instrumentalist camp. They look on nature as a storehouse of "resources" to be organized and used by people, as having no other value than the value some human gives.[3]

In describing the "yes" camp Worster characterises the term in sense 3. However, in characterising the "no's" he presupposes an understanding of the term in both senses 1 and 3. The passage assumes that to deny that natural patterns have value independently of the evaluations of humans is to grant them only instrumental value: a subjectivist meta-ethics entails that non-humans can have only instrumental value. This assumption is widespread.[4] It also underlies the claims of some critics of an environmental ethic who reject it on meta-ethical grounds thus: To claim that items in the non-human world have intrinsic values commits one to an objectivist view of values; an objectivist view of values is indefensible; hence the non-human world contains nothing of intrinsic value.[5]

The assumption that a subjectivist meta-ethics commits one to the view that non-humans have only instrumental value is false. Its apparent plausibility is founded on a confusion of claims about the source of values with claims about their object.[6] The subjectivist claims that the only sources of value are the evaluative attitudes of humans. But this does not entail that the only ultimate objects of value are the states of human beings. Likewise, to be an objectivist about the source of value, i.e., to claim that whether or not something has value does not depend on the attitudes of valuers, is compatible with a thoroughly anthropocentric view of the object of value – that the only things which do in fact have value are humans and their states, such that a world without humans would have no value whatsoever.

To enlarge, consider the emotivist as a standard example of a subjectivist. Evaluative utterances merely evince the speaker's attitudes with the purpose of changing the attitudes of the hearer. They state no facts. Within the emotivist tradition Stevenson provides an admirably clear account of intrinsic value. Intrinsic value is defined as non-instrumental value: "'intrinsically good' is roughly synonymous with 'good for its own sake, as an end, as distinct from good as a means to something else'."[7] Stevenson then offers the following account of what it is to say something has intrinsic value:

> "X is intrinsically good" asserts that the speaker approves of X intrinsically, and acts emotively to make the hearer or hearers likewise approve of X intrinsically.[8]

There are no reasons why the emotivist should not fill the X place by entities and states of the non-human world. There is nothing in the emotivist's meta-ethical position that precludes her holding basic attitudes that are biocentric. Thus let the H! operator express hurrah attitudes and B! express boo attitudes.[9] Her ultimate values might for example include the following:

H! (The existence of natural ecosystems)

B! (The destruction of natural ecosystems by humans).

There is no reason why the emotivist must assume that either egoism or humanism is true, that is that she must assign non-instrumental value only to her own or other humans' states.[10]

It might be objected, however, that there are other difficulties in holding an emotivist meta-ethics and an environmental ethic. In making humans the source of all value, the emotivist is committed to the view that a world without humans contains nothing of value. Hence, while nothing logically precludes the emotivists assigning non-instrumental value to objects in a world which contains humans, it undermines some of the considerations that have led to the belief in the need to assign such value. For example, the standard last man arguments[11] in defence of an environmental ethic fail: the last man whose last act is to destroy a rain forest could on a subjectivist account of value do no wrong, since a world without humans is without value.

This objection fails for just the same reason as did the original assumption that subjectivism entails: non-humans have only instrumental value. It confuses the source and object of value. There is nothing in emotivism that forces the emotivist to confine the objects of her attitudes to those that exist at the time at which she expresses them. Her moral utterances might evince attitudes towards events and states of affairs that might happen after her death, for example,

H! (My great grand-children live in a world without poverty).

Likewise her basic moral attitudes can range over periods in which humans no longer exist, for example,

H! (Rain forests exist after the extinction of the human species).

Like the rest of us she can deplore the vandalism of the last man. Her moral utterances might evince attitudes not only to other times but also to other possible worlds. Nothing in her meta-ethics stops her asserting with Leibniz that this world is the best of all possible worlds, or, in her despair at the destructiveness of humans, expressing the attitude that it would have been better had humans never existed:

H! (the possible world in which humans never came into existence).

That humans are the source of value is not incompatible with their assigning value to a world in which they do not exist. To conclude, nothing in the emotivist's meta-ethics dictates the content of her attitudes.

Finally it needs to be stressed that while subjectivism does not rule out non-humans having non-instrumental value, objectivism does not rule it in. To claim that moral utterances have a truth value is not to specify which utterances are true. The objectivist can hold that the moral facts are such that only the states of humans possess value in themselves: everything else has only instrumental value. Ross, for example, held that only states of conscious beings have intrinsic value:

Contemplate any imaginary universe from which you suppose mind entirely absent, and you will fail to find anything in it you can call good in itself.[12]

Moore allowed that without humans the world might have some, but only very insignificant, value.[13] It does not follow from the claim that values do not have their source in humans that they do not have humans as their sole ultimate object.

The upshot of this discussion is a very traditional one, that meta-ethical commitments are logically independent of ethical ones. However, in the realm of environmental ethics it is one that needs to be re-affirmed. No meta-ethical position is required by an environmental ethic in its basic sense, i.e., an ethic which holds that non-human entities should not be treated merely as a means to the satisfaction of human wants. In particular, one can hold such an ethic and deny objectivism. However, this is not to say that there might not be other reasons for holding an objectivist account of ethics and that some of these reasons might appear particularly pertinent when considering evaluative statements about non-humans. It has not been my purpose in this section of the paper to defend ethical subjectivism and in section IV I defend a version of objectivism about environmental values. First, however, I discuss briefly intrinsic value in its Moorean sense, intrinsic value$_2$ – for this sense of the term is again often confused with intrinsic value$_1$.

III

In its second sense intrinsic value refers to the value an object has solely in virtue of its "intrinsic properties": it is value that "depends solely on the intrinsic nature of the thing in question."[14] I suggested earlier that the intrinsic properties of an object are its non-relational properties. What is meant by "non-relational properties"? There are two interpretations that might be placed on the phrase:

(i)   The non-relational properties of an object are those that persist regardless of the existence or non-existence of other objects (weak interpretation).

(ii) The non-relational properties of an object are those that can be character-ised without reference to other objects (strong interpretation).[15]

The distinction between the two senses will not concern me further here, although a similar distinction will take on greater significance in the following section.

If any property is irreducibly relational then rarity is. The rarity of an object depends on the non-existence of other objects, and the property cannot be characterised without reference to other objects. In practical concern about the environment a special status is ascribed to rare entities. The preservation of endangered species of flora and fauna and of unusual habitats and ecological systems is a major practical environmental problem. Rarity appears to confer a special value to an object. This value is related to that of another irreducibly relational property of environmental significance, i.e., diversity. However, it has been argued that such value can have no place in an environmental ethic which places intrinsic value on natural items. The argument runs something as follows:

1   To hold an environmental ethic is to hold that natural objects have intrinsic value.
2   The values objects have in virtue of their relational properties, e.g., their rarity, cannot be intrinsic values.

Hence:

3   The values objects have in virtue of their relational properties have no place in an environmental ethic.[16]

This argument commits a fallacy of equivocation. The term "intrinsic value" is being used in its Moorean sense, intrinsic value, in the second premise, but as synonym for non-instrumental value, intrinsic value, in the first. The senses are distinct. Thus, while it may be true that if an object has only instrumental value it cannot have intrinsic value in the Moorean sense, it is false that an object of non-instrumental value is necessarily also of intrinsic value in the Moorean sense. We might value an object in virtue of its relational properties, for example its rarity, without thereby seeing it as having only instrumental value for human satisfactions.

This point can be stated with greater generality. We need to distinguish:

(1)   values objects can have in virtue of their relations to other objects;

and

(2)   values objects can have in virtue of their relations to human beings.[17]

The second set of values is a proper subset of the first. Moreover, the second set of values is still not co-extensive with

(3)   values objects can have in virtue of being instrumental for human satisfaction.

An object might have value in virtue of its relation with human beings without thereby being of only instrumental value for humans. Thus, for example, one might value wilderness in virtue of its not bearing the imprint of human activity, as when John Muir opposed the damming of the Hetch Hetchy valley on the grounds that wild mountain parks should lack "all . . . marks of man's work."[18] To say "x has value because it is untouched by humans" is to say that it has value in virtue of a relation it has to humans and their activities. Wilderness has such value in virtue of our absence. However, the value is not possessed by wilderness in virtue of its instrumental usefulness for the satisfaction of human desires. The third set of values is a proper subset of both the second and the first. Intrinsic value in the sense of non-instrumental value need not then be intrinsic in the Moorean sense.

What of the relation between Moorean intrinsic value and objective value? Is it the case that if there is value that "depends solely on the intrinsic nature of the thing in question" then subjectivism about values must be rejected? If an object has value only in virtue of its intrinsic nature, does it follow that it has value independently of human valuations? The answer depends on the interpretation given to the phrases "depends solely on" and "only in virtue of." If these are interpreted to exclude the activity of human evaluation, as I take it Moore intended, then the answer to both questions is immediately "yes." However, there is a natural subjectivist reading to the phrases. The subjectivist can talk of the valuing agent *assigning* value to objects solely in virtue of their intrinsic natures. Given a liberal interpretation of the phrases, a subjectivist can hold that some objects have intrinsic value in the Moorean sense.

IV

In section II I argued that the claim that nature has non-instrumental value does not commit one to an objectivist meta-ethics. However, I left open the question as to whether there might be other reasons particularly pertinent in the field of environmental ethics that would lead us to hold an objectivist account of value. I will show in this section that there are.

The ethical objectivist holds that the evaluative properties of objects are real properties of objects, that is, that they are properties that objects possess independently of the valuations of valuers. What is meant by "independently of the valuations of valuers"? There are two readings of the phrase which parallel the two senses of "non-relational property" outlined in the last section:

(1)   The evaluative properties of objects are properties that exist in the absence of evaluating agents. (Weak interpretation)
(2)   The evaluative properties of objects can be characterised without reference to evaluating agents. (Strong interpretation)

The distinction is a particular instance of a more general distinction between two senses in which we can talk of a property being a real property of an object:

(1)   A real property is one that exists in the absence of any being experiencing that object. (Weak interpretation)
(2)   A real property is one that can be characterised without reference to the experiences of a being who might experience the object. (Strong interpretation)

Is there anything about evaluations of the environment that make the case for objectivism especially compelling? I begin by considering the case for the weak version of objectivism. For the purpose of the rest of the discussion I will assume that only human persons are evaluating agents.

1 Weak objectivity

A popular move in recent work on environmental ethics has been to establish the objectivity of values by invoking an analogy between secondary qualities and evaluative properties in the following manner:

(1)   The evaluative properties of objects are analogous to secondary qualities. Both sets of properties are observer dependent.
(2)   The Copenhagen interpretation of quantum mechanics has shown the distinction between primary qualities and secondary qualities to be untenable. All the properties of objects are observer dependent.

Hence,

(3)   The evaluative properties of objects are as real as their primary qualities.[19]

The argument fails at every stage. In the first place the conclusion itself is too weak to support objectivism about values: it is no argument for an objectivist theory of values to show that all properties of objects are observer dependent. The second premise should in any case be rejected. Not only is it the case that the Copenhagen interpretation of quantum theory is but one amongst many,[20] it is far from clear that the Copenhagen interpretation is committed to the ontological extravagance that all properties are observer dependent. Rather it can be understood as a straightforward instrumentalist interpretation of quantum theory. As such it involves no ontological commitments about the quantum domain.[21]

More pertinent to the present discussion, there are also good grounds for rejecting the first premise. The analogy between secondary qualities and values has often been used to show that values are not real properties of objects. Thus Hume remarks:

> Vice and virtue . . . may be compared to sounds, heat and cold, which, according to modern philosophy, are not qualities in objects, but perceptions in the mind.[22]

For the Humean, both secondary qualities and evaluative properties are not real properties of objects, but, rather, illustrate the mind's "propensity to spread itself on external objects": as Mackie puts it, moral qualities are the "projection or objectification of moral attitudes."[23] The first premise of the argument assumes this Humean view of the analogy between secondary qualities and values. However, there are good grounds for inverting the analogy and that inversion promises to provide a more satisfactory argument for objectivism than that outlined above.

On the weak interpretation of the concept of a real property, secondary qualities are real properties of objects. They persist in the absence of observers. Objects do not lose their colours when we no longer perceive them. In the kingdom of the blind the grass is still green. Secondary qualities are dispositional properties of objects to appear in a certain way to ideal observers in ideal conditions. So, for example, an object is green if and only if it would appear green to a perceptually ideal observer in perceptually ideal conditions.[24] It is consistent with this characterisation of secondary qualities that an object possesses that quality even though it may never actually be perceived by an observer. Thus, while in the strong sense of the term secondary qualities are not real properties of objects – one cannot characterise the properties without referring to the experiences of possible observers – in the weak sense of the term they are.[25]

This point opens up the possibility of an inversion of the Humean analogy between secondary and evaluative qualities which has been recently exploited by McDowell and others.[26] Like the secondary qualities, evaluative qualities are real properties of objects. An object's evaluative properties are similarly dispositional properties that it has to produce certain attitudes and reactions in ideal observers in ideal conditions. Thus, we might tentatively characterise goodness thus: x is good if and only if x would produce feelings of moral approval in an ideal observer in ideal conditions. Likewise, beauty might be characterised thus: x is beautiful if and only if x would produce feelings of aesthetic delight in ideal observers in ideal conditions. Given this characterisation, an object is beautiful or good even if it never actually appears as such to an observer. The evaluative properties of objects are real in just the same sense that secondary qualities are. Both sets of properties are independent of observers in the sense that they persist in the absence of observers. The first premise of the argument outlined above should therefore be rejected. Furthermore, in rejecting this premise, one arrives at a far more convincing case for the reality of evaluative properties than that provided by excursions into quantum mechanics.

However, the promise of this line of argument for environmental ethics is, I believe, limited. There are a variety of particular arguments that might be raised against it. For example, the Humean might respond by suggesting that the analogy between secondary and evaluative properties is imperfect. The arguments for and against the analogy I will not rehearse here.[27] For even if the analogy is a good one, it is not clear to me that any point of substance about the nature of values divides the Humean and his opponent. The debate is one about preferred modes of speech, specifically about how the term "real property" is to be read. For the Humean such as Mackie, the term "real property" is understood in its strong sense. It is a property that can be characterised without reference to the experiences of an observer. Hence neither secondary qualities nor values are real properties of objects. The opponent of the Humean in employing the analogy to establish the reality of evaluative properties merely substitutes a weak interpretation of real property for the strong interpretation. There may be good reasons for doing this, but nothing about the nature of values turns on this move.[28] Moreover, there seems to be nothing about evaluative utterances concerning the natural environment which adds anything to this debate. Nothing about specifically environmental values tells for or against this argument for objectivism.

2 Strong objectivity

A more interesting question is whether there are good reasons for believing that there are objective values in the strong sense: are there evaluative properties that can be characterised without reference to the experiences of human observers? I will now argue that there are and that uses of evaluative utterances about the natural world provide the clearest examples of such values.

Consider the gardener's use of the phrase "x is good for greenfly." The term "good for" can be understood in two distinct ways. It might refer to what is conductive to the destruction of greenfly, as in "detergent sprays are good for greenfly," or it can be used to describe what causes greenfly to flourish, as in "mild winters are good for greenfly." The term "good for" in the first use describes what is instrumentally good for the gardener: given the ordinary gardener's interest in the flourishing of her rosebushes, detergent sprays satisfy that interest. The second use describes what is instrumentally good for the greenfly, quite independently of the gardener's interests. This instrumental goodness is possible in virtue of the fact that greenflies are the sorts of things that can flourish or be injured. In consequence they have their own goods that are independent of both human interests and any tendency they might have to produce in human observers feelings of approval or disapproval.[29] Such goods I will follow Von Wright in terming the "goods of X."[30]

What is the class of entities that can be said to possess such goods? Von Wright in an influential passage offers the following account;

> A being, of whose good it is meaningful to talk, is one who can meaningfully be said to be well or ill, to thrive, to flourish, be happy or miserable . . . the attributes, which go along with the meaningful use of the phrase "the good of X," may be called *biological* in a broad sense. By this I do not mean that they were terms, of which biologists make frequent use. "Happiness" and "welfare" cannot be said to belong to the professional vocabulary of biologists. What I mean by calling the terms "biological" is that they are used as attributes of beings, of whom it is meaningful to say they have a *life*. The question "What kinds or species of being have a good?" is therefore broadly identical with the question "What kinds or species of being have a life."[31]

This biological use of the terms "good for" and "good of" is at the centre of Aristotelian ethics. The distinction between "good for" and "good of" itself corresponds to the Aristotelian distinction between goods externally instrumental to a being's flourishing and those that are constitutive of a being's flourishing.[32] And the central strategy of Aristotle's ethics is to found ethical argument on the basis of this broadly biological use of the term "good." I discuss this further below.

The terms "good" and "goods" in this biological context characterise items which are real in the strong interpretation of the term. In order to characterise the conditions which are constitutive of the flourishing of a living thing one need make no reference to the experiences of human observers. The goods of an entity are given rather by the characteristic features of the kind or species of being it is. A living thing can be said to flourish if it develops those characteristics which are normal to the species to which it belongs in the normal conditions for that species. If it fails to realise such characteristics then it will be described by terms such as "defective," "stunted," "abnormal" and the like. Correspondingly, the truth of statements about what is good for a living thing, what is conducive to its flourishing, depend on no essential reference to human observers. The use of the evaluative terms in the biological context does then provide good reasons for holding that some evaluative properties are real properties on the strong interpretation of the phrase. Hence, evaluative utterances about living things do have a particular relevance to the debate about the objectivity of values. Specifically biological values tell for objectivism.

However, while the use of value terms in the specifically biological context provides the clearest examples of the existence of objective goods, the class of entities that can be meaningfully said to have such goods is not confined to the biological context. Von Wright's claim that the question "What kinds or species of being have a good?" is identical with the question "What kinds or species of being have a life?" should be rejected. The problem case for this identity claim is that of collective entities. Von Wright is willing to entertain the possibility that such entities have their own good but only if they can also be said to have their own life in a non-metaphorical sense.

But what shall we say of social units such as the family, the nation, the state. Have they got a life "literally" or "metaphorically" only? I shall not attempt to answer these questions. I doubt whether there is any other way of answering them except by pointing out existing analogies of language. It is a fact that we speak about the life and also the good (welfare) of the family, the nation and the state. This fact about the use of language we must accept and with it the idea that the social units in question *have* a life and a good. What is arguable, however, is whether the life and *a fortiori* also the good (welfare) of a social unit is not somehow "logically reducible" to the life and therefore the good of the beings – men or animals – who are its members.[33]

This passage conflates two distinct issues: whether collective entities have a life and whether they have their own goods. It does not appear to me that we can talk of collective entities having a life in anything but a metaphorical sense. They clearly lack those properties typical of living things – reproduction, growth, death and such like. However, it does make sense to talk about the conditions in which collective entities flourish and hence of their goods in a non-metaphorical sense. Correspondingly, we can meaningfully talk of what is damaging to them. Furthermore, the goods of collective entities are not reducible to the goods of their members. Thus for example we can refer to the conditions in which bureaucracy flourishes while believing this to be bad for its constituent members. Or to take another example, what is good for members of a workers' cooperative can be quite at odds with what is good for the cooperative itself: the latter is constituted by its relative competitive position in the market place, and members of cooperatives might find themselves forced to forgo the satisfaction of their own interests to realise this.[34] The question "What class of beings has a good?" is identical with the question "What class of beings can be said to flourish in a non-metaphorical sense?" The class of living things is a proper subset of this class.

This point is central to environmental questions. It makes sense to talk of the goods of collective biological entities – colonies, ecosystems and so on – in a way that is irreducible to that of its members. The realisation of the good of a colony of ants might in certain circumstances involve the death of most of its members. It is not a condition for the flourishing of an individual animal that it be eaten: it often is a condition for the flourishing of the ecosystem of which it is a part. Relatedly, a point central to Darwin's development of the theory of evolution was that living beings have a capacity to reproduce that outstrips the capacity of the environment to support them. Most members of a species die in early life. This is clearly bad for the individuals involved. But it is again essential to the flourishing of the ecosystems of which they are a part. Collective entities have their own goods. In defending this claim one need not show that they have their own life.[35]

Both individual living things and the collective entities of which they are members can be said, then, to have their own goods. These goods are quite independent of human interests and can be characterised without reference to the experiences of human observers. It is a standard at this juncture of the argument to assume that possession of goods entails moral considerability: "moral standing or considerability belongs to whatever has a good of its own."[36] This is mistaken. It is possible to talk in an objective sense of what constitutes the goods of entities, without making any claims that these ought to be realised. We can know what is "good for X" and relatedly what constitutes "flourishing for X" and yet believe that X is the sort of thing that ought not to exist and hence that the flourishing of X is just the sort of thing we ought to inhibit. The case of the gardener noted earlier is typical in this regard. The gardener knows what it is for greenfly to flourish, recognises they have their own goods, and has a practical knowledge of what is good for them. No moral injunction follows. She can quite consistently believe they ought to be done harm. Likewise one can state the conditions for the flourishing of dictatorship and bureaucracy. The anarchist can claim that "war is the health of the state." One can discover what is good both for rain forests and the AIDS virus. One can recognise that something has its own goods, and quite consistently be morally indifferent to these goods or believe one has a moral duty to inhibit their development.[37] That Y is a good of X does not entail that Y should be realised unless we have a prior reason for believing that X is the sort of thing whose good ought to be promoted. While there is not a logical gap between facts and values, in that some value statements are factual, there is a logical gap between facts and oughts. "Y is a good" does not entail "Y ought to be realised."[38]

This gap clearly raises problems for environmental ethics. The existence of objective goods was promising precisely because it appeared to show that items in the non-human world were objects of proper moral concern. The gap outlined threatens to undermine such concern. Can the gap be bridged? There are two ways one might attempt to construct such a bridge. The first is to invoke some general moral claim that linked objective goods and moral duties. One might for example invoke an objectivist version of utilitarianism: we have a moral duty to maximise the total amount of objective good in the world.[39] There are a number of problems of detail with such an approach: What are the units for comparing objective goods? How are different goods to be weighed? However, it also has a more general problem that it shares with hedonistic utilitarianism. Thus, the hedonistic utilitarian must include within his calculus pleasures that ought not to count at all e.g., those of a sadist who gets pleasure from needless suffering. The hedonistic utilitarian fails to allow that pleasures themselves are the direct objects of ethical appraisal. Similarly, there are some entities whose flourishing simply should not enter into any calculations – the flourishing of dictatorships and viruses for example. It is not the case that the goods of viruses should count, even just a very small amount. There is no reason why these goods should count at all as ends in themselves (although there are of course good *instrumental* reasons why some viruses should flourish, in that many are indispensable to the ecosystems of which they are a part). The flourishing of such entities is itself a direct object of ethical appraisal. The quasiutilitarian approach is unpromising.

A second possible bridge between objective goods and oughts is an Aristotelian one. Human beings like other entities have goods constitutive of their flourishing, and correspondingly other goods instrumental to that flourishing. The flourishing of many other living things ought to be promoted because they are constitutive of our own flourishing. This approach might seem a depressingly familiar one. It looks as if we have taken a long journey into objective value only to arrive back at a narrowly anthropocentric ethic. This however would be mistaken. It is compatible with an Aristotelian ethic that we value items in the natural world for their own sake, not simply as an external means to our own satisfaction. Consider Aristotle's account of the relationship of friendship to human flourishing.[40] It is constitutive of friendship of the best kind that we care for friends for their own sake and not merely for the pleasures or profits they might bring. To do good for a friend purely because one thought they might later return the compliment not for their own sake is to have an ill-formed friendship. Friendship in turn is a constitutive component of a flourishing life. Given the kind of beings we are, to lack friends is to lack part of what makes for a flourishing human existence. Thus the egoist who asks "why have friends?" or "why should I do good for my friends?" has assumed a narrow range of goods – "the biggest share of money, honours and bodily pleasures"[41] – and asked how friends can bring such goods. The appropriate response is to point out that he has simply misidentified what the goods of a human life are.

The best case for an environmental ethic should proceed on similar lines. For a large number of, although not all, individual living things and biological collectives, we should recognise and promote their flourishing as an end in itself.[42] Such care for the natural world is constitutive of a flourishing human life. The best human life is one that includes an awareness of and practical concern with the goods of entities in the non-human world. On this view, the last man's act of vandalism reveals the man to be leading an existence below that which is best for a human being, for it exhibits a failure to recognise the goods of non-humans. To outline such an approach is, however, only to provide a promissory note. The claim that care for the natural world for its own sake is a part of the best life for humans requires detailed defence. The most promising general strategy would be to appeal to the claim that a good human life requires a breadth of goods. Part of the problem with egoism is the very narrowness of the goods it involves. The ethical life is one that incorporates a far richer set of goods and relationships than egoism would allow. This form of argument can be made for a connection of care for the natural world with human flourishing: the recognition and promotion of natural goods as ends in themselves involves just such an enrichment.[43]

Notes

Earlier versions of this paper were read to an Open University summer school and to a philosophy seminar at Sussex University. My special thanks to Roger Crisp, Andrew Mason and Ben Gibbs for their comments on these occasions. Thanks are also due to Robin Attfield, John Benson, Stephen Clark, Terry Diffey, Alan Holland and Geoffrey Hunter for conversations on the issues discussed in this paper.

1 A. Naess, "A Defence of the Deep Ecology Movement," *Environmental Ethics*, 6 (1984), 266. However, Naess's use of the term is unstable and he sometimes uses the phrase "intrinsic value" to refer to objective value. See note 4, below.

2 G. E. Moore, "The Conception of Intrinsic Value" in *Philosophical Studies* (London: Routledge and Kegan Paul, 1922), p. 260.

3 D. Worster, *Nature's Economy* (Cambridge: Cambridge University Press, 1985), p. xi.

4 Thus, for example, Naess and Rothenberg in *Ecology, Community and Lifestyle* (Cambridge: Cambridge University Press, 1989) initially define "intrinsic value" as value which is "independent of our valuation" (ibid., p. I 1) but then in the text characterise it in terms of a contrast with instrumental value (ibid., pp. 74–75). In his own account of deep ecology Naess employs the term in the sense of noninstrumental value (see n2 and A. Naess, "The Shallow and the Deep: Long Range Ecology Movement," *Inquiry*, 16, 1973). Others are more careful. Thus, while Attfield is committed to both an objectivist meta-ethics and the view that the states of some non-humans have intrinsic value, in *A Theory of Value and Obligation* (London: Croom Helm, 1987) ch. 2, he *defines* intrinsic value as non-instrumental value and distinguishes this from his "objectivist understanding of it." Callicott in "Intrinsic Value, Quantum Theory, and Environmental Ethics," *Environmental Ethics*, 7 (1989), 257–75, distinguishes non-instrumental value from objective value, using the term "inherent value" for the former and "intrinsic value" for the latter. However, the use of these terms raises its own problems since there is little agreement in the literature as to how they are to be employed. For example, P. Taylor, *Respect for Nature* (Princeton, NJ: Princeton University Press, 1986), pp. 68–77 makes the same distinction but uses "inherent value" to describe Callicott's "intrinsic value" and "intrinsic value" to describe his "inherent value," while R. Attfield in *The Ethics of Environmental Concern* (Oxford: Blackwell, 1983), ch. 8, uses the term "inherent value" to refer to something quite different. Another exceptionally clear discussion of the meta-ethical issues surrounding environmental ethics is R. and V. Routley, "Human Chauvinism and Environmental Ethics," in D. Mannison, M. McRobbie and R. Routley (eds), *Environmental Philosophy* (Canberra: Australian National University, 1980).

5 This kind of argument is to be found in particular in the work of McCloskey. See H. J. McCloskey, "Ecological Ethics and Its Justification" in Mannison et al., op. cit., and *Ecological Ethics and Politics* (Totowa, NJ: Rowman and Littlefield, 1983).

6 Cf. D. Gauthier, *Morals by Agreement* (Oxford: Oxford University Press, 1986), pp. 46–49 and J. B. Callicott, "Intrinsic Value, Quantum Theory and Environmental Ethics," *Environmental Ethics*, 7 (1985), 257–75, who make this point quite emphatically.

7 C. L. Stevenson, *Ethics and Language* (New Haven, CT: Yale University Press, 1944).

8 Ibid., p. 178.

9 I take the operators from S. Blackburn, *Spreading the Word* (Oxford: Clarendon Press, 1984), pp. 193ff.

10 Cf. R. and V. Routley, "Human Chauvinism and Environmental Ethics," in D. Mannison, M. McRobbie and R. Routley (eds), *Environmental Philosophy* (Canberra: Australian National University, 1980).

11 See ibid., pp. 121–23.

12 W. D. Ross, *The Right and the Good* (Oxford: Clarendon Press, 1930), p. 140. Ross

held four things to have intrinsic value, virtue, pleasure, the allocation of pleasure to the virtuous, and knowledge (ibid., p. 140).

13   G. E. Moore, *Principia Ethica* (Cambridge: Cambridge University Press, 1903), pp. 28, 83ff and 188ff.

14   G. E. Moore, "The Conception of Intrinsic Value," *Philosophical Studies* (London: Routledge and Kegan Paul, 1922), p. 260.

15   I do not follow Moore's own discussion here. Moore's own use of the term is closer to the weaker than the stronger interpretation. Thus, for example, the method of isolation as a test of intrinsic value proceeds by considering if objects keep their value "if they existed *by themselves*, in absolute isolation": G. E. Moore, *Principia Ethica* (Cambridge: Cambridge University Press, 1903), p. 187.

16   A similar argument is to be found in A. Gunn, "Why Should We Care about Rare Species?," *Environmental Ethics*, 2, 1980, pp. 17–37, especially pp. 29–34.

17   J. J. Thompson partially defines intrinsic value and hence an environmental ethic in terms of a contrast with such values: "those who find intrinsic value in nature are claiming . . . that things and states which are of value are valuable for what they are in themselves and not because of their relation to us" (J. Thompson, "A Refutation of Environmental Ethics," p. 148, *Environmental Ethics*, 12 (1990), 147–60). This characterisation is inadequate, in that it rules out of an environmental ethic positions such as that of Muir who values certain parts of nature because of the absence of the marks of humans. I take it that Thompson intends a contrast to the third set of values – values objects can have in virtue of being instrumental for human satisfaction.

18   Cited in R. Dubos, *The Wooing of Earth* (London: The Athlone Press, 1980).

19   A relatively sophisticated version of the argument is to be found in Holmes Rolston, III, "Are Values in Nature Subjective or Objective?," pp. 92–95 in *Philosophy Gone Wild* (Buffalo, NY: Prometheus Books, 1989). Cf. J. B. Callicott, "Intrinsic Value, Quantum Theory and Environmental Ethics," *Environmental Ethics* (1985) 7, pp. 257–75.

20   M. Jammer, *The Philosophy of Quantum Mechanics* (New York: John Wiley, 1974) remains a good survey of the basic different interpretations of quantum theory.

21   It should also be noted that the view, popular among some Green thinkers (see, for example, F. Capra, *The Tao of Physics* [London: Wildwood House, 1975]), that the Copenhagen interpretation entails a radically new world-view that undermines the old classical Newtonian picture of the world is false. The Copenhagen interpretation is conceptually conservative and denies the possibility that we could replace the concepts of classical physics by any others (see N. Bohr, *Atomic Theory and the Description of Nature* (Cambridge: Cambridge University Press, 1934).

22   D. Hume, *A Treatise of Human Nature* (London: Fontana, 1972), Book III, sec. 1, p. 203.

23   J. Mackie, *Ethics* (Harmondsworth, England: Penguin, 1977), p. 42.

24   Cf. J. McDowell, "Values and Secondary Qualities," p. 111 in T. Honderich (ed.), *Morality and Objectivity* (London: Routledge, 1985).

25   Cf. ibid., p. 113 and J. Dancy, "Two Conceptions of Moral Realism," *Proceedings of the Aristotelian Society*, Supp. vol. 60, 1986.

26   See J. McDowell, "Values and Secondary Qualities," in T. Honderich (ed.), *Morality and Objectivity* (London: Routledge, 1985) and J. McDowell, "Aesthetic Value, Objectivity and the Fabric of the World," in E. Schaper (ed.), *Pleasure, Preference and Value* (Cambridge: Cambridge University Press, 1983). Cf. D. Wiggins, *Needs,*

Values, Truth (Oxford: Blackwell, 1987), Essays III and IV. For critical discussion of this approach see S. Blackburn, "Errors and the Phenomenology of Value," in T. Honderich (ed.), *Morality and Objectivity*; J. Dancy, "Two Conceptions of Moral Realism," *Proceedings of the Aristotelian Society*, Supp. vol. 60, 1986; C. Hookway, "Two Conceptions of Moral Realism," *Proceedings of the Aristotelian Society* Supp. vol. 60, 1986; C. Wright, "Moral Values, Projections and Secondary Qualities," *Proceedings of the Aristotelian Society*, Supp. vol. 62, 1988.

27 For such a Humean response see Blackburn, "Errors and the Phenomenology of Value," in T. Honderich (ed.), *Morality and Objectivity.*

28 I also reject Feinberg's claim that the goods of plants are reducible to those of humans with an interest in their thriving: "The Rights of Animals and Unborn Generations," in *Rights, Justice and the Bounds of Liberty* (Princeton, NJ: Princeton University Press, 1980), pp. 169–71. For a similar argument against Feinberg see P. Taylor, *Respect for Nature*, p. 68.

29 Cf. Hookway, "Two Conceptions of Moral Realism," p. 202.

30 G. H. von Wright, *The Varieties of Goodness* (London: Routledge and Kegan Paul, 1963), ch. 3.

31 Ibid., p. 50. Cf. P. Taylor, *Respect for Nature*, pp. 60–71.

32 See J. Cooper, *Reason and Human Good in Aristotle* (Cambridge, MA: Harvard University Press, 1975), pp. 19ff.

33 Von Wright, *The Varieties of Goodness*, pp. 50–51.

34 I discuss this example in more detail in J. O'Neill, "Exploitation and Workers' Councils," *Journal of Applied Philosophy*, 8 (1991), 263–67.

35 Hence, there is no need to invoke scientific hypotheses such as the Gaia hypothesis to defend the existence of such goods, as for example Goodpaster does (K. Goodpaster, "On Being Morally Considerable" p. 323, *Journal of Philosophy*, 75, 1978, pp. 308–25).

36 R. Attfield, *A Theory of Value and Obligation* (Beckenham: Croom Helm, 1987), p. 21. Cf Holmes Rolston III, *Environmental Ethics* (Philadelphia: Temple University Press, 1988), K. Goodpaster, "On Being Morally Considerable" and P. Taylor, *Respect for Nature.*

37 Compare Wiggins's point that we need to discriminate between "the (spurious) fact-value distinction and the (real) is–ought distinction" (D. Wiggins, "Truth, Invention, and the Meaning of Life," in *Needs, Values, Truth: Essays in the Philosophy of Value* (Oxford: Blackwell, 1987) p. 96). Cf. P. Taylor, Respect for Nature, pp.71–72.

38 This point undermines a common objection to objectivism, i.e., that objectivists cannot explain why value statements necessarily motivate actions. If values were objective then "someone might be indifferent to things which he regards as good or actively hostile to them" (S. Blackburn, *Spreading the Word*, p. 188). The proper reply to this is that not all value statements do motivate actions, as the example in the text reveals.

39 See R. Attfield, op. cit., for this kind of position. For a different attempt to bridge the gap between objective goods and moral oughts see P. Taylor, *Respect for Nature*, chs 2–4.

40 Aristotle, *Nicomachean Ethics*, trans. T. Irwin (Indianapolis, IN: Hackett, 1985), Books viii–ix.

41 Ibid., 1168b.

42 This would clearly involve a rejection of Aristotle's own view that animals are made for the sake of humans. (Aristotle, *Politics*, trans. J. Warrington [London: J. A. Dent and Sons, 1959], 1265b.)

43   This line of argument has the virtue of fitting well with Aristotle's own account of happiness, given an inclusive interpretation of his views. Happiness on this account is inclusive of all goods that are ends in themselves: a happy life is self-sufficient in that nothing is lacking. It is a maximally consistent set of goods. (Aristotle, *Nicomachean Ethics*, 1097b, 14–20; see J. L. Ackrill, "Aristotle on *Eudaimonia*" in A. O. Rorty (ed.), *Essays on Aristotle's Ethics* (Berkeley, CA: University of California Press, 1980) for a presentation of this interpretation.)

The Subjectivity of Values
J. L. Mackie

J. L. Mackie (1917–1981) was born in Sydney, Australia, and taught at various universities in Australia, New Zealand, and England, most recently at Oxford University. He is best known for his contributions to ethics and metaphysics. In the selection from *Ethics: Inventing Right and Wrong* that follows Mackie argues that there are no objective moral values. His arguments, together with his explanations of how we might talk as if there are objective moral values even if there are none, pose an important challenge to the moral realist.

1 Moral Scepticism

There are no objective values. This is a bald statement of the thesis of this chapter, but before arguing for it I shall try to clarify and restrict it in ways that may meet some objections and prevent some misunderstanding.

The statement of this thesis is liable to provoke one of three very different reactions. Some will think it not merely false but pernicious; they will see it as a threat to morality and to everything else that is worthwhile, and they will find the presenting of such a thesis in what purports to be a book on ethics paradoxical or even outrageous. Others will regard it as a trivial truth, almost too obvious to be worth mentioning, and certainly too plain to be worth much argument. Others again will say that it is meaningless or empty, that no real issue is raised by the question whether values are or are not part of the fabric of the world. But, precisely because there can be these three different reactions, much more needs to be said.

The claim that values are not objective, are not part of the fabric of the world, is meant to include not only moral goodness, which might be most naturally equated with moral value, but also other things that could be more loosely called moral values or disvalues – rightness and wrongness, duty, obligation, an action's being rotten and contemptible, and so on. It also includes non-moral values, notably aesthetic ones, beauty and various kinds of artistic merit. I shall not discuss these explicitly, but clearly much the same considerations apply to aesthetic and to moral values, and there would be at least some initial implausibility in a view that gave the one a different status from the other.

Since it is with moral values that I am primarily concerned, the view I am adopting may be called moral scepticism. But this name is likely to be misunderstood: "moral scepticism" might also be used as a name for either of two first order views, or perhaps for an incoherent mixture of the two. A moral sceptic might be the sort of person who says "All this talk of morality is tripe," who rejects morality and will take no notice of it. Such a person may be literally rejecting all moral judgements; he is more likely to be making moral judgements of his own, expressing a positive moral condemnation of all that conventionally passes for morality; or he may be confusing these two logically incompatible views, and saying that he rejects all morality, while he is in fact rejecting only a particular morality that is current in the society in which he has grown up. But I am not at present concerned with the merits or faults of such a position. These are first order moral views, positive or negative: the person who adopts either of them is taking a certain practical, normative, stand. By contrast, what I am discussing is a second order view, a view about the status of moral values and the nature of moral valuing, about where and how they fit into the world. These first and second order views are not merely distinct but completely independent: one could be a second order moral sceptic without being a first order one, or again the other way round. A man could hold strong moral views, and indeed ones whose content was thoroughly conventional, while believing that they were simply attitudes and policies with regard to conduct that he and other people held. Conversely, a man could reject all established morality while believing it to be an objective truth that it was evil or corrupt.

With another sort of misunderstanding moral scepticism would seem not so much pernicious as absurd. How could anyone deny that there is a difference between a kind action and a cruel one, or that a coward and a brave man behave differently in the face of danger? Of course, this is undeniable; but it is not to the point. The kinds of behaviour to which moral values and disvalues are ascribed are indeed part of the furniture of the world, and so are the natural, descriptive, differences between them; but not, perhaps, their differences in value. It is a hard fact that cruel actions differ from kind ones, and hence that we can learn, as in fact we all do, to distinguish them fairly well in practice, and to use the words "cruel" and "kind" with fairly clear descriptive meanings; but is it an equally hard fact that actions which are cruel in such a descriptive sense are to be condemned? The present issue is with regard to the objectivity specifically of value, not with regard to the objectivity of those natural, factual, differences on the basis of which differing values are assigned.

2 Subjectivism

Another name often used, as an alternative to "moral scepticism," for the view I am discussing is "subjectivism." But this too has more than one meaning. Moral subjectivism too could be a first order, normative, view, namely that everyone really ought to do whatever he thinks he should. This plainly is a (systematic) first order view; on examination it soon ceases to be plausible, but that is beside the point, for it is quite independent of the second order thesis at present under consideration. What is more confusing is that different second order views compete for the name "subjectivism." Several of these are doctrines about the meaning of moral terms and moral statements. What is often called moral subjectivism is the doctrine that, for example, "This action is right" *means* "I approve of this action," or more generally that moral judgements are equivalent to reports of the speaker's own feelings or attitudes. But the view I am now discussing is to be distinguished in two vital respects from any such doctrine as this. First, what I have called moral scepticism is a negative doctrine, not a positive one: it says what there isn't, not what there is. It says that there do not exist entities or relations of a certain kind, objective values or requirements, which many people have believed to exist. Of course, the moral sceptic cannot leave it at that. If his position is to be at all plausible, he must give some account of how other people have fallen into what he regards as an error, and this account will have to include some positive suggestions about how values fail to be objective, about what has been mistaken for, or has led to false beliefs about, objective values. But this will be a development of his theory, not its core: its core is the negation. Secondly, what I have called moral scepticism is an ontological thesis, not a linguistic or conceptual one. It is not, like the other doctrine often called moral subjectivism, a view about the meanings of moral statements. Again, no doubt, if it is to be at all plausible, it will have to give some account of their meanings, and I shall say something about this in Section 7 of this chapter and again in Chapters 2, 3, and 4. But this too will be a development of the theory, not its core.

It is true that those who have accepted the moral subjectivism which is the doctrine that moral judgements are equivalent to reports of the speaker's own feelings or attitudes have usually presupposed what I am calling moral scepticism. It is because they have assumed that there are no objective values that they have looked elsewhere for an analysis of what moral statements might mean, and have settled upon subjective reports. Indeed, if all our moral statements were such subjective reports, it would follow that, at least so far as we are aware, there are no objective moral values. If we were aware of them, we would say something about them. In this sense this sort of subjectivism entails moral scepticism. But the converse entailment does not hold. The denial that there are objective values does not commit one to any particular view about what moral statements mean, and certainly not to the view that they are equivalent to subjective reports. No doubt if moral values are not objective they are in some very broad sense subjective, and for this reason I would accept "moral subjectivism" as an alternative name to "moral scepticism." But subjectivism in this broad sense must be distinguished from the specific doctrine about meaning referred to above. Neither name is altogether satisfactory: we simply have to guard against the (different) misinterpretations which each may suggest

3 The Multiplicity of Second Order Questions

The distinctions drawn in the last two sections rest not only on the well-known and generally recognized difference between first and second order questions, but also on the more controversial claim that there are several kinds of second order moral question. Those most often mentioned are questions about the meaning and use of ethical terms, or the analysis of ethical concepts. With these go questions about the logic of moral statements: there may be special patterns of moral argument, licensed, perhaps, by aspects of the meanings of moral terms – for example, it may be part of the meaning of statements that they are universalizable. But there are also ontological, as contrasted with linguistic or conceptual, questions about the nature and status of goodness or rightness or whatever it is that first order moral statements are distinctively about. These are questions of factual rather than conceptual analysis: the problem of what goodness is cannot be settled conclusively or exhaustively by finding out what the word "good" means, or what it is conventionally used to say or to do.

Recent philosophy, biased as it has been towards various kinds of linguistic inquiry, has tended to doubt this, but the distinction between conceptual and factual analysis in ethics can be supported by analogies with other areas. The question of what perception is, what goes on when someone perceives something, is not adequately answered by finding out what words like "see" and "hear" mean, or what someone is doing in saying "I perceive . . . ," by analysing, however fully and accurately, any established concept of perception. There is a still closer analogy with colours. Robert Boyle and John Locke called colours "secondary qualities," meaning that colours as they occur in material things consist simply in patterns of arrangement and movement of minute particles on the surfaces of objects, which make them, as we would now say, reflect light of some frequencies better than others, and so enable these objects to produce colour sensations in us, but that colours as we see them do not literally belong to the surfaces of material things. Whether Boyle and Locke were right about this cannot be settled by finding out how we use colour words and what we mean in using them. Naive realism about colours might be a correct analysis not only of our pre-scientific colour concepts but also of the conventional meanings of colour words, and even of the meanings with which scientifically sophisticated people use them when they are off their guard, and yet it might not be a correct account of the status of colours.

Error could well result, then, from a failure to distinguish factual from conceptual analysis with regard to colours, from taking an account of the meanings of statements as a full account of what there is. There is a similar and in practice even greater risk of error in moral philosophy. There is another reason, too, why it would be a mistake to concentrate second order ethical discussions on questions of meaning. The more work philosophers have done on meaning, both in ethics and elsewhere, the more complications have come to light. It is by now pretty plain that no simple account of the meanings of first order moral statements will be correct, will cover adequately even the standard, conventional, senses of the main moral terms; I think, none the less, that there is a relatively clear-cut issue about the objectivity of moral values which is in danger of being lost among the complications of meaning.

4 Is Objectivity a Real Issue?

It has, however, been doubted whether there is a real issue here. I must concede that it is a rather old-fashioned one. I do not mean merely that it was raised by Hume, who argued that "The vice entirely escapes you . . . till you turn your reflexion into your own breast," and before him by Hobbes, and long before that by some of the Greek sophists. I mean rather that it was discussed vigorously in the nineteen thirties and forties, but since then has received much less attention. This is not because it has been solved or because agreement has been reached: instead it seems to have been politely shelved.

But was there ever a genuine problem? R. M. Hare has said that he does not understand what is meant by "the objectivity of values," and that he has not met anyone who does. We all know how to recognize the activity called "saying, thinking it to be so, that some act is wrong," and he thinks that it is to this activity that the subjectivist and the objectivist are both alluding, though one calls it "an attitude of disapproval" and the other "a moral intuition": these are only different names for the same thing. It is true that if one person says that a certain act is wrong and another that it is not wrong the objectivist will say that they are contradicting one another, but this yields no significant discrimination between objectivism and subjectivism, because the subjectivist too will concede that the second person is negating what the first has said, and Hare sees no difference between contradicting and negating. Again, the objectivist will say that one of the two must be wrong; but Hare argues that to say that the judgement that a certain act is wrong is itself wrong is merely to negate that judgement, and the subjectivist too must negate one or other of the two judgements, so that still no clear difference between objectivism and subjectivism has emerged. He sums up his case thus: "Think of one world into whose fabric values are objectively built; and think of another in which those values have been annihilated. And remember that in both worlds the people in them go on being concerned about the same things – there is no difference in the 'subjective' concern which people have for things, only in their 'objective' value. Now I ask, 'What is the difference between the states of affairs in these two worlds?' Can any answer be given except 'None whatever'?"

Now it is quite true that it is logically possible that the subjective concern, the activity of valuing or of thinking things wrong, should go on in just the same way whether there are objective values or not. But to say this is only to reiterate that there is a logical distinction between first and second order ethics: first order judgements are not necessarily affected by the truth or falsity of a second order view. But it does not follow, and it is not true, that there is no difference whatever between these two worlds. In the one there is something that backs up and validates some of the subjective concern which people have for things, in the other there is not. Hare's argument is similar to the positivist claim that there is no difference between a phenomenalist or Berkeleian world in which there are only minds and their ideas and the commonsense realist one in which there are also material things, because it is logically possible that people should have the same experiences in both. If we reject the positivism that would make the dispute between realists and phenomenalists a pseudo-question, we can reject Hare's similarly supported dismissal of the issue of the objectivity of values.

In any case, Hare has minimized the difference between his two worlds by considering only the situation where people already have just such subjective concern; further differences come to light if we consider how subjective concern is acquired or changed. If there were something in the fabric of the world that validated certain kinds of concern, then it would be possible to acquire these merely by finding something out, by letting one's thinking be controlled by how things were. But in the world in which objective values have been annihilated the acquiring of some new subjective concern means the development of something new on the emotive side by the person who acquires it, something that eighteenth-century writers would put under the head of passion or sentiment.

The issue of the objectivity of values needs, however, to be distinguished from others with which it might be confused. To say that there are objective values would not be to say merely that there are some things which are valued by everyone, nor does it entail this. There could be agreement in valuing even if valuing is just something that people do, even if this activity is not further validated. Subjective agreement would give intersubjective values, but intersubjectivity is not objectivity. Nor is objectivity simply universalizability: someone might well be prepared to universalize his prescriptive judgements or approvals – that is, to prescribe and approve in just the same ways in all relevantly similar cases, even ones in which he was involved differently or not at all – and yet he could recognize that such prescribing and approving were his activities, nothing more. Of course if there were objective values they would presumably belong to *kinds* of things or actions or states of affairs, so that the judgements that reported them would be universalizable; but the converse does not hold.

A more subtle distinction needs to be made between objectivism and descriptivism. Descriptivism is again a doctrine about the meanings of ethical terms and statements, namely that their meanings are purely descriptive rather than even partly prescriptive or emotive or evaluative, or that it is not an essential feature of the conventional meaning of moral statements that they have some special illocutionary force, say of commending rather than asserting. It contrasts with the view that commendation is in principle distinguishable from description (however difficult they may be to separate in practice) and that moral statements have it as at least part of their meaning that they are commendatory and hence in some uses intrinsically action-guiding. But descriptive meaning neither entails nor is entailed by objectivity. Berkeley's subjective idealism about material objects would be quite compatible with the admission that material object statements have purely descriptive meaning. Conversely, the main tradition of European moral philosophy from Plato onwards has combined the view that moral values are objective with the recognition that moral judgements are partly prescriptive or directive or action-guiding. Values themselves have been seen as at once prescriptive and objective. In Plato's theory the Forms, and in particular the Form of the Good, are eternal, extra-mental, realities. They are a very central structural element in the fabric of the world. But it is held also that just knowing them or "seeing" them will not merely tell men what to do but will ensure that they do it, overruling any contrary inclinations. The philosopher-kings in the *Republic* can, Plato thinks, be trusted with unchecked power because their education will have given them knowledge of the Forms. Being acquainted with the Forms of the Good and Justice and Beauty and the rest they will, by this knowledge alone, without any further motivation, be impelled to pursue and promote these ideals. Similarly, Kant believes that pure reason can by itself be practical, though he does not pretend to be able to explain how it can be so. Again, Sidgwick argues that if there is to be a science of ethics – and he assumes that there can be, indeed he defines ethics as "the science of conduct" – what ought to be "must in another sense have objective existence: it must be an object of knowledge and as such the same for all minds"; but he says that the affirmations of this science "are also precepts," and he speaks of happiness as "an end *absolutely* prescribed by reason." Since many philosophers have thus held that values are objectively prescriptive, it is clear that the ontological doctrine of objectivism must be distinguished from descriptivism, a theory about meaning.

But perhaps when Hare says that he does not understand what is meant by "the objectivity of values" he means that he cannot understand how values could be objective, he cannot frame for himself any clear, detailed, picture of what it would be like for values to be part of the fabric of the world. This would be a much more plausible claim; as we have seen, even Kant hints at a similar difficulty. Indeed, even Plato warns us that it is only through difficult studies spread over many years that one can approach the knowledge of the Forms. The difficulty of seeing how values could be objective is a fairly strong reason for thinking that they are not so; this point will be taken up in Section 9 . . . but it is not a good reason for saying that this is not a real issue.

I believe that as well as being a real issue it is an important one. It clearly matters for general philosophy. It would make a radical difference to our metaphysics if we had to find room for objective values – perhaps something like Plato's Forms – somewhere in our picture of the world. It would similarly make a difference to our epistemology if it had to explain how such objective values are or can be known, and to our philosophical psychology if we had to allow such knowledge, or Kant's pure practical reason, to direct choices and actions. Less obviously, how this issue is settled will affect the possibility of certain kinds of moral argument. For example, Sidgwick considers a discussion between an egoist and a utilitarian, and points out that if the egoist claims that his happiness or pleasure is objectively desirable or good, the utilitarian can argue that the egoist's happiness "cannot be more objectively desirable or more a good than the similar happiness of any other person: the mere fact . . . that *he is he* can have nothing to do with its objective desirability or goodness." In other words, if ethics is built on the concept of objective goodness, then egoism as a first order system or method of ethics can be refuted, whereas if it is assumed that goodness is only subjective it cannot. But Sidgwick correctly stresses what a number of other philosophers have missed, that this argument against egoism would require the objectivity specifically of goodness: the objectivity of what ought to be or of what it is rational to do would not be enough. If the egoist claimed that it was objectively rational, or obligatory upon him, to seek his own happiness, a similar argument about the irrelevance of the fact that he is he would lead only to the conclusion that it was objectively rational or obligatory for each other person to seek *his* own happiness, that is, to a universalized form of egoism, not to the refutation of egoism. And of course insisting on the universalizability of moral judgements, as opposed to the objectivity of goodness, would yield only the same result.

5 Standards of Evaluation

One way of stating the thesis that there are no objective values is to say that value statements cannot be either true or false. But this formulation, too, lends itself to misinterpretation. For there are certain kinds of value statements which undoubtedly can be true or false, even if, in the sense I intend, there are no objective values. Evaluations of many sorts are commonly made in relation to agreed and assumed standards. The classing of wool, the grading of apples, the awarding of prizes at sheepdog trials, flower shows, skating and diving championships, and even the marking of examination papers are carried out in relation to standards of quality or merit which are peculiar to each particular subject-matter or type of contest, which may be explicitly laid down but which, even if they are nowhere explicitly stated, are fairly well understood and agreed by those who are recognized as judges or experts in each particular field. Given any sufficiently determinate standards, it will be an objective issue, a matter of truth and falsehood, how well any particular specimen measures up to those standards. Comparative judgements in particular will be capable of truth and falsehood: it will be a factual question whether this sheep dog has performed better than that one.

The subjectivist about values, then, is not denying that there can be objective evaluations relative to standards, and these are as possible in the aesthetic and moral fields as in any of those just mentioned. More than this, there is an objective distinction which applies in many such fields, and yet would itself be regarded as a peculiarly moral one: the distinction between justice and injustice. In one important sense of the word it is a paradigm case of injustice if a court declares someone to be guilty of an offence of which it knows him to be innocent. More generally, a finding is unjust if it is at variance with what the relevant law and the facts together require, and particularly if it is known by the court to be so. More generally still, any award of marks, prizes, or the like is unjust if it is at variance with the agreed standards for the contest in question: if one diver's performance in fact measures up better to the accepted standards for diving than another's, it will be unjust if the latter is awarded higher marks or the prize. In this way the justice or injustice of decisions relative to standards can be a thoroughly objective matter, though there may still be a subjective element in the

interpretation or application of standards. But the statement that a certain decision is thus just or unjust will not be objectively prescriptive: in so far as it can
be simply true it leaves open the question whether there is any objective requirement to do what is just and to refrain from what is unjust, and equally leaves
open the practical decision to act in either way.

Recognizing the objectivity of justice in relation to standards, and of evaluative judgements relative to standards, then, merely shifts the question of the
objectivity of values back to the standards themselves. The subjectivist may try
to make his point by insisting that there is no objective validity about the choice
of standards. Yet he would clearly be wrong if he said that the choice of even the
most basic standards in any field was completely arbitrary. The standards used
in sheepdog trials clearly bear some relation to the work that sheepdogs are kept
to do, the standards for grading apples bear some relation to what people generally want in or like about apples, and so on. On the other hand, standards are not
as a rule strictly validated by such purposes. The appropriateness of standards is
neither fully determinate nor totally indeterminate in relation to independently
specifiable aims or desires. But however determinate it is, the objective appropriateness of standards in relation to aims or desires is no more of a threat to the
denial of objective values than is the objectivity of evaluation relative to standards. In fact it is logically no different from the objectivity of goodness relative to
desires. Something may be called good simply in so far as it satisfies or is such
as to satisfy a certain desire; but the objectivity of such relations of satisfaction
does not constitute in our sense an objective value.

6 Hypothetical and Categorical Imperatives

We may make this issue clearer by referring to Kant's distinction between hypothetical and categorical imperatives, though what he called imperatives are more
naturally expressed as "ought"-statements than in the imperative mood. "If you
want X, do Y" (or "You ought to do Y") will be a hypothetical imperative if it is
based on the supposed fact that Y is, in the circumstances, the only (or the best)
available means to X; that is, on a causal relation between Y and X. The reason for
doing Y lies in its causal connection with the desired end, X; the oughtness is
contingent upon the desire. But "You ought to do Y" will be a categorical imperative if you ought to do Y irrespective of any such desire for any end to which Y
would contribute, if the oughtness is not thus contingent upon any desire. But this
distinction needs to be handled with some care. An "ought"-statement is not in
this sense hypothetical merely because it incorporates a conditional clause. "If you
promised to do Y, you ought to do Y" is not a hypothetical imperative merely on
account of the stated if-clause; what is meant may be either a hypothetical or a
categorical imperative, depending upon the implied reason for keeping the supposed promise. If this rests upon some such further unstated conditional as "If you
want to be trusted another time," then it is a hypothetical imperative; if not, it is
categorical. Even a desire of the agent's can figure in the antecedent of what,
though conditional in grammatical form, is still in Kant's sense a categorical im-

perative. "If you are strongly attracted sexually to young children you ought not to go in for school teaching" is not, in virtue of what it explicitly says, a hypothetical imperative: the avoidance of school teaching is not being offered as a means to the satisfaction of the desires in question. Of course, it could still be a hypothetical imperative, if the implied reason were a prudential one; but it could also be a categorical imperative, a moral requirement where the reason for the recommended action (strictly, avoidance) does not test upon that action's being a means to the satisfaction of any desire that the agent is supposed to have. Not every conditional ought-statement or command, then, is a hypothetical imperative; equally, not every non-conditional one is a categorical imperative. An appropriate if-clause may be left unstated. Indeed, a simple command in the imperative mood, say a parade-ground order, which might seem most literally to qualify for the title of a categorical imperative, will hardly ever be one in the sense we need here. The implied reason for complying with such an order will almost always be some desire of the person addressed, perhaps simply the desire to keep out of trouble. If so, such an apparently categorical order will be in our sense a hypothetical imperative. Again, an imperative remains hypothetical even if we change the "if" to "since": the fact that the desire for X is actually present does not alter the fact that the reason for doing Y is contingent upon the desire for X by way of Y's being a means to X. In Kant's own treatment, while imperatives of skill relate to desires which an agent may or may not have, imperatives of prudence relate to the desire for happiness which, Kant assumes, everyone has. So construed, imperatives of prudence are no less hypothetical than imperatives of skill, no less contingent upon desires that the agent has at the time the imperatives are addressed to him. But if we think rather of a counsel of prudence as being related to the agent's future welfare, to the satisfaction of desires that he does not yet have – not even to a present desire that his future desires should be satisfied – then a counsel of prudence is a categorical imperative, different indeed from a moral one, but analogous to it.

A categorical imperative, then, would express a reason for acting which was unconditional in the sense of not being contingent upon any present desire of the agent to whose satisfaction the recommended action would contribute as a means – or more directly: "You ought to dance," if the implied reason is just that you want to dance or like dancing, is still a hypothetical imperative. Now Kant himself held that moral judgements are categorical imperatives, or perhaps are all applications of one categorical imperative, and it can plausibly be maintained at least that many moral judgements contain a categorically imperative element. So far as ethics is concerned, my thesis that there are no objective values is specifically the denial that any such categorically imperative element is objectively valid. The objective values which I am denying would be action-directing absolutely, not contingently (in the way indicated) upon the agent's desires and inclinations.

Another way of trying to clarify this issue is to refer to moral reasoning or moral arguments. In practice, of course, such reasoning is seldom fully explicit: but let us suppose that we could make explicit the reasoning that supports some evaluative conclusion, where this conclusion has some action-guiding force that is not contingent upon desires or purposes or chosen ends. Then what I am saying is that somewhere in the input to this argument – perhaps in one or more of the premisses, perhaps in some part of the form of the argument – there will be something which cannot be objectively validated – some premiss which is not capable of being simply true, or some form of argument which is not valid as a matter of general logic, whose authority or cogency is not objective, but is constituted by our choosing or deciding to think in a certain way.

7 The Claim to Objectivity

If I have succeeded in specifying precisely enough the moral values whose objectivity I am denying, my thesis may now seem to be trivially true. Of course, some will say, valuing, preferring, choosing, recommending, rejecting, condemning, and so on, are human activities, and there is no need to look for values that are prior to and logically independent of all such activities. There may be widespread agreement in valuing, and particular value-judgements are not in general arbitrary or isolated: they typically cohere with others, or can be criticized if they do not, reasons can be given for them, and so on; but if all that the subjectivist is maintaining is that desires, ends, purposes, and the like figure somewhere in the system of reasons, and that no ends or purposes are objective as opposed to being merely intersubjective, then this may be conceded without much fuss.

But I do not think that this should be conceded so easily. As I have said, the main tradition of European moral philosophy includes the contrary claim, that there are objective values of just the sort I have denied. I have referred already to Plato, Kant, and Sidgwick. Kant in particular holds that the categorical imperative is not only categorical and imperative but objectively so: though a rational being gives the moral law to himself, the law that he thus makes is determinate and necessary. Aristotle begins the *Nicomachean Ethics* by saying that the good is that at which all things aim, and that ethics is part of a science which he calls "politics," whose goal is not knowledge but practice; yet he does not doubt that there can be *knowledge* of what is the good for man, nor, once he has identified this as well-being or happiness, *eudaimonia*, that it can be known, rationally determined, in what happiness consists; and it is plain that he thinks that this happiness is intrinsically desirable, not good simply because it is desired. The rationalist Samuel Clarke holds that

> these eternal and necessary differences of things make it *fit and reasonable* for creatures so to act . . . even separate from the consideration of these rules being the *positive will* or *command of God*; and also antecedent to any respect or regard, expectation or apprehension, of any *particular private and personal advantage or disadvantage, reward or punishment*, either present or future.

Even the sentimentalist Hutcheson defines moral goodness as "some quality apprehended in actions, which procures approbation . . . ," while saying that the moral sense by which we perceive virtue and vice has been given to us (by the Author of nature) to direct our actions. Hume indeed was on the other side, but he is still a witness to the dominance of the objectivist tradition, since he claims that when we "see that the distinction of vice and virtue is not founded merely on the relations of objects, nor is perceived by reason," this "would subvert all the vulgar systems of morality." And Richard Price insists that right and wrong are "real characters of actions," not "qualities of our minds," and are perceived by the understanding; he criticizes the notion of moral sense on the ground that it would make virtue an affair of taste, and moral right and wrong "nothing in the objects themselves"; he rejects Hutcheson's view because (perhaps mistakenly) he sees it as collapsing into Hume's.

But this objectivism about values is not only a feature of the philosophical tradition. It has also a firm basis in ordinary thought, and even in the meanings of moral terms. No doubt it was an extravagance for Moore to say that "good" is the name of a non-natural quality, but it would not be so far wrong to say that in moral contexts it is used as if it were the name of a supposed non-natural quality, where the description "non-natural" leaves room for the peculiar evaluative, prescriptive, intrinsically action-guiding aspects of this supposed quality. This point can be illustrated by reflection on the conflicts and swings of opinion in recent years between non-cognitivist and naturalist views about the central, basic, meanings of ethical terms. If we reject the view that it is the function of such terms to introduce objective values into discourse about conduct and choices of action, there seem to be two main alternative types of account. One (which has importantly different subdivisions) is that they conventionally express either attitudes which the speaker purports to adopt towards whatever it is that he characterizes morally, or prescriptions or recommendations, subject perhaps to the logical constraint of universalizability. Different views of this type share the central thesis that ethical terms have, at least partly and primarily, some sort of non-cognitive, non-descriptive, meaning. Views of the other type hold that they are descriptive in meaning, but descriptive of natural features, partly of such features as everyone, even the non-cognitivist, would recognize as distinguishing kind actions from cruel ones, courage from cowardice, politeness from rudeness, and so on, and partly (though these two overlap) of relations between the actions and some human wants, satisfactions, and the like. I believe that views of both these types capture part of the truth. Each approach can account for the fact that moral judgements are action-guiding or practical. Yet each gains much of its plausibility from the felt inadequacy of the other. It is a very natural reaction to any non-cognitive analysis of ethical terms to protest that there is more to ethics than this, something more external to the maker of moral judgements, more authoritative over both him and those of or to whom he speaks, and this reaction is likely to persist even when full allowance has been made for the logical, formal, constraints of full-blooded prescriptivity and universalizability. Ethics, we are inclined to believe, is more a matter of knowledge and less a matter of decision than any non-cognitive analysis allows. And of course naturalism satisfies this demand. It will not be a matter of choice or decision whether an action is cruel or unjust or imprudent or whether it is likely to produce more distress than pleasure. But in satisfying this demand, it introduces a converse deficiency. On a naturalist analysis, moral judgements can be practical, but their practicality is wholly relative to desires or possible satisfactions of the person or persons whose actions are to be guided; but moral judgements seem to say more than this. This view leaves out the categorical quality of moral requirements. In fact both naturalist and non-cognitive analyses leave out the apparent authority of ethics, the one by excluding the categorically imperative aspect, the other the claim to objective validity or truth. The ordinary user of moral language means to say something about whatever it is that he characterizes morally, for example a possible action, as it is in itself, or would be if it were realized, and not about, or even simply expressive of, his, or anyone else's, attitude or relation to it. But the something he wants to say is not purely descriptive, certainly not inert, but something that involves a call for action or for the refraining from action, and one that is absolute, not contingent upon any desire or preference or policy or choice, his own or anyone else's. Someone in a state of moral perplexity, wondering whether it would be wrong for him to engage, say, in research related to bacteriological warfare, wants to arrive at some judgement about this concrete case, his doing this work at this time in these actual circumstances; his relevant characteristics will be part of the subject of the judgement, but no relation between him and the proposed action will be part of the predicate. The question is not, for example, whether he really wants to do this work, whether it will satisfy or dissatisfy him, whether he will in the long run have a pro-attitude towards it, or even whether this is an action of a sort that he can happily and sincerely recommend in all relevantly similar cases. Nor is he even wondering just whether to recommend such action in all relevantly similar cases. He wants to know whether this course of action would be wrong in itself. Something like this is the everyday objectivist concept of which talk about non-natural qualities is a philosopher's reconstruction.

The prevalence of this tendency to objectify values – and not only moral ones – is confirmed by a pattern of thinking that we find in existentialists and those influenced by them. The denial of objective values can carry with it an extreme emotional reaction, a feeling that nothing matters at all, that life has lost its purpose. Of course this does not follow; the lack of objective values is not a good reason for abandoning subjective concern or for ceasing to want anything. But the abandonment of a belief in objective values can cause, at least temporarily, a decay of subjective concern and sense of purpose. That it does so is evidence that the people in whom this reaction occurs have been tending to objectify their concerns and purposes, have been giving them a fictitious external authority. A claim to objectivity has been so strongly associated with their subjective concerns and purposes that the collapse of the former seems to undermine the latter as well.

This view, that conceptual analysis would reveal a claim to objectivity, is sometimes dramatically confirmed by philosophers who are officially on the other side. Bertrand Russell, for example, says that "ethical propositions should be expressed in the optative mood, not in the indicative"; he defends himself effectively against the charge of inconsistency in both holding ultimate ethical valuations to be subjective and expressing emphatic opinions on ethical questions. Yet at the end he admits:

> Certainly there *seems* to be something more. Suppose, for example, that some one were to advocate the introduction of bullfighting in this country. In opposing the proposal I should *feel*, not only that I was expressing my desires, but that my desires in the matter are *right*, whatever that may mean. As a matter of argument, I can, I think, show that I am not guilty of any logical inconsistency in holding to the above interpretation of ethics and at the same time expressing strong ethical preferences. But in feeling I am not satisfied.

But he concludes, reasonably enough, with the remark: "I can only say that, while my own opinions as to ethics do not satisfy me, other people's satisfy me still less."

I conclude, then, that ordinary moral judgements include a claim to objectivity, an assumption that there are objective values in just the sense in which I am concerned to deny this. And I do not think it is going too far to say that this assumption has been incorporated in the basic, conventional, meanings of moral terms. Any analysis of the meanings of moral terms which omits this claim to objective, intrinsic, prescriptivity is to that extent incomplete, and this is true of any non-cognitive analysis, any naturalist one, and any combination of the two.

If second order ethics were confined, then, to linguistic and conceptual analysis, it ought to conclude that moral values at least are objective: that they are so is part of what our ordinary moral statements mean: the traditional moral concepts of the ordinary man as well as of the main line of western philosophers are concepts of objective value. But it is precisely for this reason that linguistic and conceptual analysis is not enough. The claim to objectivity, however ingrained in our language and thought, is not self-validating. It can and should be questioned. But the denial of objective values will have to be put forward not as the result of an analytic approach, but as an "error theory," a theory that although most people in making moral judgements implicitly claim, among other things, to be pointing to something objectively prescriptive, these claims are all false. It is this that makes the name "moral scepticism" appropriate.

But since this is an error theory, since it goes against assumptions ingrained in our thought and built into some of the ways in which language is used, since it conflicts with what is sometimes called common sense, it needs very solid support. It is not something we can accept lightly or casually and then quietly pass on. If we are to adopt this view, we must argue explicitly for it. Traditionally it has been supported by arguments of two main kinds, which I shall call the argument from relativity and the argument from queerness, but these can, as I shall show, be supplemented in several ways.

8 The Argument from Relativity

The argument from relativity has as its premiss the well-known variation in moral codes from one society to another and from one period to another, and also the differences in moral beliefs between different groups and classes within a complex community. Such variation is in itself merely a truth of descriptive morality, a fact of anthropology which entails neither first order nor second order ethical views. Yet it may indirectly support second order subjectivism: radical differences between first order moral judgements make it difficult to treat those judgements as apprehensions of objective truths. But it is not the mere occurrence of disagreements that tends against the objectivity of values. Disagreement on questions in history or biology or cosmology does not show that there are no objective issues in these fields for investigators to disagree about. But such scientific disagreement results from speculative inferences or explanatory hypotheses based on inadequate evidence, and it is hardly plausible to interpret moral disagreement in the same way. Disagreement about moral codes seems to reflect people's adherence to and participation in different ways of life. The causal connection seems to be mainly that way round: it is that people approve of monogamy because they participate in a monogamous way of life rather than that they participate in a monogamous way of life because they approve of monogamy. Of course, the standards may be an idealization of the way of life from which they arise: the monogamy in which people participate may be less complete, less rigid, than that of which it leads them to approve. This is not to say that moral judgements are purely conventional. Of course there have been and are moral heretics and moral reformers, people who have turned against the established rules and practices of their own communities for moral reasons, and often for moral reasons that we would endorse. But this can usually be understood as the extension, in ways which, though new and unconventional, seemed to them to be required for consistency, of rules to which they already adhered as arising out of an existing way of life. In short, the argument from relativity has some force simply because the actual variations in the moral codes are more readily explained by the hypothesis that they reflect ways of life than by the hypothesis that they express perceptions, most of them seriously inadequate and badly distorted, of objective values.

But there is a well-known counter to this argument from relativity, namely to say that the items for which objective validity is in the first place to be claimed are not specific moral rules or codes but very general basic principles which are recognized at least implicitly to some extent in all society – such principles as provide the foundations of what Sidgwick has called different methods of ethics: the principle of universalizability, perhaps, or the rule that one ought to conform to the specific rules of any way of life in which one takes part, from which one profits, and on which one relies, or some utilitarian principle of doing what tends, or seems likely, to promote the general happiness. It is easy to show that such general principles, married with differing concrete circumstances, different existing social patterns or different preferences, will beget different specific moral rules; and there is some plausibility in the claim that the specific rules thus generated will vary from community to community or from group to group in close agreement with the actual variations in accepted codes.

The argument from relativity can be only partly countered in this way. To take this line the moral objectivist has to say that it is only in these principles that the objective moral character attaches immediately to its descriptively specified ground or subject: other moral judgements are objectively valid or true, but only derivatively and contingently – if things had been otherwise, quite different sorts of actions would have been right. And despite the prominence in recent philosophical ethics of universalization, utilitarian principles, and the like, these are very far from constituting the whole of what is actually affirmed as basic in ordinary moral thought. Much of this is concerned rather with what Hare calls "ideals" or, less kindly, "fanaticism." That is, people judge that some things are good or right, and others are bad or wrong, not because – or at any rate not only because – they exemplify some general principle for which widespread implicit acceptance could be claimed, but because something about those things arouses certain responses immediately in them, though they would arouse radically and irresolvably different responses in others. "Moral sense" or "intuition" is an initially more plausible description of what supplies many of our basic moral judgements than "reason." With regard to all these starting points of moral thinking the argument from relativity remains in full force.

9 The Argument from Queerness

Even more important, however, and certainly more generally applicable, is the argument from queerness. This has two parts, one metaphysical, the other epistemological. If there were objective values, then they would be entities or qualities or relations of a very strange sort, utterly different from anything else in the universe. Correspondingly, if we were aware of them, it would have to be by some special faculty of moral perception or intuition, utterly different from our ordinary ways of knowing everything else. These points were recognized by Moore when he spoke of non-natural qualities, and by the intuitionists in their talk about a "faculty of moral intuition." Intuitionism has long been out of favour, and it is indeed easy to point out its implausibilities. What is not so often stressed, but is more important, is that the central thesis of intuitionism is one to which any objectivist view of values is in the end committed: intuitionism merely makes unpalatably plain what other forms of objectivism wrap up. Of course the suggestion that moral judgements are made or moral problems solved by just sitting down and having an ethical intuition is a travesty of actual moral thinking. But, however complex the real process, it will require (if it is to yield authoritatively prescriptive conclusions) some input of this distinctive sort, either premises or forms of argument or both. When we ask the awkward question, how we can be aware of this authoritative prescriptivity, of the truth of these distinctively ethical premises or of the cogency of this distinctively ethical pattern of reasoning, none of our ordinary accounts of sensory perception or introspection or the framing and confirming of explanatory hypotheses or inference or logical construction or conceptual analysis, or any combination of these, will provide a satisfactory answer; a special sort of intuition is a lame answer, but it is the one to which the clearheaded objectivist is compelled to resort.

Indeed, the best move for the moral objectivist is not to evade this issue, but to look for companions in guilt. For example, Richard Price argues that it is not moral knowledge alone that such an empiricism as those of Locke and Hume is unable to account for, but also our knowledge and even our ideas of essence, number, identity, diversity, solidity, inertia, substance, the necessary existence and infinite extension of time and space, necessity and possibility in general, power, and causation. If the understanding, which Price defines as the faculty within us that discerns truth, is also a source of new simple ideas of so many other sorts, may it not also be a power of immediately perceiving right and wrong, which yet are real characters of actions?

This is an important counter to the argument from queerness. The only adequate reply to it would be to show how, on empiricist foundations, we can construct an account of the ideas and beliefs and knowledge that we have of all these matters. I cannot even begin to do that here, though I have undertaken some parts of the task elsewhere. I can only state my belief that satisfactory accounts of most of these can be given in empirical terms. If some supposed metaphysical necessities or essences resist such treatment, then they too should be included, along with objective values, among the targets of the argument from queerness.

This queerness does not consist simply in the fact that ethical statements are "unverifiable." Although logical positivism with its verifiability theory of descriptive meaning gave an impetus to non-cognitive accounts of ethics, it is not only logical positivists but also empiricists of a much more liberal sort who should find objective values hard to accommodate. Indeed, I would not only reject the verifiability principle but also deny the conclusion commonly drawn from it, that moral judgements lack descriptive meaning. The assertion that there are objective values or intrinsically prescriptive entities or features of some kind, which ordinary moral judgements presuppose, is, I hold, not meaningless but false.

Plato's Forms give a dramatic picture of what objective values would have to be. The Form of the Good is such that knowledge of it provides the knower with both a direction and an overriding motive; something's being good both tells the person who knows this to pursue it and makes him pursue it. An objective good would be sought by anyone who was acquainted with it, not because of any contingent fact that this person, or every person, is so constituted that he desires this end, but just because the end has to-be-pursuedness somehow built into it. Similarly, if there were objective principles of right and wrong, any wrong (possible) course of action would have not-to-be-doneness somehow built into it. Or we should have something like Clarke's necessary relations of fitness between situations and actions, so that a situation would have a demand for such-and-such an action somehow built into it.

The need for an argument of this sort can be brought out by reflection on Hume's argument that "reason" – in which at this stage he includes all sorts of knowing as well as reasoning – can never be an "influencing motive of the will." Someone might object that Hume has argued unfairly from the lack of influencing power (not contingent upon desires) in ordinary objects of knowledge and ordinary reasoning, and might maintain that values differ from natural objects precisely in their power, when known, automatically to influence the will. To this Hume could, and would need to, reply that this objection involves the postulating of value-entities or value-features of quite a different order from anything else with which we are acquainted, and of a corresponding faculty with which to detect them. That is, he would have to supplement his explicit argument with what I have called the argument from queerness.

Another way of bringing out this queerness is to ask, about anything that is supposed to have some objective moral quality, how this is linked with its natural features. What is the connection between the natural fact that an action is a piece of deliberate cruelty – say, causing pain just for fun – and the moral fact that it is wrong? It cannot be an entailment, a logical or semantic necessity. Yet it is not merely that the two features occur together. The wrongness must somehow be "consequential" or "supervenient"; it is wrong because it is a piece of deliberate cruelty. But just what *in the world* is signified by this "because"? And how do we know the relation that it signifies, if this is something more than such actions being socially condemned, and condemned by us too, perhaps through our having absorbed attitudes from our social environment? It is not even sufficient to postulate a faculty which "sees" the wrongness: something must be postulated which can see at once the natural features that constitute the cruelty, and the wrongness, and the mysterious consequential link between the two. Alliteratively, the intuition required might be the perception that wrongness is a higher order property belonging to certain natural properties; but what is this belonging of properties to other properties, and how can we discern it? How much simpler and more comprehensible the situation would be if we could replace the moral quality with some sort of subjective response which could be causally related to the detection of the natural features on which the supposed quality is said to be consequential.

It may be thought that the argument from queerness is given an unfair start if we thus relate it to what are admittedly among the wilder products of philosophical fancy – Platonic Forms, non-natural qualities, self-evident relations of fitness, faculties of intuition, and the like. Is it equally forceful if applied to the terms in which everyday moral judgements are more likely to be expressed – though still, as has been argued in Section 7, with a claim to objectivity – "you must do this," "you can't do that," "obligation," "unjust," "rotten," "disgraceful," "mean," or talk about good reasons for or against possible actions? Admittedly not; but that is because the objective prescriptivity, the element a claim for whose authoritativeness is embedded in ordinary moral thought and language, is not yet isolated in these forms of speech, but is presented along with relations to desired end feelings, reasoning about the means to desired ends, interpersonal demands, the injustice which consists in the violation of what are in the context the accepted standards of merit, the psychological constituents of meanness, and so on. There is nothing queer about any of these, and under cover of them the claim for moral authority may pass unnoticed. But if I am right in arguing that it is ordinarily there, and is therefore very likely to be incorporated almost automatically in philosophical accounts of ethics which systematize our ordinary thought even in such apparently innocent terms as these, it needs to be examined, and for this purpose it needs to be isolated and exposed as it is by the less cautious philosophical reconstructions.

10 Patterns of Objectification

Considerations of these kinds suggest that it is in the end less paradoxical to reject than to retain the common-sense belief in the objectivity of moral values, provided that we can explain how this belief, if it is false, has become established and is so resistant to criticisms. This proviso is not difficult to satisfy.

On a subjectivist view, the supposedly objective values will be based in fact upon attitudes which the person has who takes himself to be recognizing and responding to those values. If we admit what Hume calls the mind's "Propensity to spread itself on external objects," we can understand the supposed objectivity of moral qualities as arising from what we can call the projection or objectification of moral attitudes. This would be analogous to what is called the "pathetic fallacy," the tendency to read our feelings into their objects. If a fungus, say, fills us with disgust, we may be inclined to ascribe to the fungus itself a non-natural quality of foulness. But in moral contexts there is more than this propensity at work. Moral attitudes themselves are at least partly social in origin: socially established – and socially necessary – patterns of behaviour put pressure on individuals, and each individual tends to internalize these pressures and to join in requiring these patterns of behaviour of himself and of others. The attitudes that are objectified into moral values have indeed an external source, though not the one assigned to them by the belief in their absolute authority. Moreover, there are motives that would support objectification. We need morality to regulate interpersonal relations, to control some of the ways in which people behave towards one another, often in opposition to contrary inclinations. We therefore want our moral judgements to be authoritative for other agents as well as for ourselves: objective validity would give them the authority required. Aesthetic values are logically in the same position as moral ones; much the same metaphysical and epistemological considerations apply to them. But aesthetic values are less strongly objectified than moral ones; their subjective status, and an "error theory" with regard to such claims to objectivity as are incorporated in aesthetic judgements, will be more readily accepted, just because the motives for their objectification are less compelling.

But it would be misleading to think of the objectification of moral values as primarily the projection of feelings, as in the pathetic fallacy. More important are wants and demands. As Hobbes says, "whatsoever is the object of any man's

Appetite or Desire, that is it, which he for his part calleth *Good*"; and certainly both the adjective "good" and the noun "goods" are used in non-moral contexts of things because they are such as to satisfy desires. We get the notion of something's being objectively good, or having intrinsic value, by reversing the direction of dependence here, by making the desire depend upon the goodness, instead of the goodness on the desire. And this is aided by the fact that the desired thing will indeed have features that make it desired, that enable it to arouse a desire or that make it such as to satisfy some desire that is already there. It is fairly easy to confuse the way in which a thing's desirability is indeed objective with its having in our sense objective value. The fact that the word "good" serves as one of our main moral terms is a trace of this pattern of objectification.

Similarly related uses of words are covered by the distinction between hypothetical and categorical imperatives. The statement that someone "ought to" or, more strongly, "must" do such-and-such may be backed up explicitly or implicitly by reference to what he wants or to what his purposes and objects are. Again, there may be a reference to the purposes of someone else, perhaps the speaker: "You must do this" – "Why?" – "Because I want such-and-such." The moral categorical imperative which could be expressed in the same words can be seen as resulting from the suppression of the conditional clause in a hypothetical imperative without its being replaced by any such reference to the speaker's wants. The action in question is still required in something like the way in which it would be if it were appropriately related to a want, but it is no longer admitted that there is any contingent want upon which its being required depends. Again this move can be understood when we remember that at least our central and basic moral judgements represent social demands, where the source of the demand is indeterminate and diffuse. Whose demands or wants are in question, the agent's, or the speaker's, or those of an indefinite multitude of other people? All of these in a way, but there are advantages in not specifying them precisely. The speaker is expressing demands which he makes as a member of a community, which he has developed in and by participation in a joint way of life; also, what is required of this particular agent would be required of any other in a relevantly similar situation; but the agent too is expected to have internalized the relevant demands, to act as if the ends for which the action is required were his own. By suppressing any explicit reference to demands and making the imperatives categorical we facilitate conceptual moves from one such demand relation to another. The moral uses of such words as "must" and "ought" and "should," all of which are used also to express hypothetical imperatives, are traces of this pattern of objectification.

It may be objected that this explanation links normative ethics too closely with descriptive morality, with the mores or socially enforced patterns of behaviour that anthropologists record. But it can hardly be denied that moral thinking starts from the enforcement of social codes. Of course it is not confined to that. But even when moral judgements are detached from the mores of any actual society they are liable to be framed with reference to an ideal community of moral agents, such as Kant's kingdom of ends, which but for the need to give God a special place in it would have been better called a commonwealth of ends.

Another way of explaining the objectification of moral values is to say that ethics is a system of law from which the legislator has been removed. This might have been derived either from the positive law of a state or from a supposed system of divine law. There can be no doubt that some features of modern European moral concepts are traceable to the theological ethics of Christianity. The stress on quasi-imperative notions, on what ought to be done or on what is wrong in a sense that is close to that of "forbidden," are surely relics of divine commands. Admittedly, the central ethical concepts for Plato and Aristotle also are in a broad sense prescriptive or intrinsically action-guiding, but in concentrating rather on "good" than on "ought" they show that their moral thought is an objectification of the desired and the satisfying rather than of the commanded. Elizabeth Anscombe has argued that modern, non-Aristotelian, concepts of *moral* obligation, *moral* duty, of what is *morally* right and wrong, and of the *moral* sense of "ought" are survivals outside the framework of thought that made them really intelligible, namely the belief in divine law. She infers that "ought" has "become a word of mere mesmeric force," with only a "delusive appearance of content," and that we would do better to discard such terms and concepts altogether, and go back to Aristotelian ones.

There is much to be said for this view. But while we can explain some distinctive features of modern moral philosophy in this way, it would be a mistake to see the whole problem of the claim to objective prescriptivity as merely local and unnecessary, as a postoperative complication of a society from which a dominant system of theistic belief has recently been rather hastily excised. As Cudworth and Clarke and Price, for example, show, even those who still admit divine commands, or the positive law of God, may believe moral values to have an independent, objective but still action-guiding authority. Responding to Plato's *Euthyphro* dilemma, they believe that God commands what he commands because it is in itself good or right, not that it is good or right merely because and in that he commands it. Otherwise God himself could not be called good. Price asks, "What can be more preposterous, than to make the Deity nothing but will; and to exalt this on the ruins of all his attributes?" The apparent objectivity of moral value is a widespread phenomenon which has more than one source: the persistence of a belief in something like divine law when the belief in the divine legislator has faded out is only one factor among others. There are several different patterns of objectification, all of which have left characteristic traces in our actual moral concepts and moral language.

11 The General Goal of Human Life

The argument of the preceding sections is meant to apply quite generally to moral thought, but the terms in which it has been stated are largely those of the Kantian and post-Kantian tradition of English moral philosophy. To those who are more familiar with another tradition, which runs through Aristotle and Aquinas, it may seem wide of the mark. For them, the fundamental notion is that of the good for man, or the general end or goal of human life, or perhaps of a set of basic goods or primary human purposes. Moral reasoning consists partly in achieving a more adequate understanding of this basic goal (or set of goals), partly in working out the best way of pursuing and realizing it. But this approach is open to two radically different interpretations. According to one, to say that something is the good for man or the general goal of human life is just to say that this is what men in fact pursue or will find ultimately satisfying, or perhaps that it is something which, if postulated as an implicit goal, enables us to make sense of actual human strivings and to detect a coherent pattern in what would otherwise seem to be a chaotic jumble of conflicting purposes. According to the other interpretation, to say that something is the good for man or the general goal of human life is to say that this is man's proper end, that this is what he ought to be striving after, whether he in fact is or not. On the first interpretation we have a descriptive statement, on the second a normative or evaluative or prescriptive one. But this approach tends to combine the two interpretations, or to slide from one to the other, and to borrow support for what are in effect claims of the second sort from the plausibility of statements of the first sort.

I have no quarrel with this notion interpreted in the first way. I would only insert a warning that there may well be more diversity even of fundamental purposes, more variation in what different human beings will find ultimately satisfying, than the terminology of "*the* good for man" would suggest. Nor indeed, have I any quarrel with the second, prescriptive, interpretation, provided that it is recognized as subjectively prescriptive, that the speaker is here putting forward his own demands or proposals, or those of some movement that he represents, though no doubt linking these demands or proposals with what he takes to be already in the first, descriptive, sense fundamental human goals. In fact, I shall myself make use of the notion of the good for man, interpreted in both these ways, when I try in Chapter 8 to sketch a positive moral system. But if it is claimed that something is objectively the right or proper goal of human life, then this is tantamount to the assertion of something that is objectively categorically imperative, and comes fairly within the scope of our previous arguments. Indeed, the running together of what I have here called the two interpretations is yet another pattern of objectification: a claim to objective prescriptivity is constructed by combining the normative element in the second interpretation with the objectivity allowed by the first, by the statement that such and such are fundamentally pursued or ultimately satisfying human goals. The argument from relativity still applies: the radical diversity of the goals that men actually pursue and find satisfying makes it implausible to construe such pursuits as resulting from an imperfect grasp of a unitary true good. So too does the argument from queerness; we can still ask what this objectively prescriptive rightness of the true goal can be, and how this is linked on the one hand with the descriptive features of this goal and on the other with the fact that it is *to some extent* an actual goal of human striving. To meet these difficulties, the objectivist may have recourse to the purpose of God: the true purpose of human life is fixed by what God intended (or, intends) men to do and to be. Actual human strivings and satisfactions have some relation to this true end because God made men for this end and made them such as to pursue it – but only *some* relation, because of the inevitable imperfection of created beings.

I concede that if the requisite theological doctrine could be defended, a kind of objective ethical prescriptivity could be thus introduced. Since I think that theism cannot be defended, I do not regard this as any threat to my argument. But I shall take up the question of relations between morality and religion again in Chapter 10. Those who wish to keep theism as a live option can read the arguments of the intervening chapters hypothetically, as a discussion of what we can make of morality without recourse to God, and hence of what we can say about morality if, in the end, we dispense with religious belief.

12 Conclusion

I have maintained that there is a real issue about the status of values, including moral values. Moral scepticism, the denial of objective moral values, is not to be confused with any one of several first order normative views, or with any linguistic or conceptual analysis. Indeed, ordinary moral judgements involve a claim to objectivity which both non-cognitive and naturalist analyses fail to capture. Moral scepticism must, therefore, take the form of an error theory, admitting that a belief in objective values is built into ordinary moral thought and language, but holding that this ingrained belief is false. As such, it needs arguments to support it against "common sense." But solid arguments can be found. The considerations that favour moral scepticism are: first, the relativity or variability of some important starting points of moral thinking and their apparent dependence on actual ways of life; secondly, the metaphysical peculiarity of the supposed objective values, in that they would have to be intrinsically action-guiding and motivating; thirdly, the problem of how such values could be consequential or supervenient upon natural features; fourthly, the corresponding epistemological difficulty of accounting for our knowledge of value entities or features and of their links with the features on which they would be consequential; fifthly, the possibility of explaining, in terms of several different patterns of objectification, traces of which remain in moral language and moral concepts, how even if there were no such objective values people not only might have come to suppose that there are but also might persist firmly in that belief. These five points sum up the case for moral scepticism; but of almost equal importance are the preliminary removal of misunderstandings that often prevent this thesis from being considered fairly and explicitly, and the isolation of those items about which the moral sceptic is sceptical from many associated qualities and relations whose objective status is not in dispute.

But what if we can establish this negative conclusion, that there are no objective values? How does it help us to say anything positively about ethics? Does it not at one stroke rule out all normative ethics, laying it down that all affirmative first order judgements are false, since they include, by virtue of the very meanings of their terms, unwarranted claims to objectivity? I shall take up these questions in Chapter 5; but first I want to amplify and reinforce the conclusion of this chapter by some investigations of the meanings and logical connections of moral terms.

How to Be a Moral Realist
Richard Boyd

Richard Boyd, a Professor of Philosophy at Cornell University, is best known for his work in philosophy of science. The following article draws some important parallels between realist philosophy of science and moral realism. Boyd argues that by using the full resources of naturalistic and realistic conceptions of scientific knowledge, the moral realist can respond to typical anti-realist critiques of moral realism. In the article Boyd attempts to answer some of the serious challenges that face moral realism, such as how to account for cultural relativity and what to count as moral properties.

1 Introduction

1.1 Moral realism
Scientific realism is the doctrine that scientific theories should be understood as putative descriptions of real phenomena, that ordinary scientific methods constitute a reliable procedure for obtaining and improving (approximate) knowledge of the real phenomena which scientific theories describe, and that the reality described by scientific theories is largely independent of our theorizing. Scientific theories describe reality and reality is "prior to thought" (see Boyd 1982).

By "moral realism" I intend the analogous doctrine about moral judgments, moral statements, and moral theories. According to moral realism:

1 Moral statements are the sorts of statements which are (or which express propositions which are) true or false (or approximately true, largely false, etc.);
2 The truth or falsity (approximate truth . . .) of moral statements is largely independent of our moral opinions, theories, etc.;
3 Ordinary canons of moral reasoning – together with ordinary canons of scientific and everyday factual reasoning – constitute, under many circumstances at least, a reliable method for obtaining and improving (approximate) moral knowledge.

It follows from moral realism that such moral terms as "good," "fair," "just," "obligatory" usually correspond to real properties or relations and that our ordinary standards for moral reasoning and moral disputation – together with reliable standards for scientific and everyday reasoning – constitute a fairly reliable way of finding out which events, persons, policies, social arrangements, etc., have these properties and enter into these relations. It is *not* a consequence of moral realism that our ordinary procedures are "best possible" for this purpose – just as it is not a consequence of scientific realism that our existing scientific methods are best possible. In the scientific case, improvements in knowledge can be expected to produce improvements in method (Boyd 1980, 1982, 1983, 1985a, 1985b, 1985c), and there is no reason to exclude this possibility in the moral case.

Scientific realism contrasts with instrumentalism and its variants and with views like that of Kuhn (1970) according to which the reality which scientists study is largely constituted by the theories they adopt. Moral realism contrasts with noncognitivist metaethical theories like emotivism and with views according to which moral principles are largely a reflection of social constructs or conventions.

What I want to do in this essay is to explore the ways in which recent developments in realist philosophy of science, together with related "naturalistic" developments in epistemology and philosophy of language, can be employed in the articulation and defense of moral realism. It will not be my aim here to establish that moral realism is true. Indeed, if moral realism is to be defended along the lines I will indicate here then a thoroughgoing defense of moral realism would be beyond the scope of a single essay. Fortunately a number of extremely important defenses of moral realism have recently been published (see, e.g., Brink 1984, 1989; Gilbert 1981b, 1982, 1984b, 1986b, forthcoming; Miller 1984b; Railton 1986; Sturgeon 1984a, 1984b). What I hope to demonstrate in the present essay is that moral realism can be shown to be a more attractive and plausible philosophical position if recent developments in realist philosophy of science are brought to bear in its defense. I intend the general defense of moral realism offered here as a proposal regarding the metaphysical, epistemological, and semantic framework within which arguments for moral realism are best formulated and best understood.

In addition, l am concerned to make an indirect contribution to an important recent debate among Marxist philosophers and Marx scholars concerning the Marxist analysis of moral discourse (see, e.g. Gilbert 1981a, 1981b, 1982, 1984b, 1986a, 1986b; Miller 1979, 1981, 1982, 1983, 1984a, 1984b; Wood 1972, 1979). Two questions are central in this debate: the question of what metaethical views Marx and other Marxist figures actually held or practiced and the question of what metaethical views are appropriate to a Marxist analysis of history and in particular to a Marxist analysis of the role of class ideology in the determination of the content of moral conceptions. I have nothing to contribute to the efforts to answer the first question, which lies outside my competence. About the second, I am convinced that Marxists should be moral realists and that the admirably motivated decision by many antirevisionist Marxists to adopt a nonrealist relativist stance in metaethics represents a sectarian (if nonculpable) error. I intend the defense of moral realism presented here to be fully compatible with the recognition of the operation in the history of moral inquiry of just the sort of ideological forces which Marxist historians (among others) have emphasized. A thoroughgoing defense of this compatibility claim is not attempted in the present essay; I develop it in a forthcoming essay.

1.2 Scientific knowledge and moral skepticism

One of the characteristic motivations for anti-realistic metaethical positions – either for noncognitivist views or for views according to which moral knowledge has a strong constructive or conventional component – lies in a presumed epistemological contrast between ethics, on the one hand, and the sciences, on the other. Scientific methods and theories appear to have properties objectivity, value neutrality, empirical testability, for example – which are either absent altogether or, at any rate, much less significant in the case of moral beliefs and the procedures by which we form and criticize them. These differences make the methods of science (and of everyday empirical knowledge) seem apt for the *discovery* of facts while the "methods" of moral reasoning seem, at best, to be appropriate for the rationalization, articulation, and application of preexisting social conventions or individual preferences.

Many philosophers would like to explore the possibility that scientific beliefs and moral beliefs are not so differently situated as this presumed epistemological contrast suggests. We may think of this task as the search for a conception of "unified knowledge" which will bring scientific and moral knowledge together within the same analytical framework in much the same way as the positivists' conception of "unified science" sought to provide an integrated treatment of knowledge within the various special sciences. There are, roughly, two plausible general strategies for unifying scientific and moral knowledge and minimizing the apparent epistemological contrast between scientific and moral inquiry:

1   Show that our scientific beliefs and methods actually possess many of the features (e.g., dependence on nonobjective "values" or upon social conventions) which form the core of our current picture of moral beliefs and methods of moral reasoning.
2   Show that moral beliefs and methods are much more like our current conception of scientific beliefs and methods (more "objective," "external," "empirical," "intersubjective," for example) than we now think.

The first of these options has already been explored by philosophers who subscribe to a "constructivist" or neo-Kantian conception of scientific theorizing (see, e.g., Hanson 1958; Kuhn 1970). The aim of the present essay will be to articulate and defend the second alternative. In recent papers (Boyd 1979, 1982, 1983, 1985a, 1985b, 1985c) I have argued that scientific realism is correct, but that its adequate defense requires the systematic adoption of a distinctly naturalistic and realistic conception of knowledge, of natural kinds, and of reference. What I hope to show here is that once such a distinctly naturalistic and realistic conception is adopted, it is possible to offer a corresponding defense of moral realism which has considerable force and plausibility.

My argumentative strategy will be to offer a list of several challenges to moral realism which will, I hope, be representative of those considerations which make it plausible that there is the sort of epistemological contrast between science and ethics which we have been discussing. Next, I will present a summary of some recent work in realistic philosophy of science and related "naturalistic" theories in epistemology and the philosophy of language. Finally, I will indicate how the results of this recent realistic and naturalistic work can be applied to rebut the arguments against moral realism and to sketch the broad outlines of an alternative realistic conception of moral knowledge and of moral language.

2 Some Challenges to Moral Realism

2.1 Moral intuitions and empirical observations

In the sciences, we decide between theories on the basis of observations, which have an important degree of objectivity. It appears that in moral reasoning, moral intuitions play the same role which observations do in science: we test general moral principles and moral theories by seeing how their consequences conform (or fail to conform) to our moral intuitions about particular cases. It appears that it is the foundational role of observations in science which makes scientific objectivity possible. How could moral intuitions possibly play the same sort of foundational role in ethics, especially given the known diversity of moral judgments between people? Even if moral intuitions do provide a "foundation" for moral inquiry, wouldn't the fact that moral "knowledge" is grounded in intuitions rather than in observation be exactly the sort of fundamental episte-mological contrast which the received view postulates, especially since people's moral intuitions typically reflect the particular moral theories or traditions which they already accept, or their culture, or their upbringing? Doesn't the role of moral intuitions in moral reasoning call out for a "constructivist" metaethics? If moral intuitions don't play a foundational role in ethics and if morality is sup-posed to be epistemologically like science, *then what plays, in moral reasoning, the role played by observation in science?*

2.2 The role of "reflective equilibrium" in moral reasoning
We have already seen that moral intuitions play a role in moral reasoning which appears to threaten any attempt to assimilate moral reasoning to the model of objective empirical scientific methodology. Worse yet, as Rawls (1971) has re-minded us, what we do with our moral intuitions, our general moral principles, and our moral theories, in order to achieve a coherent moral position, is to engage in "trading-off" between these various categories of moral belief in order to achieve a harmonious "equilibrium'. Moral reasoning *begins* with moral *pre-suppositions*, general as well as particular, and proceeds by negotiating between

conflicting *presuppositions*. It is easy to see how this could be a procedure for rationalization of individual or social norms or, to put it in more elevated terms, a procedure for the "construction" of moral or ethical systems. But if ethical beliefs and ethical reasoning are supposed to be like scientific beliefs and methods, then this procedure would have to be a procedure for *discovering* moral facts! How could any procedure so presupposition-dependent be a *discovery* procedure rather than a *construction procedure*? (See Dworkin 1973.)

2.3 Moral progress and cultural variability

If moral judgments are a species of factual judgment, then one would expect to see moral progress, analogous to progress in science. Moreover, one of the characteristics of factual inquiry in science is its relative independence from cultural distortions: scientists with quite different cultural backgrounds can typically agree in assessing scientific evidence. If moral reasoning is reasoning about objective moral *facts*, then what explains our lack of progress in ethics and the persistence of cultural variability in moral beliefs?

2.4 Hard cases

If goodness, fairness, etc., are real and objective properties, then what should one say about the sorts of hard cases in ethics which we can't seem *ever* to resolve? Our experience in science seems to be that hard scientific questions are only *temporarily* rather than permanently unanswerable. Permanent disagreement seems to be very rare indeed. Hard ethical questions seem often to be permanent rather than temporary.

In such hard ethical cases, is there a fact of the matter inaccessible to moral inquiry? If so, then doesn't the existence of such facts constitute a significant epistemological difference between science and ethics? If not, if there are not facts of the matter, then isn't moral realism simply refuted by such indeterminacy?

2.5 Naturalism and naturalistic definitions

If goodness, for example, is a real property, then wouldn't it be a *natural* property? If not, then isn't moral realism committed to some unscientific and superstitious belief in the existence of non-natural properties? If goodness would be a natural property, then isn't moral realism committed to the extremely implausible claim that moral terms like "good" possess naturalistic definitions?

2.6 Morality, motivation, and rationality

Ordinary factual judgments often provide us with reasons for action: they serve as constraints on rational choice. But they do so only because of our antecedent interests or desires. If moral judgments are merely factual judgments, as moral realism requires, then the relation of moral judgments to motivation and rationality must be the same. It would be possible in principle for someone or some thinking thing, to be entirely rational while finding moral judgments motivationally neutral and irrelevant to choices of action.

If this consequence follows from moral realism, how can the moral realist account for the particularly close connection between moral judgments and judgments about what to do? What about the truism that moral judgments have commendatory force as a matter of their meaning or the plausible claim that the moral preferability of a course of action always provides a reason (even if not an overriding one) for choosing it?

2.7 The semantics of moral terms

Moral realism is an anti-subjectivist position. There is, for example, supposed to be a single objective property which we're all talking about when we use the term "good" in moral contexts. But people's moral concepts differ profoundly. How can it be maintained that our radically different concepts of "good" are really concepts of one and the same property? Why not a different property for each significantly different conception of the good? Don't the radical differences in our conceptions of the good suggest either a noncognitivist or a constructivist conception of the semantics of ethical terms?

2.8 Verificationism and anti-realism in ethics

Anti-realism in ethics, like the rejection of theoretical realism in science, is a standard positivist position. In the case of science, there is a straightforward verificationist objection to realism about alleged "theoretical entities:" they are unobservables; statements about them lie beyond the scope of empirical investigation and are thus unverifiable in principle. (See Boyd 1982 for a discussion of various formulations of this key verificationist argument.)

It is interesting to note that the challenges to moral realism rehearsed in 2.1–2.7 do not take the form of so direct an appeal to verificationism. Only in the case of the concern about non-natural moral properties (2.5) might the issue of verifiability be directly relevant, and then only if the objection to nonnatural properties is that they would be unobservable. Instead, the arguments in 2.1–2.7 constitute an *indirect* argument against moral realism: they point to features of moral beliefs or of moral reasoning for which, it is suggested, the best explanation would be one which entailed the rejection of moral realism. Moreover, what is true of the challenges to moral realism rehearsed above is typical: by and large positivists, and philosophers influenced by positivism, did not argue directly for the unverifiability of moral statements: they did not make an appeal to the unobservability of alleged moral properties or deny that moral theories had observational consequences. Instead, they seemed to take a noncognitivist view of ethics to be established by an "inductive inference to the best explanation" of the sort of facts cited in 2.1–2.7.

In this regard, then, the standard arguments against moral realism are more closely analogous to Kuhnian objections to scientific realism than they are to the standard verificationist arguments against the possibility of knowledge of "theoretical entities." Sections 2.1, 2.2, 2.3, and 2.7 rehearse arguments which are importantly similar to Kuhn's arguments from the paradigm dependence of scientific concepts and methods to a constructivist and anti-realistic conception of science. I have argued elsewhere (Boyd 1979, 1982, 1983, 1985a) that a systematic rebuttal to the verificationist epistemology and philosophy of language which form the foundations of logical positivism can in fact be extended to a defense of scientific realism against the more constructivist and neo-Kantian considerations represented by Kuhn's work. If the arguments of the present essay are successful, then this conclusion can be generalized: a realist and anti-empiricist account in the philosophy of science can be extended to a defense of *moral* realism as well, even though the challenges to moral realism are apparently only indirectly verificationist.

3 Realist Philosophy of Science

3.1 The primacy of reality

By "scientific realism" philosophers mean the doctrine that the methods of science are capable of providing (partial or approximate) knowledge of unobservable ("theoretical") entities, such as atoms or electromagnetic fields, in addition to knowledge about the behavior of observable phenomena (and of course, that the properties of these and other entities studied by scientists are largely theory-independent).

Over the past three decades or so, philosophers of science within the empiricist tradition have been increasingly sympathetic toward scientific realism and increasingly inclined to alter their views of science in a realist direction. The reasons for this realist tendency lie largely in the recognition of the extraordinary role which theoretical considerations play in actual (and patently successful) scientific practice. To take the most striking example, scientists routinely modify or extend operational "measurement" or "detection" procedures for "theoretical" magnitudes or entities on the basis of new theoretical developments. This sort of methodology is perfectly explicable on the realist assumption that the operational procedures in question really are procedures for the measurement or detection of unobservable entities and that the relevant theoretical developments reflect increasingly accurate knowledge of such "theoretical" entities. Accounts of the revisability of operational procedures which are compatible with a non-realist position appear inadequate to explain the way in which theory-dependent revisions of "measurement" and "detection" procedures make a positive methodological contribution to the progress of science.

This pattern is quite typical: The methodological contribution made by theoretical considerations in scientific methodology is inexplicable on a non-realist conception but easily explicable on the realist assumption that such considerations are a reflection of the growth of *theoretical* knowledge. (For a discussion of this point see Boyd 1982, 1983, 1985a, 1985b.) Systematic development of this realist theme has produced developments in epistemology, metaphysics, and the philosophy of language which go far beyond the mere rejection of verificationism and which point the way toward a distinctly realist conception of the central issues in the philosophy of science. These developments include the articulation of causal or naturalistic theories of reference (Kripke 1971, 1972; Putnam 1975a;

Boyd 1979, 1982), of measurement (Byerly and Lazara 1973), of "natural kinds" and scientific categories (Quine 1969a; Putnam 1975a; Boyd 1979, 1982, 1983, 1985b), of scientific epistemology generally (Boyd 1972, 1979, 1982, 1983, 1985a, 1985b, 1985c), and of causation (Mackie 1974; Shoemaker 1980; Boyd 1982, 1985b).

Closely related to these developments has been the articulation of causal or naturalistic theories of knowledge (see, e.g., Armstrong 1973; Goldman 1967, 1976; Quine 1969b). Such theories represent generalizations of causal theories of perception and reflect a quite distinctly realist stance with respect to the issue of our knowledge of the external world. What all these developments – both within the philosophy of science and in epistemology generally – have in common is that they portray as *a posteriori* and contingent various matters (such as the operational "definitions" of theoretical terms, the "definitions" of natural kinds, or the reliability of the senses) which philosophers in the modern tradition have typically sought to portray as *a priori*. In an important sense, these developments represent the fuller working out of the philosophical implications of the realist doctrine that reality is prior to thought. (For a further development of this theme see Boyd 1982, 1983, 1985a, 1985b.) It is just this *a posteriority* and contingency in philosophical matters, I shall argue, which will make possible a plausible defense of moral realism against the challenges outlined in Part 2.

In the remaining sections of Part 3 I will describe some of the relevant features of these naturalistic and realistic developments. These "results" in recent realistic philosophy are not, of course, uncontroversial, and it is beyond the scope of this essay to defend them. But however much controversy they may occasion, unlike moral realism, they do not occasion incredulity: they represent a plausible and defensible philosophical position. The aim of this essay is to indicate that, if we understand the relevance of these recent developments to issues in moral philosophy, then moral realism should, though controversial, be equally credible.

3.2 Objective knowledge from theory-dependent methods

I suggested in the preceding section that the explanation for the movement toward realism in the philosophy of science during the past two or three decades lies in the recognition of the extraordinarily theory-dependent character of scientific methodology and in the inability of any but a realist conception of science to explain why so theory-dependent a methodology should be reliable. The theoretical revisability of measurement and detection procedures, I claimed, played a crucial role in establishing the plausibility of a realist philosophy of science.

If we look more closely at this example, we can recognize two features of scientific methodology which are, in fact, quite general. In the first place, the realist's account of the theoretical revisability of measurement and detection procedures rests upon a conception of scientific research as *cumulative by successive approximations to the truth*.

Second, this cumulative development is possible because *there is a dialectical relationship between current theory and the methodology for its improvement.* The approximate truth of current theories explains why our existing measurement procedures are (approximately) reliable. That reliability, in turn, helps to explain why our experimental or observational investigations are successful in uncovering new theoretical knowledge, which, in turn, may produce improvements in experimental techniques, etc.

These features of scientific methodology are *entirely* general. Not only measurement and detection procedures but all aspects of scientific methodology – principles of experimental design, choices of research problems, standards for the assessment of experimental evidence, principles governing theory choice, and rules for the use of theoretical language – are highly dependent upon current theoretical commitments (Boyd 1972, 1973, 1979, 1980, 1982, 1983, 1985a, 1985b; Kuhn 1970; van Fraassen 1980). No aspect of scientific method involves the "presupposition-free" testing of individual laws or theories. Moreover, the theory dependence of scientific methodology *contributes* to its reliability rather than detracting from it.

The only scientifically plausible explanation for the reliability of a scientific methodology which is so theory-dependent is a thoroughgoingly realistic explanation: Scientific methodology, dictated by currently accepted theories, is reliable at producing further knowledge precisely *because, and to the extent that, currently accepted theories are relevantly approximately true.* For example, it is because our current theories are approximately true that the canons of experimental design which they dictate are appropriate for the rigorous testing of new (and potentially more accurate) theories. What the scientific method provides is a paradigm-dependent paradigm-modification strategy: a strategy for modifying or amending our existing theories in the light of further research, which is such that its methodological principles at any given time will themselves depend upon the theoretical picture provided by the currently accepted theories. If the body of accepted theories is itself relevantly sufficiently approximately true, then this methodology operates to produce a subsequent dialectical improvement both in our knowledge of the world and in our methodology itself. Both our new theories and the methodology by which we develop and test them depend upon previously acquired theoretical knowledge. It is not possible to explain even the instrumental reliability of actual scientific practice without invoking this explanation and without adopting a realistic conception of scientific knowledge (Boyd 1972, 1973, 1979, 1982, 1983, 1985a, 1985b, 1985c).

The way in which scientific methodology is theory-dependent dictates that we have a strong methodological preference for new theories which are plausible in the light of our existing theoretical commitments: this means that we prefer new theories which relevantly resemble our existing theories (where the determination of the relevant respects of resemblance is itself a theoretical issue). The reliability of such a methodology is explained by the approximate truth of existing theories, and one consequence of this explanation is that *judgments of theoretical plausibility are evidential.* The fact that a proposed theory is itself plausible in the light of previously confirmed theories is evidence for its (approximate) truth (Boyd 1972, 1973, 1979, 1982, 1983, 1985a, 1985b, 1985c). A purely conventionalistic account of the methodological role of considerations of theoretical plausibility cannot be adequate because it cannot explain the contribution which such considerations make to the instrumental reliability of scientific methodology (Boyd 1979, 1982, 1983).

The upshot is this: The theory-dependent conservatism of scientific methodology is *essential* to the rigorous and reliable testing and development of new scientific theories; on balance, theoretical "presuppositions" play neither a destructive nor a conventionalistic role in scientific methodology. They are essential to its reliability. If by the "objectivity" of scientific methodology we mean its capacity to lead to the discovery of *theory-independent reality*, then scientific methodology is objective precisely because it is *theory-dependent* (Boyd 1979, 1982, 1983, 1985a, 1985b, 1985c).

3.3 Naturalism and radical contingency in epistemology

Modern epistemology has been largely dominated by positions which can be characterized as "foundationalist:" all knowledge is seen as ultimately grounded in certain foundational beliefs which have an epistemically privileged position – they are *a priori* or self-warranting, incorrigible, or something of the sort. Other true beliefs are instances of knowledge only if they can be justified by appeals to foundational knowledge. Whatever the nature of the foundational beliefs, or whatever their epistemic privilege is suppose to consist in, it is an *a priori* question which beliefs fall in the privileged class. Similarly, the basic inferential principles which are legitimate for justifying non-foundational knowledge claims, given foundational premises, are such that they can be identified *a priori* and it can be shown *a priori* that they are rational principles of inference. We may fruitfully think of foundationalism as consisting of two parts, *premise foundationalism*, which holds that all knowledge is justifiable from an *a priori* specifiable core of foundational beliefs, and *inference foundationalism*, which holds that the principles of justifiable inference are ultimately reducible to inferential principles which can be shown *a priori* to be rational.

Recent work in "naturalistic epistemology" or "causal theories of knowing" (see e.g., Armstrong 1973; Goldman 1967, 1976; Quine 1969b) strongly suggest that the foundationalist conception of knowledge is fundamentally mistaken. For the crucial case of perceptual knowledge, there seem to be (in typical cases at least) neither premises (foundational or otherwise) nor inferences; instead, perceptual knowledge obtains when perceptual beliefs are produced by epistemically reliable mechanisms. For a variety of other cases, even where premises and inferences occur, it seems to be the reliable production of belief that distinguishes cases of knowledge from other cases of true belief. A variety of naturalistic considerations suggests that there are no beliefs which are epistemically privileged in the way foundationalism seems to require.

I have argued (see Boyd 1982, 1983, 1985a, 1985b, 1985c) that the defense of scientific realism requires an even more thoroughgoing naturalism in epistemology and, consequently, an even more thoroughgoing rejection of foundationalism.

In the first place, the fact that scientific knowledge grows cumulatively by successive approximation and the fact that the evaluation of theories is an ongoing social phenomenon require that we take the crucial causal notion in epistemology to be reliable *regulation* of belief rather than reliable belief *production*. The relevant conception of belief regulation must reflect the approximate social and dialectical character of the growth of scientific knowledge. It will thus be true that the causal mechanisms relevant to knowledge will include mechanisms, social and technical as well as psychological, for the criticism, testing, acceptance, modification, and transmission of scientific theories and doctrines. For that reason, an understanding of the role of social factors in science may be relevant not only for the sociology and history of science but for the epistemology of sciences as well. The epistemology of science is in this respect dependent upon empirical knowledge.

There is an even more dramatic respect in which the epistemology of science rests upon empirical foundations. All the significant methodological principles of scientific inquiry (except, perhaps, the rules of deductive logic, but see Boyd 1985c) are profoundly theory-dependent. They are a reliable guide to the truth *only* because, and to the extent that, the body of background theories which determines their application is relevantly approximately true. The rules of rational scientific inference are not reducible to some more basic rules whose reliability as a guide to the truth is independent of the truth of background theories. Since it is a contingent empirical matter which background theories are approximately true, the rationality of scientific principles of inference ultimately rests on a contingent matter of empirical fact, just as the epistemic role of the senses rests upon the contingent empirical fact that the senses are reliable detectors of external phenomena. Thus inference foundationalism is radically false; there are no *a priori* justifiable rules of nondeductive inference. The epistemology of empirical science is an empirical science (Boyd 1982, 1983, 1985a, 1985b, 1985c).

One consequence of this radical contingency of scientific methods is that the emergence of scientific rationality as we know it depended upon the logically, epistemically, and historically contingent emergence of a relevantly approximately true theoretical tradition. It is not possible to understand the initial emergence of such a tradition as the consequence of some more abstractly conceived scientific or rational methodology which itself is theory-independent. There is no such methodology. We must think of the establishment of the corpuscular theory of matter in the seventeenth century as the beginning of rational methodology in chemistry, not as a consequence of it (for a further discussion see Boyd 1982).

3.4 Scientific intuitions and trained judgment
Both noninferential perceptual judgments and elaborately argued explicit inferential judgments in theoretical science have a purely contingent *a posteriori* foundation. Once this is recognized, it is easy to see that there are methodologically important features of scientific practice which are intermediate between

noninferential perception and explicit inference. One example is provided by what science textbook authors often refer to as "physical intuition," "scientific maturity," or the like. One of the intended consequences of professional training in a scientific discipline (and other disciplines as well) is that the student acquire a "feel" for the issues and the actual physical materials which the science studies. As Kuhn (1970) points out, part of the role of experimental work in the training of professional scientists is to provide such a feel for the paradigms or "worked examples" of good scientific practice. There is very good reason to believe that having good physical (or biological or psychological) intuitions is important to epistemically reliable scientific practice. It is also quite clear both that the acquisition of good scientific intuitions depends on learning explicit theory, as well as on other sorts of training and practice, *and* that scientists are almost never able to make fully explicit the considerations which play a role in their intuitive judgments. The legitimate role of such "tacit" factors in science has often been taken (especially by philosophically inclined scientists) to be an especially puzzling feature of scientific methodology.

From the perspective of the naturalistic epistemology of science, there need be no puzzle. It is, of course, a question of the very greatest psychological interest just how intuitive judgments in science work and how they are related to explicit theory, on the one hand, and to experimental practice, on the other. But it seems overwhelmingly likely that scientific intuitions should be thought of as trained judgments which resemble perceptual judgments in not involving (or at least not being fully accounted for by) explicit inferences, but which resemble explicit inferences in science in depending for their reliability upon the relevant approximate truth of the explicit theories which help to determine them. This dependence upon the approximate truth of the relevant background theories will obtain even in those cases (which may be typical) in which the tacit judgments reflect a deeper understanding than that currently captured in explicit theory. It is an important and exciting fact that some scientific knowledge can be represented tacitly before it can be represented explicitly, but this fact poses no difficulty for a naturalistic treatment of scientific knowledge. Tacit or intuitive judgments in science are reliable because they are grounded in a theoretical tradition (itself partly tacit) which is, as a matter of contingent empirical fact, relevantly approximately true.

3.5 Non-Humean conceptions of causation and reduction
The Humean conception of causal relations according to which they are analyzable in terms of regularity, correlation, or deductive subsumability under laws is defensible only from a verificationist position. If verificationist criticisms of talk about unobservables are rejected – as they should be – then there is nothing more problematical about talk of causal powers than there is about talk of electrons or electromagnetic fields. There is no reason to believe that causal terms have definitions (analytic or natural) in noncausal terms. Instead, "cause" and its cognates refer to natural phenomena whose analysis is a matter for physicists, chemists, psychologists, historians, etc., rather than a matter of conceptual analysis.

In particular, it is perfectly legitimate – as a naturalistic conception of epistemology requires – to employ unreduced causal notions in philosophical analysis (Boyd 1982, 1985b; Shoemaker 1980).

One crucial example of the philosophical application of such notions lies in the analysis of "reductionism." If a materialist perspective is sound, then *in some sense* all natural phenomena are "reducible" to basic physical phenomena. The (prephilosophically) natural way of expressing the relevant sort of reduction is to say that all substances are composed of purely physical substances, all forces are composed of physical forces, all causal powers or potentialities are realized in physical substances and their causal powers, etc. This sort of analysis freely employs unreduced causal notions. If it is "rationally reconstructed" according to the Humean analysis of such notions, we get the classic analysis of reduction in terms of the syntactic reducibility of the theories in the special sciences to the laws of physics, which in turn dictates the conclusion that all natural properties must be definable in the vocabulary of physics. Such an analysis is entirely without justification from the realistic and naturalistic perspective we are considering. Unreduced causal notions are philosophically acceptable, and the Humean reduction of them mistaken. The prephilosophically natural analysis of reduction is also the philosophically appropriate one. In particular, purely physical objects, states, properties, etc. need not have definitions in "the vocabulary of physics" or in any other reductive vocabulary (see Boyd 1982).

3.6 Natural definitions

Locke speculates at several places in Book IV of the *Essay* (see, e.g., IV, iii, 25) that when kinds of substances are defined by "nominal essences," as he thinks they must be, it will be impossible to have a general science of, say, chemistry. The reason is this: nominal essences define kinds of substance in terms of sensible properties, but the factors which govern the behavior (even the observable behavior) of substances are insensible corpuscular real essences. Since there is no reason to suppose that our nominal essences will correspond to categories which reflect uniformities in microstructure, there is no reason to believe that kinds defined by nominal essences provide a basis for obtaining general knowledge of substances. Only if we could sort substances according to their hidden real essences would systematic general knowledge of substances be possible.

Locke was right. Only when kinds are defined by natural rather than conventional definitions is it possible to obtain sound scientific explanations (Putnam 1975a; Boyd 1985b) or sound solutions to the problem of "projectibility" in inductive inference in science (Quine 1969a; Boyd 1979, 1982, 1983, 1985a, 1985b, 1985c). Indeed this is true not only for the definitions of natural kinds but also for the definitions of the properties, relations, magnitudes, etc., to which we must refer in sound scientific reasoning. In particular, a wide variety of terms do not possess analytic or stipulative definitions and are instead defined in terms of properties, relations, etc., which render them appropriate to particular sorts of scientific or practical reasoning. In the case of such terms, proposed definitions are always in principle revisable in the light of new evidence or new theoretical developments. Similarly, the fact that two people or two linguistic communities apply different definitions in using a term is not, by itself, sufficient to show that they are using the term to refer to different kinds, properties, etc.

3.7 Reference and epistemic access

If the traditional empiricist account of definition by nominal essences (or "operational definitions" or "criteria! Attributes") is to be abandoned in favor of a naturalistic account of definitions (at least for some terms) then a naturalistic conception of reference is required for those cases in which the traditional empiricist semantics has been abandoned. Such a naturalistic account is provided by recent causal theories of reference (see, e.g., Feigl 1956; Kripke 1972; Putnam 1975a). The reference of a term is established by causal connections of the right sort between the use of the term and (instances of) its referent.

The connection between causal theories of reference and naturalistic theories of knowledge and of definitions is quite intimate: reference is itself an epistemic notion and the sorts of causal connections which are relevant to reference are just those which are involved in the reliable regulation of belief (Boyd 1979, 1982). *Roughly*, and for nondegenerate cases, a term t refers to a kind (property, relation, etc.) k just in case there exist causal mechanisms whose tendency is to bring it about, over time, that what is predicated of the term t will be approximately true of k (excuse the blurring of the use–mention distinction). Such mechanisms will typically include the existence of procedures which are approximately accurate for recognizing members or instances of k (at least for easy cases) and which relevantly govern the use of t, the social transmission of certain relevantly approximately true beliefs regarding k, formulated as claims about t (again excuse the slight to the use–mention distinction), a pattern of deference to experts on k with respect to the use of t, etc. (for a fuller discussion see Boyd 1979, 1982). When relations of this sort obtain, we may think of the properties of k as regulating the use of t (via such causal relations), and we may think of what is said using t as providing us with socially coordinated *epistemic access* to k; t refers to k (in nondegenerate cases) just in case the socially coordinated use of t provides significant epistemic access to k, and not to other kinds (properties, etc.) (Boyd 1979, 1982).

3.8 Homeostatic property-cluster definitions

The sort of natural definition[1] in terms of corpuscular real essences anticipated by Locke is reflected in the natural definitions of chemical kinds by molecular formulas; "water = H_2O" is by now the standard example (Putnam 1975a). Natural definitions of this sort specify necessary and sufficient conditions for membership in the kind in question. Recent non-naturalistic semantic theories in the ordinary language tradition have examined the possibility of definitions which do not provide necessary and sufficient conditions in this way. According to various property-cluster or criteria! attribute theories, some terms have definitions which are provided by a collection of properties such that the possession of an adequate number of these properties is sufficient for falling within the extension of the term. It is supposed to be a conceptual (and thus an *a priori*) matter what properties belong in the cluster and which combinations of them are sufficient for falling under the term. Insofar as different properties in the cluster are differently "weighted" in such judgments, the weighting is determined by our concept of the kind or property being defined. It is characteristically insisted, however, that our concepts of such kinds are "open textured" so that there is some indeterminacy in extension *legitimately* associated with property-cluster or criterial attribute definitions. The "imprecision" or "vagueness" of such definitions is seen as a perfectly appropriate feature of ordinary linguistic usage, in contrast to the artificial precision suggested by rigidly formalistic positivist conceptions of proper language use.

I shall argue (briefly) that – despite the Philistine antiscientism often associated with "ordinary language" philosophy – the property-cluster conception of definitions provides an extremely deep insight into the possible form of natural definitions. I shall argue that there are a number of scientifically important kinds, properties, etc., whose natural definitions are very much like the property-cluster definitions postulated by ordinary-language philosophers (for the record, I doubt that there are any terms whose definitions actually fit the ordinary-language model, because I doubt that there are any significant "conceptual truths" at all). There are natural kinds, properties, etc., whose natural definitions involve a kind of property cluster to*gether* with an associated indeterminacy in extension. Both the property-cluster form of such definitions and the associated indeterminacy are dictated by the scientific task of employing categories which correspond to inductively and explanatorily relevant causal structures. In particular, the indeterminacy in extension of such natural definitions could not be remedied without rendering the definitions unnatural in the sense of being scientifically misleading. What I believe is that the following sort of situation is commonplace in the special sciences which study complex structurally or functionally characterized phenomena:

1 There is a family F of properties which are "contingently clustered" in nature in the sense that they co-occur in an important number of cases.

2 Their co-occurrence is not, at least typically, a statistical artifact, but rather the result of what may be metaphorically (sometimes literally) described as a sort of *homeostasis*. Either the presence of some of the properties in F tends (under appropriate conditions) to favor the presence of the others, or there are underlying mechanisms or processes which tend to maintain the presence of the properties in F, or both.

3 The homeostatic clustering of the proper ties in F is causally important: there are (theoretically or practically) important effects which are produced by a conjoint occurrence of (many of) the properties in F together with (some or all of) the underlying mechanisms in question.

4 There is a kind term t which is applied to things in which the homeostatic clustering of most of the properties in F occurs.

5   This t has no analytic definition; rather all or part of the homeostatic cluster F together with some or all of the mechanisms which underlie it provides the natural definition of t. The question of just which properties and mechanisms belong in the definition of t *is* an *a posteriori* question – often a difficult theoretical one.

6   Imperfect homeostasis is nomologically possible or actual: some thing may display some but not all of the properties in F; some but not all of the relevant underlying homeostatic mechanisms may be present.

7   In such cases, the relative importance of the various properties in F and of the various mechanisms in determining whether the thing falls under t – if it can be determined at all – is a theoretical rather than an conceptual issue.

8   In cases in which such a determination is possible, the outcome will typically depend upon quite particular facts about the actual operation of the relevant homeostatic mechanisms, about the relevant background conditions and about the causal efficacy of the partial cluster of properties from F. For this reason the outcome, if any, will typically be different in different possible worlds, even when the partial property cluster is the same and even when it is unproblematical that the kind referred to by t in the actual world exists.

9   Moreover, there will be many cases of extensional vagueness which are such that they are not resolvable, even given all the relevant facts and all the true theories. There will be things which display some but not all of the properties in F (and/or in which some but not all of the relevant homeostatic mechanisms operate) such that no rational considerations dictate whether or not they are to be classed under t, assuming that a dichotomous choice is to be made.

10 The causal importance of the homeostatic property cluster F together with the relevant underlying homeostatic mechanisms is such that the kind or property denoted by t is a natural kind in the sense discussed earlier.

11 No refinement of usage which replaces t by a significantly less extensionally vague term will preserve the naturalness of the kind referred to. Any such refinement would either require that we treat as important distinctions which are irrelevant to causal explanation or to induction or that we ignore similarities which are important in just these ways.

The reader is invited to assure herself that 1 through 11 hold, for example, for the terms "healthy" and "is healthier than." Whether these are taken to be full-blown cases of natural property (relation) terms is not crucial here. They do illustrate almost perfectly the notion of a homeostatic property cluster and the correlative notion of a homeostatic cluster term. It is especially important to see *both* that *a posteriori* theoretical considerations in medicine can sometimes decide problematical cases of healthiness or of relative healthiness, often in initially counterintuitive ways *and* that nevertheless only highly artificial modifications of the notions of health and relative health could eliminate most or all of the extensional vagueness which they possess. One way to see the latter point is to consider what we would do if, for some statistical study of various medical practices, we were obliged to eliminate most of the vagueness in the notion of relative healthiness even where medical theory was silent. What we would strive to do would be to resolve the vagueness in such a way as not to bias the results of the study – not to favor one finding about the efficacy of medical practices over another. The role of natural kinds is, by contrast, precisely to *bias* (in the pejoratively neutral sense of the term) inductive generalization (Quine 1969a; Boyd 1979, 1981, 1983, 1985a, 1985b). Our concern not to bias the findings reflects our recognition that the resolution of vagueness in question would be unnatural in the sense relevant to this inquiry.

The paradigm cases of natural kinds – biological species – are examples of homeostatic cluster kinds in this sense. The appropriateness of any particular biological species for induction and explanation in biology depends upon the *imperfectly* shared and homeostatically related morphological, physiological, and behavioral features which characterize its members. The definitional role of mechanisms of homeostasis is reflected in the role of interbreeding in the modern species concept; for sexually reproducing species, the exchange of genetic material between populations is thought by some evolutionary biologists to be essential to the homeostatic unity of the other properties characteristic of the species and it is thus reflected in the species definition which they propose (see Mayr 1970). The *necessary* indeterminacy in extension of species terms is a consequence of evolutionary theory, as Darwin observed: speciation depends on the existence of populations which are intermediate between the parent species and the emerging one. Any "refinement" of classification which artificially eliminated the resulting indeterminacy in classification would obscure the central fact about heritable variations in phenotype upon which biological evolution depends. More determinate species categories would be scientifically inappropriate and misleading.

It follows that a consistently developed scientific realism *predicts* indeterminacy for those natural kind or property terms which refer to complex phenomena; such indeterminacy is a necessary consequence of "cutting the world at its (largely theory-independent) joints." Thus consistently developed scientific realism *predicts* that there will be some failures of bivalence for statements which refer to complex homeostatic phenomena (contrast, e.g., Putnam 1983 on "metaphysical realism" and vagueness). Precision in describing indeterminate or "borderline" cases of homeostatic cluster kinds (properties, etc.) consists not in the introduction of artificial precision in the definitions of such kinds but rather in a detailed description of the ways in which the indeterminate cases are like and unlike typical members of the kind (see Boyd 1982 on borderline cases of knowledge, which are themselves homeostatic cluster phenomena).

4 How to Be a Moral Realist

4.1 Moral semantics, intuitions, reflective equilibrium, and hard cases

Some philosophical opportunities are too good to pass up. For many of the more abstract challenges to moral realism, recent realistic and naturalistic work in the philosophy of science is suggestive of possible responses in its defense. Thus for example, it has occurred to many philosophers (see, e.g., Putnam 1975b) that naturalistic theories of reference and of definitions might be extended to the analysis of moral language. *If* this could be done successfully *and if* the results were favorable to a realist conception of morals, then it would be possible to reply to several anti-realist arguments. For example, against the objection that wide divergence of moral concepts or opinions between traditions or cultures indicates that, at best, a constructivist analysis of morals is possible, the moral realist might reply that differences in conception or in working definitions need not indicate the absence of shared causally fixed referents for moral terms.

Similarly, consider the objection that a moral realist must hold that goodness is a natural property, and thus commit the "naturalistic fallacy" of maintaining that moral terms possess analytic definitions in, say, physical terms. The moral realist may choose to agree that goodness is probably a physical property but deny that it has any analytic definition whatsoever. If the realist's critique of the syntactic analysis of reductionism in science is also accepted, then the moral realist can deny that it follows from the premise that goodness is a physical property or that goodness has any physical definition, analytic or otherwise.

If the moral realist takes advantage of naturalistic and realistic conceptions in epistemology as well as in semantic theory, other rebuttals to anti-realist challenges are suggested. The extent of the potential for rebuttals of this sort can best be recognized if we consider the objection that the role of reflective equilibrium in moral reasoning dictates a constructivist rather than a realist conception of morals. The moral realist might reply that the dialectical interplay of observations, theory, and methodology which, according to the realist, constitutes the *discovery* procedure for scientific inquiry *just is* the method of reflective equilibrium, so that the prevalence of that method in moral reasoning cannot by *itself* dictate a non-realist conception of morals.

If the response just envisioned to the concern over reflective equilibrium is successful, then the defender of moral realism will have established that – in moral reasoning as in scientific reasoning – the role of culturally transmitted presuppositions in reasoning does not necessitate a constructivist (or noncognitivist) rather than a realist analysis of the subject matter. *If* that is established, then the moral realist might defend the epistemic role of culturally determined intuitions in ethics by treating ethical intuitions on the model of theory-determined intuitions in science, which the scientific realist takes to be examples of epistemically reliable trained judgments.

Finally, if the moral realist is inclined to accept the anti-realist's claim that the existence of hard cases in ethics provides a reason to doubt that there is a moral fact of the matter which determines the answer in such cases (more on this later), then the scientific realist's conclusion that bivalence fails for some statements involving homeostatic cluster kind terms *might* permit the moral realist to reason that similar failures of bivalence for some ethical statements need not be fatal to moral realism.

In fact, I propose to employ just these rebuttals to the various challenges to moral realism I have been discussing. They represent the application of a coherent naturalistic conception of semantics and of knowledge against the challenges raised by the critic of moral realism. But they do not stand any chance of rebutting moral anti-realism unless they are incorporated into a broader conception of morals and of moral knowledge which meets certain very strong constraints. These constraints are the subject of the next section.

4.2 Constraints on a realist conception of moral knowledge

Suppose that a defense of moral realism is to be undertaken along the lines just indicated. What constraints does that particular defensive strategy place on a moral realist's conception of morals and of moral knowledge? Several important constraints are suggested by a careful examination of the realist doctrines in the philosophy of science whose extension to moral philosophy is contemplated.

In the first place, the scientific realist is able to argue that "reflective equilibrium" in science and a reliance on theory-dependent scientific intuitions are epistemically reliable *only* on the assumption that the theoretical tradition which governs these methodological practices contains theories which are relevantly approximately true. Indeed, the most striking feature of the consistently realistic epistemology of science is the insistence that the epistemic reliability of scientific methodology is contingent upon the establishment of such a theoretical tradition. Moreover, the possibility of offering a realist rather than a constructivist interpretation of reflective equilibrium and of intuition in science rests upon the realist's claim that observations and theory-mediated measurement and detection of "unobservables" in science represent epistemically relevant causal interactions between scientists and a theory-independent reality. Were the realist unable to treat observation and measurement as providing "epistemic access" to reality in this way, a constructivist treatment of scientific knowledge would be almost unavoidable.

Similarly, the scientific realist is able to employ a naturalistic conception of definitions and of reference only because (1) it is arguable that the nature of the subject matter of science dictates that kinds, properties, etc., be defined by nonconventional definitions and (2) it is arguable that actual scientific practices result in the establishment of "epistemic access" to the various "theoretical entities" which, the realist maintains, are (part of) the subject matter of scientific inquiry.

Finally, the realist can insist that realism not only can tolerate but implies certain failures of bivalence only because it can be argued that homeostatic cluster kinds (properties, etc.) must have indeterminacy in extension in order for reference to them to be scientifically fruitful. These considerations suggest that the following constraints must be satisfied by an account of moral knowledge if it is to be the basis for the proposed defense of moral realism:

1   It must be possible to explain how our moral reasoning *started out* with a stock of relevantly approximately true moral beliefs so that reflective

equilibrium in moral reasoning can be treated in a fashion analogous to the scientific realist's treatment of reflective equilibrium in scientific reasoning. Note that this constraint does not require that it be possible to argue that we started out with close approximations to the truth (seventeenth-century corpuscular theory was quite far from the truth). What is required is that the respects of approximation be such that it is possible to see how continued approximations would be forthcoming as a result of subsequent moral and nonmoral reasoning.

2   There must be an answer to the question "What plays, in moral reasoning, the role played by observation in science?" which can form the basis for a realist rather than a constructivist conception of the foundations of reflective equilibrium in moral reasoning.

3   It must be possible to explain why moral properties, say goodness, would require natural rather than conventional definitions.

4   It must be possible to show that our ordinary use of moral terms provides us with epistemic access to moral properties. Moral goodness must, to some extent, regulate the use of the word "good" in moral reasoning. Here again examination of the corresponding constraint in the philosophy of science indicates that the regulation need not be nearly perfect, but it must be possible to show that sufficient epistemic access is provided to form the basis for the growth of moral knowledge.

5   It must be possible to portray occasional indeterminacy in the extension of moral terms as rationally dictated by the nature of the subject matter in a way analogous to the scientific realist's treatment of such indeterminacy in the case of homeostatic cluster terms.

In the work of scientific realists, the case that the analogous constraints are satisfied has depended upon examination of the substantive findings of various of the sciences (such as, e.g., the atomic theory of matter or the Darwinian conception of speciation). It is very unlikely that an argument could be mounted in favor of the view that moral knowledge meets the constraints we are considering which does not rely in a similar way on substantive doctrines about the foundations of morals. What I propose to do instead is to *describe* one account of the nature of morals which almost ideally satisfies the constraints in question and to indicate how a defense of moral realism would proceed on the basis of this account.

It will not be my aim here to defend this account of morals against morally plausible rivals. In fact, I am inclined to think – *partly* because of the way in which it allows the constraints we are considering to be satisfied – that if there is a truth of the matter about morals (that is, if moral realism is true), then the account I will be offering is close to the truth. But my aim in this paper is merely to establish that moral realism is plausible and defensible. The substantive moral position I will consider is a plausible version of nonutilitarian consequentialism, one which – I believe – captures many of the features which make consequentialism *one* of the standard and plausible positions in moral philosophy. If moral realism is defensible on the basis of a plausible version of consequentialism, then it is a philosophically defensible position which must be taken seriously in metaethics; and that's all I'm trying to establish here.

It is, moreover, pretty clear that a variety of plausible alternative conceptions of the foundations of morals satisfy the constraints we are discussing. If I am successful here in mounting a plausible defense of moral realism, given the substantive conception I will propose, then it is quite likely that the very powerful semantic and epistemic resources of recent realist philosophy of science could be effectively employed to defend moral realism on the basis of many of the alternative conceptions. I leave it to the defenders of alternative conceptions to explore these possibilities. The defense of moral realism offered here is to be thought of as (the outline of) a "worked example" of the application of the general strategy proposed in 4.1.

One more thing should be said about the substantive conception of morals offered here. Like any naturalistic account, it rests upon potentially controversial empirical claims about human psychology and about social theory. It is a commonplace, I think, that moral realism is an optimistic position (or, perhaps, that it is typically an optimist's position). One nice feature of the substantive analysis of morals upon which my defense of moral realism will be based is that it quite obviously rests upon optimistic claims about human potential. Perhaps in that respect it is well suited to serve as a representative example of the variety of substantive moral views which would satisfy the constraints in question.

4.3 Homeostatic consequentialism
In broad outline, the conception of morals upon which the sample defense of moral realism will rest goes like this:

1   There are a number of important human goods, things which satisfy important human needs. Some of these needs are physical or medical. Others are psychological or social; these (probably) include the need for love and friendship, the need to engage in cooperative efforts, the need to exercise control over one's own life, the need for intellectual and artistic appreciation and expression, the need for physical recreation, etc. The question of just which important human needs there are is a potentially difficult and complex empirical question.

2   Under a wide variety of (actual and possible) circumstances these human goods (or rather instances of the satisfaction of them) are homeostatically clustered. In part they are clustered because these goods themselves are – when present in balance or moderation – mutually supporting. There are in addition psychological and social mechanisms which when, and to the extent to which, they are present contribute to the homeostasis. They probably include cultivated attitudes of mutual respect, political democracy, egalitarian social relations, various rituals, customs, and rules of courtesy, ready access to education and information, etc. It is a complex and difficult question in psychology and social theory just what these mechanisms are and how they work.

3   Moral goodness is defined by this cluster of goods and the homeostatic mechanisms which unify them. Actions, policies, character traits, etc. are morally good to the extent to which they tend to foster the realization of these goods or to develop and sustain the homeostatic mechanisms upon which their unity depends.

4   In actual practice, a concern for moral goodness can be a guide to action for the morally concerned because the homeostatic unity of moral goodness tends to mitigate possible conflicts between various individual goods. In part, the possible conflicts are mitigated just because various of the important human goods are mutually reinforcing. Moreover, since the existence of effective homeostatic unity among important human goods is part of the moral good, morally concerned choice is constrained by the imperative to balance potentially competing goods in such a way that homeostasis is maintained or strengthened. Finally, the improvement of the psychological and social mechanisms of homeostasis themselves is a moral good whose successful pursuit tends to further mitigate conflicts of the sort in question. In this regard, moral practice resembles good engineering practice in product design. In designing, say, automobiles there are a number of different desiderata (economy, performance, handling, comfort, durability, . . .) which are potentially conflicting but which enjoy a kind of homeostatic unity if developed in moderation. One feature of good automotive design is that it promotes these desiderata within the limits of homeostasis. The other feature of good automotive design (or, perhaps, of good automotive engineering) is that it produces technological advances which permit that homeostatic unity to be preserved at higher levels of the various individual desiderata. So it is with good moral practice as well.[2]

I should say something about how the claim that the nature of the constituents of moral goodness is an empirical matter should be understood. I mean the analogy between moral inquiry and scientific inquiry to be taken very seriously. It is a commonplace in the history of science that major advances often depend on appropriate social conditions, technological advances, and prior scientific discoveries. Thus, for example, much of eighteenth-century physics and chemistry was possible only because there had developed (a) the social conditions in which work in the physical sciences was economically supported, (b) a technology sufficiently advanced to make the relevant instrumentation possible, and (c) the theoretical legacy of seventeenth-century Newtonian physics and corpuscular chemistry.

   Via somewhat different mechanisms the same sort of dependence obtains in the growth of our knowledge of the good. Knowledge of fundamental human goods and their homeostasis represents basic knowledge about human psychological and social potential. Much of this knowledge is genuinely *experimental* knowledge and the relevant experiments are ("naturally" occurring) political and social experiments whose occurrence and whose interpretation depends both on "external" factors and upon the current state of our moral understanding. Thus, for example, we would not have been able to explore the dimensions of our needs for artistic expression and appreciation had not social and technological developments made possible cultures in which, for some classes at least, there was the leisure to produce and consume art. We would not have understood the role of political democracy in the homeostasis of the good had the conditions not arisen in which the first limited democracies developed. Only after the moral insights gained from the first democratic experiments were in hand, were we equipped to see the depth of the moral peculiarity of slavery. Only since the establishment of the first socialist societies are we even beginning to obtain the data necessary to assess the role of egalitarian social practices in fostering the good.

It is also true of moral knowledge, as it is in case of knowledge in other "special sciences," that the improvement of knowledge may depend upon theoretical advances in related disciplines. It is hard, for example, to see how deeper understanding in history or economic theory could fail to add to our understanding of human potential and of the mechanisms underlying the homeostatic unity of the good.

Let us now consider the application of the particular theory of the good presented here as a part of the strategy for the defense of moral realism indicated in the preceding section. I shall be primarily concerned to defend the realist position that moral goodness is a real property of actions, policies, states of affairs, etc., and that our moral judgments are, often enough, reflections of truths about the good. A complete realist treatment of the semantics of moral terms would of course require examining notions like obligation and justice as well. I will not attempt this examination here, in part because the aim of this essay is merely to indicate briefly how a plausible defense of moral realism might be carried out rather than to carry out the defense in detail. Moreover, on a consequentialist conception of morals such notions as obligation and justice are derivative ones, and it is doubtful if the details of the derivations are relevant to the defense of moral realism in the way that the defense of a realist conception of the good is.

In the remaining sections of the essay I shall offer a defense of homeostatic consequentialist moral realism against the representative anti-realist challenges discussed in Part 2. The claim that the term "good" in its moral uses refers to the homeostatic cluster property just described (or even the claim that there is such a property) represents a complex and controversial philosophical and empirical hypothesis. For each of the responses to anti-realist challenges which I will present, there are a variety of possible anti-realist rebuttals, both empirical and philosophical. It is beyond the scope of this essay to explore these rebuttals and possible moral realist responses to them in any detail. Instead, I shall merely indicate how plausible realist rebuttals to the relevant challenges can be defended. Once again, the aim of the present paper is not to establish moral realism but merely to establish its plausibility and to offer a general framework within which further defenses of moral realism might be understood.

4.4 Observations, intuitions, and reflective equilibrium

Of the challenges to moral realism we are considering, two are straightforwardly epistemological. They suggest that the role of moral intuitions and of reflective equilibrium in moral reasoning dictate (at best) a constructivist interpretation of morals. As we saw in Section 4.2, it would be possible for the moral realist to respond by assimilating the role of moral intuitions and reflective equilibrium to the role of scientific intuitions and theory-dependent methodological factors in the realist account of scientific knowledge, but this response is viable only if it is possible to portray many of our background moral beliefs and judgments as relevantly approximately true and only if there is a satisfactory answer to the question: "What plays, in moral reasoning, the role played in science by observation?" Let us turn first to the latter question.

I propose the answer: "Observation."

According to the homeostatic consequentialist conception of morals (indeed, according to any naturalistic conception) goodness is an ordinary natural property, and it would be odd indeed if observations didn't play the same role in the study of this property that they play in the study of all the others. According to the homeostatic consequentialist conception, goodness is a property quite similar to the other properties studied by psychologists, historians, and social scientists, and observations will play the same role in moral inquiry that they play in the other kinds of empirical inquiry about people.

It is worth remarking that in the case of any of the human sciences *some* of what must count as observation is observation of oneself, and *some* is the sort of self-observation involved in introspection. Moreover, *some* of our observations of other people will involve trained judgment and the operation of sympathy. No reasonable naturalistic account of the foundations of psychological or social knowledge or of our technical knowledge in psychology or the social sciences will fail to treat such sources of belief – when they are generally reliable – as cases of observation in the relevant sense.

It is true, of course, that both the content and the evidential assessment of observations of this sort will be influenced by theoretical considerations, but this does not distinguish observations in the human sciences from those in other branches of empirical inquiry. The theory dependence of observations and their interpretation is simply one aspect of the pervasive theory dependence of methodology in science which the scientific realist cheerfully acknowledges (since it plays a crucial role in arguments for scientific realism). It is possible to defend a realist interpretation of the human sciences because it is possible to argue that actual features in the world constrain the findings in those sciences sufficiently that the relevant background theories will be approximately true enough for theory-dependent observations to play a reliable epistemic role.

In the case of moral reasoning, observations and their interpretation will be subject to just the same sort of theory-dependent influences. This theory dependence is one aspect of the general phenomenon of theory dependence of methodology in moral reasoning which we, following Rawls, have been describing as reflective equilibrium. We will be able to follow the example of scientific realists and to treat the observations which play a role in moral reasoning as sufficiently reliable for the defense of moral realism just in case we are able to portray the theories upon which they and their interpretation depend as relevantly approximately true – that is, just in case we are able to carry out the other part of the moral realist's response to epistemic challenges and to argue that our background moral beliefs are sufficiently near the truth to form the foundations for a reliable empirical investigation of moral matters. Let us turn now to that issue.

What we need to know is whether it is reasonable to suppose that, for quite some time, we have had background moral beliefs sufficiently near the truth that they could form the basis for subsequent improvement of moral knowledge in the light of further experience and further historical developments. Assuming, as we shall, a homeostatic consequentialist conception of morals, this amounts to the question whether our background beliefs about human goods and the psychological and social mechanisms which unite them have been good enough to guide the gradual process of expansion of moral knowledge envisioned in that conception. Have our beliefs about our own needs and capacities been good enough – since, say the emergence of moral and political philosophy in ancient Greece – that we have been able to respond to new evidence and to the results of new social developments by expanding and improving our understanding of those needs and capacities even when doing so required rejecting some of our earlier views in favor of new ones? It is hard to escape the conclusion that this is simply the question "Has the rational empirical study of human kind proven to be possible?" Pretty plainly the answer is that such study has proven to be possible, though difficult. In particular we have improved our understanding of our own needs and our individual and social capacities by just the sort of historically complex process envisioned in the homeostatic consequentialist conception. I conclude therefore that there is no reason to think that reflective equilibrium – which is just the standard methodology of any empirical inquiry, social or otherwise – raises any epistemological problems for the defense of moral realism.

Similarly, we may now treat moral intuitions exactly on a par with scientific intuitions, as a species of trained judgment. Such intuitions are *not* assigned a foundational role in moral inquiry; in particular they do not substitute for observations. Moral intuitions are simply one cognitive manifestation of our moral understanding, just as physical intuitions, say, are a cognitive manifestation of physicists' understanding of their subject matter. Moral intuitions, like physical intuitions, play a limited but legitimate role in empirical inquiry *precisely because* they are linked to theory *and* to observations in a generally reliable process of reflective equilibrium.

It may be useful by way of explaining the epistemic points made here to consider very briefly how the moral realist might respond to one of the many possible anti-realist rebuttals to what has just been said. Consider the following objection: The realist treatment of reflective equilibrium requires that our background moral beliefs have been for some time relevantly approximately true. As a matter of fact, the overwhelming majority of people have probably always believed in some sort of theistic foundation of morals: moral laws are God's laws; the psychological capacities which underlie moral practice are a reflection of God's design; etc. According to the homeostatic consequentialism which we are supposed to accept for the sake of argument, moral facts are mere natural facts. Therefore, according to homeostatic consequentialism, most people have always had profoundly mistaken moral beliefs. How then can it be claimed that our background beliefs have been relevantly approximately true?

I reply that – assuming that people have typically held theistic beliefs of the sort in question – it does follow from homeostatic consequentialism that they have been *in that respect* very wrong indeed. But being wrong in that respect does not preclude their moral judgments having been relatively reliable reflections of facts about the homeostatic cluster of fundamental human goods, according to the model of the development of moral knowledge discussed earlier. Until Darwin, essentially all biologists attributed the organization and the adaptive features of the physiology, anatomy, and behavior of plants and animals to God's direct planning. That attribution did not prevent biologists from accumulating the truly astonishing body of knowledge about anatomy, physiology, and animal behavior upon which Darwin's discovery of evolution by natural selection depended; nor did it prevent their recognizing the profound biological insights of Darwin's theory. Similarly, seventeenth-century corpuscular chemistry did provide the basis for the development of modern chemistry in a way that earlier quasi-animistic renaissance naturalism in chemistry could not. Early corpuscular theory was right that the chemical properties of substances are determined by the fundamental properties of stable "corpuscles:" it was wrong about almost everything else, but what it got right was enough to point chemistry in a fruitful direction. I understand the analogy between the development of scientific knowledge and the development of moral knowledge to be very nearly exact.

There may indeed be one important respect in which the analogy between the development of scientific knowledge and the development of moral knowledge is inexact, but oddly, this respect of disanalogy makes the case for moral realism stronger. One of the striking consequences of a full-blown naturalistic and realistic conception of knowledge is that our knowledge, even our most basic knowledge, rests upon logically contingent "foundations." Our perceptual knowledge, for example, rests upon the logically contingent *a posteriori* fact that our senses are reliable detectors of certain sorts of external objects. In the case of perceptual knowledge, however, there is a sense in which it is nonaccidental, noncontingent, that our senses are reliable detectors. The approximate reliability of our senses (with respect to some applications) is explained by evolutionary theory in a quite fundamental way (Quine 1969a). By contrast, the reliability of our methodology in chemistry is much more dramatically contingent. As a matter of fact, early thinkers tried to explain features of the natural world by analogy to sorts of order they already partly understood: mathematical, psychological, and mechanical. The atomic theory of matter represents one such attempt to assimilate chemical order to the better-understood mechanical order. In several important senses it was highly contingent that the microstructure of matter turned out to be particulate and mechanical enough that the atomic (or "corpuscular") *guess* could provide the foundation for epistemically reliable research in chemistry. The accuracy of our guess in this regard is not, for example, explained by either evolutionary necessity or by deep facts about our psychology. In an important sense, the seventeenth century belief in the corpuscular theory of matter was not reliably produced. It was not produced by an antecedent generally reliable methodology: reasoning by analogy is *not* generally reliable except in contexts where a rich and approximately accurate body of theory *already* exists to guide us in finding the right respects of analogy (see Boyd 1982).

By contrast, the emergence of relevantly approximately true beliefs about the homeostatic cluster of fundamental human goods – although logically contingent – was much less strikingly "accidental." From the point of view either of evolutionary theory or of basic human psychology it is hardly accidental that we are able to recognize many of our own and others' fundamental needs. Moreover, it is probably not accidental from an evolutionary point of view that we were able to recognize some features of the homeostasis of these needs. Our initial relevantly approximately accurate beliefs about the good may well have been produced by generally reliable psychological and perceptual mechanisms and thus may have been clear instances of knowledge in a way in which our initial corpuscular beliefs were not (for a discussion of the latter point see Boyd 1982). It *is easier*, not *harder*, to explain how moral knowledge is possible than it is to explain how scientific knowledge is possible. Locke was right that we are fitted by nature for moral knowledge (in both the seventeenth- and the twentieth-century senses of the term) in a way that we are not so fitted for scientific knowledge of other sorts.

4.5 Moral semantics

We have earlier considered two objections to the moral realist's account of the semantics of moral terms. According to the first, the observed diversity of moral concepts – between cultures as well as between individuals and groups within a culture – suggests that it will not be possible to assign a single objective subject matter to their moral disputes. The divergence of concepts suggests divergence of reference of a sort which constructivist relativism is best suited to explain. According to the second objection, moral realism is committed to the absurd position that moral terms possess definitions in the vocabulary of the natural sciences. We have seen that a moral realist rebuttal to these challenges is possible which assimilates moral terms to naturalistically and nonreductively definable terms in the sciences. Such a response can be successful only if (1) there are good reasons to think that moral terms must possess natural rather than stipulative definitions and (2) there are good reasons to think that ordinary use of moral terms provides us with epistemic access to moral properties, so that, for example, moral goodness to some extent regulates our use of the word "good" in moral contexts.

The homeostatic consequentialist conception of morals provides a justification for the first of these claims. If the good is defined by a homeostatic phenomenon the details of which we still do not entirely know, then it is a paradigm case of a property whose "essence" is given by a natural rather than a stipulative definition.

Is it plausible that the homeostatic cluster of fundamental human goods has, to a significant extent, regulated the use of the term "good" so that there is a general tendency, of the sort indicated by the homeostatic consequentialist conception of the growth of moral knowledge, for what we say about the good to be true of that cluster? If what I have already said about the possibility of defending a realist conception of reflective equilibrium in moral reasoning is right, the answer must be "yes." Such a tendency is guaranteed by basic evolutionary and psychological facts, and it is just such a tendency which we can observe in the ways in which our conception of the good has changed in the light of new evidence concerning human needs and potential. Indeed, the way we ("preanalytically") recognize moral uses of the term "good" and the way we identify moral terms in other languages are precisely by recourse to the idea that moral terms are those involved in discussions of human goods and harms. We tacitly assume *something like* the proposed natural definition of "good" in the practice of translation of moral discourse. I think it will help to clarify this realist response if we consider two possible objections to it. The first objection reflects the same concern about the relation between moral and theological reasoning that we examined in the preceding section. It goes like this: How is it possible for the moral realist who adopts homeostatic consequentialism to hold that there is a general tendency for our beliefs about the good to get truer? After all, the error of thinking of the good as being defined by God's will persists unabated and is – according to the homeostatic consequentialist's conception – a very important falsehood.

I reply, first, that the sort of tendency to the truth required by the epistemic access account of reference is not such that it must preclude serious errors. Newtonians were talking about mass, energy, momentum, etc., all along, even though they were massively wrong about the structure of space-time. We might be irretrievably wrong about some other issue in physics and still use the terms of physical theory to refer to real entities, magnitudes, etc. All that is required is a significant epistemically relevant causal connection between the use of a term and its referent.

Moreover, as I suggested earlier, it is characteristic of what we recognize as moral discourse (whether in English or in some other language) that considerations of human well-being play a significant role in determining what is said to be "good." The moral realist need not deny that other considerations – perhaps profoundly false ones – also influence what we say is good. After all, the historian of biology need not deny that the term "species" has relatively constant reference throughout the nineteenth century, even though, prior to Darwin, religious considerations injected profound errors into biologists' conception of species. Remember that we do not ordinarily treat a theological theory as a theory *of* moral goodness at all unless it says something about what we independently recognize as human well-being. The role of religious considerations in moral reasoning provides a challenge for moral realists, but exactly the same challenge faces a realist interpretation of biological or psychological theorizing before the twentieth century, and it can surely be met.

The second objection I want to consider represents a criticism of moral realism often attributed to Marx (see, e.g., Wood 1972; for the record I believe that Marx's position on this matter was confused and that he vacillated between an explicit commitment to the relativist position, which Wood discusses, and a tacit commitment to a position whose reconstruction would look something like the position defended here). The objection goes like this: The moral realist – in the guise of the homeostatic consequentialist, say – holds that what regulate the use of moral terms are facts about human well-being. But this is simply not so. Consider, for example, sixteenth-century discussions of rights. One widely acknowledged "right" was the divine right of kings. Something surely regulated the use of the language of rights in the sixteenth century, but it clearly wasn't human well-being construed in the way the moral realist intends. Instead, it was the well-being of kings and of the aristocratic class of which they were a part.

I agree with the analysis of the origin of the doctrine of the divine right of kings; indeed, I believe that such class determination of moral beliefs is a commonplace phenomenon. But I do not believe that this analysis undermines the claim that moral terms refer to aspects of human well-being. Consider, for example, the psychology of thinking and intelligence. It is extremely well documented (see, e.g., Gould 1981; Kamin 1974) that the content of much of the literature in this area is determined by class interests rather than by the facts. Nevertheless, the psychological terms occurring in the most egregiously prejudiced papers refer to real features of human psychology; this is so because, in other contexts, their use is relevantly regulated by such features. Indeed – and this is the important point – if there were not such an epistemic (and thus referential) connection to real psychological phenomena, the ideological rationalization of class structures represented by the class-distorted literature would be ineffective. It's only when people come to believe, for example, that Blacks lack a trait, *familiar in other contexts as "intelligence,"* that racist theories can serve to rationalize the socioeconomic role to which Blacks are largely confined.

Similarly, I argue, in order for the doctrine of the divine right of kings to serve a class function, it had to be the case that moral language was often enough connected to issues regarding the satisfaction of real human needs. Otherwise, an appeal to such a supposed right would be ideologically ineffective. Only when rights-talk has *some* real connection to the satisfaction of the needs of nonaristocrats could this instance of rights-talk be useful to kings and their allies.

Once again, when the analogy between moral inquiry and scientific inquiry is fully exploited, it becomes possible to defend the doctrines upon which moral realism rests.

4.6 Hard cases and divergent views

Two of the challenges to moral realism we are considering are grounded in the recognition that some moral issues seem very hard to resolve. On the one hand, there seem to be moral dilemmas which resist resolution even for people who share a common moral culture. Especially with respect to the sort of possible cases often considered by moral philosophers, there often seems to be no rational way of deciding between morally quite distinct courses of action. Our difficulty in resolving moral issues appears even greater when we consider the divergence in moral views that exists between people from different backgrounds or cultures. The anti-realist proposes to explain the difficulties involved by denying that there is a common objective subject matter which determines answers to moral questions.

We have seen that – to the extent that she chooses to take the difficulties in resolving moral issues as evidence for the existence of moral statements for which bivalence fails – the moral realist can try to assimilate such failures to the failures of bivalence which realist philosophy *predicts* in the case, for example, of some statements involving homeostatic cluster terms. Such a response will work only to the extent that moral terms can be shown to possess natural definitions relevantly like homeostatic cluster definitions. Of course, according to homeostatic consequentialism, moral terms (or "good" at any rate) just are homeostatic cluster terms, so this constraint is satisfied. What I want to emphasize is that a moral realist *need not* invoke failures of bivalence in every case in which difficulties arise in resolving moral disputes.

Recall that on the conception we are considering moral inquiry is about a complex and difficult subject matter, proceeds often by the analysis of complex and "messy" naturally occurring social experiments, and is subject to a very high level of social distortion by the influence of class interests and other cultural factors. In this regard moral inquiry resembles inquiry in any of the complex and politically controversial social sciences. In such cases, even where there is no reason to expect failures of bivalence, one would predict that the resolution of some issues will prove difficult or, in some particular social setting, impossible. Thus the moral realist can point to the fact that moral inquiry is a species of social inquiry to explain much of the observed divergence in moral views and the apparent intractability of many moral issues.

Similarly, the complexity and controversiality of moral issues can be invoked to explain the especially sharp divergence of moral views often taken to obtain between different cultures. For the homeostatic consequentialist version of moral realism to be true it must be the case that in each culture in which moral inquiry takes place the homeostatically clustered human goods epistemically regulate moral discourse to an appreciable extent. On the realistic and naturalistic conception of the growth of knowledge, this will in turn require that the moral tradition of the culture in question embody some significant approximations to the truth about moral matters. It is, however, by no means required that two such cultural traditions have started with initial views which approximated the truth to the same extent or along the same dimensions, nor is it required that they have been subjected to the same sorts of social distortion, nor that they have embodied the same sorts of naturally occurring social experimentation. It would thus be entirely unsurprising if two such traditions of moral inquiry should have, about some important moral questions, reached conclusions so divergent that no resolution of their disagreement will be possible within the theoretical and methodological framework which the two traditions *currently* have in common, even though these issues may possess objective answers eventually discoverable from within either tradition or from within a broader tradition which incorporates insights from both.

In this regard it is useful to remember the plausibility with which it can be argued that, if there were agreement on all the nonmoral issues (including theological ones), then there would be no moral disagreements. I'm not sure that this is exactly right. For one thing, the sort of moral agreement which philosophers typically have in mind when they say this sort of thing probably does not include agreement that some question has an indeterminate answer, which is something predicted by homeostatic consequentialism. Nevertheless, careful philosophical examination will reveal. I believe, that agreement on nonmoral issues would eliminate *almost all* disagreement about the sorts of moral issues which arise in ordinary moral practice. Moral realism of the homeostatic consequentialist variety provides a quite plausible explanation for this phenomenon.

It is nevertheless true that, for some few real-world cases and for *lots* of the contrived cases so prevalent in the philosophical literature, there does appear to be serious difficulty in finding rational resolutions – assuming as we typically do that an appeal to indeterminacy of the extension of "good" doesn't count as a resolution. In such cases the strategy available to the moral realist *is* to insist that failures of bivalence do occur just as a homeostatic consequentialist moral realist predicts.

Philosophers often suggest that the major normative ethical theories will yield the same evaluations in almost all actual cases. Often it is suggested that this fact supports the claim that there is some sort of objectivity in ethics, but it is very difficult to see just why this should be so. Homeostatic consequentialist moral realism provides the basis for a satisfactory treatment of this question. Major theories in normative ethics have almost always sought to provide definitions for moral terms with almost completely definite extensions. This is, of course, in fact a mistake; moral terms possess homeostatic cluster definitions instead. The appearance of sharp divergence between major normative theories, with respect to the variety of possible cases considered by philosophers, arises from the fact that they offer different putative resolutions to issues which lack any resolution *at all* of the sort anticipated in those theories. The general agreement of major normative theories on almost all actual cases is explained both by the fact that the actual features of the good regulate the use of the term "good" in philosophical discourse *and* by the homeostatic character of the good: when different normative theories put different weight on different components of the good, the fact that such components are – in actual cases – linked by reliable homeostatic mechanisms tends to mitigate, in real-world cases, the effects of the differences in the weights assigned. Homeostatic consequentialism represents the common grain of truth in other normative theories.

4.7 Morality, motivation, and rationality

There remains but one of the challenges to moral realism which we are here considering. It has often been objected against moral realism that there is some sort of logical connection between moral judgments and reasons for action which a moral realist cannot account for. It might be held, for example, that the recognition that one course of action is morally preferable to another *necessarily* provides a reason (even if not a decisive one) to prefer the morally better course of action. Mere facts (especially mere *natural* facts) cannot have this sort of logical connection to rational choice or reasons for action. Therefore, so the objection goes, there cannot be moral facts; moral realism (or at least naturalistic moral realism) is impossible.

It is of course true that the naturalistic moral realist must deny that moral judgments necessarily provide reasons for action; surely, for example, there could be nonhuman cognizing systems which could understand the natural facts about moral goodness but be entirely indifferent to them in choosing how to act. Moral judgments might provide for them no reasons for action whatsoever. Moreover, it is hard to see how the naturalistic moral realist can escape the conclusion that it would be *logically possible* for there to be a human being for whom moral judgments provided no reasons for action. The moral realist must therefore deny that the connection between morality and reasons for action is so strong as the objection we are considering maintains. The appearance of an especially intimate connection must be explained in some other way.

The standard naturalist response is to explain the apparent intimacy of the connection by arguing that the natural property moral goodness is one such that for psychologically normal humans, the fact that one of two choices is morally preferable will in fact provide some reason for preferring it. The homeostatic consequentialist conception of the good is especially well suited to this response since it defines the good in terms of the homeostatic unity of fundamental human needs. It seems to me that this explanation of the close connection between moral judgments and reasons for action is basically right, but it ignores – it seems to me – one important source of the anti-realist's intuition that the connection between moral judgments and rational choice must be a necessary one. What I have in mind is the very strong intuition which many philosophers share that the person for whom moral judgments are motivationally indifferent would not only be psychologically atypical but would have some sort of *cognitive* deficit with respect to moral reasoning as well. The anti-realist diagnoses this deficit as a failure to recognize a definitional or otherwise necessary connection between moral goodness and reasons for action.

I think that there is a deep insight in the view that people for whom questions of moral goodness are irrelevant to how they would choose to act suffer a cognitive deficit. I propose that the deficit is not – as the anti-realist would have it – a failure to recognize a necessary connection between moral judgments and reasons for action. Instead, I suggest, if we adopt a naturalistic conception of moral knowledge we can diagnose in such people a deficit in the capacity to make moral judgments somewhat akin to a perceptual deficit. What I have in mind is the application of a causal theory of moral knowledge to the examination of a feature of moral reasoning which has been well understood in the empiricist tradition since Hume, that is, the role of sympathy in moral understanding.

It is extremely plausible that for normal human beings the capacity to access human goods and harms – the capacity to *recognize* the extent to which others are well or poorly off with respect to the homeostatic cluster of moral goods and the capacity to *anticipate correctly* the probable effect on others' well-being of various counterfactual circumstances depends upon their capacity for sympathy, their capacity to imagine themselves in the situation of others or even to find themselves involuntarily doing so in cases in which others are especially well or badly off. The idea that sympathy plays this sort of cognitive role is a truism of nineteenth-century faculty psychology, and it is very probably right.

It is also very probably right, as Hume insists, that the operation of sympathy is *motivationally* important: as a matter of contingent psychological fact, when we put ourselves in the place of others in imagination, the effects of our doing so include our taking pleasure in others' pleasures and our feeling distress at their misfortune, and we are thus motivated to care for the well-being of others. The psychological mechanisms by which all this takes place may be more complicated than Hume imagined, but the fact remains that one and the same psychological mechanism – sympathy – plays *both* a cognitive *and* a motivational role in normal human beings. We are now in a position to see why the morally unconcerned person, the person for whom moral facts are motivationally irrelevant, probably suffers a *cognitive* deficit with respect to moral reasoning. Such a person would have to be deficient in sympathy, because the motivational role of sympathy is precisely to make moral facts motivationally relevant. In consequence, she or he would be deficient with respect to a cognitive capacity (sympathy) which is ordinarily important for the correct assessment of moral facts. The motivational deficiency would, as a matter of contingent fact about human psychology, be a cognitive deficiency as well.

Of course it does not follow that there could not be cognizing systems which are quite capable of assessing moral facts without recourse to anything like sympathy; they might, for example, rely on the application of a powerful tacit or explicit theory of human psychology instead. Indeed it does not follow that there are not actual people – some sociopaths and con artists, for example – who rely on such theories instead of sympathy. But it is true, just as the critic of moral realism insists, that there is generally a cognitive deficit associated with moral indifference. The full resources of naturalistic epistemology permit the moral realist to acknowledge and explain this important insight of moral anti-realists.

4.8 Conclusion

I have argued that if the full resources of naturalistic and realistic conceptions of scientific knowledge and scientific language are deployed and if the right sort of positive theory of the good is advanced, then it is possible to make a plausible case for moral realism in response to typical anti-realist challenges. Two methodological remarks about the arguments I have offered may be useful. In the first place, the rebuttals I have offered to challenges to moral realism really do depend strongly upon the naturalistic and nonfoundational aspects of current (scientific) realist philosophy of science. They depend, roughly, upon the aspects of the scientific realist's program which make it plausible for the scientific realist to claim that philosophy is an empirical inquiry continuous with the sciences and with, for example, history and empirical social theory. I have argued elsewhere (Boyd 1981, 1982, 1983, 1985a, 1985b, 1985c) that these aspects of scientific realism are essential to the defense of scientific realism against powerful empiricist and constructivist arguments.

If we now ask how one should decide between scientific realism and its rivals, I am inclined to think that the answer is that the details of particular technical arguments will not be sufficient to decide the question rationally; instead, one must assess the overall conceptions of knowledge, language, and understanding which go with the rival conceptions of science (I argue for this claim in Boyd 1983). *One* important constraint on an acceptable philosophical conception in these areas is that it permit us to understand the obvious fact that moral reasoning is not nearly so different from scientific or other factual reasoning as logical positivists have led us to believe. It is initially plausible, I think, that a constructivist conception of science is favored over both empiricist and realist conceptions insofar as we confine our attention to this constraint. If what I have said here is correct, this may well not be so. Thus the successful development of the arguments presented here may be relevant not only to our assessment of moral realism but to our assessment of scientific realism as well. Here is a kind of methodological unity of philosophy analogous to (whatever it was which positivists called) "unity of science."

My second methodological point is that the arguments for moral realism presented here depend upon optimistic empirical claims both about the organic unity of human goods and about the possibility of reliable knowledge in the "human sciences" generally. Although I have not argued for this claim here, I believe strongly that any plausible defense of naturalistic moral realism would require similarly optimistic empirical assumptions. I am also inclined to believe that insofar as moral anti-realism is plausible its plausibility rests not only upon technical philosophical arguments but also upon relatively pessimistic empirical beliefs about the same issues. I suggest, therefore, that our philosophical examination of the issues of moral realism should include, in addition to the examination of technical arguments on both sides, the careful examination of empirical claims about the unity and diversity of human goods and about our capacity for knowledge of ourselves. That much of philosophy ought surely to be at least partly empirical.

Notes

An early version of this paper, incorporating the naturalistic treatments of the roles of reflective equilibrium and moral intuitions in moral reasoning and a naturalistic conception of the semantics of moral terms (but not the homeostatic property cluster formulation of consequentialism), was presented to the Philosophy Colloquium at Case-Western Reserve University in 1977. I am grateful to the audience at that colloquium for helpful criticisms which greatly influenced my formulation of later versions.

In approximately the version published here, the paper was presented at the University of North Carolina, the University of Chicago, Cornell University, the Universities of California at Berkeley and at Los Angeles, the University of Washington, Dartmouth College, and Tufts University. Papers defending the general homeostatic property cluster account of natural definitions were presented at Oberlin, Cornell, and Stanford. Extremely valuable criticisms from the audiences at these universities helped me in developing the more elaborate defense of moral realism presented in *Realism and the Moral Sciences* and summarized in Part 5 [not included in this anthology].

My interest in the question of moral realism initially arose from my involvement in the anti-Vietnam War movement of the late 1960s and was sustained in significant measure by my participation in subsequent progressive movements. I have long been interested in whether or not moral relativism played a progressive or a reactionary role in such movements; the present essay begins an effort to defend the latter alternative. I wish to acknowledge the important influence on my views of the Students for a Democratic Society (especially its Worker–Student Alliance Caucus), the International Committee against Racism, and the Progressive Labor Party. Their optimism about the possibility of social progress and about the rational capacity of ordinary people have played an important role in the development of my views.

I have benefited from discussions with many people about various of the views presented here. I want especially to thank David Brink, Norman Daniels, Philip Gasper, Paul Gomberg, Kristen Guyot, Terence Irwin, Barbara Koslowski, David Lyons, Christopher McMahon, Richard Miller, Milton Rosen, Sydney Shoemaker, Robert Stalnaker, Stephen Sullivan, Milton Wachsberg, Thomas Weston, and David Whitehouse. My thinking about homeostatic property cluster definitions owes much to conversations with Philip Gasper, David Whitehouse, and especially Kristin Guyot. I am likewise indebted to Richard Miller for discussions about the foundations of nonutilitarian consequentialism. My greatest debt is to Alan Gilbert and Nicholas Sturgeon. I wish to thank the Society for the Humanities at Cornell University for supporting much of the work reflected in Part 5.

1   This is the only section of Part 3 which advances naturalistic and realistic positions not already presented in the published literature. It represents a summary of work in progress. For some further developments see Section 5.2 [not printed in this anthology].

2   Two points of clarification about the proposed homeostatic consequentialist definition of the good are in order. In the first place, I understand the homeostatic cluster which defines moral goodness to be social rather than individual. The properties in homeostasis are to be thought of as instances of the satisfaction of particular human needs among people generally, rather than within the life of a single individual. Thus, the homeostatic consequentialist holds not (or at any rate not merely) that the satisfaction of each of the various human needs within the life of an individual contributes (given relevant homeostatic mechanisms) to the satisfaction of the others in the life of that same individual. Instead, she claims that, given the relevant homeostatic mechanisms, the satisfaction of those needs for one individual tends to be conducive to their satisfaction for others, and it is to the homeostatic unity of human need satisfaction in the society generally that she or he appeals in proposing a definition of the good.

Homeostatic consequentialism as I present it here is, thus, not a version of ethical egoism. I am inclined to think that individual well-being has a homeostatic property cluster definition and thus that a homeostatic property cluster conception of the definition of the good would be appropriate to the formulation of the most plausible versions of egoism, but I do not find even those versions very plausible and it is certainly not a version of egoism to which I mean to appeal in illustrating the proposed strategy for defending moral realism.

Second, I owe to Judith Jarvis Thomson the observation that, strictly speaking, the homeostatic consequentialist conception of the good does not conform to the more abstract account of homeostatic property cluster definitions presented in Section 3.8. According to that account, the homeostatically united properties and the definitionally relevant properties associated with the relevant mechanisms of homeostasis are all properties of the same kind of thing: organisms, let us say, in the case of the homeostatic property cluster definition of a particular biological species.

By contrast, some of the properties which characterize human well-being and the mechanisms upon which its homeostatic unity depends are (on the homeostatic consequentialist conception) in the first instance properties of individuals, whereas others are properties of personal relations between individuals and still others are properties of large-scale social arrangements. Homeostatic unity is postulated between instances of the realization of the relevant properties in objects of different logical type.

It should be obvious that the additional logical complexity of the proposed homeostatic property cluster definition of the good does not vitiate the rebuttals offered here to antirealist arguments. For the record, it seems to me that Professor Thomson's observation in fact applies to the actual case of species definitions as well: some of the homeostatically united properties and homeostatic mechanisms which define a species are in the first instance properties of individual organisms, some properties of small groups of organisms, some of larger populations (in the standard sense of that term), and some of the relations between such populations.

Bibliography

Armstrong, D. M. 1973. *Belief, Truth and Knowledge*. Cambridge: Cambridge University Press.

Boyd, R. 1972. "Determinism, Laws and Predictability in Principle." *Philosophy of Science* 39: 431–50.

Boyd, R. 1973. "Realism, Underdetermination and a Causal Theory of Evidence." *Nous* 7: 1–12.

Boyd, R. 1979. "Metaphor and Theory Change." In A. Ortony, ed., *Metaphor and Thought*. Cambridge: Cambridge University Press.

Boyd, R. 1980. "Materialism without Reductionism: What Physicalism Does Not Entail." In N. Block, ed., *Readings in Philosophy of Psychology*, vol. 1. Cambridge, Mass.: Harvard University Press.

Boyd, R. 1982. "Scientific Realism and Naturalistic Epistemology." In P. D. Asquith and R. N. Giere, eds, *PSA 1980*, vol. 2. East Lansing: Philosophy of Science Association.

Boyd, R. 1983. "On the Current Status of the Issue of Scientific Realism." *Erkenntnis* 19: 45–90.

Boyd, R. 1985a. "Lex Orendi Est Lex Credendi." In Paul Churchland and Clifford

Hooker, eds, *Images of Science: Scientific Realism Versus Constructive Empiricism*. Chicago: University of Chicago Press.

Boyd, R. 1985b. "Observations, Explanatory Power, and Simplicity." In P. Achinstein and O. Hannaway, eds, *Observation, Experiment, and Hypothesis in Modern Physical Science*. Cambridge, Mass.: MIT Press.

Boyd, R. 1985c. "The Logician's Dilemma: Deductive Logic, Inductive Inference and Logical Empiricism." *Erkenntnis* 22: 197–252.

Boyd, R. Forthcoming. *Realism and the Moral Sciences* (unpublished manuscript).

Brink, D. 1984. "Moral Realism and the Skeptical Arguments from Disagreement and Queerness." *Australasian Journal of Philosophy* 62.2: 111–25.

Brink, D. 1989. *Moral Realism and the Foundation of Ethics*. Cambridge: Cambridge University Press.

Byerly, H., and V. Lazara 1973. "Realist Foundations of Measurement." *Philosophy of Science* 40: 10–28.

Carnap, R. 1934. *The Unity of Science*. Trans. M. Black. London: Kegan Paul.

Dworkin, R. 1973. "The Original Position." *University of Chicago Law Review* 40: 500–33.

Feigl, H. 1956. "Some Major Issues and Developments in the Philosophy of Science of Logical Empiricism." In H. Feigl and M. Scriven. eds, *Minnesota Studies in the Philosophy of Science*, vol. I. Minneapolis: University of Minnesota Press.

Field, H. 1973. "Theory Change and the Indeterminacy of Reference." *Journal of Philosophy* 70: 462–81.

Gilbert, A. 1981a. *Marx's Politics: Communists and Citizens*. New Brunswick, NJ: Rutgers University Press.

Gilbert, A. 1981b. "Historical Theory and the Structure of Moral Argument in Marx," *Political Theory* 9: 173–205.

Gilbert, A. 1982. "An Ambiguity in Marx's and Engel's Account of Justice and Equality," *American Political Science Review* 76: 328–46.

Gilbert, A. 1984a. "The Storming of Heaven: Capital and Marx's Politics." In J. R. Pennock, ed., *Marxism Today*, Nomos 26. New York: New York University Press.

Gilbert, A. 1984b. "Marx's Moral Realism: Eudaimonism and Moral Progress." In J. Farr and T. Ball, eds, *After Marx*. Cambridge: Cambridge University Press.

Gilbert, A. 1986a. "Moral Realism, Individuality and Justice in War," *Political Theory* 14: 105–35.

Gilbert, A. 1986b. "Democracy and Individuality," *Social Philosophy and Policy* 3: 19–58.

Gilbert, A. Forthcoming. *Equality and Objectivity*.

Goldman A. 1967. "A Causal Theory of Knowing." *Journal of Philosophy* 64: 357–72.

Goldman A. 1976. "Discrimination and Perceptual Knowledge." *Journal of Philosophy* 73: 771–91.

Goodman, N. 1973. *Fact, Fiction, and Forecast*. 3rd edn. Indianapolis: Bobbs-Merrill.

Gould, S. J. 1981. *The Mismeasure of Man*. New York: W. W. Norton.

Hanson, N. R. 1958. *Patterns of Discovery*. Cambridge: Cambridge University Press.

Kamin L. J. 1974. *The Science and Politics of IQ*. Potomac, Md.: Lawrence Erlbaum Associates.

Kripke S. A. 1971. "Identity and Necessity." In M. K. Munitz, ed., *Identity and Individuation*. New York: New York University Press.

Kripke S. A. 1972. "Naming and Necessity." In D. Davidson and G. Hamman, eds, *The Semantics of Natural Language*. Dordrecht, Netherlands: D. Reidel.

Kuhn, T. 1970. *The Structure of Scientific Revolutions*. 2nd edn. Chicago: University of

Chicago Press.

Mackie, J. L. 1974. *The Cement of the Universe*. Oxford: Oxford University Press.

Mayr, E. 1970. *Populations, Species and Evolution*. Cambridge: Harvard University Press.

Miller, R. 1978. "Methodological Individualism and Social Explanation." *Philosophy of Science* 45: 387–414.

Miller, R. 1979. "Reason and Commitment in the Social Sciences." *Philosophy and Public Affairs* 8: 241–66.

Miller, R. 1981. "Rights and Reality." *Philosophical Review* 90: 383–407.

Miller, R. 1982. "Rights and Consequences." *Midwest Studies in Philosophy* 7: 151–74.

Miller, R. 1983. "Marx and Morality." *Nomos* 26: 3–32.

Miller, R. 1984a. *Analyzing Marx*. Princeton, NJ: Princeton University Press.

Miller, R. 1984b. "Ways of Moral Learning." *Philosophical Review* 94: 507–56.

Putnam, H. 1975a. "The Meaning of 'Meaning'." In H. Putnam, *Mind, Language and Reality*. Cambridge: Cambridge University Press.

Putnam, H. 1975b. "Language and Reality." In H. Putnam. *Mind, Language and Reality*. Cambridge: Cambridge University Press.

Putnam, H. 1983. "Vagueness and Alternative Logic." In H. Putnam. *Realism and Reason*. Cambridge: Cambridge University Press.

Quine, W. V. O. 1969a. "Natural Kinds." In W. V. O. Quine. *Ontological Relativity and Other Essays*. New York: Columbia University Press.

Quine, W. V. O. 1969b. "Epistemology Naturalized." In W. V. O. Quine, *Ontological Relativity and Other Essays*. New York: Columbia University Press.

Railton, P. 1986. "Moral Realism." *Philosophical Review* 95: 163–207.

Rawls, J. 1971. *A Theory of Justice*. Cambridge, Mass.: Harvard University Press.

Shoemaker, S. 1980. "Causality and Properties." In P. van Inwagen, ed., *Time and Cause*. Dordrecht, Netherlands: D. Reidel.

Sturgeon, N. 1984a. "Moral Explanations." In D. Copp and D. Zimmerman, eds, *Morality, Reason and Truth*. Totowa, NJ: Rowman and Allanheld.

Sturgeon, N. 1984b. "Review of P. Foot, *Moral Relativism and Virtues and Vices*." *Journal of Philosophy* 81: 326–33.

van Fraassen, B. 1980. *The Scientific Image*. Oxford: Oxford University Press.

Wood, A. 1972. "The Marxian Critique of Justice." *Philosophy and Public Affairs* 1: 244–82.

Wood, A. 1979. "Marx on Right and Justice: A reply to Husami." *Philosophy and Public Affairs* 8: 267–95.

Wood, A. 1984. "A Marxian Approach to 'The Problem of Justice.'" *Philosophica* 33: 9–32.

4

God and Evil

Introduction

As we have seen, the problem of universals and the reality of moral value has practical implications. Our moral and political judgments will be affected by our metaphysical views about the reality of moral value or the nature of universals. For many the connection between metaphysics and ethics is particularly strong when it comes to God's existence, because they believe that moral rightness and wrongness is determined by God and if God does not exist then nothing can be morally right or wrong.

But not only do metaphysical views have practical consequences, practical considerations can influence our metaphysical views. For instance, while metaphysical views about moral value can influence a philosopher's moral judgments about the environment, the influence can also go in the other direction. An environmentalist might feel very strongly that wilderness area should be preserved even if that entails economic costs, and this moral stance can influence her metaphysical views about the existence and nature of moral value.

That our moral views can influence our metaphysical views is especially clear when it comes to the question of God's existence and the simple moral observation that there is evil in the world. It takes very little reflection to reveal that the supposed coexistence of God and evil leads to a serious problem. Before we take a look at the problem we will discuss the general strategies employed when attempting to show that God exists. But first some background information.

Which God?

First of all, which god are we talking about? While some claim that there is only one god, namely God, that people talk about and relate to in different ways, the fact is that history has given us numerous gods, or in case there is just one God, at least various descriptions of God. We need to make clear what properties the god of our interest possesses.

Most religious documents and books that reveal information about people's religions talk about some of the properties the god(s) of the religion possesses. Thus, we have Homer provide information about the Greek gods, the Icelandic

Sagas provide information about the Nordic gods, Gilgamesh provide information about the gods of their culture, the Bible provide information about God, the Koran about Allah, and so on. But the descriptions are of different gods that have various and sometimes incompatible properties. The first three describe a multitude of gods who have magnified human characteristics. They are very strong without being all powerful, they know a lot without being all knowing, and many of them are far from being good. The God of the Old Testament shows many of the same characteristics. He is a jealous God who punishes those who have done nothing worse than being the offspring of someone who did not worship Him. He is not all-knowing, as is apparent, for instance, from the story of Sodom and Gomorra, when He walks around with Abraham wondering how many non-sinners there are in the cities. And while He is obviously very powerful, there are no signs in the Old Testament of Him being all-powerful. These gods, as so described, are not the ones Christians or Muslims worship. Christians and Muslims want to put their fate and faith in the hands of God or Allah. They would not be comforted by someone who might be lacking some vital piece of information, or someone who might have a mean streak. Perhaps for that reason, Christianity and Islam have come to think of God or Allah as being not just very powerful but all-powerful, not just good but all-good, and not just knowing but all-knowing. Whatever other properties God might have and whatever god we might be talking about, we are considering a god that has at least the three properties of being all-good, all-knowing, and all-powerful.

God's Properties

Now that we know the three properties we are concerned with, we need to clarify what it means for a being to have those properties. We will give a definition of what it is to have each property and then provide examples to further explain what is involved in having the property. A closer look at each of these properties shows that individually they already raise deep metaphysical questions.

First, consider the property of being all-powerful or omnipotence:

God is omnipotent $=_{df}$ God can do everything.

The definition allows God to do anything, including extraordinary things such as reviving the dead, parting seas, and other miracles that break the laws of nature (they would not be miracles unless they broke the laws of nature). However, the definition yields a paradox, the *paradox of omnipotence*.

Consider the power to make a stone so big that God cannot lift it. If God does not have this power, then God is not omnipotent because God lacks a power: the power to make a stone so big that God cannot lift it. This means that omnipotence as we defined it requires that God can make such a stone. But if God has this power, God can make a stone so big that God cannot lift it, which means that God is not omnipotent because there is a stone that God cannot lift. So omnipotence leads to a paradox. If we suppose that God is omnipotent, then God is not omnipotent. So if God is omnipotent, then God is both omnipotent and not omnipotent.

The solution to this paradox was proposed long time ago by the medieval philosopher Saint Thomas Aquinas (1224–1274). Aquinas argued that God's power does not require that God is able to do things that entail logical contradictions. Aquinas believed that the following definition better captures God's power:

God is all powerful $=_{df}$ God can do whatever is logically possible,

where something is logically possible just in case it is not self-contradictory or does not entail a logical contradiction. This revised definition takes care of the previous problem.

Let's test this definition with another example. Consider, say, the power to wiggle one's toes. Does God have the power to wiggle God's toes? If someone has the ability to wiggle her toes, she has a body. So if God has the power to wiggle God's toes, God has a body. But usually it is assumed that God does not have a body, and certainly not a body with toes like we have. So to suppose that God has the power to wiggle his toes entails a contradiction, namely that God both has and does not have a body. Wiggling God's toes, then, is something that is logically impossible for God to do given that God does not have a body with toes. Consequently, not being able to do this does not restrict God's omnipotence as defined by Aquinas.

Let us now turn to the property of being all-knowing or omniscience:

God is omniscient $=_{df}$ God knows everything that can be known.

So, God knows every little detail about what has happened, what is happening, and what will happen. We can put it this way: for every true proposition – whether it is about the past, present, or future – God knows it. If it is true that tomorrow you will get a flat tire on your bicycle exactly at noon, then God knows that tomorrow you will get a flat tire on your bicycle exactly at noon.

Finally, God is all-good or omnibenevolent. This property can be characterized as follows:

God is omnibenevolent $=_{df}$ If God knows about some evil and God can eliminate or prevent it, God prevents or eliminates it.

This understanding of God's goodness depends on understanding what evil is, but we can understand what evil is without having a definition of *evil*. We know that rape, murder, slavery, or genocide are evils even if we are not sure how to characterize the nature of evil. As we saw in chapter 1, there are many things we understand for which we do not have definitions.

Arguments for the Existence of God

There are three main types of arguments one can turn to when trying to show that God exists: design arguments, cosmological arguments, and ontological arguments. Each type of argument has been stated and restated in many versions. Our focus will not be on any particular version of the arguments. Instead, we shall focus on the underlying strategy behind each type of argument, arguing that each strategy faces insurmountable difficulties.

Design arguments

These arguments use empirical evidence to justify belief in the existence of God. The strategy of design arguments includes the following three steps:

Step 1:   arguing that nature shows all the tell-tale signs of a design.
Step 2:   showing that, since we have a design, we probably have a designer.
Step 3:   showing that this designer is God.

The first step usually involves saying something about how well the pieces of nature fit together and how the harmony and beauty found in nature show that nature is carefully thought out and pieced together. Apart from the design details found on Earth one might consider how the Earth is placed at just the right distance from the Sun so it is not too hot and not too cold, that it rotates, thus giving us night and day, that it is appropriately tilted so that we have the seasons, and how all of these work together to help sustain life. The second step typically points out that when we find some designed object such as a watch, cave drawing, or burial mounds, we correctly conclude that it is highly likely that there is a designer behind these artifacts. The final step is to argue that the designer of nature is God.

A design argument faces difficulties at all three steps. Step 1 involves showing that nature shows signs of being designed. We can reasonably assume that if something is designed then it serves some end(s), so that it is designed for a purpose. It is easy to see this in human artifacts; clocks are designed with it in mind to tell the time, cars are designed with transportation in mind, computers are designed so that certain tasks can be accomplished more effectively, dining tables serve the purpose of holding our food in a convenient place while we are eating, and so on.

How can we show that nature shows signs of being designed? Early versions of the argument focused on *parts* of nature, such as various organs (for example, eyes and ears) as well as the motion of the planets. But as time has passed, critics have pointed out that science provides better explanations of the features these objects have than does the hypothesis that there is a designer. Evolution can explain the development of the various organs, and physics can explain why the planets stay in the orbits they occupy.

Later versions of the argument have sometimes focused on more general features of nature. One can, for example, point out the beauty of nature, how it does, but does not have to, sustain life of the kind we enjoy, and how nature provides us with challenges to help us become better persons. Given this, one might argue that nature, as a whole, exhibits signs of design. Let us not discuss at this point whether or not the design is good or bad, efficient or not. These are further difficulties that have to be dealt with in step 1, and some of the issues raised will play a key role in the argument from evil, the only argument that tries to show that God does not exist. But, let us, for the sake of argument, grant that nature shows signs of design and move on to step 2.

Step 2 of design arguments attempts to show that since we have a design, we have a designer. Regardless of how one attempts to show this, we have already found a major weakness that has to be overcome. Why should we attempt to show that there is a designer and not *designers* that stand behind the design? There is ample empirical evidence for the claim that behind every design there are, not one, but many designers. How many designers, for example, does it take to design a car, a computer, a watch, etc.? Even a relatively simple human artifact such as a watch took centuries to develop, and current watch designers are reaping the benefits from the work of their predecessors. On the relatively rare occasion that someone displays genuine creativity in a design, the design is usually inspired by previous designs, and the subsequent implementation of the design, the making of the object, relies on the efforts of others. For example, one cannot sketch the design without paper and a pencil (inventions of others), and one cannot build without material and some knowledge of how to make and treat the material one is working with. The simple fact is that human artifacts, the best examples of design that we know of, heavily depend on cooperation and a high degree of specialization. Consequently, design arguments are much better suited to argue that there are *designers* rather than a designer. That is, if anything, the argument should support a conclusion to the effect that there are many gods instead of God.

The final step of design arguments argues that God is the designer of nature. Even if we grant that step 2 supports that there is a designer and not many designers of nature, what reason do we have to think that this designer is God? Surely, we would have to grant that the designer is very powerful, very knowing, and, perhaps, good. But we do not have good reasons to argue that the designer is all-knowing, all-powerful, and all-good.

Cosmological arguments

Cosmological arguments, like design arguments, start by pointing out some features of the world around us. But cosmological arguments then try to prove conclusively that God exists, while design arguments have the less ambitious goal of establishing that nature, in all likelihood, has a designer, namely God.

When discussing cosmological arguments, we need to first distinguish between *contingent* facts, existence, events, and *necessary* facts, existence, events.

When something is contingent then it could have been or not been. For example, both you and this book are contingently existing beings. The book might never have been published, and you might have died in a tragic accident at the age of five. It is also a contingent fact that you are reading this book now, for you might have opted for reading a different book or not reading at all. Most the things you see around you in nature are contingently existing things. Each individual thing might not have existed. Contrast this with something that is necessary, namely something that cannot not be, something that has to exist. God, if He exists, is such a being.

The general strategy of cosmological arguments is to first point out some contingent feature of the universe, and then argue that this contingent feature cannot be explained without the existence of a necessary being, namely God. Thus, Thomas Aquinas (1225–1274) argued that the following contingent features of the universe cannot be explained without there being a necessary being: motion, cause, contingently existing beings, gradations of value (that some things are better or worse than other), and order. In order to see how the arguments fit the pattern we have outlined we can look at his first argument for God's existence. Aquinas makes use of the contingent fact that things are in motion. He then argues that since we cannot have infinite chains of movers and things moved, we must reach a first mover who is not moved by anything else, namely God.

Cosmological arguments suffer from three serious problems. First of all, even if we can argue that there is, for example, a first mover or a first cause, that is not sufficient to establish God's existence. Why should we, for example, assume that the first mover is all-powerful, all-good, and all-knowing? And why should we assume that the first cause is all-powerful, all-good, and all-knowing. We can safely assume that if something set the universe in motion, then that was something very powerful. We do not have any reason to further assume that it was all-knowing or all-good, or even all-powerful. So, even though cosmological arguments were to succeed in proving that something exists necessarily, such as a first mover or a first cause, they provide no reason for why this necessarily existing being is God rather than something else.

The second problem is that the arguments do not deliver what they promise. As we have seen, the arguments proceed from something that is contingently true to something that is necessarily true and needed to account for contingencies. Thus, the claim is that the world of contingent facts cannot be adequately explained without this necessary fact.

The problem is that the supposedly necessary truth that God exists, or any other necessary truth, does not suffice to explain the world of contingencies. If we try to construct an explanation from a necessary fact to some contingent fact then we need an argument that has among its premises a necessary truth, namely that there is a God, and as a conclusion a contingently true statement about the contingent world. The argument, where "Q" is replaced with a statement about the contingent world and "P" is replaced with any statement that gets us the conclusion, would look like this:

It is necessary that God exists.

P is true (necessarily true or contingently true).

So, Q is contingently true.

The problem is that the second premise cannot be replaced with a necessary truth, for one cannot derive a contingent truth from nothing but necessary truths. But if the second premise is replaced with a contingent truth, then there will remain at least one contingent fact that is not explained; namely the one the second premise is about. Suppose that the second premise is not replaced with a contingent truth about nature, but rather a contingent truth about God. For example, many Christians believe that creation is a product of God's free decision to create this world. If so, then the second premise is contingently true, for God did not have to create anything, and certainly not the world we live in. But now the contingent truth that needs to be explained is God's free action. So, while cosmological arguments set out to explain the contingent world, they cannot succeed in explaining all the contingent features of the world. There will always remain some unexplained contingent facts.

The upshot of this is that cosmological arguments cannot live up to their promise, which is that the world of contingent beings can be adequately explained with the introduction of this necessary being. Given that, the motivation for introducing a necessary being is removed, for the choice now seems to stand between explaining contingencies with a mix of a necessary truth and contingent truths, and explaining contingencies with only contingent truths. Either way, we are stuck with contingent truths as playing a crucial role in the explanations of other contingent truths. We can furthermore conclude from the argument that it is very likely the case that the contingent world can never be fully accounted for and explained. Not even the introduction of a necessary being, such as God, can accomplish that.

The third difficulty cosmological arguments face is to justify a principle that they presuppose, namely the Principle of Sufficient Reason. The principle claims that there is a sufficient reason for every contingent fact; that is, for every contingency, there is a sufficient reason for why it obtains rather than not. The principle can be applied to individual contingent facts, as when you look for why you are reading this book, and it can be applied to the contingent universe as a whole.

Is the principle true? As we argued above, there are reasons to believe that some facts of the contingent universe cannot be explained. This is further supported by quantum physics, which tells us among other things that particles leave a chunk of radioactive material at random, so we cannot explain why one particle rather than the one occupying the space next to it left the chunk at some particular time. We have therefore good reasons to believe that the Principle of Sufficient Reason is false when applied to individual contingent facts. Is the principle true when applied to the universe as a whole? It is very hard to say. It is, however, important to notice that one cannot simply *assume* that the principle is true when applied to the universe as a whole. The advocate of cosmological arguments therefore has the difficult task ahead to show that the Principle of Sufficient Reason is true when applied to the universe as a whole.

Ontological arguments

Ontological arguments represent some of the most brilliant attempts to prove God's existence. These arguments attempt to show that, because of his nature, God must exist. The argument has been stated in numerous versions, and has recently been developed in light of recent advances in logic. The main idea behind ontological arguments is that since we can conceive of God as being perfect, or the greatest conceivable being, then God must exist. For, assume that God is the greatest conceivable being and that He does not exist in reality. Then one can conceive of a being just like Him who exists in reality and would therefore be greater than God. But that is impossible, for God *is* the greatest conceivable being. So, God must exist in reality.

The main challenge to ontological arguments comes from attempts to parody them; show that they work equally well to prove the existence of a ridiculous being such as the greatest conceivable unicorn, the greatest conceivable island, the dirtiest island conceivable, and so on. Take, for example, the phrase "the dirtiest conceivable island," substitute it for "God" in the argument above and, apparently, you have proved that the dirtiest conceivable island exists. If ontological arguments can show that such an island exists, then they work all too well; the proofs come too easily, for the arguments even prove things to exist that we have every reason to believe do not exist.

There is, however, an important disanalogy between the concept of God and the concept of the dirtiest conceivable island. God is *all*-knowing, *all*-good, and *all*-powerful, and so there is what we might call *an intrinsic maximum* built into the concept of God. We cannot, for example, add to God's knowledge, we cannot add to God's power, and we cannot make God a little better. The same does not seem to be true of the dirtiest conceivable island. It is hard to imagine that we cannot pollute it a little more, spread a little more garbage here and there, and add a little more dirt to it. And if that is so, then the concept of the dirtiest conceivable island is incoherent; the dirtiest conceivable island is something we cannot conceive of.

That is not so with a being we might call "Satan." Satan is a being who, just like God, is all-powerful and all-knowing. But unlike God, Satan is all-evil. Since the concept of Satan is like the concept of God in the sense that the same kind of intrinsic maximum is built into it, it certainly seems as if ontological arguments that conclude that God exists should serve equally well to conclude that Satan exists. And this is a problem for the theist who claims that God is the greatest conceivable being, for here we have a being who seems just as great as God, namely Satan. Neither can lay claim to being *the greatest*.

The theist might try to respond to the argument by claiming that evil is a manifestation or a sign of weakness and ignorance. But it is easy to see that the Satan worshipper can make the same claims about goodness, namely that it is a sign of weakness and ignorance and that the few who "have what it takes" and have the strength and wisdom to rise above the crowd are only labeled evil by the weak and envious who are left behind.

So it seems that the well known arguments for God's existence are less than successful: they fail to show that God exists. But this does not mean that God does not exist. All it shows is that we do not have good arguments for God's existence. To show that God does not exist, we need an argument whose conclusion is that God does not exist, and this is precisely the aim of *the argument from evil*.

The Argument from Evil

Evil is a problem because it does not appear to be compatible with the existence of God understood as a being who is all-powerful, all-knowing, and all-good. It is easy to see this in the following simple argument.

1   If God exists, God is omnipotent, omniscient and omnibenevolent.
2   If God is omnipotent, then God can eliminate or prevent all evils
3   If God is omniscient, God knows about all evils.
4   If God is omnibenevolent, then if God can eliminate or prevent all evils and God knows about all evils, then God prevents or eliminates all evils.
5   Therefore, if God exists, God prevents or eliminates all evils.

With this preliminary conclusion in place, the argument continues:

6   If God eliminates or prevents all evils, there is no evil in the world.
7   There is evil in the world.
8   Therefore, God does not eliminate or prevent all evils.
9   Therefore, God does not exist.

Preliminary conclusion (8) follows from (6) and (7) and the final conclusion that God does not exist follows from (8) and (5).

Needless to say, a central premise in this argument that needs a closer look is that there is evil in the world. There are some people who deny there is evil in the world, but anyone who pays closer attention to the world around us and has some knowledge of history or current events will recognize evil in the world. Rape, genocide, murder, and slavery, among many other things, are continuing and stable features of the way human beings – individually and collectively – conduct their affairs. To deny these evils is a sign of either callousness or ignorance, two vices that are themselves among the evils of this world.

Nevertheless, we need to be careful. Some evils might be necessary for greater goods. For instance, think of the evil of having children vaccinated. After all, they have to be injected several times and they obviously feel pain and often feel a little sick for a few days afterwards. But this is an evil necessary for a greater good. All we need to do is point to the good effects, both individual and societal, of vaccination, and we realize that the little discomfort the children suffer is negligible and worth it. This suggests that we need to distinguish what we might call "gratuitous evil," or evil that is not necessary for a greater good, and "non-gratuitous evil," or evil that is necessary for a greater good.

In light of this distinction, the argument from evil against God's existence has to be revised as follows:

1   If God exists, God is omnipotent, omniscient and omnibenevolent.
2   If God is omnipotent, then God can eliminate or prevent all gratuitous evils.
3   If God is omniscient, God knows about all evils.
4   If God is omnibenevolent, then if God can eliminate or prevent all gratuitous evils and God knows about all evils, then God prevents or eliminates all gratuitous evils.
5   Therefore, if God exists, God prevents or eliminates all gratuitous evils.
6   If God eliminates or prevents all gratuitous evils, there is no gratuitous evil in the world.
7   There is gratuitous evil in the world.
8   Therefore, God does not eliminate or prevent all gratuitous evils.
9   Therefore, God does not exist.

So now we know at least this much: if there is gratuitous evil in the world, then an all-knowing, all-powerful, and all-benevolent God does not exist. Is there gratuitous evil in the world?

Good and Evil as Ying and Yang

A quick popular response to the argument from evil is that we cannot have good without evil. Evil is a necessary counterpart of good. But here we need to separate two issues: the concept of evil and the existence of evil. It might well be the case that we need the *concept* of evil as a counterpart to the concept of good; that is, we might not be able to understand the concept good without understanding the concept evil. If this is what the response is based on, then the response cannot go very far against this argument. The argument focuses on the *existence* of a certain kind of evil, not the concept of evil, and it is not at all obvious that we need the existence of evil in order to experience and enjoy what is good.

Another closely related response is to suppose that no evil is gratuitous because every evil produces some good and that some of these goods could have happened only because of the evil. The basic idea is that the world's evils are lessons for others to make them better and opportunities for good actions.

For example, someone might argue that genocide such as occurred during the

Second World War was necessary so that people could come to recognize the evils of genocide or better understand human capacity for evil. It may also be argued that the evils of genocide were a necessary condition for the noble and heroic deeds of the people trying to fight the evils of genocide. Without the Nazi policy of genocide, there could not be a Warsaw uprising. The same thing might be argued for slavery. The evil of slavery, it may be argued, made possible the good deeds of abolitionists and the workers on the underground railroad that helped to free slaves. Perhaps slavery also strengthened people's resolve to recognize the rights of all human beings, and that is a good thing that might not have occurred without slavery.

Since non-gratuitous evil is evil that is necessary for some greater good, we need to ask two questions of every evil that is claimed to be non-gratuitous because it leads to some good. We need to determine (a) whether this evil is indeed necessary for the good it produces and (b) whether the good it produces is indeed a greater good; that is, whether it outweighs the evil that brought it about.

Let's ask these questions about Hitler's genocide against European Jews and Gypsies (or Romany, as they prefer to be called). Was Hitler's genocide really necessary to produce whatever good this evil produced? Did the good produced by Hitler's genocide outweigh the evil of his genocide? The answer to both questions is a resounding "No." The heroism of the uprising in the Jewish ghetto of Warsaw could have been achieved in many other ways without Hitler's genocide. For instance, an uprising that would have prevented Hitler's coming to power could have been just as heroic and it would have prevented Nazi genocide, which would give us moral heroism without Hitler's genocide. Moreover, whatever good was made possible by Hitler's genocide is decidedly not a greater good. Survivors of concentration camps point out that the hellish conditions of these camps sometimes brought out the very best in people – for instance, a very old inmate sacrificing himself to save a young parent from the gas chamber, gallows or firing squad. There is tremendous nobility in such actions, but this in no way outweighed the evils of the genocidal policies of the German Nazis. These noble actions were only droplets of good water in a toxic sea of evil, and concentration camp survivors will attest to that.

Genocide, along with all the other terrors that seem to be a mainstay of human history, cannot be dismissed as non-gratuitous on the ground that they produce other goods. This response is not very effective, and the theist needs to prepare a stronger defense.

The Free Will Defense

There is a stronger defense against the argument from evil. Many Christians will grant that the evils of genocide far outweigh any goods produced by the genocide and that the genocide was not necessary to produce these goods, but they nevertheless deny that there are gratuitous evils. What they often have in mind is that even though the goods produced by evils do not justify the evil, the evil itself is made necessary by some other greater good that has this evil as a necessary consequence. In other words, rather than seeking to find a justification for evil in some greater good among the consequences of evil, a theist can look for a greater good in the conditions that bring about the world's evil.

This is the strategy of what probably is the strongest response to the argument from evil: *the free will defense*. The free will defense, in one of its simplest forms, goes like this. God endowed humans with free will because a world with free will is better than a world without free will. Humans sometimes, as a result of having free will, make decisions that cause evil in the world. So the evil of the world is not gratuitous: its existence is necessary for a greater good, namely the existence of free will.

This response rests on the assumptions that there is free will and that it is a good thing. Whether or not there is such a thing as free will is open to debate, as we will see in chapter 7, but for the sake of argument, let's suppose that in some interesting sense there is free will. Whether or not it is good is also less than obvious, but it seems very widely accepted that free will is a good thing, whether or not we really have it, so again for the sake of argument, let's grant that this is so.

Given that there is free will and that free will is a good thing, we need to ask our two questions. (a) Is the existence of evil necessary for the existence of free will; that is, could there have been free will without evil? (b) Does the existence of freedom outweigh the evil in the world; that is, is free will indeed a greater good? Let us turn to the first question in this section, and the second question in the next section.

Could God have created a world in which there is free will, but no evil? This would be a world in which people still make free choices, but it is a world in which all the choices are good ones and do not lead to evil. Picture God pondering what world to create. God considers all the possible worlds, or possible ways in which things might turn out to be – perhaps each possible world is a long list of logically consistent propositions describing everything that is true in that world.

Some of the possible worlds will have very different natural laws than the ones that hold in our actual world – for instance, the relations between mass and energy in some worlds are completely different than the relations that hold in ours. While such possible worlds are radically different from our actual world, other possibilities are a little closer to what actually is the case. For instance, some possible worlds do not have any humans, some lack water, some have no Earth, and some do not contain any life at all. Other possible worlds God considers are even more similar to the one that was finally created. For instance, a world where today I decide to drive to school instead of ride my bicycle is different from the actual world, but it is extremely close to the actual world. A possible world still closer to our world is one where I blink my eyes a few moments later than when I actually did right now.

So imagine that God at creation has a choice of which possible world to make actual. Given that free will is a good thing, God will not even consider creating worlds in which there is no free will – perhaps worlds where human beings are very much like robots in the sense that they do not have a real choice; instead they are hardwired and without free will. The only possible worlds God considers are worlds that contain beings with free will. For the sake of simplicity we will only consider the worlds where human beings have free will. In some of these possible worlds humans have a choice between good and evil. In some of those worlds the humans sometimes choose to do what is evil. God chose to create one of the latter worlds, namely the world in which we live.

By making this one, God did not create other worlds God could have made. One kind of world God did not create is a Do-right World. These are worlds in which human beings always choose to do what is good and what does not lead to evil. Human beings still have free wills in these worlds; they still make free choices, but they always choose to do the right thing. Still another kind of world God did not create is the All-good World. While in a Do-right World humans have choices between good and evil and choose good, in an All-good World all the choices are good because there are only good options and no evil consequences.

Both Do-right Worlds and All-good Worlds are worlds without evil. The question is this: why did God not create either of these two worlds instead of the one in which we live?

The contemporary Christian philosopher Alvin Plantinga has argued that there are worlds that God could not have created and that, more specifically, God could not have created a world containing moral good but no moral evil. Plantinga's argument is difficult and deserves close attention, but the basic ideas are simple.

Consider the actual world – our world, the one God created – and let's follow Plantinga in calling it "Kronos." In Kronos there is a man, Curley, who freely does something wrong; he freely does A, some evil deed. Now, take Kronos and subtract from it Curley's free but morally evil deed A and everything that is entailed by this evil action. Let us call the part or segment of Kronos without Curley's freely doing A and what this entails "S." In addition to not containing Curley's free action A, let us make sure that S also does not include Curley freely refraining from doing A. That way Curley is left free with respect to doing A in S.

We can now consider another possible world distinct from Kronos. Call this other world "W." W is a possible world that contains S, but in addition to S, it has Curley freely refraining from doing A. We can suppose this is a Do-right World in which Curley has an evil option – doing A – but freely decides against it. Plantinga's task is to show that God could not have created W. If he can show this, then it seems he has answered our first question and shown that some evil is necessary for free will; that there cannot be a world with free will but no moral evil.

To see this, suppose that this is true:

1 If S is actual, Curley freely does A.

In other words, given the state of affairs S, Curley freely does dastardly deed A. Could God have created world W, which contains segment S but in which Curley refrains from doing A? To create W, God would have had to create S. But if (1) is true, then given that S is in W, Curley freely does A in W! So God cannot create W, which includes S but has Curley refraining from doing A. Given the truth of (1), the only kind of world God can create that includes S is one in which Curley freely does A.

Plantinga's argument raises many deep questions, but is it convincing? One thing to notice right away is that even if Plantinga's argument does work it excludes at best Do-right Worlds; that is, worlds where there are evil options but people freely refrain from choosing them. This still leaves us with All-good Worlds, and the nagging question remains why God did not create an All-good World where there are no evil options. All-good Worlds are not worlds where Curley freely refrains from doing immoral action A. Instead, these are worlds where doing A is not even an option and Curley can only do good.

Moreover, it is not even obvious that this argument excludes all Do-right Worlds. If (1) is true, then it is true that God could not create the Do-right World in which there is S and Curley refrains from doing A. But God still has other options: God could refrain either from creating Curley or from creating condition S. God could create a world with Curley that does not contain S and instead contains only situations out of which Curley freely chooses to refrain from immoral actions. Or God could have chosen not to create Curley and instead create another person with greater moral fortitude who, unlike Curley, will freely refrain from doing A even when given the option of doing A.

Finally, the free will defense is ineffective against the argument from evil because it only addresses evil produced by free will. The free will defense focuses on *moral evil* while ignoring another kind of evil, namely *natural evil*. Moral evil is evil resulting from free will, while natural evil is evil not resulting from free will. Actions for which human beings are morally responsible are typical moral evils, e.g. deliberate, premeditated murder. Natural evil includes evil inflicted upon us by nature, such as death and suffering caused by tornadoes, hurricanes, earthquakes, drought, floods, avalanches, and so on. A successful rebuttal of the argument from evil has to address both moral evil and natural evil. Even if the free will defense were to succeed, the proponent of the argument from evil could quickly point out that it is not a satisfactory reply to the argument, for the theist still has to account for natural evil.

Measuring Good and Evil

Let us remind ourselves of the other question we need to ask in order to examine the claim that the world's evil is not gratuitous because it is necessary for free will, a greater good: is free will a greater good that outweighs the evil that it brings about? The theist needs to show why the actual evils of this world – all of them – are not gratuitous, and how the existence of free will is a greater good that outweighs all the evil that in fact exists.

This is a tall order, even if we limit ourselves to moral evils. Let's grant that a world with free will is better than a world without it, that free will can exist only if there is moral evil, and that sometimes the goodness of free will outweighs moral evil. It still does not follow that it always outweighs moral evil. Consider Hitler's free will. Does the fact that he had a free will, which supposedly is a good thing, outweigh the evil of his actions? Surely the answer to this question is a resounding "No." A world without Hitler's free will is a better world, and whatever is good on account of the fact that he had a free will is puny and pathetic next to the evils he brought about and made possible.

Theists can try to simplify their task of explaining evil by not putting so much burden on free will. Perhaps free will can explain some of the world's evil, but other evils are explained in some other way. The general idea is that all the evil in the world is necessary for a greater good, and so regardless of what happens, it is all for the best.

Let us put the theist to the test with her opinion that regardless of what happens it will turn out to be for the best. We provide an example of evil, and the theist provides her explanation. Instead of going into detail about how the given evil might be necessary, we will shorten the theist's reply, for, after all, how the given evil might be necessary is in most cases pure speculation. So, here we go with a discussion between a theist and a person we can call Axel.

AXEL: A child fell and scraped its knee on my sidewalk.

THEIST: That might seem really bad, but it will turn out to be for the best.

AXEL: My son was hit by a bicycle and broke his arm.

THEIST: That might seem really bad, but it will turn out to be for the best.

AXEL: My neighbor is paralyzed from a car accident caused by a drunk driver.

THEIST: That might seem really bad, but it will turn out to be for the best.

AXEL: Five people were laid off before Christmas in order to benefit the shareholders.

THEIST: That might seem really bad, but it will turn out to be for the best.

AXEL: Ten kindergartners were trapped in a burning bus and burned to death.

THEIST: That might seem really bad, but it will turn out to be for the best.

AXEL: One hundred people were evicted from their trailer homes so that a developer could build another shopping mall.

THEIST: That might seem really bad, but it will turn out to be for the best.

AXEL: Two hundred people drowned when a mud-slide fell on their village.

THEIST: That might seem really bad, but it will turn out to be for the best.

AXEL: Six million Jews were killed in Nazi concentration camps.

THEIST: That might seem really bad, but it will turn out to be for the best.

Regardless of how big the evil seems, the theist comes back with the claim that it is evil that is necessary for a greater good. Gradually the reply starts to sound unreasonable. It starts to sound more like a cliché than an explanation. Supposing, for instance, that we are supposed to learn a lesson from the Nazi concentration camp, could not the lesson have been taught with the extermination of 5.9 million Jews instead of 6 million? And supposing that we are to benefit from children being victims of fire, do so many children have to die in that way? Shouldn't perhaps the number of tragic fatalities be tied to how well they are reported in the media, for surely in the old days, when news traveled neither fast nor far, we might have needed more tragedies to have the same impact or to affect the same number of people, as fewer tragedies do now.

The approach the theist is taking also makes one wonder what kind of morality God adheres to. It seems apparent that the theist is claiming that we need to look at the end result of an event, balance the good and the bad, and the result will inevitably be that the good outweighs the bad. Thus, the event is, on balance, a good event. This is in essence a utilitarian type of reasoning; we add up the unhappiness and we add up the happiness resulting from an event, and if there is more happiness than unhappiness the event is good. Since most theists frown at the idea that God is a utilitarian, or anything in kin with a utilitarian, she might have to reconsider her type of reply to Axel.

Conclusion

We have seen that it is difficult to reconcile an all-powerful, all-knowing, and all-good God with the existence of gratuitous evil. We have looked at two important strategies for denying the existence of gratuitous evil, but neither seems very promising. Neither the good consequences of evil nor the condition of freedom that brings about evil makes the evil of the world necessary.

What is left for the theist to do? One option is to accept the conclusion and change one's beliefs. Many people have done this in response to evil, and there are various ways in which you can accept the conclusion. You can become an atheist and simply deny the existence of God. However, you can also change your conception of God. We have seen that omniscience and omnipotence are sources of trouble and so there are good reasons for being skeptical about these supposedly divine properties. If the God of your faith is not all-powerful or all-knowing, then you do not need to worry about the compatibility of the existence of God and the existence of evil.

Each of these strategies comes with special problems, but they are all rational strategies. There is yet another kind of strategy that is very widespread among religious believers. It is simply to accept the incompatibility of God and the world's evil, and deny that either God or the religious believer is constrained by considerations of logic and reason when it comes to faith. This sort of strategy rejects rationality and embraces irrationality, including the incompatibility of the world's evil and an omniscient, omnipotent and omnibenevolent God. This is a very courageous response defended by thinkers as diverse as the Roman Christian theologian Tertullian (150–230 CE) and the Danish philosopher Soren Kierkegaard (1813–1855), both of whom believed in God just because their faith was absurd and irrational.

But it is difficult to find merit in this sort of strategy because it subverts one of the most important goods human beings can have: our capacity to reason and reason well. Surely a being who gives us this capacity to reason, gives it a central role to play in our ability to navigate through a complicated and treacherous world, and then subverts this capacity is much less than all-good and not worthy of our adoration. We should expect more from God, as well as from each other.

Selection from *Proslogion*
St Anselm of Canterbury

St Anselm of Canterbury (1033?–1109) was born in Aosta, Italy, entered the monastery and became abbot in Normandy, France, and was Archbishop of Canterbury, England. He believed that it is possible to prove that God exists as long as you have a concept of God, which St Anselm took to be the concept of the greatest possible being.

The mind stirred up to the contemplation of God

Come now, wretched man, escape for a moment from your preoccupations and draw back a little while from your seething thoughts. Lay aside for now your burdensome worries and put off your wearisome tasks. Empty yourself to God for a little while, and rest a short time in him. Enter the private chamber of your mind, shut out everything except God and whatever may help you to search for him; lock the door and seek him out. Speak now, my whole heart, and say to God "I seek thy face; thy face Lord will I seek" (Psalms 27:8).

. . . I acknowledge and give thanks, Lord, that you have created me in this your image, so that I may be mindful of you, and think of you and love you. But the image is so scraped and worn away by my vices, so darkened by the smoke of my sins, that it cannot do what it was created to do unless you renew and reform it. I will not attempt, Lord, to reach your height, for my understanding falls so far short of it. But I desire to understand your truth just a little, the truth that my heart believes and loves. I do not seek to understand in order that I may believe, but I believe in order that I may understand. For this also I believe: unless I believe, I shall not understand.

God truly exists

So, Lord, you who give understanding to those who have faith, grant me to understand, so far as you judge it fit, that you indeed exist as we believe, and that you are what we believe you to be. Now we believe that you are *something than which nothing greater can be thought*. Is there then no such being, since "the fool hath said in his heart: there is no God" (Psalms 14:1)? Yet surely this same fool, when he hears the very words I now speak – "something than which nothing greater can be thought" – understands what he hears; and what he understands exists in his understanding, even if he does not understand that it actually exists. For it is one thing for an object to exist in the understanding, and another to understand that the object exists. When an artist thinks in advance of what he is about to paint, he has it in his understanding, but does not yet understand it to exist, since he has not yet painted it. But when he has painted it, then he both has it in his understanding and also understands that it exists, since he has painted it. Hence even the fool must agree that there exists, in the understanding at least, something than which nothing greater can be thought; for when he hears this expression he understands it, and whatever is understood exists in the understanding. Yet surely *that than which a greater cannot be thought* cannot exist in the understanding alone. For once granted that it exists, if only in the understanding, it can be thought of as existing in reality, and this is greater. Hence if *that than which a greater cannot be thought* exists solely in the understanding, it would follow that the very thing than which a greater *cannot* be thought turns out to be that than which a greater *can* be thought; but this is clearly impossible. Hence something than which a greater cannot be thought undoubtedly exists both in the understanding and in reality.

God cannot be thought not to exist

And certainly this entity so truly exists that it cannot be thought not to exist. For it is possible to think of a being which cannot be thought of as not existing; and this is greater than that something which can be thought of as not existing. So if *that than which a greater cannot be thought* can be thought not to exist, it would follow that the very same thing than which a greater cannot be thought is *not* that than which a greater cannot be thought; and this is inconsistent. Hence something than which a greater cannot be thought exists so truly that it cannot even be thought not to exist.

And this being is you, O Lord our God. So truly do you exist, O Lord my God, that you cannot even be thought not to exist. And how appropriate this is. For if some mind could think of something better than you, then a created being would rise above its creator and judge its creator, which is utterly absurd. Moreover, everything there is, apart from you alone, can be thought not to exist. You alone of all things possess existence in the truest sense and to the highest degree; for whatever else there is does not exist as truly, and so possesses existence to a lesser degree. Why then is it that the fool hath said in his heart there is no God, since it is so obvious to the rational mind that you exist to the greatest degree of all? Why, except that he is indeed dull and foolish!

How the fool said in his heart what cannot be thought

But how did he come to say in his heart what he could not think; or how was it impossible for him to think what he said in his heart, given that saying in one's heart and thinking are one and the same? Did he really both think it, since he said it in his heart, and also not say it in his heart, because he could not think it? If this is so, indeed since it is so, then there is more than one sense in which something is "said in one's heart" or "thought:" a thing is thought in one sense when we think of the word signifying it, but in another sense when we understand what the thing itself is. In the former sense, then, God can be thought not to exist, but not at all in the latter sense. For no one who understands what God is can think that God does not exist, even though he may say the words in his heart without any sense, or in some strange sense. For God *is that than which a greater cannot be thought*. And if someone understands this clearly, he understands that this being exists in such a way that he cannot not exist, even in thought. Hence he who understands that God exists in this way cannot think that he does not exist.

I give you thanks, good Lord, that what I formerly believed through your gift of faith, I now understand through the light which you bestow; so much so that the truth of your existence, even if I were unwilling to believe it, is now something I cannot fail to understand.

God is whatever is better to be than not to be; he alone, existing through himself, makes all other things from nothing

What are you then, lord God, you than whom nothing greater can be thought? What are you but the supreme being, the only being who exists through itself, and the one who has made all other things from nothing? For whatever falls short of this *is less* than what can be thought, and this cannot be thought true of you. So can any good thing be lacking in the supreme good, the source of every good that exists? You are therefore just, truthful, blessed and whatever is better to be than not to be; for it is better to be just than unjust, and better to be blessed than not.

Selection from *Summa Theologica*
St Thomas Aquinas

St Thomas Aquinas (1225–1274), born near Naples, Italy, is commonly thought to be the greatest philosopher and theologian of the Middle Ages. Aquinas was a prolific writer whose works were so esteemed by the Catholic Church that in 1879 Pope Leo XIII declared Aquinas' teachings to be the official Catholic philosophy. The selection that follows is taken from *Summa Theologica*, where Aquinas proves God's existence in five different ways. The first three ways are cosmological arguments, the fourth way relies on the order of being, and the fifth way is a design argument. Aquinas' contribution to cosmological arguments was little to none. But his statement of the arguments represents the state of the art of the arguments as developed by Jewish and Islamic philosophers and theologians.

The existence of God can be proved in five ways

The first and quite obvious way is taken from a consideration of motion. It is certain and agreed on the basis of what our senses tell us that some things in this world are in motion. But whatever is in motion is moved by something else; for nothing undergoes motion except in so far as it is in a state of *potentiality* in respect of that towards which it is moved. A thing moves in the active sense, on the other hand, in so far as it is in *actuality*. For moving in this sense is simply bringing something from potentiality to actuality; but nothing can be brought into actuality except by something which is itself in actuality. For example, something which is actually hot, like fire, makes wood, which is hot in potentiality, hot in actuality, thereby moving and altering it. Now it is not possible for the same thing to be, at the same time and in the same respect, both in actuality and in potentiality (for what is actually hot cannot be at the same time potentially hot, though it may be potentially cold). So it is impossible that (in the same respect and in the same way) something should be both mover and moved, or that it should move itself. Hence whatever is in motion is moved by something else. And if this something else is itself moved, it must in turn be moved by something else, and so on. But the sequence cannot continue *ad infinitum*, since in this case there would not be any first mover, and hence nothing would move anything else, since subsequent moving things do not move unless moved by an original mover (just as a stick does not move unless moved by a hand). Hence it is necessary to arrive at a first mover which is moved by nothing else; and this everyone understands to be God.

The second way is taken from the notion of an efficient cause. In the world that we perceive around us we find an order of efficient causes, but we never find, nor is it possible that there should be, something that is the efficient cause of itself; for if there were, it would have to be prior to itself, which is impossible. But it is not possible for the series of efficient causes to go on *ad infinitum*. For in each ordered series of efficient causes, the first item is the cause of the next item, and this in turn is the cause of the final item (though there may be more than one intermediate step); and if any one cause is taken away, the effect will also be absent. Hence if there was not a first item in the series of efficient causes there will be no intermediate or final items. But if the series of efficient causes stretches back *ad infinitum*, there will be no first efficient cause, which will mean that there will be no final effect, and no intermediate efficient causes, which is patently not the case. Hence it is necessary to posit some first efficient cause; and this everyone calls "God."

The third way is taken from possibility and necessity, and goes as follows. We come across some things which are merely *possibles* – they can both be and not be; for example we find some things coming into being and passing away, and hence having the possibility of being and not being. But it is impossible for everything there is to be of this sort, since if something has the possibility of not being, then at some time or other it lacks being. So if all things have the possibility of not being, at some time there was nothing at all. But if this were the case, then there would still be nothing now, since what lacks being does not begin to be except through something which is. So if nothing was in being, it was impossible for anything to begin to be, and so there would still be nothing, which is patently not the case. Hence not all beings are possibles, but there must be something in the world which is necessary. Now everything which is necessary either has the cause of its necessity from elsewhere, or it does not. But it is not possible that a sequence of necessary beings having the cause of their necessity elsewhere should continue *ad infinitum* (as was proved in the case of efficient causes). So it is necessary to posit something which is necessary in its own right, and does not have the cause of its necessity from elsewhere but is itself the cause of necessity in other things; and this everyone calls "God."

The fourth way is taken from the gradations to be found in things. We come across some things which are more or less good, or true or noble than others, and so on. But "more" and "less" are terms used of different things by reference to how close they are to what is greatest of its kind (for example, something is "hotter" if it is closer to what is hottest). Hence there is something which is truest and best and noblest, and consequently greatest in being; for things which are truest are greatest in being, as Aristotle says in Book II of his *Metaphysics*. Now what we call the greatest in any kind is the cause of everything of that kind, just as fire, which has the greatest heat, is the cause of everything hot (as Aristotle says in the same book). Hence there is something which is the cause of being and goodness and every other perfection in things; and this we call "God."

The fifth way is taken from the manner in which things are directed or guided. We see some things that lack knowledge, namely natural bodies, working for the sake of a goal or end. This is clear from the fact that they always or often act in the same way to pursue what is best; and this shows that they reach their goal not by chance but from directedness. But things which do not have knowledge do not tend towards a goal unless they are guided by something with knowledge and intelligence, as an arrow is by the archer. Hence there is some intelligent being by whom all natural things are directed to their goal or end; and this we call "God."

Selection from *Dialogues Concerning Natural Religion*
David Hume

David Hume (1711–1776), a Scottish philosopher, did not have his work, *Dialogues Concerning Natural Religion*, published during his lifetime due to atheistic or agnostic overtones in the work. In the selection that follows he discusses the various types of misery and ills and argues that given the evil in the universe, and given that this evil could have been prevented as far as our limited understanding can judge, we cannot infer that God exists.

My sentiments, replied PHILO, are not worth being made a mystery of; and, therefore, without any ceremony, I shall deliver what occurs to me with regard to the present subject. It must, I think, be allowed that, if a very limited intelligence, whom we shall suppose utterly unacquainted with the universe, were assured, that it were the production of a very good, wise, and powerful Being, however finite, he would, from his conjectures, form *beforehand* a different notion of it from what we find it to be by experience; nor would he ever imagine, merely from these attributes of the cause, of which he is informed, that the effect could be so full of vice and misery and disorder, as it appears in this life. Supposing now, that this person were brought into the world, still assured, that it was the workmanship of such a sublime and benevolent Being; he might, perhaps, be surprised at the disappointment; but would never retract his former belief if founded on any very solid argument; since such a limited intelligence must be sensible of his own blindness and ignorance, and must allow, that there may be many solutions of those phenomena, which will forever escape his comprehension. But supposing, which is the real case with regard to man, that this creature is not antecedently convinced of a supreme intelligence, benevolent, and powerful, but is left to gather such a belief from the appearances of things; this entirely alters the case, nor will he ever find any reason for such a conclusion. He may be fully convinced of the narrow limits of his understanding; but this will not help him in forming an inference concerning the goodness of superior powers, since he must form that inference from what he knows, not from what he is ignorant of. The more you exaggerate his weakness and ignorance, the more diffident you render him, and give him the greater suspicion, that such subjects are beyond the reach of his faculties. You are obliged, therefore, to reason with him merely from the known phenomena, and to drop every arbitrary supposition or conjecture.

Did I show you a house or palace, where there was not one apartment convenient or agreeable; where the windows, doors, fires, passages, stairs, and the whole economy of the building were the source of noise, confusion, fatigue, darkness, and the extremes of heat and cold; you would certainly blame the contrivance, without any further examination. The architect would in vain display his subtilty, and prove to you, that if this door or that window were altered, greater ills would ensue. What he says, may be strictly true: The alteration of one particular, while the other parts of the building remain, may only augment the inconveniences. But still you would assert in general, that, if the architect had had skill and good intentions, he might have formed such a plan of the whole, and might have adjusted the parts in such a manner, as would have remedied all or most of these inconveniences. His ignorance, or even your own ignorance of such a plan, will never convince you of the impossibility of it. If you find many inconveniences and deformities in the building, you will always, without entering into any detail, condemn the architect.

In short, I repeat the question: Is the world, considered in general and as it appears to us in this life, different from what a man or such a limited being would, *beforehand*, expect from a very powerful, wise, and benevolent Deity? It must be strange prejudice to assert the contrary. And from thence I conclude, that, however consistent the world may be, allowing certain suppositions and conjectures with the idea of such a Deity, it can never afford us an inference concerning his existence. The consistency is not absolutely denied, only the inference. Conjectures, especially where infinity is excluded from the divine attributes, may, perhaps, be sufficient to prove a consistence; but can never be foundations for any inference.

There seem to be *four* circumstances, on which depend all, or the greatest part of the ills, that molest sensible creatures; and it is not impossible but all these circumstances may be necessary and unavoidable. We know so little beyond common life, or even of common life, that, with regard to the economy of a universe, there is no conjecture, however wild, which may not be just; nor any one, however plausible, which may not be erroneous. All that belongs to human understanding, in this deep ignorance and obscurity, is to be sceptical, or at least cautious; and not to admit of any hypothesis, whatever; much less, of any which is supported by no appearance of probability. Now this I assert to be the case with regard to all the causes of evil, and the circumstances on which it depends. None of them appear to human reason, in the least degree, necessary or unavoidable; nor can we suppose them such, without the utmost licence of imagination.

The *first* circumstance which introduces evil, is that contrivance or economy of the animal creation, by which pains, as well as pleasures, are employed to excite all creatures to action, and make them vigilant in the great work of self-preservation. Now pleasure alone, in its various degrees, seems to human understanding sufficient for this purpose. All animals might be constantly in a state of enjoyment; but when urged by any of the necessities of nature, such as thirst, hunger, weariness; instead of pain, they might feel a diminution of pleasure, by which they might be prompted to seek that object, which is necessary to their subsistence. Men pursue pleasure as eagerly as they avoid pain; at least, they might have been so constituted. It seems, therefore, plainly possible to carry on the business of life without any pain. Why then is any animal ever rendered susceptible of such a sensation? If animals can be free from it an hour, they might enjoy a perpetual exemption from it; and it required as particular a contrivance of their organs to produce that feeling, as to endow them with sight, hearing, or any of the senses. Shall we conjecture, that such a contrivance was necessary, without any appearance of reason? And shall we build on that conjecture as on the most certain truth?

But a capacity of pain would not alone produce pain were it not for the *second* circumstance, viz. the conducting of the world by general laws; and this seems nowise necessary to a perfect Being. It is true, if everything were conducted by particular volitions, the course of nature would be perpetually broken, and no man could employ his reason in the conduct of life. But might not other particular violations remedy this inconvenience? In short, might not the Deity exterminate all ill, wherever it were to be found, and produce all good, without any preparation or long progress of causes and effects?

Besides, we must consider that, according to the present economy of the world, the course of nature, though supposed exactly regular, yet to us appears not so, and many events are uncertain, and many disappoint our expectations. Health and sickness, calm and tempest, with an infinite number of other accidents, whose causes are unknown and variable, have a great influence both on the fortunes of particular persons and on the prosperity of public societies; and indeed all human life, in a manner, depends on such accidents. A Being, therefore, who knows the secret springs of the universe, might easily, by particular volitions, turn all these accidents to the good of mankind, and render the whole world happy, without discovering himself in any operation. A fleet, whose purposes were salutary to society, might always meet with a fair wind; good princes enjoy sound health and long life; persons born to power and authority be framed with good tempers and virtuous dispositions. A few such events as these, regularly and wisely conducted, would change the face of the world; and yet would no more seem to disturb the course of nature or confound human conduct than the present economy of things, where the causes are secret and variable and compounded. Some small touches, given to Caligula's brain in his infancy, might have converted him into a Trajan. One wave, a little higher than the rest, by burying Caesar and his fortune in the bottom of the ocean, might have restored liberty to a considerable part of mankind. There may, for aught we know, be good reasons, why Providence interposes not in this manner, but they are unknown to us; and, though the mere supposition, that such reasons exist, may be sufficient to *save* the conclusion concerning the divine attributes, yet surely it can never be sufficient to *establish* that conclusion.

If every thing in the universe be conducted by general laws, and if animals be rendered susceptible of pain, it scarcely seems possible but some ill must arise in the various shocks of matter, and the various concurrence and opposition of general laws; but this ill would be very rare, were it not for the *third* circumstance which I proposed to mention, viz. the great frugality with which all powers and faculties are distributed to every particular being. So well adjusted are the organs and capacities of all animals, and so well fitted to their preservation, that, as far as history or tradition reaches, there appears not to be any single species which has yet been extinguished in the universe. Every animal has the requisite endowments, but these endowments are bestowed with so scrupulous an economy, that any considerable diminution must entirely destroy the creature. Wherever one power is increased, there is a proportional abatement in the others. Animals, which excel in swiftness, are commonly defective in force. Those, which possess both, are either imperfect in some of their senses, or are oppressed with the most craving wants. The human species, whose chief excellence is reason and sagacity, is of all others the most necessitous, and the most deficient in bodily advantages; without clothes, without arms, without food, without lodging, without any convenience of life, except what they owe to their own skill and industry. In short, nature seems to have formed an exact calculation of the necessities of her creatures; and, like a *rigid master*, has afforded them little more powers or endowments than what are strictly sufficient to supply those necessities. An *indulgent parent* would have bestowed a large stock, in order to guard against accidents, and secure the happiness and welfare of the creature, in the most unfortunate concurrence of circumstances. Every course of life would not have been so surrounded with precipices, that the least departure from the true path, by mistake or necessity, must involve us in misery and ruin. Some reserve, some fund, would have been provided to ensure happiness; nor would the powers and the necessities have been adjusted with so rigid an economy. The Author of Nature is inconceivably powerful; his force is supposed great, if not altogether inexhaustible; nor is there any reason, as far as we can judge, to make him observe this strict frugality in his dealings with his creatures. It would have been better, were his power extremely limited, to have created fewer animals, and to have endowed these with more faculties for their happiness and preservation. A builder is never esteemed prudent, who undertakes a plan, beyond what his stock will enable him to finish.

In order to cure most of the ills of human life, I require not that man should have the wings of the eagle, the swiftness of the stag, the force of the ox, the arms of the lion, the scales of the crocodile or rhinoceros; much less do I demand the sagacity of an angel or cherubim. I am contented to take an increase in one single power or faculty of his soul. Let him be endowed with a greater propensity to industry and labour; a more vigorous spring and activity of mind; a more constant bent to business and application. Let the whole species possess naturally an equal diligence with that which many individuals are able to attain by habit and reflection; and the most beneficial consequences, without any allay of ill, is the immediate and necessary result of this endowment. Almost all the moral, as well as natural evils of human life arise from idleness; and were our species, by the original constitution of their frame, exempt from this vice or infirmity, the perfect cultivation of land, the improvement of arts and manufactures, the exact execution of every office and duty, immediately follow; and men at once may fully reach that state of society, which is so imperfectly attained by the best-regulated government. But as industry is a power, and the most valuable of any, nature seems determined, suitably to her usual maxims, to bestow it on men with a very sparing hand; and rather to punish him severely for his deficiency in it, than to reward him for his attainments. She has so contrived his frame, that nothing but the most violent necessity can oblige him to labour; and she employs all his other wants to overcome, at least in part, the want of diligence, and to endow him with some share of a faculty, of which she has thought fit naturally to bereave him. Here our demands may be allowed very humble, and therefore the more reasonable. If we required the endowments of superior penetration and judgment, of a more delicate taste of beauty, of a nicer sensibility to benevolence and friendship; we might be told, that we impiously pretend to break the order of nature, that we want to exalt ourselves into a higher rank of being, that the presents which we require, not being suitable to our state and condition, would only be pernicious to us. But it is hard; I dare to repeat it, it is hard, that being placed in a world so full of wants and necessities; where almost every being and element is either our foe or refuses its assistance; we should also have our own temper to struggle with, and should be deprived of that faculty which can alone fence against these multiplied evils.

The *fourth* circumstance, whence arises the misery and ill of the universe, is the inaccurate workmanship of all the springs and principles of the great machine of nature. It must be acknowledged, that there are few parts of the universe, which seem not to serve some purpose, and whose removal would not produce a visible defect and disorder in the whole. The parts hang all together; nor can one be touched without affecting the rest, in a greater or less degree. But at the same time, it must be observed, that none of these parts or principles, however useful, are so accurately adjusted, as to keep precisely within those bounds in which their utility consists; but they are, all of them, apt, on every occasion, to run into the one extreme or the other. One would imagine, that this grand production had not received the last hand of the maker; so little finished is every part, and so coarse are the strokes, with which it is executed. Thus, the winds are requisite to convey the vapours along the surface of the globe, and to assist men in navigation; but how oft, rising up to tempests and hurricanes, do they become pernicious? Rains are necessary to nourish all the plants and animals of the earth; but how often are they defective? how often excessive? Heat is requisite to all life and vegetation; but is not always found in the due proportion. On the mixture and secretion of the humours and juices of the body depend the health and prosperity of the animal; but the parts perform not regularly their proper function. What more useful than all the passions of the mind, ambition, vanity, love, anger? But how oft do they break their bounds, and cause the greatest convulsions in society? There is nothing so advantageous in the universe, but what frequently becomes pernicious, by its excess or defect; nor has nature guarded, with the requisite accuracy, against all disorder or confusion. The irregularity is never, perhaps, so great as to destroy any species; but is often sufficient to involve the individuals in ruin and misery.

On the concurrence, then, of these *four* circumstances does all or the greatest part of natural evil depend. Were all living creatures incapable of pain, or were the world administered by particular volitions, evil never could have found access into the universe; and were animals endowed with a large stock of powers and faculties, beyond what strict necessity requires; or were the several springs and principles of the universe so accurately framed as to preserve always the just temperament and medium; there must have been very little ill in comparison of what we feel at present. What then shall we pronounce on this occasion? Shall we say, that these circumstances are not necessary, and that they might easily have been altered in the contrivance of the universe? This decision seems too presumptuous for creatures so blind and ignorant. Let us be more modest in our conclusions. Let us allow, that, if the goodness of the Deity (I mean a goodness like the human) could be established on any tolerable reasons *a priori*, these phenomena, however untoward, would not be sufficient to subvert that principle; but might easily, in some unknown manner, be reconcilable to it. But let us still assert that, as this goodness is not antecedently established, but must be inferred from the phenomena, there can be no grounds for such an inference, while there are so many ills in the universe, and while these ills might so easily have been remedied, as far as human understanding can be allowed to judge on such a subject. I am sceptic enough to allow, that the bad appearances, notwithstanding all my reasonings, may be compatible with such attributes as you suppose; but surely they can never prove these attributes. Such a conclusion cannot result from scepticism; but must arise from the phenomena, and from our confidence in the reasonings which we deduce from these phenomena.

Look round this universe. What an immense profusion of beings, animated and organized, sensible and active! You admire this prodigious variety and fecundity. But inspect a little more narrowly these living existences, the only beings worth regarding. How hostile and destructive to each other! How insufficient all of them for their own happiness! How contemptible or odious to the spectator! The whole presents nothing but the idea of a blind nature, impregnated by a great vivifying principle, and pouring forth from her lap, without discernment or parental care, her maimed and abortive children!

Here the Manichaean system occurs as a proper hypothesis to solve the difficulty; and no doubt, in some respects, it is very specious, and has more probability than the common hypothesis, by giving a plausible account of the strange mixture of good and ill which appears in life. But if we consider, on the other hand, the perfect uniformity and agreement of the parts of the universe, we shall not discover in it any marks of the combat of a malevolent with a benevolent Being. There is indeed an opposition of pains and pleasures in the feelings of sensible creatures; but are not all the operations of nature carried on by an opposition of principles, of hot and cold, moist and dry, light and heavy? The true conclusion is, that the original source of all things is entirely indifferent to all these principles, and has no more regard to good above ill than to heat above cold, or to drought above moisture, or to light above heavy.

There may *four* hypotheses be framed concerning the first causes of the universe: *that* they are endowed with perfect goodness; *that* they have perfect malice; *that* they are opposite and have both goodness and malice; *that* they have neither goodness nor malice. Mixed phenomena can never prove the two former unmixed principles. And the uniformity and steadiness of general laws seem to oppose the third. The fourth, therefore, seems by far the most probable.

What I have said concerning natural evil will apply to moral, with little or no variation; and we have no more reason to infer that the rectitude of the supreme Being resembles human rectitude than that his benevolence resembles the human. Nay, it will be thought, that we have still greater cause to exclude from him moral sentiments, such as we feel them; since moral evil, in the opinion of many, is much more predominant above moral good than natural evil above natural good.

Summary of the Controversy Reduced to Formal Arguments
Gottfried Wilhelm von Leibniz

The German mathematician and philosopher Gottfried Wilhelm von Leibniz (1646–1716) is often considered to be one of the last universal geniuses. He developed the infinitesimal calculus independently of Newton and wrote extensively on science, philosophy, history, and law. He was also an inventor and diplomat. One of Leibniz's major works was *Theodicy* (a vindication of God's justice), where he tries to solve the problem of evil. In *Theodicy* Leibniz argues that the world we live in is in fact the best of all possible worlds, and that there is no gratuitous evil in the world. The excerpt that follows shows how Leibniz responds to objections to his view.

Some persons of discernment have wished me to make this addition. I have the more readily deferred to their opinion, because of the opportunity thereby gained for meeting certain difficulties, and for making observations on certain matters which were not treated in sufficient detail in the work itself.

Objection I

Whoever does not choose the best course is lacking either in power, or knowledge, or goodness.

God did not choose the best course in creating this world.

Therefore God was lacking in power, or knowledge, or goodness.

Answer

I deny the minor, that is to say, the second premiss of this syllogism, and the opponent proves it by this:

Prosyllogism

Whoever makes things in which there is evil, and which could have been made without any evil, or need not have been made at all, does not choose the best course.

God made a world wherein there is evil; a world, I say, which could have been made Without any evil or which need not have been made at all.

Therefore God did not choose the best course.

Answer

I admit the minor of this prosyllogism: for one must confess that there is evil in this world which God has made, and that it would have been possible to make a world without evil or even not to create any world, since its creation depended upon the free will of God. But I deny the major, that is, the first of the two premisses of the prosyllogism, and I might content myself with asking for its proof. In order, however, to give a clearer exposition of the matter, I would justify this denial by pointing out that the best course is not always that one which tends towards avoiding evil, since it is possible that the evil may be accompanied by a greater good. For example, the general of an army will prefer a great victory with a slight wound to a state of affairs without wound and without victory. I have proved this in further detail in this work by pointing out, through instances taken from mathematics and elsewhere, that an imperfection in the part may be required for a greater perfection in the whole. I have followed therein the opinion of St Augustine, who said a hundred times that God permitted evil in order to derive from it a good, that is to say, a greater good; and Thomas Aquinas says (in Libr. 2, *Sent. Dist.*, qu. I, art. I) that the permission of evil tends towards the good of the universe. I have shown that among older writers the fall of Adam was termed *felix culpa*, a fortunate sin, because it had been expiated with immense benefit by the incarnation of the Son of God: for he gave to the universe something more noble than anything there would otherwise have been amongst created beings. For the better understanding of the matter I added, following the example of many good authors, that it was consistent with order and the general good for God to grant to certain of his creatures the opportunity to exercise their freedom, even when He foresaw that they would turn to evil: for God could easily correct the evil, and it was not fitting that in order to prevent sin He should always act in an extraordinary way. It will therefore sufficiently refute the objection to show that a world with evil may be better than a world without evil. But I have gone still further in the work, and have even shown that this universe must be indeed better than every other possible universe.

Objection II

If there is more evil than good in intelligent creatures, there is more evil than good in all God's work.

Now there is more evil than good in intelligent creatures.

Therefore there is more evil than good in all God's work.

Answer

I deny the major and the minor of this conditional syllogism. As for the major, I do not admit it because this supposed inference from the part to the whole, from intelligent creatures to all creatures, assumes tacitly and without proof that creatures devoid of reason cannot be compared or taken into account with those that have reason. But why might not the surplus of good in the non-intelligent creatures that fill the world compensate for and even exceed incomparably the surplus of evil in rational creatures? It is true that the value of the latter is greater; but by way of compensation the others are incomparably greater in number; and it may be that the proportion of number and quantity surpasses that of value and quality.

The minor also I cannot admit, namely, that there is more evil than good in intelligent creatures. One need not even agree that there is more evil than good in the human kind. For it is possible, and even a very reasonable thing, that the glory and the perfection of the blessed may be incomparably greater than the misery and imperfection of the damned, and that here the excellence of the total good in the smaller number may exceed the total evil which is in the greater number. The blessed draw near to divinity through a divine Mediator, so far as can belong to these created beings, and make such progress in good as is impossible for the damned to make in evil, even though they should approach as nearly as may be the nature of demons. God is infinite, and the Devil is finite; good can and does go on *ad infinitum*, whereas evil has its bounds. It may be therefore, and it is probable, that there happens in the comparison between the blessed and the damned the opposite of what I said could happen in the comparison between the happy and the unhappy, namely that in the latter the proportion of degrees surpasses that of numbers, while in the comparison between intelligent and non-intelligent the proportion of numbers is greater than that of values. One is justified in assuming that a thing may be so as long as one does not prove that it is impossible, and indeed what is here put forward goes beyond assumption.

But secondly, even should one admit that there is more evil than good in the human kind, one still has every reason for not admitting that there is more evil than good in all intelligent creatures. For there is an inconceivable number of Spirits, and perhaps of other rational creatures besides: and an opponent cannot prove that in the whole City of God, composed as much of Spirits as of rational animals without number and of endless different kinds, the evil exceeds the good. Although one need not, in order to answer an objection, prove that a thing is, when its mere possibility suffices, I have nevertheless shown in this present work that it is a result of the supreme perfection of the Sovereign of the Universe that the kingdom of God should be the most perfect of all states or governments possible, and that in consequence what little evil there is should be required to provide the full measure of the vast good existing there.

Objection III

If it is always impossible not to sin, it is always unjust to punish.

Now it is always impossible not to sin, or rather all sin is necessary.

Therefore it is always unjust to punish.

The minor of this is proved as follows:

First prosyllogism

Everything predetermined is necessary.

Every event is predetermined.

Therefore every event (and consequently, sin also) is necessary.

Again this second minor is proved thus:

Second prosyllogism

That which is future, that which is foreseen, that which is involved in causes is predetermined.

Every event is of this kind.

Therefore every event is predetermined.

Answer

I admit in a certain sense the conclusion of the second prosyllogism, which is the minor of the first; but I shall deny the major of the first prosyllogism, namely that everything predetermined is necessary; taking "necessity," say the necessity to sin, or the impossibility of not sinning, or of not doing some action, in the sense relevant to the argument, that is, as a necessity essential and absolute, which destroys the morality of action and the justice of punishment. If anyone meant a different necessity or impossibility (that is, a necessity only moral or hypothetical, which will be explained presently) it is plain that we would deny him the major stated in the objections. We might content ourselves with this answer, and demand the proof of the proposition denied: but I am well pleased to justify my manner of procedure in the present work, in order to make the matter clear and to throw more light on this whole subject, by explaining the necessity that must be rejected and the determination that must be allowed. The truth is that the necessity contrary to morality, which must be avoided and which would render punishment unjust, is an insuperable necessity, which would render all opposition unavailing, even though one should wish with all one's heart to avoid the necessary action, and though one should make all possible efforts to that end. Now it is plain that this is not applicable to voluntary actions, since one would not do them if one did not so desire. Thus their provision and predetermination is not absolute, but it presupposes will: if it is certain that one will do them, it is no less certain that one will will to do them. These voluntary actions and their results will not happen whatever one may do and whether one will them or not; but they will happen because one will do, and because one will will to do, that which leads to them. That is involved in provision and predetermination, and forms the reason thereof. The necessity of such events is called conditional or hypothetical, or again necessity of consequence, because it presupposes the will and the other requisites. But the necessity which destroys morality, and renders punishment unjust and reward unavailing, is found in the things that will be whatever one may do and whatever one may will to do: in a word, it exists in that which is essential. This it is which is called an absolute necessity. Thus it avails nothing with regard to what is necessary absolutely to ordain interdicts or commandments, to propose penalties or prizes, to blame or to praise; it will come to pass no more and no less. In voluntary actions, on the contrary, and in what depends upon them, precepts, armed with power to punish and to reward, very often serve, and are included in the order of causes that make action exist. Thus it comes about that not only pains and effort but also prayers are effective, God having had even these prayers in mind before he ordered things, and having made due allowance for them. That is why the precept *Ora et labora* (Pray and work) remains intact. Thus not only those who (under the empty pretext of the necessity of events) maintain that one can spare oneself the pains demanded by affairs, but also those who argue against prayers, fall into that which the ancients even in their time called "the Lazy Sophism." So the predetermination of events by their causes is precisely what contributes to morality instead of destroying it, and the causes incline the will without necessitating it. For this reason the determination we are concerned with is not a necessitation. It is certain (to him who knows all) that the effect will follow this inclination; but this effect does not follow thence by a consequence which is necessary, that is, whose contrary implies contradiction; and it is also by such an inward inclination that the will is determined, without the presence of necessity. Suppose that one has the greatest possible passion (for example, a great thirst), you will admit that the soul can find some reason for resisting it, even if it were only that of displaying its power. Thus though one may never have complete indifference of equipoise, and there is always a predominance of inclination for the course adopted, that predominance does not render absolutely necessary the resolution taken.

Objection IV

Whoever can prevent the sin of others and does not so, but rather contributes to it, although he be fully apprised of it, is accessory thereto.

God can prevent the sin of intelligent creatures; but he does not so, and he rather contributes to it by his cooperation and by the opportunities he causes, although he is fully cognizant of it.

Therefore, etc.

Answer

I deny the major of this syllogism. It may be that one can prevent the sin, but that one ought not to do so, because one could not do so without committing a sin oneself, or (when God is concerned) without acting unreasonably. I have given instances of that, and have applied them to God himself. It may be also that one contributes to the evil, and that one even opens the way to it sometimes, in doing things one is bound to do. And when one does one's duty, or (speaking of God) when, after full consideration, one does that which reason demands, one is not responsible for events, even when one foresees them. One does not will these evils; but one is willing to permit them for a greater good, which one cannot in reason help preferring to other considerations. This is a *consequent* will, resulting from acts of *antecedent* will, in which one wills the good. I know that some persons, in speaking of the antecedent and consequent will of God, have meant by the antecedent that which wills that all men be saved, and by the consequent that which wills, in consequence of persistent sin, that there be some damned, damnation being a result of sin. But these are only examples of a more general notion, and one may say with the same reason, that God wills by his antecedent will that men sin not, and that by his consequent or final and decretory will (which is always followed by its effect) he wills to permit that they sin, this permission being a result of superior reasons. One has indeed justification for saying, in general, that the antecedent will of God tends towards the production of good and the prevention of evil, each taken in itself, and as it were detached (*particulariter et secundum quid*; Thom., I, qu. 19, art. 6) according to the measure of the degree of each good or of each evil. Likewise one may say that the consequent, or final and total, divine will tends towards the production of as many goods as can be put together, whose combination thereby becomes determined, and involves also the permission of some evils and the exclusion of some goods, as the best possible plan of the universe demands. Arminius, in his *Antiperkinsus*, explained very well that the will of God can be called consequent not only in relation to the action of the creature considered beforehand in the divine understanding, but also in relation to other anterior acts of divine will. But it is enough to consider the passage cited from Thomas Aquinas, and that from Scotus (1, dist. 46, qu. II) to see that they make this distinction as I have made it here. Nevertheless if anyone will not suffer this use of the terms, let him put "previous" in place of "antecedent" will, and "final" or "decretory" in place of "consequent" will. For I do not wish to wrangle about words.

Evil and Omnipotence
J. L. Mackie

In the following selection, Mackie discusses the argument from evil and concludes that the theist cannot adequately reply to the argument. This, Mackie says, puts the theist in the unenviable position that not only does she believe something that cannot be proven (namely, that God exists), but she must be prepared to believe something that can be disproved from other beliefs she also holds.

The traditional arguments for the existence of God have been fairly thoroughly criticised by philosophers. But the theologian can, if he wishes, accept this criticism. He can admit that no rational proof of God's existence is possible.

And he can still retain all that is essential to his position, by holding that God's existence is known in some other, non-rational way. I think, however, that a more telling criticism can be made by way of the traditional problem of evil. Here it can be shown, not that religious beliefs lack rational support, but that they are positively irrational, that the several parts of the essential theological doctrine are inconsistent with one another, so that the theologian can maintain his position as a whole only by a much more extreme rejection of reason than in the former case. He must now be prepared to believe, not merely what cannot be proved, but what can be *disproved* from other beliefs that he also holds.

The problem of evil, in the sense in which I shall be using the phrase, is a problem only for someone who believes that there is a God who is both omnipotent and wholly good. And it is a logical problem, the problem of clarifying and reconciling a number of beliefs: it is not a scientific problem that might be solved by further observations, or a practical problem that might be solved by a decision or an action. These points are obvious; I mention them only because they are sometimes ignored by theologians, who sometimes parry a statement of the problem with such remarks as "Well, can you solve the problem yourself?" or "This is a mystery which may be revealed to us later" or "Evil is something to be faced and overcome, not to be merely discussed."

In its simplest form the problem is this: God is omnipotent; God is wholly good; and yet evil exists. There seems to be sonic contradiction between these three propositions, so that if any two of them were true the third would be false. But at the same time all three are essential parts of most theological positions: the theologian, it seems, at once *must* adhere and *cannot consistently* adhere to all three. (The problem does not arise only for theists, but I shall discuss it in the form in which it presents itself for ordinary theism.)

However, the contradiction does not arise immediately; to show it we need some additional premises, or perhaps some quasi-logical rules connecting the terms "good," "evil," and "omnipotent." These additional principles are that good is opposed to evil, in such a way that a good thing always eliminates evil as far as it can, and that there are no limits to what an omnipotent thing can do. From these it follows that a good omnipotent thing eliminates evil completely, and then the propositions that a good omnipotent thing exists, and the evil exists, are incompatible.

A   Adequate Solutions

Now once the problem is fully stated it is clear that it can be solved, in the sense that the problem will not arise if one gives up at least one of the propositions that constitute it. If you are prepared to say that God is not wholly good, or not quite omnipotent, or that evil does not exist, or that good is not opposed to the kind of evil that exists, or that there are limits to what an omnipotent thing can do, then the problem of evil will not arise for you.

There are, then, quite a number of adequate solutions of the problem of evil, and some of these have been adopted, or almost adopted, by various thinkers. For example, a few have been prepared to deny God's omnipotence, and rather more have been prepared to keep the term "omnipotence" but severely to restrict its meaning, recording quite a number of things that an omnipotent being cannot do. Some have said that evil is an illusion, perhaps because they held that the whole world of temporal, changing things is an illusion, and that what we call evil belongs only to this world, or perhaps because they held that although temporal things are much as we see them, those that we call evil are not really evil. Some have said that what we call evil is merely the privation of good, that evil in a positive sense, evil that would really be opposed to good, does not exist. Many have agreed with Pope that disorder is harmony not understood, and that partial evil is universal good. Whether any of these views is true is, of course, another question. But each of them gives an adequate solution of the problem of evil in the sense that if you accept it this problem does not arise for you, though you may, of course, have other problems to face.

But often enough these adequate solutions are only almost adopted. The thinkers who restrict God's power, but keep the term "omnipotence," may reasonably be suspected of thinking, in other contexts, that his power is really unlimited. Those who say that evil is an illusion may also be thinking, inconsistently, that this illusion is itself an evil. Those who say that "evil" is merely privation of good may also be thinking, inconsistently, that privation of good is an evil. (The fallacy here is akin to some forms of the "naturalistic fallacy" in ethics, where some think, for example, that "good" is just what contributes to evolutionary progress, and that evolutionary progress is itself good.) If Pope meant what he said in the first line of his couplet, that "disorder" is only harmony not understood, the "partial evil" of the second line must, for consistency, mean "that which, taken in isolation, falsely appears to be evil," but it would more naturally mean "that which, in isolation, really is evil." The second line, in fact, hesitates between two views, that "partial evil" isn't really evil, since only the universal quality is real, and that "partial evil" is really an evil, but only a little one.

In addition, therefore, to adequate solutions, we must recognise unsatisfactory inconsistent solutions, in which there is only a half-hearted or temporary rejection of one of the propositions which together constitute the problem. In these, one of the constituent propositions is explicitly rejected, but it is covertly reasserted or assumed elsewhere in the system.

B Fallacious Solutions

Besides these half-hearted solutions, which explicitly reject but implicitly assert one of the constituent propositions, there are definitely fallacious solutions which explicitly maintain all the constituent propositions, but implicitly reject at least one of them in the course of the argument that explains away the problem of evil.

There are, in fact, many so-called solutions which purport to remove the contradiction without abandoning any of its constituent propositions. These must be fallacious, as we can see from the very statement of the problem, but it is not so easy to see in each case precisely where the fallacy lies. I suggest that in all cases the fallacy has the general form suggested above: in order to solve the problem one (or perhaps more) of its constituent propositions is given up, but in such a way that it appears to have been retained, and can therefore be asserted without qualification in other contexts. Sometimes there is a further complication: the supposed solution moves to and fro between, say, two of the constituent propositions, at one point asserting the first of these but covertly abandoning the second, at another point asserting the second but covertly abandoning the first. These fallacious solutions often turn upon some equivocation with the words "good" and "evil," or upon some vagueness about the way in which good and evil are opposed to one another, or about how much is meant by "omnipotence." I propose to examine some of these so-called solutions, and to exhibit their fallacies in detail. Incidentally, I shall also be considering whether an adequate solution could be reached by a minor modification of one or more of the constituent propositions, which would, however, still satisfy all the essential requirements of ordinary theism.

1 "Good cannot exist without evil" or "Evil is necessary as a counterpart to good."

It is sometimes suggested that evil is necessary as a counterpart to good, that if there were no evil there could be no good either, and that this solves the problem of evil. It is true that it points to an answer to the question "Why should there be evil?" But it does so only by qualifying some of the propositions that constitute the problem.

First it sets a limit to what God can do, saying that God cannot create good without simultaneously creating evil, and this means either that God is not omnipotent or that there are some limits to what an omnipotent thing can do. It may be replied that these limits are always presupposed, that omnipotence has never meant the power to do what is logically impossible, and on the present view the existence of good without evil would be a logical impossibility. This interpretation of omnipotence may, indeed, be accepted as a modification of our original account which does not reject anything that is essential to theism, and I shall in general assume it in the subsequent discussion. It is, perhaps, the most common theistic view, but I think that some theists at least have maintained that God can do what is logically impossible. Many theists, at any rate, have held that logic itself is created or laid down by God, that logic is the way in which God arbitrarily chooses to think. (This is, of course, parallel to the ethical view that morally right actions are those which God arbitrarily chooses to command, and the two views encounter similar difficulties.) And *this* account of logic is clearly inconsistent with the view that God is bound by logical necessities – unless it is possible for an omnipotent being to bind himself, an issue which we shall consider later, when we come to the Paradox of Omnipotence. This solution of the problem of evil cannot, therefore, be consistently adopted along with the view that logic is itself created by God.

But, secondly, this solution denies that evil is opposed to good in our original sense. If good and evil are counterparts, a good thing will not "eliminate evil as far as it can." Indeed, this view suggests that good and evil are not strictly qualities of things at all. Perhaps the suggestion is that good and evil are related in much the same way as great and small. Certainly, when the term "great" is used relatively as a condensation of "greater than so-and-so," and "small" is used correspondingly, greatness and smallness are counterparts and cannot exist without each other. But in this sense greatness is not a quality, not an intrinsic feature of anything; and it would be absurd to think of a movement in favour of greatness and against smallness in this sense. Such a movement would be self-defeating, since relative greatness can be promoted only by a simultaneous promotion of relative smallness. I feel sure that no theists would be content to regard God's goodness as analogous to this – as if what he supports were not the good but the better, and as if he had the paradoxical aim that all things should be better than other things.

This point is obscured by the fact that "great" and "small" seem to have an absolute as well as a relative sense. I cannot discuss here whether there is absolute magnitude or not, but if there is, there could be an absolute sense for "great," it could mean of at least a certain size, and it would make sense to speak of all things getting bigger, of a universe that was expanding all over, and therefore it would make sense to speak of promoting greatness. But in this sense great and small are not logically necessary counterparts: either quality could exist without the other. There would be no logical impossibility in everything's being small or in everything's being great.

Neither in the absolute nor in the relative sense, then, of "great" and "small" do these terms provide an analogy of the sort that would be needed to support this solution of the problem of evil. In neither case are greatness and smallness both necessary counterparts and mutually opposed forces or possible objects for support and attack.

It may be replied that good and evil are necessary counterparts in the same way as any quality and its logical opposite: redness can occur, it is suggested, only if non–redness also occurs. But unless evil is merely the privation of good, they are not logical opposites, and some further argument would be needed to show that they are counterparts in the same way as genuine logical opposites. Let us assume that this could be given. There is still doubt of the correctness of the metaphysical principle that a quality must have a real opposite: I suggest that it is not really impossible that everything should be, say, red, that the truth is merely that if everything were red we should not notice redness, and so we should have no word "red"; we observe and give names to qualities only if they have real opposites. If so, the principle that a term must have an opposite would belong only to our language or to our thought, and would not be an ontological principle, and, correspondingly, the rule that good cannot exist without evil would not state a logical necessity of a sort that God would just have to put up with. God might have made everything good, though we should not have noticed it if he had.

But, finally, even if we concede that this is an ontological principle, it will provide a solution for the problem of evil only if one is prepared to say, "Evil exists, but only just enough evil to serve as the counterpart of good." I doubt whether any theist will accept this. After all, the ontological requirement that non-redness should occur would be satisfied even if all the universe, except for a minute speck, were red, and, if there were a corresponding requirement for evil as a counterpart to good, a minute dose of evil would presumably do. But theists are not usually willing to say, in all contexts, that all the evil that occurs is a minute and necessary dose.

2 "Evil is necessary as a means to good."

It is sometimes suggested that evil is necessary for good not as a counterpart but as a means. In its simple form this has little plausibility as a solution of the problem of evil, since it obviously implies a severe restriction of God's power. It would be a *causal* law that you cannot have a certain end without a certain means, so that if God has to introduce evil as a means to good, he must be subject to at least some causal laws. This certainly conflicts with what a theist normally means by omnipotence. This view of God as limited by causal laws also conflicts with the view that causal laws are themselves made by God, which is more widely held than the corresponding view about the laws of logic. This conflict, would, indeed, be resolved if it were possible for an omnipotent being to bind himself, and this possibility has still to be considered. Unless a favourable answer can be given to this question, the suggestion that evil is necessary as a means to good solves the problem of evil only by denying one of its constituent propositions, either that God is omnipotent or that "omnipotent" means what it says.

3 "The universe is better with some evil in it than it could be if there were no evil."

Much more important is a solution which at first seems to be a mere variant of the previous one, that evil may contribute to the goodness of a whole in which it is found, so that the universe as a whole is better as it is, with some evil in it, than it would be if there were no evil. This solution may be developed in either of two ways. It may be supported by an aesthetic analogy, by the fact that contrasts heighten beauty, that in a musical work, for example, there may occur discords which somehow add to the beauty of the work as a whole. Alternatively, it may be worked out in connexion with the notion of progress, that the best possible organisation of the universe will not be static, but progressive, that the gradual overcoming of evil by good is really a finer thing than would be the eternal unchallenged supremacy of good.

In either case, this solution usually starts from the assumption that the evil whose existence gives rise to the problem of evil is primarily what is called physical evil, that is to say, pain. In Hume's rather half-hearted presentation of the problem of evil, the evils that he stresses are pain and disease, and those who reply to him argue that the existence of pain and disease makes possible the existence of sympathy, benevolence, heroism, and the gradually successful struggle of doctors and reformers to overcome these evils. In fact, theists often seize the opportunity to accuse those who stress the problem of evil of taking a low, materialistic view of good and evil, equating these with pleasure and pain, and of ignoring the more spiritual goods which can arise in the struggle against evils.

But let us see exactly what is being done here. Let us call pain and misery "first order evil" or "evil (1)." What contrasts with this, namely, pleasure and happiness, will be called "first order good" or "good (1)." Distinct from this is "second order good" or "good (2)" which somehow emerges in a complex situation in which evil (1) is a necessary component – logically, not merely causally, necessary. (Exactly how it emerges does not matter: in the crudest version of this solution good (2) is simply the heightening of happiness by the contrast with misery, in other versions it includes sympathy with suffering, heroism in facing danger, and the gradual decrease of first order evil and increase of first order good.) It is also being assumed that second order good is more important than first order good or evil, in particular that it more than outweighs the first order evil it involves.

Now this is a particularly subtle attempt to solve the problem of evil. It defends God's goodness and omnipotence on the ground that (on a sufficiently long view) this is the best of all logically possible worlds, because it includes the important second order goods, and yet it admits that real evils, namely first order evils, exist. But does it still hold that good and evil are opposed? Not, clearly, in the sense that we set out originally: good does not tend to eliminate evil in general. Instead, we have a modified, a more complex pattern. First order good (e.g. happiness) contrasts with first order evil (e.g. misery): these two are opposed in a fairly mechanical way; some second order goods (e.g. benevolence) try to maximize first order good and minimize first order evil; but God's goodness is not this, it is rather the will to maximize *second* order good. We might, therefore, call God's goodness an example of a third order goodness, or good (3). While this account is different from our original one, it might well be held to be an improvement on it, to give a more accurate description of the way in which good is opposed to evil, and to be consistent with the essential theist position.

There might, however, be several objections to this solution.

First, some might argue that such qualities as benevolence – and *a fortiori* the third order goodness which promotes benevolence – have a merely derivative value, that they are not higher sorts of good, but merely means to good (1), that is, to happiness, so that it would be absurd for God to keep misery in existence in order to make possible the virtues of benevolence, heroism, etc. The theist who adopts the present solution must, of course, deny this, but he can do so with some plausibility, so I should not press this objection.

Secondly, it follows from this solution that God is not in our sense benevolent or sympathetic: he is not concerned to minimise evil (1), but only to promote good (2); and this might be a disturbing conclusion for some theists.

But, thirdly, the fatal objection is this. Our analysis shows clearly the possibility of the existence of a *second* order evil, an evil (2) contrasting with good (2) as evil (1) contrasts with good (1). This would include malevolence, cruelty, callousness, cowardice, and states in which good (1) is decreasing and evil (1) increasing. And just as good (2) is held to be the important kind of good, the kind that God is concerned to promote, so evil (2) will, by analogy, be the important kind of evil, the kind which God, if he were wholly good and omnipotent, would eliminate. And yet evil (2) plainly exists, and indeed most theists (in other contexts) stress its existence more than that of evil (1). We should, therefore, state the problem of evil in terms of second order evil, and against this form of the problem the present solution is useless.

An attempt might be made to use this solution again, at a higher level, to explain the occurrence of evil (2): indeed the next main solution that we shall examine does just this, with the help of some new notions. Without any fresh notions, such a solution would have little plausibility: for example, we could hardly say that the really important good was a good (3), such as the increase of benevolence in proportion to cruelty, which logically required for its occurrence the occurrence of some second order evil. But even if evil (2) could be explained in this way, it is fairly clear that there would be third order evils contrasting with this third order good: and we should be well on the way to an infinite regress, where the solution of a problem of evil, stated in terms of evil (*n*), indicated the existence of an evil (*n* + 1), and a further problem to be solved.

4 "Evil is due to human free will."

Perhaps the most important proposed solution of the problem of evil is that evil is not to be ascribed to God at all, but to the independent actions of human beings, supposed to have been endowed by God with freedom of the will. This solution may be combined with the preceding one: first order evil (e.g. pain) may be justified as a logically necessary component m second order good (e.g. sympathy) while second order evil (e.g. cruelty) is not justified, but is so ascribed to human beings that God cannot be held responsible for it. This combination evades my third criticism of the preceding solution.

The free will solution also involves the preceding solution at a higher level. To explain why a wholly good God gave men free will although it would lead to some important evils, it must be argued that it is better on the whole that men should act freely, and sometimes err, than that they should be innocent automata, acting rightly in a wholly determined way. Freedom, that is to say, is now treated as a third order good, and as being more valuable than second order goods (such as sympathy and heroism) would be if they were deterministically produced, and it is being assumed that second order evils, such as cruelty, are logically necessary accompaniments of freedom, just as pain is a logically necessary pre-condition of sympathy.

I think that this solution is unsatisfactory primarily because of the incoherence of the notion of freedom of the will: but I cannot discuss this topic adequately here, although some of my criticisms will touch upon it.

First I should query the assumption that second order evils are logically necessary accompaniments of freedom. I should ask this: if God has made men such that in their free choices they sometimes prefer what is good and sometimes what is evil, why could he not have made men such that they always freely choose the good? If there is no logical impossibility in a man's freely choosing the good on one, or on several, occasions, there cannot be a logical impossibility in his freely choosing the good on every occasion. God was not, then, faced with a choice between making innocent automata and making beings who, in acting freely, would sometimes go wrong: there was open to him the obviously better possibility of making beings who would act freely but always go right. Clearly, his failure to avail himself of this possibility is inconsistent with his being both omnipotent and wholly good.

If it is replied that this objection is absurd, that the making of some wrong choices is logically necessary for freedom, it would seem that "freedom" must here mean complete randomness or indeterminacy, including randomness with regard to the alternatives good and evil, in other words that men's choices and consequent actions can be "free" only if they are not determined by their characters. Only on this assumption can God escape the responsibility for men's actions; for if he made them as they are, but did not determine their wrong choices, this can only be because the wrong choices are not determined by men as they are. But then if freedom is randomness, how can it be a characteristic of will? And, still more, how can it be the most important good? What value or merit would there be in free choices if these were random actions which were not determined by the nature of the agent?

I conclude that to make this solution plausible two different senses of "freedom" must be confused, one sense which will justify the view that freedom is a third order good, more valuable than other goods would be without it, and another sense, sheer randomness, to prevent us from ascribing to God a decision to make men such that they sometimes go wrong when he might have made them such that they would always freely go right.

This criticism is sufficient to dispose of this solution. But besides this there is a fundamental difficulty in the notion of an omnipotent God creating men with free will, for if men's wills are really free this must mean that even God cannot control them, that is, that God is no longer omnipotent. It may be objected that God's gift of freedom to men does not mean that he *cannot* control their wills, but that he always *refrains* from controlling their wills. But why, we may ask, should God refrain from controlling evil wills? Why should he not leave men free to will rightly, but intervene when he sees them beginning to will wrongly? If God could do this, but does not, and if he is wholly good, the only explanation could be that even a wrong free act of will is not really evil, that its freedom is a value which outweighs its wrongness, so that there would be a loss of value if God took away the wrongness and the freedom together. But this is utterly opposed to what theists say about sin in other contexts. The present solution of the problem of evil, then, can be maintained only in the form that God has made men so free that he *cannot* control their wills.

This leads us to what I call the Paradox of Omnipotence: can an omnipotent being make things which he cannot subsequently control? Or, what is practically equivalent to this, can an omnipotent being make rules which then bind himself? (These are practically equivalent because any such rules could be regarded as setting certain things beyond his control, and *vice versa*). The second of these formulations is relevant to the suggestions that we have already met, that an omnipotent God creates the rules of logic or causal laws, and is then bound by them.

It is clear that this is a paradox: the questions cannot be answered satisfactorily either in the affirmative or in the negative. If we answer "Yes," it follows that if God actually makes things which he cannot control, or makes rules which bind himself, he is not omnipotent once he has made them: there are then things which he cannot do. But if we answer "No," we are immediately asserting that there are things which he cannot do, that is to say that he is already not omnipotent.

It cannot be replied that the question which sets this paradox is not a proper question. It would make perfectly good sense to say that a human mechanic has made a machine which he cannot control: if there is any difficulty about the question it lies in the notion of omnipotence itself.

This, incidentally, shows that although we have approached this paradox from the free will theory, it is equally a problem for a theological determinist. No one thinks that machines have free will, yet they may well be beyond the control of their makers. The determinist might reply that anyone who makes anything determines its ways of acting, and so determines its subsequent behaviour: even the human mechanic does this by his choice of materials and structure for his machine, though he does not know all about either of these: the mechanic thus determines, though he may not foresee, his machine's actions. And since God is omniscient, and since his creation of things is total, he both determines and foresees the ways in which his creatures will act. We may grant this, but it is beside the point. The question is not whether God originally determined the future actions of his creatures, but whether he can subsequently control their actions, or whether he was able in his original creation to put things beyond his subsequent control. Even on determinist principles the answers "Yes" and "No" are equally irreconcilable with God's omnipotence.

Before suggesting a solution of this paradox, I would point out that there is a parallel Paradox of Sovereignty. Can a legal sovereign make a law restricting its own future legislative power? For example, could the British parliament make a law forbidding any future parliament to socialise banking, and also forbidding the future repeal of this law itself? Or could the British parliament, which was legally sovereign in Australia in, say, 1899, pass a valid law, or series of laws, which made it no longer sovereign in 1933? Again, neither the affirmative nor the negative answer is really satisfactory. If we were to answer "Yes," we should be admitting the validity of a law which, if it were actually made, would mean that parliament was no longer sovereign. If we were to answer "No," we should be admitting that there is a law, not logically absurd, which parliament cannot validly make, that is, that parliament is not now a legal sovereign. This paradox can be solved in the following way. We should distinguish between first order laws, that is laws governing the actions of individuals and bodies other than the legislature, and second order laws, that is laws about laws, laws governing the actions of the legislature itself. Correspondingly, we should distinguish two orders of sovereignty, first order sovereignty (sovereignty (1)) which is unlimited authority to make first order laws, and second order sovereignty (sovereignty (2)) which is unlimited authority to make second order laws. If we say that parliament is sovereign we might mean that any parliament at any time has sovereignty (1), or we might mean that parliament has both sovereignty (1) and sovereignty (2) at present, but we cannot without contradiction mean both that the present parliament has sovereignty (2) and that every parliament at every time has sovereignty (1), for if the present parliament has sovereignty (2) it may use it to take away the sovereignty (1) of later parliaments. What the paradox shows is that we cannot ascribe to any continuing institution legal sovereignty in an inclusive sense.

The analogy between omnipotence and sovereignty shows that the paradox of omnipotence can be solved in a similar way. We must distinguish between first order omnipotence (omnipotence (1)), that is unlimited power to act, and second order omnipotence (omnipotence (2)), that is unlimited power to determine what powers to act things shall have. Then we could consistently say that God all the time has omnipotence (1), but if so no beings at any time have powers to act independently of God. Or we could say that God at one time had omnipotence (2), and used it to assign independent powers to act to certain things, so that God thereafter did not have omnipotence (1). But what the paradox shows is that we cannot consistently ascribe to any continuing being omnipotence is an inclusive sense.

An alternative solution of this paradox would be simply to deny that God is a continuing being, that any times can be assigned to his actions at all. But on this assumption (which also has difficulties of its own) no meaning can be given to the assertion that God made men with wills so free that he could not control them. The paradox of omnipotence can be avoided by putting God outside time, but the free will solution of the problem of evil cannot be saved in this way, and equally it remains impossible to hold that an omnipotent God binds himself by causal or logical laws.

Conclusion

Of the proposed solutions of the problem of evil which we have examined, none has stood up to criticism. There may be other solutions which require examination, but this study strongly suggests that there is no valid solution of the problem which does not modify at least one of the constituent propositions in a way which would seriously affect the essential core of the theistic position.

Quite apart from the problem of evil, the paradox of omnipotence has shown that God's omnipotence must in any case be restricted in one way or another, that unqualified omnipotence cannot be ascribed to any being that continues through time. And if God and his actions are not in time, can omnipotence, or power of any sort, be meaningfully ascribed to him?

Was It within God's Power to Create Any Possible World He Pleased?
Alvin Plantinga

Alvin Plantinga, a theist and a philosophy professor at the University of Notre Dame, has written extensively in the areas of epistemology and philosophy of religion. In the excerpt below, Plantinga takes up the question of whether God can create any world God pleases, for if God can, then it seems that God can create a world in which we act freely and always do what is right. Plantinga argues that there are worlds that God, although all-powerful, cannot create. In particular, he argues that given that we sometimes make the wrong choice, God cannot create a world in which we always make the right choice.

This is indeed the crucial question for the Free Will Defense. If we wish to discuss it with insight and authority, we shall have to look into the idea of *possible worlds*. And a sensible first question is this: what sort of thing is a possible world? The basic idea is that a possible world is a *way things could have been*; it is a *state of affairs* of some kind. Earlier we spoke of states of affairs, in particular of good and evil states of affairs. Suppose we look at this idea in more detail. What sort of thing is a state of affairs? The following would be examples:

Nixon's having won the 1972 election

7 + 5's being equal to 12

All men's being mortal

and

Gary, Indiana's having a really nasty pollution problem.

These are *actual* states of affairs: states of affairs that do in fact *obtain*. And corresponding to each such actual state of affairs there is a true proposition – in the above cases, the corresponding propositions would be *Nixon won the 1972 presidential election, 7 + 5 is equal to 12, all men are mortal,* and *Gary, Indiana, has a really nasty pollution problem.* A proposition *p corresponds* to a state of affairs *s*, in this sense, if it is impossible that *p* be true and *s* fail to obtain and impossible that *s* obtain and *p* fail to be true.

But just as there are false propositions, so there are states of affairs that do *not* obtain or are *not* actual. *Kissinger's having swum the Atlantic* and *Hubert Horatio Humphrey's having run a mile in four minutes* would be examples. Some states of affairs that do not obtain are *impossible*: e.g., *Hubert's having drawn a square circle*, *7 + 5's being equal to 75*, and *Agnew's having a brother who was an only child*. The propositions corresponding to these states of affairs, of course, are necessarily false. So there are states of affairs that *obtain or are actual* and also states of affairs that don't obtain. Among the latter some are *impossible* and others are possible. And a possible world is a possible state of affairs. Of course not every possible state of affairs is a possible world; *Hubert's having run a mile in four minutes* is a possible state of affairs but not a possible world. No doubt it is an *element* of many possible worlds, but it isn't itself inclusive enough to be one. To be a possible world, a state of affairs must be very large – so large "as to be *complete* or *maximal.*

To get at this idea of completeness we need a couple of definitions. As we have already seen . . . a state of affairs *A includes* a state of affairs *B* if it is not possible that *A* obtain and *B* not obtain or if the conjunctive state of affairs *A but not B* – the state of affairs that obtains if and only if *A* obtains and *B* does not – is not possible. For example, *Jim Whittaker's being the first American to climb Mt Everest* includes *Jim Whittaker's being an American*. It also includes *Mt. Everest's being climbed, something's being climbed, no American's having climbed Everest before Whittaker did*, and the like. *Inclusion* among states of affairs is like *entailment* among propositions; and where a state of affairs *A* includes a state of affairs *B*, the proposition corresponding to *A* entails the one corresponding to *B*. Accordingly, *Jim Whittaker is the first American to climb Everest* entails *Mt Everest has been climbed, something has been climbed*, and *no American climbed Everest before Whittaker did*. Now suppose we say further that a state of affairs *A precludes* a state of affairs *B* if it is not possible that *both* obtain, or if the conjunctive state of affairs *A* and *B* is impossible. Thus *Whittaker's being the first American to climb Mt Everest* precludes *Luther Jerstad's being the first American to climb Everest*, as well as *Whittaker's never having climbed any mountains*. If *A* precludes *B*, then *A*'s corresponding proposition entails the denial of the one corresponding to *B*. Still further, let's say that the *complement* of a state of affairs is the state of affairs that obtains just in case *A* does not obtain. [Or we might say that the complement (call it $\bar{A}$) of *A* is the state of affairs corresponding to the *denial or negation* of the proposition corresponding to *A*.] Given these definitions, we can say what it is for a state of affairs to be *complete*: *A* is a complete state of affairs if and only if for every state of affairs *B*, either *A includes B or A precludes B*. (We could express the same thing by saying that if *A* is a complete state of affairs, then for every state of affairs *B*, either *A* includes *B* or *A* includes $\bar{B}$, the complement of *B*.) And now we are able to say what a possible world is: a possible world is any possible state of affairs that is complete. If *A* is a possible world, then it says something about everything; every state of affairs S is either included in or precluded by it.

Corresponding to each possible world W, furthermore, there is a set of propositions that I'll call *the book on W*. A proposition is in the book on W just in case the state of affairs to which it corresponds is included in W. Or we might express it like this. Suppose we say that a proposition P *is true in a world W* if and only if P *would have been true if W had been actual* – if and only if, that is, it is not possible that W be actual and P be false. Then the book on W is the set of propositions true in W. Like possible worlds, books are *complete*; *if B* is a book, then for any proposition P, either P or the denial of P will be a member of B. A book is a *maximal consistent set* of propositions; it is so large that the addition of another proposition to it always yields an explicitly inconsistent set.

Of course, for each possible world there is exactly one book corresponding to it (that is, for a given world W there is just one book B such that each member of B is true in W); and for each book there is just one world to which it corresponds. So every world has its book.

It should be obvious that exactly one possible world is actual. At *least* one must be, since the set of true propositions is a maximal consistent set and hence a book. But then it corresponds to a possible world, and the possible world corresponding to this set of propositions (since it's the set of *true* propositions) will be actual. On the other hand there is at *most* one actual world. For suppose there were two: W and W'. These worlds cannot include all the very same states of affairs; if they did, they would be the very same world. So there must be at least one state of affairs S such that W includes S and W' does not. But a possible world is maximal; W, therefore, includes the complement $\bar{S}$ of S. So if both W and W' were actual, as we have supposed, then both S and S' would be actual – which is impossible. So there can't be more than one possible world that is actual.

Leibniz pointed out that a proposition p is necessary if it is true in every possible world. We may add that p is possible if it is true in one world and impossible if true in none. Furthermore, p *entails q* if there is no possible world in which p is true and q is false, and p *is consistent with q if* there is at least one world in which both p and q are true.

A further feature of possible worlds is that people (and other things) *exist* in them. Each of us exists in the actual world, obviously; but a person also exists in many worlds distinct from the actual world. It would be a mistake, of course, to think of all of these worlds as somehow "going on" at the same time, with the same person reduplicated through these worlds and actually existing in a lot of different ways. This is not what is meant by saying that the same person exists in different possible worlds. What is meant, instead, is this: a person Paul exists in each of those possible worlds W which is such that, if W *had been actual, Paul* would have existed – actually existed. Suppose Paul had been an inch taller than he is, or a better tennis player. Then the world that does in fact obtain would not have been actual; some other world – W', let's say – would have obtained instead. If W' had been actual, Paul would have existed; so Paul exists in W'.

(Of course there are still other possible worlds in which Paul does not exist – worlds, for example, in which there are no people at all.) Accordingly, when we say that Paul exists in a world *W*, what we mean is that Paul *would have* existed had *W* been actual. Or we could put it like this: Paul exists in each world *W* that includes the state of affairs consisting in Paul's existence. We can put this still more simply by saying that Paul exists in those worlds whose books contain the proposition *Paul exists*.

But isn't there a problem here? *Many* people are named "Paul": Paul the apostle, Paul J. Zwier, John Paul Jones, and many other famous Pauls. So who goes with "Paul exists"? Which Paul? The answer has to do with the fact that books contain *propositions* – not sentences. They contain the sort of thing sentences are used to express and assert. And the same sentence – "Aristotle is wise," for example – can be used to express many different propositions. When Plato used it, he asserted a proposition predicating wisdom of his famous pupil; when Jackie Onassis uses it, she asserts a proposition predicating wisdom of her wealthy husband. These are distinct propositions (we might even think they differ in truth value); but they are expressed by the same sentence. Normally (but not always) we don't have much trouble determining which of the several propositions expressed by a given sentence is relevant in the context at hand. So in this case a given person, Paul, exists in a world *W* if and only if *W*'s book contains the proposition that says that he – that particular person – exists. The fact that the sentence we use to express this proposition can also be used to express other propositions is not relevant.

After this excursion into the nature of books and worlds we can return to our question. Could God have created just any world He chose? Before addressing the question, however, we must note that God does not, strictly speaking, *create* any possible worlds or states of affairs at all. What He creates are the heavens and the earth and all that they contain. But He has not created states of affairs. There are, for example, the state of affairs consisting in God's existence and the state of affairs consisting in His nonexistence. That is, there is such a thing as the state of affairs consisting in the existence of God, and there is also such a thing as the state of affairs consisting in the nonexistence of God, just as there are the two propositions *God exists* and *God does not exist*. The theist believes that the first state of affairs is actual and the first proposition true, the atheist believes that the second state of affairs is actual and the second proposition true. But, of course, both propositions exist, even though just one is true. Similarly, there are two states of affairs here, just one of which is actual. So both states of affairs *exist*, but only one *obtains*. And God has not created either one of them since there never was a time at which either did not exist. Nor has He created the state of affairs consisting in the earth's existence; there was a time when *the earth* did not exist, but none when the state of affairs consisting in the earth's existence didn't exist. Indeed, God did not bring into existence any states of affairs at all. What He did was to perform actions of a certain sort – creating the heavens and the earth, for example – which resulted in the *actuality of* certain states of affairs. God *actualizes* states of affairs. He actualizes the possible world that does in fact obtain; He does not create it. And while He has created Socrates, He did not create the state of affairs consisting in Socrates' existence.[1]

Bearing this in mind, let's finally return to our question. Is the atheologian right in holding that if God is omnipotent, then he could have actualized or created any possible world He pleased? Not obviously. First, we must ask ourselves whether God is a *necessary* or a *contingent* being. A *necessary* being is one that exists in every possible world – one that would have existed no matter which possible world had been actual; a contingent being exists only in some possible worlds. Now if God is not a necessary being (and many, perhaps most, theists think that He is not), then clearly enough there will be many possible worlds He could not have actualized – all those, for example, in which He does not exist. Clearly, God could not have created a world in which He doesn't even exist.

So, if God is a contingent being then there are many possible worlds beyond His power to create. But this is really irrelevant to our present concerns. For perhaps the atheologian can maintain his case if he revises his claim to avoid this difficulty; perhaps he will say something like this: if God is omnipotent, then He could have actualized any of those possible worlds *in which He exists*. So if He exists and is omnipotent, He could have actualized (contrary to the Free Will Defense) any of those possible worlds in which He exists and in which there exist free creatures who do no wrong. He could have actualized worlds containing moral good but no moral evil. Is this correct?

Let's begin with a trivial example. You and Paul have just returned from an Australian hunting expedition: your quarry was the elusive double-wattled cassowary. Paul captured an aardvark, mistaking it for a cassowary. The creature's disarming ways have won it a place in Paul's heart; he is deeply attached to it. Upon your return to the States you offer Paul $500 for his aardvark, only to be rudely turned down. Later you ask yourself, "What would he have done if I'd offered him $700?" Now what is it, exactly, that you are asking? What you're really asking in a way is whether, under a *specific set of conditions*, Paul would have sold it. These conditions include your having offered him $700 rather than $500 for the aardvark, everything else being as much as possible like the conditions that did in fact obtain. Let *S'* be this set of conditions or state of affairs. *S'* includes the state of affairs consisting in your offering Paul $700 (instead of the $500 you did offer him); of course it does not include his *accepting* your offer, and it does not include his *rejecting* it; for the rest, the conditions it includes are just like the ones that did obtain in the actual world. So, for example, *S'* includes Paul's being free to accept the offer and free to refrain; and if in fact the going rate for an aardvark was $650, then *S'* includes the state of affairs consisting in the going rate's being $650. So we might put your question by asking which of the following conditionals is true:

(1) If the state of affairs *S'* had obtained, Paul would have accepted the offer
(2) If the state of affairs *S'* had obtained, Paul would not have accepted the offer.

It seems clear that at least one of these conditionals is true, but naturally they can't both be; so exactly one is.

Now since S' includes neither Paul's accepting the offer nor his rejecting it, the antecedent of (1) and (2) does not entail the consequent of either. That is,

(3) S' obtains

does not entail either

(4) Paul accepts the offer

or

(5) Paul does not accept the offer.

So there are possible worlds in which both (3) and (4) are true, and other possible worlds in which both (3) and (5) are true.

We are now in a position to grasp an important fact. Either (1) or (2) is in fact true; and either way there are possible worlds God could not have actualized. Suppose, first of all, that (1) is true. Then it was beyond the power of God to create a world in which (1) Paul is free to sell his aardvark and free to refrain, and in which the other states of affairs included in S' obtain, and (2) Paul does not sell. That is, it was beyond His power to create a world in which (3) and (5) are both true. There is at least one possible world like this, but God, despite His omnipotence, could not have brought about its actuality. For let W be such a world. To actualize W, God must bring it about that Paul is free with respect to this action, and that the other states of affairs included in S' obtain. But (1), as we are supposing, is true; so if God had actualized S' and left Paul *free* with respect to this action, he would have sold: in which case W would not have been actual. If, on the other hand, God had *brought it about* that Paul didn't sell or had *caused him* to refrain from selling, then Paul would not have been free with respect to this action; then S' would not have been actual (since S' includes Paul's being free with respect to it), and W would not have been actual since W includes S'.

Of course if it is (2) rather than (1) that is true, then another class of worlds was beyond God's power to actualize – those, namely, in which S' obtains and Paul *sells* his aardvark. These are the worlds in which both (3) and (4) are true. But either (1) or (2) is true. Therefore, there are possible worlds God could not have actualized. If we consider whether or not God could have created a world in which, let's say, both (3) and (4) are true, we see that the answer depends upon a peculiar kind of fact; it depends upon what Paul would have freely chosen to do in a certain situation. So there are any number of possible worlds such that it is partly up to Paul whether God can create them.[2]

That was a past tense example. Perhaps it would be useful to consider a future tense case, since this might seem to correspond more closely to God's situation in choosing a possible world to actualize. At some time t in the near future Maurice will be free with respect to some insignificant action – having freeze-dried oatmeal for breakfast, let's say. That is, at time t Maurice will be free to have oatmeal but also free to take something else – shredded wheat, perhaps. Next, suppose we consider S', a state of affairs that is included in the actual world and includes Maurice's being free with respect to taking oatmeal at time t. That is, S' includes Maurice's being free at time t to take oatmeal and free to reject it. S' does not include Maurice's taking oatmeal, however; nor does it include his rejecting it. For the rest S' is as much as possible like the actual world. In particular there are many conditions that do in fact hold at time t and are *relevant* to his choice – such conditions, for example, as the fact that he hasn't had oatmeal lately, that his wife will be annoyed if he rejects it, and the like; and S' includes each of these conditions. Now God no doubt knows what Maurice will do at time t, if S obtains; He knows which action Maurice would freely perform if S were to be actual. That is, God knows that one of the following conditionals is true:

(6) If S' were to obtain, Maurice will freely take the oatmeal

or

(7) If S' were to obtain, Maurice will freely reject it.

We may not know which of these is true, and Maurice himself may not know; but presumably God does.

So either God knows that (6) is true, or else He knows that (7) is. Let's suppose it is (6). Then there is a possible world that God, though omnipotent, cannot create. For consider a possible world W' that shares S' with the actual world (which for ease of reference I'll name "Kronos") and in which Maurice does *not* take oatmeal. (We know there is such a world, since S' does not include Maurice's taking the oatmeal.) S' obtains in W' just as it does in Kronos. Indeed, everything in W' is just as it is in Kronos up to time t. But whereas in Kronos Maurice takes oatmeal at time t, in W' he does not. Now W' is a perfectly possible world; but it is not within God's power to create it or bring about its actuality. For to do so He must actualize S'. But (6) is in fact true. So if God actualizes S' (as He must to create W') and leaves Maurice free with respect to the action in question, then he will take the oatmeal; and then, of course, W' will not be actual. If, on the other hand, God causes Maurice to *refrain* from taking the oatmeal, then he is not *free* to take it. That means, once again, that W' is not actual; for in W' Maurice is free to take the oatmeal (even if he doesn't do so). So if (6) is true, then this world W' is one that God can't actualize, it is not within His power to actualize it even though He is omnipotent and it is a possible world.

Of course, if it is (7) that is true, we get a similar result; then too there are possible worlds that God can't actualize. These would be worlds which share S'

with Kronos and in which Maurice *does* take oatmeal. But either (6) or (7) *is* true; so either way there is a possible world that God can't create. If we consider a world in which *S'* obtains and in which Maurice freely chooses oatmeal at time *t*, we see that whether or not it is within God's power to actualize it depends upon what Maurice would do if he were free in a certain situation. Accordingly, there are any number of possible worlds such that it is partly up to Maurice whether or not God can actualize them. It is, of course, up to God whether or not to create Maurice and also up to God whether or not to make him free with respect to the action of taking oatmeal at time *t*. (God could, if He chose, cause him to succumb to the dreaded *equine obsession*, a condition shared by some people and most horses, whose victims find it *psychologically impossible* to refuse oats or oat products.) But if He creates Maurice and creates him free with respect to this action, then whether or not he actually performs the action is up to Maurice – not God.[3]

Now we can return to the Free Will Defense and the problem of evil. The Free Will Defender, you recall, insists on the possibility that it is not within God's power to create a world containing moral good without creating one containing moral evil. His atheological opponent – Mackie, for example – agrees with Leibniz in insisting that if (as the theist holds) God is omnipotent, then it *follows* that He could have created any possible world He pleased. We now see that this contention – call it "Leibniz' Lapse" – is a mistake. The atheologian is right in holding that there are many possible worlds containing moral good but no moral evil; his mistake lies in endorsing Leibniz' Lapse. So one of his premises – that God, if omnipotent, could have actualized just any world He Pleased – is false.

Could God Have Created a World Containing Moral Good but No Moral Evil?

Now suppose we recapitulate the logic of the situation. The Free Will Defender claims that the following is possible:

(8) God is omnipotent, and it was not within His power to create a world containing moral good but no moral evil.

By way of retort the atheologian insists that there are possible worlds containing moral good but no moral evil. He adds that an omnipotent being could have actualized any possible world he chose. So if God is omnipotent, it follows that He could have actualized a world containing moral good but no moral evil, hence (8), contrary to the Free Will Defender's claim, is not possible. What we have seen so far is that his second premise – Leibniz' Lapse – is false.

Of course, this does not settle the issue in the Free Will Defender's favor. Leibniz' Lapse (appropriately enough for a lapse) is false; but this doesn't show that (8) is possible. To show this latter we must demonstrate the possibility that among the worlds God could not have actualized are all the worlds containing moral good but no moral evil. How can we approach this question?

Instead of choosing oatmeal for breakfast or selling an aardvark, suppose we think about a morally significant action such as taking a bribe. Curley Smith, the mayor of Boston, is opposed to the proposed freeway route; it would require destruction of the Old North Church along with some other antiquated and structurally unsound buildings. L. B. Smedes, the director of highways, asks him whether he'd drop his opposition for $1 million. "Of course," he replies. "Would you do it for $2?" asks Smedes. "What do you take me for?" comes the indignant reply. "That's already established," smirks Smedes, "all that remains is to nail down your price." Smedes then offers him a bribe of $35,000; unwilling to break with the fine old traditions of Bay State politics, Curley accepts. Smedes then spends a sleepless night wondering whether he could have bought Curley for $20,000.

Now suppose we assume that Curley was free with respect to the action of taking the bribe – free to take it and free to refuse. And suppose, furthermore, that he would have taken it. That is, let us suppose that

(9) If Smedes had offered Curley a bribe of $20,000, he would have accepted it.

If (9) is true, then there is a state of affairs S' that (1) includes Curley's being offered a bribe of $20,000; (2) does not include either his accepting the bribe or his rejecting it; and (3) is otherwise as much as possible like the actual world. Just to make sure S' includes every relevant circumstance, let us suppose that it is a *maximal world segment*. That is, add to S' any state of affairs compatible with but not included in it, and the result will be an entire possible world. We could think of it roughly like this: S' is included in at least one world W in which Curley takes the bribe and in at least one world W' in which he rejects it. If S' is a maximal world segment, then S' is what remains of W when *Curley's taking the bribe* is deleted; it is also what remains of W' when *Curley's rejecting the bribe* is detected. More exactly, if S' is a maximal world segment, then every possible state of affairs that includes S', but isn't included by S', is a possible world. So if (9) is true, then there is a maximal world segment S' that (1) includes Curley's being offered a bribe of $20,000; (2) does not include either his accepting the bribe or his rejecting it; (3) is otherwise as much as possible like the actual world – in particular, it includes Curley's being free with respect to the bribe; and (4) is such that if it were actual then Curley would have taken the bribe. That is,

(10) If S' were actual, Curley would have accepted the bribe is true.

Now, of course, there is at least one possible world W' in which S' is actual and Curley does not take the bribe. But God could not have created W'; to do so, He would have been obliged to actualize S', leaving Curley free with respect to the action of taking the bribe. But under these conditions Curley, as (10) assures us, would have accepted the bribe, so that the world thus created would not have been S'.

Curley, as we see, is not above a bit of Watergating. But there may be worse to come. Of course, there are possible worlds in which he is significantly free (i.e., free with respect to a morally significant action) and never does what is wrong. But the sad truth about Curley may be this. Consider W', any of these worlds: in W' Curley is significantly free, so in W' there are some actions that are morally significant for him and with respect to which he is free. But at least one of these actions – call it A – has the following peculiar property. There is a maximal world segment S' that obtains in W' and is such that (1) S' includes Curley's being free *re* A but neither his performing A nor his refraining from A; (2) S' is otherwise as much as possible like W'; and (3) if S' had been actual, Curley would have gone wrong with respect to A.[4] (Notice that this third condition holds in fact, in the actual world; it does not hold in that world W'.)

This means, of course, that God could not have actualized W'. For to do so He'd have been obliged to bring it about that S' is actual; but then Curley would go wrong with respect to A. Since in W' he always does what is right, the world thus actualized would not be W'. On the other hand, if God *causes* Curley to go right with respect to A or *brings it about that* he does so, then Curley isn't free with respect to A; and so once more it isn't W' that is actual. Accordingly God cannot create W'. But W' was just any of the worlds in which Curley is significantly free but always does only what is right. It therefore follows that it was not within God's power to create a world in which Curley produces moral good but no moral evil. Every world God can actualize is such that if Curley is significantly free in it, he takes at least one wrong action.

Obviously Curley is in serious trouble. I shall call the malady from which he suffers *transworld depravity*. (I leave as homework the problem of comparing transworld depravity with what Calvinists call "total depravity.") By way of explicit definition:

(11) A person P suffers from transworld depravity if and only if the following holds: for every world W such that P is significantly free in W and P does only what is right in W, there is an action A and a maximal world segment S' such that

(1) S' includes A's being morally significant for P
(2) S' includes P's being free with respect to A
(3) S' is included in W and includes neither P's performing A nor P's refraining from performing A

and

(4)   If S' were actual, P would go wrong with respect to A.

(In thinking about this definition, remember that (4) is to be true in fact, in the actual world – not in that world W.)

What is important about the idea of transworld depravity is that if a person suffers from it, then it wasn't within God's power to actualize any world in which that person is significantly free but does no wrong – that is, a world in which he produces moral good but no moral evil.

We have been here considering a crucial contention of the Free Will Defender: the contention, namely, that

(8) God is omnipotent, and it was not within His power to create a world containing moral good but no moral evil.

How is transworld depravity relevant to this? As follows. Obviously it is possible that there be persons who suffer from transworld depravity. More generally, it is possible that everybody suffers from it. And if this possibility were actual, then God, though omnipotent, could not have created any of the possible worlds containing just the persons who do in fact exist, and containing moral good but no moral evil. For to do so He'd have to create persons who were significantly free (otherwise there would be no moral good) but suffered from transworld depravity. Such persons go wrong with respect to at least one action in any world God could have actualized and in which they are free with respect to morally significant actions; so the price for creating a world in which they produce moral good is creating one in which they also produce moral evil.

Notes

1   Strict accuracy demands, therefore, that we speak of God as *actualizing* rather than creating possible worlds. I shall continue to use both locutions, thus sacrificing accuracy to familiarity. For more about possible worlds see my book *The Nature of Necessity* (Oxford: The Clarendon Press, 1974), chaps 4–8.
2   For a fuller statement of this argument see Plantinga, *The Nature of Necessity*, chap. 9, secs 4–6.
3   For a more complete and more exact statement of this argument see Plantinga, *The Nature of Necessity*, chap. 9, secs 4–6.
4   A person goes wrong with respect to an action if he either wrongfully performs it or wrongfully fails to perform it.

5

Causation and Responsibility

Introduction

There is a sense in which everyone understands what is involved when we talk about cause and effect. If an airplane crashes, we understand the goal of the subsequent investigation into the cause of the crash. If a person is shot to death, we understand that the damage the bullet did caused death, and if you feel drunk, we understand that the cause is the amount of alcohol in your body. But then consider the following three scenarios.

A patient is hooked up to life support equipment in a hospital, a physician decides to turn off the machinery, and the patient dies. What caused the patient's death? There are bound to be disagreements, for some will say that the patient died from the disease or injury for which he went to the hospital in the first place, while others will point out that had it not been for the physician, the patient would not have died.

An autoworker in Michigan loses her job and is unemployed. Where do we look for the causes of her unemployment? There is no single answer to this question. Some will urge us to look at the unemployed worker: her motivation, work, education, behavior, and so on. Others will urge us to focus on the employer's motivation and behavior to find the causes of the worker's unemployment. Still others will urge us to look at the economy as a whole – the pattern of relations between labor, business, and government – to find the causes of the worker's unemployment.

A terrorist group has captured an embassy and threatens to blow it up unless the government gives in to the group's demands. The government does not budge and the terrorists explode the embassy, killing all the inhabitants. Again, some will say that the terrorists are the cause of the tragedy, while others will be quick to point out that the government has to carry its share of the blame because the tragedy would not have occurred had the government given in to the demands.

It is clear that in order to sort out these and other examples we need to get more clear on the concept of causation. Our everyday understanding of the concept is not clear or sophisticated enough to guide us when even fairly common complications arise.

Why Should We Care?

As the above examples suggest, moral responsibility and causality are closely related, and one of the reasons we care about causality is that we care about moral responsibility. Who is morally responsible for the patient's death, the worker's unemployment, or the embassy killings?

However, we need to be careful about how causal and moral responsibility are connected. Specifically, we need to distinguish between the following two connections:

1   If a person is causally responsible for something, then he or she is morally responsible for it.
2   If a person is morally responsible for something, then he or she is causally responsible for it.

Claim (1) states that causal responsibility is sufficient for moral responsibility, while (2) states that causal responsibility is necessary for moral responsibility.

A simple example will show that causal responsibility is not sufficient for moral responsibility. A tornado that causes death and destruction in a community is causally responsible for this death and destruction but it is not morally responsible because it is not a moral agent. Moral agents must have minds, and tornadoes do not have minds. But jointly having a mind and being causally responsible for something is also not sufficient for moral responsibility. You need to know what you are doing in order to be morally responsible. A toddler who plays with a loaded gun that is left laying around by a careless parent and kills a sibling is not morally responsible for this killing, although the toddler is causally responsible for the killing.

So (1) is false, but it is reasonable to assume that (2) is true and that causal responsibility is necessary for moral responsibility. You can see this by considering cases where I am not in any way causally responsible for something or, to put it more bluntly, by considering incidents that I had nothing to do with. If I had nothing to do with some event, then I cannot be morally responsible for it. For example, if a murder occurs in the next town and I had nothing whatsoever to do with it, then I cannot be morally responsible for it. But that means that if I have some moral responsibility for something happening, then I played some causal role.

Consequently, it is important to be clear about the nature of causality so that we can be clearer about how to allocate moral responsibility. In order to know who all the parties are that are morally responsible for some reprehensible event, we need to know all the parties that are causally responsible for that event. Of course, as we just saw, being causally responsible does not mean that they are morally responsible, but they are suspects we have to examine more closely to see if they are morally responsible.

Of course, there are many other reasons why we should care about causality.

Clearly the natural sciences are interested in discovering causes and effects, and consequently causal statements play a central role in scientific explanations. If it were to turn out that the concept of causality has very little objective basis in reality and is mostly a subjective projection, then surely the popular picture of science as the pursuit of objective facts would be seriously tarnished. Thus a proper assessment of the nature of science, at least as we know it today, requires some understanding of the nature of causality.

Notice that an arena where science and morality meet is in a police laboratory. Forensic scientists study blood samples, bullet wounds, or fingerprints in order to find the causes of the crime and gather evidence that can be used in court to determine who is guilty of the crime. They need to worry about not only what kinds of causes are needed to establish guilt, but also what sorts of things are needed to establish causal responsibility. Thus they need to pay special attention to the nature of causality.

This was made abundantly clear in the trial of O. J. Simpson, the US football star accused of murdering his spouse, Nicole Simpson. One of the issues of this trial was the role of statistical evidence in establishing causal responsibility. For example, is the fact that a relatively high percentage of cases involving domestic abuse lead to homicide or attempted homicide relevant to establishing O. J. Simpson's causal responsibility, granting that he was responsible for previously abusing Nicole Simpson?

This sort of issue is not unusual. For a long time, tobacco companies argued that the fact that there was a significant statistical correlation between smoking tobacco and lung cancer was not sufficient to show that tobacco smoking caused lung cancer. For example, this statistical fact about smoking, together with the fact that an individual long-term smoker contracted cancer, was, according to tobacco manufacturing firms, insufficient to establish that this person's smoking tobacco caused his cancer. They maintained that establishing causal responsibility requires more than establishing a pattern or regularity. What is needed, they argued, is showing that there is a specific causal chain from smoking to cancer in the case of this specific individual.

Clearly we need to understand something about the nature of causality to evaluate these significant claims that have great consequences on our assessments of moral responsibility.

Ontology

At the very least, we can agree that causality is a relationship between a cause and an effect. When a ball breaks a window, the causal relation is between a ball and a breaking window; when a sudden noise startles an infant, the relation is between the noise and the startling infant. The noise or ball are the causes, while the breaking window and the startled infant are the effects.

However, we still need to know what kinds of things can be causes and effects. There are various kinds of things that have concerned and continue to concern metaphysicians, and we should review them before we turn to what kinds of things can be causes and effects.

One type of thing is what Aristotle called a "substance," or what we take to be an object. These are things that, among other things, have properties, are related to other things, change, persist through time. Typical substances are physical objects: grains of wheat, blades of grass, ears of corn, trees, rocks, chairs, volcanoes, and so on. Many people believe that there are also non-physical substances: angels, gods, souls, and human minds.

In addition to substances, there are the properties and relations that objects can have. Examples of properties are *being made of wood, being red, being deciduous*, and so forth. These are properties that wooden chairs, red apples, and deciduous trees have. Relations hold between two or more things. For instance, causality is a relation between two things, as are *being in love, being taller than*, or *being larger than*. But there are also relations that hold between more than two things – for example, the number four is between three and five, and *being between x and y* is a relation that holds of three things. When you buy a sack of oranges for your daughter, you are also engaged in a relationship that involves three objects: you, a sack of oranges, and your daughter. We discussed the metaphysical issues concerning the nature of properties and relations in chapter 2 on the problem of universals.

So far we have three kinds of things – substances, properties, and relations – but there are more. Not only are there objects that have properties and are related to each other in various ways, but things happen or occur. A deciduous tree loses its leaves, an apple is eaten, a wooden chair breaks, love hurts, and so on. Such happenings and occurrences are events, and you will notice that the world is full of events: water boiling, people making tea, children running, plants growing, planets orbiting, and so forth.

We should also not forget times and places. Things happen at a certain time in certain places. The French Revolution occurred in France in 1789 and the water boiled in a pot on my stove at 24:07 hours Universal Coordinated Time. Some things can while other things cannot be in two different places at the same time. As we saw in chapter 2, it seems that properties and relations can be in two different places at the same time.

In addition to substances, properties, and relations, events, times, and places, many metaphysicians believe that there also are states of affairs. If Lucy and Desi are in love, then in addition to the two objects (Lucy and Desi), the relation (being in love), the time (1950s), the place (New York City), and relevant events that characterize being in love (teasing, arguing, kissing), there is a certain state of affairs, namely *that Lucy and Desi are in love*. Other examples of states of affairs are *that an apple is red, that there was a revolution in France in the eighteenth century*, and so on. All of these are states of affairs that are facts: they are states of affairs that actually obtain. Lucy and Desi are in love, an apple is red, and there was a revolution in France. But there are also states of affairs that are not facts; that is, states of affairs that do not obtain. It is possible that life never evolved on Earth. This state of affairs – *that life did not evolve on Earth* – might have obtained, and in that case there would be no human beings on Earth. There are many such states of affairs that could have obtained but in fact did not obtain: *that you were born in 1898, that Santa Claus flies a sled, that dinosaurs ate human beings,* and so on.

Finally, it seems that we must include sets or collections in our list of kinds of things. An apple, a loaf of bread, and a bottle of wine is not a substance, a property or relation, an event, a time, a place, or a state of affairs. Instead, it is a set consisting of three physical objects. There are also sets consisting of other kinds of things. For instance, the set of events that occurred in eighteenth-century France will include the storming of the Bastille, the beheading of Marie Antoinette, as well as events such as opening a bottle of wine, eating bread and cheese, or a breeze blowing through the guillotine. Of course, there are also sets of numbers, such as the set of all natural numbers, and it is in mathematics that we explicitly encounter sets most often.

Not all philosophers agree that this survey of the kinds of things there are is accurate. Some philosophers deny that substances are different kinds of things distinct from properties; for them substances are sets of properties related to each other in a special way. Others deny that there are substances because they think that substances are really types of events. Still other philosophers deny that there are states of affairs in addition to substances, properties and relations, and events. Some philosophers even deny that there are relations and believe that what looks like a relation is really just a property. For instance, if Romeo and Juliet are in love, there is no relation between them. Instead, Romeo has the property of loving Juliet and Juliet has the property of loving Romeo.

Nevertheless, this is a list of the kinds of things that on a first glance, without too much reflection, seem to exist, and with this list we can start looking for the sorts of things that can be causes and effects.

Causes and Effects

It seems that all the types of things we surveyed in the previous section can function as causes and effects.

When a ball breaks a window, a physical object is a cause. Here are other examples where physical objects are causes: Singh caused the accident, aspirin reduced the fever, cancer kills many people, and Auguste Rodin made *The Thinker.* Rodin and Singh are people, aspirin is a chemical substance and cancer is a kind of cell, and all four are, roughly speaking, objects that have causal effects. If gods or angels exist, then there also are non-physical substances that are causes. For instance, if the Judeo-Christian God created the universe, then a non-physical substance is a cause.

It seems objects can also be effects. When a mason builds a house, the house is an effect of the mason's activities. Similarly, we might say that a tree was brought about by a complex set of causes, and thus the tree is a physical object that is an effect of prior causes.

Properties also seem to be causes and effects. The fact that a chair has the property of being combustible caused it to burn when thrown in the fire, and a bee is attracted to the bright colors of a flower. Properties are also effects of causes. For instance, the colors of a flower are brought about by pigments in the petals of a flower, which in turn are brought about by chemical reactions during the growth of a flower. The same holds for relations: love breeds children, while hate causes war.

When a noise startles an infant, an event causes something. Other examples of events as causes are: plucking the string caused it to vibrate, breaking sharply on ice caused the car to swerve, her anxiety was due to drinking espresso all afternoon. Plucking a string, drinking beer, driving a car, stepping on your brakes, and crashing into a tree are all events, and it is these happenings or occurrences that bring about certain causal effects.

Events, of course, can also be effects. Driving while drunk causes accidents, and car accidents certainly are tragic events. A good rain together with sunshine causes plants to grow, and the growing of a plant is an event, although a slow event, at least compared to an automobile accident.

States of affairs or conditions also are causes. Here are some examples: the infection was caused by a weakened immune system, the depressed condition of the economy caused widespread labor unrest, and Tamara's alertness reduced the chances of an accident. A weakened immune system, an economic depression, and being alert are all states of affairs that bring about diverse effects under certain circumstances. States of affairs are also effects of causes: That there are three apple trees in our backyard is a state of affairs caused by many things, including that people planted them there.

It is harder to see that times, places, and sets are causes and effects, but even these kinds of things enter causal relations.

When two automobiles traveling at the same speed enter an intersection at the same time, then they will collide. That their paths crossed at the same time and place was, at least in part, the cause of this collision. Times and places can also be effects of causes if contemporary physics is correct. The spatial and temporal structure of the universe, according to contemporary cosmology, is the product of a certain event, namely the Big Bang.

The fact that effects typically are the product of causes that are complex and involve many factors suggests that sometimes sets can also be causes. For instance, the igniting of a match is not caused by one event. At least two events were involved in the cause: a combustible matchhead was struck on the side of the matchbox and sufficient oxygen was flowing in the air around the struck matchhead. Both of these events together are causing the effect, and one way of understanding this is that the cause is a set of conditions that includes these two events as members. In fact, it seems that most causes are complex sets of conditions. Just consider the set of factors that brought about your birth or all the things that had to occur for Rodin to have become a sculptor and make *The Thinker*. Similarly, sets can be effects. The set of objects in a kitchen drawer did not just happen to be there, but they were all put there by various people for various reasons, and thus this set is the effect of diverse human causes.

Many philosophers believe that although it appears that all the kinds of things mentioned can be causes and effects, as a matter of fact only events are causally related. They would argue that it is not the ball that causes the window to break, but the flying ball hitting the window – an event – that causes the window to break. Similarly, the sculptor Rodin did not cause the statue of *The Thinker*, but Rodin's creative activity – his designing and making the mold, pouring the bronze, and so on – that caused the statue.

Of course, Rodin is involved in the cause, but as a feature of the events that caused the statue. In the same manner, properties, times, and places are involved. Rodin has the property of *being sighted*, and his seeing of the mold helps to make sure he pours the bronze into the mold, and not on the floor. The fact that the statue was made in Paris in the nineteenth century is due to the fact that the events that make up Rodin's making of the statue take place in Paris in the nineteenth century. Events always occur at specific times in specific places.

Finally, even though it seems that sets can also be causes because the striking of the match and the presence of oxygen around the matchhead together cause the match to ignite, perhaps this combination of events is not really a set of events. Perhaps it is better to understand this combination not as a set, but as one complex event that is made up of other events, including the striking of the match and oxygen flowing around the matchhead.

In light of this diversity of views, it is probably best not to take a stand on what sorts of things can and cannot be causes and effects. However, we certainly won't make a mistake if in our thinking about causality we take events to be paradigm examples of causes.

Total and Partial Causes

There is a forest fire and after some investigation the authorities discover that a campfire was not properly extinguished. They declare that embers from a campfire left by careless campers were the cause of the forest fire. The definite article "the" in "the cause" suggests that the presence of embers was the only thing that caused the forest fire. But strictly speaking, this is false. If we are going to be accurate, we must include in the causes of the forest fire the fact that there was oxygen present in the atmosphere and that the forest was combustible. We focus on the embers, but, as the contemporary philosopher Hilary Putnam pointed out, if extraterrestrials were to examine the scene, they would probably blame all the oxygen in the atmosphere, and not the embers.

What this shows is that we need to distinguish between everything that is causally responsible for an effect and what we in our causal explanations identify as "the" cause of an effect. Everything that is causally responsible for an effect is the *total* cause of an event, and strictly speaking, *the* cause of an event is the total cause. The causes that we isolate and identify in our causal explanations are only *partial* causes. The embers are partial causes because they caused the forest fire not by themselves, but together with the oxygen in the air.

The fact that typically we focus on partial causes, and tend to ignore total causes, leads us to two important questions. First, why do we focus on partial causes when investigating an effect at the expense of its total cause? Second, from all the possible partial causes that are part of the total cause, why do we focus on one partial cause and not another?

The first question is relatively easy to answer. Total causes are too large. Consider the forest fire again. The total cause will have to include the Big Bang, because it is at least partially responsible that there is a solar system that includes a planet with oxygen in its atmosphere and combustible vegetation on its surface. It will also have to include evolutionary processes that are causally responsible for the emergence of intelligent forms of life on this planet that make fires. So strictly speaking, the total cause of any event will include much of the history of our planet and a good bit of the history of the universe.

Needless to say, this is quite a bit, and for this reason complete causal explanations that take into account the total cause of an effect are out of our reach. Many philosophers conclude from this that the idea of a total cause has no practical value – we cannot use it to guide our causal explanations – and consequently that the very idea of a total cause should be shunned. Perhaps this conclusion is too hasty – the knowledge that there is a total cause may at least make us more careful in isolating partial causes – but this much is true: we have good practical reasons to focus on partial causes in our causal investigations. Total causes include too much for mere mortals to contemplate.

The second question is more difficult. Given that we have to look for partial causes, why do we focus on some partial causes and not others? For example, why do we isolate the campfire as the cause of the forest fire, while extraterrestrials might focus on the oxygen present in our atmosphere?

Various answers have been given, but one thing they all have in common is that what is singled out as a cause has something to do with the interests of the persons giving the causal explanation. For example, we are interested in controlling forest fires, and for us the easiest way to control them is to control the behavior of campers. Thus we isolate the careless campers as the cause, and not the presence of oxygen in the atmosphere. The extraterrestrials are more interested in the atmosphere – perhaps because they are traveling through space looking for some good real estate – and so they focus on the oxygen rather than the careless campers.

Once human interests play a role in causal explanations, we cannot avoid ethical, social, and political questions that are raised by causal explanations. Consider the case of the unemployed worker. We can focus on worker expectations for certain benefits and pay or we can focus on employer expectations for a certain margin of profits. Which should we change? If we take worker expectations as a given that we should not or cannot change – much like we do the fact that our atmosphere has oxygen – then we will look elsewhere for the causes of unemployment, perhaps in employer expectations. If we take employer expectations as a given, then we will probably be inclined to focus on worker expectations.

Similarly, if we are not interested in changing the behavior of the government, but are interested in changing the behavior of terrorists, we will isolate the terrorists as the cause. On the other hand, if we are interested in changing the behavior of the government and assume that terrorist behavior is a given in such conditions, then we will isolate government behavior as the cause. Of course, our interests may include both government and terrorist behavior, and in that case we will probable include both government and terrorist behavior in our causal explanation.

Often when there are disputes about causes, the real dispute is over human interests. Consider the case of a patient who dies of, say, lung disease and heart failure after the doctor disconnects the life support in accordance with the wishes expressed in a living will. Clearly the total cause of death includes the doctor's actions as well as lung disease and heart failure, but nevertheless people will find themselves disputing the cause of death in such cases. What lies behind such disputes is a conflict of interests. Those that are concerned with promoting life at all costs and averting death whenever possible will focus on the doctor who turned off the life support systems. On the other hand, if for one reason or another we are interested in preserving natural causes of death and are critical of using artificial life support systems in these conditions, we will focus on lung disease and heart failure as the causes of death.

Triggering and Structuring Causes

Another important distinction, due to the philosopher and former engineer Fred Dretske, is between triggering and structuring causes. A triggering cause is a cause that initiates a chain of events that results in some effect, e.g. the flipping of a light switch is the triggering cause of a light's coming on. Similarly, the rapid increase in atmospheric pressure triggers a headache. Clearly the heart failure is a triggering cause of the patient's death, and the doctor's actions are a triggering cause of the heart failure.

To understand structuring causes, consider a thermostat. The heat that causes the bimetallic strip in a thermostat to bend is a triggering cause of the bending, while the engineers and workers that made the thermostat, specifically the ones who caused the strip to be calibrated so that it bends at certain temperatures and closes an electric circuit, are structuring causes. The electrician who wires the switch and lamp is a structuring cause: she causes the structure that includes the switch, wire, and lamp, and relates them in such a way that flipping the switch turns on the light.

Typically, it is easier to identify triggering causes than it is to identify structuring causes. Consider the forest fire again. The careless campfire triggered the forest fire, but for it to be able to trigger the forest fire, a certain structure had to be in place. This structure includes all the following and more:

1   A forest that is very combustible.
2   Sufficient amount of oxygen in the atmosphere.
3   Human beings who go into this forest and make fires.
4   Human beings who are careless.

What brought about this structure is a confluence of many factors. Evolutionary processes are responsible for the forest and fire-making human beings. Cosmological and evolutionary factors are responsible for the oxygen in the atmosphere. Cultural factors are responsible for the fact that this forest is still standing and that people visit the forest to camp. Psychological and cultural factors are responsible for carelessness. All of these factors, then, play a role in the structuring cause of this situation in which the campers trigger a forest fire.

Although it is easy to ignore structuring causes because they are more difficult to identify, they become important when we are interested in finding out about why there are certain structures or patterns. For instance, if we are interested in why certain species are able to flourish together in a certain environment, even though one feeds on the other, we need to look for the structuring causes of this region and the species that thrive in it. Clearly, biological evolution will be one of the structuring causes we will have to isolate to understand this situation.

We also must not ignore structuring causes when trying to understand social phenomena. The relationships between employers and employees are part of a social and economic structure, and to understand this we need to look for structuring causes. The fact that employers can downsize their companies and leave for cheaper labor markets is a structural feature of many economic systems, and if we are trying to understand this structure, we must look for structuring causes. The search for triggering causes in this case will not shed light on the structure.

Whether or not we focus on structuring causes in our causal explanations will have something to do with our interests. If we take the functioning of a thermostat for granted and are only interested in why the bimetallic strip did not bend in the proper way, we will focus on triggering causes. But if we start thinking about the very design of the thermostat and are interested in alternative designs – perhaps ones that do not rely on bimetallic strips – we will look to structuring causes. Similarly, if we take the economic and political structures of a society for granted (in much the same way that we take Earth's oxygen for granted), then we will ignore the causes of these structures and look for triggering causes at work within these structures. But if our interests turn to why a society has the political and economic structures it has, we will start looking at structuring causes.

The fact that interests play a role in what partial cause we highlight in our causal explanations does not mean that causes are subjective or in some other way less than real. The partial causes we isolate in our explanations – whether we are looking at one of the triggering causes or highlighting one of the structuring causes – can be as real as the other causes that are part of the total cause of the effect. What the partial causes are not are total causes, and we need to keep this in mind when we look for causes and be more aware of the interests we have in our search for partial causes.

Regularity Theories of Causality

Now that we are aware of various kinds of causality, we need to turn to one of the central questions of the metaphysics of causality. Is causality a relation that is in some sense subjective and imposed upon the world, or is it an objective relation that is, so to speak, part of the design of the universe, no matter how anyone thinks about it? Needless to say, philosophers divide into two major camps on this question. Let us begin by considering the views of David Hume, one of first philosophers to turn a critical eye to the concept of causality.

Hume was an empiricist and so he believed that all ideas have to be drawn from experience, and those ideas or features of ideas that cannot be drawn from experience are illegitimate. He applied this principle to the concept of causality and concluded that causality involves four factors. To say that A causes B is to say, Hume maintained, that (a) B comes after A (succession), (b) A and B are close in space and time (contiguity), (c) A and B repeatedly occur together (constant conjunction), and (d) A and B are necessarily connected (necessity). Whether or not succession and contiguity are required for causality is doubtful, but many philosophers believe that constant conjunction and necessity are required. In fact, that causality consists of constant conjunction and necessity, properly understood, is the core of a type of view about causality that is often labeled as the "regularity theory of causality."

The concept of constant conjunction is clear enough. When A causes B, Hume argued, what we experience is a constant conjunction of A and B; that is, A and B regularly occur together, so that when A occurs, B also occurs. For instance, to say that striking a match in proper circumstances (the match is dry, oxygen is present in the air around the matchhead, and so on) causes it to ignite is to say, among other things, that these two events:

striking a match in appropriate circumstances,

match igniting,

regularly occur together.

That constant conjunction is not sufficient for causality is easy to see. For example, Monday and Tuesday are constantly conjoined (and they are also contiguous and succeed each other), but Monday does not cause Tuesday. Similarly, there are many coincidences that are not causes. For instance, a gambler may win at some game of chance – for instance, a one-armed bandit – whenever he wears his lucky shoes. Still, this constant conjunction, by itself, is not a case of causality. Wearing his lucky shoes does not change the machine's behavior.

What is needed is necessity, and Hume recognized this. When A causes B,

Hume maintained, not only are A and B constantly conjoined, but there is a necessary connection between A and B. However, Hume believed that this necessary connection between a cause and an effect is not an objective, mind-independent connection. There is no necessity in the cause or effect. "Necessity is something, that exists in the mind, not in Objects," Hume writes, and it is a hallmark of regularity theories of causality that the necessity that causality requires is not objective, but supplied by the human mind.

Hume believed that the necessity was a psychological association. When we experience two events constantly conjoined and come to think of one of them as a cause and the other as an effect, then when we think of the one, we naturally expect the other. So if I strike a match in appropriate circumstances, a "gentle force," Hume maintains, makes me associate the effect, namely an ignited match, with the cause. This psychological association of cause and effect is all there is to the necessity that we think exists between causes and effects.

Today, most regularity theorists believe that Hume's psychological association is not good enough to account for the necessity causality requires. The kind of necessity that is involved in causality is a necessity that covers not only what as a matter of fact happens, but also what *would* happen in other possible circumstances. For example, if a match struck in appropriate circumstances causes the match to ignite, then it is also true that if a match *were* struck in appropriate circumstances, it *would* ignite. Suppose you strike a match under water and it does not ignite. This would not undermine the causal claim that a match struck in appropriate circumstances causes the match to ignite. These are not appropriate circumstances, and it is still true that if this match had been struck in appropriate circumstances (instead of under water), then it would have ignited.

Propositions that have the form "if it were the case that p, then it would be the case that q" are called *counter-factuals* or *contrary to fact conditionals*, and psychological necessity is not strong enough to support such propositions. If a match is in a box and not being struck on anything, I do not think about it igniting. Nevertheless, it is still true of it that if it were struck in appropriate circumstances, it would ignite. So what is needed is some other kind of necessity that supports contrary-to-fact conditionals.

Regularity theorists refuse to rely on some objective, natural necessity. In other words, when we claim that if A occurs, B *must* occur, the necessity mentioned with the word "must" does not refer to some feature of the facts involved: A, B, and the relation between A and B. As far as the objective facts are concerned, when A causes B, all there is to the causation is that A and B are regularly conjoined. For regularity theorists, the necessity resides in how we think about A and B. Their basic strategy is to treat the word "must" as something that indicates what kind of claim is being made, not as a word about the way the world is.

What the use of the word "must" indicates is that we are stating a law. Regularity theorists argue that we need to distinguish between accidental generalizations and laws. For example, whenever Buck wears his lucky shoes he wins at blackjack. Although as a matter of fact this is the case, it is only an accidental generalization. We do not suppose that if Buck were wearing his lucky shoes today, he would win at his favorite game of chance. However, we do suppose that it is a law that whenever Buck strikes a match in an appropriate manner, the match will ignite. Not only is it true that whenever Buck strikes a match, it ignites, but it is also true that if he now, contrary to fact, were to strike a match, it would ignite.

So according to the regularity theory of causality, we should understand the causal relationship as follows: when A causes B, A and B are regularly conjoined, and, moreover, we treat the claim that A and B are regularly conjoined as a law. It is this fact about how we think – that we treat the claim that when A occurs, B occurs as a law – that means it is also true that when A occurs, B *must* occur.

Problems with Regularity Theories of Causality

There are two important concerns about the way regularity theories treat causality.

The first worry concerns the claim that causality always involves a regularity or constant conjunction of cause and effect. A little reflection reveals that this cannot be true. Consider an airplane crash caused by a freak accident involving a malfunctioning coffee pot. This airplane went down because of a problem that had never occurred before and will never happen again. In other words, there is nothing regular about malfunctioning coffee pots and airplane crashes. Although this was a unique case of causality, it is nevertheless true that the malfunctioning coffee pot caused the disaster.

In fact, there can be true causal claims even if the cause never occurred. We know that if a comet were to hit Earth, it would cause great destruction on Earth. So far this has not happened and it is highly likely that it will never happen, but even if this never happens, it is still true that comets crashing into Earth cause tremendous destruction.

The second concern is with the way regularity theories treat the necessity involved in causality. First of all, it seems that not all causal claims are expressions of laws of nature. Consider the case of the terrorists exploding the embassy because the government did not want to give in to their demands. Assuming that the terrorists caused the explosion, it is unlikely, to say the least, that there is a law of nature that governs the situation. Given that there is no law that governs the government's and the terrorists' roles in the explosion, the regularity theorist would have to say that there is no cause of the explosion, and this seems wrong.

They caused the explosion, and given their actions and the appropriate conditions, the explosion had to happen. When the terrorists lit the fuse that was properly connected to an explosive device, and given that nothing was going to extinguish the fuse or in some other way prevent the explosion, the explosion had to happen. So here we have a cause and the necessity that is a feature of causality, but we have no law of nature that states that terrorists cause explosions.

Second, treating the necessity involved in causality as a feature of how we think about certain causal statements has the following consequence. Consider Buck, the gambler, again. Here are two sets of regularly conjoined events involving Buck:

1   Buck wears his lucky shoes. Buck wins at Blackjack.
2   Buck strikes one of his matches. Buck's match ignites.

To simplify issues, suppose that it just so happens that as a matter of fact it is true that whenever Buck wears his shoes he wins at blackjack, and that whenever he strikes one of his matches the match ignites. Buck is an excellent match striker and it so happens that Buck got to wear his lucky shoes fifteen times before he lost them, and every time he wore them, he won at blackjack.

Both cases support claims about the world's regularities. Case 1 supports the claim that whenever Buck wears his lucky shoes he wins at blackjack and case 2 supports the claim that whenever Buck strikes one of his matches his match ignites. Nevertheless, there is a difference between these two cases. Case 1 is not a case of causality while case 2 is a case of causality. Striking the match in the right way in the right situation causes the match to ignite, while wearing the lucky shoes does not cause the win at blackjack.

According to regularity theories, the difference between cases 1 and 2 is in how we view these cases. The claim that whenever Buck wears his lucky shoes he wins is treated as an accidental generalization, while the claim that whenever Buck strikes a match it ignites is treated as a law or an instance of a law that ties together the concepts of a striking a match and its ignition.

But surely the difference between the two cases extends beyond our thinking. After all, why do we treat the claim about lucky shoes as an accidental generalization and the claim about matches as a law? It seems that the reason for treating them differently is that there is something different about these two sets of events. Whenever Buck wears his lucky shoes he wins at blackjack is an accidental generalization because it is a sheer coincidence that these two events are regularly conjoined. On the other hand, it is a law that whenever a match is struck in appropriate circumstances it ignites because of something about these two events. The match must ignite on account of the way the world is, not on account of how we look at the world.

Necessity Theories of Causality

Necessity theories of causality avoid these problems of regularity theories because they assume that the necessity of causality is to be found in the way things are – it is a fact of nature – and not just an artifact of our thinking about the way things are.

On this view, there is a real difference between cases 1 and 2 that accounts for the fact that case 1 only supports accidental generalizations while case 2 supports laws. The difference is that in case 1 there is no natural necessity that ties Buck's lucky shoes and his winning at blackjack together, while in case 2 there is a natural necessity. When in appropriate circumstances Buck strikes a match, the match *must* ignite because of the way nature is structured.

The features of nature that make the igniting of the match necessary when struck appropriately are the natures of the materials from which matches are made and the powers these materials have on account of their natures. A match ignites because the friction between the phosphorus sulfide on the tip of the match and the rough surface on which it was struck raised the temperature of the phosphorus sulfide to the point where it combusted, and the flame of the burning phosphorus sulfide was hot enough to combust the wood of the match. What are at work in this situation are the natures of wood and phosphorus sulfide – their chemical structures – and the powers such chemical structures have – in this case the combustibility of wood and phosphorus sulfide.

Similarly, a copper wire conducts electricity because of the structure of a copper atom: it is an element with 29 protons and 35 neutrons in its nucleus, and 29 electrons configured around the nucleus. It is on account of this structure that it has the capacity to conduct an electric current when connected to an appropriate source of electricity on one end and to another conductive material on the other end.

Since necessity theories of causality locate the necessity of causality in nature, they are not troubled by examples of causality where we have not formulated any laws. Even if we do not have any laws for something, it can still have a nature and on account of that nature bring about changes in its environment. Phosphorus sulfide will combust under certain conditions even if our knowledge never advances to the point where we can formulate laws about phosphorus sulfide and combustibility.

In fact, according to this view not only can there be causes without laws, but there can be causes without any regularities. Even if there were only one match struck in the entire history of the universe, the striking of the match causes the match to ignite because phosphorus sulfide is combustible even if it combusts only once, or, for that matter, never. Similarly, even if there is only one case of a physician unplugging a life support system, this unplugging will be a cause of the patient's death because pulling the plug has the power of interrupting the power supply that is necessary for running the machine that is keeping the patient alive.

Of course, this view of causality is not without its problems. The main problems with this account of causality stem from trying to understand how we come to know causality.

Can we come to know that there is a necessary connection between causes and effects from experience? Hume argued that our knowledge of causal necessities cannot be based on empirical evidence. When we see a match being struck and igniting, all we see is two distinct events – the striking of the match and its ignition – and no necessary connection, power of force, between these two events. It is for this reason that Hume and regularity theorists in general seek to explain the necessity of causality in terms of how we think about causality and not in terms of how the world is.

Moreover, insofar as we do know causes and effects, it is because we have seen causes and effects regularly conjoined. For example, we are able to know that striking matches causes them to ignite, while wearing lucky shoes does not cause wins at blackjack, because we can conduct experiments that show that wearing shoes has nothing to do with the outcome of a game of blackjack. Moreover, as a matter of fact, wearing lucky shoes and winning at blackjack are *not* regularly conjoined, and that's how we know that there is no causal relation between wearing shoes and games of chance.

Many philosophers believe that these objections are strong enough to encourage us to reconsider regularity theories and fix the problems they have, without abandoning them. However, it seems to us that these objections are not so strong.

First, it seems that the powers of nature can be experienced. Certainly we feel our own powers when we are working or exercising hard. Perhaps Hume should have tried to run uphill or bale some hay in August to experience his own powers. Moreover, we certainly can feel the power of nature when exposed to a strong wind – for instance, while trying to cross a mountain ridge or navigate a sailboat. Finally, we can see nature's powers quite directly when a palm tree bends to the ground with the hurricane force winds. We see the wind bending the tree, and not, as Hume would have us believe, just two distinct events: a blowing wind and a bent palm tree.

Second, although it is true that usually we come to know causality on the basis of repeated observation, we must separate how we come to know something and what its nature is. For example, we come to know body temperature by measuring it with a thermometer, but our body temperature does not consist of how we measure it. It consists of the motion of our bodies' molecules. Similarly, we need to make repeated observations to come to know causality – for instance, that exposure to certain foods causes allergic reactions. But these observations only show us what was happening all along, namely that some properties of the food caused the allergic reactions.

However, the fact that in most cases we need repeated observations in order to know causes and effects should keep us humble about what we know, especially when it comes to something so complex as the individual and social behavior of human beings. Repeated observations of human behavior are hard to come by, especially the kind of complex behavior that interests us when we are concerned with moral responsibility. One reason for this is that societies and individuals cannot and should not be controlled in the manner events can be controlled in laboratory settings. The upshot of this is that there can be causes at work in individual and social behavior even though we will have a very difficult time knowing them.

Where Are We Now?

The fact that it is very difficult to know the causes of human behavior has a very important consequence for morality. As we saw at the beginning of our discussion of causality, causal responsibility is a necessary condition for moral responsibility. This, together with the fact that it is very difficult to know the causes of human behavior, suggests that we should be very careful and humble in our assessments of moral responsibility. Certainly we should not be as quick to praise and condemn people as is the habit of our politicians, journalists, and entertainers.

Of course, this is not the only reason for being careful about making moral judgments. Recall the distinction between total and partial causes. Which causes are relevant to assessing moral responsibility: is it the total cause or are the partial causes we isolate in our causal explanations a sufficient basis for making moral judgments? If we need to consider the total cause, then it will be extremely difficult to ascertain moral responsibility because our cognitive abilities are too limited to know total causes, especially when it comes to human behavior. If, on the other hand, partial causes are sufficient for assigning moral responsibility, then we should worry about the reasons we have for isolating some causes in our explanations while ignoring others. For instance, do I focus on triggering causes and ignore structuring causes in my explanation of some human behavior because this promotes my own welfare by taking for granted the structures that benefit me?

This is a question rooted in metaphysical reflection, but it is the sort of question that makes for an examined life: a life that is not only critical, but self-critical. Too often we rush to make moral judgments of other people and then proceed to act on these hasty judgments, but just a little attention to the metaphysics of causality reveals that we are being way too careless and judgmental. Metaphysics will slow us down and force us to be more careful, and we are convinced that today this can only be a good thing.

Selection from *Enquiry Concerning Human Understanding*
David Hume

David Hume (1711–1776), born in Edinburgh, Scotland, is one of the major British empiricist philosophers, whose writings also played a role in the emergence of psychology. He theorized about how we obtain and process information, paying special attention to the operations of the mind. In the following selection from *Enquiry Concerning Human Understanding*, Hume discusses the concept of causation and argues that the idea of necessary causal connection cannot be drawn from our observations of the external world. Instead, the idea must be derived from the felt force of the habitual association of ideas in our minds. We then project this notion of cause/effect onto the world as if the causal connections are real.

Section IV   Sceptical Doubts Concerning the Operations of the Understanding

Part I

ALL the objects of human reason or enquiry may naturally be divided into two kinds, to wit, *Relations of Ideas, and Matters of Fact.* Of the first kind are the sciences of Geometry, Algebra, and Arithmetic; and in short, every affirmation, which is either intuitively or demonstratively certain. *That the square of the hypothenuse is equal to the square of the two sides,* is a proposition, which expresses a relation between these figures. *That three times five is equal to the half of thirty,* expresses a relation between these numbers. Propositions of this kind are discoverable by the mere operation of thought, without dependence on what is any where existent in the universe. Though there never were a circle or triangle in nature, the truths, demonstrated by EUCLID, would for ever retain their certainty and evidence.

Matters of fact, which are the second objects of human reason, are not ascertained in the same manner; nor is our evidence of their truth, however great, of a like nature with the foregoing. The contrary of every matter of fact is still possible; because it can never imply a contradiction, and is conceived by the mind with the same facility and distinctness, as if ever so conformable to reality. *Thatt the sun will not rise to-morrow* is no less intelligible a proposition, and implies no more contradiction, than the affirmation, *that it will rise.* We should in vain, therefore, attempt to demonstrate its falsehood. Were it demonstratively false, it would imply a contradiction, and could never be distinctly conceived by the mind.

It may, therefore, be a subject worthy of curiosity, to enquire what is the nature of that evidence, which assures us of any real existence and matter of fact, beyond the present testimony of our senses, or the records of our memory. This part of philosophy, it is observable, has been little cultivated, either by the ancients or moderns; and therefore our doubts and errors, in the prosecution of so important an enquiry, may be the more excusable; while we march through such difficult paths, without any guide or direction. They may even prove useful, by exciting curiosity, and destroying that implicit faith and security, which is the bane of all reasoning and free enquiry. The discovery of defects in the common philosophy, if any such there be, will not, I presume, be a discouragement, but rather an incitement, as is usual, to attempt something more full and satisfactory, than has yet been proposed to the public.

All reasonings concerning matter of fact seem to be founded on the relation of *Cause and Effect.* By means of that relation alone we can go beyond the evidence of our memory and senses. If you were to ask a man, why he believes any matter of fact, which is absent; for instance, that his friend is in the country, or in

FRANCE; he would give you a reason; and this reason would be some other fact; as a letter received from him, or the knowledge of his former resolutions and promises. A man, finding a watch or any other machine in a desert island, would conclude, that there had once been men in that island. All our reasonings concerning fact are of the same nature. And here it is constantly supposed, that there is a connexion between the present fact and that which is inferred from it. Were there nothing to bind them together, the inference would be entirely precarious. The hearing of an articulate voice and rational discourse in the dark assures us of the presence of some person: Why? because these are the effects of the human make and fabric, and closely connected with it. If we anatomize all the other reasonings of this nature, we shall find, that they are founded on the relation of cause and effect, and that this relation is either near or remote, direct or collateral. Heat and light are collateral effects of fire, and the one effect may justly be inferred from the other.

If we would satisfy ourselves, therefore, concerning the nature of that evidence, which assures us of matters of fact, we must enquire how we arrive at the knowledge of cause and effect.

I shall venture to affirm, as a general proposition, which admits of no exception, that the knowledge of this relation is not, in any instance, attained by reasonings *a priori* but arises entirely from experience, when we find, that any particular objects are constantly conjoined with each other. Let an object be presented to a man of ever so strong natural reason and abilities; if that object be entirely new to him, he will not be able, by the most accurate examination of its sensible qualities, to discover any of its causes or effects. ADAM, though his rational faculties be supposed, at the very first, entirely perfect, could not have inferred from the fluidity, and transparency of water that it would suffocate him, or from the light and warmth of fire, that it would consume him. No object ever discovers, by the qualifiers which appear to the senses, either the causes which produced it, or the effects which will arise from it; nor can our reason, unassisted by experience, ever draw any inference concerning real existence and matter of fact.

This proposition, *that causes and effects are discoverable, not by reason, but by experience*, will readily be admitted with regard to such objects, as we remember to have once been altogether unknown to us; since we must be conscious of the utter inability, which we then lay under, of foretelling, what would arise from them. Present two smooth pieces of marble to a man, who has no tincture of natural philosophy; he will never discover, that they will adhere together, in such a manner as to require great force to separate them in a direct line, while they make so small a resistance to a lateral pressure. Such events, as bear little analogy to the common course of nature, are also readily confessed to be known only by experience; nor does any man imagine that the explosion of gunpowder, or the attraction of a loadstone, could ever be discovered by arguments *a priori*. In like manner, when an effect is supposed to depend upon an intricate machinery or secret structure of parts, we make no difficulty in attributing all our knowledge of it to experience. Who will assert, that he can give the ultimate reason, why milk or bread is proper nourishment for a man, not for a lion or a tiger?

But the same truth may not appear, at first sight, to have the same evidence with regard to events, which have become familiar to us from our first appearance in the world, which bear a close analogy to the whole course of nature, and which are supposed to depend on the simple qualities of objects, without any secret structure of parts. We are apt to imagine, that we could discover these effects by the mere operation of our reason, without experience. We fancy, that were we brought, on a sudden, into this world, we could at first have inferred, that one Billiard-ball would communicate motion to another upon impulse; and that we needed not to have waited for the event, in order to pronounce with certainty concerning it. Such is the influence of custom, that, where it is strongest, it not only covers our natural ignorance, but even conceals itself, and seems not to take place, merely because it is found in the highest degree.

But to convince us, that all the laws of nature, and all the operations of bodies without exception, are known only by experience, the following reflections may, perhaps, suffice. Were any object presented to us, and were we required to pronounce concerning the effect, which will result from it, without consulting past observation; after what manner, I beseech you, must the mind proceed in this operation? It must invent or imagine some event, which it ascribes to the object as its effect; and it is plain that this invention must be entirely arbitrary. The mind can never possibly find the effect in the supposed cause, by the most accurate scrutiny and examination. For the effect is totally different from the cause, and consequently can never be discovered in it. Motion in the second Billiard-ball is a quite distinct event from motion in the first; nor is there any thing in the one to suggest the smallest hint of the other. A stone or piece of metal raised into the air, and left without any support, immediately falls: But to consider the matter *a priori*, is there any thing we discover in this situation, which can beget the idea of a downward, rather than an upward, or any other motion, in the stone or metal?

And as the first imagination or invention of a particular effect, in all natural operations, is arbitrary, where we consult not experience; so must we also esteem the supposed tie or connexion between the cause and effect, which binds them together, and renders it impossible, that any other defect could result from the operation of that cause. When I see, for instance, a Billiard-ball moving in a straight line towards another; even suppose motion in the second ball should by accident be suggested to me, as the result of their contact or impulse; may I not conceive, that a hundred different events might as well follow from that cause? May not both these balls remain at absolute rest? May not the first ball return in a straight line, or leap off from the second in any line or direction? All these suppositions are consistent and conceivable. Why then should we give the preference to one, which is no more consistent or conceivable than the rest? All our reasonings *a priori* will never be able to show us any foundation for this preference.

In a word, then, every effect is a distinct event from its cause. It could not, therefore, be discovered in the cause, and the first invention or conception of it, *a priori*, must be entirely arbitrary. And even after it is suggested, the conjunction of it with the cause must appear equally arbitrary; since there are always many other effects, which, to reason, must seem fully as consistent and natural. In vain, therefore, should we pretend to determine any single event, or infer any cause or effect, without the assistance of observation and experience.

. . .

There are no ideas, which occur in metaphysics, more obscure and uncertain, than those of *power, force, energy, or necessary connexion*, of which it is every moment necessary for us to treat in all our disquisitions. We shall, therefore, endeavour, in this section, to fix, if possible, the precise meaning of these terms, and thereby remove some part of that obscurity, which is so much complained of in this species of philosophy.

. . .

It seems a proposition, which will not admit of much dispute, that all our ideas are nothing but copies of our impressions, or, in other words, that it is impossible for us to *think* of any thing, which we have not antecedently *felt*, either by our external or internal senses. I have endeavoured to explain and prove this proposition, and have expressed my hopes, that, by a proper application of it, men may reach a greater clearness and precision in philosophical reasonings, than what they have hitherto been able to attain. Complex ideas may, perhaps, be well known by definition, which is nothing but an enumeration of those parts or simple ideas, that compose them. But when we have pushed up definitions to the most simple ideas, and find still some ambiguity and obscurity; what resource are we then possessed of? By what invention can we throw light upon these ideas, and render them altogether precise and determinate to our intellectual view? Produce the impressions or original sentiments, from which the ideas are copied. These impressions are all strong and sensible. They admit not of ambiguity. They are not only placed in a full light themselves, but may throw light on their correspondent ideas, which lie in obscurity. And by this means, we may, perhaps, attain a new microscope or species of optics, by which, in the moral sciences, the most minute, and most simple ideas may be so enlarged as to fall readily under our apprehension, and be equally known with the grossest and most sensible ideas, that can be the object of our enquiry.

To be fully acquainted, therefore, with the idea of power or necessary connexion, let us examine its impression; and in order to find the impression with greater certainty, let us search for it in all the sources, from which it may possibly be derived.

When we look about us towards external objects, and consider the operation of causes, we are never able, in a single instance, to discover any power or necessary connexion; any quality, which binds the effect, to the cause, and renders the one an infallible consequence of the other. We only find, that the one does actually, in fact, follow the other. The impulse of one billiard-ball is attended with motion in the second. This is the whole that appears to the *outward senses*. The mind feels no sentiment or *inward* impression from this succession of objects: Consequently, there is not, in any single, particular instance of cause and effect, any thing which can suggest the idea of power or necessary connexion.

From the first appearance of an object, we never can conjecture what effect will result from it. But were the power or energy of any cause discoverable by the mind, we could foresee the effect, even without experience; and might, at first, pronounce with certainty concerning it, by the mere dint of thought and reasoning.

In reality, there is no part of matter, that does ever, by its sensible qualities, discover any power or energy, or give us ground to imagine, that it could produce any thing, or be followed by any other object, which we could denominate its effect. Solidity, extension, motion; these qualities are all complete in themselves, and never point out any other event which may result from them. The scenes of the universe are continually shifting, and one object follows another in an uninterrupted succession; but the power or force, which actuates the whole machine, is entirely concealed from us, and never discovers itself in any of the sensible qualities of body. We know, that, in fact, heat is a constant attendant of flame; but what is the connexion between them, we have no room so much as to conjecture or imagine. It is impossible, therefore, that the idea of power can be derived from the contemplation of bodies, in single instances of their operation; because no bodies ever discover any power, which can be the original of this idea.

Part II

But to hasten to a conclusion of this argument, which is already drawn out to too great a length: We have sought in vain for an idea of power or necessary connexion, in all the sources from which we could suppose it to be derived. It appears, that, in single instances of the operation of bodies, we never can, by our utmost scrutiny, discover any thing but one event following another; without being able to comprehend any force or power, by which the cause operates, or any connexion between it and its supposed effect. The same difficulty occurs in contemplating the operations of mind on body; where we observe the motion of the latter to follow upon the volition of the former; but are not able to observe or conceive the tie, which binds together the motion and volition, or the energy by which the mind produces this effect. The authority of the will over its own faculties and ideas is not a whit more comprehensible: So that, upon the whole, there appears not, throughout all nature, any one instance of connexion, which is conceivable by us. All events seem entirely loose and separate. One event follows another; but we never can observe any tie between them. They *seem conjoined*, but never *connected*. And as we can have no idea of any thing, which never appeared to our outward sense or inward sentiment, the necessary conclusion *seems* to be, that we have no idea of connexion or power at all, and that these words are absolutely without any meaning, when employed either in philosophical reasonings, or common life.

But there still remains one method of avoiding this conclusion, and one source which we have not yet examined. When any natural object or event is presented, it is impossible for us, by any sagacity or penetration, to discover, or even conjecture, without experience, what event will result from it, or to carry our foresight beyond that object, which is immediately present to the memory and senses. Even after one instance or experiment, where we have observed a particular event to follow upon another, we are not entitled to form a general rule, or foretell what will happen in like cases; it being justly esteemed an unpardonable temerity to judge of the whole course of nature from one single experiment, however accurate or certain. But when one particular species of event has always, in all instances, been conjoined with another, we make no longer any scruple of foretelling one upon the appearance of the other, and of employing that reasoning, which can alone assure us of any matter of fact or existence. We then call the one object, *Cause*, the other, *Effect*. We suppose, that there is some connexion between them; some power in the one, by which it infallibly produces the other, and operates with the greatest certainty and strongest necessity.

It appears, then, that this idea of a necessary connexion among events arises from a number of similar instances, which occur, of the constant conjunction of these events; nor can that idea ever be suggested by any one of these instances, surveyed in all possible lights and positions. But there is nothing in a number of instances, different from every single instance, which is supposed to be exactly similar; except only, that after a repetition of similar instances, the mind is carried by habit, upon the appearance of one event, to expect its usual attendant, and to believe that it will exist. This connexion, therefore, which we *feel* in the mind, this customary transition of the imagination from one object to its usual attendant, is the sentiment or impression, from which we form the idea of power or necessary connexion. Nothing farther is in the case. Contemplate the subject on all sides; you will never find any other origin of that idea. This is the sole difference between one instance, from which we can never receive the idea of connexion, and a number of similar instances, by which it is suggested. The first time a man saw the communication of motion by impulse, as by the shock of two billiard-balls, he could not pronounce that the one event was *connected*: but only that it was *conjoined* with the other. After he has observed several instances of this nature, he then pronounces them to be *connected*. What alteration has happened to give rise to this new idea of *connexion?* Nothing but that he now *feels* these events to be *connected* in his imagination, and can readily foretell the existence of one from the appearance of the other. When we say, therefore, that one object is connected with another, we mean only, that they have acquired a connexion in our thought, and give rise to this inference, by which they become proofs of each other's existence: A conclusion, which is somewhat extraordinary; but which seems founded on sufficient evidence. Nor will its evidence be weakened by any general diffidence of the understanding, or sceptical suspicion concerning every conclusion, which is new and extraordinary. No conclusions can be more agreeable to scepticism than such as make discoveries concerning the weakness and narrow limits of human reason and capacity.

And what stronger instance can be produced of the surprising ignorance and weakness of the understanding, than the present? For surely, if there be any relation among objects, which it imports to us to know perfectly, it is that of cause and effect. On this are founded all our reasonings concerning matter of fact or existence. By means of it alone we attain any assurance concerning objects, which are removed from the present testimony of our memory and senses. The only immediate utility of all sciences, is to teach us, how to control and regulate future events by their causes. Our thoughts and enquiries are, therefore, every moment, employed about this relation: Yet so imperfect are the ideas which we form concerning it, that it is impossible to give any just definition of cause, except what is drawn from something extraneous and foreign to it. Similar objects are always conjoined with similar. Of this we have experience. Suitably to this experience, therefore, we may define a cause to be *an object, followed by another, and where all the objects, similar to the first, are followed by objects similar to the second.* Or in other words, *where, if the first object had not been, the second never had existed.* The appearance of a cause always conveys the mind, by a customary transition, to the idea of the effect. Of this also we have experience. We may, therefore, suitably to this experience, form another definition of cause; and call it, *an object followed by another, and whose appearance always conveys the thought to that other.* But though both these definitions be drawn from circumstances foreign to the cause, we cannot remedy this inconvenience, or attain any more perfect definition, which may point out that circumstance in the cause, which gives it a connexion with its effect. We have no idea of this connexion; nor even any distinct notion what it is we desire to know, when we endeavour at a conception of it. We say, for instance, that the vibration of this string is the cause of this particular sound. But what do we mean by that affirmation? We either mean, *that this vibration is followed by this sound, and that all similar vibrations have been followed by similar sounds*: Or, *that this vibration is followed by this sound, and that upon the appearance of one, the mind anticipates the senses, and forms immediately an idea of the other.* We may consider the relation of cause and effect in either of these two lights; but beyond these, we have no idea of it.

To recapitulate, therefore, the reasonings of this section: Every idea is copied from some preceding impression or sentiment; and where we cannot find any impression, we may be certain that there is no idea. In all single instances of the operation of bodies or minds, there is nothing that produces any impression, nor consequently can suggest any idea, of power or necessary connexion. But when many uniform instances appear, and the same object is always followed by the same event; we then begin to entertain the notion of cause and connexion. We then *feel* a new sentiment or impression, to wit, a customary connexion in the thought or imagination between one object and its usual attendant; and this sentiment is the original of that idea which we seek for. For as this idea arises from a number of similar instances, and not from any single instance; it must arise from that circumstance, in which the number of instances differ from every individual instance. But this customary connexion or transition of the imagination is the only circumstance, in which they differ. In every other particular they are alike. The first instance which we saw of motion, communicated by the shock of two billiard-balls (to return to this obvious illustration) is exactly similar to any instance that may, at present, occur to us; except only, that we could not, at first, *infer* one event from the other; which we are enabled to do at present, after so long a course of uniform experience. I know not, whether the reader will readily apprehend this reasoning. I am afraid, that, should I multiply words about it, or throw it into a greater variety of lights, it would only become more obscure and intricate. In all abstract reasonings, there is one point of view, which, if we can happily hit, we shall go farther towards illustrating the subject, than by all the eloquence and copious expression in the world. This point of view we should endeavour to reach, and reserve the flowers of rhetoric for subjects which are more adapted to them.

A Third View of Causality
Edward H. Madden

Edward H. Madden is a Professor of Philosophy at the State University of New York at Buffalo.

There have been a number of alternatives offered to the Humean position on causality but they have not seemed very satisfactory, trying, as they usually do, to prove too much and ignoring much of value in what the historical Hume had to say. In what follows I will sketch a third view of causal necessity that seems more plausible to me than either the Humean or entailment theories we are generally offered as the only reasonable alternatives. I will show also what I take to be insurmountable difficulties in the contemporary Humean analysis of "nomic necessity," as well as trying to rebut certain objections that are bound to arise against my own view.

I

To begin with, there is a conceptual necessity implied in the very concept of cause itself, and in all concepts that have a causal element; and this definitional "must," far from being conventional or arbitrary, reflects the natural necessity of those physical systems which in fact constitute the nature of our universe.[1] The conceptual necessity of the concept of cause can be pointed up in the following way. Assume that we have good reason for saying at t_0 that f, g, h, and i are jointly sufficient to E and hence C of E. What would we say at t_1 if f, g, h, and i occurred but not E? We would clearly not say then, or ever, that while ordinarily these conditions are jointly sufficient for E, this time they were not; rather we would say that somehow we were mistaken in thinking that f, g, h, and i at t_1 were identical (except for location in space and time) with f, g, h, and i at t_1. We might have been mistaken in either of two ways. We might have mis-identified one of the conditions at t_1, erroneously thinking, say, that p was an f; or one or more of the conditions might have had its nature altered, losing some capacity or power it once had. In either case, we would withdraw the claim at t_1 that C was the cause of E. Since we would withdraw the use of C at t_1 and would never admit that f, g, h, and i at any t, if genuine instances of f, g, h, and i, would not produce E, we are clearly using C in such a way that actually producing E is part of its meaning. On the assumption that the conditions are genuinely the same (except for location in space and time), it follows, so to speak, from the principle of identity that they must produce the same effect.

So far we have seen how the concept of cause involves conceptual necessity, but the question immediately arises whether this necessity is only stipulative and conventional in nature or whether it actually tells us something about the nature of physical systems. The latter, it seems to me, is clearly the case if we take seriously our ordinary ways of thinking and see no compelling reason to depart from them. These ways have been taken seriously by such *prima facie* diverse thinkers as Aristotle, American radical empiricists, and certain Oxonian analysts, all of whom produce interestingly similar, though not identical, concepts of physical systems.[2]

To see that the conceptual necessity of "cause" reflects the necessity of physical systems, consider the ease of a suction pump. Let us say that the pressure of the air on the reservoir and the partial vacuum in the cylinder of the pump are the conditions jointly sufficient for raising the water up the pump and out the spigot. Ordinarily we would say that the atmosphere has the ability or power to push the water up the cylinder, when there is no counteracting pressure there, and that the water has the capacity, or disposition, to be pushed up the cylinder in the absence of air there. The power or ability of the atmosphere, in turn, would be explained by referring to the nature of the atmosphere – the atmosphere is a blanket of air around the surface of the earth; air has weight and so exerts pressure; and the farther down in the blanket of air the greater the weight and the greater the pressure, etc. While the power or ability of the atmosphere to raise water is understood by referring to its nature, such reference does not explain away the power. A Jaguar XK-E has the ability (is able, has the power) to do 120 m.p.h., and this ability is explained in terms of its having six cylinders, a certain kind of fuel injection pump, etc. – that is, in terms of the nature of the car.[3] But such explanations in terms of the nature of the car scarcely eliminate the notion that the car has power. "Power," "ability," and "nature" are intimately interwoven and any effort to assign ontological priorities among them is as futile as trying to assign priorities among the concepts of particulars, properties, and relations. The ineliminability of "power" and "ability" shows up again on the highest level of explanation where one can only ascribe power without any understanding of a nature that helps explicate that power. Confining ourselves to classical physics, we would say, e.g., that the masses of the earth and the atmosphere have the power of attracting each other but we do not know anything in the nature of the masses that explains the ability of mutual attraction. The ineliminable but non-mysterious powers and abilities of particular things, then, and not an ontological "tie that binds" causes and effects together is what the conceptual necessity of "cause" reflects. The power is in the atmosphere, though it will not produce an effect unless the partial vacuum in the cylinder exists, just as the power is in the attraction of the barn and the earth when the former collapses, though this effect would not have occurred unless the center beam had been removed. Running out of gasoline and the friction of tires on pavement are jointly sufficient for stopping the car, though it was the latter that had the power to stop the car, just as previously it was the exploding of the gasoline in the cylinder that provided the power to overcome that of friction.[4]

The concept "x has the power to do y," it is interesting to note, catches what might be called the strong sense of "potentiality," namely, "what would automatically happen if interfering conditions were absent or taken away." As long as gasoline is exploding in the cylinders, power is produced to overcome the normal operation of friction; and as long as the center beam is intact the attraction of the barn and earth is kept in check. But as soon as the gasoline runs out or the beam rots, the operation of these powers, a function of the structural and basic nature of our universe, comes into play. They finally produce the effect which had been held in abeyance by interfering conditions. Since interfering conditions cannot last forever, such potential events must eventually occur, though if the removal of the obstacles is under the control of man, the events need not occur at any given time.

In addition to the conceptual necessity involved in the concept of cause itself, there is conceptual necessity built into any concept whatever that has a causal component. Take, for example, the case of "copper."[5] For the scientist this term refers to something having the properties malleability, fusibility, ductility, electric conductivity, density 8.92, atomic weight 63.54, and atomic number 29 (properties both dispositional and explanatory in nature, be it noted). If an O lacked any of these features it would not be called C, or, if one thought O was C but it turned out not to have one of these features one would withdraw the ascription of C. In short, the ascription of C to O at any given time necessarily implies the presence of a cluster of properties. The reason for this conceptual necessity is clear: all the dispositional properties are interwoven closely with the concepts of atomic structure and hence with each other, so that if any part were missing the whole conceptual framework would be vitiated and the ascription of the concept C would be pointless. Again, this conceptual necessity, far from being stipulative in nature, has important ontological implications.

The first thing to note is that we are dealing here with capacities to undergo rather than abilities to do, with dispositions to react in certain ways under given conditions rather than powers to act in certain ways when the occasion arises. The copper wire has a disposition to flatten out when struck by a hammer, to melt when heated to 1,083 °C, and to conduct an electric charge. Yet the dispositional concepts of malleability, fusibility, and conductivity are just as much explained by the atomic structure of copper as the power of the atmosphere to raise water is explained by the nature of the atmosphere. Capacities just as much as powers, what particulars or substances are able to undergo as well as what they are able to do, are explained as dimensions of what the thing is itself.[6] Both what particulars are able to undergo and to do are determined by their natures – or, better, are manifestations of their natures – and hence to talk about particulars remaining the same and yet lacking their capacities and powers is to assert and deny at once that O has nature C. If we had compelling reason to believe we were not mistaken in identifying O as continuous from t_0 to t_1, but at t_1 O was not malleable, then we would correctly conclude that O had different capacities and powers at t_1 and hence had undergone a change in nature and was no longer the particular C it was at t_0. It is physically impossible for a substance to act or react incompatibly with its own nature. It is not impossible for O to act and react differently at t_1 than at t_0, but what is impossible is for it to do so and remain the same substance. In short, there is a natural necessity between what a thing is and what it is capable of doing and undergoing, and it is this natural necessity that the conceptual necessity of "copper" reflects.

There seems, however, to be an immediate problem with this view, since some individuals do gain or lose certain capacities or powers but do not thereby lose their identity – they still have the same nature.[7] A drug may lose its effectiveness over a period of time, photographic paper will not make prints after a while, and a person may lose his capacity to remember names; but the drug, paper, and person do not thereby lose their identities. This is only a *prima facie* problem, however, since such changes in powers and capacities themselves occur in some theoretical ambit within which they are explained, and hence the overall theory provides the invariable and identical nature of x which continues constant throughout the changes while explaining them. Such theoretical structures also presuppose what might be called the nature of some "fundamental particulars," space and time, etc., in the sense that their natures are taken as unchanging in order to explain those particulars which are held to be identical through changes.

II

The notion of causal or physical necessity is far from simple in nature and needs to be seen from different angles to be fully understood. Two new angles will be introduced in the present section – the direct experience of causal power or efficacy, on the one hand, and an examination of the nature of scientific explanation, on the other. There is a vast literature on both questions, so I will restrict myself severely to clarifying what I take to be fundamental issues.

To begin with, there is a great deal of confusion surrounding the claim that we are sometimes directly aware of causal power or efficacy. Critics often dismiss the claim out of hand because no one, including Hume, they say, denies we have an experience of causal connection – the question is: what is the correct philosophical analysis of this fact?[8] Critics are also suspicious of the claim because it seems to lead inevitably to pan-psychism or animism.[9] However, both of these criticisms are misguided and reflect a lack of appreciation of what a sophisticated formulation of the direct-experience-of-causality view would be.

Hume, it is true, never doubted that we have an experience of causal connectedness, and provided the following philosophical analysis of it. Since we do not have the idea of necessary connection between events, it must be derived somehow from experience. However, we are unable to find the original of this idea either in the impressions of the senses or in the internal impressions of volition. Since we do not see, feel, or hear causal necessity the idea of it cannot be derived from the impressions of our senses. Nor can it be traced to any single "internal impression," not even to our consciousness of the influence of the will. We are never able, after all, to predict with certainty that an act of willing will have its expected results. Moreover, we are not directly aware of the causal power that raises the arm because the cause includes, besides willing to raise the arm, many other neural and muscular conditions and events with which we cannot be directly acquainted. Hume concludes that the original of the idea of necessary connection, since it does not arise from a single impression, must arise from a repetition of similar instances which produces the habit or customary transition of the imagination from one object to its usual attendant. One comes to *feel* the events to be connected, though they are not, for all that, shown to be actually connected.

The advocate of direct experience claims that Hume's analysis is faulty and provides an alternate one of his own – where "analysis," however, is not equivalent to "providing a definition."[10] In briefest of outlines the strategy of the most sophisticated direct-experience advocate has three parts. First, he rejects Hume's associationistic explanation of how we come to have an idea of necessary connection. This part of Hume's thesis is factual in nature and can be seen to be clearly mistaken in the light of modern psychological investigations of the origin of the concept of causality. Second, he rejects Hume's claim that "internal impressions" cannot yield the concept of physical necessity. In the case of voluntarily raising my arm I do experience directly a power of will involved in producing the effect. It is true that I do not experience a power relation between the whole set of conditions jointly sufficient to moving my arm, but Hume's assumption that if power is to be experienced at all it must be experienced between all necessary conditions and the effect is simply unwarranted – just as Hume's assumption that the only legitimate sense of "cause" is "set of conditions jointly sufficient for e" is unwarranted. Third, the advocate of direct perception must avoid the claim that only in volitional cases is he directly aware of causal power. If he does not avoid the "inferential predicament" he will inevitably land in panpsychism and animism. One gets into the inferential predicament by arguing in the following way. I feel the force of the wind bending me and conclude that it must also be the force of the wind bending the slanting tree. There is, however, much psychological and common-sense evidence (including the use of causal expressions) to suggest that we directly apprehend the operation of power between objects and events even before we experience it between objects or events and ourselves. The paradigm for direct experience of power is wind-bending-tree not wind-bending-me. It is instructive to compare the inferential predicament in causality with its counterpart in the causal theory of perception, where one has a visual impression, a factual impression, and so on, and then "infers" somehow the physical object which causes all the impressions. The "inference" here, however, is just as evanescent and unlocated as the supposed inference in causal experience from wind-bending-me to wind-bending-tree.

Now let us turn our attention briefly to the nature of scientific explanation and see what implications it has for the concept of causal necessity. Recall again the power of the atmosphere to raise water in the cylinder of a pump. Call gravitational theory U′ and the water going up the pump U. U must occur relative to U′, we say, because the latter, plus information to the effect that there is a partial vacuum in the cylinder, explains why U happens rather than something else, say, the water's turning purple. If something else like this could have happened, we would not have succeeded in explaining why U happened rather than it. Conversely, we have good reason for believing that U′ is the case because it is indirectly and independently established by various U sets of events and laws that it conceptually unites. Hence, the necessity in a body of knowledge follows from what must be the case if U′ is true, and we have good reason for believing that U′ is the case. It does not follow, however, that U′ is necessarily true in the sense that its meaning entails its existence. U′ is not necessarily true in the sense that it is the only possible physical framework. Rather the point is that given U′, certain U's are "hypothetically necessary" in the sense that, given U′, the denial of these statements would produce inconsistencies in the theory. Even though this universe is not the only possible one, the unifications of U's suggest that it is the actual one, and the adequacy of the theory means that it reflects the nature of *this* universe. Insofar as this theory is adequate, it is necessary, since a change in the physical universe would involve a change in the nature of the particulars of that universe; and, supposing such a change to occur, there would be a new universe with a new nature, a new adequate theory, etc. So there is a necessity corresponding to the nature of the actual, though this necessity does not imply that the actual is itself necessary in the sense that its denial is self-contradictory.

III

The contemporary Humean himself believes that there are "nomic universals" which are more than mere generalizations over time, but insists that such universals can be analyzed adequately within his own frame of reference without requiring the concept of physical necessity.[11] I believe he does not sustain the claim, and in principle cannot, though it will take a bit of digging to show why not.

Roughly stated, the dominant contemporary Humean account of a particular causal statement would be: "x is the cause of y" means "there is a set of initial conditions x, a set of subsequent conditions y, and there is a law or set of laws L, and a set of meaning postulates M (definitions, semantical rules, etc.), such that L · M · x entails y and y is not entailed by any of the following: x, M, L, x · M, x · L, M · L, or z · M · L, where z is any proper subset of x." If statistical laws are included in L, then L · M · x entails only "y is probable" or "y is highly probable." L, in turn, is characterized as a "nomic universal" and distinguished from accidental and summative universals in the following way. Nomic universals are those which in addition to being true are *lawlike*; and universals are lawlike whenever in addition to being true they share some intrinsic characteristic like "contain only purely qualitative predicates," "are unrestricted in scope," "have a scope not closed to further argumentation," and "the evidence for which does not coincide with the scope of predication'; or when they have certain epistemic relations to some corpus of scientific or common-sense knowledge. While nomic universals of this sort give the required sense of universality beyond mere generality over time, they do not commit one to any non-Humean concept of physical or causal necessity. One has, so to speak, the cash equivalent of "necessity" without any ontological mortgages.

There are, however, a number of difficulties with this contemporary formulation of the Humean thesis, some of which, like difficulties with the deduction requirement, have been pointed out endlessly. There are also difficulties with the proposed definition-in-use because it confuses the meaning of a causal assertion with certain reasons that legitimately might be given for saying that some x is the cause of y. It is also perfectly legitimate in various prudential, legal, and scientific contexts to single out one of the antecedent conditions as cause, though this is no striking criticism since essentially the same Humean analysis could be reformulated to fit such contexts.[12] The criticism I am interested in pressing centers rather around the concepts of "nomic universal" and "lawlikeness." The latter concept is itself untenable and hence no adequate substitute for the former. Conclusive counter-examples have been given for all the intrinsic characteristics which have been suggested as the common factor of nomic universals, and various counter-examples destructive of different strands in the epistemic characteristic have been offered.[13] It is sometimes argued against the latter counter-examples that they are inadequate because no theoretical terms are involved in their "higher-order laws," but Murray Kitely and I have constructed in detail a hypothetico-deductive system with theoretical terms which, nevertheless, has no vestige of "nomic universality" about it.[14]

The overall result of these discussions is that the whole concept of lawlikeness is hopeless. Every criterion proposed has a counter-example which eliminates it as the characteristic which all laws, plus being true, have in common. To be sure, it is possible that there are other criteria, but one has a tired feeling that they too would have counter-examples. The plain truth of the matter is that there is nothing that all laws have in common which, plus being true, makes them nomic universals. There is no set of necessary and sufficient conditions which a universal must meet before it can be called a "nomic universal." Some universals are called laws by scientists for a variety of reasons, none of which is necessary and any one of which may be sufficient if it does not conflict with the others. Some of these reasons are partially related, others mutually independent. Universals are sometimes called laws, depending upon the context, e.g., when they fit into an established body of knowledge or connect well with what we already know, when they have predictive or explanatory power, when they contain theoretical terms or are logically related to an assertion that does, when they occur in a model theory, when their initial conditions fill in spatio-temporal gaps, when different types of instances confirm them, and even when only the multiplication of instances confirms them, if they do not conflict with any of the other criteria. The presumption, in short, is that any generalization counts as a law unless there is good counter-evidence. Epistemic relations in a given context, thus, are important in deciding not only what counts as a law but what counts as an accidental universal also.

The contemporary Humean might reply by saying that he is convinced that searching for what all laws have in common is a mistake and will abandon the concept of lawlikeness. He also agrees that a body of knowledge is necessary both to characterize a universal as accidental and as a law. But given the fact that in specific contexts we *can* distinguish laws from accidents we have, he says, all the Humean needs. Such laws are nomic universals and support counter-factual inferences while accidental universals do not.

Although this new position would be a great improvement over the previous one, nevertheless it is not without difficulties itself. Take the case of the suction pump again. Here we say that "whenever there is a partial vacuum, water goes up the cylinder" is a nomic universal because it can be inferred from what we know about atmospheric pressure and gravitational attraction. However, as we indicated, there are counter-examples from which we can infer non-nomic universals from a body of integrated knowledge, whether or not theoretical terms are involved in the higher-order "laws." Now what distinguishes the pump case as genuinely nomic as contrasted with the counter-examples? It is that the counter-examples have no power to explain in fact why any particular conclusion must follow rather than something else. The counter-examples are destructive only of alleged formal characteristics shared by all instances of "law"; they are not counter-examples of genuine laws. The only counter-example of a law would be to show that in fact there was some negative case, and we did not have a law after all. In a genuine case of nomic universality like that of the pump, however, there is an actual explanation in terms of the powers, capacities, and natures of substances why one result rather than another had to be the case – why, that is, the water must go up the cylinder rather than turning purple. But if a common-sense or scientific explanation genuinely shows why something must be the case rather than something else, then the Humean position must be abandoned as inadequate for explicating "nomic necessity."

Humeans sometimes try to salvage the concept of nomic necessity by giving a sense of "must" with one hand and taking it away with the other. It is true, they say, that x has to occur, or "must" occur, rather than something else because some system of knowledge requires or explains it. However, the most fundamental hypothesis of all, whatever constitutes the framework in which this "must" relation gets its meaning, is itself not necessary but only contingent and hence the whole system ultimately is contingent and not causally or physically necessary.

Here certainly the effort to get the cash value of nomic necessity without onto-logical mortgages is most jarring. The major error of the Humean consists in thinking that because the whole system is contingent what happens within the system is also contingent. But the latter is a non sequitur. It is true that there is an infinite number of possible universes and a contingent fact that we happen to have the one we do. To say our universe is contingent is to say that there is nothing about its nature that renders its existence necessary. But from the fact that our universe is not a necessary one it does not follow that, given our universe, what happens within it is not necessary. If something else could happen within it, then our actual universe would have a different constitution than it does have. And if something else than what must happen could happen within any system, then no explanation within that system could ever occur because one would not have succeeded in explaining the occurrence of one event rather than another.

IV

We have rejected the Humean analysis of "nomic necessity" as in principle untenable and have put in its place the concept of physical or causal necessity, a notion, we have claimed, which is internally sound and dovetails with our intuitions, common sense, and the structure of scientific explanation. However, there can be little doubt that contemporary Humeans would return the compliment by rejecting the present analysis as not simply false in detail but unsound in princi-ple. So it is necessary for me to meet these complaints before it can be said I have mounted anything like an adequate defense of my third view of causality. What criticism the Humean would offer is not difficult to guess, since any notion of physical necessity goes against what he sees as eternal verities – principles which, he feels, have been established beyond doubt by now.

(i) In principle there can be no concept of necessity in the causal relation because the conjunction of C & E is never self-contradictory. This insight sup-posedly applies to all efforts to show that physical necessity is an irreducible concept. There is no self-contradiction in saying that water in the reservoir turns purple instead of going up the cylinder when a partial vacuum is created there, or that water freezes when heated, or that air pressure decreases with depth, no matter how unexpected these results might be. The reason that asserting C & E is never self-contradictory is that the notion of a change in the course of nature is not self-contradictory.

The question immediately arises of what a Humean means by "a change in the course of nature is not self-contradictory." The only plausible answer is this: there are logically consistent systems of statements of the form *if x, then y*, which do not conform to the way things are, and there is nothing in these systems and in the system U′ which does fit our universe which *entails* the falsity of each other. But there is nothing in this analysis which counts against my position. The fact that all possible U′s do not entail the falsity of each other is equivalent to saying that no U′ is necessarily true in the sense that its meaning entails its existence. Not only does this view not conflict with what I hold, but indeed I have urged this point myself. However, while it is perfectly true that there is nothing self-contradictory about the notion of a change in the course of nature, there is something self-contradictory in the conjunction of C & E unless one puts double quotes around C to indicate that while "C" & E is not self-contradictory the notion of x as C of E has been relinquished. If "C" & E occurred there was a change in the nature of x, and it is no longer C. It *would be* self-contradictory to say that x has nature y which explains the occurrence of E, and hence is C of E, and yet x still has nature y when E occurs without C. All of these points can be applied in detail to the example of "copper" by the reader. There is a conceptual and physical necessity between the nature of O and how it acts and reacts, so that if the latter changes so has the former. Hence it is quite true that physical systems must always produce their results, though the Humean would be quite right in insisting that there is nothing self-contradictory in the concept of a change in the nature of a fundamental particular. There is nothing in what I have said that entails the necessity of the nature of any O remaining unchanged throughout time.

(ii) Even if the notion of causal necessity were acceptable, nothing could ever be known to be so related, since it is always logically possible to be mistaken whatever causal claim is made. There may be good evidence that eating strawberries caused my rash, but then I discover a case of "C" & E and conclude that it was not strawberries after all. There seems to be good evidence now that C is some ingredient found in several foods, one of which was always eaten before the rash appeared. But it is always possible that this causal claim too is false, since others like it for which there seemed to be good evidence have turned out to be false (the rash, after all, always appeared after eating strawberries before t_1), and so on, until the limit is reached – it is logically possible that every claim to the effect that x is the cause of y may be mistaken, no matter what x and y may be. Now it does not follow that because it is always possible to be mistaken about causal claims, that x and y are not necessarily related; but it does follow that they can never be known to be so related.

This argument, seemingly dependent only on the Humean insight that "C & E" is never self-contradictory, in fact proves too much, and leads to skepticism about any knowledge claims whatever.[15] The isomorphs of this type argument are unlimited. Even though there are accepted techniques for distinguishing veridical and illusory perception, it is always possible that the allegedly veridical ones are illusory or hallucinatory beyond the range of the accepted techniques to discover. While it would not follow that because it is always possible to be mistaken about perceptual claims that there are no physical objects, it would follow that they could never be known to exist. Again, even though there are accepted techniques for distinguishing a fair sample from a biased one, it is always possible that the allegedly fair sample is biased beyond the range of the accepted sampling techniques to discover. While it would not follow from this argument that there are no fair samples, it would follow that one could never know he had one.

To the assumption in this argument that "to know x" is equivalent to "being able to demonstrate x," a tempting but nevertheless mistaken reply is often given, though less frequently in recent years. According to this reply, key terms of the "skeptic's" argument are being used in a self-contradictory way. This type of reply has many variants of which the following is one extremely condensed variation.[16] Take the case of "fair sample." Though the specifications in the definiens are far from definite and precise, and though it is over-simplified in other ways, this definition of "fair sample" is apparently correct: "sample that has been randomly selected, stratified, etc." Now if the skeptic uses "fair sample" in this regular sense, he is referring to a kind of sample revealed by one of the vague requirements or some refinement thereof. If he does utilize this meaning, but also talks about a "fair sample" which one can never know he has, or have good reason to believe he has, no matter how many or refined the requirements it meets, then his use of the term is self-inconsistent, meaning that at once it both does and does not satisfy the regular requirements of a fair sample. If the use of the term is to avoid self-inconsistency, it must function in some new sense. Since no new sense is provided, however, if it is not self-inconsistent, it is vacuous.

The decisive difficulty with this reply, it is important to see, is one that it shares, strangely enough, with the Humean tradition itself, namely, the confusion between the meaning of a term and evidence for its justifiable application. Except for one who wants to prove a point, "fair sample" does not mean "sample that has been stratified . . ." but rather "sample that reflects the ratio of "x's to y's in the whole population." Random selection and stratification, then, can be seen as reasons for claiming that any given sample is a fair one. By identifying the meanings of "fair sample" and "sample that is stratified . . .," a person would be unable to give as a reason why a given sample is a fair one the facts that it has been stratified, randomly selected, etc.; but this, of course, is precisely what one wants to be able to do.

The beginning of a more appropriate reply to the Humean consists in pointing out that the possibility of being mistaken is no good reason for thinking one is mistaken. Recall the problem of distinguishing between accidental and nomic universals. Any universal counts as a law unless there is counter-evidence which shows why it must be construed as accidental. And so it is with any fundamental distinction, whether it be between accidental and nomic universals, veridical and illusory experiences, or fair and biased samples – a body of knowledge is presupposed in which the distinctions themselves make sense. To call x accidental, illusory, or biased, and to call x nomic, veridical, or fair, all require positive reasons drawn from this frame of reference; simply pointing out that it is logically possible to be mistaken wholly leaves open the question whether one is or not, just as simply pointing out that it is logically possible one is correct wholly leaves open the question whether one is or not. One fears he has been shown to be wrong in his basic beliefs by the skeptic's argument, but he has only been shown that it is impossible to *demonstrate* their correctness. But we are reassured when we remember that a framework is presupposed for saying either that x is mistaken or is correct.

The historical Hume, it must be noted finally, can be interpreted in such a way that he is both an epistemic skeptic and yet draws back from this position partially by arguments similar to the one above. According to this interpretation of Hume, he is only claiming that constant conjunction is all we *perceive* of the causal relation, not that this constitutes the ontological *nature* of the relation. Hume rejects the principle that "nothing exists but experience" but concludes that what "cause" might denote beyond constant conjunction must forever remain unknown. Although we ordinarily mean "necessary connection" when we use the concept of causation, and believe that such a connection has ontological status, neither the definition nor the belief can be justified by reason or experience. And yet, Hume says, just as one believes in the existence of the external world by instinct, so nature has seen fit to set up within one's thought processes a habit or custom which impels one to accept causation as necessary. The reasonings concerning cause and effect thus are "more properly an art of the sensitive than of the cognitive part of our natures." And though reason is unequal to the task of proving that the external world exists and that there are necessary connections between objects and events, still it is equally incapable of proving these things impossible. This, plus the fact that the instinct which compels us to believe these things is useful, shows that it would be foolhardy to believe otherwise.

The moral of this historical excursion is twofold. It suggests that Hume himself would not accept the last "in principle" argument against my position and that, in general, Hume would not make a good contemporary Humean. It should be clear that, given this interpretation of Hume, my views on causality are no further from this historical Hume on one side than contemporary Humeans are from him on the other.

Notes

Revised version of a paper read at the Dartmouth College Philosophy Colloquium April 12, 1968. Discussions with Barry Cohen, James Humber, Kevin Traynor, and Eric Dayton were a help to me in formulating my ideas.

1   Cf. E. H. Madden, "Causality and the Notion of Necessity," in forthcoming volume of *Boston Studies in the Philosophy of Science*.
2   Among the radical empiricists, I have in mind particularly Sterling P. Lamprecht and among the Oxonian analysts Rom Harre and M. R. Ayers. See Lamprecht's *The Metaphysics of Naturalism* (New York, 1967), pp. 1–33, 112–145, and his "Of a Curious Reluctance to Recognize Causal Efficacy," *The Philosophical Review*, Vol. XXXIX (1930), pp. 403–414; Ayers' *The Refutation of Determinism* (London, 1968); C. Ducasse's *Nature, Mind, and Death* (La Salle, Ill., 1951), Chapter 8; and Richard Taylor's *Action and Purpose* (Englewood Cliffs, NJ, 1966).
3   Ayers, *The Refutation of Determinism*, pp. 84ff.
4   It is this point which illuminates the discussions between Lemprecht and Ducasse. Cf. Lamprecht, *The Metaphysics of Naturalism*, p. 141, and Ducasse, "Of the Spurious Mystery in Causal Connections," *Philosophical Review*, Vol. XXXIX (1930), pp. 398–403.
5   I am indebted here to Professor Ducasse's letters in the Ducasse–Dickinson Miller correspondence in my possession.
6   Cf. Rom Harré, "Powers and Qualities," part of a full scale work in production. I

am indebted to Professor Harré for letting me see this article.

7 Ibid. Cf. Ayers, *The Refutation of Determinism*, pp. 84–89.

8 T. R. Miles, "Michotte's Experiments and the Views of Hume," in A. Michotte, *The Perception of Causality* (New York, 1963), pp. 410–415; and D. W. Hamlyn, *The Psychology of Perception* (London, 1957), pp. 76ff.

9 A. J. Ayer, *The Foundations of Empirical Knowledge* (London, 1964). SML edition, pp. 183–199.

10 Lamprecht and Ducasse are the most sophisticated of the direct-experience-of-causality advocates. William James states the position well but cannot see how to avoid pan-psychism. Alfred North Whitehead also defends this view and unenthusiastically accepts certain pan-psychic implications.

11 In what follows, by "contemporary Humean" I mean especially Professors Hempel and Nagel.

12 Cf. Bernard Berofsky, "Causality and General Laws," *Journal of Philosophy*, Vol. LXIII (1966), p. 150.

13 Roderick M. Chisholm, "Law Statements and Counterfactual Inference," *Analysis*, Vol. XV (1955), pp. 97–105; Edward H. Madden, "Definition and Reduction," *Philosophy of Science*, Vol. 28 (1961), particularly pp. 390–394, and "Discussion: Ernest Nagel's *The Structure of Science*," *Philosophy of Science*, Vol. 30 (1963), pp. 64–70.

14 Edward H. Madden and Murray Kiteley, "Postulates and Meaning," *Philosophy of Science*, Vol. 29 (1962), pp. 66–78.

15 Madden, *The Structure of Scientific Thought* (Boston, 1960), pp. 340–342.

16 *Ibid.*, pp. 291–292, 312–317.

The Ethics of Explanation
Alan Garfinkel

Alan Garfinkel was educated at Yale University and is the author of *Forms of Explanation: Rethinking the Questions in Social Theory*, from which the following section is excerpted. Garfinkel argues that science is not value free and that the very nature of causality, which is a product of our causal explanations, involves the values and interests of those who are giving the explanation.

Value-free Social Science

It is commonly said that social science can and should be value free. In fact the idea of value freedom is often held to be synonymous with being objective and/or identified with the essence of the scientific spirit itself. We often hear the call for a "scientific" social science, and generally the view that lies behind it is that science is objective in that it is value free.

In philosophy, this view is associated with the logical positivism that dominated the philosophy of science in the first half of this century. But it is more common these days among working social scientists than among philosophers. In fact something of an anomaly now exists. Positivist doctrines are reaching the height of their popularity in certain areas of social science at the same time as their final rejection by philosophers of science.

The ideal of value freedom has several sources. Partly it stems from a desire to build social science on the model of natural science; the ideal is of value-free inquiry "just like in physics."

But let us leave aside the question of whether physics really is value free. Let us also leave aside the question of whether the natural and social sciences, in view of the difference in their subject matter, could possibly have the same methods. I want to examine the philosophical foundations of this claim to value neutrality, foundations which lie in some form or other of empiricism. If we were to press the question of how social science can possibly be value free, the usual answer would be some version of the empiricist view of science. We would be told that value-free objectivity is possible because theories can be tested, confirmed, and disconfirmed by means of objective observations These theory-neutral and pure observations serve as the standards against which theories can be tested. Consequently, the argument runs, theories can be accepted or rejected purely on the basis of objective observation and formal logic, sanitized of the corruption of values.

This view is familiar enough. Even in this extreme form one can find explicit exponents, and in one or another modified form it commands a respectable audience in academic social science. This is in spite of the fact that the main development in the philosophy of science in the last twenty-five years has been the thoroughgoing refutation of just these empiricist doctrines. Unfortunately, very little of the philosophical writing has been absorbed or even noticed by the social scientists. The work of philosophers like Quine, Putnam, Hanson, and Toulmin is not well known outside professional philosophy. Kuhn's *Structure of Scientific Revolutions* has had a certain vogue but even that is not well understood. It is surprising how little social scientists know about the difficulties of the simple model of observation and the confirmation of theories. For example, the work of Putnam, Hanson, and Toulmin has helped to show that observation is inevitably theory laden, and Quine and Rudner have argued that the confirmation of theories necessarily involves values. Very little notice has been taken of these arguments.

My concern here, however, is not to argue these issues but rather to make a parallel argument in the theory of explanation. For there is another basic source for the idea of value-free social science, another empiricist doctrine, this one about the nature of causality and causal explanation.

Its essence lies in a certain way of looking at the relation between social science on the one hand and social policy on the other. The idea is that the "factual" aspects of the policy decision can be separated and distinguished from the "value-laden" aspects. In this view pure science comes packaged as causal statements which, by their nature as causal statements, are value free. The values are then added by the policymaker. If there are complaints about some application of the scientific statement, those complaints should be addressed to the policymaker or adviser, the one who made the practical decision, not the scientist.

This is, for example, the line taken by Hempel in *Aspects of Scientific Explanation*. In the chapter called "Science and Human Values" he says that science yields only instrumental judgments, that an action M is good or appropriate as a means to a goal G. But to say this is tantamount to asserting either that, in the circumstances at hand, course of action M will definitely (or probably) lead to the attainment of G or that failure to embark on course of action M will definitely (or probably) lead to the nonattainment of G. In other words, the instrumental value judgment asserts either that M is a (definitely or probably) sufficient means for attaining the end or goal G, or that it is a (definitely or probably) necessary means for attaining it. Thus, a relative, or instrumental, judgment of value can be reformulated as a statement which expresses a universal or probabilistic kind of means–end relationship, and which contains no term of moral discourse – such as "good," "better," "ought to" – at all.[1]

The idea is clear enough. Science gives us only conditional statements of the form "If . . ., then . . . ." These statements are perfectly value free, and the only place that values enter into the picture is when a policymaker decides to detach an "if" in order to get a desired "then." This view of the value neutrality of causal explanation is widely held; it is the conventional wisdom among social scientists, who often invoke the comparison to physics: "Physics tells us only that an atom bomb, for example, is *possible*. It doesn't tell us whether or not to build one. It simply reports the true statement that certain causal relations hold in the physical world." It is a view summarized by a famous dictum of Max Weber's (which Hempel cites approvingly): "Science is like a map; it can tell us how to get to a given place, but it cannot tell us where to go." The basic claim is that a certain division of labor can be effected. The causal reasoning is done by the value-free scientist, and the value judgments are made by the policymaker. The syllogism representing the practical judgment can thus be analyzed into a purely factual means–end premise and a purely evaluative end. The examples of Hempel and others have as their general form:

A causes B. (science)

B is desirable. (value)

Do A. (policy)

or

A causes B. (science)

B is undesirable. (value)

Avoid A. (policy)

There is a great deal that can be said about when inferences of such forms are valid or invalid. I will not attempt to do a general study of such practical syllogisms. My purpose here is to ask whether this division of labor can really be effected and whether the fact that the scientist makes causal judgments means that the scientific premise is value free.

Suppose for a moment it is true that practical reasoning can be represented as the sum of a causal premise and an evaluative one. Does this mean that the maker of the causal premise is engaged in value-free activity? There is reason to think not. Look again at the quotation from Hempel; notice what he says at the very end, when he is asserting that the causal premise is value free: he says that certain *words* – "good," "ought," and so on – do not appear in the causal statement. The implication is that a statement in which those words do not appear does not have any values in it. This is false. Someone can do wrong by making statements in certain contexts which contain no moral words and are causal in form.

For example, if you know that Anne Frank is hiding in the attic, it is morally wrong to utter the statement, "If you look in the attic, you'll find Anne Frank" in the presence of Nazi search parties. It is absolutely no defense in such a case to object that you were merely making a causal and therefore value-neutral statement. Thus, even if a statement has no value words it does not mean that making the statement in a particular context is necessarily a value-free act.

Simple as it is, this point seems to be missed by many people. Positivist philosophers missed it because of their emphasis on syntax over pragmatics. But others miss the point for more self-serving reasons: scientists who want to forget about, or encourage other people to forget about, the social contexts in which their research is being applied. The division of labor argument was very popular, for example, during the Vietnam War, when certain scientists were criticized for doing war-related research. "Look," they would say, "all I'm doing is abstract research on the relative effectiveness of defoliants (or the stability of helicopter gunship platforms, or the structure of field communication among the Vietcong). If you have some objection to what the Army is doing, shouldn't you take it up with them directly?"

I think we can reject this argument on the principle that someone who knowingly supplies a bad cause with scientific know-how, like someone who supplies it with guns, does wrong in doing so. There will be clear cases for this principle in highly applied sciences, as in the examples above. The situation gets more and more difficult to evaluate as the application gets more remote and as the science itself gets more abstract. Actually, any fact may end up aiding some evil cause. So what are we to do? It may seem natural to object that the values in cases like these still arise outside science itself and that the "pure inquiry" does not embody values. Consider the simple statement "A causes B." Is that statement, taken by itself, value free? I suggest that it is not.

Partial Causality

It has been noted at least since Mill that if we look at the causal explanations that actually occur in science and in practical life, we see that they are, in a sense, *incomplete*. Explanations typically will mention only one or two causal factors of an event, yet cite them as *the* cause. We say, for example, that the striking of a match caused it to light. But the striking of the match is only one of a set of factors all of which had to occur in order for the match to light. All those additional factors, like the presence of oxygen and the dryness of the match, are somehow relegated to the background or otherwise taken for granted. What makes us choose one factor instead of another as "the" cause of an event? One answer is found in Collingwood's *Essay on Metaphysics*, where he points out that a number of systematic *pragmatic* principles function to select out "the" cause. The main one is that the factors we cite as the cause are those over which we have some practical control. We typically will cite a factor which "it is in our power to produce or prevent, and by producing or preventing which we can produce or prevent that whose cause it is said to be."[2]

> Thus, if my car fails to climb a steep hill, and I wonder why, I shall not consider my problem solved by a passer-by who tells me that the top of the hill is farther away from the earth's centre than its bottom, and consequently more power is needed to take a car uphill than to take her along the level. . . . But suppose a man comes along, opens the bonnet, holds up a loose high-tension lead, and says: "Look here, sir, you're running on three cylinders." My problem is now solved. I know the cause of the stoppage. . . . It has been correctly identified as the thing that I can put right, after which the car will go properly. If I had been a person who could flatten out hills by stamping on them the passer-by would have been right to call my attention to the hill as the cause of the stoppage; not because the hill was a hill but because I was able to flatten it out. (pp. 302–3)

So the element which is brought into the foreground as "the" cause is the element over which we have practical control, while the rest is relegated to a background which is taken for granted or presupposed. It follows that in other contexts, different practical situations may call for different factors to be selected as the cause of the same phenomenon. Samuel Gorovitz, in an extension of Collingwood's discussion, talks about the example of the striking of the match and offers another sort of context, in which a nonstandard factor would be cited as the cause:

> A match, having been pulled from the assembly line in a match factory, is struck in a supposedly evacuated chamber, the purpose being to test the hardness of the match head. But the chamber has not been properly sealed, and the match lights. . . . The cause can reasonably be said to be the presence of oxygen, and not the striking.[3]

Thus, we have two different causal models, which we could represent as

striking [oxygen . . .] match lights

and

oxygen present [striking . . .] match lights

Collingwood also remarks on the dependence of cause on context and says, in effect, that when there are different handles on the phenomenon, we may have different explanations; he calls this "the relativity of causes":

> For example, a car skids while cornering at a certain point, strikes the kerb, and turns turtle. From the car-driver's point of view the cause of the accident was cornering too fast, and the lesson is that one must drive more carefully. From the county-surveyor's point of view, the cause was a defect in the surface or camber of the road, and the lesson is that greater care must be taken to make roads skid-proof. From the motor manufacturer's point of view the cause was defective design in the car, and the lesson is that one must place the centre of gravity lower. (p. 304)

The point is clear but there is something odd about his story. The characters in the auto accident would shame Sartre in their insistence on their own responsibility. Real people in auto accidents do not tend to be existential heroes. In fact the opposite is true. In a real accident the driver would jump out of the car and blame the auto manufacturer and/or the road builder. The road builder, of course, would reply: "You idiot. The roads are fine. It's the junk cars they're making today." Perhaps, in the absence of the manufacturer, they could agree that *given* the present state of the roads and *given* the driver's tendency to take corners fast, the cause of the accident was the poor design of the car. Of course the manufacturer will say, "What can you do? When people drive like that. . . ."

The relation between causality and practical control is more complicated than Collingwood and the others have imagined. In certain cases the principle "Select as the cause those things over which you have control" is replaced by "Minimize your own role in all this by selecting as the cause those things over which you do *not* have control." The standard accounts of causal selection do not acknowledge this inversion of practicality. But it is clear enough that it happens.

Sometimes, of course, the standard criterion is invoked, where the practical demands of the situation require an explanation in terms of certain variables. Suppose, for example, that you are hired by a team as a strategist. Your job is to explain to the team why it won or lost each game. If the team loses, you will not be doing your job if you say something like "We lost because they have that great half-back, who ran all over us, and scored three touchdowns." Here Collingwood is right. Your employers will say to you, "Don't tell us that. Tell us what we could have done, but failed to do, to stop him." The principle "Don't blame the other team; explain wins and losses in terms of team policy variables" is a sound principle for an in-house strategist. What the team's publicist says can be quite different since the purpose in that case might be to shift the focus away from the team's weaknesses.

And so, if a causal model separates the causal factors into foreground causes and background conditions, it is evident that the choice of a specific model may be motivated by a desire to locate responsibility in one place rather than another. But the important thing is this: Even if this desire is absent, it can still make sense to speak of a causal model as loaded or biased, independently of anyone's motivations. This enables us to avoid the question of the intentions of the scientist, for we can say that a causal model is loaded in and of itself. This is crucial for understanding the role of such models in situations where the motives of the scientists may be obscure or controversial. What I am suggesting is that motives are irrelevant to the assessment of the ideological "load" in a particular causal model. The value ladenness is a fact about the explanation not its proponents. It is value laden insofar as it insists, as a prescientific requirement, that change come from this sector rather than that.

This is how ideology becomes possible. A woman goes to a psychiatrist and says that she has been having fights with her husband. The psychiatrist says something like this: "You are having fights with your husband. Let us see what you are doing that contributes to these fights. There must be *something*, for after all, it takes two to have a fight. So we have to work on whatever it is that you're doing." Obviously, the burden of change has been placed on the woman, for the psychiatrist has written the causal model

wife's actions [husband] fight

Such a choice of framework, I want to say, stands in need of justification, and we have not so far been given one. Why has one causal factor been let off the hook? Sometimes, this will be justified by the statement that it is the woman, after all, who is the patient, not the husband, and one must work where one can; or it may be accompanied by fashionable admonitions to the woman to "take responsibility." But the end result is the same. Employing this framework amounts, in practice, to exempting the husband from responsibility.

Even at this very simple level we can find examples of this phenomenon at work in social science. Consider the case of the wage–price spiral. We are told that the cause of the rise in prices is a rise in wages. Writing this as

wages rise [???] prices rise,

we may ask, What factors are being absolved from causal responsibility? Obviously, one of the factors being held constant is the rate of profit. If profits were allowed to fall, a rise in wages would not produce a rise in prices. When this is pointed out, the response will be some further reason why profits *ought not* to decrease. In other words the defense of a particular framework will be explicitly in ethical terms. Something like "profits are necessary for growth" will be suggested as the defense of this background condition, or perhaps "investors deserve profit as a reward for investing." I am not concerned here with the exact nature of such defenses or with actually evaluating them. I want only to point out that they are required. In the typical case such justifications are not offered or are offered only in response to objections. The student is simply told that a certain causal relation holds. The fact that such justifications are usually omitted is doubly significant, for the choice of framework amounts to a choice of who is to bear responsibility.

Consequently, if the "scientific" premise, the statement "A causes B" is a statement of partial causality and cites only some of the causal factors, the whole syllogism will suffer. In such a case, drawing the conclusion "avoid A" from the premises "A causes B" and "B is undesirable" is simply fallacious, as in the case of the psychiatrist above. (We could call the fallacy the *argu-mentum ad valium*). If the woman's conduct, A, is something like "wanting to take an evening class," then the result of the practical syllogism will be that this must be avoided. Obviously, this advice is heavily loaded and not at all value free.

So this is a clear case of what we had set out to look for: a situation in which the causal premise itself was not value free. We could try to eliminate this value ladenness by taking a certain way out. Because examples like these are generated by seizing on one factor and holding it up as *the* cause, it seems natural to think that when we have brought *all* the factors up into the foreground and suppressed nothing, we will have achieved the kind of causal explanation necessary for value-free social science.

The idea that we must eliminate partial causes is very common among writers on the subject. The tradition begins with Mill himself, who laments the tendency

> to give the name of cause to almost any one of the conditions of a phenomenon, or any portion of the whole number, arbitrarily selected. . . . It will probably be admitted without longer discussion, that no one of the conditions has more claim to that title than another, and that the real cause of the phenomenon is the assemblage of all its conditions.[4]

There is almost universal agreement that the way out of this unfortunate value-ladenness is to fill out the partial causal model to the full causal explanation, in Mill's terms, "the sum total of the conditions . . . which, being realized, the consequent invariably follows."

This is the sort of explanation which the positivist writers, especially Hempel, cherished as the archetype of scientific explanation. The key feature is that, to rule out any partial causes, the thing cited as the cause must really be sufficient for the effect. In Hempel's model this sufficiency becomes complete logical sufficiency; the explanation logically entails the thing to be explained. Because of this it is not susceptible to the sort of fallacious usage that we saw in the case of the psychiatrist. If A really entails B, and B really is undesirable, then we really must avoid A. (Supposing, of course, that other conditions have been met. There may, for example, be means–end problems, or problems about balancing competing considerations.)

So it looks as if the way to avoid the hidden ethics lurking in the causal premise is to use the Hempelian model of explanation. The model presupposes that there is, in some statable form, the "full" cause of a given event. I suggest that there is no such thing and that there really is no way out of this ethics of explanation.

Are There Complete, Presuppositionless Explanations?

We are looking for an explanation which gives us the full cause and therefore is not subject to charges that it has arbitrarily (or worse) selected one causal factor. In order to see why such explanations are impossible, we must return to the earlier discussion of explanatory relativity, and ask: the full explanation *of what?* We might be tempted to say: of the event or state of affairs in question. But this is not so easy as it seems. Suppose the event in question is the auto accident I had yesterday. What is the full explanation of it? As we saw, if the object of explanation is that very accident, there is no such thing as the full explanation of it, for it would involve the whole history of the world, back through Henry Ford, the discovery of America, etc. If the object in question is a concrete particular, there is in some sense a "bad infinity" of causal factors.

To avoid this bad infinity, we had to introduce another piece of structure into the object of explanation: a sense of what will count as a relevant (or an irrelevant) difference from the event in question. Why this auto accident – rather than what? Rather than another ten feet down the road? Rather than no accident at all? Rather than one which was fatal? Each requires a different explanation.

Lacking this sense of what is to count as a relevant difference, there is no single explanation "of E." In the typical cases in which it looks as if we have a full explanation, we can find an implicit contrast space and we will have the explanation of why E rather than the contrast.

The effect of these contrast spaces is similar in a way to the suppressed causal antecedents. Both of them raise ethical problems.

Recall the Willie Sutton example. Sutton was asked why he robbed banks and gave as an answer, "Well, that's where the money is." Sutton's answer was really an answer to why he robs banks *as against robbing some other kind of thing*. It does not explain why he robs banks as against not robbing things, which was the priest's real question. The contrast space builds into its structure what is to count as a relevant alternative to the phenomenon, and the explanation explains E only as against the limited alternatives in the contrast space. The consequence of this is that once again certain possibilities are being excluded *a priori* from consideration. This will stand in need of justification.

The way in which the contrast space can slant the analysis is already obvious in the Willie Sutton case, and it is worth looking at its function in more serious cases. Explanations of unemployment seek to explain unemployment by citing factors which differentiate employed people from unemployed people, saying that S is unemployed because S has property F. Such explanations do not, in fact cannot, explain why there is unemployment at all. Rather, they explain why, given that someone is to be unemployed, it is S instead of someone else. To put it another way, all the elements in the contrast space had some people being unemployed; they differed only as to whom.

When we use explanations like that in practical reasoning, it has the obvious consequences. Because the existence of unemployed people is common to every element in the contrast space, it is presupposed by the explanation and therefore it is taken as unavoidable, practically speaking. All advice generated by this contrast space takes for granted that someone is to be unemployed; its problematic is limited to shifting around the names of the unemployed.

Such a constrast space allows us to ask only certain questions about unemployment and prevents us from asking others. As a consequence the judicious choice of a contrast space, as in the Sutton case, has an effect similar to the suppression of antecedents. Both limit the field of possibilities by what amount to prescientific requirements.

It will be clearer how such a limitation of possibility is value laden if we recall how explanations function in practical reasoning. Their role is to give us information on how we can produce or prevent the object in question. But then it follows that what exactly is taken to be a relevant alternative to the object in question is going to have a profound effect on what sort of methods will be allowable ways of producing and preventing it.

The point is this: since an explanatory framework allows only certain alternatives to B, any advice which the theory generates will be advice only on navigating among its recognized alternatives. And so an explanatory framework can be value laden by having a truncated or deformed sense of possibility. This feature plays the same role as the suppression of antecedents in the case of the woman and the psychiatrist in requiring that change come from this factor rather than that.

This phenomenon is deeper than the value ladenness associated with the Collingwood–Gorovitz model and its suppressed antecedents. The way out of *that* relativity appeared to be the insistence on the *complete* antecedent. Whether or not there is such a thing and whatever it might look like if there is, such a move does not work against explanatory relativity. For, if I am right, we can speak only of the complete antecedent of B-relative-to-X, where X is some definite range of alternatives. The relativity to a contrast space (or more elaborate form of explanation space) is an additional dimension of relativity, distinct from the suppression of antecedents.

Nevertheless, one might be tempted to take a similar line in response to it. That is, one might try to derelativize the object of explanation: Why not try to get the full explanation of E as the explanation of why E-rather-than-not-E? Such an explanation would not be subject to explanatory relativity.

The problem is that there is no such full explanation. In order for a why question to be determinate, some nontrivial contrast space must be supplied. If E is the event being explained, then the "full" question Why E-rather-than-not-E? has as its answer the totality of history up to that point. As we saw, in order to get a manageable explanation we have to supply a contrast as an additional piece of structure. This means that there is an inescapable way in which explanations are value laden.

Notes

1   C. Hempel, *Aspects of Scientific Explanation* (New York: Free Press, 1965), pp. 84–85.
2   R. G. Collingwood, *An Essay on Metaphysics* (Oxford: Oxford University Press. 1940), p. 296.
3   S. Gorovitz, "Causal Judgements and Causal Explanations," *Journal of Philosophy* 62 (1965): 695.
4   J. S. Mill, *A System of Logic* (New York: Longmans, Green, 1936), bk. 3, chap. 5, sec. 3, p. 403.

6

Mind and Morality

Introduction

Veterinarians need to know how to perform surgery on animals, and so this is something veterinary students have to learn while in veterinary school. To learn this, veterinary students have to practice surgery on live animals. For this reason, large veterinary teaching hospitals twenty years ago used to use live animals for practice surgery over and over again, even several times in one day, without any analgesia or anesthesia. Sometimes they would damage the animals – for instance, fracturing a dog's femur – just so students would have an opportunity to practice surgery.

This activity was justified on the basis of the belief that animals do not feel pain, and this belief was widely shared in the scientific community. Over the past two decades, this has changed. Veterinary teaching hospitals now use analgesia and anesthesia when performing surgeries, and animals are given a chance to recuperate before they are used again for surgery. In general, animal experimentation is now subject to more constraints and animal experimenters have to show greater concern for the welfare of their subjects than they did twenty years ago. The reason for this is that now the belief that animals do not feel pain is not widely shared by the scientific community, and thus the scientific community has come to recognize that it has some moral obligations toward animals.

Whether or not animals feel pain is relevant to the moral treatment of animals, because we have an obligation to avoid inflicting pain unless this pain is necessary for some greater good. So if surgery on an animal can be performed just as well with analgesia and anesthesia, we have an obligation to use these methods of suppressing pain. But whether or not animals feel pain is a question that cannot be answered without doing some metaphysics. We need to understand what it is to feel pain, and that is a topic in the philosophy of mind, which is a branch of metaphysics. Metaphysics tries to understand what it is to have a mind and to have mental states, and feeling pain is a mental state.

So over the past twenty years the veterinary community changed its philosophy of mind, particularly its philosophy of animal minds, and this brought about important changes in the way veterinarians treat non-human animals. Many have argued that this recognition that animals have minds and should be treated appropriately follows the same path set by our recognition of racism and sexism. The maltreatment of other races and sexes was and still is grounded in the belief that other races and sexes have lesser minds than one's own group, and that the struggle against this injustice was and still is a struggle against conceptions of mind that feed sexual and racial prejudice.

If our treatment of others and, we should hasten to add, ourselves depends on our views about what the mind is, we need to make sure we have accurate views about the nature of the mind. This means we need to have an accurate philosophy of mind, arguably one of the most fertile areas of metaphysics today. In this chapter we will survey the major views, particularly the divide between materialism and dualism, and draw a conclusion about the nature of the mind that takes both science and morality seriously.

Mind and Behavior

Consider the smile of a newborn infant. Young fathers and mothers are inclined to think that their child is showing affection and joy, while the infant's pediatrician will tell the (probably annoyed) parents that this is really not a smile, but a contortion of facial muscles in response to the pressure of intestinal gas. Wait one or two months and you will see a smile, they will say.

What we have here are two competing explanations of the infant's behavior. The parents give a psychological explanation; that is, an explanation in terms of the infant's mental life – the infant is happy and likes the parents, and thus it smiles. The pediatrician believes that this psychological explanation is not appropriate for this behavior, and instead explains it in terms of intestinal gas and mindless contortions of the infant's facial muscles.

Although we might disagree about how to explain the newborn's behavior, it is clear that at some point the infant does really smile and behave in lots of ways that require psychological explanations. Infants will turn their heads because they *hear* and *recognize* a voice, they move their eyes because they *see* a moving object, they cry because they *feel pain*, *are hungry*, or *are frightened*. Hearing, seeing, recognizing, feeling pain, and being hungry or frightened are all mental states that we use to explain much human and other animal behavior.

Some behavior needs to be explained in terms of mental states and other behavior does not. A smile that expresses joy or affection is explained in terms of mental states, while a mindless grimace or muscular twitch is not. To say that a person turned a page because she finished reading one page and wanted to read the next is to explain her behavior – turning a page – in terms of her mental states, e.g. that she is reading and wants to continue reading. To say that a person turned the page because she walked by it and the breeze her walking generated flipped the page is to explain the turning of the page in terms of something that is not mental. An epileptic seizure is not explained in terms of mental states, while convulsions due to severe pain are explained in mental terms.

The behavior that interests us is behavior that needs to be explained in terms of mental or psychological states, and we can call this kind of behavior "psychological behavior." Various mental states are used to explain psychological behavior

– for example, sensations such as smells, tastes, tickles, and pains. Visual and auditory stimulations also belong to this category. In addition to sensations there are various cognitive states: perception, memory, belief, doubt, attention, intention, reasoning, creativity, and awareness, among other things. We not only gather and process information about the world, but we also have emotional responses to it and desire certain things about it. These emotions and desires are conative or motivational states, and needless to say, these play a very important role in explaining psychological behavior.

This classification into sensation, cognition, and conation is very rough, and should not obscure the fact that many if not most mental states are mixed. For instance, a visual perception of a lake combines visual sensations, beliefs, memory, attention, and some conative elements, e.g. wanting to fish in the lake. Intending to stay and camp by the lake also combines cognition, conation, and sensation. Many claim that a belief – for instance, believing that many mountain lakes were formed by glaciers – is not just a cognitive state, but can also include certain sensations and motivations.

Awareness or consciousness is an especially interesting state because it seems that it can accompany any of the other mental states we have just discussed. Sometimes we believe something without being aware of it, while at other times we are very conscious of what we believe. When driving on an empty stretch of a highway, you might find yourself thinking about something without being aware of the road. Nevertheless, you were perceiving the road – you avoided the shoulder and stayed in your lane – although you were not consciously perceiving the road. If the founder of psychoanalysis, Sigmund Freud, is right, we have many disturbing desires of which we are not aware but that nevertheless motivate our behavior. One of the main objectives of psychoanalysis is to become conscious of these desires.

All of these states – from sensations to full consciousness – are a part of the mental life of a creature with a mind, and all of these states play a role in psychological explanations. They play a role in common-sense psychological explanations as well as in scientific explanations of behavior. When you explain that someone is absent from class because he or she wanted to stay an extra day camping in the mountains, you are giving a psychological explanation of a behavior: absence from class is a case of behavior and wanting to stay an extra day in the mountains is a mental state. When a psychologist maintains that we move our eyes back and forth because we need to have stable perceptions of our environment and we can acquire such perceptions only by scanning it with a quick succession of eye motions, she is giving a psychological explanation of a piece of behavior: eye movement.

The Mind/Body Problem

The reason all this finds its way to the desk of a metaphysician is that explanations come with commitments about what there is. If we explain the behavior of a light switch in terms of electrical currents, we are committed to the existence of electrical currents. If we explain a fever and a rash in terms of a virus, we are committed to the existence of this virus. If we explain why a rock falls to Earth in terms of gravity, we are committed to the existence of gravity. After all, it would not make much sense to claim that the boulder tumbled down from the top of the ridge on account of gravity without supposing that there is such a thing as gravity. In the same way, explanations of psychological behavior in terms of mental states come with commitments to the existence of mental states.

If the proper explanation of psychological behavior is in terms of my beliefs and desires, then there are beliefs and desires. However, the day might come when we conclude that explanations of behavior in terms of beliefs and desires are not very helpful and about as inappropriate as explaining thunderclaps as acts of an angry god, and instead explain human behavior in terms of other kinds of states, such as special kinds of information processing states of the kind we find in a computer. If that day ever comes, then our explanations will not commit us to the existence of beliefs and desires any more.

Mental states have at least one feature in common with other entities that puzzle metaphysicians, such as properties, values, God, or causality. If you are asked to locate an apple or a lake you would probably not have too much difficulty doing so. You can see these objects, point to them, and even eat them or swim in them. But try locating properties, values, God, or causality. It is difficult, if not impossible, to point to these things, and after a while you might even begin to think that perhaps there is something wrong with the request.

You know that you have beliefs and other mental states but you might be hard-pressed to locate these beliefs and mental states. Where is love and where is your desire to hike across a mountain pass? Pains and other sensations might at first seem less problematic, for if you drop something on your toes it appears that the pain is in the toes because your toes hurt. However, given what we know about pains, it is not at all clear that the pain is in your toes. For example, people whose legs have been amputated often complain of pain in their toes, or should we perhaps say that they complain of a sensation that is as if they have pain in their toes?

Consider phantom limb pain. For example, people whose legs have been amputated often complain of pain in their toes. Clearly the pain cannot be located in their toes because they do not have any toes! But if the phantom limb pain is not located in the limb, then we have good reason to believe that the pain we feel when we drop an object on our toes is also not in the toes. So where is the pain if not in the toes?

One answer is that it is in the brain, but that answer is not without its problems. In the brain we have electrical and chemical states. An active brain consists of brain cells, or neurons, which transmit spikes from one to another. A spike is a change in electrical potential or voltage that passes through the nerve cell until it comes to a synapse, which is a tiny gap (about one-fortieth of a micrometer) between neurons. There the electric current causes chemicals, "neurotransmitters," to be released into this gap, and these chemicals, under

Table 1 Mental states and physical states

Mental states	Physical states
Pain	Mass
Tickle	Velocity
Hunger	Momentum
Seeing	Acceleration
Hearing	Energy
Feeling	Heat
Smelling	Density
Consciousness	Spin
Tasting	Charge
Belief	Motion
Doubt	Flow
Memory	Pressure
Imagination	Resonance
Recognition	Photosynthesis
Attention	Excretion
Intention	Absorpiton
Deliberation	Oxidation
Desire	Circulation
Fear	Reproduction
Love	Contraction
Irresolution	Behavior

certain conditions, bring about changes in the electrical potential in the neurons on the other side of the gap.

So if a pain is not in the foot but in the brain instead, it seems that the pain must be an active brain cell or a network of active brain cells. But this is difficult to accept. Neurons, collections of neurons, or the whole brain do not hurt when you hurt your foot, so how can the pain be in the brain?

In this respect, pains are no different from other mental states – for example, hearing a violin. Soundwaves cause the eardrum to vibrate and this vibration is passed along through the middle ear by three small bones. These small bones exert pressure on the fluids in a small snail-shaped canal in the inner ear called the *cochlea*. The pressure changes in the cochlea affect the neurons of the auditory nerve, and the neural spikes caused by the changing pressure produce the sensation of hearing. Nevertheless, there is no sound in the cochlea, auditory nerve or anywhere in the brain. The ear is not like a microphone transducing sound into electrical impulses that in turn cause sound to be reproduced in some mental loudspeaker. There is no loudspeaker in the brain. So again, how can we say that hearing a sound is in the brain when there are no sounds in the brain?

The fact that it is hard to locate and point to mental states suggests that they might not be a part of the physical world. The difficulty in locating mental states indicates at the very least that we are not sure how they fit into the physical world. If mental states would fit easily into the physical world we should probably be able to locate them without too much difficulty. We might even be able to measure them, weigh them, describe their velocity, how they refract light, what color they seem to have, and so on. But we cannot do any of these, and that leaves us with a problem: are mental states part of the physical world, and if so how?

You can see the problem clearly if you fold a sheet of paper lengthwise, and on one side make a list of all the kinds of mental states we use in explaining behavior. On the other side make a list of all the physical objects and states that are well understood by the natural sciences. You might come up with two columns that look like those in table 1.

Although we put mental and physical states in separate columns, this does not mean that mental states are not physical states. What this list does show is that it is not obvious how these two kinds of things are related to each other. Are doubt and desire resonances, pressures, or excretions? Are they motions of the body? Or are they something completely distinct from anything we would ever list in the right-hand column? This, in a nutshell, is the mind/body problem.

Mind/Body Dualism

One solution to the mind/body problem is to maintain that the two columns in table 1 represent a fundamental divide in reality. Reality is divided into two distinct realms: a physical realm consisting of physical objects, properties, events, processes, and so on, and a realm of mental things, properties, events, processes, and so on. On this view, mental states are not physical and we will never be able to identify a mental state such as doubt, desire, or consciousness with something physical. This view – called "mind/body dualism" or "dualism" for short – has deep roots in the history of philosophy. We saw in the *Phaedo* that Socrates argued that mind and body are distinct. In the modern era the French philosopher René Descartes has come to be seen as the paradigm dualist philosopher.

Descartes became a dualist for a number of reasons. One reason he does not mention often but that played an important role in his thinking is that he could not understand how the mechanical processes that were known at his time could explain mental processes. Descartes lived during a time before chemistry became a science and electricity was understood. In fact, Descartes lived during a time when the concepts of force and energy were in disrepute, and many physicists, including Descartes, thought that the physical world should be understood without appealing to forces. So for Descartes the physical world literally consisted only of matter in motion, and the human body was best understood as a clock or a hydraulic system of pumps and canals. Descartes could not see how matter in motion could account for human thinking, and so for these empirical reasons, he defended dualism. If thinking cannot be explained in material terms, the alternative is to explain it in spiritual terms.

Another argument Descartes gave that some philosophers still find convincing goes like this. Descartes argued that he can know with absolute certainty that he is thinking – for instance, that he doubts, believes, perceives, and so on. However, he does not know with absolute certainty that he has a body or that his body is in certain physical states. For example, he can know for sure that it seems to him that he is walking, but he does not know for sure that he is actually walking. Perhaps he is only dreaming that he is walking, Descartes argues. Consequently, his thinking is not identical to his body or any physical states of his body.

Think about it. You now know that you are reading and thinking about what you are reading. You believe what you are reading, or you doubt what you are reading, or you are just trying to understand what you are reading and reserving judgment about the issue for some other time. But you do not know what your brain is doing. Even if you know quite a bit about the brain, you do not know exactly and with any significant degree of confidence what is going on in your central nervous system right now as you are understanding and believing, doubting, or reserving judgment.

Thus how can your understanding and any of the other mental states that accompany your understanding be one of these physical states of your body? If thinking is a state of your nervous system and you know that you are thinking right now, then it seems that it follows that you know what state of the nervous system you are in right now. But you don't know that, so one of the premises of this argument is false. Either you do not know that you are thinking right now or thinking is not a state of the nervous system. Since it is absurd to deny that you are thinking right now, the other premise must be false and thinking is not a state of the nervous system.

In order to get this conclusion we have to rely on a metaphysical principle known as the *Indiscernibility of Identicals*. It states that if you can find even one property that object *a* has and object *b* does not have, then *a* and *b* are two different objects. So if Descartes is right that his thoughts have the property of being known with absolute certainty by him while his body does not have this property, then given the Principle of the Indiscernibility of Identicals, his thoughts cannot be identified with his body.

The above two arguments for dualism are perhaps Descartes' strongest arguments for dualism. A third powerful argument for dualism can be found in the writings of Leibniz, a rationalist philosopher who came after Descartes.

Leibniz agreed with Descartes that thinking cannot be identified with bodily behavior because a mechanical puppet can behave in a very lifelike manner, but not have thoughts and feelings. But if thinking is not behavior, perhaps it is something physical that can be found inside the body. Leibniz considers this possibility and argues that this too cannot be true. He asks us to imagine enlarging a thinking machine – for example, the human body – so that we can walk into it and stroll along its parts. He maintains that all we would see are pieces that push and pull one another, but no thoughts. From this thought-experiment he concludes that thoughts cannot be any physical things inside the body either.

We can update this thought-experiment by imagining that we actually become small enough to enter the brain and observe one of its 10^{10} or 10^{11} neurons (that is, brain cells), as many as there are stars in our galaxy. Let's imagine that we are inside the central nervous system, watching a neural spike travelling along one of the long "tails" of a neuron, called "axons." We see charged atoms along the thin walls of axons, and some of them are moving in and out of the axon through special gates in the axon's thin insulating wall or membrane. As these atoms move in and out of the axon, the electrical potential of the axon's wall changes. When the electrical charge of this membrane increases at certain points in the axon, we will see a neural spike: the atoms along the membrane will move in and out down the axon, increasing the charge of the membrane, until the spike comes to where the axon terminates at a synapse. There we will observe gluta-mate, a neurotransmitter, being released into the synaptic cleft. These neurotransmitters then sometimes cause the neurons on the other side of the synaptic cleft to have a spike, and so it goes throughout the brain.

Would we see thoughts or perceptions on such a trip? It seems that here too Leibniz would argue that such a trip into the nervous system would not reveal thoughts to us. We will not see belief or doubt or the feeling of pain there amidst the tangle of neurons that make up the brain. So these mental states cannot be identified with any of these features inside the body. Since mental states are neither physical states of the whole body nor physical states inside the body, dualism must be true.

A fourth argument for dualism is inspired by the question "What is it like to be a bat?" The bat has certain objective properties: it has a certain anatomy, a special nervous system that finds and avoids objects using echolocation, and certain ways in which it navigates through the environment. Suppose we know all these objective features of bats; that is, suppose we have a complete science of bats. We can locate exactly the parts of the brain that are active when bats echolocate, the parts that are involved in flight and how echolocation and flight interact in a bat, and so on. Nevertheless, this knowledge of the bat's objective features will be incomplete. What will be missing are the subjective features of a bat; that is, what it is like to be a bat. We have an objective perspective on bats, but this does not reveal to us their subjective perspective.

The same is true of blindness. We know the objective conditions that bring with them blindness, but knowing them does not tell us what it is like to be blind; that is, the subjective perspective on blindness. Suppose we try to remedy that. We can blindfold you and have you walk around with a cane for a day. But that will not give you the subjective perspective on blindness. At most it tells you what it is like *pretending* to be blind for a day.

In much the same way, it has been argued that human perception, and thought in general, cannot be identified with the objective physical processes that behavioral scientists and neuroscientists come to know and describe. Consider tasting an apple. We can have a complete description of how people behave when they taste an apple (they bite a piece off, chew, and respond with comments or special looks), the chemical reactions in the mouth, what happens to certain cells on the tongue, how these reactions change the nerve cells on the tongue as well as in the back of the nose, and how all this brings about a chain reaction that changes the activity of the central nervous system. People who know all this will still not know everything there is to know about tasting apples. What they will miss is what it is like to taste an apple; that is, the actual experience of tasting the apple.

Consequently, the physical aspects of tasting apples, all of which are objective, do not exhaust what it is to taste apples. In addition to all the physical aspects of this mental state, there are its subjective features, and so it goes for all mental states. There is more to the world than matter and physical processes. Hence, dualism is true.

Problems for Dualism

These are four powerful arguments for mind/body dualism, but dualism is not immune from problems. There are three areas where dualism seems to run into problems: (1) the interaction between mind and body, (2) the laws of physics, and (3) the dependence of mind on nature.

Interaction

If dualism is true, we need to understand how our non-physical minds can have an effect on the physical world and how the physical world can have effects on our minds. That mind and body interact seems obvious. If you want to go for a bicycle ride and you believe that you left your bicycle on the back porch then you walk to the back porch to look for it. Your walking to the back porch is clearly physical, but your belief and your desire are, according to dualism, not physical. So here is a case of something mental – your belief and desire – bringing about something physical – your walking. When you fall off your bicycle and feel the resulting pain, then we have a case of the physical world clearly making a difference to your mental life.

The problem for dualism is that it is not clear how mind and body can interact. The most obvious way to account for this interaction is to say that mental states can cause changes in the physical environment and the physical environment can cause mental states to change. Unfortunately, causation is typically between physical events. A hurricane's velocity causes trees to snap, striking a match causes the match to ignite, and so on. Since the causality that holds between mind and body is not a relation between physical events, it seems that dualism requires a different kind of causality from ordinary causality studied by the natural sciences. In addition to the physical causality, we also need mental causality. Physical causality holds between physical events and mental causality holds between mental events as well as between mental and physical events.

This is problematic for two reasons. First, it raises the specter of Occam's razor: does dualism unnecessarily multiply entities? Not only do we have minds and bodies, but now we also have two kinds of causation. Second, how are we to understand mental causation? We have a pretty good understanding of physical causes and we have built our scientific success around that understanding. But it is unclear how useful they are for understanding mental causation because the two kinds of causation seem significantly different. For one, they do not even take place in the same medium. So, dualism saddles us with mental causes of which we have virtually no understanding.

Laws of physics

Given that mind and body interact, it seems that dualism is forced to deny two laws of physics. One is the Law of the Conservation of Energy, which is that the sum total of all physical energy in the universe remains constant. Energy cannot be created or destroyed, although it can be changed from one physical form to another – for example, from electrical energy to mechanical energy. So if there is an increase in energy somewhere, there has to be a decrease of energy elsewhere. The other is the Law of the Conservation of Momentum, which says that when two or more objects collide, the total momentum before the impact equals the total momentum after the impact. So when two billiard balls hit one another and change direction and speed, the total momentum of the two balls before the collision is the same as the momentum after the collision.

The reason why conservation of energy is violated is that if the mind acts on the body, there is an increase of energy in the body. Suppose a person decides to lift her arm. The lifting of the arm involves an increase of energy in the universe, but given that this was brought about by mental states that are not in any way physical – a desire to lift the arm, for instance – there is no corresponding loss of energy in the universe.

The reason dualism violates the conservation of momentum is that it follows from dualism that minds can increase or decrease the total momentum of a system. For instance, suppose that without the influence of any mental states a neural spike would travel down an axon and release neurotransmitters into the synaptic cleft, which in turn bring about another spike in the next neuron. This chain of spikes connected by the chemical activity in the synapse will have a certain amount of momentum. Now, suppose that there is a mental state that intervenes and stops the neurotransmitters from being released. Now there is a decrease of momentum that is not accounted for anywhere else in the brain or the physical universe. In much the same way the mind can increase momentum. Consider a neuron that is at rest at about -70 millivolts, and assume that there is nothing in the physical universe that now will bring about a change in the resting potential of this neuron. If dualism is true it would be possible for this potential to change on account of the influence of a mental state. If I want to lift my arm and lifting my arm requires that this neuron becomes active, then my desire would activate this neuron to, say, -40 millivolts, and this would be an increase in the total momentum of materials in the brain. In fact, it would be an increase of the total momentum in the whole physical universe!

So if dualism is true, well confirmed laws of physics are false. Of course, it is possible that the laws of physics are false, but it is also possible that dualism is false. What we need to do here is to decide if the reasons for believing that mind/body dualism is true are stronger than the reasons for believing in the fundamental laws of physics. It will certainly seem to many that dualism is fighting an uphill battle if one cannot accept it without giving up some of the fundamental laws of physics.

Physical dependence

One thing is clear: your mental capacities depend on your brain. Brain damage has serious consequences for how we feel, perceive, remember, reason. The capacity to recognize family and friends or move a part of a limb that is fully intact can be curtailed by a stroke that damages the brain. Alzheimer's disease afflicts the brain and affects a wide range of cognitive capacities, including memory, perception, and the ability to speak. Military combat and sexual abuse can cause stress disorders, such as severe dissociation, which includes feelings of detachment from one's self, and these stress disorders have been linked to a smaller than normal hippocampus, a part of the brain that regulates memory.

Not only do external forces change our minds by changing our brains, but sometimes people alter their own brains voluntarily in order to change their mental states. Pain killers such as aspirin or morphine are used to relieve people of their pain. People use depressants to calm down or fall asleep, stimulants to increase alertness or to produce feelings of excitement or euphoria, or even hallucinogens to alter perceptions of shape and color. Drugs that alter the brain's physical states are also used to control disorders and dysfunctions such as Tourette's syndrome, Alzheimer's disease, alcoholism, or depression.

There is also an evolutionary dependence of our minds on the physical world. Our mental abilities are the product of natural history. Before there were creatures with minds, Earth was a mindless planet. Although it was without minds, there were processes in place that made the evolution of creatures with minds possible. So somehow our mental capacities had to evolve out of non-mental processes, and it is difficult to see how dualists can make sense of this evolution of mind from purely physical processes. Dualists have tried to make sense of this by maintaining that mind *emerges* from sufficiently complex matter, but the details of this emergence of mental stuff from physical stuff remain obscure.

Given these problems for dualism, we should take a second look at the arguments we presented for dualism. All of them have serious problems.

The argument that dualism is warranted because we do not know enough about matter to make sense of mind in physical terms suffers from two defects. First, it is possible that the person making the claim does not know enough about the physical world and that the argument is only an expression of his personal ignorance and not the present state of knowledge. Second, even if in fact we do not know enough to make complete sense of mental states in physical terms, it may be that enough progress has been made to warrant the belief that eventually we will know enough.

The second argument, according to which dualism is true because we know for sure that we are thinking but do not know for sure what state our bodies are in, is invalid. Consider this analogous argument. I know for sure that my barber is cutting my hair, but I do not know for sure that a Christian fundamentalist is cutting my hair; consequently, my barber is not a Christian fundamentalist. The conclusion can be false – my barber might be a fundamentalist – while the premises are all true. So this argument is invalid, and the argument about our knowledge of brain states and mental states is invalid for the same reason. What we know about the world and what it really is are distinct things. Similarly, what we can or cannot doubt about the world and how it is are distinct things.

The problem here is that the Principle of the Indiscernibility of Identicals does not hold for mental states: beliefs, doubts, thinks, is certain that, and so on. Descartes' premises are about what he can know and cannot know – that is mental states – and consequently when the law is applied in intentional contexts we cannot trust that its conclusion is true.

The third argument for dualism involved a trip into the brain, where we observed mechanical, chemical, and electrical interactions, but no mental states. Here there are several errors at work. If you were to take a picture of someone and enlarge it to the size of Earth you would not recognize what it is of. Nevertheless, the picture would still be there and it would still be a picture of the same object. In much the same way, if you were small enough to travel into the molecular structure of water you would have difficulty recognizing water and its liquidity. But that lack of recognition does not change the fact that water is H_2O and a liquid. The lesson here is that if one focuses only on the details, one might miss larger patterns that are relevant. Sitting by the shore of the Mississippi River, I cannot see how it flows through the plain. In fact, I might not even know that it is a river; it could also be a large, elongated lake from where I am sitting. Nevertheless, it is a river that flows through the plains, and in order to see that, I need to move from my spot and travel along the shore or get a bird's eye view so that I can see a larger segment of the river. The same goes for the brain.

The final argument, the "What is it like to be a bat?" argument – is a subtle one, but it too is open to objections. Materialists argue that we need to distinguish different ways of knowing something, including knowing our own bodies and its brain states. Knowing a pain by having it is different from knowing a pain by seeing it. In the same way, knowing a brain state by having it is different from knowing it by observing it. So when I feel a pain or see a tree, my body is in a certain state and I know this state by undergoing it or having it. I could also know it in some other way, e.g. by looking at it, but this is not typically how we know our mental states. We know them simply by having them.

The situation here is analogous to playing music. There is a difference between the way a performer experiences her musical performance and the way a spectator hears it, and often this difference is very sharp. Sometimes a performer will "lose herself" in the performance and cease to be fully aware of the music that she is playing. She is fully concentrated on playing rather than listening. A spectator, on the other hand, is not playing the music but is fully concentrated on listening to it, and that way of knowing the music that is being played is different from the knowledge the performer has. In the same way, a materialist will say, when we know a physical state that is a mental state subjectively, we know it in the way performers know their music, but when we observe it objectively, we know it in the way the audience knows the music that is being played. Nevertheless, what we know in these two different ways is the same thing: a kind of physical state.

Mind/Body Materialism

The problems for dualism suggest that perhaps the mental is not distinct from the physical, and that mental states are physical states. This alternative to mind/body dualism is mind/body materialism (or physicalism, as it is sometimes called). Materialism comes in various forms, but the fundamental idea is that all the mental states, from pain to consciousness, are physical states if they are anything at all. As we will see, materialists differ on exactly what sorts of physical states mental states are, but they all deny that mental states belong to a realm of reality that is distinct from the realm of physical objects, properties, processes, or events.

The best arguments for materialism are the problems that dualism has with interaction, the laws of physics and the physical dependence of mind on the physical world. Another important argument in favor of materialism is to appeal to Occam's razor, and argue that materialism offers a simpler explanation for minds and mental capacities than dualism. While dualism needs two distinct realms, including, as we saw, two distinct kinds of causation, materialism only needs one realm and one kind of causation. Instead of trying to deal with interactions between spiritual matter and physical matter, materialists are only concerned with physical and biochemical interactions in physical matter.

From the materialist's point of view, dualists are like the farmers in a story told by the English materialist philosopher Gilbert Ryle. A group of farmers, when confronted with a locomotive for the first time, want to find out what powers the engine has. Naturally, they look for the explanation they expect to find, namely that there are horses hidden within the engine. They look for the horses and fail to find them. The engineer tells them that there are no horses in the engine and explains to them how the fire burning in the engine heats water, which then turns into steam, which then turns the wheels. The farmers listen, but do not accept the purely mechanical explanation of how the machine moves. They insist on a living thing moving the machine, and when they fail to find one, they postulate that there is a ghost that moves the machine in addition to the engine the engineer told them about. This is a violation of Occam's razor. The farmers explain the motion of the locomotive with two things – the mechanical processes of an engine plus a ghost – when, in fact, a proper understanding of the mechanical processes in the locomotive is all that is needed. Ryle argues that those who postulate an independent mind are in the same situation with regard to the mind/body problem as the farmers with regard to the locomotive; they fail to understand and appreciate the physical and materialistic explanations of the functions of the body, and violate Occam's razor by postulating that there are mental states distinct from and in addition to physical states.

The success of this argument against dualism depends on an important assumption: that there are good physical explanations for all mental states that exist. The farmers seem silly to us because we accept and appreciate the engineer's explanation that the locomotive moves on account of the operations of the engine. Dualists, however, vehemently reject that they are as silly as the farmers in Ryle's story. They are not convinced that there are adequate physical explanations for all mental phenomena. They challenge materialists to show us that there are explanations for mental phenomena such as consciousness that are as clear and satisfactory as the engineer's explanation of why a locomotive moves. Occam's razor commands us that we should not multiply entities without necessity, and dualists argue that dividing reality into two realms, one mental and one physical, is not multiplying entities without necessity.

Do we need two realms? Is the materialist right that in order to understand mental states we do not need to suppose that they are not physical states? Or is the dualist right that an adequate understanding of mental states requires that we postulate a mental realm in addition to the physical world? To better begin answering these questions, we need to be familiar with the various strategies materialists have offered for explaining mental phenomena.

Varieties of Materialism

Mind/body materialists do not agree on what mental states are and what the best strategies are for understanding the nature of mental states, but most agree that the various kinds of mental states really are various kinds of physical states, and we will focus on these kinds of materialists. So in each of the theories we will discuss in this section, feeling pain will be identified with a certain kind of physical state.

A label for this kind of materialism is "type–type identity theories," indicating that they identify *types* of mental states with *types* of physical states. An example of a type of mental state is pain. It is a kind of mental state that is common to people who burn themselves, scrape their knees, break their ankles, and so on. In addition to pain as a mental type, there are particular instances or *tokens* of pain: the pain I felt when I fell off my bicycle, the pain you felt when you fell playing soccer, and so on. What type–type identity theorists promise us is that not only are particular tokens of a mental state identical to tokens of a physical state, but every type of mental state that exists is identical to a certain type of physical state. So pain will turn out to be a certain kind of physical state, believing will turn out to be another kind of physical state, imagining still a third kind of physical state, and so on.

These positions have also been called "reductive" because by identifying mental types with physical types they reduce mental states to physical states. Familiar examples of reductions are the claims that lightning is an atmospheric electric discharge or that light and electromagnetic waves are identical. These are examples of successful reductions in the natural sciences and all of the following materialist views on the mind/body problem are attempts to equally reduce mental states to physical states.

Behaviorism

We will begin with the materialist philosophy of mind that had the most influence in psychology and philosophy during the first half of the twentieth century: behaviorism.

At the turn of the nineteenth and twentieth centuries, psychologists were committed to the studying of internal mental states. Their primary mode of observation was introspection; that is, the observation of one's own mental states. For instance, in order to discover what consciousness is, a psychologist would attend to his or her own conscious states and use this information to construct and test hypotheses about the nature of consciousness. Needless to say, experiments involving introspection were not easily repeatable and led to many contradictory accounts. For example, psychologists using introspection could not agree how many different attributes or features are essential to consciousness. This confusion in psychology caused many people to doubt that psychology was really a science.

Behaviorism was a critical reaction to introspectionist psychology and its primary goal was to make psychology a respectable science. Behaviorists rejected the introspectionist view that the primary object of psychology was the experiences of a person from his or her own point of view. Moreover, inner states, whatever they might be, were deemed irrelevant to psychology. Instead, they maintained, behavior as observed by others, particularly behavior in response to observable stimuli, is what psychologists should study. These principles about what psychology should study – behavior as observed by others and no inner mental states – came to be known as *methodological behaviorism.*

Another behaviorist view became popular in philosophical circles as *logical or analytical behaviorism.* Logical behaviorism was a view about what mental terms and phrases such as "believes," "hurts," or "thinks" mean. For example, when an English speaker says "Linda believes that $7 + 5 = 12$," she is not referring to some special state inside Linda, but only to a certain kind of behavior.

Strictly speaking, neither methodological behaviorism nor logical behaviorism is a metaphysical view because they do not say anything about the nature of mental states. While methodological behaviorism was a view about what psychologists should study and what they can safely ignore, logical behaviorism was a view about the meaning of language. However, methodological behaviorism was often rooted in a metaphysical view about mental states, namely reductive behaviorism.

Reductive behaviorism identifies the different kinds of mental states with patterns of observable behavior and dispositions to behave in certain observable ways in response to stimuli from the environment. Consider Chang's belief that there is an apple in the refrigerator. According to this view, this belief might be identical to these patterns of behavior:

1   When asked "Is there an apple in the refrigerator?" Chang responded affirmatively.
2   When given the request "Please bring me an apple," Chang opened the refrigerator.
3   If Chang were asked to list all available foodstuffs in the refrigerator, Chang would include "apple" on that list.
4   If Chang were hungry for an apple, Chang would look in the refrigerator for one.

Cases (1) and (2) are examples of observable behavior. Here Chang actually did something in response to a question and a request. Cases (3) and (4) are examples of dispositions to behave in certain ways. Chang was not actually asked to list all the available foods and she was not hungry, but Chang *would* have behaved in this manner if she *had* been asked this or if she *had* been hungry.

Of course, this list is not exhaustive because there are many different ways of behaving associated with the belief that there is an apple in the refrigerator. If Chang wants to draw an apple, pack one for lunch, smell one, show one to a child, and so on, she might also go to the refrigerator to get it. There are many more patterns of behavior that come with believing that an apple is in the refrigerator, but the reductive behaviorist believes that this is not a problem. According to the behaviorist, the task of psychology is to find out what all these patterns are and how they are connected in lawlike ways to other mental states.

We can express the reductive behaviorists' position on what mental states are with the model shown in figure 2. This model captures an important feature of behaviorism, namely that on this view a mental state is not just a static thing but a kind of event: it is a kind of response to environmental stimuli. Moreover, this model captures the fact that according to behaviorists we do not need to look inside the body to find mental states. Mental states are constituted by the whole body and how it responds and is disposed to respond to the environment.

On this view, a pain is a kind of behavior and disposition to behave. For instance, it will include pulling away from an object, yelling "Ouch!" or crying, being disposed to avoid the object in the future, affirming that it hurt when asked if it hurt, and so on. On this view, pain is not a feeling that is internal to the person in pain; it simply is a pattern of behaviors and dispositions to behave. Strangely enough, many behaviorists denied that animals feel pain even though animals certainly exhibited pain behavior in certain conditions: they would whine or yelp, writhe, foam at the mouth, try to pull away from the apparently painful

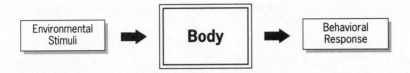

Figure 2 The reductive behaviorist's position on mental states.

object. But many behaviorists were inclined to suppose that in order to feel pain you have to have the ability to speak – e.g. say "Ouch!" and state that you are in pain – and non-human animals typically do not have any linguistic abilities.

One of the problems with reductive behaviorism is that it was extremely difficult to explain all mental states in terms only of behavior and behavioral dispositions. Whenever behaviorists started listing all the ways of behaving that are relevant to a mental state, they would always include some mental states that they have not yet explained. For instance, look back at the list of behaviors associated with Chang's belief that there is an apple in the refrigerator. Each one of those assumes something mental about Chang. When asked "Is there an apple in the refrigerator?" Chang responded affirmatively, but her response is relevant only if it is accompanied with the further mental processes involved in *understanding* the question.

Moreover, it seemed clear that there was more to pain and other sensations than behavior or dispositions to behave. An actor on a stage might not be in pain but could despite that be disposed to show the pain behavior that the script calls for. And, more seriously, behaviorism did not acknowledge that other mental states, such as desires and wants, can cause behavior. If I am thirsty I drink, but only if I have a desire to quench the thirst. Here the desire, or the lack of desire, to quench the thirst plays a significant role in explaining my behavior and it causally contributes to my behavior. But since behaviorism is ultimately only concerned with facts about stimulus and response, it has a hard time accounting for mental causation. These problems led materialists to look inside the body and identify mental states with the body's internal states.

Central state identity theory

Clearly the nervous system, particularly the central nervous system, is an obvious place to look for mental states, and in response to the problems of behaviorism materialists identified mental types with types of states of the central nervous system.

This view, often called "central state identity theory" or "identity theory" for short, identifies Chang's belief with certain kinds of neural states or patterns of neural activity. If Chang is sad when she discovers that her belief is false, her sadness is not just a sad kind of behavior, as the behaviorist would have it, but a state of her nervous system – for instance, her neurotransmitters are decreasing the rate of synaptic firings in certain parts of the brain. The feeling of sadness

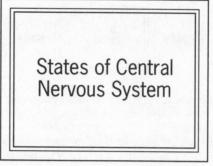

Figure 3   The central state identity theory.

just is this decrease in the activity of neurotransmitters that excite neurons and an increase in the activity of neurotransmitters that inhibit neurons. We can capture the central state identity theory with the simple model shown in figure 3.

Here mental states simply are something internal to the body, namely states of the brain. This brain-based view of mental states has an important predecessor in the English philosopher Thomas Hobbes. Hobbes rejected Descartes' dualism and tried to understand mental states such as sensations, dreams, perceptions, imagination, and reasoning in terms of the motions of small bodies or corpuscles internal to us. Of course, Hobbes knew next to nothing about the brain and the nervous system, but as far as central state identity theorists are concerned, he was on the right track.

Recent work on consciousness offers us a glimpse of how one might go about trying to reduce a type of mental state to a state of the brain. One kind of consciousness is visual awareness, such as consciously perceiving a dog in front of you. It seems that visual awareness is a complex phenomenon that involves attention, short-term memory, and an ability to attend to more than one feature of an object at the same time – for instance, seeing the shape as well as the movement of a dog at once. If attention can be located in one set of electrical and chemical neural activities, short-term memory with another, and attending to various things at the same time to another, then the central state identity theorist has a strategy for reducing visual awareness to states of the brain.

What might such a reduction look like? Consider the third feature of visual awareness: attending to various objects at the same time. It turns out that a visually aware cat has neurons in the part of the brain that handles vision – the visual cortex – that fire at very regular intervals between 35 and 75 Hertz (or cycles per second), and on average at 40 Hertz (that is, every 25 milliseconds). To many neuroscientists, this suggests that the way we can be aware of the various features of an object at the same time (e.g. seeing the dog's shape and movement simultaneously) is that the neurons involved in seeing these various aspects are all firing at the same rate. A central state identity theorist would take this to be evidence that we are discovering what visual awareness really is, namely a kind of brain state that includes the firing of neurons simultaneously in the 35–75 Hertz range.

If this turns out to be the case, the question of animal pain can be decided very easily. If an animal has the neural activity that has been identified with pain and the neurons involved in this fire in the vicinity of 40 Hertz, then we know that animals are conscious of pain and that we need to take this into account when we think about the moral standing of animals.

Good as this looks, the central state identity theory faces serious problems. Because types of mental states are identified with types of brain states, the theory is too restrictive. If something does not have a brain, it does not have mental states. Since a brain is just a collection of neurons interconnected by synaptic clefts, anything that does not have neurons and synapses does not have mental states. This means that if there are any beings in this universe that are not made of cells, they cannot have any mental states. A creature in another solar system that is not made out of carbon-based matter will not have mental states even if it behaves in extremely intelligent ways.

But we do not need to look for aliens to find problems with the central state identity theory. What are we to do if we find an animal that exhibits pain behavior but does not have the neural activity that we have identified with pain? Its brain might differ significantly from our brains, and we might not find any neural firings in the requisite frequency range. The proper conclusion would not be to deny that the creature suffers pain, but rather that pain can be identified with a certain type of brain state.

Machine functionalism

That mental states cannot be identified with states of the nervous system received much support from powerful computers and artificial intelligence. Computers perform many tasks that seem very intelligent. They can play chess better than most chess players and they are a good match for the world's best chess players. Computers can prove theorems, parse sentences, write stories, compose music, and even move about and find objects. Computers can see and hear, and they can even learn from past mistakes.

These and many other advances in artificial intelligence and robotics suggested to many people that it is at least possible that computers think and have mental states. Even if they do not have these mental capacities now, many workers in artificial intelligence believe that we are taking the first steps to develop true artificial minds, even artificial persons. It is supposed that these intelligent machines will not have brains – they will be made of much the same type of non-living material that you already find in your personal computer – but they will nevertheless be able to remember, perceive, reason, doubt, believe, imagine, and even feel.

If computers can have mental states, then mental states cannot be identified with states of the nervous system. If computers and other non-biological beings can have minds, the materialist needs to find some other way of reducing mental states that will not tie it to one kind of particular stuff, and the computer suggested how this could be done.

One of the basic building blocks in a computer is a logic gate. A logic gate for exclusive "or" represents the truth-table for the exclusive "or" (see table 2). With

Table 2   Truth-table for exclusive "or"

p	*q*	*p or q*
True	True	False
True	False	True
False	True	True
False	False	False

this truth-table in mind, we can build a logic gate, but instead of using "true" and "false," it will have electrical states of being on and being off. These on and off states will be the inputs for the logic gate, and it will have one output that depends on what the two inputs are. Since we are building a logic gate for exclusive "or," the output will be on just in case only one of the inputs is on. We can summarize this as in table 3.

With this table in mind, we can build the logic gate for exclusive "or." The logic gate will not be a table, but it will be a device that has two inputs and one output, and its output will be determined by the inputs as described by the on/off table for the exclusive "or." We could picture a logic gate as in figure 4. In this case, the first input is on while the second input is off and, consequently, the output is on. If the two inputs were both on, the output would have been off.

A computer is built out of such simple logic gates, and incredibly complex tasks, such as winning a chess game against a grandmaster, are accomplished on the basis of such simple operations. What is even more fascinating is that this logic gate can be characterized without saying anything about the material out of which it is made. Typically, the on and off states are electrical states, but that is not essential to a logic gate. If it were practical we could make logic gates out of incoming and outgoing water channels. A hydraulic logic gate for exclusive "or" would not let any water go out if neither or both channels have incoming water.

What characterizes the logic gate is a *function*. It is an input/output function that yields certain outputs given certain inputs, and what kind of material executes that function is not essential to the function. All that is required is that it is something that has the causal power to transform given inputs into specific outputs in accordance with a table like our table for the logic gate for the exclusive "or."

It is important to notice that the same function can be accomplished in vari-

Table 3   Table for logic gate for exlusive "or"

Input 1	*Input 2*	*Output*
On	On	Off
On	Off	On
Off	On	On
Off	Off	Off

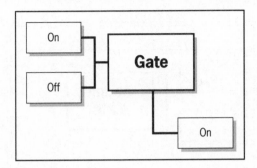

Figure 4 A logic gate for exclusive "or."

ous ways. Not only can the material used in a contraption that performs the function be different, it can be put together in more than one way. A mousetrap has a function that, as with all functions, is characterized by an input and an output. Something that takes mice for input and yields captured mice as output is a mousetrap. But mousetraps can be built from various materials, such as wood or plastic, and they can perform the function in various ways. For example, some traps yield a dead mouse while others yield a live mouse. Still, the outcome is a captured mouse.

The sort of functions that machine functionalists care most about are computational functions; that is, functions that have symbols or representations for inputs and outputs. Consider a logic gate again. It has on and off states for inputs and outputs, but these states represent something. In the example we were considering, the on and off states are symbols for truth and falsehood. When a state is on it represents something true, and when it is off it represents something false. Of course, the logic gate could also represent something else, and what it represents depends on how the computer is used. The beauty of a computer is that it is a general purpose machine, so a logic gate can be used to represent anything as long as it conforms to the way it processes inputs and outputs.

What else could be taken as input and output? Machine functionalists can limit themselves just to symbols, but many allow for other inputs and outputs besides symbols. Typically, they believe that stimuli from the environment and other mental states can be inputs, and behavior as well as other mental states can be outputs. On this more liberal view, mental states turn out to be kinds of functions that take as input stimuli from the environment, symbols, and mental states, and have as outputs symbols, other mental states, and behavior.

Of course, the functions of a person are very complex, even more complex than all the functions of the best chess-playing computer, but the machine functionalists says they are all built out of very simple functions such as our logic gate for the exclusive "or." This means that, according to a functionalist, all the mental states of a person could be completely characterized as input/output functions that transform certain input states into output states. This functionalist view of the mind can be illustrated with the model shown in figure 5. This

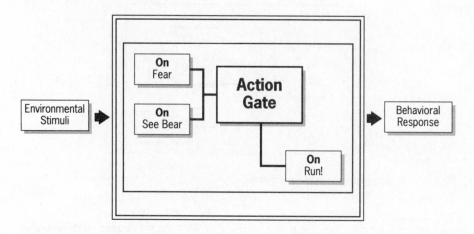

Figure 5   The functionalist view of the mind.

model shows that functionalism combines features from both behaviorism and the central state identity theory. The environmental stimuli and the behavioral responses that the behaviorists focused on are a part of the model, as are the internal states and processes that the central state identity theorist focused on.

However, while the central state identity theory tied mental states to brain processes, functionalism abstracts mental states from the brain. What is important for the functionalist is not the central nervous system, but the functions it performs. What makes something a mental state is a certain complex function it performs, no matter what it is made of. Thus an artificial machine can have mental states as a human being can, even though the machine does not have a brain, but a central processor that can perform the same functions as the brain.

It is important to keep in mind that, for a functionalist, such an artificially intelligent machine does not just *simulate* intelligence in the way that a computer simulates a surgery. In order to avoid using live animals for beginning surgery students, veterinary teaching hospitals let students operate on virtual animals. This simulation of a live animal does not consist of arteries, veins, a pumping heart, and blood, but only of representations of the animal's internal organs, their relationships, and what happens if you move one organ but not another. A functionalist maintains that an artificially intelligent machine will actually *replicate* mental states. Thus an artificial machine can have the same mental states as a human being as long as it can perform the same functions as the brain.

A consequence of this is that machines can have a moral status. We respect people because they are conscious, they reason, have plans and projects, can be disappointed or happy, and so on. If the functionalist is right, an artificial machine can have all those states. Consequently, we would have to respect these machines as much as we respect human beings. The day might come when we cannot turn off a computer without wondering about the moral implications of terminating its internal activities.

Problems for Materialism

Do we need two realms to understand the nature of the mind, as the dualist maintains, or can we get by with just one realm, as the materialist maintains? If materialism were without major problems the case would be closed: materialism wins. Unfortunately, all three of the materialist positions we discussed have important problems.

We have already discussed problems for reductive materialism and the central state identity theory. An important problem for functionalism is that it seems that not all mental states can be understood as functions; that is, as relations between inputs and outputs. It seems that some mental states have some intrinsic features – for example, pain. Of course it is true that pain is a response to certain inputs (e.g. a sharp kick to your ankle while playing soccer), and it leads to other things: you fall and hold your ankle, you worry that you have a broken ankle, you cry out for help, and so on. But all this leaves something out, namely the subjective features of feeling pain.

Another problem is that a computer does not understand anything. A logic gate transforms on and off states, but it does not understand that these states represent truth and falsehood. A computer manipulates symbols, but it has no idea what these symbols mean. Consequently, our mental states cannot simply be characterized in terms of a computer's functions because we, but not the computer, understand what we are processing.

The problems raised for behaviorism, the central state identity theory, and machine functionalism are serious philosophical problems. But these materialist positions also have serious empirical problems. For instance, behaviorism could not account very well for learning. Behaviorists wanted to avoid all reference to internal mental states, which meant that for them all learning was a process in which certain patterns of behavior are reinforced by stimuli from the environment, e.g. a reward or a punishment. This view of learning ran into trouble when trying to account for how human beings learn a language. The number of sentences that a normal human being can use and understand is too large to be learned simply through reinforcement of certain patterns of behavior. It would take too long to hear or see all of them and we can understand and use sentences without having ever heard or seen them. It seemed that to account for language learning we had to suppose that humans can learn from behavior because they *already* know something before they start observing and responding to behavior.

The central state identity theory ran against a significant body of evidence that showed that the same kind of mental activity does not have to take place in exactly the same parts of people's brains. There is a certain degree of plasticity to the central nervous system that lets various parts of the brain perform the same function. In fact, young people who lose a mental function due to permanent damage to some part of their brains can sometimes regain the function when a different part of their brains takes over that job.

Machine functionalism ran into trouble with tasks such as recognizing familiar faces. The problem with this kind of task is that it seems that it cannot be broken down into simple input/output functions that can be fully described using a table like the one we had for the logic gate for the exclusive "or." There are too many contingencies and exceptions that we master when we recognize a face, but that cannot be specified in terms of simple input/output operations. When workers in artificial intelligence tried to program computers to recognize faces, they had to use much more memory than is available to human beings, and this suggested that our ability to recognize faces cannot be identified with the way a computer recognizes faces.

In sum, every major attempt to identify mental kinds with physical kinds seems to face significant difficulty. It is therefore not at all clear what sorts of physical things minds are. This plays into the hands of dualists, who challenge the materialists to show them how mental states can be identified with anything physical. If materialists do not have a clear answer, dualists can at least find some comfort in the fact that although dualism has problems, materialists have not met the dualist challenge to show us what kinds of physical things mental states are.

Where Do We Go from Here?

It seems that we have reached an impasse. Although there are arguments for dualism, they are not fully convincing. Either they have to be rejected or they have to be fixed. Moreover, both dualist and materialist accounts of mind are not wholly adequate. Dualism has problems with interaction, the laws of physics, and the fact of physical dependence. Materialists have problems identifying mental states with physical states: behavior, brain states, or functional states do not seem to do the job. So where do we go from here?

Assuming that all that has been said so far is correct, there are several options open to us. One option is skepticism. Given the impasse between dualism and materialism, we could suspend judgment for now and just wait to see how things turn out in the future. Perhaps psychology, cognitive science, neuroscience, biology, and all the other sciences that study minds and their capacities will evolve to a point when it will be obvious to everyone with a desire to know what sorts of physical states mental states are. On the other hand, perhaps the mind will continue to elude scientists, so that dualism will begin to seem more and more plausible. Perhaps dualists will discover a knock-down argument for their view that mind and body are distinct.

Another option is to stick with your position and work on addressing the problems of your position. Dualists can try to strengthen the arguments for their position and iron out the problems of dualism. For instance, perhaps dualism can be formulated in such a way that it avoids contradicting well established laws of physics, or perhaps contemporary physics gives us reason to doubt these laws. Dualists can also try to refine their positions in various ways to avoid problems. Descartes was a *substance dualist* who believed that mind and body are distinct objects or substances, much like apples and oranges. Mind and body happened to be in the same place, but they were still distinct objects; mental properties belonged to the mind and physical properties belonged to the body.

But not all dualists agree with Descartes on this issue. There are *property dualists* who believe that there is only one kind of substance, but this substance has both mental and physical properties. Furthermore, these properties are distinct and not to be identified with each other. Property dualists differ about what this substance is. Some property dualists believe that it is physical, but happens to have distinct mental and physical properties. Others believe that the substance is neither physical nor mental, but neutral, and it is this neutral substance that has distinct mental and physical properties. In either case, property dualists maintain that a complete description of the physical components of a being is bound to be an incomplete description, for it leaves out some mental properties.

Materialists can also try to strengthen their position. Since a major source of materialist problems is that apparently not all mental states can be identified with physical states, materialists have tried to treat this problem by treating mental states as less than real. *Eliminative materialists* argue that mental states such as believing, fearing, or thinking really do not exist. These mental states are a part of a discredited world view, much like witches, magical powers, phlogiston, or ether, and a scientific conception of human nature, including the human mind, does not need to account for all our unscientific ways of describing people.

Others are more tolerant. They argue that it is useful to describe many things as if they have mental states even if they do not have any. For example, it is useful for me to think that the chess program I am playing against takes its time to think and believes that I will move my queen when in fact everyone, including machine functionalists, agrees that the current state-of-the-art home computers do not think or believe anything. It is useful because treating the computer as if it believes that I will move my queen allows me to accurately predict its behavior. In the same way, describing human beings as if they have mental states such as beliefs and desires is useful because it allows us to predict human behavior, even if a scientific description of human beings will not say anything about beliefs and desires.

It is not easy to decide which of these routes to follow, and we, the authors, ourselves do not agree on how to solve the mind/body problem. Needless to say, readers will also be pulled in many directions on this issue, which is one of the most difficult issues in metaphysics. Nevertheless, it seems that we can reach agreement on two things, and we offer them to the reader for consideration.

We must take morality seriously. Morality plays an important role in our lives, and it should play an important role in all our important decisions. Without morality, life would truly become, as Thomas Hobbes had maintained, nasty, poor, brutish, solitary and short. But a moral assessment of someone makes sense only if there are beliefs, desires, intentions, thoughts, and all the other things we are concerned with when we worry about moral responsibility. We do not morally blame a tree that falls across a road, causing an accident, because trees do not have beliefs and desires. In the same way, we could not morally evaluate people if it turned out that they do not have any mental states. So the existence of a successful practice of morality and moral assessment strongly suggests that there really are mental states.

On the other hand, materialism has this edge over dualism: suppose that we never come up with an adequate science of mind that treats minds wholly as physical states. In other words, suppose that there will always be important mental states or aspects of mental states left unexplained by a materialist science of the mind. Even if this were the case there still would be very good reasons for being a materialist. Science has been very successful at explaining too many phenomena by relying simply on physical properties, processes, and states. Force, energy, magnetism, gravity, heat, light, and life, among many other things, have come to be understood as physical phenomenal, not magical phenomena belonging to some non-physical realm. This success is very good evidence that mental states, including consciousness, are also physical phenomena, even if we cannot successfully account for them scientifically.

Of course, if it should turn out that an adequate science of the mind eludes us, materialists will have to explain why this is so, and it is not difficult to imagine some plausible hypotheses that are compatible with materialism. One hypothesis why mental states, unlike light or life, elude our scientific understanding is simply that the brain is too complicated for us to understand. Another hypothesis is that there are good evolutionary and biological reasons why we cannot come to have adequate scientific knowledge of our mental states. It would not be surprising if we flourish individually and collectively when we know ourselves best subjectively and are protected from too much objective knowledge about our minds. It is not too difficult to imagine how such complete objective knowledge and the power that comes with it could undermine the diversity in human types that is necessary for proper flourishing.

Conclusion

In sum, we have good reasons to believe that there really are mental states and we have good reason to believe that materialism is true. This means that mental states indeed are kinds of physical states. Although scientists today are working hard to understand what mental states are, including such important states as consciousness, whether we will discover what they are is still an open question. The chances are still good that the science of mind will be successful in identifying what sorts of physical states mental states are, but so far the chances that science will fail and will itself reveal the limits of what we can know about ourselves are not negligible. So, given that we have good reasons to be mind/body materialists, we should continue our efforts to find out what sorts of physical states mental states are, but we should proceed with care and be aware of the fact that there are limits to our knowledge.

This has an important consequence for how we treat others. Given that human beings cannot be confident in their understanding of exactly how to fit mind into nature, human beings need to be very careful about their judgments about who thinks and who does not, who feels pain and who does not, who is conscious and who is not. Since it is much more dangerous morally to deny that someone thinks and feels when in fact he or she does than to affirm that something thinks and feels when it does not, it is best to err on the side of caution and treat others as if they have minds when there is any uncertainty about this. This means that as long as human beings are not sure whether or not non-human animals have thoughts and feel pains, they should treat them as if they do until they have better evidence. The limits of human knowledge should set limits to how human beings act.

Selections from *Principles of Philosophy* and *Passions of the Soul*
René Descartes

The French philosopher René Descartes (1596–1650) is regarded as the founder of modern philosophy. His view that the problems of knowledge, particularly the problem of skepticism, were the most fundamental problems of all of philosophy defined philosophy for centuries. The following selection from *Principles of Philosophy* shows how Descartes' philosophy of mind rose from his theory of knowledge; material beings have epistemic properties that the soul lacks. The selection from *The Passions of the Soul* further discusses the nature of the soul and physical bodies, and how the mind and the body are connected.

Principles of Philosophy

Part I: The Principles of Human Knowledge
1 The seeker after truth must, once in the course of his life, doubt everything, as far as is possible

Since we began life as infants, and made various judgements concerning the things that can be perceived by the senses before we had the full use of our reason, there are many preconceived opinions that keep us from knowledge of the truth. It seems that the only way of freeing ourselves from these opinions is to make the effort, once in the course of our life, to doubt everything which we find to contain even the smallest suspicion of uncertainty.

2 What is doubtful should even be considered as false

Indeed, it will even prove useful, once we have doubted these things, to consider them as false, so that our discovery of what is most certain and easy to know may be all the clearer.

3 This doubt should not meanwhile be applied to ordinary life

This doubt, while it continues, should be kept in check and employed solely in connection with the contemplation of the truth. As far as ordinary life is concerned, the chance for action would frequently pass us by if we waited until we could free ourselves from our doubts, and so we are often compelled to accept what is merely probable. From time to time we may even have to make a choice between two alternatives, even though it is not apparent that one of the two is more probable than the other.

4 The reasons for doubt concerning the things that can be perceived by the senses

Given, then, that our efforts are directed solely to the search for truth, our initial doubts will be about the existence of the objects of sense perception and imagination. The first reason for such doubts is that from time to time we have caught out the senses when they were in error, and it is prudent never to place too much trust in those who have deceived us even once. The second reason is that in our sleep we regularly seem to have sensory perception of, or to imagine, countless things which do not exist anywhere; and if our doubts are on the scale just outlined, there seem to be no marks by means of which we can with certainty distinguish being asleep from being awake.

5 The reasons for doubting even mathematical demonstrations

Our doubt will also apply to other matters which we previously regarded as most certain, even the demonstrations of mathematics and even the principles which we hitherto considered to be self evident. One reason for this is that we have sometimes seen people make mistakes in such matters and accept as most certain and self evident things which seemed false to us. Secondly, and most importantly, we have been told that there is an omnipotent God who created us. Now we do not know whether he may have wished to make us beings of the sort who are always deceived even in those matters which seem to us supremely evident; for such constant deception seems no less a possibility than the occasional deception which, as we have noticed on previous occasions, does occur. We may of course suppose that our existence derives not from a supremely powerful God but either from ourselves or from some other source; but in that case, the less powerful we make the author of our coming into being, the more likely it will be that we are so imperfect as to be deceived all the time.

6 We have free will, enabling us to withhold our assent in doubtful matters and hence avoid error

But whoever turns out to have created us, and however powerful and however deceitful he may be, in the meantime we nonetheless experience within us the kind of freedom which enables us always to refrain from believing things which are not completely certain and thoroughly examined. Hence we are able to take precautions against going wrong on any occasion.

7 It is not possible for us to doubt that we exist while we are doubting; and this is the first thing we come to know when we philosophize in an orderly way

In rejecting and even imagining to be false everything which we can in any way doubt, it is easy for us to suppose that there is no God and no heaven, and that there are no bodies, and even that we ourselves have no hands or feet, or indeed any body at all. But we cannot for all that suppose that we, who are having such thoughts, are nothing. For it is a contradiction to suppose that what thinks does not, at the very time when it is thinking, exist. Accordingly, this piece of knowledge, *I am thinking, therefore I exist*, is the first and most certain of all to occur to anyone who philosophizes in an orderly way.

8 In this way we discover the distinction between soul and body, or between a thinking thing and a corporeal thing

This is the best way to discover the nature of the mind and the distinction between the mind and the body. For if we, who are supposing that everything which is distinct from us is false, examine what we are, we see very clearly that neither extension nor shape nor local motion, nor anything of this kind which is attributable to a body, belongs to our nature, but that thought alone belongs to it. So our knowledge of our thought is prior to, and more certain than, our knowledge of any corporeal thing; for we have already perceived it, although we are still in doubt about other things.

9 What is meant by "thought"

By the term "thought," I understand everything which we are aware of as happening within us, in so far as we have awareness of it. Hence, thinking is to be identified here not merely with understanding, willing and imagining, but also with sensory awareness. For if I say "I am seeing, or I am walking, therefore I exist," and take this as applying to vision or walking as bodily activities, then the conclusion is not absolutely certain. This is because, as often happens during sleep, it is possible for me to think I am seeing or walking, though my eyes are closed and I am not moving about; such thoughts might even be possible if I had no body at all. But if I take "seeing" or "walking" to apply to the actual sense or awareness of seeing or walking, then the conclusion is quite certain, since it relates to the mind, which alone has the sensation or thought that it is seeing or walking.

10 Matters which are very simple and self-evident are only rendered more obscure by logical definitions, and should not be counted as items of knowledge which it takes effort to acquire

I shall not here explain many of the other terms which I have already used or will use in what follows, because they seem to me to be sufficiently self evident. I have often noticed that philosophers make the mistake of employing logical definitions in an attempt to explain what was already very simple and self evident; the result is that they only make matters more obscure. And when I said that the proposition I am thinking, therefore I exist is the first and most certain of all to occur to anyone who philosophizes in an orderly way, I did not in saying that deny that one must first know what thought, existence and certainty are, and that it is impossible that that which thinks should not exist, and so forth. But because these are very simple notions, and ones which on their own provide us with no knowledge of anything that exists, I did not think they needed to be listed.

11 How our mind is better known than our body

In order to realize that the knowledge of our mind is not simply prior to and more certain than the knowledge of our body, but also more evident, we should notice something very well known by the natural light: nothingness possesses no attributes or qualities. It follows that, wherever we find some attributes or qualities, there is necessarily some thing or substance to be found for them to belong to; and the more attributes we discover in the same thing or substance, the clearer is our knowledge of that substance. Now we find more attributes in our mind than in anything else, as is manifest from the fact that whatever enables us to know anything else cannot but lead us to a much surer knowledge of our own mind. For example, if I judge that the earth exists from the fact that I touch it or see it, this very fact undoubtedly gives even greater support for the judgement that my mind exists. For it may perhaps be the case that I judge that I am touching the earth even though the earth does not exist at all; but it cannot be that, when I make this judgement, my mind which is making the judgement does not exist. And the same applies in other cases regarding all the things that come into our mind, namely that we who think of them exist, even if they are false or have no existence.

12 Why this fact does not come to be known to all alike

Disagreement on this point has come from those who have not done their philosophizing in an orderly way; and the reason for it is simply that they have never taken sufficient care to distinguish the mind from the body. Although they may have put the certainty of their own existence before that of anything else, they failed to realize that they should have taken "themselves" in this context to mean their minds alone. They were inclined instead to take "themselves" to mean only their bodies the bodies which they saw with their eyes and touched with their hands, and to which they incorrectly attributed the power of sense perception; and this is what prevented them from perceiving the nature of the mind.

Passions of the Soul

27 Definitions of the passions of the soul

After having considered in what respects the passions of the soul differ from all its other thoughts, it seems to me that we may define them generally as those perceptions, sensations or emotions of the soul which we refer particularly to it, and which are caused, maintained and strengthened by some movement of the spirits.

28 Explanation of the first part of this definition

We may call them "perceptions" if we use this term generally to signify all the thoughts which are not actions of the soul or volitions, but not if we use it to signify only evident knowledge. For experience shows that those who are the most strongly agitated by their passions are not those who know them best, and that the passions are to be numbered among the perceptions which the close alliance between the soul and the body renders confused and obscure. We may also call them "sensations," because they are received into the soul in the same way as the objects of the external senses, and they are not known by the soul any differently. But it is even better to call them "emotions" of the soul, not only because this term may be applied to all the changes which occur in the soul, that is, to all the various thoughts which come to it, but more particularly because, of all the kinds of thought which the soul may have, there are none that agitate and disturb it so strongly as the passions.

29 Explanation of the other part of the definition

I add that they refer particularly to the soul, in order to distinguish them from other sensations, some referred to external objects (e.g. smells, sounds and colours) and others to our body (e.g. hunger, thirst and pain). I also add that they are caused, maintained and strengthened by some movement of the spirits, both in order to distinguish them from our volitions (for these too may be called "emotions of the soul which refer to it," but they are caused by the soul itself), and also in order to explain their ultimate and most proximate cause, which distinguishes them once again from other sensations.

30 The soul is united to all the parts of the body conjointly

But in order to understand all these things more perfectly, we need to recognize that the soul is really joined to the whole body, and that we cannot properly say that it exists in any one part of the body to the exclusion of the others. For the body is a unity which is in a sense indivisible because of the arrangement of its organs, these being so related to one another that the removal of any one of them renders the whole body defective. And the soul is of such a nature that it has no relation to extension, or to the dimensions or other properties of the matter of which the body is composed: it is related solely to the whole assemblage of the body's organs. This is obvious from our inability to conceive of a half or a third of a soul, or of the extension which a soul occupies. Nor does the soul become any smaller if we cut off some part of the body, but it becomes completely separate from the body when we break up the assemblage of the body's organs.

31 There is a little gland in the brain where the soul exercises its functions more particularly than in the other parts of the body

We need to recognize also that although the soul is joined to the whole body, nevertheless there is a certain part of the body where it exercises its functions more particularly than in all the others. It is commonly held that this part is the brain, or perhaps the heart – the brain because the sense organs are related to it, and the heart because we feel the passions as if they were in it. But on carefully examining the matter I think I have clearly established that the part of the body in which the soul directly exercises its functions is not the heart at all, or the whole of the brain. It is rather the innermost part of the brain, which is a certain very small gland situated in the middle of the brain's substance and suspended above the passage through which the spirits in the brain's anterior cavities communicate with those in its posterior cavities. The slightest movements on the part of this gland may alter very greatly the course of these spirits, and conversely any change, however slight, taking place in the course of the spirits may do much to change the movements of the gland.

32 How we know that this gland is the principal seat of the soul

Apart from this gland, there cannot be any other place in the whole body where the soul directly exercises its functions. I am convinced of this by the observation that all the other parts of our brain are double, as also are all the organs of our external senses – eyes, hands, ears and so on. But in so far as we have only one simple thought about a given object at any one time, there must necessarily be some place where the two images coming through the two eyes, or the two impressions coming from a single object through the double organs of any other sense, can come together in a single image or impression before reaching the soul, so that they do not present to it two objects instead of one. We can easily understand that these images or other impressions are unified in this gland by means of the spirits which fill the cavities of the brain. But they cannot exist united in this way in any other place in the body except as a result of their being united in this gland.

33 The seat of the passions is not in the heart

As for the opinion of those who think that the soul receives its passions in the heart, this is not worth serious consideration, since it is based solely on the fact that the passions make us feel some change in the heart. It is easy to see that the only reason why this change is felt as occurring in the heart is that there is a small nerve which descends to it from the brain – just as pain is felt as in the foot by means of the nerves in the foot, and the stars are perceived as in the sky by means of their light and the optic nerves. Thus it is no more necessary that our soul should exercise its functions directly in the heart in order to feel its passions there, than that it should be in the sky in order to see the stars there.

34 How the soul and the body act on each other

Let us therefore take it that the soul has its principal seat in the small gland located in the middle of the brain. From there it radiates through the rest of the body by means of the animal spirits, the nerves, and even the blood, which can take on the impressions of the spirits and carry them through the arteries to all the limbs. Let us recall what we said previously about the mechanism of our body. The nerve fibres are so distributed in all the parts of the body that when the objects of the senses produce various different movements in these parts, the fibres are occasioned to open the pores of the brain in various different ways. This, in turn, causes the animal spirits contained in these cavities to enter the muscles in various different ways. In this manner the spirits can move the limbs in all the different ways they are capable of being moved. And all the other causes that can move the spirits in different ways are sufficient to direct them into different muscles. To this we may now add that the small gland which is the principal seat of the soul is suspended within the cavities containing these spirits, so that it can be moved by them in as many different ways as there are perceptible differences in the objects. But it can also be moved in various different ways by the soul, whose nature is such that it receives as many different impressions, that is, it has as many different perceptions as there occur different movements in this gland. And conversely, the mechanism of our body is so constructed that simply by this gland's being moved in any way by the soul or by any other cause, it drives the surrounding spirits towards the pores of the brain, which direct them through the nerves to the muscles; and in this way the gland makes the spirits move the limbs.

35 Example of the way in which the impressions of objects are united in the gland in the middle of the brain

Thus, for example, if we see some animal approaching us, the light reflected from its body forms two images, one in each of our eyes; and these images form two others, by means of the optic nerves, on the internal surface of the brain facing its cavities. Then, by means of the spirits that fill these cavities, the images radiate towards the little gland which the spirits surround: the movement forming each point of one of the images tends towards the same point on the gland as the movement forming the corresponding point of the other image, which represents the same part of the animal. In this way, the two images in the brain form only one image on the gland, which acts directly upon the soul and makes it see the shape of the animal.

36 Example of the way in which the passions are aroused in the soul

If, in addition, this shape is very strange and terrifying – that is, if it has a close relation to things which have previously been harmful to the body – this arouses the passion of anxiety in the soul, and then that of courage or perhaps fear and terror, depending upon the particular temperament of the body or the strength of the soul, and upon whether we have protected ourselves previously by defence or by flight against the harmful things to which the present impression is related. Thus in certain persons these factors dispose their brain in such a way that some of the spirits reflected from the image formed on the gland proceed from there to the nerves which serve to turn the back and move the legs in order to flee. The rest of the spirits go to nerves which expand or constrict the orifices of the heart, or else to nerves which agitate other parts of the body from which blood is sent to the heart, so that the blood is rarefied in a different manner from usual and spirits are sent to the brain which are adapted for maintaining and strengthening the passion of fear – that is, for holding open or reopening the pores of the brain which direct the spirits into these same nerves. For merely by entering into these pores they produce in the gland a particular movement which is ordained by nature to make the soul feel this passion. And since these pores are related mainly to the little nerves which serve to contract or expand the orifices of the heart, this makes the soul feel the passion chiefly as if it were in the heart.

Selection from *Conversation between d'Alembert and Diderot*
Denis Diderot

Denis Diderot (1713–1784) was a French philosopher, playwright, and one of the leading figures of the Enlightenment. He studied the influences of the senses on the acquisition of ideas, argued for a materialistic interpretation of nature, and spent five months in prison because of the atheistic overtones of his works. In the following selection, Diderot argues that the mind arises out of properly organized material and that we are not composed of two different substances. As Diderot said, quoting the Bible, "dust thou art, to dust thou shalt return."

D'ALEMBERT: I confess that a Being who exists somewhere and yet corresponds to no point in space, a Being who, lacking extension, yet occupies space; who is present in his entirety in every part of that space, who is essentially different from matter and yet is one with matter, who follows its motion, and moves it, without himself being in motion, who acts on matter and yet is subject to all its vicissitudes, a Being about whom I can form no idea; a Being of so contradictory a nature, is an hypothesis difficult to accept. But other problems arise if we reject it; for if this faculty of sensation which you propose as substitute, is a general and essential quality of matter, then stone must be sensitive.

DIDEROT: Why not?

D'ALEMBERT: It's hard to believe.

DIDEROT: Yes, for him who cuts, chisels, and crushes it, and does not hear it cry out.

D'ALEMBERT: I'd like you to tell me what difference there is, according to you between a man and a statue, between marble and flesh.

DIDEROT: Not much. Flesh can be made from marble, and marble from flesh.

D'ALEMBERT: But one is not the other.

DIDEROT: In the same way that what you call animate force is not the same as inanimate force.

D'ALEMBERT: I don't follow you.

DIDEROT: I'll explain. The transference of a body from one place to another is not itself motion, it is the consequence of motion. Motion exists equally in the body displaced and in the body that remains stationary.

D'ALEMBERT: That's a new way of looking at things.

DIDEROT: True none the less. Take away the obstacle that prevents the displacement of a stationary body, and it will be transferred. Suddenly rarefy the air that surrounds the trunk of this huge oak, and the water contained in it, suddenly expanding, will burst it into a hundred thousand fragments. I say the same of your own body.

D'ALEMBERT: That may be so. But what relation is there between motion and the faculty of sensation? Do you, by any chance, distinguish between an active and an inactive sensitiveness, as between animate and inanimate force? An animate force which is revealed by displacement, an inanimate force which manifests itself by pressure; an active sensitiveness which would be characterized by a certain recognizable behaviour in the animal and perhaps in the plant, while your inactive sensitiveness only makes itself known when it changes over to the active state?

DIDEROT: Precisely; just as you say.

D'ALEMBERT: So, then, the statue merely has inactive sensitiveness and man, animals, perhaps even plants, are endowed with active sensitiveness.

DIDEROT: There is undoubtedly that difference between the marble block and living tissue; but you can well imagine that's not the only one.

D'ALEMBERT: Of course. Whatever likeness there may be in outward form between a man and a statue, there is no similarity in their internal organization. The chisel of the cleverest sculptor cannot make even an epidermis. But there is a very simple way of transforming an inanimate force into an animate one – the experiment is repeated a hundred times a day before our eyes; whereas I don't quite see how a body can be made to pass from the state of inactive to that of active sensitiveness.

DIDEROT: Because you don't want to see it. It is just as common a phenomenon.

D'ALEMBERT: And what is this common phenomenon, if you please?

DIDEROT: I'll tell you, since you want to be put to shame; it occurs every time you eat.

D'ALEMBERT: Every time I eat!

DIDEROT: Yes, for what do you do when you eat? You remove obstacles that prevented the food from possessing active sensitiveness. You assimilate it, you turn it into flesh, you make it animal, you give it the faculty of sensation; and, what you do to this foodstuff, I can do, when I please, to marble.

D'ALEMBERT: And how?

DIDEROT: How? I shall make it edible.

D'ALEMBERT: Make marble edible? That doesn't seem easy to me.

DIDEROT: It's my business to show you the process. I take the statue you see there, I put it in a mortar, then with great blows from a pestle . . .

D'ALEMBERT: Careful, please; that's Falconet's masterpiece! If it were only by Huez or some one like that . . .

DIDEROT: Falconer won't mind; the statue is paid for, and Falconer cares little for present respect and not at all for that of posterity.

D'ALEMBERT: Go on then, crush it to powder.

DIDEROT: When the block of marble is reduced to impalpable powder, I mix it with humus or leaf-mould; I knead them well together; I water the mixture, I let it decompose for a year or two or a hundred, time doesn't matter to me. When the whole has turned into a more or less homogeneous substance, into humus, do you know what I do?

D'ALEMBERT: I'm sure you don't eat humus.

DIDEROT: No; but there is a means of connection, of assimilation, a link, between the humus and myself, a *latus* as the chemist would say.

D'ALEMBERT: And that is plant life?

DIDEROT: Quite right, I sow peas, beans, cabbages, and other vegetables; these plants feed on the soil and I feed on the plants.

D'ALEMBERT: Whether it's true or false, I like this passage from marble into humus, from humus to the vegetable kingdom, from the vegetable to the animal kingdom, to flesh.

DIDEROT: So, then, I make flesh, or soul as my daughter said, an actively sensitive substance; and if I do not thus solve the problem you set me, at any rate I get pretty near solving it; for you will admit that a piece of marble is much further removed from a being that can feel, than a being that can feel is from a being that can think.

D'ALEMBERT: I agree. But nevertheless the feeling being is not yet the thinking being.

DIDEROT: Before going one step further let me tell you the history of one of the greatest geometricians in Europe. What was this wonderful creature to begin with? Nothing.

D'ALEMBERT: What, nothing? Nothing comes from nothing.

DIDEROT: You take my words too literally. I mean to say that, before his mother, the beautiful and wicked Madame de Tencin, had reached the age of puberty, and before the adolescence of the soldier La Touche, the molecules which were to form the first rudiments of our geometrician were scattered throughout the frail, young bodies of these two, filtering through with the lymph, circulating with the blood, till at last they reached the vessels whence they were destined to unite, the germ cells of his father and mother. The precious germ, then, is formed; now according to the common belief, it is brought through the Fallopian tubes to the womb, it is attached to the womb by a long cord; it grows gradually and develops into a fetus; now comes the moment for it to leave the dark prison; it is born, abandoned on the steps of Saint-Jean-le-Rond, whence it receives its name; now, taken from the foundlings home, it is put to the breast of good Madame Rousseau, the glazier's wife; it is given suck, it grows in body and mind, becomes a man of letters, an engineer, a geometrician. How was all this done? Just through eating and other purely mechanical operations. Here, in four words you have the general formula: Eat, digest, distil *in vasi licito, et fiat home secundum artem.*[1] And to expound before the Academy the process of the formation of a man or an animal, one need employ only material agents, the successive results of which would be an inert being, a feeling being, a thinking being, a being solving the problem of the precession of the equinoxes, a sublime being, a marvellous being, a being growing old, fading away, dying, dissolved and given back to the soil.

D'ALEMBERT: You don't believe, then, in preexistent germs?

DIDEROT: No.

D'ALEMBERT: Ah, how glad I am of that.

DIDEROT: Such a theory is against reason and experiment: against experiment, since you would seek in vain for these germs in the egg or in most animals before a certain age; against reason, since, although the mind may conceive of matter as infinitely divisible, it is not so in nature, and it is unreasonable to imagine an elephant wholly formed within an atom, and within that elephant another wholly formed, and so on to infinity.

D'ALEMBERT: But without these preexistent germs, how can we account for the first generation of animals?

DIDEROT: If you're worried by the question "which came first, the hen or the egg", it's because you suppose that animals were originally the same as they are now. What madness! We can no more tell what they were originally than what they will become. The tiny worm, wriggling in the mud, may be in process of developing into a large animal; the huge animal, that terrifies us by its size, is perhaps on the way to becoming a worm, is perhaps a particular and transient production of this planet.

D'ALEMBERT: What's that you are saying?

DIDEROT: I was saying to you . . . But it'll take us away from our original discussion.

D'ALEMBERT: What does that matter? We can get back to it or not, as we please.

DIDEROT: Will you allow me to skip ahead a few million years in time?

D'ALEMBERT: Why not? Time is nothing for nature.

DIDEROT: Will you consent to my extinguishing our sun?

D'ALEMBERT: The more readily, since it will not be the first to have gone out.

DIDEROT: Once the sun has been extinguished what will be the result? Plants will perish, animals will perish, the earth will become desolate and silent. Light up that star once more, and you immediately restore the necessary cause whereby an infinite number of new species will be generated, among which I cannot swear whether, in the course of centuries, the plants and animals we know to-day will or will not be reproduced.

D'ALEMBERT: And why should the same scattered elements coming together again not give the same results?

DIDEROT: Because everything is connected in nature, and if you imagine a new phenomenon or bring back a moment of the past, you are creating a new world.

D'ALEMBERT: Anyone who thinks deeply cannot deny that. But, to come back to man, since the general order of things required his existence; remember, you left me where the feeling being is about to become the thinking being.

DIDEROT: I remember.

D'ALEMBERT: Frankly, I'd be very grateful if you would get me over that transition; I'm eager to begin thinking.

DIDEROT: Even if I should not accomplish it, what effect could that have against a sequence of incontrovertible facts?

D'ALEMBERT: None, unless we stopped short there.

DIDEROT: And in order to go further, would it be permissible for us to invent an agent whose attributes should be self-contradictory, a meaningless and unintelligible word?

D'ALEMBERT: No.

DIDEROT: Can you tell me what constitutes the existence of a perceiving being, for that being itself?

D'ALEMBERT: The consciousness of continued identity from the first moment of reflection to the present.

DIDEROT: And on what is this consciousness based?

D'ALEMBERT: On the memory of its actions.

DIDEROT: And without this memory?

D'ALEMBERT: Without this memory it would have no identity, since, realizing its existense only at the instant of receiving an impression, it would have no life-story. Its life would be an interrupted series of sensations with nothing to connect them.

DIDEROT: Very good. And what is this memory? Whence does it spring?

D'ALEMBERT: From a certain organization, which develops, grows weaker, and is sometimes lost entirely.

DIDEROT: Then, if a being that can feel, and that possesses this organization that gives rise to memory, connects up the impressions it receives, forms through this connection a story which is that of its life, and so acquires consciousness of its identify, it can then deny, affirm, conclude and think.

D'ALEMBERT: So it appears to me; there is only one more difficulty.

DIDEROT: You are wrong; there are many more.

D'ALEMBERT: But one chief one; that is, it seems to me that we can only think of one thing at a time, and that to form even a simple proposition, let alone those vast chains of reasoning that embrace in their course thousands of ideas, one would need to have at least two things present – the object, which seems to remain in the mind's eye while that mind considers the quality which it is to attribute or to deny to that object.

DIDEROT: I think that is so; that has made me sometimes compare the fibres of our organs to sensitive vibrating strings which vibrate and resound long after they have been plucked. It is this vibration, this kind of inevitable resonance, which holds the object present, while the mind is busied about the quality that belongs to that object. But vibrating strings have yet another property, that of making other strings vibrate; and that is how the first idea recalls a second, the two of them a third, these three a fourth and so on, so that there is no limit to the ideas awakened and interconnected in the mind of the philosopher, as he meditates and hearkens to himself amid silence and darkness. This instrument makes surprising leaps, and an idea once aroused may sometimes set vibrating an harmonic at an inconceivable distance. If this phenomenon may be observed between resonant strings that are lifeless and separate, why should it not occur between points that are alive and connected, between fibres that are continuous and sensitive?

D'ALEMBERT: Even if it's not true, that is at least very ingenious. But I am inclined to think that you are, without realizing it, slipping into a difficulty that you wished to avoid.

DIDEROT: What is that?

D'ALEMBERT:You are opposed to making a distinction between the two substances.

DIDEROT: I don't deny it.

D'ALEMBERT: And if you look closer, you'll see that you are making of the philosopher's mind a being distinct from the instrument, a musician as it were, who listens to the vibrating strings and decides as to their harmony or dissonance.

DIDEROT: I may have laid myself open to this objection, but you might not have made it if you had considered the difference between the instrument philosopher and the instrument harpsichord. The philosopher is an instrument that has the faculty of sensation; he is, at the same time, both the musician and the instrument. As he can feel, he is immediately conscious of the sound he gives forth; as he is an animal he retains a memory of it. This faculty of the organism, connecting up the sounds within him, produces and preserves the melody there. Just suppose that your harpsichord has the power to feel and to remember, and tell me if it will not know and repeat of its own accord the airs that you have played on its keys. We are instruments endowed with feeling and memory; our senses are so many keys that are struck by surrounding nature, and that often strike themselves. This is all, in my opinion, that happens in a harpsichord which is organized like you or me. An impression is created by some cause either within or outside the instrument, a sensation is aroused by this impression, a sensation that persists, since you cannot imagine it arising and dying instantaneously; another impression follows, which equally has its cause either within or outside the animal, a second sensation, and voices to indicate them by natural or conventional sounds.

D'ALEMBERT: I understand. So then, if this harpsichord were not only sensitive and animate but were further endowed with the faculty of feeding and reproducing itself, it would live and breed of itself, or with its female, little harpsichords, also living and vibrating.

DIDEROT: Undoubtedly. In your opinion, what, other than this, is a chaffinch, a nightingale, a musician or a man? And what other difference do you find between a bird and a bird-organ?[2] Do you see this egg? With this you can overthrow all the schools of theology, all the churches of the earth. What is this egg? An unperceiving mass, before the germ is introduced into it; and after the germ is introduced, what is it then? Still only an unperceiving mass, for this germ itself is only a crude inert fluid. How will this mass develop into a different organization, to sensitiveness, to life? By means of heat. And what will produce the heat? Motion. What will be the successive effects of this motion? Instead of answering me, sit down and let's watch them from moment to moment. First there's a dot that quivers, a little thread that grows longer and takes on colour; tissue is formed; a beak, tiny wings, eyes, feet appear; a yellowish material unwinds and produces intestines; it is an animal. This animal moves, struggles, cries out; I hear its cries through the shell; it becomes covered with down; it sees. The weight of its head, shaking about, brings its beak constantly up against the inner wall of its prison; now the wall is broken; it comes out, it walks about, flies, grows angry, runs away, comes near again, complains, suffers, loves, desires, enjoys; it has the same affections as yourself, it performs the same actions. Are you going to assert with Descartes that it is a purely imitative machine? Little children will laugh at you, and philosophers will retort that if this be a machine then you, too, are a machine. If you admit that between the animal and yourself the difference is merely one of organization, you will be showing good sense and reason, you will be honest; but from this there will be drawn the conclusion that refutes you; namely that, from inert matter, organized in a certain way, and impregnated with other inert matter, and given heat and motion, there results the faculty of sensation, life, memory, consciousness, passion and thought. You have only two courses left to take: either to imagine within the inert mass of the egg a hidden element that awaited the egg's development before revealing its presence, or to assume that this invisible element crept in through the shell at a definite moment in the development. But what is this element? Did it occupy space or did it not? How did it come, or did it escape without moving? What was it doing there or elsewhere? Was it created at the instant it was needed? Was it already in existence? Was it waiting for a home? If it was homogeneous it was material; if heterogeneous, one cannot account for its previous inertia nor its activity in the developed animal. Just listen to yourself, and you will be sorry for yourself; you will perceive that, in order to avoid making a simple supposition that explains everything, namely the faculty of sensation as a general property of matter or a product of its organization, you are giving up common sense and plunging headlong into an abyss of mysteries, contradictions and absurdities.

D'ALEMBERT: A supposition! It pleases you to say so. But suppose this quality is in its essence incompatible with matter?

DIDEROT: And how do you know that the faculty of sensation is essentially incompatible with matter, you who do not know the essence of anything, either of matter or of sensation? Do you understand the nature of motion any better, how it comes to exist in a body, and its transmission from one to another?

D'ALEMBERT: Without understanding the nature of sensation or that of matter, I can see that the faculty of sensation is a simple quality, entire, indivisible, and incompatible with a subject or substratum which is divisible.

DIDEROT: Metaphysico-theological nonsense! What! don't you see that all the qualities, all the forms by which nature becomes perceptible to our senses, are essentially indivisible? You cannot have more or less impenetrability. There is half a round body, but there is not a half of roundness; you can have motion to a greater or less degree, but either there is motion or there is not. You cannot have half, or a third, or a quarter of a head, an ear, a finger, any more than half, a third, or a quarter of a thought. If in the universe no one particle is like another, in a particle no one point like another, acknowledge that the atom itself possesses an indivisible quality or form; acknowledge that division is incompatible with the essence of forms, since it destroys them. Be a physicist, and acknowledge the produced character of an effect when you see it produced, even if you cannot explain all the steps that led from the cause to the effect. Be logical, and do not substitute for a cause which exists and which explains everything, another cause which cannot be comprehended, whose connection with the effect is even more difficult to grasp, which engenders an infinite number of difficulties and solves not one of them.

D'ALEMBERT: But what if I give up this cause?

DIDEROT: There is only one substance in the universe, in man and in the animal. The bird-organ is made of wood, man of flesh. The bird is of flesh, the musician of flesh differently organized; but both of them have the same origin, the same formation, the same functions and the same end.

D'ALEMBERT: And how is the convention of sounds established between your two harpsichords?

DIDEROT: Since an animal is a perceiving instrument, resembling any other in all respects, having the same structure, being strung with the same chords, stimulated in the same way by joy, pain, hunger, thirst, colic, wonder, terror, it is impossible that at the Pole and at the Equator it should utter different sounds. And so you will find that interjections are about the same in all languages, living and dead. The origin of conventional sounds must be ascribed to need and to proximity. The instrument endowed with the faculty of sensation, or the animal, has discovered by experience that when it uttered a certain sound a certain result followed outside it, feeling instruments like itself or other animals drew nearer, went away, asked or offered things, hurt or caressed it. All these consequences became connected in its memory and in that of others with the utterance of these sounds; and note that human intercourse consists only of sounds and actions. And, to appreciate the power of my system, notice further that it is subject to the same insurmountable difficulty that Berkeley brought against the existence of bodies. There came a moment of madness when the feeling harpsichord thought that it was the only harpsichord in the world, and that the whole harmony of the universe resided in it.

D'ALEMBERT: There's a lot to be said on all that.

DIDEROT: True.

D'ALEMBERT: For instance, your system doesn't make it clear how we form syllogisms or draw inferences.

DIDEROT: We don't draw them; they are all drawn by nature. We only state the existence of connected phenomena, which are known to us practically, by experience, whose existence may be either necessary or contingent; necessary in the case of mathematics, physics, and other exact sciences; contingent in ethics, politics and other conjectural sciences.

D'ALEMBERT: Is the connection between phenomena less necessary in one case than in another?

DIDEROT: No, but the cause undergoes too many particular vicissitudes which escape our observation, for us to be able to count with certainty upon the result that will ensue. Our certainty that a violent-tempered man will grow angry at all insult is not the same as our certainty that one body striking a smaller body set it in motion.

D'ALEMBERT: What about analogy?

DIDEROT: Analogy, in the most complex cases, is only a rule of three working out in the feeling instrument. If a familiar natural phenomenon is followed by another familiar natural phenomenon, what will be the fourth phenomenon that will follow a third either provided by nature or imagined in imitation of nature? If the lance of an ordinary warrior is ten feet long, how long will the lance of Ajax be? If I can throw a stone weighing four pounds Diomedes must be able to shift a large block of rock. The strides of gods and the leaps of their horses will correspond to the imagined proportion between gods and men. You have here a fourth chord in harmony with and proportional to three others; and the animal awaits its resonance, which always occurs within itself, though not always in nature. The poet doesn't mind about that, it doesn't affect his kind of truth. But it is otherwise with the philosopher; he must proceed to examine nature which often shows him a phenomenon quite different from what he had supposed, and then he perceives that he had been seduced by an analogy.

D'ALEMBERT: Farewell, my friend, good evening and good night to you.

DIDEROT: You're joking: but you will dream on your pillow about this conversation, and if it doesn't take on substance there, so much the worse for you; for you will be obliged to adopt far more absurd hypotheses.

D'ALEMBERT: You're wrong there; I shall go to bed a sceptic, and a sceptic I shall arise.

DIDEROT: Sceptic! Is there such a thing as a sceptic?

D'ALEMBERT: That's a good one! Are you going to tell me, now, that I'm no sceptic? Who should know about that better than I?

DIDEROT: Wait a moment.

D'ALEMBERT: Hurry up, for I'm anxious to get to sleep.

DIDEROT: I'll be brief. Do you believe there is a single debated question, on which a man can halt with a strictly equal measure of reason *for* and *against*?

D'ALEMBERT: No, that would be like Buridan's ass.

DIDEROT: In that case, there's no such being as the sceptic, since, apart from mathematical questions which admit of no uncertainty, there is for and against in all questions. The scales, then, are never even, and it is impossible that they should not hang more heavily on the side that seems to us to have most probability.

D'ALEMBERT: But probability appears to me on the right hand in the morning, on the left in the afternoon.

DIDEROT: That is to say, you are dogmatic *for* in the morning and dogmatic *against* in the afternoon.

D'ALEMBERT: And in the evening, when I recall this rapid change in my judgments, I believe neither the morning's nor the afternoon's.

DIDEROT: That is to say, you don't remember which preponderated of the two opinions between which you wavered; that this preponderance appears to you too slight to settle your feelings definitely, and that you decide to cease worrying over such problematic subjects, to leave the discussion of them to others and to contest them no further.

D'ALEMBERT: That may be so.

DIDEROT: But if someone drew you aside, and asked you in a friendly way to tell him honestly, which of the two alternatives seemed to you to present fewer difficulties, would you really be at a loss to answer, and would you realize Buridan's ass in your own person?

D'ALEMBERT: I think not.

DIDEROT: Come, my friend, if you think over it well, you will find that, in everything, our true feeling is not that about which we have never vacillated, but that to which we have most constantly returned.

D'ALEMBERT: I believe you're right.

DIDEROT: And so do I. Good night, my friend, and remember that "dust thou art, to dust thou shalt return."

D'ALEMBERT: That is sad.

DIDEROT: And yet necessary. Grant man, I don't say immortality, but merely a double span of life, and you'll see what will happen.

D'ALEMBERT: And what do you expect to happen? . . . But what do I care? Let happen what may. I want to sleep, so good night to you.

Notes

1 "into the appropriate vessels and in this way let man be made."
2 Mechanical musical-box to teach a canary tunes.

What Is It Like to Be a Bat?
Thomas Nagel

Thomas Nagel, a Professor of Philosophy at New York University, is best known for his work in ethics and philosophy of mind. The following article discusses the nature of conscious experience, or the subjective character of experience. Nagel argues that we might be able to find out all objective facts about conscious beings, but the objective facts would not provide us with information about the subjective character of experience. Thus, even though a biologist could gather all "objective" information about bats, she still would not know what it is like to be a bat. What it is like to be a bat is only captured in the subjective character of experience. So, some mental properties cannot be reduced to physical properties.

Consciousness is what makes the mind–body problem really intractable. Perhaps that is why current discussions of the problem give it little attention or get it obviously wrong. The recent wave of reductionist euphoria has produced several analyses of mental phenomena and mental concepts designed to explain the possibility of some variety of materialism, psychophysical identification, or reduction.[1] But the problems dealt with are those common to this type of reduction and other types, and what makes the mind–body problem unique, and unlike the water–H$_2$O problem or the Turing machine–IBM machine problem or the lightning–electrical discharge problem or the gene–DNA problem or the oak tree–hydrocarbon problem, is ignored.

Every reductionist has his favorite analogy from modern science. It is most unlikely that any of these unrelated examples of successful reduction will shed light on the relation of mind to brain. But philosophers share the general human weakness for explanations of what is incomprehensible in terms suited for what is familiar and well understood, though entirely different. This has led to the acceptance of implausible accounts of the mental largely because they would permit familiar kinds of reduction. I shall try to explain why the usual examples do not help us to understand the relation between mind and body – why, indeed, we have at present no conception of what an explanation of the physical nature of a mental phenomenon would be. Without consciousness the mind–body problem would be much less interesting. With consciousness it seems hopeless. The most important and characteristic feature of conscious mental phenomena is very poorly understood. Most reductionist theories do not even try to explain it. And careful examination will show that no currently available concept of reduction is applicable to it. Perhaps a new theoretical form can be devised for the purpose, but such a solution, if it exists, lies in the distant intellectual future.

Conscious experience is a widespread phenomenon. It occurs at many levels of animal life, though we cannot be sure of its presence in the simpler organisms, and it is very difficult to say in general what provides evidence of it. (Some extremists have been prepared to deny it even of mammals other than man.) No doubt it occurs in countless forms totally unimaginable to us, on other planets in other solar systems throughout the universe. But no matter how the form may vary, the fact that an organism has conscious experience *at all* means, basically, that there is something it is like to *be* that organism. There may be further implications about the form of the experience; there may even (though I doubt it) be implications about the behavior of the organism. But fundamentally an organism has conscious mental states if and only if there is something that it is like to *be* that organism – something it is like *for* the organism.

We may call this the subjective character of experience. It is not captured by any of the familiar, recently devised reductive analyses of the mental, for all of them are logically compatible with its absence. It is not analyzable in terms of any explanatory system of functional states, or intentional states, since these could be ascribed to robots or automata that behaved like people though they experienced nothing.[2] It is not analyzable in terms of the causal role of experiences in relation to typical human behavior – for similar reasons.[3] I do not deny that conscious mental states and events cause behavior, nor that they may be given functional characterizations. I deny only that this kind of thing exhausts their analysis. Any reductionist program has to be based on an analysis of what is to be reduced. If the analysis leaves something out, the problem will be falsely posed. It is useless to base the defense of materialism on any analysis of mental phenomena that fails to deal explicitly with their subjective character. For there is no reason to suppose that a reduction which seems plausible when no attempt is made to account for consciousness can be extended to include consciousness. Without some idea, therefore, of what the subjective character of experience is, we cannot know what is required of physicalist theory.

While an account of the physical basis of mind must explain many things, this appears to be the most difficult. It is impossible to exclude the phenomenological features of experience from a reduction in the same way that one excludes the phenomenological features of an ordinary substance from a physical or chemical reduction of it – namely, by explaining them as effects on the minds of human observers.[4] If physicalism is to be defended, the phenomenological features must themselves be given a physical account. But when we examine their subjective character it seems that such a result is impossible. The reason is that every subjective phenomenon is essentially connected with a single point of view, and it seems inevitable that an objective, physical theory will abandon that point of view.

Let me first try to state the issue somewhat more fully than by referring to the relation between the subjective and the objective, or between the *pour soi* and the *en soi*. This is far from easy. Facts about what it is like to be an X are very peculiar, so peculiar that some may be inclined to doubt their reality, or the significance of claims about them. To illustrate the connexion between subjectivity and a point of view, and to make evident the importance of subjective features, it will help to explore the matter in relation to an example that brings out clearly the divergence between the two types of conception, subjective and objective.

I assume we all believe that bats have experience. After all, they are mammals, and there is no more doubt that they have experience than that mice or pigeons or whales have experience. I have chosen bats instead of wasps or flounders because if one travels too far down the phylogenetic tree, people gradually shed their faith that there is experience there at all. Bats, although more closely related to us than those other species, nevertheless present a range of activity and a sensory apparatus so different from ours that the problem I want to pose is exceptionally vivid (though it certainly could be raised with other species). Even without the benefit of philosophical reflection, anyone who has spent some time in an enclosed space with an excited bat knows what it is to encounter a fundamentally *alien* form of life.

I have said that the essence of the belief that bats have experience is that there is something that it is like to be a bat. Now we know that most bats (the microchiroptera, to be precise) perceive the external world primarily by sonar, or echolocation, detecting the reflections, from objects within range, of their own rapid, subtly modulated, high-frequency shrieks. Their brains are designed to correlate the outgoing impulses with the subsequent echoes, and the information thus acquired enables bats to make precise discriminations of distance, size, shape, motion, and texture comparable to those we make by vision. But bat sonar, though clearly a form of perception, is not similar in its operation to any sense that we possess, and there is no reason to suppose that it is subjectively like anything we can experience or imagine. This appears to create difficulties for the notion of what it is like to be a bat. We must consider whether any method will permit us to extrapolate to the inner life of the bat from our own case,[5] and if not, what alternative methods there may be for understanding the notion.

Our own experience provides the basic material for our imagination, whose range is therefore limited. It will not help to try to imagine that one has webbing on one's arms, which enables one to fly around at dusk and dawn catching insects in one's mouth; that one has very poor vision, and perceives the surrounding world by a system of reflected high-frequency sound signals; and that one spends the day hanging upside down by one's feet in an attic. Insofar as I can imagine this (which is not very far), it, tells me only what it would be like for *me* to behave as a bat behaves. But that is not the question. I want to know what it is like for a *bat* to be a bat. Yet if I try to imagine this, I am restricted to the resources of my own mind, and those resources are inadequate to the task. I cannot perform it either by imagining additions to my present experience, or by imagining segments gradually subtracted from it, or by imagining some combination of additions, subtractions, and modifications.

To the extent that I could look and behave like a wasp or a bat without changing my fundamental structure, my experiences would not be anything like the experiences of those animals. On the other hand, it is doubtful that any meaning can be attached to the supposition that I should possess the internal neurophysiological constitution of a bat. Even if I could by gradual degrees be transformed into a bat, nothing in my present constitution enables me to imagine what the experiences of such a future stage of myself thus metamorphosed would be like. The best evidence would come from the experiences of bats, if we only knew what they were like.

So if extrapolation from our own case is involved in the idea of what it is like to be a bat, the extrapolation must be incompletable. We cannot form more than a schematic conception of what it is like. For example, we may ascribe general *types* of experience on the basis of the animal's structure and behavior. Thus we describe bat sonar as a form of three-dimensional forward perception; we believe that bats feel some versions of pain, fear, hunger, and lust, and that they have other, more familiar types of perception besides sonar. But we believe that these experiences also have in each case a specific subjective character, which it is beyond our ability to conceive. And if there is conscious life elsewhere in the universe, it is likely that some of it will not be describable even in the most general experiential terms available to us.[6] (The problem is not confined to exotic cases, however, for it exists between one person and another. The subjective character of the experience of a person deaf and blind from birth is not accessible to me, for example, nor presumably is mine to him. This does not prevent us each from believing that the other's experience has such a subjective character.)

If anyone is inclined to deny that we can believe in the existence of facts like this whose exact nature we cannot possibly conceive, he should reflect that in contemplating the bats we are in much the same position that intelligent bats or Martians[7] would occupy if they tried to form a conception of what it was like to be us. The structure of their own minds might make it impossible for them to succeed, but we know they would be wrong to conclude that there is not anything precise that it is like to be us: that only certain general types of mental state could be ascribed to us (perhaps perception and appetite would be concepts common to us both; perhaps not). We know they would be wrong to draw such a skeptical conclusion because we know what it is like to be us. And we know that while it includes an enormous amount of variation and complexity, and while we do not possess the vocabulary to describe it adequately, its subjective character is highly specific, and in some respects describable in terms that can be understood only by creatures like us. The fact that we cannot expect ever to accommodate in our language a detailed description of Martian or bat phenomenology should not lead us to dismiss as meaningless the claim that bats and Martians have experiences fully comparable in richness of detail to our own. It would be fine if someone were to develop concepts and a theory that enabled us to think about those things; but such an understanding may be permanently denied to us by the limits of our nature. And to deny the reality or logical significance of what we can never describe or understand is the crudest form of cognitive dissonance.

This brings us to the edge of a topic that requires much more discussion than I can give it here: namely, the relation between facts on the one hand and conceptual schemes or systems of representation on the other. My realism about the subjective domain in all its forms implies a belief in the existence of facts beyond the reach of human concepts. Certainly it is possible for a human being to believe that there are facts which humans never *will* possess the requisite concepts to represent or comprehend. Indeed, it would be foolish to doubt this, given the finiteness of humanity's expectations. After all, there would have been transfinite numbers even if everyone had been wiped out by the Black Death before Cantor discovered them. But one might also believe that there are facts which *could* not ever be represented or comprehended by human beings, even if the species lasted for ever – simply because our structure does not permit us to operate with concepts of the requisite type. This impossibility might even be observed by other beings, but it is not clear that the existence of such beings, or the possibility of their existence, is a precondition of the significance of the hypothesis that there are humanly inaccessible facts. (After all, the nature of beings with access to humanly inaccessible facts is presumably itself a humanly inaccessible fact.) Reflection on what it is like to be a bat seems to lead us, therefore, to the conclusion that there are facts that do not consist in the truth of propositions expressible in a human language. We can be compelled to recognize the existence of such facts without being able to state or comprehend them.

I shall not pursue this subject, however. Its bearing on the topic before us (namely, the mind–body problem) is that it enables us to make a general observation about the subjective character of experience. Whatever may be the status of facts about what it is like to be a human being, or a bat, or a Martian, these appear to be facts that embody a particular point of view.

I am not adverting here to the alleged privacy of experience to its possessor. The point of view in question is not one accessible only to a single individual. Rather it is a *type*. It is often possible to take up a point of view other than one's own, so comprehension of such facts is not limited to one's own case. There is a sense in which phenomenological facts are perfectly objective: one person can know or say of another what the quality of the other's experience is. They are subjective, however, in the sense that even this objective ascription of experience is possible only for someone sufficiently similar to the object of ascription to be able to adopt his point of view – to understand the ascription in the first person as well as in the third, so to speak. The more different from oneself the other experiencer is, the less success one can expect with this enterprise. In our own case we occupy the relevant point of view, but we will have as much difficulty understanding our own experience properly if we approach it from another point of view as we would if we tried to understand the experience of another species without taking up *its* point of view.[8]

This bears directly on the mind–body problem. For if the facts of experience – facts about what it is like *for* the experiencing organism – are accessible only from one point of view, then it is a mystery how the true character of experiences could be revealed in the physical operation of that organism. The latter is a domain of objective facts *par excellence* – the kind that can be observed and understood from many points of view and by individuals with differing perceptual systems. There are no comparable imaginative obstacles to the acquisition of knowledge about bat neurophysiology by human scientists, and intelligent bats or Martians might learn more about the human brain than we ever will.

This is not by itself an argument against reduction. A Martian scientist with no understanding of visual perception could understand the rainbow, or lightning, or clouds as physical phenomena, though he would never be able to understand the human concepts of rainbow, lightning, or cloud, or the place these things occupy in our phenomenal world. The objective nature of the things picked out by these concepts could be apprehended by him because, although the concepts themselves are connected with a particular point of view and a particular visual phenomenology, the things apprehended from that point of view are not: they are observable from the point of view but external to it; hence they can be comprehended from other points of view also, either by the same organisms or by others. Lightning has an objective character that is not exhausted by its visual appearance, and this can be investigated by a Martian without vision. To be precise, it has a *more* objective character than is revealed in its visual appearance. In speaking of the move from subjective to objective characterization, I wish to remain noncommittal about the existence of an end point, the completely objective intrinsic nature of the thing, which one might or might not be able to reach. It may be more accurate to think of objectivity as a direction in which the understanding can travel. And in understanding a phenomenon like lightning, it is legitimate to go as far away as one can from a strictly human viewpoint.[9]

In the case of experience, on the other hand, the connexion with a particular point of view seems much closer. It is difficult to understand what could be meant by the *objective* character of an experience, apart from the particular point of view from which its subject apprehends it. After all, what would be left of what it was like to be a bat if one removed the viewpoint of the bat? But if experience does not have, in addition to its subjective character, an objective nature that can be apprehended from many different points of view, then how can it be supposed that a Martian investigating my brain might be observing physical processes which were my mental processes (as he might observe physical processes which were bolts of lightning), only from a different point of view? How, for that matter, could a human physiologist observe them from another point of view?[10]

We appear to be faced with a general difficulty about psychophysical reduction. In other areas the process of reduction is a move in the direction of greater objectivity, toward a more accurate view of the real nature of things. This is accomplished by reducing our dependence on individual or species-specific points of view toward the object of investigation. We describe it not in terms of the impressions it makes on our senses, but in terms of its more general effects and of properties detectable by means other than the human senses. The less it depends on a specifically human viewpoint, the more objective is our description. It is possible to follow this path because although the concepts and ideas we employ in thinking about the external world are initially applied from a point of view that involves our perceptual apparatus, they are used by us to refer to things beyond themselves – toward which we *have* the phenomenal point of view. Therefore we can abandon it in favor of another, and still be thinking about the same things.

Experience itself, however, does not seem to fit the pattern. The idea of moving from appearance to reality seems to make no sense here. What is the analogue in this case to pursuing a more objective understanding of the same phenomena by abandoning the initial subjective viewpoint toward them in favor of another that is more objective but concerns the same thing? Certainly it *appears* unlikely that we will get closer to the real nature of human experience by leaving behind the particularity of our human point of view and striving for a description in terms accessible to beings that could not imagine what it was like to be us. If the subjective character of experience is fully comprehensible only from one point of view, then any shift to greater objectivity – that is, less attachment to a specific viewpoint – does not take us nearer to the real nature of the phenomenon: it takes us farther away from it.

In a sense, the seeds of this objection to the reducibility of experience are already detectable in successful cases of reduction; for in discovering sound to be, in reality, a wave phenomenon in air or other media, we leave behind one viewpoint to take up another, and the auditory, human or animal viewpoint that we leave behind remains unreduced. Members of radically different species may both understand the same physical events in objective terms, and this does not require that they understand the phenomenal forms in which those events appear to the senses of members of the other species. Thus it is a condition of their referring to a common reality that their more particular viewpoints are not part of the common reality that they both apprehend. The reduction can succeed only if the species-specific viewpoint is omitted from what is to be reduced.

But while we are right to leave this point of view aside in seeking a fuller understanding of the external world, we cannot ignore it permanently, since it is the essence of the internal world, and not merely a point of view on it. Most of the neobehaviorism of recent philosophical psychology results from the effort to substitute an objective concept of mind for the real thing, in order to have nothing left over which cannot be reduced. If we acknowledge that a physical theory of mind must account for the subjective character of experience, we must admit that no presently available conception gives us a clue how this could be done. The problem is unique. If mental processes are indeed physical processes, then there is something it is like, intrinsically,[11] to undergo certain physical processes. What it is for such a thing to be the case remains a mystery.

What moral should be drawn from these reflections, and what should be done next? It would be a mistake to conclude that physicalism must be false. Nothing is proved by the inadequacy of physicalist hypotheses that assume a faulty objective analysis of mind. It would be truer to say that physicalism is a position we cannot understand because we do not at present have any conception of how it might be true. Perhaps it will be thought unreasonable to require such a conception as a condition of understanding. After all, it might be said, the meaning of physicalism is clear enough: mental states are states of the body; mental events are physical events. We do not know which physical states and events they are, but that should not prevent us from understanding the hypothesis. What could be clearer than the words "is" and "are"?

But I believe it is precisely this apparent clarity of the word "is" that is deceptive. Usually, when we are told that X is Y we know *how* it is supposed to be true, but that depends on a conceptual or theoretical background and is not conveyed by the "is" alone. We know how both "X" and "Y" refer, and the kinds of things to which they refer, and we have a rough idea how the two referential paths might converge on a single thing, be it an object, a person, a process, an event or whatever. But when the two terms of the identification are very disparate it may not be so clear how it could be true. We may not have even a rough idea of how the two referential paths could converge, or what kind of things they might converge on, and a theoretical framework may have to be supplied to enable us to understand this. Without the framework, an air of mysticism surrounds the identification.

This explains the magical flavor of popular presentations of fundamental scientific discoveries, given out as propositions to which one must subscribe without really understanding them. For example, people are now told at an early age that all matter is really energy. But despite the fact that they know what "is" means, most of them never form a conception of what makes this claim true, because they lack the theoretical background.

At the present time the status of physicalism is similar to that which the hypothesis that matter is energy would have had if uttered by a pre-Socratic philosopher. We do not have the beginnings of a conception of how it might be true. In order to understand the hypothesis that a mental event is a physical event, we require more than an understanding of the word "is." The idea of how a mental and a physical term might refer to the same thing is lacking, and the usual analogies with theoretical identification in other fields fail to supply it. They fail because if we construe the reference of mental terms to physical events on the usual model, we either get a reappearance of separate subjective events as the effects through which mental reference to physical events is secured, or else we get a false account of how mental terms refer (for example, a causal behaviorist one).

Strangely enough, we may have evidence for the truth of something we cannot really understand. Suppose a caterpillar is locked in a sterile safe by someone unfamiliar with insect metamorphosis, and weeks later the safe is reopened, revealing a butterfly. If the person knows that the safe has been shut the whole time, he has reason to believe that the butterfly is or was once the caterpillar, without having any idea in what sense this might be so. (One possibility is that the caterpillar contained a tiny winged parasite that devoured it and grew into the butterfly.)

It is conceivable that we are in such a position with regard to physicalism. Donald Davidson has argued that if mental events have physical causes and effects, they must have physical descriptions. He holds that we have reason to believe this even though we do not – and in fact *could not* – have a general psychophysical theory.[12] His argument applies to intentional mental events, but I think we also have some reason to believe that sensations are physical processes, without being in a position to understand how. Davidson's position is that certain physical events have irreducibly mental properties, and perhaps some view describable in this way is correct. But nothing of which we can now form a conception corresponds to it; nor have we any idea what a theory would be like that enabled us to conceive of it.[13]

Very little work has been done on the basic question (from which mention of the brain can be entirely omitted) whether any sense can be made of experiences' having an objective character at all. Does it make sense, in other words, to ask what my experiences are *really* like, as opposed to how they appear to me? We cannot genuinely understand the hypothesis that their nature is captured in a physical description unless we understand the more fundamental idea that they *have* an objective nature (or that objective processes can have a subjective nature).[14]

I should like to close with a speculative proposal. It may be possible to approach the gap between subjective and objective from another direction. Setting aside temporarily the relation between the mind and the brain, we can pursue a more objective understanding of the mental in its own right. At present we are completely unequipped to think about the subjective character of experience without relying on the imagination – without taking up the point of view of the experiential subject. This should be regarded as a challenge to form new concepts and devise a new method – an objective phenomenology not dependent on empathy or the imagination. Though presumably it would not capture everything, its goal would be to describe, at least in part, the subjective character of experiences in a form comprehensible to beings incapable of having those experiences.

We would have to develop such a phenomenology to describe the sonar experiences of bats; but it would also be possible to begin with humans. One might try, for example, to develop concepts that could be used to explain to a person blind from birth what it was like to see. One would reach a blank wall eventually, but it should be possible to devise a method of expressing in objective terms much more than we can at present, and with much greater precision. The loose intermodal analogies – for example, "Red is like the sound of a trumpet" – which crop up in discussions of this subject are of little use. That should be clear to anyone who has both heard a trumpet and seen red. But structural features of perception might be more accessible to objective description, even though something would be left out. And concepts alternative to those we learn in the first person may enable us to arrive at a kind of understanding even of our own experience which is denied us by the very ease of description and lack of distance that subjective concepts afford.

Apart from its own interest, a phenomenology that is in this sense objective may permit questions about the physical[15] basis of experience to assume a more intelligible form. Aspects of subjective experience that admitted this kind of objective description might be better candidates for objective explanations of a more familiar sort. But whether or not this guess is correct, it seems unlikely that any physical theory of mind can be contemplated until more thought has been given to the general problem of subjective and objective. Otherwise we cannot even pose the mind–body problem without sidestepping it.

Notes

1   Examples are J. J. C. Smart, *Philosophy and Scientific Realism* (London: Routledge & Kegan Paul, 1963); David K. Lewis, "An Argument for the Identity Theory," *Journal of Philosophy*, LXII (1966), reprinted with addenda in David M. Rosenthal, *Materialism and the Mind–Body Problem* (Engelwood Cliffs, N.J: Prentice Hall, 1971); Hilary Putnam, "Psychological Predicates," in *Art, Mind, and Religion*, ed. W. H. Capitan and D. D. Merrill (Pittsburgh: University of Pittsburgh Press, 1967), reprinted in *Materialism*, ed. Rosenthal, as "The Nature of Mental States"; D. M. Armstrong, *A Materialist Theory of the Mind* (London: Routledge and Kegan Paul, 1968); D. C. Dennett, *Content and Consciousness* (London: Routledge and Kegan Paul, 1969). I have expressed earlier doubts in "Armstrong on the Mind," *Philosophical Review*, LXIX (1972); and "Brain Bisection and the Unity of Consciousness," *Synthese*, XX (1972). See also Saul Kripke, "Naming and Necessity," in *Semantics of Natural Language*, ed. D. Davidson and G. Harman (Dordrecht: Reidel, 1972), esp. pp. 334–42; and M. T. Thornton, "Ostensive Terms and Materialism," *The Monist*, LVI (1972), 193–214.

2   Perhaps there could not actually be such robots. Perhaps anything complex enough to behave like a person would have experiences. But that, if true, is a fact which cannot be discovered merely by analyzing the concept of experience.

3   It is not equivalent to that about which we are incorrigible, both because we are not incorrigible about experience and because experience is present in animals lacking language and thought, who have no beliefs at all about their experiences.

4   Cf. Richard Rorty, "Mind–Body Identity, Privacy, and Categories', *Review of Metaphysics*, xix (1965), esp. 37–8.

5   By "our own case" I do not mean just "my own case," but rather the mentalistic ideas that we apply unproblematically to ourselves and other human beings.

6   Therefore the analogical form of the English expression "what it is *like*" is misleading. It does not mean "what (in our experience) it *resembles*," *but* rather "how it is for the subject himself."

7   Any intelligent extraterrestrial beings totally different from us.

8   It may be easier than I suppose to transcend inter-species barriers with the aid of the imagination. For example, blind people are able to detect objects near them by a form of sonar, using vocal clicks or taps of a cane. Perhaps if one knew what that was like, one could by extension imagine roughly what it was like to possess the much more refined sonar of a bat. The distance between oneself and other persons

and other species can fall anywhere on a continuum. Even for other persons the understanding of what it is like to be them is only partial, and when one moves to species very different from oneself, a lesser degree of partial understanding may still be available. The imagination is remarkably flexible. My point, however, is not that we cannot *know* what it is like to be a bat. I am not raising that epistemological problem. My point is rather that even to form *a conception* of what it is like to be a bat (and *a fortiori* to know what it is like to be a bat) one must take up the bat's point of view. If one can take it up roughly, or partially, then one's conception will also be rough or partial. Or so it seems in our present state of understanding.

9 The problem I am going to raise can therefore be posed even if the distinction between more subjective and more objective descriptions or viewpoints can itself be made only within a larger human point of view. I do not accept this kind of conceptual relativism, but it need not be refuted to make the point that psychophysical reduction cannot be accommodated by the subjective-to-objective model familiar from other cases.

10 The problem is not just that when I look at the *Mona Lisa*, my visual experience has a certain quality, no trace of which is to be found by someone looking into my brain. For even if he did observe there a tiny image of the *Mona Lisa*, he would have no reason to identify it with the experience.

11 The relation would therefore not be a contingent one, like that of a cause and its distinct effect. It would be necessarily true that a certain physical state felt a certain way. Saul Kripke in *Semantics of Natural Language* (ed. Davidson and Harman) argues that causal behaviorist and related analyses of the mental fail because they construe, e.g., "pain" as a merely contingent name of pains. The subjective character of an experience ("its immediate phenomenological quality" Kripke calls it (p. 340)) is the essential property left out by such analyses, and the one in virtue of which it is, necessarily, the experience it is. My view is closely related to his. Like Kripke, I find the hypothesis that a certain brain state should *necessarily* have a certain subjective character incomprehensible without further explanation. No such explanation emerges from theories which view the mind–brain relation as contingent, but perhaps there are other alternatives, not yet discovered.

A theory that explained how the mind–brain relation was necessary would still leave us with Kripke's problem of explaining why it nevertheless appears contingent. That difficulty seems to me surmountable, in the following way. We may imagine something by representing it to ourselves either perceptually, sympathetically, or symbolically. I shall not try to say how symbolic imagination works, but part of what happens in the other two cases is this. To imagine something perceptually, we put ourselves in a conscious state resembling the state we would be in if we perceived it. To imagine something sympathetically, we put ourselves in a conscious state resembling the thing itself. (This method can be used only to imagine mental events and states – our own or another's.) When we try to imagine a mental state occurring without its associated brain state, we first sympathetically imagine the occurrence of the mental state: that is, we put ourselves into a state that resembles it mentally. At the same time, we attempt perceptually to imagine the nonoccurrence of the associated physical state, by putting ourselves into another state unconnected with the first: one resembling that which we would be in if we perceived the nonoccurrence of the physical state. Where the imagination of physical features is perceptual and the imagination of mental features is sympathetic, it appears to us that we can imagine any experience occurring without its associated brain state, and vice versa. The relation between them will appear contingent even if it is necessary, because of the independence of the disparate types of imagination.

(Solipsism, incidentally, results if one misinterprets sympathetic imagination as if it worked like perceptual imagination: it then seems impossible to imagine any experience that is not one's own.)

12   See "Mental Events" in *Experience and Theory*, ed. Lawrence Foster and J. W. Swanson (Amherst: University of Massachusetts Press, 1970); though I do not understand the argument against psychophysical laws.

13   Similar remarks apply to my paper "Physicalism," *Philosophical Review*, LXXIV (1965), 339–56, reprinted with postscript in *Modern Materialism*, ed. John O'Connor (New York: Harcourt Brace Jovanovich, 1969).

14   This question also lies at the heart of the problem of other minds, whose close connection with the mind–body problem is often overlooked. If one understood how subjective experience could have an objective nature, one would understand the existence of subjects other than oneself.

15   I have not defined the term "physical." Obviously it does not apply just to what can be described by the concepts of contemporary physics, since we expect further developments. Some may think there is nothing to prevent mental phenomena from eventually being recognized as physical in their own right. But whatever else may be said of the physical, it has to be objective. So if our idea of the physical ever expands to include mental phenomena, it will have to assign them an objective character – whether or not this is done by analyzing them in terms of other phenomena already regarded as physical. It seems to me more likely, however, that mental–physical relations will eventually be expressed in a theory whose fundamental terms cannot be placed clearly in either category.

Is the Brain's Mind a Computer Program?
John R. Searle

John Searle, a Professor of Philosophy at the University of California, Berkeley, has published extensively in philosophy of language and philosophy of mind. In the following article he discusses whether or not a machine can think in virtue of implementing a computer program. His answer is a resounding "No." While machines can manipulate symbols – that is, while they can perform syntactic operations – they lack understanding of what they symbols are about – that is, they do not grasp the semantic meaning of the symbols which is essential for understanding.

Can a machine think? Can a machine have conscious thoughts in exactly the same sense that you and I have? If by "machine" one means a physical system capable of performing certain functions (and what else can one mean?), then humans are machines of a special biological kind, and humans can think, and so of course machines can think. And, for all we know, it might be possible to produce a thinking machine out of different materials altogether – say, out of silicon chips or vacuum tubes. Maybe it will turn out to be impossible, but we certainly do not know that yet.

In recent decades, however, the question of whether a machine can think has been given a different interpretation entirely. The question that has been posed in its place is, Could a machine think just by virtue of implementing a computer program? Is the program by itself constitutive of thinking? This is a completely different question because it is not about the physical, causal properties of actual or possible physical systems but rather about the abstract, computational properties of formal computer programs that can be implemented in any sort of substance at all, provided only that the substance is able to carry the program.

A fair number of researchers in artificial intelligence (AI) believe the answer to the second question is yes; that is, they believe that by designing the right programs with the right inputs and outputs, they are literally creating minds. They believe furthermore that they have a scientific test for determining success or failure: the Turing test devised by Alan M. Turing, the founding father of artificial intelligence. The Turing test, as currently understood, is simply this: if a computer can perform in such a way that an expert cannot distinguish its performance from that of a human who has a certain cognitive ability – say, the ability to do addition or to understand Chinese – then the computer also has that ability. So the goal is to design programs that will simulate human cognition in such a way as to pass the Turing test. What is more, such a program would not merely be a model of the mind; it would literally be a mind, in the same sense that a human mind is a mind.

By no means does every worker in artificial intelligence accept so extreme a view. A more cautious approach is to think of computer models as being useful in studying the mind in the same way that they are useful in studying the weather, economics or molecular biology. To distinguish these two approaches, I call the first strong AI and the second weak AI. It is important to see just how bold an approach strong AI is. Strong AI claims that thinking is merely the manipulation of formal symbols, and that is exactly what the computer does: manipulate formal symbols. This view is often summarized by saying, "The mind is to the brain as the program is to the hardware."

Strong AI is unusual among theories of the mind in at least two respects: it can be stated clearly, and it admits of a simple and decisive refutation. The refutation is one that any person can try for himself or herself. Here is how it goes. Consider a language you don't understand. In my case, I do not understand Chinese. To me Chinese writing looks like so many meaningless squiggles. Now suppose I am placed in a room containing baskets full of Chinese symbols. Suppose also that I am given a rule book in English for matching Chinese symbols with other Chinese symbols. The rules identify the symbols entirely by their shapes and do not require that I understand any of them. The rules might say such things as, "Take a squiggle-squiggle sign from basket number one and put it next to a squoggle-squoggle sign from basket number two."

Imagine that people outside the room who understand Chinese hand in small bunches of symbols and that in response I manipulate the symbols according to the rule book and hand back more small bunches of symbols. Now, the rule book is the "computer program." The people who wrote it are "programmers," and I am the "computer." The baskets full of symbols are the "data base," the small bunches that are handed in to me are "questions" and the bunches I then hand out are "answers."

Now suppose that the rule book is written in such a way that my "answers" to the "questions" are indistinguishable from those of a native Chinese speaker. For example, the people outside might hand me some symbols that unknown to me mean, "What's your favorite color?" and I might after going through the rules give back symbols that, also unknown to me, mean, "My favorite is blue, but I also like green a lot." I satisfy the Turing test for understanding Chinese. All the same, I am totally ignorant of Chinese. And there is no way I could come to understand Chinese in the system as described, since there is no way that I can learn the meanings of any of the symbols. Like a computer, I manipulate symbols, but I attach no meaning to the symbols.

The point of the thought experiment is this: if I do not understand Chinese solely on the basis of running a computer program for understanding Chinese, then neither does any other digital computer solely on that basis. Digital computers merely manipulate formal symbols according to rules in the program.

What goes for Chinese goes for other forms of cognition as well. Just manipulating the symbols is not by itself enough to guarantee cognition, perception, understanding, thinking and so forth. And since computers, qua computers, are symbol-manipulating devices, merely running the computer program is not enough to guarantee cognition.

This simple argument is decisive against the claims of strong AI. The first premise of the argument simply states the formal character of a computer program. Programs are defined in terms of symbol manipulations, and the symbols are purely formal, or "syntactic." The formal character of the program, by the way, is what makes computers so powerful. The same program can be run on an indefinite variety of hardwares, and one hardware system can run an indefinite range of computer programs. Let me abbreviate this "axiom" as

Axiom 1. *Computer programs are formal (syntactic).*

This point is so crucial that it is worth explaining in more detail. A digital computer processes information by first encoding it in the symbolism that the computer uses and then manipulating the symbols through a set of precisely stated rules. These rules constitute the program. For example, in Turing's early theory of computers, the symbols were simply 0's and 1's, and the rules of the program said such things as, "Print a 0 on the tape, move one square to the left and erase a 1." The astonishing thing about computers is that any information that can be stated in a language can be encoded in such a system, and any information-processing task that can be solved by explicit rules can be programmed.

Two further points are important. First, symbols and programs are purely abstract notions: they have no essential physical properties to define them and can be implemented in any physical medium whatsoever. The 0's and 1's, qua symbols, have no essential physical properties and a fortiori have no physical, causal properties. I emphasize this point because it is tempting to identify computers with some specific technology – say, silicon chips – and to think that the issues are about the physics of silicon chips or to think that syntax identifies some physical phenomenon that might have as yet unknown causal powers, in the way that actual physical phenomena such as electromagnetic radiation or hydrogen atoms have physical, causal properties. The second point is that symbols are manipulated without reference to any meanings. The symbols of the program can stand for anything the programmer or user wants. In this sense the program has syntax but no semantics.

The next axiom is just a reminder of the obvious fact that thoughts, perceptions, understandings and so forth have a mental content. By virtue of their content they can be about objects and states of affairs in the world. If the content involves language, there will be syntax in addition to semantics, but linguistic understanding requires at least a semantic framework. If, for example, I am thinking about the last presidential election, certain words will go through my mind, but the words are about the election only because I attach specific meanings to these words, in accordance with my knowledge of English. In this respect they are unlike Chinese symbols for me. Let me abbreviate this axiom as

Axiom 2. *Human minds have mental contents (semantics).*

Now let me add the point that the Chinese room demonstrated. Having the symbols by themselves – just having the syntax – is not sufficient for having the semantics. Merely manipulating symbols is not enough to guarantee knowledge of what they mean. I shall abbreviate this as

Axiom 3. *Syntax by itself is neither constitutive of nor sufficient for semantics.*

At one level this principle is true by definition. One might, of course, define the terms syntax and semantics differently. The point is that there is a distinction between formal elements, which have no intrinsic meaning or content, and those phenomena that have intrinsic content. From these premises it follows that

Conclusion 1. *Programs are neither constitutive of nor sufficient for minds.*

And that is just another way of saying that strong AI is false.

It is important to see what is proved and not proved by this argument.

First, I have not tried to prove that "a computer cannot think." Since anything that can be simulated computationally can be described as a computer, and since our brains can at some levels be simulated, it follows trivially that our brains are computers and they can certainly think. But from the fact that a system can be simulated by symbol manipulation and the fact that it is thinking, it does not follow that thinking is equivalent to formal symbol manipulation.

Second, I have not tried to show that only biologically based systems like our brains can think. Right now those are the only systems we know for a fact can think, but we might find other systems in the universe that can produce conscious thoughts, and we might even come to be able to create thinking systems artificially. I regard this issue as up for grabs.

Third, strong AI's thesis is not that, for all we know, computers with the right programs might be thinking, that they might have some as yet undetected psychological properties; rather it is that they must be thinking because that is all there is to thinking.

Fourth, I have tried to refute strong AI so defined. I have tried to demonstrate that the program by itself is not constitutive of thinking because the program is purely a matter of formal symbol manipulation – and we know independently that symbol manipulations by themselves are not sufficient to guarantee the presence of meanings. That is the principle on which the Chinese room argument works.

I emphasize these points here partly because it seems to me the Churchlands [see following article, "Could a Machine Think?"] have not quite understood the issues. They think that strong AI is claiming that computers might turn out to think and that I am denying this possibility on common-sense grounds. But that is not the claim of strong AI, and my argument against it has nothing to do with common sense.

I will have more to say about their objections later. Meanwhile I should point out that, contrary to what the Churchlands suggest, the Chinese room argument also refutes any strong AI claims made for the new parallel technologies that are inspired by and modeled on neural networks. Unlike the traditional von Neumann computer, which proceeds in a step-by-step fashion, these systems have many computational elements that operate in parallel and interact with one another according to rules inspired by neurobiology. Although the results are still modest, these "parallel distributed processing," or "connectionist," models raise useful questions about how complex, parallel network systems like those in brains might actually function in the production of intelligent behavior.

The parallel, "brainlike" character of the processing, however, is irrelevant to the purely computational aspects of the process. Any function that can be computed on a parallel machine can also be computed on a serial machine. Indeed, because parallel machines are still rare, connectionist programs are usually run on traditional serial machines. Parallel processing, then, does not afford a way around the Chinese room argument.

What is more, the connectionist system is subject even on its own terms to a variant of the objection presented by the original Chinese room argument. Imagine that instead of a Chinese room, I have a Chinese gym: a hall containing many monolingual, English-speaking men. These men would carry out the same operations as the nodes and synapses in a connectionist architecture as described by the Churchlands, and the outcome would be the same as having one man manipulate symbols according to a rule book. No one in the gym speaks a word of Chinese, and there is no way for the system as a whole to learn the meanings of any Chinese words. Yet with appropriate adjustments, the system could give the correct answers to Chinese questions.

There are, as I suggested earlier, interesting properties of connectionist nets that enable them to simulate brain processes more accurately than traditional serial architecture does. But the advantages of parallel architecture for weak AI are quite irrelevant to the issues between the Chinese room argument and strong AI.

The Churchlands miss this point when they say that a big enough Chinese gym might have higher-level mental features that emerge from the size and complexity of the system, just as whole brains have mental features that are not had by individual neurons. That is, of course, a possibility, but it has nothing to do with computation. Computationally, serial and parallel systems are equivalent: any computation that can be done in parallel can be done in serial. If the man in the Chinese room is computationally equivalent to both, then if he does not understand Chinese solely by virtue of doing the computations, neither do they. The Churchlands are correct in saying that the original Chinese room argument was designed with traditional AI in mind but wrong in thinking that connectionism is immune to the argument. It applies to any computational system. You can't get semantically loaded thought contents from formal computations alone, whether they are done in serial or in parallel; that is why the Chinese room argument refutes strong AI in any form.

Many people who are impressed by this argument are nonetheless puzzled about the differences between people and computers. If humans are, at least in a trivial sense, computers, and if humans have a semantics, then why couldn't we give semantics to other computers? Why couldn't we program a Vax or a Cray so that it too would have thoughts and feelings? Or why couldn't some new computer technology overcome the gulf between form and content, between syntax and semantics? What, in fact, are the differences between animal brains and computer systems that enable the Chinese room argument to work against computers but not against brains?

The most obvious difference is that the processes that define something as a computer – computational processes – are completely independent of any reference to a specific type of hardware implementation. One could in principle make a computer out of old beer cans strung together with wires and powered by windmills.

But when it comes to brains, although science is largely ignorant of how brains function to produce mental states, one is struck by the extreme specificity of the anatomy and the physiology. Where some understanding exists of how brain processes produce mental phenomena – for example, pain, thirst, vision, smell – it is clear that specific neurobiological processes are involved. Thirst, at least of certain kinds, is caused by certain types of neuron firings in the hypothalamus, which in turn are caused by the action of a specific peptide, angiotensin II. The causation is from the "bottom up" in the sense that lower-level neuronal processes cause higher-level mental phenomena. Indeed, as far as we know, every "mental" event, ranging from feelings of thirst to thoughts of mathematical theorems and memories of childhood, is caused by specific neurons firing in specific neural architectures.

But why should this specificity matter? After all, neuron firings could be simulated on computers that had a completely different physics and chemistry from that of the brain. The answer is that the brain does not merely instantiate a formal pattern or program (it does that, too), but it also causes mental events by virtue of specific neurobiological processes. Brains are specific biological organs, and their specific biochemical properties enable them to cause consciousness and other sorts of mental phenomena. Computer simulations of brain processes provide models of the formal aspects of these processes. But the simulation should not be confused with duplication. The computational model of mental processes is no more real than the computational model of any other natural phenomenon.

One can imagine a computer simulation of the action of peptides in the hypothalamus that is accurate down to the last synapse. But equally one can imagine a computer simulation of the oxidation of hydrocarbons in a car engine or the action of digestive processes in a stomach when it is digesting pizza. And the simulation is no more the real thing in the case of the brain than it is in the case of the car or the stomach. Barring miracles, you could not run your car by doing a computer simulation of the oxidation of gasoline, and you could not digest pizza by running the program that simulates such digestion. It seems obvious that a simulation of cognition will similarly not produce the effects of the neurobiology of cognition.

All mental phenomena, then, are caused by neurophysiological processes in the brain. Hence,

Axiom 4. *Brains cause minds.*

In conjunction with my earlier derivation, I immediately derive, trivially,

Conclusion 2. *Any other system capable of causing minds would have to have causal powers (at least) equivalent to those of brains.*

This is like saying that if an electrical engine is to be able to run a car as fast as a gas engine, it must have (at least) an equivalent power output. This conclusion says nothing about the mechanisms. As a matter of fact, cognition is a biological phenomenon: mental states and processes are caused by brain processes. This does not imply that only a biological system could think, but it does imply that any alternative system, whether made of silicon, beer cans or whatever, would have to have the relevant causal capacities equivalent to those of brains. So now I can derive

Conclusion 3. *Any artifact that produced mental phenomena, any artificial brain, would have to be able to duplicate the specific causal powers of brains, and it could not do that just by running a formal program.*

Furthermore, I can derive an important conclusion about human brains:

Conclusion 4. *The way that human brains actually produce mental phenomena cannot be solely by virtue of running a computer program.*

I first presented the Chinese room parable in the pages of *Behavioral and Brain Sciences* in 1980, where it appeared, as is the practice of the journal, along with peer commentary, in this case, 26 commentaries. Frankly, I think the point it makes is rather obvious, but to my surprise the publication was followed by a further flood of objections that – more surprisingly – continues to the present day. The Chinese room argument clearly touched some sensitive nerve.

The thesis of strong AI is that any system whatsoever – whether it is made of beer cans, silicon chips or toilet paper – not only might have thoughts and feelings but *must* have thoughts and feelings, provided only that it implements the right program, with the right inputs and outputs. Now, that is a profoundly antibiological view, and one would think that people in AI would be glad to abandon it. Many of them, especially the younger generation, agree with me, but I am amazed at the number and vehemence of the defenders. Here are some of the common objections.

a. In the Chinese room you really do understand Chinese, even though you don't know it. It is, after all, possible to understand something without knowing that one understands it.
b. You don't understand Chinese, but there is an (unconscious) subsystem in you that does. It is, after all, possible to have unconscious mental states, and there is no reason why your understanding of Chinese should not be wholly unconscious.
c. You don't understand Chinese, but the whole room does. You are like a single neuron in the brain, and just as such a single neuron by itself cannot understand but only contributes to the understanding of the whole system, you don't understand, but the whole system does.
d. Semantics doesn't exist anyway; there is only syntax. It is a kind of prescientific illusion to suppose that there exist in the brain some mysterious "mental contents," "thought processes" or "semantics." All that exists in the brain is the same sort of syntactic symbol manipulation that goes on in computers. Nothing more.
e. You are not really running the computer program – you only think you are. Once you have a conscious agent going through the steps of the program, it ceases to be a case of implementing a program at all.
f. Computers would have semantics and not just syntax if their inputs and outputs were put in appropriate causal relation to the rest of the world. Imagine that we put the computer into a robot, attached television cameras to the robot's head, installed transducers connecting the television messages to the computer and had the computer output operate the robot's arms and legs. Then the whole system would have a semantics.

g. If the program simulated the operation of the brain of a Chinese speaker, then it would understand Chinese. Suppose that we simulated the brain of a Chinese person at the level of neurons. Then surely such a system would understand Chinese as well as any Chinese person's brain.

And so on.

All of these arguments share a common feature: they are all inadequate because they fail to come to grips with the actual Chinese room argument. That argument rests on the distinction between the formal symbol manipulation that is done by the computer and the mental contents biologically produced by the brain, a distinction I have abbreviated – I hope not misleadingly – as the distinction between syntax and semantics. I will not repeat my answers to all of these objections, but it will help to clarify the issues if I explain the weaknesses of the most widely held objection, argument c – what I call the systems reply. (The brain simulator reply, argument g, is another popular one, but I have already addressed that one in the previous section.)

The systems reply asserts that of course *you* don't understand Chinese but the whole system – you, the room, the rule book, the bushel baskets full of symbols – does. When I first heard this explanation, I asked one of its proponents, "Do you mean the room understands Chinese?" His answer was yes. It is a daring move, but aside from its implausibility, it will not work on purely logical grounds. The point of the original argument was that symbol shuffling by itself does not give any access to the meanings of the symbols. But this is as much true of the whole room as it is of the person inside. One can see this point by extending the thought experiment. Imagine that I memorize the contents of the baskets and the rule book, and I do all the calculations in my head. You can even imagine that I work out in the open. There is nothing in the "system" that is not in me, and since I don't understand Chinese, neither does the system.

The Churchlands in their companion piece produce a variant of the systems reply by imagining an amusing analogy. Suppose that someone said that light could not be electromagnetic because if you shake a bar magnet in a dark room, the system still will not give off visible light. Now, the Churchlands ask, is not the Chinese room argument just like that? Does it not merely say that if you shake Chinese symbols in a semantically dark room, they will not give off the light of Chinese understanding? But just as later investigation showed that light was entirely constituted by electromagnetic radiation, could not later investigation also show that semantics are entirely constituted of syntax? Is this not a question for further scientific investigation?

Arguments from analogy are notoriously weak, because before one can make the argument work, one has to establish that the two cases are truly analogous. And here I think they are not. The account of light in terms of electromagnetic radiation is a causal story right down to the ground. It is a causal account of the physics of electromagnetic radiation. But the analogy with formal symbols fails because formal symbols have no physical, causal powers. The only power that symbols have, qua symbols, is the power to cause the next step in the program when the machine is running. And there is no question of waiting on further research to reveal the physical, causal properties of 0's and 1's. The only relevant properties of 0's and 1's are abstract computational properties, and they are already well known.

The Churchlands complain that I am "begging the question" when I say that uninterpreted formal symbols are not identical to mental contents. Well, I certainly did not spend much time arguing for it, because I take it as a logical truth. As with any logical truth, one can quickly see that it is true, because one gets inconsistencies if one tries to imagine the converse. So let us try it. Suppose that in the Chinese room some undetectable Chinese thinking really is going on. What exactly is supposed to make the manipulation of the syntactic elements into specifically Chinese thought contents? Well, after all, I am assuming that the programmers were Chinese speakers, programming the system to process Chinese information.

Fine. But now imagine that as I am sitting in the Chinese room shuffling the Chinese symbols, I get bored with just shuffling the – to me – meaningless symbols. So, suppose that I decide to interpret the symbols as standing for moves in a chess game. Which semantics is the system giving off now? Is it giving off a Chinese semantics or a chess semantics, or both simultaneously? Suppose there is a third person looking in through the window, and she decides that the symbol manipulations can all be interpreted as stock-market predictions. And so on. There is no limit to the number of semantic interpretations that can be assigned to the symbols because, to repeat, the symbols are purely formal. They have no intrinsic semantics.

Is there any way to rescue the Churchlands' analogy from incoherence? I said above that formal symbols do not have causal properties. But of course the program will always be implemented in some hardware or another, and the hardware will have specific physical, causal powers. And any real computer will give off various phenomena. My computers, for example, give off heat, and they make a humming noise and sometimes crunching sounds. So is there some logically compelling reason why they could not also give off consciousness? No. Scientifically, the idea is out of the question, but it is not something the Chinese room argument is supposed to refute, and it is not something that an adherent of strong AI would wish to defend, because any such giving off would have to derive from the physical features of the implementing medium. But the basic premise of strong AI is that the physical features of the implementing medium are totally irrelevant. What matters are programs, and programs are purely formal.

The Churchlands' analogy between syntax and electromagnetism, then, is confronted with a dilemma; either the syntax is construed purely formally in terms of its abstract mathematical properties, or it is not. If it is, then the analogy breaks down, because syntax so construed has no physical powers and hence no physical, causal powers. If, on the other hand, one is supposed to think in terms of the physics of the implementing medium, then there is indeed an analogy, but it is not one that is relevant to strong AI.

Because the points I have been making are rather obvious – syntax is not the same as semantics, brain processes cause mental phenomena – the question arises, How did we get into this mess? How could anyone have supposed that a computer simulation of a mental process must be the real thing? After all, the whole point of models is that they contain only certain features of the modeled domain and leave out the rest. No one expects to get wet in a pool filled with Ping-Pong-ball models of water molecules. So why would anyone think a computer model of thought processes would actually think?

Part of the answer is that people have inherited a residue of behaviorist psychological theories of the past generation. The Turing test enshrines the temptation to think that if something behaves as if it had certain mental processes, then it must actually have those mental processes. And this is part of the behaviorists' mistaken assumption that in order to be scientific, psychology must confine its study to externally observable behavior. Paradoxically, this residual behaviorism is tied to a residual dualism. Nobody thinks that a computer simulation of digestion would actually digest anything, but where cognition is concerned, people are willing to believe in such a miracle because they fail to recognize that the mind is just as much a biological phenomenon as digestion. The mind, they suppose, is something formal and abstract, not a part of the wet and slimy stuff in our heads. The polemical literature in AI usually contains attacks on something the authors call dualism, but what they fail to see is that they themselves display dualism in a strong form, for unless one accepts the idea that the mind is completely independent of the brain or of any other physically specific system, one could not possibly hope to create minds just by designing programs.

Historically, scientific developments in the West that have treated humans as just a part of the ordinary physical, biological order have often been opposed by various rearguard actions. Copernicus and Galileo were opposed because they denied that the earth was the center of the universe; Darwin was opposed because he claimed that humans had descended from the lower animals. It is best to see strong AI as one of the last gasps of this antiscientific tradition, for it denies that there is anything essentially physical and biological about the human mind. The mind according to strong AI is independent of the brain. It is a computer program and as such has no essential connection to any specific hardware.

Many people who have doubts about the psychological significance of AI think that computers might be able to understand Chinese and think about numbers but cannot do the crucially human things, namely – and then follows their favorite human specialty – falling in love, having a sense of humor, feeling the angst of postindustrial society under late capitalism, or whatever. But workers in AI complain – correctly – that this is a case of moving the goalposts. As soon as an AI simulation succeeds, it ceases to be of psychological importance. In this debate both sides fail to see the distinction between simulation and duplication. As far as simulation is concerned, there is no difficulty in programming my computer so that it prints out, "I love you, Suzy"; "Ha ha"; or "I am suffering the angst of postindustrial society under late capitalism." The important point is that simulation is not the same as duplication, and that fact holds as much import for thinking about arithmetic as it does for feeling angst. The point is not that the computer gets only to the 40-yard line and not all the way to the goal line. The computer doesn't even get started. It is not playing that game.

Could a Machine Think?
Paul M. Churchland and Patricia S. Churchland

Patricia and Paul Churchland are Professors of Philosophy at the University of California, La Jolla. Patricia Churchland also received the prestigious MacArthur 'genius' grant and is a fellow at the Salk Institute. Both have defended eliminative materialism in the philosophy of mind and have argued that connectionism, or parallel processing, is the correct approach when creating intelligence. In the following article they reply to John Searle (see previous selection), while explaining some of the virtues of connectionism.

Artificial-intelligence research is undergoing a revolution. To explain how and why, and to put John R. Searle's argument in perspective, we first need a flashback.

By the early 1950s the old, vague question, Could a machine think? had been replaced by the more approachable question, Could a machine that manipulated physical symbols according to structure-sensitive rules think? This question was an improvement because formal logic and computational theory had seen major developments in the preceding half-century. Theorists had come to appreciate the enormous power of abstract systems of symbols that undergo rule-governed transformations. If those systems could just be automated, then their abstract computational power, it seemed, would be displayed in a real physical system. This insight spawned a well-defined research program with deep theoretical underpinnings.

Could a machine think? There were many reasons for saying yes. One of the earliest and deepest reasons lay in two important results in computational theory. The first was Church's thesis, which states that every effectively computable function is recursively computable. Effectively computable means that there is a "rote" procedure for determining, in finite time, the output of the function for a given input. Recursively computable means more specifically that there is a finite set of operations that can be applied to a given input, and then applied again and again to the successive results of such applications, to yield the function's output in finite time. The notion of a rote procedure is nonformal and intuitive; thus, Church's thesis does not admit of a formal proof. But it does go to the heart of what it is to compute, and many lines of evidence converge in supporting it.

The second important result was Alan M. Turing's demonstration that any recursively computable function can be computed in finite time by a maximally simple sort of symbol-manipulating machine that has come to be called a universal Turing machine. This machine is guided by a set of recursively applicable rules that are sensitive to the identity, order and arrangement of the elementary symbols it encounters as input.

These two results entail something remarkable, namely that a standard digital computer, given only the right program, a large enough memory and sufficient time, can compute *any* rule-governed input–output function. That is, it can display any systematic pattern of responses to the environment whatsoever.

More specifically, these results imply that a suitably programmed symbol-manipulating machine (hereafter, SM machine) should be able to pass the Turing test for conscious intelligence. The Turing test is a purely behavioral test for conscious intelligence, but it is a very demanding test even so. (Whether it is a fair test will be addressed below, where we shall also encounter a second and quite different "test" for conscious intelligence.) In the original version of the Turing test, the inputs to the SM machine are conversational questions and remarks typed into a console by you or me, and the outputs are type written responses from the SM machine. The machine passes this test for conscious intelligence if its responses cannot be discriminated from the type-written responses of a real, intelligent person. Of course, at present no one knows the function that would produce the output behavior of a conscious person. But the Church and Turing results assure us that, whatever that (presumably effective) function might be, a suitable SM machine could compute it.

This is a significant conclusion, especially since Turing's portrayal of a purely teletyped interaction is an unnecessary restriction. The same conclusion follows even if the SM machine interacts with the world in more complex ways: by direct vision, real speech and so forth. After all, a more complex recursive function is still Turing-computable. The only remaining problem is to identify the undoubtedly complex function that governs the human pattern of response to the environment and then write the program (the set of recursively applicable rules) by which the SM machine will compute it. These goals form the fundamental research program of classical AI.

Initial results were positive. SM machines with clever programs performed a variety of ostensibly cognitive activities. They responded to complex instructions, solved complex arithmetic, algebraic and tactical problems, played checkers and chess, proved theorems and engaged in simple dialogue. Performance continued to improve with the appearance of larger memories and faster machines and with the use of longer and more cunning programs. Classical, or "program-writing," AI was a vigorous and successful research effort from almost every perspective. The occasional denial that an SM machine might eventually think appeared uninformed and ill motivated. The case for a positive answer to our title question was overwhelming.

There were a few puzzles, of course. For one thing, SM machines were admittedly not very brainlike. Even here, however, the classical approach had a convincing answer. First, the physical material of any SM machine has nothing essential to do with what function it computes. That is fixed by its program. Second, the engineering details of any machine's functional architecture are also irrelevant, since different architectures running quite different programs can still be computing the same input–output function.

Accordingly, AI sought to find the input–output *function* characteristic of intelligence and the most efficient of the many possible programs for computing it. The idiosyncratic way in which the brain computes the function just doesn't matter, it was said. This completes the rationale for classical AI and for a positive answer to our title question.

Could a machine think? There were also some arguments for saying no. Through the 1960s interesting negative arguments were relatively rare. The objection was occasionally made that thinking was a nonphysical process in an immaterial soul. But such dualistic resistance was neither evolutionarily nor explanatorily plausible. It had a negligible impact on AI research.

A quite different line of objection was more successful in gaining the AI community's attention. In 1972 Hubert L. Dreyfus published a book that was highly critical of the parade-case simulations of cognitive activity. He argued for their inadequacy as simulations of genuine cognition, and he pointed to a pattern of failure in these attempts. What they were missing, he suggested, was the vast store of inarticulate background knowledge every person possesses and the commonsense capacity for drawing on relevant aspects of that knowledge as changing circumstance demands. Dreyfus did not deny the possibility that an artificial physical system of some kind might think, but he was highly critical of the idea that this could be achieved solely by symbol manipulation at the hands of recursively applicable rules.

Dreyfus's complaints were broadly perceived within the AI community, and within the discipline of philosophy as well, as shortsighted and unsympathetic, as harping on the inevitable simplifications of a research effort still in its youth. These deficits might be real, but surely they were temporary. Bigger machines and better programs should repair them in due course. Time, it was felt, was on AI's side. Here again the impact on research was negligible.

Time was on Dreyfus's side as well: the rate of cognitive return on increasing speed and memory began to slacken in the late 1970s and early 1980s. The simulation of object recognition in the visual system, for example, proved computationally intensive to an unexpected degree. Realistic results required longer and longer periods of computer time, periods far in excess of what a real visual system requires. This relative slowness of the simulations was darkly curious; signal propagation in a computer is roughly a million times faster than in the brain, and the clock frequency of a computer's central processor is greater than any frequency found in the brain by a similarly dramatic margin. And yet, on realistic problems, the tortoise easily outran the hare.

Furthermore, realistic performance required that the computer program have access to an extremely large knowledge base. Constructing the relevant knowledge base was problem enough, and it was compounded by the problem of how to access just the contextually relevant parts of that knowledge base in real time. As the knowledge base got bigger and better, the access problem got worse. Exhaustive search took too much time, and heuristics for relevance did poorly. Worries of the sort Dreyfus had raised finally began to take hold here and there even among AI researchers.

At about this time (1980) John Searle authored a new and quite different criticism aimed at the most basic assumption of the classical research program: the idea that the appropriate manipulation of structured symbols by the recursive application of structure-sensitive rules could constitute conscious intelligence.

Searle's argument is based on a thought experiment that displays two crucial features. First, he describes a SM machine that realizes, we are to suppose, an input–output function adequate to sustain a successful Turing test conversation conducted entirely in Chinese. Second, the internal structure of the machine is such that, however it behaves, an observer remains certain that neither the machine nor any part of it understands Chinese. All it contains is a monolingual English speaker following a written set of instructions for manipulating the Chinese symbols that arrive and leave through a mail slot. In short, the system is supposed to pass the Turing test, while the system itself lacks any genuine understanding of Chinese or real Chinese semantic content [see preceding article, "Is the Brain's Mind a Computer Program?" by John R. Searle].

The general lesson drawn is that any system that merely manipulates physical symbols in accordance with structure-sensitive rules will be at best a hollow mock-up of real conscious intelligence, because it is impossible to generate "real semantics" merely by cranking away on "empty syntax." Here, we should point out, Searle is imposing a nonbehavioral test for consciousness: the elements of conscious intelligence must possess real semantic content.

One is tempted to complain that Searle's thought experiment is unfair because his Rube Goldberg system will compute with absurd slowness. Searle insists, however, that speed is strictly irrelevant here. A slow thinker should still be a real thinker. Everything essential to the duplication of thought, as per classical AI, is said to be present in the Chinese room.

Searle's paper provoked a lively reaction from AI researchers, psychologists and philosophers alike. On the whole, however, he was met with an even more hostile reception than Dreyfus had experienced. In his companion piece in this volume, Searle forthrightly lists a number of these critical responses. We think many of them are reasonable, especially those that "bite the bullet" by insisting that, although it is appallingly slow, the overall system of the room-plus-contents does understand Chinese.

We think those are good responses, but not because we think that the room understands Chinese. We agree with Searle that it does not. Rather they are good responses because they reflect a refusal to accept the crucial third axiom of

Searle's argument: "*Syntax by itself is neither constitutive of nor sufficient for semantics.*" Perhaps this axiom is true, but Searle cannot rightly pretend to know that it is. Moreover, to assume its truth is tantamount to begging the question against the research program of classical AI, for that program is predicated on the very interesting assumption that if one can just set in motion an appropriately structured internal dance of syntactic elements, appropriately connected to inputs and outputs, it can produce the same cognitive states and achievements found in human beings.

The question-begging character of Searle's axiom 3 becomes clear when it is compared directly with his conclusion 1: "*Programs are neither constitutive of nor sufficient for minds.*" Plainly, his third axiom is already carrying 90 percent of the weight of this almost identical conclusion. That is why Searle's thought experiment is devoted to shoring up axiom 3 specifically. That is the point of the Chinese room.

Although the story of the Chinese room makes axiom 3 tempting to the unwary, we do not think it succeeds in establishing axiom 3, and we offer a parallel argument below in illustration of its failure. A single transparently fallacious instance of a disputed argument often provides far more insight than a book full of logic chopping.

Searle's style of skepticism has ample precedent in the history of science. The 18th-century Irish bishop George Berkeley found it unintelligible that compression waves in the air, by themselves, could constitute or be sufficient for objective sound. The English poet-artist William Blake and the German poet-naturalist Johann W. von Goethe found it inconceivable that small particles by themselves could constitute or be sufficient for the objective phenomenon of light. Even in this century, there have been people who found it beyond imagining that inanimate matter by itself, and however organized, could ever constitute or be sufficient for life. Plainly, what people can or cannot imagine often has nothing to do with what is or is not the case, even where the people involved are highly intelligent.

To see how this lesson applies to Searle's case, consider a deliberately manufactured parallel to his argument and its supporting thought experiment.

Axiom 1. *Electricity and magnetism are forces.*

Axiom 2. *The essential property of light is luminance.*

Axiom 3. *Forces by themselves are neither constitutive of nor sufficient for luminance.*

Conclusion 1. *Electricity and magnetism are neither constitutive of nor sufficient for light.*

Imagine this argument raised shortly after James Clerk Maxwell's 1864 suggestion that light and electromagnetic waves are identical but before the world's full appreciation of the systematic parallels between the properties of light and the properties of electromagnetic waves. This argument could have served as a compelling objection to Maxwell's imaginative hypothesis, especially if it were accompanied by the following commentary in support of axiom 3.

> Consider a dark room containing a man holding a bar magnet or charged object. If the man pumps the magnet up and down, then, according to Maxwell's theory of artificial luminance (AL), it will initiate a spreading circle of electromagnetic waves and will thus be luminous. But as all of us who have toyed with magnets or charged balls well know, their forces (or any other forces for that matter), even when set in motion, produce no luminance at all. It is inconceivable that you might constitute real luminance just by moving forces around.

How should Maxwell respond to this challenge? He might begin by insisting that the "luminous room" experiment is a misleading display of the phenomenon of luminance because the frequency of oscillation of the magnet is absurdly low, too low by a factor of 10^{15}. This might well elicit the impatient response that frequency has nothing to do with it, that the room with the bobbing magnet already contains everything essential to light, according to Maxwell's own theory.

In response Maxwell might bite the bullet and claim, quite correctly, that the room really is bathed in luminance, albeit a grade or quality too feeble to appreciate. (Given the low frequency with which the man can oscillate the magnet, the wavelength of the electromagnetic waves produced is far too long and their intensity is much too weak for human retinas to respond to them.) But in the climate of understanding here contemplated – the 1860s – this tactic is likely to elicit laughter and hoots of derision. "Luminous room, my foot, Mr Maxwell. It's pitch-black in there!"

Alas, poor Maxwell has no easy route out of this predicament. All he can do is insist on the following three points. First, axiom 3 of the above argument is false. Indeed, it begs the question despite its intuitive plausibility. Second, the luminous room experiment demonstrates nothing of interest one way or the other about the nature of light. And third, what is needed to settle the problem of light and the possibility of artificial luminance is an ongoing research program to determine whether under the appropriate conditions the behavior of electromagnetic waves does indeed mirror perfectly the behavior of light.

This is also the response that classical AI should give to Searle's argument. Even though Searle's Chinese room may appear to be "semantically dark," he is in no position to insist, on the strength of this appearance, that rule-governed symbol manipulation can never constitute semantic phenomena, especially when people have only an uninformed commonsense understanding of the semantic and cognitive phenomena that need to be explained. Rather than exploit one's understanding of these things, Searle's argument freely exploits one's ignorance of them.

With these criticisms of Searle's argument in place, we return to the question of whether the research program of classical AI has a realistic chance of solving the problem of conscious intelligence and of producing a machine that thinks. We believe that the prospects are poor, but we rest this opinion on reasons very different from Searle's. Our reasons derive from the specific performance failures of the classical research program in AI and from a variety of lessons learned from the biological brain and a new class of computational models inspired by its structure. We have already indicated some of the failures of classical AI regarding tasks that the brain performs swiftly and efficiently. The emerging consensus on these failures is that the functional architecture of classical SM machines is simply the wrong architecture for the very demanding jobs required.

What we need to know is this: How does the brain achieve cognition? Reverse engineering is a common practice in industry. When a new piece of technology comes on the market, competitors find out how it works by taking it apart and divining its structural rationale. In the case of the brain, this strategy presents an unusually stiff challenge, for the brain is the most complicated and sophisticated thing on the planet. Even so, the neurosciences have revealed much about the brain on a wide variety of structural levels. Three anatomic points will provide a basic contrast with the architecture of conventional electronic computers.

First, nervous systems are parallel machines, in the sense that signals are processed in millions of different pathways simultaneously. The retina, for example, presents its complex input to the brain not in chunks of eight, 16 or 32 elements, as in a desktop computer, but rather in the form of almost a million distinct signal elements arriving simultaneously at the target of the optic nerve (the lateral geniculate nucleus), there to be processed collectively, simultaneously and in one fell swoop. Second, the brain's basic processing unit, the neuron, is comparatively simple. Furthermore, its response to incoming signals is analog, not digital, inasmuch as its output spiking frequency varies continuously with its input signals. Third, in the brain, axons projecting from one neuronal population to another are often matched by axons returning from their target population. These descending or recurrent projections allow the brain to modulate the character of its sensory processing. More important still, their existence makes the brain a genuine dynamical system whose continuing behavior is both highly complex and to some degree independent of its peripheral stimuli.

Highly simplified model networks have been useful in suggesting how real neural networks might work and in revealing the computational properties of parallel architectures. For example, consider a three-layer model consisting of neuronlike units fully connected by axonlike connections to the units at the next layer. An input stimulus produces some activation level in a given input unit, which conveys a signal of proportional strength along its "axon" to its many "synaptic" connections to the hidden units. The global effect is that a pattern of activations across the set of input units produces a distinct pattern of activations across the set of hidden units.

The same story applies to the output units. As before, an activation pattern across the hidden units produces a distinct activation pattern across the output units. All told, this network is a device for transforming any one of a great many possible input vectors (activation patterns) into a uniquely corresponding output vector. It is a device for computing a specific function. Exactly which function it computes is fixed by the global configuration of its synaptic weights.

There are various procedures for adjusting the weights so as to yield a network that computes almost any function – that is, any vector-to-vector transformation – that one might desire. In fact, one can even impose on it a function one is unable to specify, so long as one can supply a set of examples of the desired input–output pairs. This process, called "training up the network," proceeds by successive adjustment of the network's weights until it performs the input–output transformations desired.

Although this model network vastly oversimplifies the structure of the brain, it does illustrate several important ideas. First, a parallel architecture provides a dramatic speed advantage over a conventional computer, for the many synapses at each level perform many small computations simultaneously instead of in laborious sequence. This advantage gets larger as the number of neurons increases at each layer. Strikingly, the speed of processing is entirely independent of both the number of units involved in each layer and the complexity of the function they are computing. Each layer could have four units or a hundred million; its configuration of synaptic weights could be computing simple one-digit sums or second-order differential equations. It would make no difference. The computation time would be exactly the same.

Second, massive parallelism means that the system is fault-tolerant and functionally persistent; the loss of a few connections, even quite a few, has a negligible effect on the character of the overall transformation performed by the surviving network.

Third, a parallel system stores large amounts of information in a distributed fashion, any part of which can be accessed in milliseconds. That information is stored in the specific configuration of synaptic connection strengths, as shaped by past learning. Relevant information is "released" as the input vector passes through – and is transformed by – that configuration of connections.

Parallel processing is not ideal for all types of computation. On tasks that require only a small input vector, but many millions of swiftly iterated recursive computations, the brain performs very badly, whereas classical SM machines excel. This class of computations is very large and important, so classical machines will always be useful, indeed, vital. There is, however, an equally large class of computations for which the brain's architecture is the superior technology. These are the computations that typically confront living creatures: recognizing a predator's outline in a noisy environment; recalling instantly how to avoid its gaze, flee its approach or fend off its attack; distinguishing food from nonfood and mates from nonmates; navigating through a complex and ever-changing physical/social environment; and so on.

Finally, it is important to note that the parallel system described is not manipulating symbols according to structure-sensitive rules. Rather symbol manipulation appears to be just one of many cognitive skills that a network may or may not learn to display. Rule-governed symbol manipulation is not its basic mode of operation. Searle's argument is directed against rule-governed SM machines; vector transformers of the kind we describe are therefore not threatened by his Chinese room argument even if it were sound, which we have found independent reason to doubt.

Searle is aware of parallel processors but thinks they too will be devoid of real semantic content. To illustrate their inevitable failure, he outlines a second thought experiment, the Chinese gym, which has a gymnasium full of people organized into a parallel network. From there his argument proceeds as in the Chinese room.

We find this second story far less responsive or compelling than his first. For one, it is irrelevant that no unit in his system understands Chinese, since the same is true of nervous systems: no neuron in my brain understands English, although my whole brain does. For another, Searle neglects to mention that his simulation (using one person per neuron, plus a fleet-footed child for each synaptic connection) will require at least 10^{14} people, since the human brain has 10^{11} neurons, each of which averages over 10^3 connections. His system will require the entire human populations of over 10,000 earths. One gymnasium will not begin to hold a fair simulation.

On the other hand, if such a system were to be assembled on a suitably cosmic scale, with all its pathways faithfully modeled on the human case, we might then have a large, slow, oddly made but still functional brain on our hands. In that case the default assumption is surely that, given proper inputs, it would think, not that it couldn't. There is no guarantee that its activity would constitute real thought, because the vector-processing theory sketched above may not be the correct theory of how brains work. But neither is there any a priori guarantee that it could not be thinking. Searle is once more mistaking the limits on his (or the reader's) current imagination for the limits on objective reality.

The brain is a kind of computer, although most of its properties remain to be discovered. Characterizing the brain as a kind of computer is neither trivial nor frivolous. The brain does compute functions, functions of great complexity, but not in the classical AI fashion. When brains are said to be computers, it should not be implied that they are serial, digital computers, that they are programmed, that they exhibit the distinction between hardware and software or that they must be symbol manipulators or rule followers. Brains are computers in a radically different style.

How the brain manages meaning is still unknown, but it is clear that the problem reaches beyond language use and beyond humans. A small mound of fresh dirt signifies to a person, and also to coyotes, that a gopher is around; an echo with a certain spectral character signifies to a bat the presence of a moth. To develop a theory of meaning, more must be known about how neurons code and transform sensory signals, about the neural basis of memory, learning and emotion and about the interaction of these capacities and the motor system. A neurally grounded theory of meaning may require revision of the very intuitions that now seem so secure and that are so freely exploited in Searle's arguments. Such revisions are common in the history of science.

Could science construct an artificial intelligence by exploiting what is known about the nervous system? We see no principled reason why not. Searle appears to agree, although he qualifies his claim by saying that "any other system capable of causing minds would have to have causal powers (at least) equivalent to those of brains." We close by addressing this claim. We presume that Searle is not claiming that a successful artificial mind must have *all* the causal powers of the brain, such as the power to smell bad when rotting, to harbor slow viruses such as kuru, to stain yellow with horseradish peroxidase and so forth. Requiring perfect parity would be like requiring that an artificial flying device lay eggs.

Presumably he means only to require of an artificial mind all of the causal powers relevant, as he says, to conscious intelligence. But which exactly are they? We are back to quarreling about what is and is not relevant. This is an entirely reasonable place for a disagreement, but it is an empirical matter, to be tried and tested. Because so little is known about what goes into the process of cognition and semantics, it is premature to be very confident about what features are essential. Searle hints at various points that every level, including the biochemical, must be represented in any machine that is a candidate for artificial intelligence. This claim is almost surely too strong. An artificial brain might use something other than biochemicals to achieve the same ends.

This possibility is illustrated by Carver A. Mead's research at the California Institute of Technology. Mead and his colleagues have used analog VLSI techniques to build an artificial retina and an artificial cochlea. (In animals the retina and cochlea are not mere transducers: both systems embody a complex processing network.) These are not mere simulations in a mini-computer of the kind that Searle derides; they are real information-processing units responding in real time to real light, in the case of the artificial retina, and to real sound, in the case of the artificial cochlea. Their circuitry is based on the known anatomy and physiology of the cat retina and the barn owl cochlea, and their output is dramatically similar to the known output of the organs at issue.

These chips do not use any neurochemicals, so neurochemicals are clearly not necessary to achieve the evident results. Of course, the artificial retina cannot be said to see anything, because its output does not have an artificial thalamus or cortex to go to. Whether Mead's program could be sustained to build an entire artificial brain remains to be seen, but there is no evidence now that the absence of biochemicals renders it quixotic.

We, and Searle, reject the Turing test as a sufficient condition for conscious intelligence. At one level our reasons for doing so are similar: we agree that it is also very important how the input–output function is achieved; it is important that the right sorts of things be going on inside the artificial machine. At another level, our reasons are quite different. Searle bases his position on commonsense intuitions about the presence or absence of semantic content. We base ours on the specific behavioral failures of the classical SM machines, and on the specific virtues of machines with a more brainlike architecture. These contrasts show that certain computational strategies have vast and decisive advantages over others where typical cognitive tasks are concerned, advantages that are empirically inescapable. Clearly, the brain is making systematic use of these computational advantages. But it need not be the only physical system capable of doing so. Artificial intelligence, in a nonbiological but massively parallel machine, remains a compelling and discernible prospect.

7

Freedom and Responsibility

Introduction

Several years ago a jury in Arizona acquitted an accused rapist on account of the fact that the victim had begged him to use a condom before he raped her, which he agreed to use. The jury believed that she had submitted freely to the man because she wanted him to use a condom and he used it. So, they concluded, the man's action was really not a case of rape. This is a particularly dramatic case of how their view about the nature of freedom – a metaphysical view – had definite practical consequences. The jurors believed that the victim's wanting to do something, in this case her wanting to be raped with a condom given her alternatives, was sufficient to show that she was not being coerced and that she acted freely.

As we will see in this chapter, the jury was deeply confused and mistaken about the nature of freedom, and so their legal decision was based on an error. For this reason it is extremely important to be clear about the nature of freedom, one of the central issues in metaphysics.

Voluntary Actions and Free Actions

Typically, my actions are things I want or choose to do. If I go running, I want to go running, if I go and play the violin, I choose to play the violin, and so on. Of course, this does not mean that I am always happy about what I do. I might go and run somewhat grudgingly because I also have a strong desire to sit on the couch and listen to music, but in the end my desire for the benefits of running trump my lazy desires, and the simple fact is that I want to go running, no matter how much I hate it.

Actions that we do and want or choose to do are voluntary actions. Of course, sometimes I do things I do not want to do, and these are involuntary actions. If someone pushes me out the door, my leaving the room is involuntary. If I try to leave the room but all the doors and windows are locked from the outside, then my stay in the room is involuntary. Involuntary actions are very much like things that just happen to me: feeling pain, getting sick, growing old, and, eventually, dying. Nevertheless, it is useful to distinguish involuntary actions, which still involve some doing on my part, and things that simply happen to me. After all, there is a difference between being transported out of a room while asleep and being forcibly removed from a room while fully conscious. The latter is an involuntary action, while the former is also involuntary, but it is not an action.

The fact that we have a clear contrast between voluntary and involuntary actions might suggest to us that the contrast between voluntary and involuntary actions just is the contrast between free and unfree actions. We might find some support for this in the fact that it seems quite clear that all free actions are voluntary actions. You act voluntarily just in case you do what you want to do, and surely if your action is free, you are doing what you want to do. But this does not mean that all voluntary actions are free actions. It is possible that all free actions are voluntary while not all voluntary actions are free. Are all voluntary actions free?

Consider the following case. You are driving a very nice car, your pride and joy, but you are held up at gun-point by a thief who demands your car or your life. You quickly consider the alternatives and give him your car. You want to give him your car because you prefer that over your death, so your action is voluntary. Nevertheless, you are coerced to hand over your car, and it would be a misuse of words to say that you did this freely. After all, this is a robbery and no court would acquit the thief on account of the fact that you gave up your car voluntarily.

However, notice the similarities between the robbery case and the Arizona rape case. Both victims prefer what happened to them to the given alternatives: you prefer to be robbed of your car to being shot to death and the rape victim preferred to be raped with a condom than without one. Thus both act voluntarily: given the alternatives, you want to hand over your car and the rape victim wanted to be raped with a condom. Nevertheless, both were coerced and not acting freely.

The need to distinguish between voluntary actions and free actions was noticed in the seventeenth century by the English philosopher John Locke (1632–1704). Locke writes about a man who is carried while fast asleep into a room where he is locked in so that he cannot leave. Fortunately, when he awakes, he finds that he is in the company of a good friend with whom he wants to spend some time and talk. So he wants to stay in the room, which means that he is voluntarily staying in the room, but his action of staying in the room is not free. He is locked up in the room and cannot leave if he wants to leave. Locke rightly concludes from this example that there is a difference between a voluntary and a free action.

This case, as well as the robbery and rape examples, show that a free action will involve something more than a voluntary action, and finding what this something else is – determining what, if anything, is the special feature that turns a voluntary action into a free action – is one of the difficult tasks of metaphysics. However, we already have a clear result. Although given her alternatives the woman wanted to be raped with a condom, it does not follow that she freely submitted to the rapist. As Locke noted over 200 years ago, there is a difference between free and voluntary actions.

Freedom and Causation

What else, then, is involved in a free action? This question is difficult to answer, in part because it requires us to come to terms with the tension that seems to exist between freedom and causality.

On the one hand, it seems very clear to us that sometimes we act freely. For instance, suppose you are deliberating about whether or not to stay in school. Both alternatives seem available to you: although your performance in school is not stellar, you are not forced to leave, and you have enough skills and contacts to find good work when not in school. So you carefully weigh the pros and cons of your available alternatives, decide on a course of action, and do it. What you do clearly seems to be up to you, your deliberations and decision made a difference to how you acted, and you were not forced to act in one way or another. If you decided to leave school, it was equally in your power to stay in school. No matter how you decided to act, you could have acted on your decision.

On the other hand, this self-image of us as free beings seems to conflict with the scientific image of reality, according to which every event is causally determined. Why did the *Titanic* sink? We believe that this accident was causally determined by a complex set of events and conditions that included most prominently the *Titanic*'s running into an iceberg. Given that all these events and conditions occurred, the *Titanic* had to sink; that is, it could not have failed to sink. Why did the *Challenger* explode? Again, we look for the causes that determined that the *Challenger* exploded, and we now know that a faulty rubber ring and frigid weather together played an important role in causing the explosion.

In the behavioral and social sciences we extend this search for causes to human beings. Why does a person get drunk? Because he drank alcohol, which enters the body and affects the normal functioning of the brain. Why does a person drink alcohol? Again, we look for the causes that determined a person to drink, perhaps a sad event, a celebration following a happy event, peer pressure, force of habit, or a gene that causes people to have strong desires for alcohol, to name a few of the causal factors that might enter the picture.

So on the one hand we have a self-image according to which some of our actions are free, while on the other hand we have a scientific conception of the world according to which all events, including human actions, are causally determined. If both of these conceptions true, then it must be possible for an action to be free as well as causally determined. Can an action be both free and causally determined? We need to think about this question as we consider what else a free action might be besides being a voluntary action.

Incompatibilism

Many philosophers believe that an action cannot be both free and causally determined because they maintain that freedom, properly understood, consists of being able to do other than what one in fact did. That is, a free action is not just an action that is voluntary, but the agent could have done otherwise in exactly the same circumstances.

What the "could have done otherwise" clause means is that given all the events that occur prior to a free action, the agent nevertheless could have refrained from doing what he or she in fact did. Consider the act of picking up a book and reading it. Prior to this act, many things happened. Some of these events are part of the reader's history: the reader was born, raised, and educated in a certain way and in a certain culture. Other events occurred immediately prior to reading the book: perhaps the reader saw the book, considered various alternatives, weighed the consequences, and so on. Incompatibilists believe that this act of picking up a book and reading it is free only if, given all of these prior events, she still could have done something else and refrained from picking up the book and reading it. That is, just as it is possible that all those prior events occur and the agent picks up a book and reads it, it is possible that all those prior events occur and the agent does not pick up the book and read it.

Clearly, this conception of freedom is not compatible with causal determinism. If an event is causally determined, then it must occur given all the causes of that event; that is, it is impossible that all those prior causal events occur and the effect does not occur. So, if an action is a causally determined event, then given everything that happened prior to the action, the agent could *not* have done otherwise. But if an action is free only if the agent could have done otherwise in those same circumstances, it is a contradiction to say that an action is both free and causally determined. On this conception of freedom, a free and causally determined action is an action that is both causally determined and not causally determined, a manifest contradiction.

If freedom and causal determinism are incompatible, then it seems that we are left with two options. We can either affirm that all events are causally determined and deny that there are free actions or we can affirm that some actions are free and deny that all events are causally determined. The first option is called "hard determinism" and the second option is called "indeterminism" or "libertarianism."

Hard determinists deny that given all the events that occurred prior to an action, the agent could have done otherwise. They believe that there is no evidence that this is a possibility and significant evidence that all events, including everything we do, are causally determined. Just as there are causal laws about what our natural hair or eye color must be given the genes we have, there are causal laws about all human behavior, including what we take to be free actions. The aim of the behavioral sciences, including psychology and neuroscience, is to discover the causal factors that determine our behavior, and hard determinists believe that the behavioral sciences have made and continue to make sufficient progress to warrant the view that everything human beings do is causally determined.

While we might have thought that the alcoholic began to drink regularly on account of a free decision, as a matter of fact, evidence suggests that at least for some people the taste of alcohol together with the relevant genes determine that they seek to satisfy their powerful cravings for alcohol. Similarly, you may think that your decision to get another bar of chocolate was a free one when in fact, if current research is accurate, you could be addicted to it. Chocolate appears to contains a compound (anadamide) that induces euphoria and some chemicals that prolong this effect in the brain, and we can develop an overpowering need for this compound.

Similarly, you might think that you remembered a word, say on a vocabulary test, because you tried hard to remember it, when in fact it seems that before your conscious and deliberate effort the brain was already at work retrieving the word. This suggests that we are already determined to do a certain something before we make the effort to do it, as does the following case. Subjects who are asked to choose between two different decks of cards have skin responses to the two decks that indicate that they favor one deck over the other before they consciously decide to choose a deck. In fact, evidence suggests that our conscious deliberations have little to do with what we actually do. People in a shopping mall who were asked to examine and rank four identical nylon pantyhose typically favored the rightmost pantyhose. These subjects thought that they chose the rightmost pantyhose on the grounds that these looked and felt better than the others, but in fact all the pantyhose looked and felt alike. In fact, their choice was simply based on relative position and a bias for objects on the right.

Hard determinists argue that the behavioral sciences continue to provide us with evidence that all of human behavior is causally determined by the confluence of our internal biological nature and the external forces in the human environment. Just as a match has to light given that it is struck in appropriate conditions, given the current state of our bodies and our social and natural environments, we cannot do other than what we will do next. In other words, according to hard determinism, what we do next is not free, but causally determined.

Indeterminists are not moved by the hard determinists' reasons in affirming that some human actions are free and that consequently not all events are causally determined. For many indeterminists, if that means we have to deny a cherished principle of science, so much the worse for science. Many indeterminists believe that some things escape the domain of science, and human actions are such things.

Others are not hostile to science and in fact find support for their position not only in ordinary experience, where it seems that sometimes we are free and could have done otherwise, but also in science itself. They argue that the claim that every event is causally determined is part of an incomplete and outmoded conception of the universe due to the English physicist Isaac Newton.

In Newtonian physics, every event is indeed causally determined, and consequently the present, including human action, is fully determined by what happened in the past, but in quantum physics this is not so.

Consider a chunk of a radioactive material. Newtonian physics tells us that, given enough knowledge, we can determine when a specific atom in the chunk, call it Kirstin, leaves the chunk. But quantum physics denies that we can have such knowledge. While we know the half-life of the substance, we do not know when individual atoms will leave the chunk. In particular, we do not know when Kirstin leaves the chunk. We can know how many atoms will leave the chunk over a period of time, but we cannot know which atoms leave over that time period. While there is regularity in the number of atoms that leave over a period of time, individual atoms leave at random.

Since the universe at its foundations is not determined, according to the indeterminist, there is no problem in supposing that human beings, who are made up of atomic particles, are not determined. Just as the atom could have left the chunk at a different time than it in fact did, even though all the previous conditions are exactly the same, sometimes we could have done otherwise in exactly the same circumstances. Perhaps the best evidence for this is that sometimes it seems that we have a choice and that we can do exactly the opposite of what is expected of us just to make the point that we in fact can do otherwise.

Incompatibilism and Moral Responsibility

Hard determinism and libertarianism have a problem with making sense of moral responsibility, which is an important feature of morality. We praise and blame people when they are morally responsible for their actions and we refrain from making such moral judgments when it comes to people and other animals that are not morally responsible for what they do. For example, working at a local soup kitchen or shelter for the homeless is morally praiseworthy in someone who decides to volunteer her time in this way, but the utensils and machines that are used in the kitchen or shelter are not praised. The reason is simple: people are morally responsible for their actions, while machines and utensils cannot be morally responsible.

But moral responsibility requires freedom. Someone is morally responsible for an action only if the action is free. A person who is coerced to work in the homeless shelter is not worthy of moral praise. Similarly, a machine that works in the shelter – for instance the dishwasher in the kitchen – cannot be morally responsible because it is not free. So a position that cannot make sense of freedom cannot make sense of moral responsibility.

Clearly, hard determinism has no room for moral responsibility. Hard determinists simply deny that any actions are free, and consequently they have to deny that there is such a thing as moral responsibility. Some hard determinists are willing to live with this conclusion and even see morality as an outmoded and unscientific human institution. Morally blaming and praising people is just a way of manipulating people to behave in certain ways, and there are much more efficient ways of causing people to behave in desirable ways. Others believe that we can make sense of moral responsibility without freedom because the practice of morally praising and blaming people can be justified on the grounds that it in fact it is a very efficient means for controlling people's behavior.

In either case, we are left without real moral responsibility, namely responsibility based on freedom. The moral responsibility hard determinists talk about is only a ruse: we act as if people are morally responsible and assign moral blame and praise because this is a way to manipulate people's behavior. Moreover, there is something very troubling and immoral about such a stance toward other people. This is the stance of someone who manipulates people, and not someone who treats others with dignity and respect.

Most people, including hard determinists, as a matter of fact do not just try to manipulate other people but find themselves treating people, particularly themselves, with respect and hence as if they were really free. At least when it comes to their own cases, hard determinists will assume that their actions are free. The assumption that some of our actions are free is deeply ingrained in us, and hard determinists, along with everyone else, cannot avoid making this assumption in their day-to-day activities. Even if they call freedom an illusion, they will be laboring under this illusion in their daily lives.

Theoretical beliefs that cannot be sustained in practice should be treated with suspicion. It seems that good theory and practice are compatible, and so if we deny our practical assumptions in favor of new theoretical considerations, we had better have some good alternative practices available to us that are compatible with our new theory and at least as successful as were old habits and customs we dropped. So far, hard determinism has not shown us how we can be hard determinists in practice. Hard determinists have not shown us how we can sustain the belief that hard determinism is true while we are deciding about the future of ourselves and of our family and friends.

Indeterminists allow for freedom, so they avoid the contradictions that hard determinists have to live with, but they still have problems making sense of moral responsibility. If quantum indeterminacy is our model of freedom, then this is a freedom that is useless to morality. Suppose that my actions are brought about by decaying plutonium in my brain. Every time certain atoms leave this radioactive element at a certain time and in a certain region, I have certain wants and desires and act accordingly. Given quantum physics, my actions are not determined and I could have done otherwise because the atoms could have left at different rates and in different places, but it is hard to see how I could be morally responsible for these actions.

Moral responsibility requires actions that are free in the sense of being under our control and that we bring about on account of our deliberations and choices. A puppet that behaves randomly is not free, and in the same way behavior that is brought about by quantum indeterminacy is not free. We can choose to call actions that result from quantum indeterminacy "free," but then we should be careful to distinguish this kind of freedom from the freedom we are after, namely the freedom that gives us moral responsibility.

That quantum indeterminacy does not help us to understand human freedom should not be surprising. Quantum indeterminacy is a feature of very small and fast-moving particles, while human beings are medium-sized objects that move much much more slowly. Moreover, we do not have good reasons for claiming that the indeterminacy that exists at the micro level percolates up to the level of human beings, the macro level. It is bad reasoning to argue that since indeterminacy reigns at the micro level, and since humans are composed of atoms, indeterminacy also reigns at the macro level, for objects often have properties different from the properties of the particles they are composed of.

It is much more promising to argue that since reasoning, deliberation, and behavior of the kind we are concerned with takes place in medium-sized objects, it is very likely that the random behavior we find at the micro level is absorbed into the macro level without any noticeable effect. The result might be somewhat akin to the effects of a single raindrop falling into the Pacific Ocean. The effect is minimal, and it will certainly not cause flooding in California. It is therefore quite possible that indeterminacy reigns at the quantum level while Newtonian determinacy rules for mid-sized objects.

Can indeterminists who do not rely on quantum indeterminacy make sense of the idea that our actions are under our control and that we bring them about on account of our deliberations and choices? There is a danger indeterminists have to face. The danger is that the claim that our actions are not causally determined suggests that our deliberations and choices do not play a role in bringing about our actions. If that is the case, it seems that a free action is not under our control and not something for which we can be morally responsible.

Indeterminists can try to avoid this danger by distinguishing the two components of causal determinacy: causality and determinism. If one event A causally determines another event B, then (1) A causes B and (2) given A, B must occur. Perhaps some human actions are caused but not determined. Since they are not determined, they can be considered free, but they are still under our control because they are caused by our deliberations and choices.

The idea is that our deliberations and choices might sway us in one direction rather than another without closing any options. Consider how I proceed before casting my vote in an election. I might have a choice between three candidates, candidates A, B, and C. I listen to their campaign speeches, read about their views, and decide that while there is not much difference between the three on the issues that matter to me, I slightly prefer candidate C over the others. The incompatibilist will insist that when I go into the voting booth and cast my vote, the reasons I have for favoring C over the others are strong enough to cause me to vote for C without being so strong that I could not have done otherwise and voted for A or B instead.

So, we act on reasons and the reasons sway us to do one thing rather than another without leaving us without options. And we are morally responsible for our actions precisely because they were caused by our deliberations and choices.

There are three important difficulties indeterminists who take this route have to overcome. First, since they maintain that there are free human actions that are caused but not causally determined, they are committed to the idea that something can be a cause without determining the effect. In other words, on this view, causality does not involve necessity, and as we saw in the chapter on causality, there are good reasons for supposing that causality does involve necessity.

Second, it will seem to many that this view does not do justice to the scientific conception of the world, according to which all events, at least at the macroscopic level, are subject to laws of nature. Events that obey the laws of nature are causally determined by antecedent events. For example, if someone gets cancer in the future and this falls under a law of nature, then it will be determined by the confluence of several events, including, say, his life-long smoking habit, how he smoked, other aspects of his lifestyle, the degree of pollution in his environment, and the structure and disposition of his body. If free actions are not causally determined, they do not obey the laws of nature, and hence the scientific image is false and not all macroscopic events are subject to nature's laws.

Third, it seems that this view does not do justice to our self-image, particularly the idea that our actions are under the control of our deliberations and choices. Consider the election again. I deliberate about the candidates and conclude that C is better, however slightly, than the other candidates. Believing that I should act on my preference, however slight it might be, I decide to vote for C instead of A or B, and vote for C. If these deliberations about the candidates and my decision did not causally determined my vote, then the following is possible: I deliberated exactly as I did, concluding that C is better, however slightly, than the other candidates, and my decision remains the same: I decide to vote for C because I believe that I should act on my preference, however slight it might be. But I do not vote for C, and vote for A or B instead. If this is possible, it seems that my vote is not under my control, but more like the outcome of a gamble. When I toss a coin, the outcome is not under my control, and in the same way, on this view, our actions are also never under the control of our deliberations and decisions.

In sum, if my deliberations and choices do not causally determine my actions, then I could have done something different even though my deliberations and choices remain the same. This is hard to square with the idea that I control my actions. My actions are under my control, it seems, when my deliberations and choices to act in a certain way determine what I do, but indeterminism denies that free actions can be determined. Consequently, indeterminism has a hard time making sense of moral responsibility.

Compatibilism

The alternative to incompatibilism is the view that an action can be both free and causally determined; that is, compatibilism. If freedom and causal determinism are compatible, then it seems that the problems of hard determinism and libertarianism can be avoided. Science and our self-image can coexist peacefully, and we can make sense of moral responsibility.

The ruling idea of compatibilism is that all the psychological factors that go into a decision and seem to guide our free actions are also causes of these actions. When I decide to act in a certain way, I deliberate, weigh the consequences, evaluate my wants and desires, decide on a course of action, and then act accordingly. This is why the action seems to be up to me, and the compatibilist affirms that free actions are up to us. A free action is causally determined by all these psychological factors, which we can think of as constituents of our will to act.

According to compatibilists, a free act is causally determined by our volition. But we know this cannot be the whole story. Although free actions are voluntary actions, not all voluntary actions are free. Freedom requires something more than the involvement of the will. As we saw, incompatibilists believe that what is required in addition to volition is that the agent could have done otherwise, but compatibilists cannot go along with incompatibilists on this issue. For compatibilists, a free action will be both free and causally determined, and if the action is causally determined, the agent could not do otherwise given all the prior causal factors, which include the agent's deliberations and decisions.

Soft determinism

Compatibilists do not agree on what needs to be added. Soft determinists are compatibilists who suggest that we try to capture the nature of a free action by adding the following feature to a voluntary action. A free action is not only a voluntary action, but an action the agent could have done otherwise *if the agent had willed otherwise*. While the incompatibilist maintains that a free action is such that the agent could have done otherwise, the soft determinist qualifies this and maintains that a person's action is free if she could have refrained from this action if she had wanted to. In other words, agents act freely only if they have the power to act or not to act, depending on what they want to do.

For example, consider Locke's prisoner. His act of staying in the room is voluntary because he wants to stay there and converse with his acquaintance. However, he does not, to use Locke's words, have the "Power of doing, or of forbearing to do, according as the Mind shall choose or direct." If the prisoner had wanted to leave the room, he could not have left it, and hence he was not free to stay in the room even though he stayed in the room voluntarily. In the same way, the Arizona woman's participation in the rape was not free. She could not have refrained from being raped and she was going to be raped no matter what she wanted.

Unfortunately, soft determinists have to face a very important challenge. It does not seem to be true that an action is free if the action is voluntary and the agent could have done otherwise if he or she wanted to. Consider Locke's prisoner again, except that now he is not locked in the room, but instead he has been given a drug that causes the prisoner to want to stay in the room and not go anywhere else. He could leave the room if he wanted to and he willingly is staying in the room, but his stay in the room is not free.

The reason his action is not free is that his will is not free. His case is no different from a case of brainwashing where the victim comes to want and desire to do the things that the captors want her to do. Similarly, totalitarian societies are societies where a significant portion of the population is manipulated to want to do things that the rulers of the society want people to do. Addiction is also a

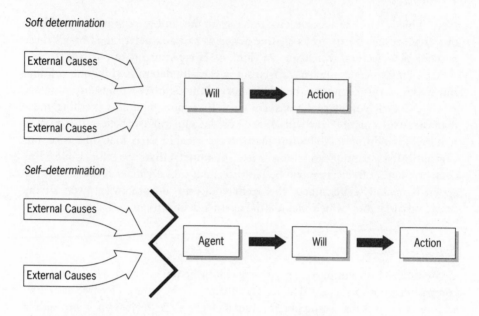

Figure 6   Soft determinist and self-determinist views on freedom.

case in point. An addict wants to consume a drug, say alcohol, and he could refrain from drinking alcohol if he wanted to. But as a matter of fact, he is addicted and cannot refrain from wanting to consume the drug in a way that makes his will unfree. Hence his drug use is not a case of a free action.

Self-determinism

It seems, then, that a free action has to be brought about by a free will. But what makes a will free? Self-determinists argue that what makes a will free is that it is determined by an agent who is not causally determined to will in this way. A free action is determined by a free will, and a free will is determined only by the agent herself. The brainwashed captive or totalitarian victim have wills that were determined by forces external to them, and hence, according to the self-determinist, their wills and their actions are not free.

Self-determinists believe that soft determinism cannot make sense of self-determination, and that for soft determinists there can be no relevant difference between brainwashed captives and ordinary people whose wants are also determined by their social and natural environments. For soft determinists, to will is an event causally determined by other events, which in turn are again causally determined by still other events. Such a chain of causal determination will eventually take us to natural and social forces external to us. The self-determinist believes that a free action stops with the agent.

We can contrast the soft determinist and self-determinist views on freedom with the model shown in figure 6, where the arrows indicate causal relations. While, for a soft determinist, the will, even when it is free, is determined by causes which in turn are determined by other causes, the self-determinist maintains that a free will is determined by an undetermined agent. You can see from figure 6 that we, as free agents, are (in the words of the self-determinist Roderick Chisholm) like God because "each of us, when we act, is a prime mover unmoved. In doing what we do, we cause certain events to happen, and nothing – or no one – causes us to cause those events to happen."

Although self-determinism allows for something that is not caused by other events, namely the agent, strictly speaking it does not violate the principle of universal causation. The principle of universal causation is that every *event* is causally determined, but an agent, according to self-determinists, is not an event. It is a special kind of object, namely one that can bring about changes in itself and the world without being determined to do this by other causes. So there is no conflict between the claim that every event is causally determined and the claim that agents are not causally determined.

Agency and Causality

It would be very nice if we could stop here. Incompatibilism is flawed because it cannot account for moral responsibility, soft determinism is flawed because it seems unable to make sense of freedom of the will, and so we are left with self-determinism. Self-determinism accounts for free action, is compatible with the principle of universal causation, and has a good account of what a free will is. A free action is a voluntary action brought about by a free will, and a free will is one that is determined by an agent. Moral responsibility lies with agents who determine their own wills and act according to their self-determined wills.

Unfortunately, there is a fly in the ointment. Self-determinism is not without its problems. The first problem is that it seems to be committed to an infinite regress that seems vicious. When the agent determines her will, it seems that this will be an event. When the agent makes a decision to act, say, to press charges against someone, she determines her will to act in this way. Perhaps she says to herself, "I am going to press charges if this is the last thing I do," and proceeds to call the police. But determining her will in this way requires some effort, it seems. But exerting effort to determine her will is something that happens – it is an event – and self-determinists believe that every event is causally determined.

So, exerting effort to determine her will is something that happens – it is an event – and self-determinists believe that every event is causally determined. Consequently, exerting power over the will is causally determined, and according to self-determinism, it is free only if this event is determined by the free will of an agent. That means that her effort to determine her will to press charges is free only if she wills to exert this effort to determine her will to press charges, and this new will – the will to exert this power over her will – is brought about by her as an agent. We can show this with the model in figure 7.

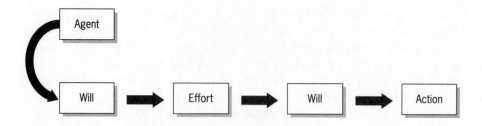

Figure 7   The will to will in self-determinism.

Unfortunately, this cannot be the end of the story for the self-determinist. Just as the agent had to exert effort over her will to determine it to act, she now has to exert effort over her will to determine it to exert effort over will to determine it to act, assuming that her will is free. But this new effort, if it is free, also has to be determined by a will that is determined by an agent, and we can see that we are generating an infinite regress. We generate this regress simply by applying the self-determinist's account of freedom to the action of exerting effort over the will to determine it to do something. Figure 8 illustrates the regress. This regress is vicious because in order for the agent to act and press those charges, she has to go through an infinite chain of volitions and exertions of effort over the will, and hence will never succeed in actually completing her action.

A second problem for self-determinism is that it seems to involve a strange kind of causation. In addition to events being causes, we also have agents being causes, and this is odd because typically causality – the kind of causality we study in the natural sciences – is between events. *Striking a match* in appropriate circumstances causes it to ignite, *ingesting aspirin* brings about relief from headaches, *lightning striking the tree* split it down the middle, *dropping air pressure* caused the high winds, and so on. The underlined phrases refer to causes and the causes are all events. But an agent is not an event, and so when the agent causes something to happen, this effect occurs without any *event* that is causally responsible for it. Something happens without anything happening that causes it. Of course, the effect of agency is not uncaused: it is caused by the agent. But it is not caused by another event, and so it appears that the agent can cause things without doing anything. This seems very strange. Ordinarily, events occur because of other events, but here we have things happen simply in virtue of an agent who can bring things about without doing anything.

The oddity of agent causality comes out when we remind ourselves that one thing causes another at certain specific times. The match ignited a little after midnight because the match was struck exactly at midnight, my headache just ceased because I took a couple of aspirins about half an hour ago. The effect occurs at a certain time, and when the effect occurs depends on when the cause occurred. For instance, if the cause had occurred earlier and the circumstances were still appropriate, the effect would have occurred a little earlier. This is not

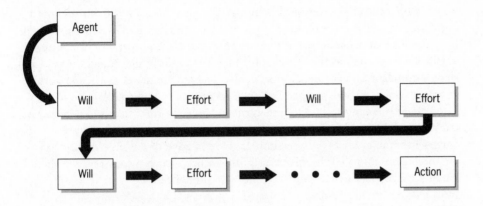

Figure 8 The infinite regress in self-determinism.

true of agent causation. Of course, an agent exists for some time, let's say from June 1976 until 2058, but this does not explain why the agent decided to press charges at a certain time, say in the last week of May in 2001 rather than the first week of June. The agent existed in May as well as June.

It seems, then, that agent causality is really a kind of causality that does not fit very easily into what we know about causality in the natural world. Where agent causation makes sense is in the way we appear to ourselves. When I think about my own actions, it does seem that self-determinism has the right picture. From my point of view as the actor, not the spectator, I am the one who brings about the decision to act, say to go for a walk. I don't think of my decision as the effect of some prior events inside me or external to me. Even my deliberations prior to the decision do not seem to be causes of my decision. It seems to me that if there is a cause, it is me, the agent. I think about what to do, but then I make the decision: I brought it about, not my deliberations or anything else that happened anywhere in the universe.

Thus self-determinism leaves us with precisely the kind of conflict it sought to avoid. Compatibilism seeks to resolve the conflict between the scientific image of the world and our own self-images, but self-determinism fails to do this. The self-determinist replaces the duality of freedom and causation with the duality of agent and event causation. While agent causation seems plausible when we think about how our decisions and actions seem to us, it is difficult to find a place for it in the scientific study of nature, where event causation rules.

Soft Determinism and Freedom of the Will

Perhaps this is just the way it is. Perhaps agents do not fit smoothly into the natural world. After all, whether or not human beings are part of the natural world is the central metaphysical issue we addressed in chapter 6, on the mind/body problem. If human minds are distinct from human bodies, then it should be expected that agents cause things in ways that have no parallel in nature.

But we concluded in the last chapter that it is unlikely that human beings, or some significant human capacity or faculty such as the mind, transcend nature. It seems very likely that we just are physical creatures, and so self-determinism, insofar as it is committed to placing agents outside the realm of natural causality, is likely to be false. Moreover, even if we are not convinced that materialism is true, we should at least try to see how far we can go with the simple idea that we are intelligent animals fully integrated into nature, which means that we should try to see if we can defend our freedom without concluding that we are distinct from nature.

How far can we go with the idea that we are wholly natural organisms *and* that we are free? As we just saw, we cannot get very far with self-determinism because it preserves human freedom by removing human beings from the natural order. Soft determinism, on the other hand, has trouble making sense of freedom of the will, and that leaves us with nothing to work with unless we find a way to fix soft determinism so that it can handle freedom of the will.

The problem with soft determinism was that there are cases where a person is doing what she wants and she could have done otherwise if she had wanted to do something else, but she still is coerced. Remember the robbery and rape cases at the beginning of this chapter. When the thief demands your car or your life, you have alternatives. You could have done something else if you had wanted to. For instance, if you wanted to refuse to turn over your car, you could have done that and accepted the lethal consequences. Nevertheless, you are being robbed and coerced to give the thief your car. Similarly, the woman in the Arizona rape case could have done otherwise if she wanted to. She could have made the mistake of resisting the rapist, thus endangering her life. Nevertheless, even though she could have done something else if she wanted to, this was a case of coercion – rape – and not a free action.

A promising treatment of these cases that soft determinists have worried about begins with the idea that we not only have desires and wants about how to act in the world, but also desires and wants about our character and who we want to be. In other words, we not only want to do things, but we also want to have certain wants and desires. For instance, consider people who are fighting nicotine addiction. They have strong desires to smoke cigarettes and these desires lead to action: smoking cigarettes. At the same time, they are trying to break their habits and for many this involves wanting not to have the desire to smoke.

These wants and desires about what wants and desires one should have are second-order volitions and desires because they are volitions and desires about what volitions and desires to have. Having wants about what one wants is essential to the examined life. Should I be the kind of person that wants to study right now or should I be the kind of person who prefers to go do something outdoors? Do I want to have this desire to smoke or do I prefer not to have it? We will ask these kinds of questions if we reflect on and evaluate our wants and desires, and someone who does not raise such questions lives an undisciplined life driven by unexamined wants and desires.

Soft determinists have suggested that we can use second-order volitions to distinguish a free will from a coerced will. The robbery victim wants to surrender his car to the thief, but he does not want to have this want. He rejects it in much the same way that the nicotine addict who rejects his addiction does not want to want to smoke. In the same manner, the rape victim wants the rapist to wear a condom, but she rejects this want of hers, which has been forced upon her by the rapist. So a free will is a will that we want to have, and an unfree will is one that we do not want to have.

Another way of putting this is that voluntary acts are free when the agents identify with their wills. A free smoker, on this account, is a person who wants to smoke and who identifies with this want: he makes this desire to smoke part of his character and part of his ideal of who he is. This distinguishes him from the unfree smoker, who wants to smoke, but does not identify with this want and wishes to banish it from his character.

Freedom and Society

This account is on the right track, but it is incomplete. It is not too difficult to imagine situations where people are not free even when they identify with their wants and desires. Many slaves coped with their condition by affirming their lot in life. In fact, they, along with everyone else, were taught that the good life consists of accepting one's given position in life and fulfilling as well as possible the duties assigned to one's station in life. That meant that if you were born a slave, the good life meant that you accepted your condition and aimed to be a good slave.

So many slaves would want to obey their masters and identified with this want. A good slave not only wanted to obey the master, but wanted to want to obey the master, rather than harbor secret resentments. These slaves may have been happier than their counterparts who rejected their place in society, but they were hardly free. They were socialized to have appropriate second-order volitions – to want to want to obey their masters – and this socialization undermined their freedom. There was something about how slaves were trained and made to fit into a slave society that undermined their freedom.

We can see from this that a full account of freedom will have to look at how we are socialized and distinguish between socialization that undermines freedom and socialization that is compatible with human freedom. This is a difficult task, because in part what we are being asked to do is to think about what a free society is – that is, a society that does not through its institutions and practices undermine human freedom – and to treat this issue properly we need to move from metaphysics to social and political philosophy.

However, we can at least try to point in the right direction. We are looking for forms of socialization that do not stunt and subvert people's abilities to use their minds and live an examined life. Socialization that does not undermine freedom is socialization that nourishes human reasoning, reflection, perception, and imagination. These are the capacities that allow us to know who we are, what we could be, and what we should be. These are also the capacities that allow us to know the nature of the world around us, and how it could and should be, and these are all things we need to know if we are to be free in our thoughts and actions.

Conclusion

It seems, then, that freedom and determinism are compatible only if free societies are possible, and free societies are possible only if there can be societies that do not stunt and undermine people's capacities to use their minds, particularly their capacities to reason, reflect, and imagine. The difficulty of determining whether such societies are possible and what forms they can take must not be underestimated. We certainly should not simply assume that our own societies are free. However, it seems that our discussion of freedom suggests important features that free societies will have. They will be societies where critical reflection and debate about the nature of free societies is widespread and the society as a whole manifests a deep concern for avoiding forms of socialization that stunt reason and undermine freedom. They are societies that are committed to what Immanuel Kant called the motto of Enlightenment: "*Sapere aude!* Have courage, to use your *own* understanding!" These are societies where people dare to use their own reason without always relying on the guidance of others and where, as Kant put it, people are not treated like domestic cattle, taught to obey and threatened with punishment for thinking on their own.

Selection from *The System of Nature,* Appendix
Paul Henri Thiry d'Holbach

D'Holbach (1723–1789) was a philosopher of the French Enlightenment and a personal friend of Diderot and Jean-Jacques Rousseau. He was an outspoken defender of both materialism and determinism, and believed that these were compatible with morality. He is also remembered as a sharp critic of religious and educational institutions for corrupting the natural instincts of human beings.

Chapter XI

Man is a physical being, subject to nature, and consequently to necessity. Born without our consent, our organization is independent of us, and our ideas come to us involuntarily. Action is the sequel of an impulse communicated by a sensible object.

I am thirsty, and see a well; can I hinder myself from wishing to drink of it? But I am told the water is poisoned, and I abstain from drinking. Will it be said, that in this case I am free? Thirst necessarily determined me to drink; the discovery of poison necessarily determines me not to drink. The second motive is stronger that the first, and I abstain from drinking. But an imprudent man, it may be said, will drink. In this case his first impulse will be strongest. In either case, the action is necessary. He who drinks is a madman; but the actions of madmen are not less necessary than those of other men.

A debauchee may be persuaded to change his conduct. This circumstance does not prove that he is free; but only, that motives can be found, sufficient to counteract the effect of those which formerly acted upon him.

Choice by no means proves liberty; since hesitation only finishes when the will is determined by sufficient motives; and man cannot hinder motives from acting upon his will. Can he prevent himself from wishing to possess what he thinks desirable? No; but we are told he can resist the desire, by reflecting upon its consequences. But has he the power of reflecting? Human actions are never free; they necessarily proceed from constitution, and from received ideas, strengthened by example, education, and experience. The motive which determines man is always beyond his power.

Notwithstanding the system of human liberty, men have universally founded their systems upon necessity along. If motives were thought incapable of influencing the will, why make use of morality, education, legislation, and even religion? We establish institutions to influence the will; a clear proof of our conviction, that they must act upon it. These institutions are necessity demonstrated to man.

The necessity that governs the physical, governs also the moral world, where every thing is also subject to the same law.

Chapter XII

Examination of the Opinions which maintain the System of Necessity to be Dangerous.

If men's actions are necessary, by what right, it is asked, are crimes punished, since involuntary actions are never the objects of punishment?

Society is an assemblage of sensible beings, susceptible of reason, who love pleasure, and hate pain. Nothing more is necessary to engage their concurrence to the general welfare. Necessity is calculated to impress all men. The wicked are madmen against whom others have a right to defend themselves. Madness is an involuntary and necessary state, yet madmen are confined. But society should never excite desires, and afterwards punish them. Robbers are often those whom society has deprived of the means of subsistence.

By ascribing all to necessity, we are told the ideas of just and unjust, of good and evil, are destroyed. No; though no man acts from necessity, his actions are just and good relative to the society whose welfare he promotes. Every man is sensible that he is compelled to love a certain mode of conduct in his neighbour. The ideas of pleasure and pain, vice and virtue, are founded upon our own essence.

Fatalism neither emboldens crime, nor stifles remorse, always felt by the wicked. They have long escaped blame or punishment, they are not on that account better satisfied with themselves. Amidst perpetual pangs, struggles, and agitations, they can neither find repose nor happiness. Every crime costs them bitter torments and sleepless nights. The system of fatality establishes morality, by demonstrating its necessity.

Fatality, it is said, discourages man, paralyzes his mind, and breaks the ties that connect him with society. But does the possession of sensibility depend upon myself? My sentiments are necessary, and founded upon nature. Though I know that all men must die, am I on that account, the less affected by the death of a wife, a child, a father, or a friend?

Fatalism ought to inspire man with a useful submission and resignation to his fate. The opinion, that all is necessary, will render him tolerant. He will lament and pardon his fellowmen. He will be humble and modest from knowing that he has received every thing which he possesses.

Fatalism, it is said, degrades man into a mere machine. Such language is the invention of ignorance, respecting what constitutes his true dignity. Every machine is valuable, when it performs well the functions to which it is destined. Nature is but a machine, of which the human species makes a part. Whether the soul be mortal or immortal, we do not the less admire its grandeur and sublimity in a Socrates.

The opinion of fatalism is advantageous to man. It prevents useless remorse from disturbing his mind. It teaches him the propriety of enjoying with moderation, as pain, ever accompanies excess. He will follow the paths of virtue, since everything shows its necessity for rendering him estimable to others and contented with himself.

Has the Self "Free Will"?
C. A. Campbell

C. A. Campbell (1897–1974) was a Professor of Philosophy at Cambridge University and a stalwart opponent of both hard determinism and compatibilism. He believed that human beings are free and that the agent performing a free action is the sole author of that action. According to Campbell, people are morally responsible only for their actions that are self-determined in this way. Campbell acknowledges that we have habits and dispositions, or what is often called "character," but he argues that a person's character is distinct from the person's self and that the character does not determine the self's choices. It is the self that has authentic and creative power to issue its own actions.

1. . . . It is something of a truism that in philosophic enquiry the exact formulation of a problem often takes one a long way on the road to its solution. In the case of the Free Will problem I think there is a rather special need of careful formulation. For there are many sorts of human freedom; and it can easily happen that one wastes a great deal of labour in proving or disproving a freedom which has almost nothing to do with the freedom which is at issue in the traditional problem of Free Will. The abortiveness of so much of the argument for and against Free Will in contemporary philosophical literature seems to me due in the main to insufficient pains being taken over the preliminary definition of the problem. . . .

Fortunately we can at least make a beginning with a certain amount of confidence. It is not seriously disputable that the kind of freedom in question is the freedom which is commonly recognised to be in some sense a precondition of moral responsibility. Clearly, it is on account of this integral connection with moral responsibility that such exceptional importance has always been felt to attach to the Free Will problem. But in what precise sense is free will a precondition of moral responsibility, and thus a postulate of the moral life in general? This is an exceedingly troublesome question; but until we have satisfied ourselves about the answer to it, we are not in a position to state, let alone decide, the question whether "Free Will" in its traditional, ethical, significance is a reality.

Our first business, then, is to ask, exactly what kind of freedom is it which is required for moral responsibility? And as to method of procedure in this inquiry, there seems to me to be no real choice. I know of only one method that carries with it any hope of success; viz. the critical comparison of those acts for which, on due reflection, we deem it proper to attribute moral praise or blame to the agents, with those acts for which, on due reflection, we deem such judgments to be improper. The ultimate touchstone, as I see it, can only be our moral consciousness as it manifests itself in our more critical and considered moral judgments. . . .

2. The first point to note is that the freedom at issue (as indeed the very name "Free *Will* Problem" indicates) pertains primarily not to overt acts but to inner acts. The nature of things has decreed that, save in the case of one's self, it is only overt acts which one can directly observe. But a very little reflection serves to show that in our moral judgments upon others their overt acts are regarded as significant only insofar as they are the expression of inner acts. We do not consider the acts of a robot to be morally responsible acts; nor do we consider the acts of a man to be so save insofar as they are distinguishable from those of a robot by reflecting an inner life of choice. Similarly, from the other side, if we are satisfied (as we may on occasion be, at least in the case of ourselves) that a person has definitely elected to follow a course which he believes to be wrong, but has been prevented by external circumstances from translating his inner choice into an overt act, we still regard him as morally blameworthy. Moral freedom, then, pertains to *inner* acts.

The next point seems at first sight equally obvious and controversial; but, as we shall see, it has awkward implications if we are in real earnest with it (as almost nobody is). It is the simple point that the act must be one of which the person judged can be regarded as the *sole* author. It seems plain enough that if there are any *other* determinants of the act, external to the self, to that extent the act is not an act which the *self* determines, and to that extent not an act for which the self can be held morally responsible. The self is only part-author of the act, and his moral responsibility can logically extend only to those elements within the act (assuming for the moment that these can be isolated) of which he is the *sole* author.

The awkward implications of this apparent truism will be readily appreciated. For, if we are mindful of the influences exerted by heredity and environment, we may well feel some doubt whether there is any act of will at all of which one can truly say that the self is sole author, sole determinant. No man has a voice in determining the raw material of impulses and capacities that constitute his hereditary endowment, and no man has more than a very partial control of the material and social environment in which he is destined to live his life. Yet it would be manifestly absurd to deny that these two factors do constantly and profoundly affect the nature of a man's choices. That this is so we all of us recognise in our moral judgments when we "make allowances," as we say, for a bad heredity or a vicious environment, and acknowledge in the victim of them a diminished moral responsibility for evil courses. Evidently we do *try*, in our moral judgments, however crudely, to praise or blame a man only in respect of that of which we can regard him as *wholly* the author. And evidently we do recognise that, for a man to be the author of an act in the full sense required for moral responsibility, it is not enough merely that he "wills" or "chooses" the act: since even the most unfortunate victim of heredity or environment does, as a rule, "will" what he does. It is significant, however, that the ordinary man, though well enough aware of the influence upon choices of heredity and environment, does not feel obliged thereby to give up his assumption that moral predicates *are* somehow applicable. Plainly he still believes that there is *something* for which a man is morally responsible, something of which we can fairly say that he is the sole author. *What is this something?* To that question common-sense is not ready with an explicit answer – though an answer is, I think, implicit in the line which its moral judgments take. I shall do what I can to give an explicit answer later in this lecture. Meantime it must suffice to observe that, if we are to be true to the deliverances of our moral consciousness, it is very difficult to deny that *sole* authorship is a necessary condition of the morally responsible act.

Thirdly we come to a point over which much recent controversy has raged. We may approach it by raising the following question. Granted an act of which the agent is sole author, does this "sole authorship" suffice to make the act a morally free act? We may be inclined to think that it does, until we contemplate the possibility that an act of which the agent is sole author might conceivably occur as a necessary expression of the agent's nature; the way in which, e.g. some philosophers have supposed the Divine act of creation to occur. This consideration excites a legitimate doubt, for it is far from easy to see how a person can be regarded as a proper subject for moral praise or blame in respect of an act which *he cannot help* performing – even if it be his own "nature" which necessitates it. Must we not recognise it as a condition of the morally free act that the agent "could have acted otherwise" than he in fact did? It is true, indeed, that we sometimes praise or blame a man for an act about which we are prepared to say, in the light of our knowledge of his established character, that he "could no other." But I think that a little reflection shows that in such cases we are not praising or blaming the man strictly for what he does *now* (or at any rate we ought not to be), but rather for those past acts of his which have generated the firm habit of mind from which his *present* act follows "necessarily." In other words, our praise and blame, so far as justified, are really retrospective, being directed not to the agent *qua* performing *this* act, but to the agent *qua* performing those past acts which have built up his present character, and in respect to which we presume that *he could* have acted otherwise, that there really *were* open possibilities before him. These cases, therefore, seem to me to constitute no valid exception to what I must take to be the rule, viz. that a man can be morally praised or blamed for an act only if he could have acted otherwise.

Now philosophers today are fairly well agreed that it is a postulate of the morally responsible act that the agent "could have acted otherwise" in *some* sense of that phrase. But sharp differences of opinion have arisen over the way in which the phrase ought to be interpreted. There is a strong disposition to water down its apparent meaning by insisting that it is not (as a postulate of moral responsibility) to be understood as a straightforward categorical proposition, but rather as a disguised hypothetical proposition. All that we really require to be assured of, in order to justify our holding X morally responsible for an act, is, we are told, that X could have acted otherwise *if* he had *chosen* otherwise (Moore, Stevenson); or perhaps that X could have acted otherwise *if* he had had a different character, or *if* he had been placed in different circumstances.

I think it is easy to understand, and even, in a measure, to sympathise with, the motives which induce philosophers to offer these counter-interpretations. It is not just the fact that "X could have acted otherwise," as a bald categorical statement, is incompatible with the universal sway of causal law – though this is, to some philosophers, a serious stone of stumbling. The more widespread objection is that it at least looks as though it were incompatible with that causal continuity of an agent's character with his conduct which is implied when we believe (surely with justice) that we can often tell the sort of thing a man will do from our knowledge of the sort of man he is.

We shall have to make our accounts with that particular difficulty later. At this stage I wish merely to show that neither of the hypothetical propositions suggested – and I think the same could be shown for any hypothetical alternative – is an acceptable substitute for the categorical proposition "X could have acted otherwise" as the presupposition of moral responsibility.

Let us look first at the earlier suggestion – "X could have acted otherwise *if* he had chosen otherwise." Now clearly there are a great many acts with regard to which we are entirely satisfied that the agent is thus situated. We are often perfectly sure that – for this is all it amounts to – if X had chosen otherwise, the circumstances presented no external obstacle to the translation of that choice into action. For example, we often have no doubt at all that X, who in point of fact told a lie, could have told the truth *if* he had so chosen. But does our confidence on this score allay all legitimate doubts about whether X is really blameworthy? Does it entail that X is free in the sense required for moral responsibility? Surely not. The obvious question immediately arises: "But *could* X have *chosen* otherwise than he did?" It is doubt about the true answer to *that* question which leads most people to doubt the reality of moral responsibility. Yet on this crucial question the hypothetical proposition which is offered as a sufficient statement of the condition justifying the ascription of moral responsibility gives us no information whatsoever.

Indeed this hypothetical substitute for the categorical "X could have acted otherwise" seems to me to lack all plausibility unless one contrives to forget why it is, after all, that we ever come to feel fundamental doubts about man's moral responsibility. Such doubts are born, surely, when one becomes aware of certain reputable worldviews in religion or philosophy, or of certain reputable scientific beliefs, which in their several ways imply that man's actions are necessitated, and thus could not be otherwise than they in fact are. But clearly a doubt so based is not even touched by the recognition that a man could very often act otherwise *if* he so chose. That proposition is entirely compatible with the necessitarian theories which generate our doubt: indeed it is this very compatibility that has recommended it to some philosophers, who are reluctant to give up either moral responsibility or Determinism. The proposition which we *must* be able to affirm if moral praise or blame of X is to be justified is the categorical proposition that X could have acted otherwise because – not if – he could have chosen otherwise; or, since it is essentially the inner side of the act that matters, the proposition simply that X could have chosen otherwise.

For the second of the alternative formulae suggested we cannot spare more than a few moments. But its inability to meet the demands it is required to meet is almost transparent. "X could have acted otherwise," as a statement of a precondition of X's moral responsibility, really means (we are told) "X could have acted otherwise *if* he were differently constituted, or *if* he had been placed in different circumstances." It seems a sufficient reply to this to point out that the person whose moral responsibility is at issue is X; a specific individual, in a specific set of circumstances. It is totally irrelevant to X's moral responsibility that we should be able to say that some person differently constituted from X, or X in a different set of circumstances, could have done something different from what X did.

3. Let me, then, briefly sum up the answer at which we have arrived to our question about the kind of freedom required to justify moral responsibility. It is that a man can be said to exercise free will in a morally significant sense only insofar as his chosen act is one of which he is the sole cause or author, and only

if – in the straightforward, categorical sense of the phrase – he "could have chosen otherwise."

I confess that this answer is in some ways a disconcerting one. Disconcerting, because most of us, however objective we are in the actual conduct of our thinking, would *like* to be able to believe that moral responsibility is real: whereas the freedom required for moral responsibility, on the analysis we have given, is certainly far more difficult to establish than the freedom required on the analyses we found ourselves obliged to reject. If, e.g. moral freedom entails only that I could have acted otherwise *if* I had chosen otherwise, there is no real "problem" about it at all. I am "free" in the normal case where there is no external obstacle to prevent my translating the alternative choice into action, and not free in other cases. Still less is there a problem if all that moral freedom entails is that I could have acted otherwise *if* I had been a differently constituted person, or been in different circumstances. Clearly I am *always* free in *this* sense of freedom. But, as I have argued, these so-called "freedoms" fail to give us the pre-conditions of moral responsibility, and hence leave the freedom of the traditional free-will problem, the freedom that people are really concerned about, precisely where it was.

. . .

5. That brings me to the second, and more constructive, part of this lecture. From now on I shall be considering whether it is reasonable to believe that man does in fact possess a free will of the kind specified in the first part of the lecture. If so, just how and where within the complex fabric of the volitional life are we to locate it? – for although free will must presumably belong (if any-where) to the volitional side of human experience, it is pretty clear from the way in which we have been forced to define it that it does not pertain simply to volition as such; not even to all volitions that are commonly dignified with the name of "choices." It has been, I think, one of the more serious impediments to profitable discussion of the Free Will problem that Libertarians and Determin-ists alike have so often failed to appreciate the comparatively narrow area within which the free will that is necessary to "save" morality is required to operate. It goes without saying that this failure has been gravely prejudicial to the case for Libertarianism. I attach a good deal of importance, therefore, to the problem of locating free will correctly within the volitional orbit. Its solution forestalls and annuls, I believe, some of the more tiresome clichés of Determinist criticism.

We saw earlier that Common Sense's practice of "making allowances" in its moral judgments for the influence of heredity and environment indicates Com-mon Sense's conviction, both that a just moral judgment must discount determi-nants of choice over which the agent has no control, and also (since it still accepts moral judgments as legitimate) that *something* of moral relevance survives which can be regarded as genuinely self-originated. We are now to try to dis-cover what this "something" is. And I think we may still usefully take Common Sense as our guide. Suppose one asks the ordinary intelligent citizen *why* he deems it proper to make allowances for X, whose heredity and/or environment are unfortunate. He will tend to reply, I think, in some such terms as these: that X has more and stronger temptations to deviate from what is right than Y or Z, who are normally circumstanced, so that he must put forth a *stronger moral effort* if he is to achieve the same level of external conduct. The intended implication seems to be that X is just as morally praiseworthy as Y or Z *if* he exerts an equivalent moral effort, even though he may not thereby achieve an equal success in conforming his will to the "concrete" demands of duty. And this implies, again, Common Sense's belief that *in moral effort* we have something for which a man is responsible *without qualification*, something that is *not* affected by heredity and environment but depends *solely* upon the self itself.

Now in my opinion Common Sense has here, in principle, hit upon the one and only defensible answer. Here, and here alone, so far as I can see, in the act of deciding whether to put forth or withhold the moral effort required to resist temptation and rise to duty, is to be found an act which is free in the sense required for moral responsibility; an act of which the self is sole author, and of which it is true to say that "it could be" (or, after the event, "could have been") "otherwise." Such is the thesis which we shall now try to establish.

6. The species of argument appropriate to the establishment of a thesis of this sort should fall, I think, into two phases. First, there should be a consideration of the evidence of the moral agent's own inner experience. What *is* the act of moral decision, and what does it imply, from the standpoint of the actual participant? Since there is no way of knowing the act of moral decision – or for that matter any other form of activity – except by actual participation in it, the evidence of the subject, or agent, is on an issue of this kind of palmary importance. It can hardly, however, be taken as in itself conclusive. For even if that evidence should be overwhelmingly to the effect that moral decision does have the characteristics required by moral freedom, the question is bound to be raised – and in view of considerations from other quarters pointing in a contrary direction is *rightly* raised – Can we *trust* the evidence in inner experience? That brings us to what will be the second phase of the argument. We shall have to go on to show, if we are to make good our case, that the extraneous considerations so often supposed to be fatal to the belief in moral freedom are in fact innocuous to it.

In the light of what was said [previously] about the self's experience of moral decision as a *creative* activity, we may perhaps be absolved from developing the first phase of the argument at any great length. The appeal is throughout to one's own experience in the actual taking of the moral decision in the situation of moral temptation. "Is it possible," we must ask, "for anyone so circumstanced to *dis*believe that he could be deciding otherwise?" The answer is surely not in doubt. When we decide to exert moral effort to resist a temptation, we feel quite certain that we *could* withhold the effort; just as, if we decide to withhold the effort and yield to our desires, we feel quite certain that we *could* exert it – otherwise we should not blame ourselves afterwards for having succumbed. It may be, indeed, that this conviction is mere self-delusion. But that is not at the moment our concern. It is enough at present to establish that the act of deciding to exert or to withhold moral effort, as we know it from the inside in actual moral living, belongs to the category of acts which "could have been otherwise."

Mutatis mutandis, the same reply is forthcoming if we ask, "Is it possible for the moral agent in the taking of his decision to disbelieve that he is the *sole* author of that decision?" Clearly he cannot disbelieve that it is *he* who takes the decision. That, however, is not in itself sufficient to enable him, on reflection, to regard himself as *solely* responsible for the act. For his "character" as so far formed might conceivably be a factor in determining it, and no one can suppose that the constitution of his "character" is uninfluenced by circumstances of heredity and environment with which he has nothing to do. But as we pointed out . . . , the very essence of the moral decision as it is experienced is that it is a decision whether or not to *oppose* our character. I think we are entitled to say, therefore, that the act of moral decision is one in which the self is for itself not merely "author" but "sole author."

7. We may pass on, then, to the second phase of our constructive argument; and this will demand more elaborate treatment. Even if a moral agent *qua* making a moral decision in the situation of "temptation" cannot help believing that he has free will in the sense at issue – a moral freedom between real alternatives, between genuinely open possibilities – are there, nevertheless, objections to a freedom of this kind so cogent that we are bound to distrust the evidence of "inner experience"?

I begin by drawing attention to a simple point whose significance tends, I think, to be underestimated. If the phenomenological analysis we have offered is substantially correct, no one while functioning as a moral agent can help believing that he enjoys free will. Theoretically he may be completely convinced by Determinist arguments, but when actually confronted with a personal situation of conflict between duty and desire he is quite certain that it lies with him here and now whether or not he will rise to duty. It follows that if Determinists could produce convincing theoretical arguments against a free will of this kind, the awkward predicament would ensue that man has to deny as a theoretical being what he had to assert as a practical being. Now I think the Determinist ought to be a good deal more worried about this than he usually is. He seems to imagine that a strong case on general theoretical grounds is enough to prove that the "practical" belief in free will, even if inescapable for us as practical beings, is mere illusion. But in fact it proves nothing of the sort. There is no reason whatever why a belief that we find ourselves obliged to hold *qua* practical beings should be required to give way before a belief which we find ourselves obliged to hold *qua* theoretical beings; or, for that matter, vice versa. All that the theoretical arguments of Determinism can prove, unless they are reinforced by a refutation of the phenomenological analysis that supports Libertarianism, is that there is a radical conflict between the theoretical and the practical sides of man's nature, an antinomy at the very heart of the self. And this is a state of affairs with which no one can easily rest satisfied. I think therefore that the Determinist ought to concern himself a great deal more than he does with phenomenological analysis, in order to show, if he can, that the assurance of free will is not really an inexpungable element in man's practical consciousness. There is just as much obligation upon him, convinced though he may be of the soundness of his theoretical arguments, to expose the errors of the Libertarian's phenomenological analysis, as there is upon us, convinced though we may be of the soundness of the Libertarian's phenomenological analysis, to expose the errors of the Determinist's theoretical arguments.

8. However, we must at once begin the discharge of our own obligation. The rest of this lecture will be devoted to trying to show that the arguments which seem to carry most weight with Determinists are, to say the least of it, very far from compulsive.

Fortunately a good many of the arguments which at an earlier time in the history of philosophy would have been strongly urged against us make almost no appeal to the bulk of philosophers today, and we may here pass them by. That applies to any criticism of "open possibilities" based on a metaphysical theory about the nature of the universe as a whole. Nobody today *has a* metaphysical theory about the nature of the universe as a whole! It applies also, with almost equal force, to criticisms based upon the universality of causal law as a supposed postulate of science. There have always been, in my opinion, sound philosophic reasons for doubting the validity, as distinct from the convenience, of the causal postulate in its universal form, but at the present time, when scientists themselves are deeply divided about the need for postulating causality even within their own special field, we shall do better to concentrate our attention upon criticisms which are more confidently advanced. I propose to ignore also, on different grounds, the type of criticism of free will that is sometimes advanced from the side of religion, based upon religious postulates of Divine Omnipotence and Omniscience. So far as I can see, a postulate of human freedom is every bit as necessary to meet certain religious demands (e.g. to make sense of the "conviction of sin"), as postulates of Divine Omniscience and Omnipotence are to meet certain other religious demands. If so, then it can hardly be argued that religious experience as such tells more strongly against than for the position we are defending; and we may be satisfied, in the present context, to leave the matter there. It will be more profitable to discuss certain arguments which contemporary philosophers do think important, and which recur with a somewhat monotonous regularity in the literature of anti-Libertarianism.

These arguments can, I think, be reduced in principle to no more than two: first, the argument from "predictability"; second, the argument from the alleged meaninglessness of an act supposed to be the self's act and yet not an expression of the self's character. Contemporary criticism of free will seems to me to consist almost exclusively of variations on these two themes. I shall deal with each in turn.

9. On the first we touched in passing at an earlier stage. Surely it is beyond question (the critic urges) that when we know a person intimately we can foretell with a high degree of accuracy how he will respond to at least a large number of practical situations. One feels safe in predicting that one's dog-loving friend will not use his boot to repel the little mongrel that comes yapping at his heels; or again that one's wife will not pass with incurious eyes (or indeed pass at all) the new hat-shop in the city. So to behave would not be (as we say) "in character." But, so the criticism runs, you with your doctrine of "genuinely open possibilities," of a free will by which the self can diverge from its own character, remove all rational basis from such prediction. You require us to make the absurd supposition that the success of countless predictions of the sort in the past has been mere matter of chance. If you *really* believed in your theory, you would not be surprised if tomorrow your friend with the notorious horror of strong drink should suddenly exhibit a passion for whisky and soda, or if your friend whose taste for reading has hitherto been satisfied with the sporting columns of the newspapers should be discovered on a fine Saturday afternoon poring over the works of Hegel. But of course you *would* be surprised. Social life would be sheer chaos if there were not well-grounded social expectations; and social life is not sheer chaos. Your theory is hopelessly wrecked upon obvious facts.

Now whether or not this criticism holds good against some versions of Libertarian theory I need not here discuss. It is sufficient if I can make it clear that against the version advanced in this lecture according to which free will is localised in a relatively narrow field of operation, the criticism has no relevance whatsoever.

Let us remind ourselves briefly of the setting within which, on our view, free will functions. There is X, the course which we believe we ought to follow, and Y, the course towards which we feel our desire is strongest. The freedom which we ascribe to the agent is the freedom to put forth or refrain from putting forth the moral effort required to resist the pressure of desire and do what he thinks he ought to do.

But then there is surely an immense range of practical situations – covering by far the greater part of life – in which there is no question of a conflict within the self between what he most desires to do and what he thinks he ought to do? Indeed such conflict is a comparatively rare phenomenon for the majority of men. Yet over that whole vast range there is nothing whatever in our version of Libertarianism to prevent our agreeing that character determines conduct. In the absence, real or supposed, of any "moral" issue, what a man chooses will be simply that course which, after such reflection as seems called for, he deems most likely to bring him what he most strongly desires; and that is the same as to say the course to which his present character inclines him.

Over by far the greater area of human choices, then, our theory offers no more barrier to successful prediction on the basis of character than any other theory. For where there is no clash of strongest desire with duty, the free will we are defending has no business. There is just nothing for it to do.

But what about the situations – rare enough though they may be – in which there *is* this clash and in which free will does therefore operate? Does our theory entail that there at any rate, as the critic seems to suppose, "anything may happen"?

Not by any manner of means. In the first place, and by the very nature of the case, the range of the agent's possible choices is bounded by what he thinks he ought to do on the one hand, and what he most strongly desires on the other. The freedom claimed for him is a freedom of decision to make or withhold the effort required to do what he thinks he ought to do. There is no question of a freedom to act in some "wild" fashion, out of all relation to his characteristic beliefs and desires. This so-called "freedom of caprice," so often charged against the Libertarian, is, to put it bluntly, a sheer figment of the critic's imagination, with no *habitat* in serious Libertarian theory. Even in situations where free will does come into play it is perfectly possible, on a view like ours, given the appropriate knowledge of a man's character, to predict within certain limits how he will respond.

But "probable" prediction in such situations can, I think, go further than this. It is obvious that where desire and duty are at odds, the felt "gap" (as it were) between the two may vary enormously in breadth in different cases. The moderate drinker and the chronic tippler may each want another glass, and each deem it his duty to abstain, but the felt gap between desire and duty in the case of the former is trivial beside the great gulf which is felt to separate them in the case of the latter. Hence it will take a far harder moral effort for the tippler than for the moderate drinker to achieve the same external result of abstention. So much is matter of common agreement. And we are entitled, I think, to take it into account in prediction, on the simple principle that the harder the moral effort required to resist desire the less likely it is to occur. Thus in the example taken, most people would predict that the tippler will very probably succumb to his desires, whereas there is a reasonable likelihood that the moderate drinker will make the comparatively slight effort needed to resist them. So long as the prediction does not pretend to more than a measure of probability, there is nothing in our theory which would disallow it.

I claim, therefore, that the view of free will I have been putting forward is consistent with predictability of conduct on the basis of character over a very wide field indeed. And I make the further claim that the field will cover all the situations of life concerning which there is any empirical evidence that successful prediction is possible.

10. Let us pass on to consider the second main line of criticism. This is, I think, much the more illuminating of the two, if only because it compels the Libertarian to make explicit certain concepts which are indispensable to him, but which, being desperately hard to state clearly, are apt not to be stated at all. The critic's fundamental point might be stated somewhat as follows:

"Free will as you describe it is completely unintelligible. On your own showing no *reason* can be given, because there just *is* no reason, why a man decides to exert rather than to withhold moral effort, or vice versa. But such an act – or more properly, such an 'occurrence' – it is nonsense to speak of as an act of a *self*. If there is nothing in the self's character to which it is, even in principle, in any way traceable, the self has nothing to do with it. Your so-called 'freedom,' therefore, so far from supporting the self's moral responsibility, destroys it as surely as the crudest Determinism could do."

If we are to discuss this criticism usefully, it is important, I think, to begin by getting clear about two different senses of the word "intelligible."

If, in the first place, we mean by an "intelligible" act one whose occurrence is in principle capable of being inferred, since it follows necessarily from something (though we may not know in fact from what), then it is certainly true that the Libertarian's free will is unintelligible. But that is only saying, is it not, that the Libertarian's "free" act is not an act which follows necessarily from something! This can hardly rank as a *criticism* of Libertarianism. It is just a description of it. That there can be nothing unintelligible in *this* sense is precisely what the Determinist has got to *prove*.

Yet it is surprising how often the critic of Libertarianism involves himself in this circular mode of argument. Repeatedly it is urged against the Libertarian, with a great air of triumph, that on his view he can't say *why* I now decide to rise to duty, or now decide to follow my strongest desire in defiance of duty. Of course he can't. If he could he wouldn't *be* a Libertarian. To "account for" a "free" act is a contradiction in terms. A free will is *ex hypothesi* the sort of thing of which the request for an *explanation* is absurd. The assumption that an explanation must be in principle possible for the act of moral decision deserves to rank as a classic example of the ancient fallacy of "begging the question."

But the critic usually has in mind another sense of the word "unintelligible." He is apt to take it for granted that an act which is unintelligible in the *above* sense (as the morally free act of the Libertarian undoubtedly is) is unintelligible in the *further* sense that we can attach no meaning to it. And this is an altogether more serious matter. If it could really be shown that the Libertarian's "free will" were unintelligible in this sense of being meaningless, that, for myself at any rate, would be the end of the affair. Libertarianism would have been conclusively refuted.

But it seems to me manifest that this can *not* be shown. The critic has allowed himself, I submit, to become the victim of a widely accepted but fundamentally vicious assumption. He has assumed that whatever is meaningful must exhibit its meaningfulness to those who view it from the standpoint of external observation. Now if one chooses thus to limit one's self to the rôle of external observer, it is, I think, perfectly true that one can attach no meaning to an act which is the act of something we call a "self" and yet follows from nothing in that self's character. But then *why should we* so limit ourselves, when what is under consideration is a subjective activity? For the apprehension of subjective acts there is *another* standpoint available, that of *inner experience*, of the practical consciousness in its actual functioning. If our free will should turn out to be something to which we can attach a meaning from *this* standpoint, no more is required. And no more ought to be expected. For I must repeat that only from the inner standpoint of living experience *could* anything of the nature of "activity" be directly grasped. Observation from without is in the nature of the case impotent to apprehend the active *qua* active. We can from without observe sequences of states. If into these we read activity (as we sometimes do), this can only be on the basis of what we discern in ourselves from the inner standpoint. It follows that if anyone insists upon taking his criterion of the meaningful simply from the standpoint of external observation, he is really deciding in advance of the evidence that the notion of activity, and a fortiori the notion of a free will, is "meaningless." He looks for the free act through a medium which is in the nature of the case incapable of revealing it, and then, because inevitably he doesn't find it, he declares that it doesn't exist!

But if, as we surely ought in this context, we adopt the inner standpoint, then (I am suggesting) things appear in a totally different light. From the inner standpoint, it seems to me plain, there is no difficulty whatever in attaching meaning to an act which is the self's act and which nevertheless does not follow from the self's character. So much I claim has been established by the phenomenological analysis . . . of the act of moral decision in face of moral temptation. It is thrown into particularly clear relief where the moral decision is to make the moral effort required to rise to duty. For the very function of moral effort, as it appears to the agent engaged in the act, is to enable the self to act against the line of least resistance, against the line to which his character as so far formed most strongly inclines him. But if the self is thus conscious here of *combating* his formed character, he surely cannot possibly suppose that the act, although his own act, *issues from* his formed character? I submit, therefore, that the self knows very well indeed – from the inner standpoint – what is meant by an act which is the *self's* act and which nevertheless does not follow from the self's *character*.

What this implies – and it seems to me to be an implication of cardinal importance for any theory of the self that aims at being more than superficial – is that the nature of the self is for itself something more than just its character as so far formed. The "nature" of the self and what we commonly call the "character" of the self are by no means the same thing, and it is utterly vital that they should not be confused. The "nature" of the self comprehends, but is not without remainder reducible to, its "character"; it must, if we are to be true to the testimony of our experience of it, be taken as including *also* the authentic creative power of fashioning and re-fashioning "character."

The misguided, and as a rule quite uncritical, belittlement, of the evidence offered by inner experience has, I am convinced, been responsible for more bad argument by the opponents of Free Will than has any other single factor. How often, for example, do we find the Determinist critic saying, in effect, "*Either* the act follows necessarily upon precedent states, *or* it is a mere matter of chance and accordingly of no moral significance." The disjunction is invalid, for it does not exhaust the possible alternatives. It seems to the critic to do so only because he *will* limit himself to the standpoint which is proper, and indeed alone possible, in dealing with the physical world, the standpoint of the external observer. If only he would allow himself to assume the standpoint which is not merely proper for, but necessary to, the apprehension of subjective activity, the inner standpoint of the practical consciousness in its actual functioning, he would find himself obliged to recognise the falsity of his disjunction. Reflection upon the act of moral decision as apprehended from the inner standpoint would force him to recognise a *third* possibility, as remote from chance as from necessity, that, namely, of *creative activity*, in which (as I have ventured to express it) nothing determines the act save the agent's doing of it.

11. There we must leave the matter. But as this lecture has been, I know, somewhat densely packed, it may be helpful if I conclude by reminding you, in bald summary, of the main things I have been trying to say. Let me set them out in so many successive theses.

1 The freedom which is at issue in the traditional Free Will problem is the freedom which is presupposed in moral responsibility.

2 Critical reflection upon carefully considered attributions of moral responsibility reveals that the only freedom that will do is a freedom which permits to inner acts of choice, and that these acts must be acts (*a*) of which the self is *sole* author, and (*b*) which the self could have performed otherwise.

3 From phenomenological analysis of the situation of moral temptation we find that the self as engaged in this situation is inescapably convinced that it possesses a freedom of precisely the specified kind, located in the decision to exert or withhold the moral effort needed to rise to duty where the pressure of its desiring nature is felt to urge it in a contrary direction.

4 Of the two types of Determinist criticism which seem to have most influence today, that based on the predictability of much human behaviour fails to touch a Libertarianism which confines the area of free will as above indicated. Libertarianism so understood is compatible with all the predictability that the empirical facts warrant. And:

5 The second main type of criticism, which alleges the "meaninglessness" of an act which is the self's act and which is yet not determined by the self's character, is based on a failure to appreciate that the standpoint of inner experience is not only legitimate but indispensable where what is at issue is the reality and nature of a subjective activity. The creative act of moral decision is inevitably meaningless to the mere external observer; but from the inner standpoint it is as real, and as significant, as anything in human experience.

Two Concepts of Freedom
William L. Rowe

William L. Rowe is Professor of Philosophy at Purdue University in Indiana. He has published influential essays in the philosophy of religion, metaphysics, and the history of modern philosophy. In the essay "Two Concepts of Freedom" he lays out two competing concepts of freedom and sets out to defend self-determinism and the idea that agents can be uncaused causes.

In his life of Samuel Johnson, Boswell reports Johnson as saying: "All theory is against freedom of the will; all experience for it." The first part of this remark would be agreeable to many eighteenth century philosophers: those believing that certain theoretical principles concerning explanation or causality support the doctrine of necessity. But the second part, that experience is on the side of free will, would be somewhat puzzling to those eighteenth century philosophers who hold that free will is a power and that a power, as opposed to an activity, is not something we can directly experience or be conscious of.[1] In his journal, however, which presumably was written shortly after the actual conversation with Johnson, Boswell reports Johnson's remark differently. There he has Johnson saying: "All theory against freedom of will, all practice for it."[2] Here the second part makes better philosophical sense, for that our practice of moral praise and blame is on the side of free will was a standard theme among eighteenth century advocates of free will, and it is perfectly understandable, therefore, that Johnson would have cited practice as on the side of freedom. But what is the *concept* of freedom that lies behind this remark by Johnson? And more generally, what *conceptual issues* were at the center of the controversy over freedom and necessity that occupied the last half of the seventeenth and most of the eighteenth century, a controversy bringing forward as its champions, on one side or another, such formidable figures as Hobbes, Locke, Samuel Clarke, Leibniz, Hume, and Thomas Reid? I want to answer these questions, not simply in order to deepen our understanding of this historical episode in the controversy over freedom and necessity, as important as that may be, but because I believe a clear understanding of this episode in the controversy can help us in our current thinking about the problem of freedom and necessity.

My belief is that when all is said and done there are two fundamentally different conceptions of freedom that occupy center stage in the controversy that we may arbitrarily date as beginning with Thomas Hobbes and Bishop Bramhall (in the second half of the seventeenth century) and ending with Thomas Reid and Joseph Priestley (in the late eighteenth century). Vestiges of these two conceptions are very much alive in the twentieth century. I intend, however, to examine these two conceptions in their earlier setting, analyzing and evaluating them in the light of criticisms advanced against them, both then and now. The first of these conceptions, of which John Locke is a major advocate, I will call *Lockean freedom*. The other conception, of which Thomas Reid is the leading advocate, I will call *Reidian freedom*. The history of the controversy in the period we are considering is fundamentally a dispute over which of these two concepts of freedom is more adequate to our commonsense beliefs about freedom and our general metaphysical and scientific principles.

Before we begin with Locke's conception of freedom, it is best to note that all participants in the controversy embraced what has come to be known as the volitional theory of action. Since this theory is common to the controversy we are examining, it plays no significant role in the controversy itself. Nevertheless, some brief description of it will help us understand certain points that emerge in the controversy. According to this theory, actions are of two sorts: those that involve thoughts and those that involve motions of the body. What makes the occurrence of a certain thought or bodily motion an *action* is its being preceded by a certain act of will (a volition) which brings about the thought or motion. Volitions, then, are "action starters." On the other hand, they are also themselves referred to as "actions." Of course, if we do classify volitions as actions, we cannot say that *every* action must be preceded by a volition. For then no action could occur unless it were preceded by an absolutely infinite number of volitions. But we still can say that thoughts and bodily motions are actions only if *they* are preceded by volitions that cause them. It is not clear whether volitions that start actions are viewed as distinct from the actions started, or as a part of the actions. It is also unclear just what the agent wills when his volition starts (or is part of) a certain action. These uncertainties, however, will have little bearing on our examination of the two conceptions of freedom that dominated eighteenth century thought.

I. Lockean Freedom

Locke distinguished between a free action and a voluntary action. For your action to be voluntary all that is required is that you will to do that action and perform it, presumably as a result of your willing to do it. Suppose you are sitting in your chair and someone invites you to go for a walk. You reject the idea, choosing instead to remain just where you are. Your so remaining, Locke would say, is a voluntary act. But was it a free act? This is a further question for Locke, and it depends on whether you could have done otherwise had you so willed. If I had injected you with a powerful drug, so that at the time – perhaps without your being aware of it – your legs were paralyzed, then your act of remaining in the chair was voluntary but not free, for you could not have got up and walked had you willed to do so. A free act, says Locke, is not just a voluntary act.[3] An act is free if it is voluntary *and* it is true that had you willed to do otherwise you would have been able to do otherwise. For Locke, then, we can say that you are free with respect to a certain action provided it is in your power to do it if you will to do it *and* in your power to refrain from doing it if you should will to refrain. Locke tells us that a man who is chained in prison does not stay in prison freely – even if that is what he wants to do – because it is not in his power to leave if he should will to leave. But if the prison doors are thrown open, and his chains are removed, he is free to leave and free to stay – for he can do either, depending on his will.

So far, of course, little or nothing has been said about the question of whether the will is free. And this was what Locke preferred, thinking on the whole that the question of freedom is the question of whether you are free *to do* what you will; much confusion, he thought, results from asking whether you are free *to will* what you will. But the chief merit of Locke's conception of freedom, or so it seemed to many, is that it fits nicely with the belief that our acts of will are causally necessitated by prior events and circumstances. Anthony Collins, Locke's friend and follower, took up this topic in his book, *A Philosophical Inquiry Concerning Human Liberty*, published in London in 1717. Collins argued that all our actions are subject to causal necessity; he argued, that is, that our actions are so determined by the causes preceding them that, given the causes and circumstances, no other actions were possible. What are the causes of our actions? Well, the immediate cause of the action is your decision or act of will to perform that action. What is the cause of your making that decision? According to Locke and Collins, the cause of that act of will is your desires, judgments, and the circumstances that prevailed just prior to that decision. Given your desires and judgments at the time, and given the circumstances that prevailed, it was impossible for you not to will as you did. And given the desires, judgments, circumstances, and the act of will, it was impossible for you not to act as you did. Now this impossibility of willing and acting otherwise does not conflict with Lockean freedom. For Lockean freedom does not require that *given the causes*, we somehow could have acted differently. All it requires is that *if* we had decided or willed differently *then* we could have acted differently. Indeed, Locke is careful to note that the absolute determination of the will or preference of the mind does not preclude freedom so far as the action flowing from the will or preference of the mind is concerned. He remarks:

> But though the preference of the Mind be always determined . . . ; yet the Person who has the power, in which alone consists liberty to act, or not to act, according to such preference, is nevertheless free; such determination abridges not that Power. He that has his Chains knocked off, and the Prison doors set open to him, is perfectly at liberty, because he may either go or stay as he best likes; though his preference be determined to stay by the darkness of the Night, or illness of the Weather, or want of other Lodging. He ceases not to be free; though that which at that time appears to him the greater Good absolutely determines his preference, and *makes* him stay in his Prison.[4]

Let us call those who believe both that we have Lockean freedom and that our actions and acts of will are subject to causal necessity, "necessitarians." It is likely that Locke was a necessitarian; Hobbes and Collins most certainly were. Those who, like Clarke and Reid, hold that necessity and freedom are really inconsistent with one another do not disagree with the necessitarians concerning the consistency of *Lockean freedom* with the causal necessity of our actions and acts of will. What they reject is the whole notion of Lockean freedom. Before we state their conception of freedom, however, we had best consider what their objections are to the Lockean idea of freedom.[5]

Lockean freedom, as we saw, exists solely at the level of *action*: *you* are free with respect to some action provided that you have the power to do the act if you will to do it, and have the power not to do it if you will not to do it. But what about the *will*? What if you don't have the power to will the action, or don't have the power not to will it? To see the difficulty here, let's return to our example where you are sitting down, someone asks you get up and walk over to the window to see what is happening outside, but you are quite satisfied where you are and choose to remain sitting. We earlier supposed that I had injected you with a powerful drug so that you can't move your legs. Here Locke would say that you don't sit freely, since it was not in your power to do otherwise if you had willed otherwise – say, to get up and walk to the window. But let's now suppose that instead of paralyzing your legs I had hooked up a machine to your brain so that I can and do cause you to will to sit, thus depriving you of the *capacity* to will to do otherwise. It's still true that you have the power to get up and walk if you should will to do so – I haven't taken away your physical capacity to walk, as I did when I paralyzed your legs. Here the problem is that you can't *will* to do anything other than sit. In this case, it seems clear that you sit of necessity, not freely. You can't do otherwise than sit, not because you lack the power to get up and walk if you should manage to choose to do that, but because you lack the power to *choose* to get up and walk. On Locke's account of freedom, however, it remains true that you sit freely and not of necessity. And this being so, we must conclude that Locke's account of freedom is simply inadequate. It is not sufficient that you have the power to do otherwise if you so will; it must also be true that you have the power to will to do otherwise. Freedom that is worth the name, therefore, must include power *to will*, not simply power *to do if we will*.

There is a second objection to Lockean freedom, an objection based on the fact that Lockean freedom is consistent with the causal necessity of our actions and decisions. According to the necessitarians, you are totally determined to will and act as you do by your motives and circumstances. Indeed, Leibniz quotes with favor Bayle's comparison of the influence of motives on an agent to the influence of weights on a balance. Referring to Bayle, Leibniz remarks: "According to him, one can explain what passes in our resolutions by the hypothesis that the will of man is like a balance which is at rest when the weights of its two pans are equal, and which always inclines either to one side or the other according to which of the pans is the more heavily laden."[6] Bayle's idea is that just as the heavier weight determines the movement of the balance, so does the stronger motive determine the movement of your will. If your motive to get up and walk to the window is stronger than whatever motive you have to remain sitting, then it determines you to will to get up and walk to the window. Given the respective strength of these motives, it is no more possible for you to will to remain sitting than it is possible for a balance to stay even when a heavier weight is placed in one of its pans than in the other. Motives, on this view, are determining causes of the decisions of our will in precisely the way in which weights are the determining causes of the movements of the balance. But if all this is so, claim the opponents of the necessitarians, then no one acts freely, no one has power over his will. For it was generally agreed that our motives are determined by factors largely beyond our control, and if these motives determine our acts of will as weights determine the movement of a balance, then we can no more control our will than the balance can control its movements. Just as a balance has no freedom of movement, so the person would have no freedom of will. Freedom would be an illusion if our will is subjected to causal necessity by motives and circumstances. Since Lockean freedom is consistent with such causal necessity, Lockean freedom is really not freedom at all.[7]

We've looked at two major objections to Lockean freedom. According to Locke, freedom to do a certain thing is (roughly) the power to do that thing if we will to do it. Our first objection is that we might have the power to do something if we willed to do it and yet lack the power to will to do it. Surely, freedom must include the power to will, and not just the power to do *if* we will. Our second objection is against the necessitarian view that our acts of will are causally necessitated by prior events and circumstances. If that is so then we *now* have no more control over what we will to do than a balance has over how it moves once the weights are placed in its pans. Causal necessitation of our acts of will denies to us any real power over the determinations of our will. And without such power we do not act freely. To be told, as Locke would tell us, that we could have done something else if we had so willed, is of course interesting, and perhaps not unimportant. But if we are totally determined to will as we do and cannot will otherwise, then it is absurd to say we act freely simply because had we willed otherwise – which we could not do – we could have acted otherwise.

I believe these objections to Lockean freedom are in the end totally convincing. Indeed, it puzzles me that the notion of Lockean freedom continues to survive in the face of such utterly devastating objections. But before passing on to the second concept of freedom, *Reidian freedom*, we should note an attempt or two to defend or amend Lockean freedom so that it will appear less implausible.

At the level of action we are free, for Locke, provided we could have done otherwise if we had chosen or willed to do otherwise. Basically, our objections to Lockean freedom point out the need to supplement freedom at the level of action with freedom at the level of the will. The problem for the necessitarian is how to do this without abandoning the causal necessitation of the will by our motives and circumstances. Now one might be tempted to suggest that at the level of the will we are free provided we could have willed to do otherwise *if* we had been in different circumstances or had different motives – a thesis that in no way conflicts with the act of will being causally necessitated by our actual motives and circumstances. Such a suggestion of what it means to have free will fully merits, I believe, the contempt and ridicule that Kant meant when he spoke of a "wretched subterfuge" and William James meant when he spoke of "a quagmire of evasion."[8] If Lockean freedom is to be saved, we need a better account of free will than this suggestion provides.

In his discussion of Locke's account of freedom, Leibniz generally endorses Locke's view but points out its failure to provide any account of free will. He suggests two accounts of free will, one in contrast to the bondage of the passions, an account drawn from the Stoics; a second in contrast to necessity, an account that is Leibniz's own.[9] Although neither account removes the causal necessitation of the will, the first account does appear to soften the blow. Leibniz remarks: "the Stoics said that only the wise man is free; and one's mind is indeed not free when it is possessed by a great passion, for then one cannot will as one should, i.e., with proper deliberation. It is in that way that God alone is perfectly free, and that created minds are free only in proportion as they are above passion; . . ."[10] Here we have a nice amendment to Lockean freedom. For an action to be free it must not only be willed and such that we could have done otherwise if we had willed otherwise, but also the act of will must have been free in the sense of resulting at least partially from the proper exercise of reason. If the passions totally determine the act of will and the consequent action, we need not say that the person acts freely. However, if the judgments of reason and our circumstances totally determine our will so that given those judgments and circumstances no other act of will was possible, we can still say that we act freely, provided we could have done otherwise had we chosen or willed to do otherwise, for as rational beings we are willing as we should. This amendment, I believe, softens the necessitarian view; but it fails to solve the basic problem. For to will as we should is one thing, and to will freely is another. The problem with Lockean freedom is not that it fails to rule out necessitation of the will *by the passions*; the problem is that it fails to rule out the necessitation of the will *period*. It is time to turn to our second concept of freedom.

II. Reidian Freedom

The clearest statement of our second concept of freedom is by the Scottish philosopher, Thomas Reid. Here is what Reid says.

> By the *liberty* of a moral agent, I understand, a power over the determinations of his own will.
>
> If, in any action, he had power to will what he did, or not to will it, in that action he is free. But if, in every voluntary action, the determination of his will be the necessary consequence of something involuntary in the state of his mind, or of something in his external circumstances, he is not free; he has not what I call the liberty of a moral agent, but is subject to necessity.[11]

It is helpful, I believe, to divide Reid's view of freedom into two themes: a negative thesis and a positive thesis. The negative thesis is this: if some action of ours is free then our decision or act of will to do that action cannot have been causally necessitated by any prior events, whether they be internal or external. If I have a machine hooked up to your brain in such a manner that my flip of a switch causally necessitates your decision to get up and walk across the room, it follows that you are not free in your action of getting up and walking across the room. In this case your decision to do that action is causally necessitated by some prior *external* event, the flipping of the switch. On the other hand, if your decision to do the act was causally necessitated by your motives and circumstances, then the causally necessitating event is *internal*, and the action again is not free. You are free in some action only if your decision to do that act is not causally necessitated by any involuntary event, whether internal or external. This is the negative thesis.

All too often, it is assumed that this second concept of freedom, which I have called *Reidian freedom*, consists in nothing more than this negative thesis. And the major objection of the necessitarians to Reidian freedom is based on this assumption. According to Reid, our free acts of will are not caused by any prior events, whether external or internal. And the difficulty with this, so the objection goes, is that it conflicts with the view that every event has a cause, a view that most eighteenth century philosophers, including Reid, accepted. What this objection reveals, however, is that the necessitarians hold to only one sort of causation, causation by prior events. Thus once it was denied that our free acts of will are caused by any prior events, the necessitarians concluded that the advocates of Reidian freedom were committed to the view that our free acts of will are totally uncaused events. But Reid, following Samuel Clarke, Edmund Law, and others, believed in another sort of causation, causation by persons or agents. And what they affirmed in their positive thesis is that free acts of will are caused by the agent whose acts they are. Reid, then, no less than the necessitarians affirmed that all events, including our free acts of will, are caused. As he remarks: "I grant, then, that an effect uncaused is a contradiction, and that an event uncaused is an absurdity. The question that remains is whether a volition, undetermined by motives, is an event uncaused. This I deny. The cause of the volition is the man that willed it."[12]

What we've just seen is that the advocates of Reidian freedom agree with the necessitarians in holding that every event has a cause. What they deny is that every event has an event-cause. In the case of our free acts of will the cause is not some prior event but the agent whose acts they are. To understand Reidian freedom, therefore, we need to look at the foundation on which it rests, the idea of agent causation.

Reid believed that the original notion of "cause" is that of an agent who brings about changes in the world by *acting*. To be such a cause Reid held that a thing or substance must satisfy three conditions: first, it must have the power to bring about the change in the world; second, it must exert its power to bring about that change; third, it must have the power not to bring about the change. It will help us understand and appreciate his view if we contrast two examples. Suppose a piece of zinc is dropped into some acid, and the acid dissolves the zinc. In this example, we might say that the acid has the power to bring about a certain change in the zinc. We might also be willing to say that in this instance the acid *exerted* its power to bring about this change, it *exerted* its power to dissolve the zinc. But can we reasonably say that the acid had the power not to bring about this change? Clearly we cannot. The acid has no power to refrain from dissolving the zinc. When the conditions are right, the acid must dissolve the zinc. So Reid's third condition is not satisfied. The acid, therefore, is not an agent-cause of the zinc's dissolving. Turning to our second example, suppose I invite you to write down the word "cause." Let's suppose that you have the power to do so and that you exert that power with the result that a change in the world occurs, and the world "cause" is written on a piece of paper. Here, when we look at Reid's third condition, we believe that it does obtain. We believe that you had the power to refrain from initiating your action of writing down the word "cause." The acid had no power to refrain from dissolving the zinc, but you had the power not to bring about your action of writing down the word "cause." If these things are so, then in this instance you are a true agent-cause of a certain change in the world, for you had the power to bring about that change, you exerted that power by acting, and finally, you had the power not to bring about that change.

There is one very important point to note concerning Reid's idea of agent causation. We sometimes speak of causing someone to cause something else. But if we fully understand Reid's notion of agent causation we can see, I think, that no event or agent can cause someone to agent-cause some change. And this, again, is because of Reid's third condition of agent causation, the condition that requires that you have the power to refrain from bringing about the change. Suppose an event occurs that causes you to cause something to happen – some boiling water spills on your hand, say, causing you to drop the pot of boiling water. Now if the spilling of the boiling water on your hand really does cause you to bring about your dropping the pot, if it causally necessitates you to cause your dropping of the pot, then given the spilling of the boiling water on your hand it wasn't in your power not to bring about your dropping tie pot. But you are the agent-cause of some change only if it was in your power at the time not to cause that change. This being so, it is quite impossible that anything should ever cause you to agent-cause some change. Since having the power not to cause a change is required for you to be the agent-cause of some change, and since being caused to cause some change implies that you cannot refrain from causing that change, it follows that no one can be caused to agent-cause a change. If you are the agent-cause of some change, it follows that you were not caused to agent-cause that change.

Having taken a brief look at Reid's notion of agent causation, we can return to what I have been calling Reidian freedom. According to Reidian freedom, any action we perform as a result of our act of will to do that action is a free action, provided that we were the agent-cause of the act of will to perform that action. And since to agent-cause an act of will includes the power not to cause it, we can say that every act of will resulting in *a free* action is an act of will we had power to produce and power not to produce. As Reid says: "If, in any action, he had power to will what he did, or not to will it, in that action he is free."

Suppose someone wills to perform a certain action, say revealing a secret of great importance that he has been entrusted with. Since his act of will must have a cause, either it is caused by the agent himself – in which case he is the agent-cause of that act of will and his action is free – or something else causes his act of will and his action, although voluntary, is not free. In some cases, it will not be difficult to decide the matter. Suppose our person has been offered a small bribe and, as a result, reveals the important secret. Here, we would judge that the person does act freely, believing that the desire for the bribe is not sufficient of itself to cause the agent to will as he did. On the other hand, if our agent is placed on the rack and made to suffer intensely over a period of time and finally, after much pain, divulges the secret, we would all judge that the intense pain was such as to cause directly the volition to reveal the important secret. The volition was not agent-caused and the action of revealing the secret was not *free*. But these are the easy cases. Clearly, between these two extremes there is a continuum of cases in which we would find the judgment between agent-cause and other cause extraordinarily difficult to make with any assurance. To help us here, we need to note another important element in Reid's theory of human freedom.

Reid believes that freedom is a *power*, a power over the determinations of our will. Now power is something that can come in degrees: you may have more or less of it. Presumably, under torture on the rack, your power over your will may be reduced to zero and your freedom thereby destroyed. On the other hand, your desire for a small bribe is unlikely to diminish significantly your power not to will to reveal the secret. Between these two extremes the mounting strength of your desires and passions will make it increasingly difficult for you to refrain from willing to reveal the secret. But so long as their strength is not irresistible, if you do will to reveal it, you will be at least a *partial agent-cause* of your act of will, and, therefore, will act with a certain degree of freedom and a corresponding degree of responsibility. Of course, people may differ considerably in terms of the power they possess over their wills. So a desire of a given strength may overwhelm one person while only slightly diminishing another person's power over his will. Therefore, in order to determine whether a person acted freely and with what degree of freedom, we need to judge two things: we need to judge the degree of power over the will that the person possesses *apart* from the influence of his desires and passions; and we need to judge the strength of his desires and passions. Clearly these are matters about which at best only reasonable or probable judgments can be made.

Leibniz once remarked concerning a version of the free will doctrine: "What is asserted is impossible, but if it came to pass it would be harmful."[13] This remark nicely captures most of the objections to the view of Reid and other free will advocates. For these objections divide into those that argue that the view is impossible because it is internally inconsistent or inconsistent with some well-established principle of causality or explanation, and those that argue that the possession of free will would be harmful because the agent's actions would then be capricious, uninfluenced by motives, rewards or punishment. I want here to look at two different objections that fall into the first category. The first of these, and by far the most popular, is, I believe, a spurious objection. Since it is spurious, I will bury it in a footnote.[14] The second, however, is a very serious objection, revealing, I believe, a real difficulty in Reid's agent-cause account of freedom.

The second objection (the serious one), like the first, arrives at the absurd conclusion that any action requires an infinite series of antecedent events, each produced by the agent who produces the action. This absurd conclusion, I believe, does follow from Reid's view of agent-causation in conjunction with the principle that every event has a cause. I propose here to explain how this absurdity is embedded in Reid's theory and what can be done to remove it.

On Reid's theory, when an agent wills some action, the act of will is itself an event and, as such, requires a cause. If the act of will is free, its cause is not some event, it is the agent whose act of will it is. Being the cause of the act of will, the agent must satisfy Reid's three conditions of agent-causation. Thus the agent must have had the power to bring about the act of will as well as the power to refrain from bringing about the act of will, and she must have *exerted* her power to bring about the act of will. It is the last of these conditions that generates an infinite regress of events that an agent must cause if she is to cause her act of will. For what it tells us is that to produce the act of will the agent must *exert* her power to bring about the act of will. Now an exertion of power is itself an event. As such, it too must have a cause. On Reid's view the cause must again be the agent herself. But to have caused this exertion the agent must have had the power to bring it about and must have *exerted* that power. Each exertion of power is itself an event which the agent can cause only by having the power to cause it and by *exerting* that power. As Reid reminds us, "In order to the production of any effect, there must be in the cause, not only power, but the exertion of that power: for power that is not exerted produces no effect."[15] The result of this principle, however, is that in order to produce any act of will whatever, the agent must cause an infinite number of exertions. Reid's theory of agent-causation, when conjoined with the principle that every event has a cause, leads to the absurdity of an infinite regress of agent-produced exertions for every act of will the agent produces.

It is remarkable that Reid appears never to have seen this difficulty in his theory. Occasionally he joins the causal principle and his view of agent-causation into a single remark, with the result that the difficulty fairly leaps up from the page. For example, in discussing Leibniz's view that every action has a sufficient reason, Reid remarks: "If the meaning of the question be, was there a cause of the action? Undoubtedly there was: of every event there must be a cause, that had power sufficient to produce it, and that exerted that power for the purpose."[16] If exertions of power are events – and what else could they be? – the infinite regress of exertions produced by the agent who performs any action is abundantly apparent in this remark. Perhaps Reid didn't see the problem because he always had in mind the basic distinction between the *effects* agents produce by their actions and the *actions* of the agents by which they produce those effects. With this distinction in mind, it is natural to suppose that *everything* an agent causes (the effects) she causes not simply by virtue of having a certain power but by acting, by exerting that power. Put this way, Reid's notion that an agent can cause something only by acting, by *exerting* her power, is intuitively attractive – so attractive, perhaps, that one may be blind to the difficulty that appears when actions themselves are held to be among the things that an agent causes.

One solution to the difficulty requires that we view some acts of the agent as caused by the agent, but not caused by some *exertion* of the agent's power to produce them. Perhaps we should think of the act of will as in some way a special sort of action, a *basic act*. A basic act of an agent is one that she causes but not by any exertion of power or any other act. Short of some such view, it seems that we must either accept the absurdity of the infinite regress, view some act of the agent as itself uncaused (thus abandoning the causal principle), or take the view that an act of will is not itself an event and, therefore, does not fall under the causal principle. This last move, however, would leave the act of will as a surd in Reid's theory and plainly conflicts with his stated position that acts of will are effects. "I consider the determination of the will as an effect."[17]

The solution I've proposed requires a significant change in Reid's view of agent-causation. Not every act of the agent can be produced by the agent only by the agent's *exerting* her power to produce it. Acts of will that are produced by the agent whose acts they are, we shall say, are such that the agent causes them but not by any other act or any exertion of the power she has to produce the acts of will. We thus can halt the regress of acts of exertions that is implied by the conjunction of the causal principle and Reid's analysis of what it is to be a cause "in the strict and proper sense." The price, of course, is a significant modification of Reid's account of agent-causation.

Can we afford this price? Many philosophers would agree with Jonathan Edwards in holding that it is simply impossible that the agent should *cause* his act of will without an *exertion* of his power to produce that act of will, an exertion that is *distinct* from the act of will that is produced.[18]

The answer to Edwards is that although some actions (moving one's arm, e.g.) can be caused by the agent only by the agent exerting his power to produce his action of moving his arm, other actions such as acts of will are produced directly by the agent and not by means of exertions that are distinct from the acts of will produced. To deny the possibility of the latter is simply to claim that ultimately only events can be causes of events – thus if there is no exertion of power by the agent (and no other event causes the volition), no act of will can be produced. But the whole idea of agent-causation is that agents are causes of events, that in addition to event-causes there are causes of a wholly different kind – agents. If we take the view that persons really are active, rather than passive, in the production of their acts, then the modification I've suggested is precisely what one might expect the theory of agency embraced by Reid ultimately to imply. For, on the one hand, it is Reid's view that events and circumstances and other agents do not cause the person to agent-cause his acts of will. If other agents or prior events cause the person to do something, then the person lacks power to refrain and, therefore, is not the agent-cause of those doings: he is in fact passive with respect to his actions. And, on the other hand, if the person is the agent-cause of some act of his then on pain of infinite regress there must be some exertion or act he brings about without engaging in some other exertion or act in order to bring it about. In short, once we fully grasp the idea of agent-causation we can see, I believe, that it implies that when an agent causes his action there is some event (an act of will, perhaps) that the agent causes without bringing about any other event as a means to producing it.[19]

III. Reidian Freedom and Responsibility

We started with Johnson's remark that although all theory is against free will, all experience or practice is for it. Among the several arguments Reid advanced in favor of free will, his argument from our *practice of* holding persons morally responsible for their actions and decisions is undoubtedly the strongest. I believe that Reid's argument from the fact of moral responsibility to the existence of Reidian freedom merits careful examination. But I have no time here to do that. Instead, I want to sharpen our grasp of Reidian freedom by considering just what it implies with respect to the vexing question of whether the agent could have done or willed otherwise. For there are, I believe, good reasons to doubt the traditional claim that an agent is morally responsible for doing A only if she could have avoided doing A. And there appear to be good reasons to doubt the claim that an agent is morally responsible for doing A only if she could have refrained from willing to do A. Now if this should be so, then if Reidian freedom implies either of these claims, it will *not* be true that an agent is morally responsible only if she possesses Reidian freedom – Reid's strongest argument for Reidian freedom will stand refuted.

According to Locke, the agent freely does A only if she could have refrained from doing A had she so willed. Reid says that freedom must include power over the determinations of our will. Perhaps then, Reidian freedom is simply Lockean freedom with the addition of the power to will to do A and the power to will to refrain from doing A.[20] If so, I'm afraid that moral responsibility does not entail Reidian freedom. For moral responsibility does not entail Lockean freedom. One of Locke's examples is of a man who wills to stay in a room, not knowing that he is locked in. We may hold such a person responsible even though he would not have been able to avoid staying in the room had he willed not to stay in the room. For the agent who willingly does what he does, believing it to be in his power to do otherwise, must be distinguished from the person who stays in the room unwillingly because he is unable to leave. And if such a person is morally accountable for what he does, moral responsibility does not entail Reidian freedom *if* Reidian freedom is correctly understood as Lockean freedom with the addition of power over the will. But a careful look at Reid's account of a free action shows that it is a mistake so to understand Reidian freedom. What he says is this: "if, in any action, he had power to will what he did, or not to will it, in that action he is free." There is nothing in Reid's account to suggest that the agent must have had the power to do otherwise had he so willed. What Reid says is that if a person wills to perform some action and does so, then he performs that action freely provided he had the power not to will to do that action.

An interesting challenge to the idea that we are morally responsible for our action only if we could have refrained from willing it has been advanced by Frankfurt and Nozick.[21] To see the challenge, consider the following example. Suppose a mad scientist has gained access to your volitional capacity and not only can tell what act of will you are about to bring about but, worse yet, can send electrical currents into your brain that will cause a particular act of will to occur even though it is not the act of will that you would have brought about if left to your own devices. We will suppose that you are deliberating on a matter of great concern: killing Jones. Our mad scientist happens to be interested in Jones's going on to his reward, but he wants Jones to die by your hand. His complicated machinery tells him that you are about to conclude your deliberations by willing *not* to kill Jones. Quickly, he pushes the buttons sending certain currents into your brain with the result that the volition to kill Jones occurs in you and results, let us say, in your actually killing Jones. Clearly you are not here morally accountable for your act of will and subsequent action of killing Jones. Were matters left to you, you would have willed not to kill Jones and would not have killed him. Although on Reid's account of this case it would be true that you willed to kill Jones, it is also true that you were not the agent-cause of your act of will and are therefore not morally accountable for your willing and your action.

Our second case is similar to, but also crucially different from, the first case. The mad scientist is intent on seeing to it that Jones is killed by your hand. But rather than activate the machine to cause your act of will to kill Jones, he would prefer that you bring about that act of will and the subsequent action of killing Jones. This time, however, your deliberations result in your act of will to kill Jones. The mad scientist could and would have caused that act of will in you had you been going to will not to kill Jones. But no such action on his part was necessary. There is a process in place (the machine, etc.) that assures that you shall will to kill Jones. But the process is activated *only if* you are not going to initiate your act of will to kill Jones. Given the machine, it was not in your power to avoid willing to kill Jones. But this fact *played no role* in what actually led to your willing to kill Jones and the actual killing that resulted. In this case, we do wish to hold you morally responsible for your act of will and the resulting action. And this is so even though it was not in your power to prevent your willing to kill Jones and not in your power to refrain from killing Jones.

Frankfurt argues that the fact that there are circumstances that make it impossible for an agent to avoid performing a certain action diminishes or extinguishes moral accountability for the action only if those circumstances in some way *bring it about* that the agent performs the action in question. This is true in our first case, where the mad scientist pushes the buttons that send the current causing your volition to kill Jones. Here the circumstances that prevent you from *not* willing to kill Jones *bring about* your volition to kill Jones. But in the second case, the circumstances that make it impossible for you not to will to kill Jones *play no role* in bringing it about that you willed to kill Jones. As Frankfurt remarks: "For those circumstances, by hypothesis, actually had nothing to do with his having done what he did. He would have done precisely the same thing, . . . , even if they had not prevailed."[22] It is because these circumstances play no role in what the agent willed and did that the agent bears moral responsibility for his volition and act even though it was not in his power to refrain from doing what he did. I believe Frankfurt is right about this matter. What remains to be seen, however, is whether Reid's basic intuition of a necessary connection between moral accountability and power over the will is unable to accommodate the case in which the agent is morally accountable but cannot prevent willing to kill Jones.

The second mad scientist example shows that an agent may be morally accountable for an act of will to do A even though it is not in the agent's power not to will that action. This certainly *appears* to conflict with Reid's theory. But we need to recall here that what is *crucial for* Reid's view of moral accountability is that the person be the *agent-cause* of her volition to do A. His view is that the agent is morally accountable for her voluntary action only if she is the agent-cause of her volition to do A. Now we already have seen that she may be the agent-cause of her volition to do A and not have it in her power not to will that action. This is what we learned, in part, from our second mad scientist case. But here, I believe, we need to distinguish between

1 It was in the agent's power not to will doing A.

and

2 It was in the agent's power *not* to cause her volition to do A.

In our second mad scientist case, (1) is false. But (2) is not false. The agent does have the power not to cause her volition to do A. The mad scientist has so arranged matters that the machine automatically causes the volition to do A in our agent if, but only if, the agent is about not to will to do A. This being so, (1) is clearly false. The agent cannot prevent her willing to do A; for if she does not cause her willing to do A the machine will cause her act of will to do A. But it still may be up to the agent whether *she* shall be the cause of her volition to do A. This power, Reid would argue, depends on a number of factors: the will of God, the continued existence of the agent, the absence of prior internal events and circumstances determining the occurrence of the volition to do A, etc. It also depends on the mad scientist's decision to activate the machine *only if* the agent is about not to will to do A. The scientist can cause our agent to will to do A. He does this by causing that act of will in the agent.[23] But if he does so then the agent does not agent-cause her volition to do A. The real agent-cause is the scientist. So if the agent has the power to cause her volition to do A she also has the power *not to cause* that volition. If she does not cause the volition and the machine activates, she, nevertheless, wills to do A – but *she* is not the cause of that act of will. I propose, therefore, the following as representing Reid's basic intuition concerning the connection between moral accountability and power:

(P) A person is morally accountable for his action A only if he causes the volition to do A and it was in his power not to cause his volition to do A.[24]

(I believe this principle expresses Reid's view of our moral accountability for volitions as well. Simply replace "action A" with "volition to do A.")

Principle P accords with our intuitions concerning both of the mad scientist's cases. In the first case, when the machinery causes the volition to kill Jones, we do not wish to hold the agent morally accountable for the volition and its causal products. After all, if left to himself he would have willed to refrain from killing Jones. In the second case, where the machinery is not activated, we do hold the agent responsible for the volition and the action of killing Jones. And this is just what principle P will support. For the agent caused his volition to kill Jones and had it in his power not to cause that volition. I suggest, therefore, that the Frankfurt–Nozick examples do not refute the thesis that moral responsibility for a voluntary action implies Reidian freedom with respect to that action.[25]

Conclusion

Some philosophical questions eventually yield to fairly definitive answers, answers which succeeding generations of philosophers accept, thereby contributing to our sense of progress in the discipline. Other philosophical questions seem to defy progress in the sense of definitive answers that are commonly accepted. Progress regarding them consists largely in deeper understanding and clarity concerning the questions and their possible answers. These are the deep philosophical questions. My conviction is that the question of human freedom is of the latter sort. I know that by setting forth the two concepts of freedom that were at the center of the eighteenth century controversy over freedom and necessity, and by criticizing the one, Lockean freedom, and recommending the other, Reidian freedom, I have not contributed to philosophical progress in the first sense. I haven't given any definitive answer. And in these compatibilist days, I certainly haven't given any answer that would be commonly accepted in my own department, let alone the discipline. My hope is that I have made some of these issues clearer and more understandable and have thereby contributed to philosophical progress in the second sense, helping us to grasp more clearly the philosophical question of human freedom and its relation both to causality and to moral responsibility.

Notes

1   Thus Thomas Reid remarks: "Power is not an object of any of our external senses, nor even an object of consciousness" (*Essays on the Active Powers of Man*, IV, ch. 1, p. 512; references are to the 1983 printing by Georg Olms Verlag of *The Works of Thomas Reid DD*, 8th ed., edited by Sir William Hamilton [James Thin, 1895]).

2   I am grateful to the distinguished Johnson scholar, Donald Green, for pointing this out to me.

3   Don Locke in "Three Concepts of Free Action," *Proceedings of the Aristotelian Society* (suppl., 1975), p. 96. fails to see that John Locke distinguishes between a voluntary and a free act. Thus he wrongly interprets Locke as holding "that to act freely is to act as you want to: the man who wants to get out of a locked room does not remain there freely but, Locke insists, a man who wants to stay there, to speak to a friend, does stay freely, even if the door is locked."

4   *An Essay Concerning Human Understanding*, Peter H. Nidditch, ed. (Oxford: Clarendon Press, 1975), bk. II, section 33.

5   There is an objection by J. L. Austin that also should be considered, since it attacks

a point that is assumed by the other objections. Locke and Collins, as we just saw, took the view that given the causes of your action A, you could not have done anything other than A. Yet this does not preclude it being true that you could have done something else if you had willed to do something else. For with a difference in the causes, we might expect a difference in our powers. Now this nice harmony of causal necessity and freedom of action presupposes that the "if" in statements of the form "S could have done X if S had chosen or willed to do X" is an "if" of causal condition. And Austin had an apparently devastating argument to show that the "if" in "S could have done X if S had chosen or willed to do X" is not the "if" of causal condition. (See "Ifs and Cans," *Proceedings of the British Academy*, 42 (1956), pp. 107–32.) The argument is this: if we consider an "if" of causal condition, as in the statement "This zinc will dissolve if placed in that acid," we can note two points. First, it will follow that if this zinc does not dissolve then it has not been placed in that acid. Second, it will not follow simpliciter that this zinc will dissolve. Just the opposite holds, however, of statements of the form "S could have done X if S had chosen or willed to do X." First, it will not follow that if S could not have done X, then S has not chosen or willed to do X. And second, it will follow simpliciter that S could have done X. From these premises Austin concludes that the "if" in "S could have done X if S had chosen or willed to do X" is not the "if" of causal condition. But all that really follows from these premises is that the "if" in "S could have done X if S had chosen or willed to do X" does not present a condition of the *main clause*, "S could have done X." It may still be, for all Austin has shown, an "if" of causal condition of something else. What else? Clearly, as Kurt Baler has argued, it would have to be of S's doing X ("Could and Would," *Analysis*, 13 [suppl., 1963], pp. 20–29). The "if" in "S could have done X if S had chosen or willed to do X" is an "if" of causal condition of the doing of X by S. What statements of this form tell us is that a set of conditions necessary for S's doing X obtained at the time in question, and had S chosen or willed to do X there would then have been a set of conditions sufficient for S's doing X. On this account, "S could have done X if S had chosen or willed to do X" implies the genuinely conditional statement form, "S would have done X if S had chosen or willed to do X." So Austin's argument fails to establish that Locke and Collins were wrong to suppose that the "if" in "S could have done X if S had chosen or willed to do X" is an "if" of condition.

6 *Theodicy*, Austin Farrer, ed., and E. M. Huggard, trans. (LaSalle, IL: Open Court, 1985), para. 324.

7 These two objections, and others, are expressed by Reid, Clarke, and Edmund Law. Perhaps their most forceful presentation is contained in Clarke's stinging attack on Collin's work. See *Remarks upon a Book, entitled, A Philosophical Enquiry Concerning Human Liberty* (1717), in Samuel Clarke, *The Works* (1738), vol. 4. The 1738 edition has been reprinted by Garland Publishing, 1978.

8 See Kant's *Critique of Practical Reason*, Lewis W. Beck, trans. (Indianapolis: Bobbs-Merrill Co., 1956), p. 99. Also see W. James's "The Dilemma of Determinism," in *The Writings of William James*, John J. McDermott, ed. (Chicago: The University of Chicago Press, 1977), p. 590.

9 In his second account of free will, Leibniz insists that the act of will must be free in the sense of not being necessitated by the motives and circumstances that give rise to it. His often repeated dictum on this matter is that motives "incline without necessitating." This remark has the appearance of giving the free will advocate just what he wants, the power to have willed otherwise even though the motives and

circumstances be unchanged. But Leibniz meant no such thing. The motive that inclines most determines the will and the action, just as the weight that is heaviest determines the movement of the balance. Motives and circumstances necessitate the act of will in the sense that it is logically or causally impossible that those motives and circumstances should obtain and the act of will not obtain. Leibniz's claim that they don't necessitate the act of will means only that the act of will *itself* is not thereby rendered an absolute or logical necessity. Since Spinoza, Hobbes, and Collins held that the act of will is itself absolutely necessary, Leibniz's point is well taken. But, as we noted, it does nothing to remove the causal necessity of the act of will.

10   *New Essays on Human Understanding*, P. Remnant and J. Bennett, trans. and ed. (Cambridge: Cambridge University Press, 1982), bk. II, ch. xxi, sect 8.

11   *Active Powers*, IV, ch. 1, p. 599.

12   Letter to Dr James Gregory, 1793, in Hamilton, *Works*, p. 87.

13   "Observations on the book concerning 'The Origin of Evil'," in *Theodicy*, p. 406.

14   The spurious objection is that the doctrine of the freedom of the will implies that each act of will that is free is itself the result of a prior act of will, ad infinitum. According to the free will position, an action is free provided it is willed and the agent freely determined or brought about that act of will. But, so the spurious objection goes, to determine freely an act of will is to will freely that act of will. So an act of will is freely determined only if it is freely chosen. But an agent freely chooses an act of will only if his choice of that act of will is itself freely determined by the agent, in which case the choice of the act of will is itself the result of a prior free choice by the agent. And so we are off to the races, each determination of the will by the agent being preceded by an infinite series of determinations of the will by the agent. This objection fails, however, because it supposes that what it is for the agent to determine his will (that is, bring it about that he wills X, rather than something else) is for the agent to *will* that his will be determined in a certain manner. (See, for example, Jonathan Edwards, *Freedom of the Will*, Paul Ramsey, ed. [New Haven, CT: Yale University Press, 1957], p. 172). But it is very doubtful that any free will advocate held this view. Many free will advocates attributed to the agent a power of self-determination, a selfmoving principle. But by this they meant only that when the volitional act is produced by the self-moving principle, it is produced by the agent himself and not by any other thing or agent. (See "Unpublished Letters of Thomas Reid to Lord Kames, 1762–1782," collected by Ian Simpson Ross, *Texan Studies in Literature and Language* 7 [1965], p. 51.) They did not mean that in causing his volition the agent first chose or willed to produce that volition. To attribute such a view to them is to misunderstand what they claimed. According to the free will advocates, the soul or mind determines the will but does not do so by choosing or willing that the mind will, rather than some other act. This objection, therefore, fails.

15   *Active Powers*, TV, ch. II, p. 603.

16   Ibid., ch. IX, p. 625.

17   Ibid., ch. I, p. 602.

18   See Edwards, *Freedom of the Will*, pp. 175–76.

19   The solution I present in the text requires a major modification of Reid's theory of agent causation: dropping the requirement that the agent must *exercise* his power to bring about an act of will if the agent is to *cause* that act of will. There is, however, a way of solving the problem of the infinite regress that leaves Reid's

theory intact. The whole problem vanishes if we take the view that the *exercise* of the agent's power (in order to produce his volition) is not itself an *event*. Not being an event, we require no cause of it, thus preventing the regress from starting. Is there any basis for such a view? Perhaps so. First, we must note that on Reid's view an event is a *change* in a substance. (Actually, Reid also includes the coming into existence of a substance as an event.) The occurrence of a volition in the agent is an event. The agent causes that event by exercising his power to cause it. What then of the agent's *exercise of power*? Here we may turn to Aristotle and his view of a *self-mover*. A self-mover is distinguished from a moved-mover. The latter (for example, a stick moving a stone) has a capacity to bring about movement in something else (the stone), but the exercise of that capacity is itself a movement. The *exercise* of the moved-mover's capacity to bring about motion in another is, therefore, an event. But the agent who causes the stick to move must be an unmoved mover – the exercise of its capacity to cause movement in another is *not itself a movement*. Not being a movement, it is not a change in a substance and is, therefore, not an event. Thus Aristotle holds that a *self-mover* has a part that is moved (undergoes a change) and a part that moves but is not itself in motion (does not undergo a change). The part that moves but is not itself in motion must, of course, *exercise* its capacity to produce motion in the part that is moved. But this *exercise* of the unmoved part's capacity to produce motion is not itself a change in the part that is not itself in motion (not itself a change in the part that is an unmoved mover; see Aristotle's *Physics*, bk. viii, sections 4 and 5). Following Aristotle, we might take Reid to hold that the exercise of the agent's power to produce the volition to do A is *not itself* a change in the agent, it is not a change the agent undergoes. Now the causal principle, as Reid interprets it, holds that every event (every change in a substance) has a cause. The exertion of power to produce a *basic* change (e.g., an act of will), however, is not itself a change the substance undergoes. Therefore, it is not an event, and, therefore, does not require a cause. It would be an interesting and important addition to historical scholarship to see if Reid's theory can bear this interpretation.

20   For such an account of Reid, see Timothy Duggan's essay, "Active Power and the Liberty of Moral Agents," in Stephen F. Barker and Tom L. Beauchamp, eds, *Thomas Reid: Critical Interpretations* (Philadelphia: Philosophical Monographs, 1976), p. 106.

21   See Harry G. Frankfurt's "Alternate Possibilities and Moral Responsibility," *Journal of Philosophy*, 66 (1969), pp. 829–39.

22   Frankfurt, "Responsibility," p. 837.

23   I take Reid to hold (rightly) that causing a volition to do A in an agent is to cause *the agent's willing to do A*. Thus, when an agent wills to do A we can raise the question of whether the cause of his so willing is the agent himself or something else.

24   Of course, we hold persons accountable for actions that they do not will. If I will to open my car door and do so, with the result that I knock you off your bicycle, I may be accountable for what I did through culpable ignorance – knocking you off your bicycle – even though I did not will to do it. But we may take Reid's account of freedom as what is entailed by those *voluntary* actions for which we are morally responsible.

25   Could not a supersophisticated scientist so arrange his machine that if the agent were about not to cause his volition to do A the machine would activate, causing

him to *cause* his volition to do A? If so, and if our agent does cause his volition, with the result that the machine is not activated, isn't our agent responsible even though it is not in his power *not to cause* his volition? The Reidian reply to this is that it is *conceptually impossible* to cause an *agent* to cause (in Reid's sense) his volition. For an agent has active power to cause only if he has power not to cause. This last is a conceptual truth for Reid. "Power to produce any effect, implies power not to produce it" (*Active Powers*, IV, ch. I, p. 523).

Freedom of the Will and the Concept of a Person
Harry G. Frankfurt

Harry G. Frankfurt is a Professor of Philosophy at Princeton University and best known for his work on Descartes and freedom and determinism. Frankfurt is a compatibilist who notes that the free will discussion has focused very little on the problem of free will. Frankfurt argues that persons, unlike animals, have not only first-order desires, such as the desire to smoke, but also second-order desires, namely desires about the first-order desires. I might, for example, desire not to have the desire to smoke. According to Frankfurt we act freely if and only if we do as we desire to and, in addition, have a second-order desire to act on that desire.

What philosophers have lately come to accept as analysis of the concept of a person is not actually analysis of *that* concept at all. Strawson, whose usage represents the current standard, identifies the concept of a person as "the concept of a type of entity such that *both* predicates ascribing states of consciousness *and* predicates ascribing corporeal characteristics . . . are equally applicable to a single individual of that single type."[1] But there are many entities besides persons that have both mental and physical properties. As it happens – though it seems extraordinary that this should be so – there is no common English word for the type of entity Strawson has in mind, a type that includes not only human beings but animals of various lesser species as well. Still, this hardly justifies the misappropriation of a valuable philosophical term.

Whether the members of some animal species are persons is surely not to be settled merely by determining whether it is correct to apply to them, in addition to predicates ascribing corporeal characteristics, predicates that ascribe states of consciousness. It does violence to our language to endorse the application of the term "person" to those numerous creatures which do have both psychological and material properties but which are manifestly not persons in any normal sense of the word. This misuse of language is doubtless innocent of any theoretical error. But although the offense is "merely verbal," it does significant harm. For it gratuitously diminishes our philosophical vocabulary, and it increases the likelihood that we will overlook the important area of inquiry with which the term "person" is most naturally associated. It might have been expected that no problem would be of more central and persistent concern to philosophers than that of understanding what we ourselves essentially are. Yet this problem is so generally neglected that it has been possible to make off with its very name almost without being noticed and, evidently, without evoking any widespread feeling of loss.

There is a sense in which the word "person" is merely the singular form of "people" and in which both terms connote no more than membership in a certain biological species. In those senses of the word which are of greater philosophical interest, however, the criteria for being a person do not serve primarily to distinguish the members of our own species from the members of other species. Rather, they are designed to capture those attributes which are the subject of our most humane concern with ourselves and the source of what we regard as most important and most problematical in our lives. Now these attributes would be of equal significance to us even if they were not in fact peculiar and common to the members of our own species. What interests us most in the human condition would not interest us less if it were also a feature of the condition of other creatures as well.

Our concept of ourselves as persons is not to be understood, therefore, as a concept of attributes that are necessarily species-specific. It is conceptually possible that members of novel or even of familiar nonhuman species should be persons; and it is also conceptually possible that some members of the human species are not persons. We do in fact assume, on the other hand, that no member of another species is a person. Accordingly, there is a presumption that what is essential to persons is a set of characteristics that we generally suppose – whether rightly or wrongly – to be uniquely human.

It is my view that one essential difference between persons and other creatures is to be found in the structure of a person's will. Human beings are not alone in having desires and motives, or in making choices. They share these things with the members of certain other species, some of whom even appear to engage in deliberation and to make decisions based upon prior thought. It seems to be peculiarly characteristic of humans, however, that they are able to form what I shall call "second-order desires" or "desires of the second order."

Besides wanting and choosing and being moved *to do* this or that, men may also want to have (or not to have) certain desires and motives. They are capable of wanting to be different, in their preferences and purposes, from what they are. Many animals appear to have the capacity for what I shall call "first-order desires" or "desires of the first order," which are simply desires to do or not to do one thing or another. No animal other than man, however, appears to have the capacity for reflective self-evaluation that is manifested in the formation of second-order desires.[2]

I

The concept designated by the verb "to want" is extraordinarily elusive. A statement of the form "*A* wants to *X*" – taken by itself, apart from a context that serves to amplify or to specify its meaning – conveys remarkably little information. Such a statement may be consistent, for example, with each of the following statements: (a) the prospect of doing X elicits no sensation or introspectible emotional response in A; (b) A is unaware that he wants to X; (c) A believes that he does not want to X; (d) A wants to refrain from X-ing; (e) A wants to Y and believes that it is impossible for him both to Y and to X; (f) A does not "really" want to X; (g) *A would rather die than X*; and so on. It is therefore hardly sufficient to formulate the distinction between first-order and second-order desires, as I have done, by suggesting merely that someone has a first-order desire when he wants to do or not to do such-and-such, and that he has a second-order desire when he wants to have or not to have a certain desire of the first order.

As I shall understand them, statements of the form "A wants to X" cover a rather broad range of possibilities.[3] They may be true even when statements like (a) through (g) are true: when A is unaware of any feelings concerning X-ing, when he is unaware that he wants to X, when he deceives himself about what he wants and believes falsely that he does not want to X, when he also has other desires that conflict with his desire to X, or when he is ambivalent. The desires in question may be conscious or unconscious, they need not be univocal, and A may be mistaken about them. There is a further source of uncertainty with regard to statements that identify someone's desires, however, and here it is important for my purposes to be less permissive.

Consider first those statements of the form "A wants to X" which identify first-order desires – that is, statements in which the term "to X" refers to an action. A statement of this kind does not, by itself, indicate the relative strength of A's desire to X. It does not make it clear whether this desire is at all likely to play a decisive role in what A actually does or tries to do. For it may correctly be said that A wants to X even when his desire to X is only one among his desires and when it is far from being paramount among them. Thus, it may be true that A wants to X when he strongly prefers to do something else instead; and it may be true that he wants to X despite the fact that, when he acts, it is not the desire to X that motivates him to do what he does. On the other hand, someone who states that A wants to X may mean to convey that it is this desire that is motivating or moving A to do what he is actually doing or that A will in fact be moved by this desire (unless he changes his mind) when he acts.

It is only when it is used in the second of these ways that, given the special usage of "will" that I propose to adopt, the statement identifies A's will. To identify an agent's will is either to identify the desire (or desires) by which he is motivated in some action he performs or to identify the desire (or desires) by which he will or would be motivated when or if he acts. An agent's will, then, is identical with one or more of his first-order desires. But the notion of the will, as I am employing it, is not coextensive with the notion of first-order desires. It is not the notion of something that merely inclines an agent in some degree to act in a certain way. Rather, it is the notion of an *effective* desire – one that moves (or will or would move) a person all the way to action. Thus the notion of the will is not coextensive with the notion of what an agent intends to do. For even though someone may have a settled intention to do X, he may nonetheless do something else instead of doing X because, despite his intention, his desire to do X proves to be weaker or less effective than some conflicting desire.

Now consider those statements of the form "A wants to X" which identify second-order desires – that is, statements in which the term "to X" refers to a desire of the first order. There are also two kinds of situation in which it may be true that A wants to want to X. In the first place, it might be true of A that he wants to have a desire to X despite the fact that he has a univocal desire, altogether free of conflict and ambivalence, to refrain from X-ing. Someone might want to have a certain desire, in other words, but univocally want that desire to be unsatisfied.

Suppose that a physician engaged in psychotherapy with narcotics addicts believes that his ability to help his patients would be enhanced if he understood better what it is like for them to desire the drug to which they are addicted. Suppose that he is led in this way to want to have a desire for the drug. If it is a genuine desire that he wants, then what he wants is not merely to feel the sensations that addicts characteristically feel when they are gripped by their desires for the drug. What the physician wants, insofar as he wants to have a desire, is to be inclined or moved to some extent to take the drug.

It is entirely possible, however, that, although he wants to be moved by a desire to take the drug, he does not want this desire to be effective. He may not want it to move him all the way to action. He need not be interested in finding out what it is like to take the drug. And insofar as he now wants only to *want* to take it, and not to *take* it, there is nothing in what he now wants that would be satisfied by the drug itself. He may now have, in fact, an altogether univocal desire *not* to take the drug; and he may prudently arrange to make it impossible for him to satisfy the desire he would have if his desire to want the drug should in time be satisfied.

It would thus be incorrect to infer, from the fact that the physician now wants to desire to take the drug, that he already does desire to take it. His second-order desire to be moved to take the drug does not entail that he has a first-order desire to take it. If the drug were now to be administered to him, this might satisfy no desire that is implicit in his desire to want to take it. While he wants to want to take the drug, he may have *no* desire to take it; it may be that *all* he wants is to taste the desire for it. That is, his desire to have a certain desire that he does not have may not be a desire that his will should be at all different than it is.

Someone who wants only in this truncated way to want to X stands at the margin of preciosity, and the fact that he wants to want to X is not pertinent to the identification of his will. There is, however, a second kind of situation that may be described by "A wants to want to X"; and when the statement is used to describe situations of this second kind, then it does pertain to what A wants his will to be. In such cases the statement means that A wants the desire to X to be the desire that moves him effectively to act. It is not merely that he wants the desire to X to be among the desires by which, to one degree or another, he is moved or inclined to act. He wants this desire to be effective – that is, to provide the motive in what he actually does. Now when the statement that A wants to want to X is used in this way, it does entail that A already has a desire to X. It could not be true both that A wants the desire to X to move him into action and that he does not want to X. It is only if he does want to X that he can coherently want the desire to X not merely to be one of his desires but, more decisively, to be his will.[4]

Suppose a man wants to be motivated in what he does by the desire to concentrate on his work. It is necessarily true, if this supposition is correct, that he already wants to concentrate on his work. This desire is now among his desires. But the question of whether or not his second-order desire is fulfilled does not turn merely on whether the desire he wants is one of his desires. It turns on whether this desire is, as he wants it to be, his effective desire or will. If, when the chips are down, it is his desire to concentrate on his work that moves him to do what he does, then what he wants at that time is indeed (in the relevant sense) what he wants to want. If it is some other desire that actually moves him when he acts, on the other hand, then what he wants at that time is not (in the relevant sense) what he wants to want. This will be so despite the fact that the desire to concentrate on his work continues to be among his desires.

II

Someone has a desire of the second order either when he wants simply to have a certain desire or when he wants a certain desire to be his will. In situations of the latter kind, I shall call his second-order desires "second-order volitions" or "volitions of the second order." Now it is having second-order volitions, and not having second-order desires generally, that I regard as essential to being a person. It is logically possible, however unlikely, that there should be an agent with second-order desires but with no volitions of the second order. Such a creature, in my view, would not be a person. I shall use the term "wanton" to refer to agents who have first-order desires but who are not persons because, whether or not they have desires of the second order, they have no second-order volitions.[5]

The essential characteristic of a wanton is that he does not care about his will. His desires move him to do certain things, without its being true of him either that he wants to be moved by those desires or that he prefers to be moved by other desires. The class of wantons includes all nonhuman animals that have desires and all very young children. Perhaps it also includes some adult human beings as well. In any case, adult humans may be more or less wanton; they may act wantonly, in response to first-order desires concerning which they have no volitions of the second order, more or less frequently.

The fact that a wanton has no second-order volitions does not mean that each of his first-order desires is translated heedlessly and at once into action. He may have no opportunity to act in accordance with some of his desires. Moreover, the translation of his desires into action may be delayed or precluded either by conflicting desires of the first order or by the intervention of deliberation. For a wanton may possess and employ rational faculties of a high order. Nothing in the concept of a wanton implies that he cannot reason or that he cannot deliberate concerning how to do what he wants to do. What distinguishes the rational wanton from other rational agents is that he is not concerned with the desirability of his desires themselves. He ignores the question of what his will is to be. Not only does he pursue whatever course of action he is most strongly inclined to pursue, but he does not care which of his inclinations is the strongest.

Thus a rational creature, who reflects upon the suitability to his desires of one course of action or another, may nonetheless be a wanton. In maintaining that the essence of being a person lies not in reason but in will, I am far from suggesting that a creature without reason may be a person. For it is only in virtue of his rational capacities that a person is capable of becoming critically aware of his own will and of forming volitions of the second order. The structure of a person's will presupposes, accordingly, that he is a rational being.

The distinction between a person and a wanton may be illustrated by the difference between two narcotics addicts. Let us suppose that the physiological condition accounting for the addiction is the same in both men, and that both succumb inevitably to their periodic desires for the drug to which they are addicted. One of the addicts hates his addiction and always struggles desperately, although to no avail, against its thrust. He tries everything that he thinks might enable him to overcome his desires for the drug. But these desires are too powerful for him to withstand, and invariably, in the end, they conquer him. He is an unwilling addict, helplessly violated by his own desires.

The unwilling addict has conflicting first-order desires: he wants to take the drug, and he also wants to refrain from taking it. In addition to these first-order desires, however, he has a volition of the second order. He is not a neutral with regard to the conflict between his desire to take the drug and his desire to refrain from taking it. It is the latter desire, and not the former, that he wants to constitute his will; it is the latter desire, rather than the former, that he wants to be effective and to provide the purpose that he will seek to realize in what he actually does.

The other addict is a wanton. His actions reflect the economy of his first-order desires, without his being concerned whether the desires that move him to act are desires by which he wants to be moved to act. If he encounters problems in obtaining the drug or in administering it to himself, his responses to his urges to take it may involve deliberation. But it never occurs to him to consider whether he wants the relations among his desires to result in his having the will he has. The wanton addict may be an animal, and thus incapable of being concerned about his will. In any event he is, in respect of his wanton lack of concern, no different from an animal.

The second of these addicts may suffer a first-order conflict similar to the first-order conflict suffered by the first. Whether he is human or not, the wanton may (perhaps due to conditioning) both want to take the drug and want to refrain from taking it. Unlike the unwilling addict, however, he does not prefer that one of his conflicting desires should be paramount over the other; he does not prefer that one first-order desire rather than the other should constitute his will. It would be misleading to say that he is neutral as to the conflict between his desires, since this would suggest that he regards them as equally acceptable. Since he has no identity apart from his first-order desires, it is true neither that he prefers one to the other nor that he prefers not to take sides.

It makes a difference to the unwilling addict, who is a person, which of his conflicting first-order desires wins out. Both desires are his, to be sure; and whether he finally takes the drug or finally succeeds in refraining from taking it, he acts to satisfy what is in a literal sense his own desire. In either case he does something he himself wants to do, and he does it not because of some external influence whose aim happens to coincide with his own but because of his desire to do it. The unwilling addict identifies himself, however, through the formation of a second-order volition, with one rather than with the other of his conflicting first-order desires. He makes one of them more truly his own and, in so doing, he withdraws himself from the other. It is in virtue of this identification and withdrawal, accomplished through the formation of a second-order volition, that the unwilling addict may meaningfully make the analytically puzzling statements that the force moving him to take the drug is a force other than his own, and that it is not of his own free will but rather against his will that this force moves him to take it.

The wanton addict cannot or does not care which of his conflicting first-order desires wins out. His lack of concern is not due to his inability to find a convincing basis for preference. It is due either to his lack of the capacity for reflection or to his mindless indifference to the enterprise of evaluating his own desires and motives.[6] There is only one issue in the struggle to which his first-order conflict may lead: whether the one or the other of his conflicting desires is the stronger. Since he is moved by both desires, he will not be altogether satisfied by what he does no matter which of them is effective. But it makes no difference to *him* whether his craving or his aversion gets the upper hand. He has no stake in the conflict between them and so, unlike the unwilling addict, he can neither win nor lose the struggle in which he is engaged. When a *person* acts, the desire by which he is moved is either the will he wants or a will he wants to be without. When a *wanton* acts, it is neither.

III

There is a very close relationship between the capacity for forming second-order volitions and another capacity that is essential to persons – one that has often been considered a distinguishing mark of the human condition. It is only because a person has volitions of the second order that he is capable both of enjoying and of lacking freedom of the will. The concept of a person is not only, then, the concept of a type of entity that has both first-order desires and volitions of the second order. It can also be construed as the concept of a type of entity for whom the freedom of its will may be a problem. This concept excludes all wantons, both infrahuman and human, since they fail to satisfy an essential condition for the enjoyment of freedom of the will. And it excludes those suprahuman beings, if any, whose wills are necessarily free.

Just what kind of freedom is the freedom of the will? This question calls for an identification of the special area of human experience to which the concept of freedom of the will, as distinct from the concepts of other sorts of freedom, is particularly germane. In dealing with it, my aim will be primarily to locate the problem with which a person is most immediately concerned when he is concerned with the freedom of his will.

According to one familiar philosophical tradition, being free is fundamentally a matter of doing what one wants to do. Now the notion of an agent who does what he wants to do is by no means an altogether clear one: both the doing and the wanting, and the appropriate relation between them as well, require elucidation. But although its focus needs to be sharpened and its formulation refined I believe that this notion does capture at least part of what is implicit in the idea of an agent who *acts* freely. It misses entirely, however, the peculiar content of the quite different idea of an agent whose *will* is free.

We do not suppose that animals enjoy freedom of the will, although we recognize that an animal may be free to run in whatever direction it wants. Thus, having the freedom to do what one wants to do is not a sufficient condition of having a free will. It is not a necessary condition either. For to deprive someone of his freedom of action is not necessarily to undermine the freedom of his will. When an agent is aware that there are certain things he is not free to do, this doubtless affects his desires and limits the range of choices he can make. But suppose that someone, without being aware of it, has in fact lost or been deprived of his freedom of action. Even though he is no longer free to do what he wants to do, his will may remain as free as it was before. Despite the fact that he is not free to translate his desires into actions or to act according to the determinations of his will, he may still form those desires and make those determinations as freely as if his freedom of action had not been impaired.

When we ask whether a person's will is free we are not asking whether he is in a position to translate his first-order desires into actions. That is the question of whether he is free to do as he pleases. The question of the freedom of his will does not concern the relation between what he does and what he wants to do. Rather, it concerns his desires themselves. But what question about them is it?

It seems to me both natural and useful to construe the question of whether a person's will is free in close analogy to the question of whether an agent enjoys freedom of action. Now freedom of action is (roughly, at least) the freedom to do what one wants to do. Analogously, then, the statement that a person enjoys freedom of the will means (also roughly) that he is free to want what he wants to want. More precisely, it means that he is free to will what he wants to will, or to have the will he wants. Just as the question about the freedom of an agent's action has to do with whether it is the action he wants to perform, so the question about the freedom of his will has to do with whether it is the will he wants to have.

It is in securing the conformity of his will to his second-order volitions, then, that a person exercises freedom of the will. And it is in the discrepancy between his will and his second-order volitions, or in his awareness that their coincidence is not his own doing but only a happy chance, that a person who does not have this freedom feels its lack. The unwilling addict's will is not free. This is shown by the fact that it is not the will he wants. It is also true, though in a different way, that the will of the wanton addict is not free. The wanton addict neither has the will he wants nor has a will that differs from the will he wants. Since he has no volitions of the second order, the freedom of his will cannot be a problem for him. He lacks it, so to speak, by default.

People are generally far more complicated than my sketchy account of the structure of a person's will may suggest. There is as much opportunity for ambivalence, conflict, and self-deception with regard to desires of the second order, for example, as there is with regard to first-order desires. If there is an unresolved conflict among someone's second-order desires, then he is in danger of having no second-order volition; for unless this conflict is resolved, he has no preference concerning which of his first-order desires is to be his will. This condition, if it is so severe that it prevents him from identifying himself in a sufficiently decisive way with *any* of his conflicting first-order desires, destroys him as a person. For it either tends to paralyze his will and to keep him from acting at all, or it tends to remove him from his will so that his will operates without his participation. In both cases he becomes, like the unwilling addict though in a different way, a helpless bystander to the forces that move him.

Another complexity is that a person may have, especially if his second-order desires are in conflict, desires and volitions of a higher order than the second. There is no theoretical limit to the length of the series of desires of higher and higher orders; nothing except common sense and, perhaps, a saving fatigue prevents an individual from obsessively refusing to identify himself with any of his desires until he forms a desire of the next higher order. The tendency to generate such a series of acts of forming desires, which would be a case of humanization run wild, also leads toward the destruction of a person.

It is possible, however, to terminate such a series of acts without cutting it off arbitrarily. When a person identifies himself *decisively* with one of his first-order desires, this commitment "resounds" throughout the potentially endless array of higher orders. Consider a person who, without reservation or conflict, wants to be motivated by the desire to concentrate on his work. The fact that his second-order volition to be moved by this desire is a decisive one means that there is no room for questions concerning the pertinence of desires or volitions of higher orders. Suppose the person is asked whether he wants to want to want to concentrate on his work. He can properly insist that this question concerning a third-order desire does not arise. It would be a mistake to claim that, because he has not considered whether he wants the second-order volition he has formed, he is indifferent to the question of whether it is with this volition or with some other that he wants his will to accord. The decisiveness of the commitment he has made means that he has decided that no further question about his second-order volition, at any higher order, remains to be asked. It is relatively unimportant whether we explain this by saying that this commitment implicitly generates an endless series of confirming desires of higher orders, or by saying that the commitment is tantamount to a dissolution of the pointedness of all questions concerning higher orders of desire.

Examples such as the one concerning the unwilling addict may suggest that volitions of the second order, or of higher orders, must be formed deliberately and that a person characteristically struggles to ensure that they are satisfied. But the conformity of a person's will to his higher-order volitions may be far more thoughtless and spontaneous than this. Some people are naturally moved by kindness when they want to be kind, and by nastiness when they want to be nasty, without any explicit forethought and without any need for energetic self-control. Others are moved by nastiness when they want to be kind and by kindness when they intend to be nasty, equally without forethought and without active resistance to these violations of their higher-order desires. The enjoyment of freedom comes easily to some. Others must struggle to achieve it.

IV

My theory concerning the freedom of the will accounts easily for our disinclination to allow that this freedom is enjoyed by the members of any species inferior to our own. It also satisfies another condition that must be met by any such theory, by making it apparent why the freedom of the will should be regarded as desirable. The enjoyment of a free will means the satisfaction of certain desires – desires of the second or of higher orders – whereas its absence means their frustration. The satisfactions at stake are those which accrue to a person of whom it may be said that his will is his own. The corresponding frustrations are those suffered by a person of whom it may be said that he is estranged from himself, or that he finds himself a helpless or a passive bystander to the forces that move him.

A person who is free to do what he wants to do may yet not be in a position to have the will he wants. Suppose, however, that he enjoys both freedom of action and freedom of the will. Then he is not only free to do what he wants to do; he is also free to want what he wants to want. It seems to me that he has, in that case, all the freedom it is possible to desire or to conceive. There are other good things in life, and he may not possess some of them. But there is nothing in the way of freedom that he lacks.

It is far from clear that certain other theories of the freedom of the will meet these elementary but essential conditions: that it be understandable why we desire this freedom and why we refuse to ascribe it to animals. Consider, for example, Roderick Chisholm's quaint version of the doctrine that human freedom entails an absence of causal determination.[7] Whenever a person performs a free action, according to Chisholm, it's a miracle. The motion of a person's hand, when the person moves it, is the outcome of a series of physical causes; but some event in this series, "and presumably one of those that took place within the brain, was caused by the agent and not by any other events" (18). A free agent has, therefore, "a prerogative which some would attribute only to God: each of us, when we act, is a prime mover unmoved" (23).

This account fails to provide any basis for doubting that animals of subhuman species enjoy the freedom it defines. Chisholm says nothing that makes it seem less likely that a rabbit performs a miracle when it moves its leg than that a man does so when he moves his hand. But why, in any case, should anyone *care* whether he can interrupt the natural order of causes in the way Chisholm describes? Chisholm offers no reason for believing that there is a discernible difference between the experience of a man who miraculously initiates a series of causes when he moves his hand and a man who moves his hand without any such breach of the normal causal sequence. There appears to be no concrete basis for preferring to be involved in the one state of affairs rather than in the other.[8]

It is generally supposed that, in addition to satisfying the two conditions I have mentioned, a satisfactory theory of the freedom of the will necessarily provides an analysis of one of the conditions of moral responsibility. The most common recent approach to the problem of understanding the freedom of the will has been, indeed, to inquire what is entailed by the assumption that someone is morally responsible for what he has done. In my view, however, the relation between moral responsibility and the freedom of the will has been very widely misunderstood. It is not true that a person is morally responsible for what he has done only if his will was free when he did it. He may be morally responsible for having done it even though his will was not free at all.

A person's will is free only if he is free to have the will he wants. This means that, with regard to any of his first-order desires, he is free either to make that desire his will or to make some other first-order desire his will instead. Whatever his will, then, the will of the person whose will is free could have been otherwise; he could have done otherwise than to constitute his will as he did. It is a vexed question just how "he could have done otherwise" is to be understood in contexts such as this one. But although this question is important to the theory of freedom, it has no bearing on the theory of moral responsibility. For the assumption that a person is morally responsible for what he has done does not entail that the person was in a position to have whatever will he wanted.

This assumption *does* entail that the person did what he did freely, or that he did it of his own free will. It is a mistake, however, to believe that someone acts freely only when he is free to do whatever he wants or that he acts of his own free will only if his will is free. Suppose that a person has done what he wanted to do, that he did it because he wanted to do it, and that the will by which he was moved when he did it was his will because it was the will he wanted. Then he did it freely and of his own free will. Even supposing that he could have done otherwise, he would not have done otherwise; and even supposing that he could have had a different will, he would not have wanted his will to differ from what it was. Moreover, since the will that moved him when he acted was his will because he wanted it to be, he cannot claim that his will was forced upon him or that he was a passive bystander to its constitution. Under these conditions, it is quite irrelevant to the evaluation of his moral responsibility to inquire whether the alternatives that he opted against were actually available to him.[9]

In illustration, consider a third kind of addict. Suppose that his addiction has the same physiological basis and the same irresistible thrust as the addictions of the unwilling and wanton addicts, but that he is altogether delighted with his condition. He is a willing addict who would not have things any other way. If the grip of his addiction should somehow weaken, he would do whatever he could to reinstate it; if his desire for the drug should begin to fade, he would take steps to renew its intensity.

The willing addict's will is not free, for his desire to take the drug will be effective regardless of whether or not he wants this desire to constitute his will. But when he takes the drug, he takes it freely and of his own free will. I am inclined to understand his situation as involving the overdetermination of his first-order desire to take the drug. This desire is his effective desire because he is physiologically addicted. But it is his effective desire also because he wants it to be. His will is outside his control, but, by his second-order desire that his desire for the drug should be effective, he has made this will his own. Given that it is therefore not only because of his addiction that his desire for the drug is effective, he may be morally responsible for taking the drug.

My conception of the freedom of the will appears to be neutral with regard to the problem of determinism. It seems conceivable that it should be causally determined that a person is free to want what he wants to want. If this is conceivable, then it might be causally determined that a person enjoys a free will. There is no more than an innocuous appearance of paradox in the proposition that it is determined, ineluctably and by forces beyond their control, that certain people have free wills and that others do not. There is no incoherence in the proposition that some agency other than a person's own is responsible (even *morally* responsible) for the fact that he enjoys or fails to enjoy freedom of the will. It is possible that a person should be morally responsible for what he does of his own free will and that some other person should also be morally responsible for his having done it.[10]

On the other hand, it seems conceivable that it should come about by chance that a person is free to have the will he wants. If this is conceivable, then it might be a matter of chance that certain people enjoy freedom of the will and that certain others do not Perhaps it is also conceivable, as a number of philosophers believe, for states of affairs to come about in a way other than by chance or as the outcome of a sequence of natural causes. If it is indeed conceivable for the relevant states of affairs to come about in some third way, then it is also possible that a person should in that third way come to enjoy the freedom of the will.

Notes

1   P. F. Strawson, *Individuals* (London: Methuen, 1959), pp. 101–102. Ayer's *usage of* "person" is similar: "it is characteristic of persons in this sense that besides having

various physical properties . . . they are also credited with various forms of consciousness" [A. J. Ayer, *The Concept of a Person* (New York: St Martin's, 1963), p. 82]. What concerns Strawson and Ayer is the problem of understanding the relation between mind and body, rather than the quite different problem of understanding what it is to he a creature that not only has a mind and a body but is also a person.

2   For the sake of simplicity, I shall deal only with what someone wants or desires, neglecting related phenomena such as choices and decisions. I propose to use the verbs "to want" and "to desire" interchangeably, although they are by no means perfect synonyms. My motive in forsaking the established nuances of these words arises from the fact that the verb "to want," which suits my purposes better so far as its meaning is concerned, does not lend itself so readily to the formation of nouns as does the verb "to desire." It is perhaps acceptable, albeit graceless, to speak in the plural of someone's "wants." But to speak in the singular of someone's "want" would be an abomination.

3   What I say in this paragraph applies not only to cases in which "to X" refers to a possible action or inaction. It also applies to cases in which "to X" refers to a first-order desire and in which the statement that "A wants to X" is therefore a shortened version of a statement – "A wants to want to X" – that identifies a desire of the second order.

4   It is not so clear that the entailment relation described here holds in certain kinds of cases, which I think may fairly be regarded as nonstandard, where the essential difference between the standard and the nonstandard cases lies in the kind of description by which the first-order desire in question is identified. Thus, suppose that A admires B so fulsomely that, even though he does not know what B wants to do, he wants to be effectively moved by whatever desire effectively moves B without knowing what B's will is; in other words, A wants his own will to be the same. It certainly does not follow that A already has, among his desires, a desire like the one that constitutes B's will. I shall not pursue here the questions of whether there are genuine counterexamples to the claim made in the text or of how, if there are, that claim should be altered.

5   Creatures with second-order desires but no second-order volitions differ significantly from brute animals, and, for some purposes, it would be desirable to regard them as persons. My usage, which withholds the designation "person" from them, is thus somewhat arbitrary. I adopt it largely because it facilitates the formulation of some of the points I wish to make. Hereafter, whenever I consider statements of the form "A wants to want to X," I shall have in mind statements identifying second-order volitions and not statements identifying second-order desires that are not second-order volitions.

6   In speaking of the evaluation of his own desires and motives as being characteristic of a person, I do not mean to suggest that a person's second-order volitions necessarily manifest a *moral* stance on his part toward his first-order desires. It may not be from the point of view of morality that the person evaluates his first-order desires. Moreover, a person may be capricious and irresponsible in forming his second-order volitions and give no serious consideration to what is at stake. Second-order volitions express evaluations only in the sense that they are preferences. There is no essential restriction on the kind of basis, if any, upon which they are formed.

7   "Freedom and Action," in K. Lehrer, ed., *Freedom and Determinism* (New York: Random House, 1966), pp. 11–44.

8   I am not suggesting that the alleged difference between these two states of affairs is

unverifiable. On the contrary, physiologists might well be able to show that Chisholm's conditions for a free action are not satisfied, by establishing that there is no relevant brain event for which a sufficient physical cause cannot be found.

9   For another discussion of the considerations that cast doubt on the principle that a person is morally responsible for what he has done only if he could have done otherwise, see my "Alternate Possibilities and Moral Responsibility," *Journal of Philosophy*, 1969: 829–839.

10 There is a difference between being *fully* responsible and being *solely* responsible. Suppose that the willing addict has been made an addict by the deliberate and calculated work of another. Then it may be that both the addict and this other person are fully responsible for the addict's taking the drug while neither of them is solely responsible for it. That there is a distinction between full moral responsibility and sole moral responsibility is apparent in the following example. A certain light can be turned on or off by flicking either of two switches, and each of these switches is simultaneously flicked to the "on" position by a different person, neither of whom is aware of the other. Neither person is solely responsible for the light's going on, nor do they share the responsibility in the sense that each is partially responsible; rather, each of them is fully responsible.

Sanity and the Metaphysics of Responsibility
Susan Wolf

Susan Wolf is Professor of Philosophy at Johns Hopkins University. Her published work is primarily on the relation between freedom, reason, and moral responsibility. She believes that human beings are both natural creatures and free, but that their freedom depends on reason and sanity.

Philosophers who study the problems of free will and responsibility have an easier time than most in meeting challenges about the relevance of their work to ordinary, practical concerns. Indeed, philosophers who study these problems are rarely faced with such challenges at all, since questions concerning the conditions of responsibility come up so obviously and so frequently in everyday life. Under scrutiny, however, one might question whether the connections between philosophical and nonphilosophical concerns in this area are real.

In everyday contexts, when lawyers, judges, parents, are concerned with issues of responsibility, they know, or think they know, what in general the conditions of responsibility are. Their questions are questions of application: Does this or that particular person meet this or that particular condition? Is he mature enough, or informed enough, or sane enough to be responsible? Was he acting under posthypnotic suggestion or under the influence of a mind-impairing drug? It is assumed, in these contexts, that normal, fully developed adult human beings are responsible beings. The questions have to do with whether a given individual falls within the normal range.

By contrast, philosophers tend to be uncertain about the general conditions of responsibility, and they care less about dividing the responsible from the nonresponsible agents than about determining whether, and if so why, any of us are ever responsible for anything at all.

In the classroom, we might argue that the philosophical concerns grow out of the nonphilosophical ones, that they take off where the nonphilosophical questions stop. In this way, we might convince our students that even if they are not plagued by the philosophical worries, they ought to be. If they worry about whether a person is mature enough, informed enough, and sane enough to be responsible, then they should worry about whether he is metaphysically free enough, too.

The argument I shall make in this essay, however, goes in the opposite direction. My aim is not to convince people who are interested in the apparently nonphilosophical conditions of responsibility that they should go on to worry about the philosophical conditions as well, but rather to urge those who already worry about the philosophical problems not to leave the more mundane, philosophical problems behind. In particular, I shall suggest that the mundane recognition that *sanity* is a condition of responsibility has more to do with the murky and apparently metaphysical problems that surround the issue of responsibility than at first meets the eye. Once the significance of the condition of sanity is fully appreciated, at least some of the apparently insuperable metaphysical aspects of the problem of responsibility will dissolve.

My strategy will be to examine a recent trend in philosophical discussions of responsibility, a trend that tries, but I think ultimately fails, to give an acceptable analysis of the conditions of responsibility and that fails due to what at first appear to be deep and irresolvable metaphysical problems. It is here that I shall suggest that the condition of sanity comes to the rescue. What at first appears to be an impossible requirement for responsibility – namely, the requirement that the responsible agent must have created himself – turns out to be the vastly more mundane and noncontroversial requirement that the responsible agent must, in a fairly standard sense, be sane.

1 Frankfurt, Watson, and Taylor

The trend I have in mind is exemplified by the writings of Harry Frankfurt, Gary Watson, and Charles Taylor. I shall briefly discuss each of their separate proposals, and then offer a composite view that, while lacking the subtlety of any of the separate accounts, will highlight some important insights and some important blindspots that they share.

In his seminal article, "Freedom of the Will and the Concept of a Person,"[1] Harry Frankfurt notes a distinction between freedom of action and freedom of the will. A person has freedom of action, he points out, if she has the freedom to do whatever she wills to do – the freedom to walk or sit, to vote liberal or conservative, to publish a book or open a store, in accordance with her strongest desires. Even a person who has freedom of action may fail to be responsible for her actions, however, if the wants or desires she has the freedom to convert into action are themselves not subject to her control. Thus, the person who acts under posthypnotic suggestion, the victim of brainwashing, the kleptomaniac might all possess freedom of action. In the standard contexts in which these examples are raised, it is assumed that none of the individuals are locked up or bound. Rather, these individuals are understood to act on what, at one level at least, must be called *their own desires*. Their exemption from responsibility stems from the fact that their own desires (or, at least the ones governing their actions) are not up to them. These cases may be described in Frankfurt's terms as cases of people who possess freedom of action but who fail to be responsible agents because they lack freedom of the will.

Philosophical problems about the conditions of responsibility naturally focus on an analysis of this latter kind of freedom: What *is* freedom of the will, and under what conditions can we reasonably be thought to possess it? Frankfurt's proposal is to understand freedom of the will by analogy to freedom of action. As freedom of action is the freedom to do whatever one wills to do, freedom of the will is the freedom to will whatever one wants to will. To make this point clearer, Frankfurt introduces a distinction between first-order and second-order desires. First-order desires are desires to do or to have various things, second-order desires are desires about what desires to have or what desires to make effective in action. In order for an agent to have both freedom of action and freedom of the will, she must be capable of governing her actions by her first-order desires *and* capable of governing her first-order desires by her second order desires.

Gary Watson's view of free agency[2] – free and responsible agency, that is – is similar to Frankfurt's in holding that an agent is responsible for an action only if the desires expressed by that action are of a particular kind. While Frankfurt identifies the right kind of desires as desires that are supported by second-order desires, Watson draws a distinction between "mere" desires, so to speak, and desires that are *values*. According to Watson, the difference between free action and unfree action cannot be analyzed by reference to the logical form of the desires from which these various actions arise, but rather must relate to a difference in the quality of their source. Whereas some of my desires are just appetites or conditioned responses which I find myself "stuck with," others are expressions of judgments on my part that the objects I desire are good. Insofar as my actions can be governed by the latter type of desire – governed, that is, by my values or valuational system – they are actions that I perform freely and for which I am responsible.

Both Frankfurt's and Watson's accounts offer ways of cashing out the intuition that in order to be responsible for one's actions, one must be responsible for the self that performs these actions. Charles Taylor, in an article entitled "Responsibility for Self,"[3] discusses the same intuition. While Taylor does not describe his view in terms of different levels or types of desire, his view is related, for he claims that our freedom and responsibility depends on our ability to reflect on, criticize, and revise ourselves. Like Frankfurt and Watson, Taylor seems to believe that if the characters from which our actions flowed were simply and permanently *given* to us, implanted by heredity, environment, or God, then we would be mere vehicles through which the causal forces of the world traveled – no more responsible than dumb animals or young children or machines. But like the others, he points out that, for most of us, our characters and desires are not so brutely implanted – or, at any rate, if they are, they are subject to revision by our own reflecting, valuing, or second-order desiring selves. We human beings – and as far as we know, only we human beings – have the ability to step back from ourselves and decide whether we are the selves we want to be. Because of this, these philosophers think, we are responsible for ourselves and for the actions that we produce.

Although there are subtle and interesting differences among the accounts of Frankfurt, Watson, and Taylor, my concern is with features of their views that are common to them all. All share the idea that responsible agency involves something more than intentional agency. All agree that if we are responsible agents, it is not just because our actions are within the control of our wills, but because, in addition, our wills are not just psychological states in us, but expressions of characters that come *from* us, or that at any rate are acknowledged and affirmed *by* us. For Frankfurt, this means that our wills must be ruled by our second-order desires; for Watson, that our wills must be governable by our system of values; for Taylor, that our wills must issue from selves that are subject to self-assessment and redefinition in terms of a vocabulary of worth. In one way or another, all these philosophers seem to be saying that the key to responsibility lies in the fact that responsible agents are those for whom it is not just the case that their actions are within the control of their wills, but also the case that their wills are within the control of their *selves* in some deeper sense. Because, at one level, the differences among Frankfurt, Watson, and Taylor may be understood as differences in the analysis or interpretation of what it is for an action to be under the control of this deeper self, we may speak of their separate positions as variations of one basic view about responsibility, the Deep Self View.

2 The Deep Self View

Much more must be said about the notion of a deep self before a fully satisfactory account of this view can be given. Providing a careful, detailed analysis of that notion poses an interesting, important, and difficult task in its own right. The degree of understanding achieved by abstraction from the views of Frankfurt, Watson, and Taylor, however, should be sufficient to allow us to recognize some important virtues as well as some important drawbacks of the Deep Self View.

One virtue is that this view explains a good portion of our pretheoretical intuitions about responsibility. It explains why kleptomaniacs, victims of brain-washing, and people acting under posthypnotic suggestion may not be responsible for their actions, although most of us typically are. In the cases of people in these special categories, the connection between the agents' deep selves and their wills is dramatically severed – their wills are governed, not by their deep selves, but by forces external to and independent from them. A different intuition is that we adult human beings can be responsible for our actions in a way that dumb animals, infants, and machines cannot be. Here the explanation is not in terms of a split between these beings' deep selves and their wills – rather the point is that these beings *lack* deep selves altogether. Kleptomaniacs and victims of hypnosis exemplify individuals whose selves are *alienated* from their actions; lower animals and machines, on the other hand, don't have the sorts of selves from which actions *can* be alienated, and so they don't have the sort of selves from which, in the happier cases, actions can responsibly flow.

At a more theoretical level, the Deep Self View has another virtue: It responds to at least one way in which the fear of determinism presents itself.

A naive reaction to the idea that everything we do is completely determined by a causal chain that extends backwards beyond the times of our births involves thinking that in that case we would have no control over our behavior whatsoever. If everything is determined, it is thought, then what happens, happens, whether we want it to or not. A common, and proper, response to this concern points out that determinism does not deny the causal efficacy an agent's desires might have on her behavior. On the contrary, determinism in its more plausible forms tends to affirm this connection, merely adding that as one's behavior is determined by one's desires, so one's desires are determined by something else.[4]

Those who were initially worried that determinism implied fatalism, however, are apt to find their fears merely transformed rather than erased. If our desires are governed by something else, they might say, they are not *really* ours after all – or, at any rate, they are ours in only a superficial sense.

The Deep Self View offers an answer to this transformed fear of determinism, for it allows us to distinguish cases in which desires are determined by forces foreign to oneself from desires which are determined by one's self – by one's "real," or second-order-desiring, or valuing, or deep self, that is. Admittedly, there are cases, like that of the kleptomaniac or the victim of hypnosis, in which the agent acts on desires that "belong to" her in only a superficial sense. But the proponent of the Deep Self View will point out that even if determinism is true, ordinary adult human action can be distinguished from this. Determinism implies that the desires that govern our actions are in turn governed by something else, but that something else will, in the fortunate cases, be our own deeper selves.

This account of responsibility thus offers a response to our fear of determinism. But it is a response with which many will remain unsatisfied. For, even if my actions are governed by my desires and my desires are governed by my own deeper self, there remains the question, who, or what, is responsible for this deeper self? The above response seems only to have pushed the problem further back.

Admittedly, some versions of the Deep Self View – namely, Frankfurt's and Taylor's – seem to anticipate this question by providing a place for the ideal that an agent's deep self may be governed by a still deeper self. Thus, for Frankfurt, second-order desires may themselves be governed by third-order desires, third-order desires by fourth-order desires, and so on. And Taylor points out that, as we can reflect and evaluate our prereflective selves, so we can reflect and evaluate the selves who are doing the first reflecting and evaluating, and so on. But this capacity to recursively create endless levels of depth ultimately misses the criticism's point.

First of all, even if there is no *logical* limit to the number of levels of reflection or depth a person may have, there is certainly a psychological limit: it is virtually impossible to imaginatively conceive a fourth-, much less an eighth-order desire. More importantly, no matter how many levels of self we posit, there will still, in any individual case, be a last level – a deepest self about whom the question, "What governs it?" will arise as problematic as ever. If determinism is true, it implies that even if my actions are governed by my desires, and my desires are governed by my deepest self, my deepest self will still be governed by something that must, logically, be external to myself altogether. Though I can step back from the values my parents and teachers have given me and ask whether these are the values I really want, the "I" that steps back will itself be a product of the parents and teachers I am questioning.

The problem seems even worse when one sees that one fares no better if determinism is false. For if my deepest self is not determined by something external to myself, it will still not be determined by *me*. Whether I am a product of carefully controlled forces or a result of random mutations, whether there is a complete explanation of my origin or no explanation at all, I am not, in any case, responsible for my existence. I am not in control of my deepest self.

Thus, though the claim that an agent is responsible for only those actions that are within the control of her deep self correctly identifies a necessary condition for responsibility – a condition that separates the hypnotized and the brainwashed, the immature and the lower animals from ourselves, for example – it fails to provide a sufficient condition of responsibility that puts all fears of determinism to rest. For one of the fears invoked by the thought of determinism seems to be connected to its implication that we are but intermediate links in a causal chain, rather than ultimate, self-initiating sources of movement and change. From the point of view of one who has this fear, the Deep Self View seems merely to add loops to the chain, complicating the picture but not really improving it. From the point of view of one who has this fear, responsibility seems to require being a prime mover unmoved, whose deepest self is itself neither random *nor* externally determined but is rather determined *by* itself – who is, in other words, self-created.

At this point, however, proponents of the Deep Self View may wonder whether this fear is legitimate. For although people evidently can be brought to the point where they feel that responsible agency requires them to be ultimate sources of power, to the point where it seems that nothing short of self-creation will do, a return to the internal standpoint of the agent whose responsibility is in question makes it hard to see what good this metaphysical status is supposed to provide or what evil its absence is supposed to impose.

From the external standpoint, which discussions of determinism and indeterminism encourage us to take up, it may appear that a special metaphysical status is required to distinguish us significantly from other members of the natural world. But proponents of the Deep Self View will suggest that this is an illusion that a return to the internal standpoint should dispel. The possession of a deep self that is effective in governing one's actions is a sufficient distinction, they will say. For while other members of the natural world are not in control of the selves that they are, we, possessors of effective deep selves, are in control. We can reflect on what sorts of beings we are, and on what sorts of marks we make on the world. We can change what we don't like about ourselves and keep what we do. Admittedly, we do not create ourselves from nothing. But as long as we can revise ourselves, they will suggest, it is hard to find reason to complain. Harry Frankfurt writes that a person who is free to do what he wants to do and also free to want what he wants to want has "all the freedom it is possible to desire or to conceive."[5] This suggests a rhetorical question: If you are free to control your actions by your desires, and free to control your desires by your deeper desires, and free to control those desires by still deeper desires, what further kind of freedom can you want?

3 The Condition of Sanity

Unfortunately, there is a further kind of freedom we can want, which it is reasonable to think necessary for responsible agency. The Deep Self View fails to be convincing when it is offered as a complete account of the conditions of responsibility. To see why, it will be helpful to consider another example of an agent whose responsibility is in question.

JoJo is the favorite son of Jo the First, an evil and sadistic dictator of a small undeveloped country. Because of his father's special feelings for the boy, JoJo is given a special education and is allowed to accompany his father often and observe his daily routine. In light of this treatment, it is not surprising that little JoJo takes his father as a role-model and develops values very much like his dad's. As an adult, he does many of the same sorts of things his father did, including sending people to prison or to death or to torture chambers on the basis of the slightest of his whims. He is not *coerced* to do these things, he acts according to his own desires. Moreover, these are desires that he wholly wants to have. When he steps back and asks, "Do I really want to be this sort of person?" his answer is resoundingly Yes, for this way of life expresses a crazy sort of power that forms part of his deepest ideal.

In light of JoJo's heritage and upbringing – both of which he was powerless to control – it is dubious at best that he should be regarded as responsible for what he does. For it is unclear whether anyone with a childhood such as his could have developed into anything but the twisted and perverse sort of person that he has become. But note that JoJo is someone whose actions are controlled by his desires and whose desires are the desires he wants to have. That is, his actions are governed by desires that are governed by and expressive of his deepest self.

The Frankfurt–Watson–Taylor strategy that allowed us to differentiate our normal selves from the victims of hypnosis and brainwashing will not allow us to differentiate ourselves from the son of Jo the First. In the case of these earlier victims, we were able to say that although the actions of these individuals were, at one level, in control of the individuals themselves, these individuals themselves, *qua* agents, were not the selves they more deeply wanted to be. In this respect, these people were unlike our happily more integrated selves. But we cannot say of JoJo that his self, *qua* agent, is not the self he wants it to be. From the inside, he feels as integrated, free, and responsible as we do.

Our judgment that JoJo is not a responsible agent is one that we can only make from the outside – from reflecting on the fact, it seems, that his deepest self is not up to him. Looked at from the outside, however, our situation seems no different from his. For in the last analysis, it is not up to any of us to have the deepest selves we do. Once more, the problem seems metaphysical – and not just metaphysical, but insuperable. For, as I mentioned before, the problem is independent of the truth of determinism. Whether we are determined or undetermined, we cannot have created our deepest selves. Literal self-creation is not just empirically, but logically impossible.

If JoJo is not responsible because his deepest self is not up to him, then we are not responsible either. Indeed, in that case responsibility would be impossible for anyone ever to achieve. But I believe that the appearance that literal self-creation is required for freedom and responsibility is itself mistaken.

The Deep Self View was right in pointing out that freedom and responsibility requires us to have certain distinctive types of control over our behavior and ourselves. Specifically, our actions need to be under the control of ourselves, and our (superficial) selves need to be under the control of our deep selves. Having seen that these types of control are not enough to guarantee us the status of responsible agents, we are tempted to go on to suppose that we must have yet another kind of control to assure us that even our deepest selves are somehow up to us. But not all the things necessary for freedom and responsibility must be types of power and control. We may need simply to *be* a certain way, even though it is not within our power to determine whether we are that way or not.

Indeed, it becomes obvious that at least one condition of responsibility is of this form as soon as one remembers what, in everyday contexts, we have known all along – namely, that in order to be responsible, an agent must be *sane*. It is not ordinarily in our power to determine whether we are or are not sane. Most of us, it would seem, are lucky, but some of us are not. Moreover, being sane does not necessarily mean that one has any type of power or control that an insane person lacks. All to our distress, some insane people, like JoJo and some actual political leaders who resemble him, may have complete control of their actions, and even complete control of their acting selves. The desire to be sane is thus not a desire for another form of control. It is rather a desire that one's self be connected to the world in a certain way – we could even say it is a desire that one's self be *controlled by* the world in certain ways and not in others.

This becomes clear if we attend to the criteria for sanity that have historically been dominant in legal questions about responsibility. According to the M'Naughten Rule, a person is sane if (1) he knows what he's doing and (2) he knows that what he's doing is, as the case may be, right or wrong. Insofar as one's desire to be sane involves a desire to know what one's doing – or more generally, a desire to live in the Real World – it is a desire to be controlled – to have, in this case, one's *beliefs* controlled – by perceptions and sound reasoning that produce an accurate conception of the world rather than by blind or distorted forms of response. The same goes for the second constituent of sanity – only, in this case, one's hope is that one's *values* be controlled by processes that afford an accurate conception of the world.[6] Putting these two conditions together, we may understand sanity, then, as the minimally sufficient ability to cognitively and normatively recognize and appreciate the world for what it is.

There are problems with this definition of sanity, at least some of which will become obvious in what follows, that make it ultimately unacceptable either as a gloss on or an improvement of the meaning of the term in many of the contexts in which it is used. The definition offered does seem to bring out the interest sanity has for us in connection with issues of responsibility, however, and some pedagogical as well as stylistic purposes will be served if we use sanity hereafter in this admittedly specialized sense.

4 The Sane Deep Self View

So far I have argued that the conditions of responsible agency offered by the Deep Self View are necessary but not sufficient. Moreover, the gap left open by the Deep Self View seems to be one that can only be filled by a metaphysical, and as it happens, metaphysically impossible addition. I now wish to argue, however, that the condition of sanity, as characterized above, is sufficient to fill the gap. In other words, the Deep Self View, supplemented by the condition of sanity, provides a satisfying conception of responsibility. The conception of responsibility I am proposing, then, agrees with the Deep Self View in requiring that a responsible agent be able to govern her actions by her desires and to govern her desires by her deep self. In addition, my conception insists that the agent's deep self be sane and claims that this is all that is needed for responsible agency. By contrast to the plain Deep Self View, let us call this new proposal the Sane Deep Self View.

It is worth noting, to begin with, that this new proposal deals with the case of JoJo and related cases of deprived childhood victims, in ways that better match our pretheoretical intuitions. Unlike the plain Deep Self View, the Sane Deep Self View offers a way of explaining why JoJo is not responsible for his actions without throwing our own responsibility into doubt. For, although like us, JoJo's actions flow from desires that flow from his deep self, unlike us, JoJo's deep self is itself insane. Sanity, remember, involves the ability to know the difference between right and wrong, and a person who, even on reflection, can't see that having someone tortured because he failed to salute you is wrong plainly lacks the requisite ability.

Less obviously, but quite analogously, this new proposal explains why we give less than full responsibility to persons who, though acting badly, act in ways that are strongly encouraged by their societies – the slaveowners of the 1850s, the

German Nazis of the 1930s, and many male chauvinists of our fathers' generation, for example. These are people, we imagine, who falsely believe that the ways they are acting are morally acceptable, and so, we may assume, their behavior is expressive of or at least in accordance with these agents' deep selves. But their false beliefs in the moral permissibility of their actions and the false values from which these beliefs derived may have been inevitable given the social circumstances in which they developed. If we think that the agents could not help but be mistaken about their values, we do not blame them for the actions which those values inspired.[7]

It would unduly distort ordinary linguistic practice to call the slaveowner, the Nazi, or the male chauvinist even partially or locally insane. Nonetheless the reason for withholding blame from them is at bottom the same as the reason for withholding it from JoJo. Like JoJo, they are, at the deepest level, unable to cognitively and normatively recognize and appreciate the world for what it is. In our sense of the term, their deepest selves are not fully sane.

The Sane Deep Self View thus offers an account of why victims of deprived childhood as well as victims of misguided societies may not be responsible for their actions without implying that we are not responsible for ours. The actions of these others are governed by mistaken conceptions of value that the agents in question cannot help but have. Since, as far as we know, our values are not, like theirs, unavoidably mistaken, the fact that these others are not responsible for their actions need not force us to conclude that we are not responsible for ours.

But it may not yet be clear why sanity, in this special sense, should make such a difference; why, in particular, the question of whether someone's values are unavoidably *mistaken* should have any bearing on their status as responsible agents. The fact that the Sane Deep Self View implies judgments that match our intuitions about the difference in status between characters like JoJo and ourselves provides little support for it if it cannot also defend these intuitions. So we must consider an objection that comes from the point of view we earlier considered that rejects the intuition that a relevant difference can be found.

Earlier, it seemed that the reason JoJo was not responsible for his actions was that although his actions were governed by his deep self, his deep self was not up to him. But this had nothing to do with his deep self's being mistaken or not mistaken, evil or good, insane or sane. If JoJo's values are unavoidably mistaken, our values, even if not mistaken, appear to be just as unavoidable. When it comes to freedom and responsibility, isn't it the unavoidability rather than the mistakenness, that matters?

Before answering this question, it is useful to point out a way in which it is ambiguous: the concepts of avoidability and mistakenness are not unequivocally distinct. One may, to be sure, construe the notion of avoidability in a purely metaphysical way. Whether an event or state of affairs is unavoidable under this construal depends, as it were, on the tightness of the causal connections, so to speak, that bear on the event's or state of affairs' coming about. In this sense, our deep selves do seem as unavoidable for us as JoJo's and the others' are for them. For presumably we are just as influenced by our parents, our cultures, and our schooling as they are influenced by theirs. In another sense, however, our characters are not similarly unavoidable.

In particular, in the cases of JoJo and the others, there are certain features of their characters that they cannot avoid *even though these features are seriously mistaken, misguided, or bad*. This is so because, in our special sense of the term, these characters are less than fully sane. Since these characters lack the ability to know right from wrong, they are unable to revise their characters on the basis of right and wrong, and so their deep selves lack the resources and the reasons that might have served as a basis for self-correction. Since the deep selves we unavoidably have, however, are sane deep selves – deep selves, that is, that unavoidably *contain* the ability to know right from wrong, we unavoidably do have the resources and reasons on which to base self-correction. What this means is that though in one sense we are no more in control of our deepest selves than JoJo and others, it does not follow in our case, as it does in theirs, that we would be the way we are, even if it is a bad or wrong way to be. But, if this does not follow, it seems to me, our absence of control at the deepest level should not upset us.

Consider what the absence of control at the deepest level amounts to for us: Whereas JoJo is unable to control the fact that, at the deepest level, he is not fully sane, we are not responsible for the fact that, at the deepest level, we are. It is not up to us to *have* minimally sufficient abilities to cognitively and normatively recognize and appreciate the world for what it is. Also, presumably, it is not up to us to have lots of other properties, at least to begin with – a fondness for purple, perhaps, or an antipathy for beets. As the proponents of the plain Deep Self View have been at pains to point out, however, we do, if we are lucky, have the ability to revise ourselves in terms of the values that are held by or constitutive of our deep selves. If we are lucky enough both to have this ability and to have our deep selves be sane, it follows that although there is much in our characters that we did not choose to have, there is nothing irrational or objectionable in our characters that we are compelled to keep.

Being sane, we are able to understand and evaluate our characters in a reasonable way, to notice what there is reason to hold on to, what there is reason to eliminate, and what, from a rational and reasonable standpoint, we may retain or get rid of as we please. Being able as well to govern our superficial selves by our deep selves, then, we are able to change the things that we find there is reason to change. This being so, it seems that although we may not be *metaphysically* responsible for ourselves – for, after all, we did not create ourselves from nothing – we are *morally* responsible for ourselves, for we are able to understand and appreciate right and wrong, and to change our characters and our actions accordingly.

5 Self-creation, Self-revision, and Self-correction

At the beginning of this chapter, I claimed that recalling that sanity was a condition of responsibility would dissolve at least some of the appearance that responsibility was metaphysically impossible. To see how this is so, and to get a fuller sense of the Sane Deep Self View, it may be helpful to put that view into perspective by comparing it to the other views we have discussed along the way.

As Frankfurt, Watson, and Taylor showed us, in order to be free and responsible, we need not only to be able to control our actions in accordance with our desires, we need to be able to control our desires in accordance with our deepest selves. We need, in other words, to be able to *revise* ourselves – to get rid of some desires and traits, and perhaps replace them with others on the basis of our deeper desires or values or reflections. Consideration of the fact that the selves who are doing the revising might themselves be either brute products of external forces or arbitrary outputs of random generation made us wonder whether the capacity for self-revision was enough to assure us of responsibility, however, and the example of JoJo added force to the suspicion that it was not. If the ability to revise ourselves is not enough, however, the ability to create ourselves does not seem necessary either. Indeed, when you think of it, it is unclear why anyone should want self-creation. Why should anyone be disappointed at having to accept the idea that one has to get one's start somewhere? It is an idea that most of us have lived with quite contentedly all along. What we do have reason to want, then, is something more than the ability to revise ourselves but less than the ability to create ourselves. Implicit in the Sane Deep Self View is the idea that what is needed is the ability to *correct* (or approve) ourselves.

Recognizing that in order to be responsible for our actions, we have to be responsible for ourselves, the Sane Deep Self View analyzes what is necessary in order to be responsible for our selves as (1) the ability to evaluate ourselves sensibly and accurately and (2) the ability to transform ourselves insofar as our evaluation tells us to do so. We may understand the exercise of these abilities as a process whereby we *take* responsibility for the selves that we are but did not ultimately create. The condition of sanity is intrinsically connected to the first ability; the condition that we be able to control our superficial selves by our deep selves is intrinsically connected to the second.

The difference between the plain Deep Self View and the Sane Deep Self View, then, is the difference between the requirement of the capacity for self-revision and the requirement of the capacity for self-correction. Anyone with the first capacity can *try* to take responsibility for herself. Only someone with a sane deep self, however, a deep self that can see and appreciate the world for what it is, can evaluate herself sensibly and accurately. And so, although insane serves can try to take responsibility for themselves, only sane selves will properly be accorded responsibility.

6 Two Objections Considered

At least two problems with the Sane Deep Self View are so glaring as to have certainly struck many of my readers, and, in closing, I shall briefly address them. First, some will be wondering how, in light of my specialized use of the term "sanity," I can be so sure that "we" are any saner than the nonresponsible individuals I have discussed. What justifies my confidence that, unlike the slaveowners, Nazis, and male chauvinists, not to mention JoJo himself, we are able to understand and appreciate the world for what it is? The answer to this is that nothing justifies this except widespread intersubjective agreement and the considerable success we have in getting around in the world and satisfying our needs. These are not sufficient grounds for the smug assumption that we are in a position to see the truth about all aspects of ethical and social life. Indeed, it seems more reasonable to expect that time will reveal blindspots in our cognitive and normative outlook, just as it has revealed errors in the outlooks of those who have lived before. But our judgments of responsibility can only be made from here, on the basis of the understandings and values that we can develop by exercising the abilities we do possess as well and as fully as possible.

If some have been worried that my view implicitly expresses an overconfidence in the assumption that we are sane and therefore right about the world, others will be worried that my view too closely connects sanity with being right about the world and fear that my view implies that anyone who acts wrongly or has false beliefs about the world is therefore insane and so not responsible for his actions. This seems to me to be a more serious worry, which I am sure I cannot answer to everyone's satisfaction.

First, it must be admitted that the Sane Deep Self View embraces a conception of sanity that is explicitly normative. But this seems to me a strength of that view rather than a defect. Sanity *is* a normative concept, in its ordinary as well as in its specialized sense, and severely deviant behavior, such as that of a serial murderer or a sadistic dictator, does constitute evidence of a psychological defect in the agent. The suggestion that the most horrendous, stomach-turning crimes could only be committed by an insane person – an inverse of Catch-22, as it were – must be regarded as a serious possibility, despite the practical problems that would accompany general acceptance of that conclusion.

But, it will be objected, there is no justification, on the Sane Deep Self View, for regarding only horrendous and stomach-turning crimes as evidence of insanity in its specialized sense. If sanity is the ability to cognitively and normatively understand and appreciate the world for what it is, then *any* wrong action or false belief will count as evidence of the absence of that ability. This point may also be granted, but we must be careful about what conclusion to draw. To be sure, when someone acts in a way that is not in accordance with acceptable standards of rationality and reasonableness, it is always appropriate to look for an explanation of why she acted that way. The hypothesis that she was unable to understand and appreciate that her action fell outside acceptable bounds will always be a possible explanation. Bad performance on a math test always suggests the possibility that the test taker is stupid. Typically, however, other explanations will be possible, too – for example, that the agent was too lazy to consider whether her action was acceptable, or too greedy to care, or in the case of the math test taker, that she was too occupied with other interests to attend class or study. Other facts about the agent's history will help us decide among these hypotheses.

This brings out the need to emphasize that sanity, in the specialized sense, is defined as the *ability* to cognitively and normatively understand and appreciate the world for what it is. According to our commonsense understandings, having this ability is one thing and exercising it is another – at least some wrong-acting, responsible agents presumably fall within the gap. The notion of "ability" is notoriously problematic, however, and there is a long history of controversy about whether the truth of determinism would show our ordinary ways of thinking to be simply confused on this matter. At this point, then, metaphysical concerns may voice themselves again – but at least they will have been pushed into a narrower, and perhaps a more manageable corner.

The Sane Deep Self View does not, then, solve all the philosophical problems connected to the topics of free will and responsibility, and if anything, it highlights some of the practical and empirical problems rather than solves them. It may, however, resolve some of the philosophical, and particularly, some of the metaphysical problems, and reveal how intimate are the connections between the remaining philosophical problems and the practical ones.

Notes

1 Harry G. Frankfurt, "Freedom of the Will and the Concept of a Person," *Journal of Philosophy* 68 (1971), 5–20; see ch. 4 above.
2 Gary Watson, "Free Agency," *Journal of Philosophy* 72 (1975), 205–20; see ch. 7 above.
3 Charles Taylor, "Responsibility for Self," in A. E. Rorty, ed., *The Identities of Persons* (Berkeley: University of California Press, 1976), 281–99.
4 See, e.g., David Hume, *A Treatise of Human Nature* (Oxford: Oxford University Press, 1967), 399–406, and R. E. Hobart, "Free Will as Involving Determination and Inconceivable Without It," *Mind* (1934).
5 Frankfurt, "Freedom of the Will," p. 72.
6 Strictly speaking, perception and sound reasoning may not be enough to ensure the ability to achieve an accurate conception of what one is doing and especially to achieve a reasonable normative assessment of one's situation. Sensitivity and exposure to certain realms of experience may also be necessary for these goals. For the purposes of this essay, I shall understand "sanity" to include whatever it takes to enable one to develop an adequate conception of one's world. In other contexts, however, this would be an implausibly broad construal of the term.
7 Admittedly, it is open to question whether these individuals were in fact unable to help having mistaken values, and indeed, whether recognizing the errors of their society would even have required exceptional independence or strength of mind. This is presumably an empirical question, the answer to which is extraordinarily hard to determine. My point here is simply that *if* we believe that they are unable to recognize that their values are mistaken, we do not hold them responsible for the actions that flow from these values, and *if* we believe that their ability to recognize their normative errors is impaired, we hold them less than fully responsible for the relevant actions.

8

Against Metaphysics

Introduction

Can we do without metaphysics? The discussion so far suggests that metaphysics lurks in areas that are crucial to our lives. When thinking about the state and our allegiance to it, we make assumptions about the nature of the state and how individuals are related to it, and these, as Plato saw, quickly take us to the metaphysical problem of universals. Human beings have strong feelings about what should and should not be done, and today one of the most pressing concerns is what to do about the steady deterioration of our natural environment. But when we start to argue about this we will soon run against suspicions that morality may all be just a matter of opinion, and whether or not this is so is a metaphysical issue.

Today most people cannot get by without thinking about God at some time or another. Many people think their nations are sanctioned by God and public policy around the globe is made in God's name, but whether God exists is an old metaphysical issue that refuses to die. The concept of cause is no less central to our lives than the concept of God. We all know that it plays a role in science and medicine, but we also use it when discussing moral and legal responsibility. People or institutions cannot be morally or legally responsible for something they did not cause, which means that we need to understand causality to properly assign moral responsibility. But the nature of causality is in the domain of metaphysics, as is the question whether causality is real or mostly an artifact of the human mind.

Whether a creature has a mind and how much of a mind it has makes a difference to our beliefs about how we should treat animals – whether we should eat them or invite them for dinner – but the nature of mind is a metaphysical puzzle and continues to be a puzzle even in the face of tremendous progress in the brain and behavioral sciences. Finally, although we value freedom very highly and appeal to it in politics, law, and morality, it is no less puzzling than universals, value, God, causality, or mind. This too is not just an academic puzzle. People make decisions based on their ideas about freedom and a thorough reflection on the nature of freedom forces us to think about how our societies are organized.

In short, how we treat others and organize our communities will be informed by our views about freedom, mind, causality, God, value, and universality, but all of these views are metaphysical views! Thus it is surprising that metaphysics has quite frankly at times been scoffed, ridiculed, and buried. The attacks on metaphysics have not constituted one unified war, but have rather been battles and scrimmages that have been fought at various times and launched by various individuals, schools, and positions. The scope of the attacks has also differed. Some attacks have tried to eliminate all of metaphysics, when the attackers argued that the conceptual foundations of metaphysics were faulty. Other attacks have tried to show that metaphysics is not a necessary part of our lives, particularly our moral and political activities. Logical positivism as well as postmodernism are examples of the first kind of critique of metaphysics, while the contemporary moral and political philosopher John Rawls has advanced the second line of thought about the value of metaphysics.

Logical Positivist Critiques of Metaphysics

"Logical positivism" is a name given to a set of ideas and attitudes espoused by the Vienna Circle, a discussion group that was formed in 1925 in Vienna, Austria. Philosophers and scientists were members of this discussion group, including Moritz Schlick, Otto Neurath, Herbert Feigl, Edgar Zilsel, Kurt Gödel, Rudolf Carnap, and Felix Kaufman, as well as A. J. Ayer, Ludwig Wittgenstein, and Karl Popper. The ideas of this group spread quickly from Vienna throughout Europe, and to North America, particularly when many of the members of the Vienna Circle, including Carnap, Feigl, and Gödel, emigrated to the United States to escape European fascism.

There was a strong strand against all philosophy among the members of the Vienna Circle. One of its members who today is classified as a philosopher, Ernst Mach, actually denied that he was a philosopher. Rudolf Carnap thought that philosophy ought to be destroyed, and claimed that the Vienna Circle gave no answers to philosophical questions and instead rejected all philosophical questions, whether in ethics, epistemology, or metaphysics.

The Vienna Circle's anti-philosophical stance was a reaction to several trends in nineteenth-century European philosophy, particularly idealism and various forms of relativism. These trends had in common a suspicion of the idea that human beings represent the world around us as it truly is. Philosophy as it evolved during the scientific revolution in the seventeenth century assigned a place of honor to science. Science was seen as the culmination of the human quest to find better and better representations of the physical world around us. Nineteenth-century European philosophy had shifted its focus away from representing the world to the activities of expressing and asserting oneself in the world. Philosophers of this period, which was marked by great social, political, and cultural changes, began to take seriously activities of artists, who often seek to express, rather than represent, their aspirations and emotions, or politicians and businessmen, who aim to assert themselves in governments and marketplaces.

In fact, nineteenth-century philosophers started to think of human self-expression and self-assertion as fundamental to everything human beings do, including science. Science, according to philosophers such as Hegel or Nietzsche, is better understood not as an attempt to represent the physical world, but as an attempt of scientists and the people for whom they work to express or assert themselves. Scientists may think that they are merely seeking better representations of the world around them, but in fact they are really seeking to express their own inner natures or pursuing agendas for enhancing their power. This was not seen as a problem, but as something worthy of praise.

The Vienna Circle sought to revive the ideal of human beings seeking better and better representations of the world, particularly in the sciences. They were encouraged in this by the revolutionary progress physics had made during the early part of the twentieth century. In fact, they placed physics on a pedestal as a model of the progress human beings can make in their pursuit of improved representations of the world. Philosophy, on the other hand, was seen as mostly a form of poetry or literature that was either irrelevant to the human quest for knowledge or a hindrance to it, because it spread confusing nonsense that kept people from pursuing truth.

With sciences as its model, logical positivism focused on verification and truth conditions of sentences, and empirical criteria for words. If no criterion of application of a word is known or provided, then that word is cognitively meaningless, and if the method of verification of a sentence was not known or, which amounts to the same thing, its truth conditions were not known, then the sentence is cognitively meaningless. A few examples will clarify this.

Suppose I am comparing CD players and I describe one as being transparent and the other as not being transparent, but as being veiled. When you ask me what it is for a CD player to sound transparent, I have no clear answers for you. There are no clear-cut signs of transparency, I claim. In fact, when pressed further, I am unable to provide a reason for why I say that one player sounds transparent while another sounds veiled. Moreover, there does not seem to be any discernible difference in the sound of the player that I claim sounds transparent and ones I claim do not sound transparent. In the absence of criteria for properly using the word "transparent" in describing CD players, this word used in that way appears to be cognitively meaningless. Logical positivists argued that words that allegedly refer to something beyond experience, such as the words "mind" and "God," are prime examples of cognitively meaningless words. Since the words refer to something beyond experience, they cannot have an empirical criteria of application, and thus are meaningless.

The statements in which cognitively meaningless words occur are mere pseudo-statements and are also cognitively meaningless. This is not to say that I do not associate some feelings or emotions with the word, but the word does not become cognitively meaningful because of that. It might acquire an emotional meaning through such association, as, for example, ethical terms do, but not cognitive meaning which comes with some criteria of application. For instance, saying that a CD player sounds transparent may be a way of expressing your feelings of well-being while listening to it, but this is emotional meaning, not cognitive meaning. In the same way, since the words "good" and "God" lack cognitive meaning, the sentences "Being kind to children is good" and "God is forgiving" also lack cognitive meaning, although they can be rich in emotional meaning.

There are other ways in which sentences can be cognitively meaningless. For example, "He neither runs" is not a grammatical sentence and that is why you cannot make any sense of it. Others are grammatical, but are still meaningless, such as "Green ideas sleep furiously" or "I am the walrus." Although all the words are meaningful and the structure is grammatical, you still have no idea what the criteria of application are for such sentences.

The logical positivists charged metaphysics with committing various errors resulting in metaphysical statements lacking cognitive meaning. As we saw in chapter 3, on values, logical positivists asserted that meaningful statements are either analytic – that is, true in virtue of the meaning of their words – in which case they say nothing about reality, or empirical, in which case they belong to the domain of the empirical sciences. And since the statements of metaphysics fall into neither the analytic nor the empirical category, they are meaningless.

There are various ways of dealing with the logical positivists' criticism of philosophy and metaphysics. If we, for a moment, grant the logical positivists the claim that all statements are either analytic or empirical, then there is clearly still room for at least some metaphysics. One of the legacies of logical positivism is behaviorism, which attempted to inform us of the nature of the mind and thus clearly is a metaphysical position. And after behaviorism there follow various kinds of materialistic theories of the mind, many of which have an active empirical research component.

The logical positivists presented an atomistic account of word and sentence meaning. Individual words, if they were cognitively meaningful, had criteria of application, and individual sentences, if meaningful, could be verified. This account of word meaning and sentence meaning has come under a strong attack from philosophers who argue that one cannot cut a word and its meaning from the network it belongs to; namely the language as a whole. The meaning of a word, they argue, does not come only from a criteria of application, but also from its connections with other words in the language and its use in the language. On these views the language is like a web and individual words and sentences belong to the language, and thus have a meaning only when they form a part of the web.

Finally, the distinction between the analytic and the empirical has come under attack. The logical positivists assumed that every statement is knowable either with experience or without experience, and further, that those that were knowable without experience were uninformative. If a statement was analytic it was assumed to be both necessarily true and knowable without experience, and if it was either of these it was called uninformative.

Recent analytic philosophy has become very suspicious of the word "analytic" due to the many uses it was put to. The word was sometimes used when philosophers intended to call a statement necessary, sometimes it was used to call something knowable without experience, sometimes it was used to say that a statement was true in virtue of the meanings of the words used to make the statement, and sometimes it was used to indicate that a statement was not informative.

Subsequent work has, for example, pointed out that when we talk of something as being necessarily true, we are talking about metaphysics, and when we talk about something as being knowable without experience, we are talking about epistemology. Furthermore, it is now acknowledged that even if a statement is either necessarily true or knowable without experience, it does not mean that it is uninformative. Statements in mathematics and logic, as well as definitions, are commonly viewed as being informative despite being either necessarily true or knowable without experience, or both. So, contrary to what the logical positivists thought, informative statements are not limited to empirically verifiable statements. In the end, logical positivism did not eliminate metaphysics. But it certainly had serious effects on the direction taken when dealing with certain metaphysical problems. It suffices to point to its effect on the treatment of the mind/body problem, where logical positivism motivated behaviorism.

Postmodern Critiques of Metaphysics

Postmodernism is an important trend in recent philosophy. Postmodern thinkers refuse to place physics or any science on a pedestal and reject logical positivism's pursuit of the ideal of objective, scientific knowledge. In general, they are suspicious of appeals to the ideals of truth and objectivity. Instead, postmodernists extol the human capacity to make or construct things, whether in the pursuit of power or just for fun, and believe that everything is a human construction, including what physicists and other scientists talk about.

Postmodernists identify metaphysics with a commitment to certain distinctions that they reject as mere human constructions. They are particularly concerned with the distinction between appearance and reality. The idea that some things are objective and real while others are mere subjective appearances seems pernicious to postmodernists. It is seen as an artificial distinction that people make primarily to serve their own or their community's interests. Things that do not serve these interests are branded as mere appearances, while things that serve these interests are anointed with the mark of reality.

These critics of modern culture take many of their cues from the nineteenth-century German philosopher and critic of metaphysics, Friedrich Nietzsche. Nietzsche's writing style is very literary, full of irony and metaphor, but there is a philosophical purpose to his style of writing. Nietzsche denied that there was such a thing as literal and objective truth. All claims, whether in physics, politics, poetry or philosophy, are subjective and metaphorical. They are all expressions and products of human drives and needs, particularly the drive to control and exercise power over our environment. The pursuit of objective and scientific knowledge, for instance, is nothing more than an attempt to assert ourselves over others. For, Nietzsche, good science is not an improved representation of the world, but an improved means of exercising power over others, and how successful a science is in this has nothing to do with the truth or objectivity of its claims.

Nietzsche rejects the very idea of an objective reality; that is, a realm of objects or processes that are independent of our minds. For Nietzsche, everything is a product of our perspective, and our perspective is an expression of our needs and desires for power. He believes that there is no objective component to our perspective. Although we may be inclined to believe that at least sometimes there is something objective or real that is the object of our perspective and independent of it, Nietzsche believes that this belief is a mere prejudice and an expression of our will to power. To claim that your perspective is objective and of something real is just a maneuver in a battle to preserve or enhance your power.

Nietzsche's basic strategy is to offer psychological explanations for key ideas and distinctions. He notices that many things people do are motivated by their psychological desires and needs, he believes that most of these desires and needs are for self-aggrandizement, and he tries to explain as much as he can in terms of this *will to power.*

Psychological explanations, which have become very powerful and popular in the twentieth century, have a special advantage over what we might call objectivist explanations. All other things being equal, a psychological explanation is simpler than an objectivist explanation. Remember our discussion of universals or moral value. Explaining universals or moral value in terms of how we think has the advantage that it is simpler than an objectivist account that maintains that there really are objective universals or moral values. This is also true for psychological accounts of God. Explaining God in terms of our subjective needs is much simpler than explaining God in terms of the real, objective existence of God.

Similarly, explaining the appearance/reality distinction in terms of our psychological needs and drives has the advantage of simplicity over an objectivist interpretation of this distinction. Instead of having two kinds of things – subjective appearances and objective reality – the psychological explanation commits us only to have human drives and needs and makes the appearance/reality distinction into a figment of our power-hungry thinking.

Of course, simplicity is not the only criterion for evaluating an explanation. Very often, better explanations are more complex than less successful explanations. A good explanation also has to account for all the facts, and Nietzsche's psychological account of the appearance/reality distinction is better than competing accounts that make this into a real, objective distinction only if it in fact accounts for all the different ways in which we draw and use that distinction. We leave it as an open question whether Nietzsche (or a Nietzschean account) can give a successful psychological explanation of the appearance/reality distinction. Our concern is to see if Nietzsche succeeds in debunking metaphysics.

Suppose for the sake of argument that Nietzsche's psychological account of the appearance/reality distinction is successful and is better than any objectivist explanation according to which there really is a distinction between appearance and reality. Suppose that this distinction is indeed only a product of human desires for self-aggrandizement. Would this spell the end of metaphysics?

Metaphysics is concerned with what there is and the structure or nature of what there is. In giving a psychological explanation of the distinction between appearance and reality, Nietzsche makes some commitments to what there is and its nature or structure. He maintains that there are psychological drives and needs – particularly the will to power – and he tries to explain as much as possible as an expression of the will to power. To put it simply, Nietzsche is telling us something about reality: that it consists of the will to power and that there is nothing that exists apart from will to power. This is a metaphysical position.

Similarly, contemporary postmodernism cannot escape metaphysics. Postmodernists today have tried to avoid the metaphysical commitments Nietzsche makes concerning the existence of needs, desires, and the will to power. They have suggested that Nietzsche still aims at what might be called a "grand narrative" or all-encompassing story about what there is and is not. He still weaves a grandiose story about the will to power as the root of all there is, they would argue. They aim to avoid all this by arguing that there are no credible grand narratives; all we have are many local narratives that cannot be woven together into one large story.

This too does not spell an end to metaphysics. The metaphysics of postmodernism includes two important ideas. First, there are narratives or stories, and everything from fairy tales to your text in physics is best understood as a kind of narrative. Second, there is no overarching grand narrative that weaves all other narratives together into one complex story about reality. These are claims about what there is and its structure: that there are narratives and that things are such that there cannot be a unifying narrative.

Metaphysics and Political Philosophy

John Rawls is arguably the greatest moral and political philosopher of the twentieth century. In his major work, *A Theory of Justice*, Rawls develops and defends the idea of justice in terms of fairness. He argues that there are two principles of justice:

1 *Principle of Equal Liberty.* Every person is to have an equal right to the most extensive amount of liberty compatible with similar liberty for everyone else.
2 *Principle of Difference.* Social and economic inequalities must be arranged so that (a) everyone has an opportunity to acquire these unequally distributed goods and (b) the inequalities are to everyone's advantage, including the least advantaged members of society.

According to the first principle, everyone will be able to do whatever they want as long as they do not diminish others' ability to do what they want. The second principle aims to guarantee that there is an equality of opportunity and that even the poorest and most powerless members of society are better off under this arrangement than under alternative arrangements. In case there is a conflict between the two principles, the first principle takes precedence over the second principle.

Rawls argues that these are the principles of justice we would accept if we think about justice in an unbiased and fair way. Can human beings think about anything in an unbiased and fair way? Rawls believes that we can, and devises a scheme that promotes such thinking. He suggests that we have to think about justice as behind a *veil of ignorance*. Behind the veil of ignorance we do not know how society's goods are distributed. We do not know what our economic or political status is in society and we do not know how natural talents and abilities are distributed. For instance, we do not know if we are rich or poor in relation to other people in our society, how much political power we wield over others, and how intelligent we are compared to others. In sum, we do not know what advantages or disadvantages we have with respect to our fellow human beings.

Nevertheless, we do know a few things behind the veil of ignorance. We know that we are rational and that we care about our own well-being. We also know that we cannot make it on our own and that we need to cooperate with other people. Moreover, we know that cooperation is possible; that is, that human beings can work together to achieve common goals. Finally, we are aware of the fact that we want to have principles of justice, and we intend to stick by these principles as long as others are also committed to justice. With this in mind, behind the veil of ignorance, Rawls argues, we would want everyone to have as much liberty as is compatible with everyone having the same amount, and we would want to distribute goods in a way that is to everyone's mutual advantage. In other words, we would commit ourselves to the Principle of Equal Liberty and the Principle of Difference.

Is Rawls working with some metaphysical assumptions in his political philosophy? It certainly looks as if he is making metaphysical assumptions. For instance, it seems that he assumes that behind the veil of ignorance we are still persons. This is a significant claim, because behind the veil of ignorance we do not know or even have beliefs about our social, economic, and political positions with respect to other people. We do not know what social or economic class we belong to, what our loyalties and allegiances are, who our adversaries or competitors are, and so on. Can we be persons and not know or have beliefs about our specific attachments and loyalties to other people, say our family or community?

To answer this question is to engage in some metaphysics about the nature of persons. Individualists will agree with Rawls and argue that there is a core to one's personality that does not include any knowledge or beliefs about where we stand in society. On the other hand, communitarians will deny that there is such a core. To be a person is not only to have social ties and a place in society, but to have thoughts about specific people, one's place in society and the interests that we have as a result of our social position.

Of course, even if it were true that as persons we will always have a conception of our place in society, perhaps sometimes we can try to abstract from or somehow ignore this conception. Maybe this is all Rawls is suggesting: when we think about what the principles of justice are, we should abstract away from all these social beliefs and not use any of them in our reasoning about justice. So, if you are an upper middle-class young woman from Nigeria studying in Canada and you are reasoning about what justice is, do not use the fact that you are an upper middle-class young woman from Nigeria studying in Canada in your reasoning. Can a person perform such a feat of abstraction? Certainly it looks like a noble and praiseworthy aim – to ignore all these social facts about us – but whether or not we can will involve some thinking about what it is to be a person and what sort of thinking a person is capable of, and these are metaphysical issues.

Another place where metaphysics seems to appear in Rawls's political philosophy is in his assumption that when thinking about justice we think of ourselves as free. We have the power to think freely about what is good and just and take responsibility for the aims and aspirations we have in our lives. This conception of us as being free persons has metaphysical consequences, and this is easy to see. If this conception is accurate, hard determinism is false, and if hard determinism is true, this conception is false. As we saw, hard determinists deny that we are free.

The view that we are free is a metaphysical view no matter what the origins of this view. Many children first encounter the view that we are free in a religious context, because they are taught morality and personal responsibility through religion. But this does not mean that this is only a religious claim. Just as the claim that God exists is a religious as well as a metaphysical claim, the idea that we are free belongs to both religion and metaphysics. Rawls is probably right that for many the idea that we are free is rooted in the political arena, and consequently for many the view that we are free is political. However, that the idea that we are free belongs in the political arena does not preclude it from also belonging to metaphysics and being subject to metaphysical scrutiny.

Conclusion

Metaphysical views are found in all aspects of our practical lives, including in our political lives, and for this reason we cannot do without metaphysics. This should not be surprising. Metaphysics is concerned with what there is and the nature or structure of what there is, and all of our activities are guided by basic assumptions about what there is and what structure it has. Of course, we do not always reflect on these assumptions, but sooner or later thinking people will find themselves thinking about these metaphysical assumptions.

We will find ourselves thinking about these issues because we will encounter fundamental political, moral, legal, or social conflicts that will involve diverging metaphysical views. Whether we are engaging in these conflicts as partisans or simply trying to understand them, we will run into views about what there is or the nature or structure of what there is. We will see that views about universality, value, divinity, causality, mind or freedom permeate the differences and conflicts that sooner or later emerge for all human beings.

Conflicts will force us to think about metaphysics, but conflicts are not required for us to seek out metaphysics and reflect about metaphysical issues. We want lives that are worthwhile. Nobody is happy knowing that he or she is living a worthless life. But an unexamined life is not worth living, as Socrates maintained before his death. Not taking everything for granted all the time and finding the time and energy to re-examine even our most cherished convictions is the mark of a life lived with care and attention to detail. For this reason, reflective human beings will seek out metaphysics, the subject where we carefully examine the fundamental assumptions about reality that guide us in theory and in practice.

The Elimination of Metaphysics through Logical Analysis of Language
Rudolf Carnap *(Translated by Arthur Pap)*

Rudolf Carnap (1891–1970) was an Austrian philosopher who taught in Vienna and Prague before he moved to the United States in 1935. He first taught at the University of Chicago and then until his retirement in 1961 at the University of California at Los Angeles. Carnap was one of the founders and one of the strongest advocates of logical positivism. He believed that when properly analyzed, metaphysical problems were mere pseudo-problems, and that metaphysical statements were cognitively meaningless. Progress in philosophy, Carnap argued, needed scientific analysis of its concepts and, as he argues in the following selection, metaphysical concepts do not lend themselves to such analysis.

1 Introduction

There have been many *opponents of metaphysics* from the Greek skeptics to the empiricists of the 19th century. Criticisms of very diverse kinds have been set forth. Many have declared that the doctrine of metaphysics is *false*, since it contradicts our empirical knowledge. Others have believed it to be *uncertain*, on the ground that its problems transcend the limits of human knowledge. Many antimetaphysicians have declared that occupation with metaphysical questions is *sterile*. Whether or not these questions can be answered, it is at any rate unnecessary to worry about them; let us devote ourselves entirely to the practical tasks which confront active men every day of their lives!

The development of *modern logic* has made it possible to give a new and sharper answer to the question of the validity and justification of metaphysics. The researches of applied logic or the theory of knowledge, which aim at clarifying the cognitive content of scientific statements and thereby the meanings of the terms that occur in the statements, by means of logical analysis, lead to a positive and to a negative result. The positive result is worked out in the domain of empirical science; the various concepts of the various branches of science are clarified; their formal-logical and epistemological connections are made explicit. In the domain of *metaphysics*, including all philosophy of value and normative theory, logical analysis yields the negative result *that the alleged statements in this domain are entirely meaningless*. Therewith a radical elimination of metaphysics is attained, which was not yet possible from the earlier antimetaphysical standpoints. It is true that related ideas may be found already in several earlier trains of thought, e.g. those of a nominalistic kind; but it is only now when the development of logic during recent decades provides us with a sufficiently sharp tool that the decisive step can be taken.

In saying that the so-called statements of metaphysics are *meaningless*, we intend this word in its strictest sense. In a loose sense of the word a statement or a question is at times called meaningless if it is entirely sterile to assert or ask it. We might say this for instance about the question "what is the average weight of those inhabitants of Vienna whose telephone number ends with '3'?" or about a statement which is quite obviously false like "in 1910 Vienna had 6 inhabitants" or about a statement which is not just empirically, but logically false, a contradictory statement such as "persons A and B are each a year older than the other." Such sentences are really meaningful, though they are pointless or false; for it is only meaningful sentences that are even divisible into (theoretically) fruitful and sterile, true and false. In the strict sense, however, a sequence of words is *meaningless if* it does not, within a specified language, constitute a statement. It may happen that such a sequence of words looks like a statement at first glance; in that case we call it a *pseudo-statement*. Our thesis, now, is that logical analysis reveals the alleged statements of metaphysics to be pseudo-statements.

A language consists of a vocabulary and a syntax, i.e. a set of words which have meanings and rules of sentence formation. These rules indicate how sentences may be formed out of the various sorts of words. Accordingly, there are two kinds of pseudo-statements: either they contain a word which is erroneously believed to have meaning, or the constituent words are meaningful, yet are put together in a counter-syntactical way, so that they do not yield a meaningful statement. We shall show in terms of examples that pseudo-statements of both kinds occur in metaphysics. Later we shall have to inquire into the reasons that support our contention that metaphysics in its entirety consists of such pseudo-statements.

2 The Significance of a Word

A word which (within a definite language) has a meaning, is usually also said to designate a concept; if it only seems to have a meaning while it really does not, we speak of a "pseudo-concept." How is the origin of a pseudo-concept to be explained? Has not every word been introduced into the language for no other purpose than to express something or other, so that it had a definite meaning from the very beginning of its use? How, then, can a traditional language contain meaningless words? To be sure, originally every word (excepting rare cases which we shall illustrate later) had a meaning. In the course of historical development a word frequently changes its meaning. And it also happens at times that a word loses its old sense without acquiring a new one. It is thus that a pseudo-concept arises.

What, now, is *the meaning of a word?* What stipulations concerning a word must be made in order for it to be significant? (It does not matter for our investigation whether these stipulations are explicitly laid down, as in the case of some words and symbols of modern science, or whether they have been tacitly agreed upon, as is the case for most words of traditional language.) First, the *syntax* of the word must be fixed, i.e. the mode of its occurrence in the simplest sentence form in which it is capable of occurring; we call this sentence form its *elementary sentence*. The elementary sentence form for the word "stone" e.g. is "x is a stone"; in sentences of this form some designation from the category of things occupies the place of "x," e.g. "this diamond," "this apple." Secondly, for an elementary sentence S containing the word an answer must be given to the following question, which can be formulated in various ways:

(1)   What sentences is S *deducible* from, and what sentences are deducible from S?
(2)   Under what conditions is S supposed to be true, and under what conditions false?
(3)   How is S to be *verified?*
(4)   What is the *meaning* of S?

(1) is the correct formulation; formulation (2) accords with the phraseology of logic, (3) with the phraseology of the theory of knowledge, (4) with that of philosophy (phenomenology). Wittgenstein has asserted that (2) expresses what philosophers mean by (4): the meaning of a sentence consists in its truth-condition. ((1) is the "metalogical" formulation; it is planned to give elsewhere a detailed exposition of metalogic as the theory of syntax and meaning, i.e. relations of deducibility.)

In the case of many words, specifically in the case of the overwhelming majority of scientific words, it is possible to specify their meaning by reduction to other words ("constitution," definition). E.g. "'arthropods' are animals with segmented bodies and jointed legs." Thereby the above-mentioned question for the elementary sentence form of the word "arthropods," that is for the sentence form "the thing x is an arthropod," is answered: it has been stipulated that a sentence of this form is deducible from premises of the form "x is an animal," "x has a segmented body," "x has jointed legs," and that conversely each of these sentences is deducible from the former sentence. By means of these stipulations about deducibility (in other words: about the truth-condition, about the method of verification, about the meaning) of the elementary sentence about "arthropods" the meaning of the word "arthropods" is fixed. In this way every word of the language is reduced to other words and finally to the words which occur in the so-called "observation sentences" or "protocol sentences." It is through this reduction that the word acquires its meaning.

For our purposes we may ignore entirely the question concerning the content and form of the primary sentences (protocol sentences) which has not yet been definitely settled. In the theory of knowledge it is customary to say that the primary sentences refer to "the given"; but there is no unanimity on the question what it is that is given. At times the position is taken that sentences about the given speak of the simplest qualities of sense and feeling (e.g. "warm," "blue," "joy" and so forth); others incline to the view that basic sentences refer to total experiences and similarities between them; a still different view has it that even the basic sentences speak of things. Regardless of this diversity of opinion it is certain that a sequence of words has a meaning only if its relations of deducibility to the protocol sentences are fixed, whatever the characteristics of the protocol sentences may be; and similarly, that a word is significant only if the sentences in which it may occur are reducible to protocol sentences.

Since the meaning of a word is determined by its criterion of application (in other words: by the relations of deducibility entered into by its elementary sentence-form, by its truth-conditions, by the method of its verification), the stipulation of the criterion takes away one's freedom to decide what one wishes to "mean" by the word. If the word is to receive an exact meaning, nothing less than the criterion of application must be given; but one cannot, on the other hand, give more than the criterion of application, for the latter is a sufficient determination of meaning. The meaning is implicitly contained in the criterion; all that remains to be done is to make the meaning explicit.

Let us suppose, by way of illustration, that someone invented the new word "teavy" and maintained that there are things which are teavy and things which are not teavy. In order to learn the meaning of this word, we ask him about its criterion of application: how is one to ascertain in a concrete case whether a given thing is teavy or not? Let us suppose to begin with that we get no answer from him: there are no empirical signs of teavyness, he says. In that case we would deny the legitimacy of using this word. If the person who uses the word says that all the same there are things which are teavy and there are things which are not teavy, only it remains for the weak, finite intellect of man an eternal secret which things are teavy and which are not, we shall regard this as empty verbiage. But perhaps he will assure us that he means, after all, something by the word "teavy." But from this we only learn the psychological fact that he associates some kind of images and feelings with the word. The word does not acquire a meaning through such associations. If no criterion of application for the word is stipulated, then nothing is asserted by the sentences in which it occurs, they are but pseudo-statements.

Secondly, take the case when we are given a criterion of application for a new word, say "toovy"; in particular, let the sentence "this thing is toovy" be true if and only if the thing is quadrangular (it is irrelevant in this context whether the criterion is explicitly stated or whether we derive it by observing the affirmative and the negative uses of the word). Then we will say: the word "toovy" is synonymous with the word "quadrangular." And we will not allow its users to tell us that nevertheless they "intended" something else by it than "quadrangular"; that though every quadrangular thing is also toovy and conversely, this is only because quadrangularity is the visible manifestation of toovyness, but that the latter itself is a hidden, not itself observable property. We would reply that after the criterion of application has been fixed, the synonymy of "toovy" and "quadrangular" is likewise fixed, and that we are no further at liberty to "intend" this or that by the word.

Let us briefly summarize the result of our analysis. Let "a" be any word and "S(a)" the elementary sentence in which it occurs. Then the sufficient and necessary condition for "a" being meaningful may be given by each of the following formulations, which ultimately say the same thing:

1   The *empirical criteria* for a are known.
2   It has been stipulated from what protocol sentences "S(a)" *is deducible*.
3   The *truth-conditions* for "S(a)" are fixed.
4   The method of *verification* of "S(a)" is known.[1]

3 Metaphysical Words without Meaning

Many words of metaphysics, now, can be shown not to fulfill the above requirement, and therefore to be devoid of meaning.

Let us take as an example the metaphysical term "principle" (in the sense of principle of being, not principle of knowledge or axiom). Various metaphysicians offer an answer to the question which is the (highest) "principle of the world" (or of "things," of "existence," of "being"), e.g. water, number, form, motion, life, the spirit, the idea, the unconscious, activity, the good, and so forth. In order to discover the meaning of the word "principle" in this metaphysical question we must ask the metaphysician under what conditions a statement of the form "x is the principle of y" would be true and under what conditions it would be false. In other words: we ask for the criteria of application or for the definition of the word "principle." The metaphysician replies approximately as follows: "x is the principle of y" is to mean "y arises out of x," "the being of y rests on the being of x," "y exists by virtue of x" and so forth. But these words arc ambiguous and vague. Frequently they have a clear meaning; e.g., we say of a thing or process y that it "arises out of" x when we observe that things or processes of kind x are frequently or invariably followed by things or processes of kind y (causal connection in the sense of a lawful succession). But the metaphysician tells us that he does not mean this empirically observable relationship. For in that case his metaphysical theses would be merely empirical propositions of the same kind as those of physics. The expression "arising from" is not to mean here a relation of temporal and causal sequence, which is what the word ordinarily means. Yet, no criterion is specified for any other meaning. Consequently, the alleged "metaphysical" meaning, which the word is supposed to have here in contrast to the mentioned empirical meaning, does not exist. If we reflect on the original meaning of the word "principium" (and of the corresponding Greek word "ἀρχή"), we notice the same development. The word is explicitly deprived of its original meaning "beginning"; it is not supposed to mean the temporally prior any more, but the prior in some other, specifically metaphysical, respect. The criteria for this "metaphysical respect," however, are lacking. In both cases, then, the word has been deprived of its earlier meaning without being given a new meaning; there remains the word as an empty shell. From an earlier period of significant use, it is still associatively connected with various mental images; these in turn get associated with new mental images and feelings in the new context of usage. But the word does not thereby become meaningful; and it remains meaningless as long as no method of verification can be described.

Another example is the word "God." Here we must, apart from the variations of its usage within each domain, distinguish the linguistic usage in three different contexts or historical epochs, which however overlap temporally. In its *mythological* use the word has a clear meaning. It, or parallel words in other languages, is sometimes used to denote physical beings which are enthroned on Mount Olympus, in Heaven or in Hades, and which are endowed with power, wisdom, goodness and happiness to a greater or lesser extent. Sometimes the word also refers to spiritual beings which, indeed, do not have manlike bodies, yet manifest themselves nevertheless somehow in the things or processes of the visible world and are therefore empirically verifiable. In its *metaphysical* use, on the other hand, the word "God" refers to something beyond experience. The word is deliberately divested of its reference to a physical being or to a spiritual being that is immanent in the physical. And as it is not given a new meaning, it becomes meaningless. To be sure, it often looks as though the word "God" had a meaning even in metaphysics. But the definitions which are set up prove on closer inspection to be pseudo-definitions. They lead either to logically illegitimate combinations of words (of which we shall treat later) or to other metaphysical words (e.g. "primordial basis," "the absolute," "the unconditioned," "the autonomous," "the self-dependent" and so forth), but in no case to the truth-conditions of its elementary sentences. In the case of this word not even the first requirement of logic is met, that is the requirement to specify its syntax, i.e. the form of its occurrence in elementary sentences. An elementary sentence would here have to be of the form "x is a God"; yet, the metaphysician either rejects this form entirely without substituting another, or if he accepts it he neglects to indicate the syntactical category of the variable x. (Categories are, for example, material things, properties of things, relations between things, numbers etc.)

The *theological* usage of the word "God" falls between its mythological and its metaphysical usage. There is no distinctive meaning here, but an oscillation from one of the mentioned two uses to the other. Several theologians have a clearly empirical (in our terminology, "mythological") concept of God. In this case there are no pseudo-statements; but the disadvantage for the theologian lies in the circumstance that according to this interpretation the statements of theology are empirical and hence are subject to the judgment of empirical science. The linguistic usage of other theologians is clearly metaphysical. Others again do not speak in any definite way, whether this is because they follow now this, now that linguistic usage, or because they express themselves in terms whose usage is not clearly classifiable since it tends towards both sides.

Just like the examined examples "principle" and "God," most of the other *specifically metaphysical terms are devoid of meaning*, e.g. "the Idea," "the Absolute," "the Unconditioned," "the Infinite," "the being of being," "non-being," "thing in itself," "absolute spirit," "objective spirit," "essence," "being-in-it-self," "being-in-and-for-itself," "emanation," "manifestation," "articulation," "the Ego," "the non-Ego," etc. These expressions are in the same boat with "teavy," our previously fabricated example. The metaphysician tells us that empirical truth-conditions cannot be specified; if he adds that nevertheless he "means" something, we know that this is merely an allusion to associated images and feelings which, however, do not bestow a meaning on the word. The alleged statements of metaphysics which contain such words have no sense, assert nothing, are mere pseudo-statements. Into the explanation of their historical origin we shall inquire later.

4 The Significance of a Sentence

So far we have considered only those pseudo-statements which contain a meaningless word. But there is a second kind of pseudo-statement. They consist of meaningful words, but the words are put together in such a way that nevertheless no meaning results. The syntax of a language specifies which combinations of words are admissible and which inadmissible. The grammatical syntax of natural languages, however, does not fulfill the task of elimination of senseless combinations of words in all cases. Let us take as examples the following sequences of words:

1 "Caesar is and"
2 "Caesar is a prime number"

The word sequence (1) is formed countersyntactically; the rules of syntax require that the third position be occupied, not by a conjunction, but by a predicate, hence by a noun (with article) or by an adjective. The word sequence "Caesar is a general," e.g., is formed in accordance with the rules of syntax. It is a meaningful word sequence, a genuine sentence. But, now, word sequence (2) is likewise syntactically correct, for it has the same grammatical form as the sentence just mentioned. Nevertheless (2) is meaningless. "Prime number" is a predicate of numbers; it can be neither affirmed nor denied of a person. Since (2) looks like a statement yet is not a statement, does not assert anything, expresses neither a true nor a false proposition, we call this word sequence a "pseudo-statement." The fact that the rules of grammatical syntax are not violated easily seduces one at first glance into the erroneous opinion that one still has to do with a statement, albeit a false one. But "a is a prime number" is false if and only if a is divisible by a natural number different from a and from 1; evidently it is illicit to put here "Caesar" for "a." This example has been so chosen that the nonsense is easily detectable. Many so-called statements of metaphysics are not so easily recognized to be pseudo-statements. The fact that natural languages allow the formation of meaningless sequences of words without violating the rules of grammar, indicates that grammatical syntax is, from a logical point of view, inadequate. If grammatical syntax corresponded exactly to logical syntax, pseudo-statements could not arise. If grammatical syntax differentiated not only the word-categories of nouns, adjectives, verbs, conjunctions etc., but within each of these categories made the further distinctions that are logically indispensable, then no pseudo-statements could be formed. If, e.g., nouns were grammatically subdivided into several kinds of words, according as they designated properties of physical objects, of numbers etc., then the words "general" and "prime number" would belong to grammatically different word-categories, and (2) would be just as linguistically incorrect as (1). In a correctly constructed language, therefore, all nonsensical sequences of words would be of the kind of example (1). Considerations of grammar would already eliminate them as it were automatically; i.e. in order to avoid nonsense, it would be unnecessary to pay attention to the meanings of the individual words over and above their syntactical type (their "syntactical category," e.g. thing, property of things, relation between things, number, property of numbers, relation between numbers, and so forth). It follows that if our thesis that the statements of metaphysics are pseudo-statements is justifiable, then metaphysics could not even be expressed in a logically constructed language. This is the great philosophical importance of the task, which at present occupies the logicians, of building a logical syntax.

5 Metaphysical Pseudo-statements

Let us now take a look at some examples of metaphysical pseudo-statements of a kind where the violation of logical syntax is especially obvious, though they accord with historical-grammatical syntax. We select a few sentences from that metaphysical school which at present exerts the strongest influence in Germany.[2]

"What is to be investigated is being only and – nothing else; being alone and further – *nothing*; solely being, and beyond being – *nothing*. *What about this Nothing?* . . . *Does the Nothing exist only because the Not, i.e. the Negation, exists? Or is it the other way around? Does Negation and the Not exist only because the Nothing exists?* . . . We assert: *the Nothing is prior to the Not and the Negation.* . . . Where do we seek the Nothing? How do we find the Nothing. . . . We know the Nothing. . . . *Anxiety reveals the Nothing.* . . . That for which and because of which we were anxious, was 'really' – nothing. Indeed: the Nothing itself – as such – was present. . . . *What about this Nothing? – The Nothing itself nothings.*"

In order to show that the possibility of forming pseudo-statements is based on a logical defect of language, we set up the schema opposite – Table X. The sentences under I are grammatically as well as logically impeccable, hence meaningful. The sentences under II (excepting B3) are in grammatical respects perfectly analogous to those under I. Sentence form IIA (as question and answer) does not, indeed, satisfy the requirements to be imposed on a logically correct language. But it is nevertheless meaningful, because it is translatable into correct language. This is shown by sentence IIIA, which has the same meaning as IIA. Sentence form IIA then proves to be undesirable because we can be led from it, by means of grammatically faultless operations, to the meaningless sentence forms IIB, which are taken from the above quotation. These forms cannot even be constructed in the correct language of Column III. Nonetheless, their nonsensicality is not obvious at first glance, because one is easily deceived by the analogy with the meaningful sentences IB. The fault of our language identified here lies, therefore, in the circumstance that, in contrast to a logically correct language, it admits of the same grammatical form for meaningful and meaningless word sequences. To each sentence in words we have added a corresponding formula in the notation of symbolic logic; these formulae facilitate recognition of the undesirable analogy between IA and IIA and therewith of the origin of the meaningless constructions IIB.

On closer inspection of the pseudo-statements under IIB, we also find some differences. The construction of sentence (1) is simply based on the mistake of employing the word "nothing" as a noun, because it is customary in ordinary language to use it in this form in order to construct a negative existential statement (see IIA). In a correct language, on the other hand, it is not a particular *name*, but a certain *logical form* of the sentence that serves this purpose (see IIIA). Sentence IIB2 adds something new, viz. the fabrication of the meaningless word "to nothing." This sentence, therefore, is senseless for a twofold reason. We pointed out before that the meaningless words of metaphysics usually owe their origin to the fact that a meaningful word is deprived of its meaning through its metaphorical use in metaphysics. But here we confront one of those rare cases where a new word is introduced which never had a meaning to begin with. Likewise sentence IIB3 must be rejected for two reasons. In respect of the error of using the word "nothing" as a noun, it is like the previous sentences. But in addition it involves a contradiction. For even if it were admissible to introduce "nothing" as a name or description of an entity, still the existence of this entity would be denied in its very definition, whereas sentence (3) goes on to affirm its existence. This sentence, therefore, would be contradictory, hence absurd, even if it were not already meaningless.

In view of the gross logical errors which we find in sentences IIB, we might be led to conjecture that perhaps the word "nothing" has in Heidegger's treatise a meaning entirely different from the customary one. And this presumption is further strengthened as we go on to read there that anxiety reveals the Nothing,

Table X

I.	II.	III.
Meaningful Sentences of Ordinary Language	Transition from Sense to Nonsense in Ordinary Language	Logically Correct Language
A. What is outside? Ou(?) Rain is outside Ou(r)	A. What is outside? Ou(?) Nothing is outside Ou(no)	A. There is nothing (does not exist anything) which is outside ~(Ex).Ou(x)
B. What about this rain? (i.e. what does the rain do? Or: what else can be said about this rain?) ?(r)	B. "What about this Nothing?" ?(no)	B. None of these forms can ever be constructed
1. We know the rain. K(r)	1. "We seek the Nothing" "We find the Nothing" "We know the Nothing" K(no)	
2. The rain rains R(r)	2. "The Nothing nothings" No(no)	
	3. "The Nothing exists only because . . ." Ex(no)	

that the Nothing itself is present as such in anxiety. For here the word "nothing" seems to refer to a certain emotional constitution, possibly of a religious sort, or something or other that underlies such emotions. If such were the case, then the mentioned logical errors in sentences IIB would not be committed. But the first sentence of the quotation at the beginning of this section proves that this interpretation is not possible. The combination of "only" and "nothing else" shows unmistakably that the word "nothing" here has the usual meaning of a logical particle that serves for the formulation of a negative existential statement. This introduction of the word "nothing" is then immediately followed by the leading question of the treatise: "What about this Nothing?"

But our doubts as to a possible misinterpretation get completely dissolved as we note that the author of the treatise is clearly aware of the conflict between his questions and statements, and logic. "*Question and answer* in regard to the

Nothing are equally *absurd* in themselves. . . . The fundamental rule of thinking commonly appealed to, the law of prohibited contradiction, general '*logic*,' destroys this question." All the worse for logic! We must abolish its sovereignty: "If thus the power of the *understanding* in the field of questions concerning Nothing and Being is broken, then the fate of the sovereignty of 'logic' within philosophy is thereby decided as well. The very idea of 'logic' dissolves in the whirl of a more basic questioning." But will sober science condone the whirl of counterlogical questioning? To this question too there is a ready answer: "The alleged sobriety and superiority of science becomes ridiculous if it does not take the Nothing seriously." Thus we find here a good confirmation of our thesis; a metaphysician himself here states that his questions and answers are irreconcilable with logic and the scientific way of thinking.

The difference between our thesis and that of the *earlier antimetaphysicians* should now be clear. We do not regard metaphysics as "mere speculation" or "fairy tales." The statements of a fairy tale do not conflict with logic, but only with experience; they are perfectly meaningful, although false. Metaphysics is not "*superstition*"; it is possible to believe true and false propositions, but not to believe meaningless sequences of words. Metaphysical statements are not even acceptable as "*working hypotheses*"; for an hypothesis must be capable of entering into relations of deducibility with (true or false) empirical statements, which is just what pseudo-statements cannot do.

With reference to the so-called *limitation of human knowledge* an attempt is sometimes made to save metaphysics by raising the following objection: metaphysical statements are not, indeed, verifiable by man nor by any other finite being; nevertheless they might be construed as conjectures about the answers which a being with higher or even perfect powers of knowledge would make to our questions, and as such conjectures they would, after all, be meaningful. To counter this objection, let us consider the following. If the meaning of a word cannot be specified, or if the sequence of words does not accord with the rules of syntax, then one has not even asked a question. (Just think of the pseudo-questions: "Is this table teavy?", "is the number 7 holy?", "which numbers are darker, the even or the odd ones?") Where there is no question, not even an omniscient being can give an answer. Now the objector may say: just as one who can see may communicate new knowledge to the blind, so a higher being might perhaps communicate to us metaphysical knowledge, e.g. whether the visible world is the manifestation of a spirit. Here we must reflect on the meaning of "new knowledge." It is, indeed, conceivable that we might encounter animals who tell us about a new sense. If these beings were to prove to us Fermat's theorem or were to invent a new physical instrument or were to establish a hitherto unknown law of nature, then our knowledge would be increased with their help. For this sort of thing we can test, just the way even a blind man can understand and test the whole of physics (and therewith any statement made by those who can see). But if those hypothetical beings tell us something which we cannot verify, then we cannot understand it either; in that case no information has been communicated to us, but mere verbal sounds devoid of meaning though possibly associated with images. It follows that our knowledge can only be quantitatively enlarged by other beings, no matter whether they know more or less or everything, but no knowledge of an essentially different kind can be added. What we do not know for certain, we may come to know with greater certainty through the assistance of other beings; but what is unintelligible, meaningless for us, cannot become meaningful through someone else's assistance, however vast his knowledge might be. Therefore no god and no devil can give us metaphysical knowledge.

6 Meaninglessness of All Metaphysics

The examples of metaphysical statements which we have analyzed were all taken from just one treatise. But our results apply with equal validity, in part even in verbally identical ways, to other metaphysical systems. That treatise is completely in the right in citing approvingly a statement by Hegel ("pure Being and pure Nothing, therefore, are one and the same"). The metaphysics of Hegel has exactly the same logical character as this modern system of metaphysics. And the same holds for the rest of the metaphysical systems, though the kind of phraseology and therewith the kind of logical errors that occur in them deviate more or less from the kind that occurs in the examples we discussed.

It should not be necessary here to adduce further examples of specific metaphysical sentences in diverse systems and submit them to analysis. We confine ourselves to an indication of the most frequent kinds of errors.

Perhaps the majority of the logical mistakes that are committed when pseudo-statements are made, are based on the logical faults infecting the use of the word "to be" in our language (and of the corresponding words in other languages, at least in most European languages). The first fault is the ambiguity of the word "to be." It is sometimes used as copula prefixed to a predicate ("I am hungry"), sometimes to designate existence ("I am"). This mistake is aggravated by the fact that metaphysicians often are not clear about this ambiguity. The second fault lies in the form of the verb in its second meaning, the meaning of *existence*. The verbal form feigns a predicate where there is none. To be sure, it has been known for a long time that existence is not a property (cf. Kant's refutation of the ontological proof of the existence of God). But it was not until the advent of modern logic that full consistency on this point was reached: the syntactical form in which modern logic introduces the sign for existence is such that it cannot, like a predicate, be applied to signs for objects, but only to predicates (cf. e.g. sentence IIIA in the above table). Most metaphysicians since antiquity have allowed themselves to be seduced into pseudo-statements by the verbal, and therewith the predicative form of the word "to be," e.g. "I am," "God is."

We meet an illustration of this error in Descartes' "cogito, ergo sum." Let us disregard here the material objections that have been raised against the premise – viz. whether the sentence "I think" adequately expresses the intended state of affairs or contains perhaps an hypostasis – and consider the two sentences only from the formal-logical point of view. We notice at once two essential logical mistakes. The first lies in the conclusion "I am." The verb "to be" is undoubtedly meant in the sense of existence here; for a copula cannot be used without predicate; indeed, Descartes' "I am" has always been interpreted in this sense. But in that case this sentence violates the above-mentioned logical rule that existence can be predicated only in conjunction with a predicate, not in conjunction with a name (subject, proper name). An existential statement does not have the form "a exists" (as in "I am," i.e. "I exist"), but "there exists something of such and such a kind." The second error lies in the transition from "I think" to "I exist." If from the statement "P(a)" ("a has the property P") an existential statement is to be deduced, then the latter can assert existence only with respect to the predicate P, not with respect to the subject a of the premise. What follows from "I am a European" is not "I exist," but "a European exists." What follows from "I think" is not "I am" but "there exists something that thinks."

The circumstance that our languages express existence by a verb ("to be" or "to exist") is not in itself a logical fault; it is only inappropriate, dangerous. The verbal form easily misleads us into the misconception that existence is a predicate. One then arrives at such logically incorrect and hence senseless modes of expression as were just examined. Likewise such forms as "Being" or "Not-Being," which from time immemorial have played a great role in metaphysics, have the same origin. In a logically correct language such forms cannot even be constructed. It appears that in the Latin and the German languages the forms "ens" or "das Seiende" were, perhaps under the seductive influence of the Greek example, introduced specifically for use by metaphysicians; in this way the language deteriorated logically whereas the addition was believed to represent an improvement.

Another very frequent violation of logical syntax is the so-called *"type confusion"* of concepts. While the previously mentioned mistake consists in the predicative use of a symbol with non-predicative meaning, in this case a predicate is, indeed, used as predicate yet as predicate of a different type. We have here a violation of the rules of the so-called theory of types. An artificial example is the sentence we discussed earlier: "Caesar is a prime number." Names of persons and names of numbers belong to different logical types, and so do accordingly predicates of persons (e.g. "general") and predicates of numbers ("prime number"). The error of type confusion is, unlike the previously discussed usage of the verb "to be," not the prerogative of metaphysics but already occurs very often in conversational language also. But here it rarely leads to nonsense. The typical ambiguity of words is here of such a kind that it can be easily removed.

Example: 1. 'This table is larger than that." 2. "The height of this table is larger than the height of that table." Here the word "larger" is used in (1) for a relation between objects, in (2) for a relation between numbers, hence for two distinct syntactical categories. The mistake is here unimportant; it could, e.g., be eliminated by writing "larger1" and "larger2"; "larger1" is then defined in terms of "larger2" by declaring statement form (1) to be synonymous with (2) (and others of a similar kind).

Since the confusion of types causes no harm in conversational language, it is usually ignored entirely. This is, indeed, expedient for the ordinary use of language, but has had unfortunate consequences in metaphysics. Here the conditioning by everyday language has led to confusions of types which, unlike those in everyday language, are no longer translatable into logically correct form. Pseudo-statements of this kind are encountered in especially large quantity, e.g., in the writings of Hegel and Heidegger. The latter has adopted many peculiarities of the Hegelian idiom along with their logical faults (e.g. predicates which should be applied to objects of a certain sort are instead applied to predicates of these objects or to "being" or to "existence" or to a relation between these objects).

Having found that many metaphysical statements are meaningless, we confront the question whether there is not perhaps a core of meaningful statements in metaphysics which would remain after elimination of all the meaningless ones.

Indeed, the results we have obtained so far might give rise to the view that there are many dangers of falling into nonsense in metaphysics, and that one must accordingly endeavor to avoid these traps with great care if one wants to do metaphysics. But actually the situation is that meaningful metaphysical statements are impossible. This follows from the task which metaphysics sets itself: to discover and formulate a kind of knowledge which is not accessible to empirical science.

We have seen earlier that the meaning of a statement lies in the method of its verification. A statement asserts only so much as is verifiable with respect to it. Therefore a sentence can be used only to assert an empirical proposition, if indeed it is used to assert anything at all. If something were to lie, in principle, beyond possible experience, it could be neither said nor thought nor asked.

(Meaningful) statements are divided into the following kinds. First there are statements which are true solely by virtue of their form ("tautologies" according to Wittgenstein; they correspond approximately to Kant's "analytic judgments"). They say nothing about reality. The formulae of logic and mathematics are of this kind. They are not themselves factual statements, but serve for the transformation of such statements. Secondly there are the negations of such statements (*"contradictions"*). They are self-contradictory, hence false by virtue of their form. With respect to all other statements the decision about truth or falsehood lies in the protocol sentences. They are therefore (true or false) *empirical statements* and belong to the domain of empirical science. Any statement one desires to construct which does not fall within these categories becomes automatically meaningless. Since metaphysics does not want to assert analytic propositions, nor to fall within the domain of empirical science, it is compelled to employ words for which no criteria of application are specified and which are therefore devoid of sense, or else to combine meaningful words in such a way that neither an analytic (or contradictory) statement nor an empirical statement is produced. In either case pseudo-statements are the inevitable product.

Logical analysis, then, pronounces the verdict of meaninglessness on any alleged knowledge that pretends to reach above or behind experience. This verdict hits, in the first place, any speculative metaphysics, any alleged knowledge by *pure thinking* or by *pure intuition* that pretends to be able to do without experience. But the verdict equally applies to the kind of metaphysics which, starting from experience, wants to acquire knowledge about that which *transcends experience* by means of special *inferences* (e.g. the neo-vitalist thesis of the directive presence of an "entelechy" in organic processes, which supposedly cannot be understood in terms of physics; the question concerning the "essence of causality," transcending the ascertainment of certain regularities of succession; the talk about the "thing in itself"). Further, the same judgment must be passed on all *philosophy of norms*, or *philosophy of value*, on any ethics or esthetics as a normative discipline. For the objective validity of a value or norm is (even on the view of the philosophers of value) not empirically verifiable nor deducible from empirical statements; hence it cannot be asserted (in a meaningful statement) at all. In other words: Either empirical criteria are indicated for the use of "good" and "beautiful" and the rest of the predicates that are employed in the normative sciences, or they are not. In the first case, a statement containing such a predicate turns into a factual judgment, but not a value judgment; in the second case, it becomes a pseudo-statement. It is altogether impossible to make a statement that expresses a value judgment.

Finally, the verdict of meaninglessness also hits those metaphysical movements which are usually called, improperly, epistemological movements, that is *realism* (insofar as it claims to say more than the empirical fact that the sequence of events exhibits a certain regularity, which makes the application of the inductive method possible) and its opponents: subjective *idealism*, solipsism, phenomenalism, and *positivism* (in the earlier sense).

But what, then, is left over for *philosophy*, if all statements whatever that assert something are of an empirical nature and belong to factual science? What remains is not statements, nor a theory, nor a system, but only a *method*: the method of logical analysis. The foregoing discussion has illustrated the negative application of this method: in that context it serves to eliminate meaningless words, meaningless pseudo-statements. In its positive use it serves to clarify meaningful concepts and propositions, to lay logical foundations for factual science and for mathematics. The negative application of the method is necessary and important in the present historical situation. But even in its present practice, the positive application is more fertile. We cannot here discuss it in greater detail. It is the indicated task of logical analysis, inquiry into logical foundations, that is meant by *"scientific philosophy"* in contrast to metaphysics.

The question regarding the logical character *of* the statements which we obtain as the result of a logical analysis, e.g. the statements occurring in this and other logical papers, can here be answered only tentatively: such statements are partly analytic, partly empirical. For these statements about statements and parts of statements belong in part to pure *metalogic* (e.g. "a sequence consisting of the existence-symbol and a noun, is not a sentence"), in part to descriptive metalogic (e.g. "the word sequence at such and such a place in such and such a book is meaningless"). Metalogic will be discussed Elsewhere. It will also be shown there that the metalogic which speaks about the sentences of a given language can be formulated in that very language itself.

7 Metaphysics as Expression of an Attitude toward Life

Our claim that the statements of metaphysics are entirely meaningless, that they do not assert anything, will leave even those who agree intellectually with our results with a painful feeling of strangeness: how could it be explained that so many men in all ages and nations, among them eminent minds, spent so much energy, nay veritable fervor, on metaphysics if the latter consisted of nothing but mere words, nonsensically juxtaposed? And how could one account for the fact that metaphysical books have exerted such a strong influence on readers up to the present day, if they contained not even errors, but nothing at all? These doubts are justified since metaphysics does indeed have a content; only it is not theoretical content. The (pseudo)statements of metaphysics do not serve for the *description of states of affairs*, neither existing ones (in that case they would be true statements) nor non-existing ones (in that case they would be at least false statements). They serve for the *expression of the general attitude of a person towards life* ("Lebenseinstellung, Lebensgefühl") .

Perhaps we may assume that metaphysics originated from *mythology*. The child is angry at the "wicked table" which hurt him. Primitive man endeavors to conciliate the threatening demon of earthquakes, or he worships the deity of the fertile rains in gratitude. Here we confront personifications of natural phenomena, which are the quasi-poetic expression of man's emotional relationship to his environment. The heritage of mythology is bequeathed on the one hand to poetry, which produces and intensifies the effects of mythology on life in a deliberate way; on the other hand, it is handed down to theology, which develops mythology into a system. Which, now, is the historical role of metaphysics? Perhaps we may regard it as a substitute for theology on the level of systematic, conceptual thinking. The (supposedly) transcendent sources of knowledge of theology are here replaced by natural, yet supposedly trans-empirical sources of knowledge. On closer inspection the same content as that of mythology is here still recognizable behind the repeatedly varied dressing: we find that metaphysics also arises from the need to give expression to a man's attitude in life, his emotional and volitional reaction to the environment, to society, to the tasks to which he devotes himself, to the misfortunes that befall him. This attitude manifests itself, unconsciously as a rule, in everything a man does or says. It also impresses itself on his facial features, perhaps even on the character of his gait. Many people, now, feel a desire to create over and above these manifestations a special expression of their attitude, through which it might become visible in a more succinct and penetrating way. If they have artistic talent they are able to express themselves by producing a work of art. Many writers have already clarified the way in which the basic attitude is manifested through the style and manner of a work of art (e.g. Dilthey and his students). [In this connection the term "world view"

("Weltanschauung") is often used; we prefer to avoid it because of its ambiguity, which blurs the difference between attitude and theory, a difference which is of decisive importance for our analysis.] What is here essential for our considerations is only the fact that art is an adequate, metaphysics an inadequate means for the expression of the basic attitude. Of course, there need be no intrinsic objection to one's using any means of expression one likes. But in the case of metaphysics we find this situation: through the form of its works it pretends to be something that it is not. The form in question is that of a system of statements which are apparently related as premises and conclusions, that is, the form of a theory. In this way the fiction of theoretical content is generated, whereas, as we have seen, there is no such content. It is not only the reader, but the metaphysician himself who suffers from the illusion that the metaphysical statements say something, describe states of affairs. The metaphysician believes that he travels in territory in which truth and falsehood are at stake. In reality, however, he has not asserted anything, but only expressed something, like an artist. That the metaphysician is thus deluding himself cannot be inferred from the fact that he selects language as the medium of expression and declarative sentences as the form of expression; for lyrical poets do the same without succumbing to self-delusion. But the metaphysician supports his statements by arguments, he claims assent to their content, he polemicizes against metaphysicians of divergent persuasion by attempting to refute their assertions in his treatise. Lyrical poets, on the other hand, do not try to refute in their poem the statements in a poem by some other lyrical poet; for they know they are in the domain of art and not in the domain of theory.

Perhaps music is the purest means of expression of the basic attitude because it is entirely free from any reference to objects. The harmonious feeling or attitude, which the metaphysician tries to express in a monistic system, is more clearly expressed in the music of Mozart. And when a metaphysician gives verbal expression to his dualistic-heroic attitude towards life in a dualistic system, is it not perhaps because he lacks the ability of a Beethoven to express this attitude in an adequate medium? Metaphysicians are musicians without musical ability. Instead they have a strong inclination to work within the medium of the theoretical, to connect concepts and thoughts. Now, instead of activating, on the one hand, this inclination in the domain of science, and satisfying, on the other hand, the need for expression in art, the metaphysician confuses the two and produces a structure which achieves nothing for knowledge and something inadequate for the expression of attitude.

Our conjecture that metaphysics is a substitute, albeit an inadequate one, for art, seems to be further confirmed by the fact that the metaphysician who perhaps had artistic talent to the highest degree, viz. Nietzsche, almost entirely avoided the error of that confusion. A large part of his work has predominantly empirical content. We find there, for instance, historical analyses of specific artistic phenomena, or an historical-psychological analysis of morals. In the work, however, in which he expresses most strongly that which others express through metaphysics or ethics, in *Thus Spake Zarathustra*, he does not choose the misleading theoretical form, but openly the form of art, of poetry.

Remarks by the Author (1957)

To section 1, "metaphysics." This term is used in this paper, as usually in Europe, for the field of alleged knowledge of the essence of things which transcends the realm of empirically founded, inductive science. Metaphysics in this sense includes systems like those of Fichte, Schelling, Hegel, Bergson, Heidegger. But it does not include endeavors towards a synthesis and generalization of the results of the various sciences.

To section 1, "meaning." Today we distinguish various kinds of meaning, in particular cognitive (designative, referential) meaning on the one hand, and non-cognitive (expressive) meaning components, e.g. emotive and motivative, on the other. In the present paper, the word "meaning" is always understood in the sense of "cognitive meaning." The thesis that the sentences of metaphysics are meaningless, is thus to be understood in the sense that they have no cognitive meaning, no assertive content. The obvious psychological fact that they have expressive meaning is thereby not denied; this is explicitly stated in section 7.

To section 6, "metalogic." This term refers to the theory of expressions of a language and, in particular, of their logical relations. Today we would distinguish between logical syntax as the theory of purely formal relations and semantics as the theory of meaning and truth-conditions.

To section 6, realism and idealism. That both the affirmative and the negative theses concerning the reality of the external world are pseudo-statements, I have tried to show in the monograph *Scheinprobleme in der Philosophie: Das Fremdpsychische und der Realismusstreit*, Berlin, 1928. The similar nature of the ontological theses about the reality or unreality of abstract entities, e.g., properties, relations, propositions, is discussed in "Empiricism, Semantics, and Ontology," *Revue intern. de Philos.* 4, 1950, 20–40, reprinted in: *Meaning and Necessity*, second edition, Chicago, 1956.

Notes

1. For the logical and epistemological conception which underlies our exposition, but can only briefly be intimated here, cf. Wittgenstein, *Tractatus Logico-Philosophicus*, 1922, and Carnap, *Der logische Aufbau der Welt*, 1928.
2. The following quotations (original italics) are taken from M. Heidegger, *Was Ist Metaphysik?*, 1929. We could just as well have selected passages from any other of the numerous metaphysicians of the present or of the past; yet the selected passages seem to us to illustrate our thesis especially well.

The Four Great Errors
Friedrich Nietzsche

Friedrich Nietzsche (1844–1900), a German philosopher, was a ruthless critic of the philosophical tradition and considered by some to be the forefather of existentialism and postmodernism. In this selection he attacks some of the key metaphysical concepts and argues that philosophers have created the world on the basis of these concepts, which, in fact, are either hopelessly confused or do not describe or apply to anything.

1 The error of confusing cause and effect

There is no more dangerous error than that of mistaking the effect for the cause: I call it the real corruption of reason. Yet this error belongs among the most ancient and recent habits of mankind: it is even hallowed among us and goes by the name of "religion" or "morality." Every single sentence which religion and morality formulate contains it; priests and legislators of moral codes are the originators of this corruption of reason.

I give an example. Everybody knows the book of the famous Cornaro in which he recommends his slender diet as a recipe for a long and happy life – a virtuous one too. Few books have been read so much; even now thousands of copies are sold in England every year. I do not doubt that scarcely any book (except the Bible, as is meet) has done as much harm, has *shortened* as many lives, as this well-intentioned *curiosum*. The reason: the mistaking of the effect for the cause. The worthy Italian thought his diet was the *cause* of his long life, whereas the precondition for a long life, the extraordinary slowness of his metabolism, the consumption of so little, was the cause of his slender diet. He was not free to eat little *or* much; his frugality was not a matter of "free will": he became sick when he ate more. But whoever is no carp not only does well to eat properly, but needs to. A scholar in our time, with his rapid consumption of nervous energy, would simply destroy himself with Cornaro's diet. *Crede experto.*[1]

2

The most general formula on which every religion and morality is founded is: "Do this and that, refrain from this and that – then you will be happy! Otherwise . . ." Every morality, every religion, is this imperative; I call it the great original sin of reason, the *immortal unreason*. In my mouth, this formula is changed into its opposite – first example of my "revaluation of all values": a well-turned-out human being, a "happy one," must perform certain actions and shrinks instinctively from other actions; he carries the order, which he represents physiologically, into his relations with other human beings and things. In a formula: his virtue is the *effect* of his happiness. A long life, many descendants –

this is not the wages of virtue; rather virtue itself is that slowing down of the metabolism which leads, among other things, also to a long life, many descendants – in short, to *Cornarism*.

The church and morality say: "A generation, a people, are destroyed by license and luxury." My *recovered* reason says: when a people approaches destruction, when it degenerates physiologically, then license and luxury *follow* from this (namely, the craving for ever stronger and more frequent stimulation, as every exhausted nature knows it). This young man turns pale early and wilts; his friends say: that is due to this or that disease. I say: that he became diseased, that he did not resist the disease, was already the effect of an impoverished life or hereditary exhaustion. The newspaper reader says: this party destroys itself by making such a mistake. My *higher* politics says: a party which makes such mistakes has reached its end; it has lost its sureness of instinct. Every mistake in every sense is the effect of the degeneration of instinct, of the disintegration of the will: one could almost define what is bad in this way. All that is good is instinct – and hence easy, necessary, free. Laboriousness is an objection; the god is typically different from the hero. (In my language: light feet are the first attribute of divinity.)

3 The error of a false causality

People have believed at all times that they knew what a cause is; but whence did we take our knowledge – or more precisely, our faith that we had such knowledge? From the realm of the famous "inner facts," of which not a single one has so far proved to be factual. We believed ourselves to be causal in the act of willing: we thought that here at least we caught causality in the act. Nor did one doubt that all the antecedents of an act, its causes, were to be sought in consciousness and would be found there once sought – as "motives": else one would not have been free and responsible for it. Finally, who would have denied that a thought is caused? that the ego causes the thought?

Of these three "inward facts" which seem to guarantee causality, the first and most persuasive is that of the will as cause. The conception of a consciousness ("spirit") as a cause, and later also that of the ego as cause (the "subject"), are only afterbirths: first the causality of the will was firmly accepted as given, as *empirical*.

Meanwhile we have thought better of it. Today we no longer believe a word of all this. The "inner world" is full of phantoms and will-o'-the-wisps: the will is one of them. The will no longer moves anything, hence does not explain anything either – it merely accompanies events; it can also be absent. The so-called *motive:* another error. Merely a surface phenomenon of consciousness, something alongside the deed that is more likely to cover up the antecedents of the deeds than to represent them. And as for the *ego!* That has become a fable, a fiction, a play on words: it has altogether ceased to think, feel, or will!

What follows from this? There are no mental causes at all. The whole of the allegedly empirical evidence for that has gone to the devil. That is what follows! And what a fine abuse we had perpetrated with this "empirical evidence"; we *created* the world on this basis as a world of causes, a world of will, a world of spirits. The most ancient and enduring psychology was at work here and did not do anything else: all that happened was considered a doing, all doing the effect of a will; the world became to it a multiplicity of doers; a doer (a "subject") was slipped under all that happened. It was out of himself that man projected his three "inner facts" – that in which he believed most firmly, the will, the spirit, the ego. He even took the concept of being from the concept of the ego; he posited "things" as "being," in his image, in accordance with his concept of the ego as a cause. Small wonder that later he always found in things only that *which he had put into them.* The thing itself, to say it once more, the concept of thing is a mere reflex of the faith in the ego as cause. And even your atom, my dear mechanists and physicists – how much error, how much rudimentary psychology is still residual in your atom! Not to mention the "thing-in-itself," the *horrendum puderutum* of the metaphysicians! The error of the spirit as cause mistaken for reality! And made the very measure of reality! And called God!

4 The error of imaginary causes

To begin with dreams: *ex post facto*, a cause is slipped under a particular sensation (for example, one following a far-off cannon shot) – often a whole little novel in which the dreamer turns up as the protagonist. The sensation endures meanwhile in a kind of resonance: it waits, as it were, until the causal instinct permits it to step into the foreground – now no longer as a chance occurrence, but as "meaning." The cannon shot appears in a *causal* mode, in an apparent reversal of time. What is really later, the motivation, is experienced first – often with a hundred details which pass like lightning – and the shot *follows*. What has happened? The representations which were *produced* by a certain state have been misunderstood as its causes.

In fact, we do the same thing when awake. Most of our general feelings – every kind of inhibition, pressure, tension, and explosion in the play and counterplay of our organs, and particularly the state of the *nerous sympathicus* – excite our causal instinct: we want to have a reason for feeling this way or that – for feeling bad or for feeling good. We are never satisfied merely to state the fact that we feel this way or that: we admit this fact only – become conscious of it only – when we have furnished some kind of motivation. Memory, which swings into action in such cases, unknown to us, brings up earlier states of the same kind, together with the causal interpretations associated with them – not their real causes. The faith, to be sure, that such representations, such accompanying conscious processes, are the causes, is also brought forth by memory. Thus originates a habitual acceptance of a particular causal interpretation, which, as a matter of fact, inhibits any investigation into the real cause – even precludes it.

5 The psychological explanation of this

To derive something unknown from something familiar relieves, comforts, and satisfies, besides giving a feeling of power. With the unknown, one is confronted with danger, discomfort, and care; the first instinct is to abolish these painful states. First principle: any explanation is better than none. Since at bottom it is merely a matter of wishing to be rid of oppressive representations, one is not too particular about the means of getting rid of them: the first representation that explains the unknown as familiar feels so good that one "considers it true." The proof of pleasure ("of strength") as a criterion of truth.

The causal instinct is thus conditional upon, and excited by, the feeling of fear. The "why?" shall, if at all possible, not give the cause for its own sake so much as for *a particular kind of cause* – a cause that is comforting, liberating, and relieving. That it is something already familiar, experienced, and inscribed in the memory, which is posited as a cause, that is the first consequence of this need. That which is new and strange and has not been experienced before, is excluded as a cause. Thus one searches not only for some kind of explanation to serve as a cause, but for a particularly selected and preferred kind of explanation – that which has most quickly and most frequently abolished the feeling of the strange, new, and hitherto unexperienced: the *most habitual* explanations. Consequence: one kind of positing of causes predominates more and more, is concentrated into a system, and finally emerges as *dominant*, that is, as simply precluding other causes and explanations. The banker immediately thinks of "business," the Christian of "sin," and the girl of her love.

6 The whole realm of morality and religion belongs under this concept of imaginary causes

The "explanation" of *disagreeable* general feelings. They are produced by beings that are hostile to us (evil spirits: the most famous case – the misunderstanding of the hysterical as witches). They are produced by acts which cannot be approved (the feeling of "sin," of "sinfulness," is slipped under a physiological discomfort; one always finds reasons for being dissatisfied with oneself). They are produced as punishments, as payment for something we should not have done, for what we should not have *been* (impudently generalized by Schopenhauer into a principle in which morality appears as what it really is – as the very poisoner and slanderer of life: "Every great pain, whether physical or spiritual, declares what we deserve; for it could not come to us if we did not deserve it." *World as Will and Representation* II, 666). They are produced as effects of ill-considered actions that turn out badly. (Here the affects, the senses, are posited as causes, as "guilty"; and physiological calamities are interpreted with the help of other calamities as "deserved.")

The "explanation" of *agreeable* general feelings. They are produced by trust in God. They are produced by the consciousness of good deeds (the so-called "good conscience" – a physiological state which at times looks so much like good digestion that it is hard to tell them apart). They are produced by the successful termination of some enterprise (a naive fallacy: the successful termination of some enterprise does not by any means give a hypochondriac or a Pascal agreeable general feelings). They are produced by faith, charity, and hope – the Christian virtues.

In truth, all these supposed explanations are resultant states and, as it were, translations of pleasurable or unpleasurable feelings into a false dialect: one is in a state of hope *because* the basic physiological feeling is once again strong and rich; one trusts in God *because* the feeling of fullness and strength gives a sense of rest. Morality and religion belong altogether to the *psychology of error:* in every single case, cause and effect are confused; or truth is confused with the effects of *believing* something to be true; or a state of consciousness is confused with its causes.

7 The error of free will

Today we no longer have any pity for the concept of "free will": we know only too well what it really is – the foulest of all theologians' artifices, aimed at making mankind "responsible" in their sense, that is, *dependent upon them.* Here I simply supply the psychology of all "making responsible."

Wherever responsibilities are sought, it is usually the instinct of wanting to judge and punish which is at work. Becoming has been deprived of its innocence when any being-such-and-such is traced back to will, to purposes, to acts of responsibility: the doctrine of the will has been invented essentially for the purpose of punishment, that is, because one wanted to impute guilt. The entire old psychology, the psychology of will, was conditioned by the fact that its originators, the priests at the head of ancient communities, wanted to create for themselves the right to punish – or wanted to create this right for God. Men were considered "free" so that they might be judged and punished – so that they might become guilty: consequently, every act had to be considered as willed, and the origin of every act had to be considered as lying within the consciousness (and thus the most fundamental counterfeit in *psychologicis* was made the principle of psychology itself).

Today, as we have entered into the reverse movement and we immoralists are trying with all our strength to take the concept of guilt and the concept of punishment out of the world again, and to cleanse psychology, history, nature, and social institutions and sanctions of them, there is in our eyes no more radical opposition than that of the theologians, who continue with the concept of a "moral world-order" to infect the innocence of becoming by means of "punishment" and "guilt." Christianity is a metaphysics of the hangman.

8

What alone can be our doctrine? That no one gives man his qualities – neither God, nor society, nor his parents and ancestors, nor he himself. (The nonsense of the last idea was taught as "intelligible freedom" by Kant – perhaps by Plato already.) No one is responsible for man's being there at all, for his being such-and-such, or for his being in these circumstances or in this environment. The fatality of his essence is not to be disentangled from the fatality of all that has been and will be. Man is not the effect of some special purpose, of a will, and end; nor is he the object of an attempt to attain an "ideal of humanity" or an "ideal of happiness" or an "ideal of morality." It is absurd to wish to devolve one's essence on some end or other. We have invented the concept of "end": in reality there is no end.

One is necessary, one is a piece of fatefulness, one belongs to the whole, one is in the whole; there is nothing which could judge, measure, compare, or sentence our being, for that would mean judging, measuring, comparing, or sentencing the whole. But there is nothing besides the whole. That nobody is held responsible any longer, that the mode of being may not be traced back to a *causa prima*, that the world does not form a unity either as a sensorium or as "spirit" – that alone is the great liberation; with this alone is the innocence of becoming restored. The concept of "God" was until now the greatest objection to existence. We deny God, we deny the responsibility in God: only thereby do we redeem the world.

Note

1   "Believe him who has tried!"

Justice as Fairness: Political not Metaphysical
John Rawls

John Rawls is Emeritus Professor of Philosophy at Harvard University. His book *Theory of Justice* (1971) established him as one of the most important political and moral philosophers of the twentieth century. Rawls defends an egalitarian view of justice that builds on the classical social contract theories of John Locke, Jean-Jacques Rousseau, and Immanuel Kant. In this essay Rawls responds to the criticism that his moral and political philosophy depends on metaphysical views about freedom and the nature of a person. He argues that his views do not depend on metaphysical assumptions.

In this discussion I shall make some general remarks about how I now understand the conception of justice that I have called "justice as fairness" (presented in my book *A Theory of Justice*).[1] I do this because it may seem that this conception depends on philosophical claims I should like to avoid, for example, claims to universal truth, or claims about the essential nature and identity of persons. My aim is to explain why it does not. I shall first discuss what I regard as the task of political philosophy at the present time and then briefly survey how the basic intuitive ideas drawn upon in justice as fairness are combined into a political conception of justice for a constitutional democracy. Doing this will bring out how and why this conception of justice avoids certain philosophical and metaphysical claims. Briefly, the idea is that in a constitutional democracy the public conception of justice should be, so far as possible, independent of controversial philosophical and religious doctrines. Thus, to formulate such a conception, we apply the principle of toleration to philosophy itself: the public conception of justice is to be political, not metaphysical. Hence the title.

I want to put aside the question whether the text of *A Theory of Justice* supports different readings than the one I sketch here. Certainly on a number of points I have changed my views, and there are no doubt others on which my views have changed in ways that I am unaware of.[2] I recognize further that certain faults of exposition as well as obscure and ambiguous passages in *A Theory of Justice* invite misunderstanding; but I think these matters need not concern us and I shan't pursue them beyond a few footnote indications. For our purposes here, it suffices first, to show how a conception of justice with the structure and content of justice as fairness can be understood as political and not metaphysical, and second, to explain why we should look for such a conception of justice in a democratic society.

I

One thing I failed to say in *A Theory of Justice*, or failed to stress sufficiently, is that justice as fairness is intended as a political conception of justice. While a political conception of justice is, of course, a moral conception, it is a moral conception worked out for a specific kind of subject, namely, for political, social, and economic institutions. In particular, justice as fairness is framed to apply to what I have called the "basic structure" of a modern constitutional democracy.[3] (I shall use "constitutional democracy" and "democratic regime," and similar phrases interchangeably.) By this structure I mean such a society's main political, social, and economic institutions, and how they fit together into one unified system of social cooperation. Whether justice as fairness can be extended to a general political conception for different kinds of societies existing under different historical and social conditions, or whether it can be extended to a general moral conception, or a significant part thereof, are altogether separate questions. I avoid prejudging these larger questions one way or the other.

It should also be stressed that justice as fairness is not intended as the application of a general moral conception to the basic structure of society, as if this structure were simply another case to which that general moral conception is applied.[4] In this respect justice as fairness differs from traditional moral doctrines, for these are widely regarded as such general conceptions. Utilitarianism is a familiar example, since the principle of utility, however it is formulated, is usually said to hold for all kinds of subjects ranging from the actions of individuals to the law of nations. The essential point is this: as a practical political matter no general moral conception can provide a publicly recognized basis for a conception of justice in a modern democratic state. The social and historical conditions of such a state have their origins in the Wars of Religion following the Reformation and the subsequent development of the principle of toleration, and in the growth of constitutional government and the institutions of large industrial market economies. These conditions profoundly affect the requirements of a workable conception of political justice: such a conception must allow for a diversity of doctrines and the plurality of convicting, and indeed incommensurable, conceptions of the good affirmed by the members of existing democratic societies.

Finally, to conclude these introductory remarks, since justice as fairness is intended as a political conception of justice for a democratic society, it tries to draw solely upon basic intuitive ideas that are embedded in the political institutions of a constitutional democratic regime and the public traditions of their interpretation. Justice as fairness is a political conception in part because it starts from within a certain political tradition. We hope that this political conception of justice may at least be supported by what we may call an "overlapping consensus," that is, by a consensus that includes all the opposing philosophical and religious doctrines likely to persist and to gain adherents in a more or less just constitutional democratic society.[5]

II

There are, of course, many ways in which political philosophy may be understood, and writers at different times, faced with different political and social circumstances, understand their work differently. Justice as fairness I would now understand as a reasonably systematic and practicable conception of justice for a constitutional democracy, a conception that offers an alternative to the dominant utilitarianism of our tradition of political thought. Its first task is to provide a more secure and acceptable basis for constitutional principles and basic rights and liberties than utilitarianism seems to allow.[6] The need for such a political conception arises in the following way.

There are periods, sometimes long periods, in the history of any society during which certain fundamental questions give rise to sharp and divisive political controversy, and it seems difficult, if not impossible, to find any shared basis of political agreement. Indeed, certain questions may prove intractable and may never be fully settled. One task of political philosophy in a democratic society is to focus on such questions and to examine whether some underlying basis of agreement can be uncovered and a mutually acceptable way of resolving these questions publicly established. Or if these questions cannot be fully settled, as may well be the case, perhaps the divergence of opinion can be narrowed sufficiently so that political cooperation on a basis of mutual respect can still be maintained.[7]

The course of democratic thought over the past two centuries or so makes plain that there is no agreement on the way basic institutions of a constitutional democracy should be arranged if they are to specify and secure the basic rights and liberties of citizens and answer to the claims of democratic equality when citizens are conceived as free and equal persons (as explained in the last three paragraphs of Section III). A deep disagreement exists as to how the values of liberty and equality are best realized in the basic structure of society. To simplify, we may think of this disagreement as a conflict within the tradition of democratic thought itself, between the tradition associated with Locke, which gives greater weight to what Constant called "the liberties of the moderns," freedom of thought and conscience, certain basic rights of the person and of property, and the rule of law, and the tradition associated with Rousseau, which gives greater weight to what Constant called "the liberties of the ancients," the equal political liberties and the values of public life. This is a stylized contrast and historically inaccurate, but it serves to fix ideas.

Justice as fairness tries to adjudicate between these contending traditions first, by proposing two principles of justice to serve as guidelines for how basic institutions are to realize the values of liberty and equality, and second, by specifying a point of view from which these principles can be seen as more appropriate than other familiar principles of justice to the nature of democratic citizens viewed as free and equal persons. What it means to view citizens as free and equal persons is, of course, a fundamental question and is discussed in the following sections. What must be shown is that a certain arrangement of the basic structure, certain institutional forms, are more appropriate for realizing the values of liberty and equality when citizens are conceived as such persons, that is (very briefly), as having the requisite powers of moral personality that enable them to participate in society viewed as a system of fair cooperation for mutual advantage. So to continue, the two principles of justice (mentioned above) read as follows:

1   Each person has an equal right to a fully adequate scheme of equal basic rights and liberties, which scheme is compatible with a similar scheme for all.
2   Social and economic inequalities are to satisfy two conditions: first, they must be attached to offices and positions open to all under conditions of fair equality of opportunity; and second, they must be to the greatest benefit of the least advantaged members of society.

Each of these principles applies to a different part of the basic structure; and both are concerned not only with basic rights, liberties, and opportunities, but also with the claims of equality; while the second part of the second principle underwrites the worth of these institutional guarantees.[8] The two principles together, when the first is given priority over the second, regulate the basic institutions which realize these values.[9] But these details, although important, are not our concern here.

We must now ask: how might political philosophy find a shared basis for settling such a fundamental question as that of the most appropriate institutional forms for liberty and equality? Of course, it is likely that the most that can be done is to narrow the range of public disagreement. Yet even firmly held convictions gradually change: religious toleration is now accepted, and arguments for persecution are no longer openly professed; similarly, slavery is rejected as inherently unjust, and however much the aftermath of slavery may persist in social practices and unavowed attitudes, no one is willing to defend it. We collect such settled convictions as the belief in religious toleration and the rejection of slavery and try to organize the basic ideas and principles implicit in these convictions into a coherent conception of justice. We can regard these convictions as provisional fixed points which any conception of justice must account for if it is to be reasonable for us. We look, then, to our public political culture itself, including its main institutions and the historical traditions of their interpretation, as the shared fund of implicitly recognized basic ideas and principles. The hope is that these ideas and principles can be formulated clearly enough to be combined into a conception of political justice congenial to our most firmly held convictions. We express this by saying that a political conception of justice, to be acceptable, must be in accordance with our considered convictions, at all levels of generality, on due reflection (or in what I have called "reflective equilibrium").[10]

The public political culture may be of two minds even at a very deep level. Indeed, this must be so with such an enduring controversy as that concerning the most appropriate institutional forms to realize the values of liberty and equality. This suggests that if we are to succeed in finding a basis of public agreement, we must find a new way of organizing familiar ideas and principles into a conception of political justice so that the claims in conflict, as previously understood, are seen in another light. A political conception need not be an original creation but may only articulate familiar intuitive ideas and principles so that they can be recognized as fitting together in a somewhat different way than before. Such a conception may, however, go further than this: it may organize these familiar ideas and principles by means of a more fundamental intuitive idea within the complex structure of which the other familiar intuitive ideas are then systematically connected and related. In justice as fairness, as we shall see in the next section, this more fundamental idea is that of society as a system of fair social cooperation between free and equal persons. The concern of this section is how we might find a public basis of political agreement. The point is that a conception of justice will only be able to achieve this aim if it provides a reasonable way of shaping into one coherent view the deeper bases of agreement embedded in the public political culture of a constitutional regime and acceptable to its most firmly held considered convictions.

Now suppose justice as fairness were to achieve its aim and a publicly acceptable political conception of justice is found. Then this conception provides a publicly recognized point of view from which all citizens can examine before one another whether or not their political and social institutions are just. It enables them to do this by citing what are recognized among them as valid and sufficient reasons singled out by that conception itself. Society's main institutions and how they fit together into one scheme of social cooperation can be examined on the same basis by each citizen, whatever that citizen's social position or more particular interests. It should be observed that, on this view, justification is not regarded simply as valid argument from listed premises, even should these premises be true. Rather, justification is addressed to others who disagree with us, and therefore it must always proceed from some consensus, that is, from premises that we and others publicly recognize as true; or better, publicly recognize as acceptable to us for the purpose of establishing a working agreement on the fundamental questions of political justice. It goes without saying that this agreement must be informed and uncoerced, and reached by citizens in ways consistent with their being viewed as free and equal persons.[11]

Thus, the aim of justice as fairness as a political conception is practical, and not metaphysical or epistemological. That is, it presents itself not as a conception of justice that is true, but one that can serve as a basis of informed and willing political agreement between citizens viewed as free and equal persons. This agreement when securely founded in public political and social attitudes sustains the goods of all persons and associations within a just democratic regime. To secure this agreement we try, so far as we can, to avoid disputed philosophical, as well as disputed moral and religious, questions. We do this not because these questions are unimportant or regarded with indifference,[12] but because we think them too important and recognize that there is no way to resolve them politically. The only alternative to a principle of toleration is the autocratic use of state power. Thus, justice as fairness deliberately stays on the surface, philosophically speaking. Given the profound differences in belief and conceptions of the good at least since the Reformation, we must recognize that, just as on questions of religious and moral doctrine, public agreement on the basic questions of philosophy cannot be obtained without the state's infringement of basic liberties. Philosophy as the search for truth about an independent metaphysical and moral order cannot, I believe, provide a workable and shared basis for a political conception of justice in a democratic society.

We try, then, to leave aside philosophical controversies whenever possible, and look for ways to avoid philosophy's longstanding problems. Thus, in what I have called "Kantian constructivism," we try to avoid the problem of truth and the controversy between realism and subjectivism about the status of moral and political values. This form of constructivism neither asserts nor denies these doctrines.[13] Rather, it recasts ideas from the tradition of the social contract to achieve a practicable conception of objectivity and justification founded on public agreement in judgment on due reflection. The aim is free agreement, reconciliation through public reason. And similarly, as we shall see (in Section V), a conception of the person in a political view, for example, the conception of citizens as free and equal persons, need not involve, so I believe, questions of philosophical psychology or a metaphysical doctrine of the nature of the self. No political view that depends on these deep and unresolved matters can serve as a public conception of justice in a constitutional democratic state. As I have said, we must apply the principle of toleration to philosophy itself. The hope is that, by this method of avoidance, as we might call it, existing differences between contending political views can at least be moderated, even if not entirely removed, so that social cooperation on the basis of mutual respect can be maintained. Or if this is expecting too much, this method may enable us to conceive how, given a desire for free and uncoerced agreement, a public understanding could arise consistent with the historical conditions and constraints of our social world. Until we bring ourselves to conceive how this could happen, it can't happen.

III

Let's now survey briefly some of the basic ideas that make up justice as fairness in order to show that these ideas belong to a political conception of justice. As I have indicated, the overarching fundamental intuitive idea, within which other basic intuitive ideas are systematically connected, is that of society as a fair system of cooperation between free and equal persons. Justice as fairness starts from this idea as one of the basic intuitive ideas which we take to be implicit in the public culture of a democratic society.[14] In their political thought, and in the context of public discussion of political questions, citizens do not view the social order as a fixed natural order, or as an institutional hierarchy justified by religious or aristocratic values. Here it is important to stress that from other points of view, for example, from the point of view of personal morality, or from the point of view of members of an association, or of one's religious or philosophical doctrine, various aspects of the world and one's relation to it, may be regarded in a different way. But these other points of view are not to be introduced into political discussion.

We can make the idea of social cooperation more specific by noting three of its elements:

1   Cooperation is distinct from merely socially coordinated activity, for example, from activity coordinated by orders issued by some central authority. Cooperation is guided by publicly recognized rules and procedures which those who are cooperating accept and regard as properly regulating their conduct.

2   Cooperation involves the idea of fair terms of cooperation: these are terms that each participant may reasonably accept, provided that everyone else likewise accepts them. Fair terms of cooperation specify an idea of reciprocity or mutuality: all who are engaged in cooperation and who do their part as the rules and procedures require, are to benefit in some appropriate way as assessed by a suitable benchmark of comparison. A conception of political justice characterizes the fair terms of social cooperation. Since the primary subject of justice is the basic structure of society, this is accomplished in justice as fairness by formulating principles that specify basic rights and duties within the main institutions of society, and by regulating the institutions of background justice over time so that the benefits produced by everyone's efforts are fairly acquired and divided from one generation to the next.

3   The idea of social cooperation requires an idea of each participant's rational

advantage, or good. This idea of good specifies what those who are engaged in cooperation, whether individuals, families, or associations, or even nation-states, are trying to achieve, when the scheme is viewed from their own standpoint.

Now consider the idea of the person.[15] There are, of course, many aspects of human nature that can be singled out as especially significant depending on our point of view. This is witnessed by such expressions as *homo politicus*, *homo oeconomicus*, *homo faber*, and the like. Justice as fairness starts from the idea that society is to be conceived as a fair system of cooperation and so it adopts a conception of the person to go with this idea. Since Greek times, both in philosophy and law, the concept of the person has been understood as the concept of someone who can take part in, or who can play a role in, social life, and hence exercise and respect its various rights and duties. Thus, we say that a person is someone who can be a citizen, that is, a fully cooperating member of society over a complete life. We add the phrase "over a complete life" because a society is viewed as a more or less complete and self-sufficient scheme of cooperation, making room within itself for all the necessities and activities of life, from birth until death. A society is not an association for more limited purposes; citizens do not join society voluntarily but are born into it, where, for our aims here, we assume they are to lead their lives.

Since we start within the tradition of democratic thought, we also think of citizens as free and equal persons. The basic intuitive idea is that in virtue of what we may call their moral powers, and the powers of reason, thought, and judgment connected with those powers, we say that persons are free. And in virtue of their having these powers to the requisite degree to be fully cooperating members of society, we say that persons are equal.[16] We can elaborate this conception of the person as follows. Since persons can be full participants in a fair system of social cooperation, we ascribe to them the two moral powers connected with the elements in the idea of social cooperation noted above: namely, a capacity for a sense of justice and a capacity for a conception of the good. A sense of justice is the capacity to understand, to apply, and to act from the public conception of justice which characterizes the fair terms of social cooperation. The capacity for a conception of the good is the capacity to form, to revise, and rationally to pursue a conception of one's rational advantage, or good. In the case of social cooperation, this good must not be understood narrowly but rather as a conception of what is valuable in human life. Thus, a conception of the good normally consists of a more or less determinate scheme of final ends, that is, ends we want to realize for their own sake, as well as of attachments to other persons and loyalties to various groups and associations. These attachments and loyalties give rise to affections and devotions, and therefore the flourishing of the persons and associations who are the objects of these sentiments is also part of our conception of the good. Moreover, we must also include in such a conception a view of our relation to the world – religious, philosophical, or moral – by reference to which the value and significance of our ends and attachments are understood.

In addition to having the two moral powers, the capacities for a sense of justice and a conception of the good, persons also have at any given time a particular conception of the good that they try to achieve. Since we wish to start from the idea of society as a fair system of cooperation, we assume that persons as citizens have all the capacities that enable them to be normal and fully cooperating members of society. This does not imply that no one ever suffers from illness or accident; such misfortunes are to be expected in the ordinary course of human life; and provision for these contingencies must be made. But for our purposes here I leave aside permanent physical disabilities or mental disorders so severe as to prevent persons from being normal and fully cooperating members of society in the usual sense.

Now the conception of persons as having the two moral powers, and therefore as free and equal, is also a basic intuitive idea assumed to be implicit in the public culture of a democratic society. Note, however, that it is formed by idealizing and simplifying in various ways. This is done to achieve a clear and uncluttered view of what for us is the fundamental question of political justice: namely, what is the most appropriate conception of justice for specifying the terms of social cooperation between citizens regarded as free and equal persons, and as normal and fully cooperating members of society over a complete life. It is this question that has been the focus of the liberal critique of aristocracy, of the socialist critique of liberal constitutional democracy, and of the conflict between liberals and conservatives at the present time over the claims of private property and the legitimacy (in contrast to the effectiveness) of social policies associated with the so-called welfare state.

IV

I now take up the idea of the original position.[17] This idea is introduced in order to work out which traditional conception of justice, or which variant of one of those conceptions, specifies the most appropriate principles for realizing liberty and equality once society is viewed as a system of cooperation between free and equal persons. Assuming we had this purpose in mind, let's see why we would introduce the idea of the original position and how it serves its purpose.

Consider again the idea of social cooperation. Let's ask: how are the fair terms of cooperation to be determined? Are they simply laid down by some outside agency distinct from the persons cooperating? Are they, for example, laid down by God's law? Or are these terms to be recognized by these persons as fair by reference to their knowledge of a prior and independent moral order? For example, are they regarded as required by natural law, or by a realm of values known by rational intuition? Or are these terms to be established by an undertaking among these persons themselves in the light of what they regard as their mutual advantage? Depending on which answer we give, we get a different conception of cooperation.

Since justice as fairness recasts the doctrine of the social contract, it adopts a form of the last answer: the fair terms of social cooperation are conceived as agreed to by those engaged in it, that is, by free and equal persons as citizens who are born into the society in which they lead their lives. But their agreement, like any other valid agreement, must be entered into under appropriate conditions. In particular, these conditions must situate free and equal persons fairly and must not allow some persons greater bargaining advantages than others. Further, threats of force and coercion, deception and fraud, and so on, must be excluded.

So far so good. The foregoing considerations are familiar from everyday life. But agreements in everyday life are made in some more or less clearly specified situation embedded within the background institutions of the basic structure. Our task, however, is to extend the idea of agreement to this background framework itself. Here we face a difficulty for any political conception of justice that uses the idea of a contract, whether social or otherwise. The difficulty is this: we must find some point of view, removed from and not distorted by the particular features and circumstances of the all-encompassing background framework, from which a fair agreement between free and equal persons can be reached. The original position, with the feature I have called "the veil of ignorance," is this point of view.[18] And the reason why the original position must abstract from and not be affected by the contingencies of the social world is that the conditions for a fair agreement on the principles of political justice between free and equal persons must eliminate the bargaining advantages which inevitably arise within background institutions of any society as the result of cumulative social, historical, and natural tendencies. These contingent advantages and accidental influences from the past should not influence an agreement on the principles which are to regulate the institutions of the basic structure itself from the present into the future.

Here we seem to face a second difficulty, which is, however, only apparent. To explain: from what we have just said it is clear that the original position is to be seen as a device of representation and hence any agreement reached by the parties must be regarded as both hypothetical and nonhistorical. But if so, since hypothetical agreements cannot bind, what is the significance of the original position?[19] The answer is implicit in what has already been said: it is given by the role of the various features of the original position as a device of representation. Thus, that the parties are symmetrically situated is required if they are to be seen as representatives of free and equal citizens who are to reach an agreement under conditions that are fair. Moreover, one of our considered convictions, I assume, is this: the fact that we occupy a particular social position is not a good reason for us to accept, or to expect others to accept, a conception of justice that favors those in this position. To model this conviction in the original position the parties are not allowed to know their social position; and the same idea is extended to other cases. This is expressed figuratively by saying that the parties are behind a veil of ignorance. In sum, the original position is simply a device of representation: it describes the parties, each of whom are responsible for the essential interests of a free and equal person, as fairly situated and as reaching an agreement subject to appropriate restrictions on what are to count as good reasons.[20]

Both of the above mentioned difficulties, then, are overcome by viewing the original position as a device of representation: that is, this position models what we regard as fair conditions under which the representatives of free and equal persons are to specify the terms of social cooperation in the case of the basic structure of society; and since it also models what, for this case, we regard as acceptable restrictions on reasons available to the parties for favoring one agreement rather than another, the conception of justice the parties would adopt identifies the conception we regard – *here and now* – as fair and supported by the best reasons. We try to model restrictions on reasons in such a way that it is perfectly evident which agreement would be made by the parties in the original position as citizens' representatives. Even if there should be, as surely there will be, reasons for and against each conception of justice available, there may be an overall balance of reasons plainly favoring one conception over the rest. As a device of representation the idea of the original position serves as a means of public reflection and self-clarification. We can use it to help us work out what we now think, once we are able to take a clear and uncluttered view of what justice requires when society is conceived as a scheme of cooperation between free and equal persons over time from one generation to the next. The original position serves as a unifying idea by which our considered convictions at all levels of generality are brought to bear on one another so as to achieve greater mutual agreement and self-understanding.

To conclude: we introduce an idea like that of the original position because there is no better way to elaborate a political conception of justice for the basic structure from the fundamental intuitive idea of society as a fair system of cooperation between citizens as free and equal persons. There are, however, certain hazards. As a device of representation the original position is likely to seem somewhat abstract and hence open to misunderstanding. The description of the parties may seem to presuppose some metaphysical conception of the person, for example, that the essential nature of persons is independent of and prior to their contingent attributes, including their final ends and attachments, and indeed, their character as a whole. But this is an illusion caused by not seeing the original position as a device of representation. The veil of ignorance, to mention one prominent feature of that position, has no metaphysical implications concerning the nature of the self; it does not imply that the self is ontologically prior to the facts about persons that the parties are excluded from knowing. We can, as it were, enter this position any time simply by reasoning for principles of justice in accordance with the enumerated restrictions. When, in this way, we simulate being in this position, our reasoning no more commits us to a metaphysical doctrine about the nature of the self than our playing a game like Monopoly commits us to thinking that we are landlords engaged in a desperate rivalry, winner take all.[21] We must keep in mind that we are trying to show how the idea of society as a fair system of social cooperation can be unfolded so as to specify the most appropriate principles for realizing the institutions of liberty and equality when citizens are regarded as free and equal persons.

V

I just remarked that the idea of the original position and the description of the parties may tempt us to think that a metaphysical doctrine of the person is presupposed. While I said that this interpretation is mistaken, it is not enough simply to disavow reliance on metaphysical doctrines, for despite one's intent they may still be involved. To rebut claims of this nature requires discussing them in detail and showing that they have no foothold. I cannot do that here.[22]

I can, however, sketch a positive account of the political conception of the person, that is, the conception of the person as citizen (discussed in Section III), involved in the original position as a device of representation. To explain what is meant by describing a conception of the person as political, let's consider how citizens are represented in the original position as free persons. The representation of their freedom seems to be one source of the idea that some metaphysical doctrine is presupposed. I have said elsewhere that citizens view themselves as free in three respects, so let's survey each of these briefly and indicate the way in which the conception of the person used is political.[23]

First, citizens are free in that they conceive of themselves and of one another as having the moral power to have a conception of the good. This is not to say that, as part of their political conception of themselves, they view themselves as inevitably tied to the pursuit of the particular conception of the good which they affirm at any given time. Instead, as citizens, they are regarded as capable of revising and changing this conception on reasonable and rational grounds, and they may do this if they so desire. Thus, as free persons, citizens claim the right to view their persons as independent from and as not identified with any particular conception of the good, or scheme of final ends. Given their moral power to form, to revise, and rationally to pursue a conception of the good, their public identity as free persons is not affected by changes over time in their conception of the good. For example, when citizens convert from one religion to another, or no longer affirm an established religious faith, they do not cease to be, for questions of political justice, the same persons they were before. There is no loss of what we may call their public identity, their identity as a matter of basic law. In general, they still have the same basic rights and duties; they own the same property and can make the same claims as before, except insofar as these claims were connected with their previous religious affiliation. We can imagine a society (indeed, history offers numerous examples) in which basic rights and recognized claims depend on religious affiliation, social class, and so on. Such a society has a different political conception of the person. It may not have a conception of citizenship at all; for this conception, as we are using it, goes with the conception of society as a fair system of cooperation for mutual advantage between free and equal persons.

It is essential to stress that citizens in their personal affairs, or in the internal life of associations to which they belong, may regard their final ends and attachments in a way very different from the way the political conception involves. Citizens may have, and normally do have at any given time, affections, devotions, and loyalties that they believe they would not, and indeed could and should not, stand apart from and objectively evaluate from the point of view of their purely rational good. They may regard it as simply unthinkable to view themselves apart from certain religious, philosophical, and moral convictions, or from certain enduring attachments and loyalties. These convictions and attachments are part of what we may call their "nonpublic identity." These convictions and attachments help to organize and give shape to a person's way of life, what one sees oneself as doing and trying to accomplish in one's social world. We think that if we were suddenly without these particular convictions and attachments we would be disoriented and unable to carry on. In fact, there would be, we might think, no point in carrying on. But our conceptions of the good may and often do change over time, usually slowly but sometimes rather suddenly. When these changes are sudden, we are particularly likely to say that we are no longer the same person. We know what this means: we refer to a profound and pervasive shift, or reversal, in our final ends and character; we refer to our different nonpublic, and possibly moral or religious, identity. On the road to Damascus Saul of Tarsus becomes Paul the Apostle. There is no change in our public or political identity, nor in our personal identity as this concept is understood by some writers in the philosophy of mind.[24]

The second respect in which citizens view themselves as free is that they regard themselves as self-originating sources of valid claims. They think their claims have weight apart from being derived from duties or obligations specified by the political conception of justice, for example, from duties and obligations owed to society. Claims that citizens regard as founded on duties and obligations based on their conception of the good and the moral doctrine they affirm in their own life are also, for our purposes here, to be counted as self-originating. Doing this is reasonable in a political conception of justice for a constitutional democracy; for provided the conceptions of the good and the moral doctrines citizens affirm are compatible with the public conception of justice, these duties and obligations are self-originating from the political point of view.

When we describe a way in which citizens regard themselves as free, we are describing how citizens actually think of themselves in a democratic society should questions of justice arise. In our conception of a constitutional regime, this is an aspect of how citizens regard themselves. That this aspect of their freedom belongs to a particular political conception is clear from the contrast with a different political conception in which the members of society are not viewed as self-originating sources of valid claims. Rather, their claims have no weight except insofar as they can be derived from their duties and obligations owed to society, or from their ascribed roles in the social hierarchy justified by religious or aristocratic values. Or to take an extreme case, slaves are human beings who are not counted as sources of claims, not even claims based on social duties or obligations, for slaves are not counted as capable of having duties or obligations. Laws that prohibit the abuse and maltreatment of slaves are not founded on claims made by slaves on their own behalf, but on claims originating either from slaveholders, or from the general interests of society (which does not include the interests of slaves). Slaves are, so to speak, socially dead: they are not publicly recognized as persons at all.[25] Thus, the contrast with a political conception which allows slavery makes clear why conceiving of citizens as free persons in virtue of their moral powers and their having a conception of the good, goes with a particular political conception of the person. This conception of persons fits into a political conception of justice founded on the idea of society as a system of cooperation between its members conceived as free and equal.

The third respect in which citizens are regarded as free is that they are regarded as capable of taking responsibility for their ends and this affects how their various claims are assessed.[26] Very roughly, the idea is that, given just background institutions and given for each person a fair index of primary goods (as required by the principles of justice), citizens are thought to be capable of adjusting their aims and aspirations in the light of what they can reasonably expect to provide for. Moreover, they are regarded as capable of restricting their claims in matters of justice to the kinds of things the principles of justice allow. Thus, citizens are to recognize that the weight of their claims is not given by the strength and psychological intensity of their wants and desires (as opposed to their needs and requirements as citizens), even when their wants and desires are rational from their point of view. I cannot pursue these matters here. But the procedure is the same as before: we start with the basic intuitive idea of society as a system of social cooperation. When this idea is developed into a conception of political justice, it implies that, viewing ourselves as persons who can engage in social cooperation over a complete life, we can also take responsibility for our ends, that is, that we can adjust our ends so that they can be pursued by the means we can reasonably expect to acquire given our prospects and situation in society. The idea of responsibility for ends is implicit in the public political culture and discernible in its practices. A political conception of the person articulates this idea and fits it into the idea of society as a system of social cooperation over a complete life.

To sum up, I recapitulate three main points of this and the preceding two sections:

First, in Section III persons were regarded as free and equal in virtue of their possessing to the requisite degree the two powers of moral personality (and the powers of reason, thought, and judgment connected with these powers), namely, the capacity for a sense of justice and the capacity for a conception of the good. These powers we associated with two main elements of the idea of cooperation, the idea of fair terms of cooperation and the idea of each participant's rational advantage, or good.

Second, in this section (Section V), we have briefly surveyed three respects in which persons are regarded as free, and we have noted that in the public political culture of a constitutional democratic regime citizens conceive of themselves as free in these respects.

Third, since the question of which conception of political justice is most appropriate for realizing in basic institutions the values of liberty and equality has long been deeply controversial within the very democratic tradition in which citizens are regarded as free and equal persons, the aim of justice as fairness is to try to resolve this question by starting from the basic intuitive idea of society as a fair system of social cooperation in which the fair terms of cooperation are agreed upon by citizens themselves so conceived. In Section IV, we saw why this approach leads to the idea of the original position as a device of representation.

. . .

Notes

Beginning in November of 1983, different versions of this paper were presented at New York University, the Yale Law School Legal Theory Workshop, the University of Illinois, and the University of California at Davis. I am grateful to many people for clarifying numerous points and for raising instructive difficulties; the paper is much changed as a result. In particular, I am indebted to Donald Davidson, B. J. Diggs, Catherine Elgin, Owen Fiss, Stephen Holmes, Norbert Hornstein, Thomas Nagel, George Priest, and David Sachs; and especially to Burton Dreben who has been of very great help throughout. Indebtedness to others on particular points is indicated in the footnotes.

1 Cambridge, MA: Harvard University Press, 1971.
2 A number of these changes, or shifts of emphasis, are evident in three lectures entitled "Kantian Constructivism in Moral Theory," *Journal of Philosophy*, 77 (September 1980).
3 *Theory*, Sec. a, and see the index; see also "The Basic Structure as Subject," in *Values and Morals*, eds Alvin Goldman and Jaegwon Kim (Dordrecht: Reidel, 1978), pp. 47–71.
4 See "Basic Structure as Subject," ibid., pp. 48–50.
5 This idea was introduced in *Theory*, pp. 387f, as a way to weaken the conditions for the reasonableness of civil disobedience in a nearly just democratic society. Here and later in Secs VI and VII it is used in a wider context.
6 *Theory*, Preface, p. viii.
7 Ibid., pp. 582f. On the role of a conception of justice in reducing the divergence of opinion, see pp. 44f, 53, 314, and 564. At various places the limited aims in developing a conception of justice are noted: see p. 364 on not expecting too much of an account of civil disobedience; pp. 200f on the inevitable indeterminacy of a conception of justice in specifying a series of points of view from which questions of justice can be resolved; pp. 89f. on the social wisdom of recognizing that perhaps only a few moral problems (it would have been better to say: problems of political justice) can be satisfactorily settled, and thus of framing institutions so that intractable questions do not arise; on pp. 53, 87ff., 320f the need to accept simplifications is emphasized. Regarding the last point, see also "Kantian Constructivism," pp. 560–64.
8 The statement of these principles differs from that given in *Theory* and follows the statement in "The Basic Liberties and Their Priority," *Tanner Lectures on Human Values*, Vol. III (Salt Lake City: University of Utah Press, 1982), p. 5. The reasons for the changes are discussed at pp. 4–55 of that lecture. They are important for the revisions made in the account of the basic liberties found in *Theory* in the attempt to answer the objections of H. L. A. Hart; but they need not concern us here.

9   The idea of the worth of these guarantees is discussed ibid., pp. 40f.

10 *Theory*, pp. 20f., 48–51, and 120f.

11 Ibid., pp. 580–83.

12 Ibid., pp. 214f.

13 On Kantian constructivism, see especially the third lecture referred to in footnote 2.

14 Although *Theory* uses this idea from the outset (it is introduced on p. 4), it does not emphasize, as I do here and in "Kantian Constructivism," that the basic ideas of justice as fairness are regarded as implicit or latent in the public culture of a democratic society.

15 It should be emphasized that a conception of the person, as I understand it here, is a normative conception, whether legal, political, or moral, or indeed also philosophical or religious, depending on the overall view to which it belongs. In this case the conception of the person is a moral conception, one that begins from our everyday conception of persons as the basic units of thought, deliberation and responsibility, and adapted to a political conception of justice and not to a comprehensive moral doctrine. It is in effect a political conception of the person, and given the aims of justice as fairness, a conception of citizens. Thus, a conception of the person is to be distinguished from an account of human nature given by natural science or social theory. On this point, see "Kantian Constructivism," pp. 534f.

16 *Theory*, Sec. 77.

17 Ibid., Sec. 4, Ch. 3, and the index.

18 On the veil of ignorance, see ibid., Sec. 24, and the index.

19 This question is raised by Ronald Dworkin in the first part of his very illuminating, and to me highly instructive, essay "Justice and Rights" (1973), reprinted in *Taking Rights Seriously* (Cambridge, MA: Harvard University Press, 1977).

20 The original position models a basic feature of Kantian constructivism, namely, the distinction between the Reasonable and the Rational, with the Reasonable as prior to the Rational. (For an explanation of this distinction, see "Kantian Constructivism," pp. 528f., and passim.)

21 *Theory*, pp. 138f., 147. The parties in the original position are said (p. 147) to be theoretically defined individuals whose motivations are specified by the account of that position and not by a psychological view about how human beings are actually motivated. This is also part of what is meant by saying (p. 121) that the acceptance of the particular principles of justice is not conjectured as a psychological law or probability but rather follows from the full description of the original position. Although the aim cannot be perfectly achieved, we want the argument to be deductive, "a kind of moral geometry." In "Kantian Constructivism" (p. 532) the parties are described as merely artificial agents who inhabit a construction. Thus I think R. B. Brandt mistaken in objecting that the argument from the original position is based on defective psychology. See his A *Theory of the Good and the Right* (Oxford: Clarendon Press, 1979), pp. 239–42. Of course, one might object to the original position that it models the conception of the person and the deliberations of the parties in ways that are unsuitable for the purposes of a political conception of justice; but for these purposes psychological theory is not directly relevant. On the other hand, psychological theory is relevant for the account of the stability of a conception of justice, as discussed in *Theory*, Pt. III. . . . Similarly, I think Michael Sandel mistaken in supposing that the original position involves a conception of the self ". . . shorn of all its contingently-given attributes," a self that "assumes a kind of supra-empirical status, . . . and given prior to its ends, a pure subject of agency

and possession, ultimately thin." See *Liberalism and the Limits of Justice* (Cambridge: Cambridge University Press, 1982), pp. 93–95. I cannot discuss these criticisms in any detail. The essential point (as suggested in the introductory remarks) is not whether certain passages in *Theory* call for such an interpretation (I doubt that they do), but whether the conception of justice as fairness presented therein can be understood in the light of the interpretation I sketch in this article and in the earlier lectures on constructivism, as I believe it can be.

22 Part of the difficulty is that there is no accepted understanding of what a metaphysical doctrine is. One might say, as Paul Hoffman has suggested to me, that to develop a political conception of justice without presupposing, or explicitly using, a metaphysical doctrine, for example, some particular metaphysical conception of the person, is already to presuppose a metaphysical thesis: namely, that no particular metaphysical doctrine is required for this purpose. One might also say that our everyday conception of persons as the basic units of deliberation and responsibility presupposes, or in some way involves, certain metaphysical theses about the nature of persons as moral or political agents. Following the method of avoidance, I should not want to deny these claims. What should be said is the following. If we look at the presentation of justice as fairness and note how it is set up, and note the ideas and conceptions it uses, no particular metaphysical doctrine about the nature of persons, distinctive and opposed to other metaphysical doctrines, appears among its premises, or seems required by its argument. If metaphysical presuppositions are involved, perhaps they are so general that they would not distinguish between the distinctive metaphysical views – Cartesian, Leibnizian, or Kantian; realist, idealist, or materialist – with which philosophy traditionally has been concerned. In this case, they would not appear to be relevant for the structure and content of a political conception of justice one way or the other. I am grateful to Daniel Brudney and Paul Hoffman for discussion of these matters.

23 For the first two respects, see "Kantian Constructivism," pp. 544f. (For the third respect, see footnote 26 below.) The account of the first two respects found in those lectures is further developed in the text above and I am more explicit on the distinction between what I call here our "public" versus our "nonpublic or moral identity." The point of the term "moral" in the latter phrase is to indicate that personal conceptions of the (complete) good are nominally an essential element in characterizing their nonpublic (or nonpolitical) identity, and these conceptions are understood as nominally containing important moral elements, although they include other elements as well, philosophical and religious. The term "moral" should be thought of as a stand-in for all these possibilities. I am indebted to Elizabeth Anderson for discussion and clarification of this distinction.

24 Here I assume that an answer to the problem of personal identity tries to specify the various criteria (for example, psychological continuity of memories and physical continuity of body, or some part thereof) in accordance with which two different psychological states, or actions (or whatever), which occur at two different times may be said to be states or actions of the same person who endures over time; and it also tries to specify how this enduring person is to be conceived, whether as a Cartesian or a Leibnizian substance, or as a Kantian transcendental ego, or as a continuant of some other kind, for example, bodily or physical. See the collection of essays edited by John Perry, *Personal Identity* (Berkeley, CA: University of California Press, 1975), especially Perry's introduction, pp. 3–30; and Sydney Shoemaker's essay in *Personal Identity* (Oxford: Basil Blackwell, 1984), both of which consider a

number of views. Sometimes in discussions of this problem, continuity of fundamental aims and aspirations is largely ignored, for example, in views like H. P. Grice's (included in Perry's collection) which emphasizes continuity of memory. Of course, once continuity of fundamental aims and aspirations is brought in, as in Derek Parfit's *Reasons and Persons* (Oxford: Clarendon Press, 1984), Pt. III, there is no sharp distinction between the problem of persons' nonpublic or moral identity and the problem of their personal identity. This latter problem raises profound questions on which past and current philosophical views widely differ, and surely will continue to differ. For this reason it is important to try to develop a political conception of justice which avoids this problem as far as possible.

25   For the idea of social death, see Orlando Patterson, *Slavery and Social Death* (Cambridge, MA: Harvard University Press, 1982), esp. pp. 5–9, 38–45, 337. This idea is interestingly developed in this book; and has a central place in the author's comparative study of slavery.

26   See "Social Unity and Primary Goods," in *Utilitarianism and Beyond*, eds Amartya Sen and Bernard Williams (Cambridge: Cambridge University Press, 1982), Sec. IV, pp. 167–70.

Glossary

a posteriori knowledge: knowledge that can be had only as a consequence of experiences. For example, it is only knowable *a posteriori* that birds lay eggs or that the Earth circles the sun. See also *a priori knowledge*.

a priori knowledge: knowledge that can be had independently of experience. Typically, it is something that can be known by reason alone. For example, the propositions that all oak trees are trees and that all bachelors are unmarried adult males are knowable *a priori*. See also *a posteriori knowledge*.

agnosticism: the belief that it is not known whether God exists.

analytic proposition: (a) a proposition that is true in virtue of meaning or concepts alone; (b) a proposition that is derivable only from logic and definitions. For example, "No bachelor is married" expresses an analytic proposition because it can be derived from the logical truth "No bachelor is not a bachelor" and the definition of "bachelor." See also *synthetic proposition*.

anti-realism: anti-realism is used in the context of a controversy where the existence, or reality, of something is under consideration. Anti-realism is the view that what is in question does not exist and, typically, that it is a construction, creation, or projection of the human mind. For example, ethical anti-realism is the view that there are no moral properties, and mathematical anti-realism is the view that numbers do not exist. See *realism*.

Aristotelian realism: a view about the nature of *universals*, namely that universals are real, distinct from any particular individual, but cannot exist independently of individuals. For example, on this view the universal Redness can exist only if there are individual red objects. See also *Platonic realism* and *nominalism*.

atheism: the belief that there is no God.

behaviorism: see *logical behaviorism*, *methodological behaviorism*, and *reductive behaviorism*.

central state identity theory: a materialist view of the mind, namely that the mind is identical to states of the central nervous system. Type–type identity theories hold that types of mental states are identical to types of states of the nervous system. Token–token identity theories only hold that particular tokens of mental states are identical to particular tokens of states of the nervous system.

correspondence theory of truth: theories according to which a statement is true just in case what is stated to be the case as a matter of fact is the case. See *epistemic theories of truth*.

coherence theory of truth: a theory according to which the truth of a statement or a belief depends on whether or not it coheres with the rest of what we individually or collectively believe.

compatibilism: the view that an action can be both free and causally determined.

concept nominalism: see *nominalism*.

contingent: an adjective used to describe objects, facts, and propositions. Objects or facts are contingent if it is possible that they do not exist. A true proposition is contingent if it is possible that it is false. See *necessary*.

cultural relativism: the view that moral values depend on cultural or social norms, so that an action is morally right just in the case that it is approved of by the society or culture in which it is performed.

determinism: the view that every event is determined by prior causes. See also *hard determinism* and *compatibilism, incompatibilism*.

dualism: (a) see *mind/body dualism*; (b) the view that reality consists of two distinct fundamental kinds of substances or things, typically mental and material substances. See also *monism, pluralism*, and *substance*.

eliminative materialism: the view that mental states such as believing, fearing, or thinking really do not exist. These mental states are a part of a discredited world view, much like witches, magical powers, phlogiston, or ether, and a scientific conception of human nature, including the human mind, does not need to account for all of our unscientific ways of describing people.

empirical knowledge: see *a posteriori knowledge*.

empirical verifiability: a statement is empirically verifiable if it can, at least in principle, be shown to be true on the basis of observation.

empiricism: a view about the nature of knowledge, namely that all human knowledge comes from sensory experience. It also denies that reason alone, without experience, can be a source of knowledge. See *rationalism*.

epistemic theories of truth: theories according to which 'truth' and 'is true' are defined in terms of justification and evidence, so that a statement is true just in case it is properly justified or warranted. See *correspondence theory of truth*.

error theory: the view that all statements about some particular subject matter are false. An error theory in ethics is the view that all statements in ethics are false, and an error theory in philosophy of religion is the view that all statements about God are false. Typically, error theories also explain why these false statements are accepted as true by so many people.

essence: the essence, or the essential properties of an object, is the properties the object has to have in order to exist and be the kind of thing it is. It is, for example, an essential property of triangles to have three sides.

ethical cognitivism: the view that moral statements are either true or false; see also *moral realism* and ethical *error theory*.

forms: also called "Platonic Ideas"; these are the unchanging universals that Plato believed were real, while the natural world we experience was a mere appearance that consisted of imperfect replicas of the forms.

free will defense: a response to the argument from evil against God's existence, namely that evil is caused by free will, and that it is so good to have free will that it outweighs the evil that results from it.

functionalism: a kind of mind/body materialism, namely that mental states are defined by their functions, specifically their causal roles with stimuli as well as with other mental states.

gratuitous evil: evil that is not necessary for a greater good. Some think, for example, that while going for the dentist for a biannual checkup is an example of non-gratuitous evil, while rapes are examples of gratuitous evil.

hard determinism: the view that all human actions are causally determined and that no human actions are free. See *indeterminism* and *soft determinism*.

idealism: the view that only minds and the properties of minds exist; denies the existence of matter distinct from mind. See *materialism*.

incompatibilism: the position that an action cannot be both free and causally determined. See *hard determinism* and *indeterminism*.

indeterminism: the view that some human actions are free and not causally determined; sometimes also called "libertarianism."

indiscernibility of identicals: the principle of the indiscernibility of identicals states that if you can find even one property that object *a* has and object *b* does not have, then *a* and *b* are two different objects.

instrumentalism: the view that theoretical claims, or claims of an explanation, should not be understood as being literally true about the world, but rather as an instrument for making predictions. For example, talk in physics about sub-atomic particles would not be understood as being about those particles, but rather as a part of a theory that helps us predict what happens in certain experiments.

logical behaviorism: a view about the meaning of psychological terms, namely that they can be analyzed in terms of behavior and dispositions to behave. See *reductive behaviorism* and *methodological behaviorism*.

materialism: The view that only matter and the properties of matter exist. See *idealism* and *mind/body materialism*.

mind/body materialism: the view that the mind and all mental states, processes, and events are material or physical states, processes, and events. See *behaviorism*, *central state identity theory*, and *functionalism*.

methodological behaviorism: the view that psychology should rely only on observable behavior for evidence in psychological research. Methodological behaviorists opposed the introspective study of the mind that was popular during the second half of the nineteenth century. Methodological behaviorists need not be *reductive behaviorists* or *logical behaviorists*.

mind/body dualism: a view about the nature of the mind, namely that the mind or the properties or states of the mind are distinct from the body or any material state. There are two varieties of mind/body dualism. (a) Substance dualism is the view that mind and body are two distinct substances. (b) Property dualism is the view that mental properties are distinct from physical properties, even if they belong to the same substance. See also *materialism*.

monism: the view that there is only one kind of substance. *Materialism* and *idealism* are examples of monism. See also *dualism* and *pluralism* and *substance*.

moral subjectivism: the view that something has a moral value only if there is someone who values it.

naturalism: (a) see *materialism*; (b) the view that all that exists can be explained and studied with the empirical methods of the natural sciences.

naturalistic fallacy: (a) the view that it is a mistake to identify a moral property with a natural property; (b) the view that moral conclusions cannot be derived from non-moral premises.

necessary: something is necessary if it could not have been otherwise. On most accounts it is necessary that $2 + 2 = 4$, and it is necessary that all bachelors are unmarried. According to Leibniz, if something is necessarily true, then it is true in all *possible worlds*, and if necessarily false, then it is false in all *possible worlds*. See also *contingent*.

necessity theories of causality: theories about the nature of causality according to which there is a necessary connection between cause and effect and this necessity is a feature of the way the world is and not projected or constructed by human beings. See *regularity theory of causality.*

neutral monism: the view that there is only one kind of substance, and it is neither mental nor physical.

nominalism: the view that there are no *universals* over and above particular individuals. There are several varieties of nominalism, depending on how nominalists explain common properties. Predicate nominalism is the view that common properties are a product of the common names and predicates of our language. Concept nominalism is the view that properties are a product of human thinking. Resemblance nominalism is the view that common properties are due to resemblances between particular individuals.

Occam's razor: a principle which tells us that when choosing among two or more theories or explanations, we should, all other things being equal, choose the one that is simpler. The principle is often couched in terms of ontological economy, telling us not to multiply entities beyond necessity.

partial cause: one of many causal factors that make up the *total cause* of an effect.

Platonic realism: a view about the nature of *universals*, namely that universals are real, distinct from all particular individuals, and exist independently of them. On this view the universal Redness can exist even if there are no red individuals. See also *Aristotelian realism* and *nominalism.*

pluralism: in metaphysics the view that reality consists of various distinct kinds of fundamental substances. Typically, pluralists believe that in addition to physical and mental kinds of objects and processes, there are others, such as moral or aesthetic objects, that are neither mental nor physical. See also *dualism, monism,* and *substance.*

possible world: a maximally consistent set of possible situations. Philosophers use possible world talk when discussing what might or might not be the case. For example, in a possible world the Beatles broke up without ever recording an album, and in a possible world the Holocaust never took place. One possible world has the distinction of also being actual, namely the world we live in. See also *contingent* and *necessary.*

pragmatic theory of truth: a theory according to which a statement or belief is true just in the case that it is warranted by the available evidence (John Dewey) or it is good for definite and assignable reasons (William James).

predicate nominalism: See *nominalism.*

qualia: what we seem to be immediately aware of when we are having a conscious experience, as distinct from the properties in the environment that cause or correspond to the experience. For example, the perceived red when we see a ripe tomato is a qualia, and is distinct from the properties of the tomato.

rationalism: a view about the nature of knowledge, namely that reason alone is a source of knowledge. See also *empiricism.*

realism: a term used in the context of a controversy where the existence, or reality, of something is under consideration. Realism affirms the existence or reality of whatever it is whose existence or reality is being debated. Traditionally, realism was the view that universals exist, and was contrasted with *nominalism.* Today, realism in the philosophy of mathematics is the view that numbers exist, realism in ethics is the view that moral properties or objects exist, and realism in the philosophy of science is the view that the theoretical entities described by science exist. See also *instrumentalism.*

realist theories of truth: theories of truth that define truth in terms of mind-independent features of the world, and not in terms of human properties or activities. See *correspondence theories of truth* and *epistemic theories of truth.*

reductionism: the view that phenomena in one domain can be completely explained in terms of the phenomena of another domain.

reductive behaviorism: a view that identifies the different kinds of mental states with patterns of observable behavior and dispositions to behave in certain observable ways in response to stimuli from the environment.

regularity theories of causality: theories about the nature of causality according to which if A causes B, events of type A and B are regularly conjoined, and the necessary connection between cause and effect is an artifact of how we think about A and B, not a feature of A and B. See *necessity theories of causality*.

resemblance nominalism: see *nominalism*.

self-determinism: the view that an action is free when it is produced by a free will, and a will is free when it is determined by an agent who is not causally determined to will in this way.

soft determinism: a view according to which an action can be both free and causally determined, and that it is free if the agent could have done otherwise had he or she wanted to. See *compatibilism* and *hard determinism*.

solipsism: (a) the view that there is nothing else besides me; (b) the view that there is nothing else I can know besides me.

structuring cause: the cause of causal relationships or structures. For example, if turning a switch causes a light to turn on, then the structuring cause is what brought it about that turning the switch will cause the light to turn on. In this case, it is the electrician who placed the switch, wire and lamp in such a way that turning the switch turns on the light. See *triggering cause*.

substance: that which is capable of independent existence or that has properties and relations. Materialists believe that physical matter is the only thing that qualifies as a substance. Dualists, such as Descartes, believed that there are two kinds of substances, material and immaterial. Neutral monists, such as Spinoza, believed that there was one substance and that mental and material things were aspects of that substance. Idealists believe that mind is the only kind of substance.

synthetic proposition: a proposition that is true in virtue of the way the world is, not simply true in virtue of meanings or concepts. Typically, *empirical knowledge* consists of synthetic propositions. See also *analytic proposition*.

theism: the belief that there is a God.

tokens: individual instances of a certain *type*. Socrates is a token of the type human being. The book you are holding in your hands is a token of the type *Beginning Metaphysics*.

total cause: all the factors involved that are causally responsible for a given effect. See also *partial cause*.

triggering cause: a cause that initiates a chain of events that results in some effect. For example, the flipping of a light switch is the triggering cause of a light's coming on. See also *structuring cause*.

type: set of *tokens*.

universals: that which distinct individual things have in common. Kinds, such as the kind cow, and properties, such as the property of being red, are universals. Nominalists claim that universals are just names we give things that resemble each other, and that universals do not exist over and above particulars. See also *nominalism*.

verification principle: a theory of meaning held in high regard by the logical positivists. The principle stated that a statement is cognitively meaningful if, and only if, it is either analytic or empirically verifiable.

Index